# Lecture Notes in Computer Science 16083

Founding Editors

Gerhard Goos
Juris Hartmanis

The series Lecture Notes in Computer Science (LNCS), including its subseries Lecture Notes in Artificial Intelligence (LNAI) and Lecture Notes in Bioinformatics (LNBI), has established itself as a medium for the publication of new developments in computer science and information technology research, teaching, and education.

LNCS enjoys close cooperation with the computer science R & D community, the series counts many renowned academics among its volume editors and paper authors, and collaborates with prestigious societies. Its mission is to serve this international community by providing an invaluable service, mainly focused on the publication of conference and workshop proceedings and postproceedings. LNCS commenced publication in 1973.

Davide Taibi · Darja Smite

Editors

# Software Engineering and Advanced Applications

51st Euromicro Conference, SEAA 2025
Salerno, Italy, September 10–12, 2025
Proceedings, Part III

 Springer

*Editors*
Davide Taibi 🆔
University of Oulu
Oulu, Finland

Darja Smite 🆔
Blekinge Institute of Technology
Karlskrona, Sweden

ISSN 0302-9743          ISSN 1611-3349 (electronic)
Lecture Notes in Computer Science
ISBN 978-3-032-04206-4          ISBN 978-3-032-04207-1 (eBook)
https://doi.org/10.1007/978-3-032-04207-1

# Preface

These three LNCS volumes contain the papers presented at SEAA 2025, the *51st Euromicro Conference Series on Software Engineering and Advanced Applications*, held on September 10–12, 2025, in Salerno, Italy.

SEAA serves as a long-standing international forum for researchers, practitioners, and students to share and discuss the latest innovations, emerging trends, practical experiences, and ongoing challenges and concerns in the field of software engineering and advanced information technology applications for software-intensive systems.

To address this mission, the 2025 edition of SEAA once again brought together a vibrant community through a diverse program. This year, the conference featured nine specialized tracks, each led by a team of co-chairs. These tracks spanned a wide range of topics and reflected the truly multidisciplinary nature of software engineering research and practice.

This year, SEAA received a record high number of 177 research submissions over nine thematic tracks. Each submission underwent a rigorous single-blinded peer-review process. Every paper was assigned to at least three and up to five independent reviewers, selected based on topic expertise. Reviewers were each asked to evaluate 2–3 papers. They assessed submissions according to criteria such as scientific soundness, originality, relevance to the SEAA community and the track theme, clarity of presentation, and contribution to the field. In cases where reviews yielded divergent scores or conflicting recommendations, track chairs actively moderated discussions to facilitate consensus. Conflicts of interest with the track chairs were further handled by the PC Chairs.

Following this process, a total of 62 full papers (including two vision papers) and 20 short papers were selected for inclusion in the proceedings. The diverse set of contributions reflects the high quality and breadth of work being conducted in the SEAA community.

The final program would not have been possible to complete without the effort, commitment, and invaluable contribution of the track chairs. From managing submissions and overseeing the peer-review process, to assisting in completing the exciting program, the track chairs were central to SEAA 2025's quality and relevance. We express our sincere appreciation to the track chairs as listed below.

1. **Cyber-Physical Systems** (CPS): V. Klös (Carl von Ossietzky University of Oldenburg, Germany), and S. Mubeen (Mälardalen University, Sweden)
2. **Data-and AI-Driven Engineering** (DAIDE): J. Bosch (Chalmers & Gothenburg University, Sweden), and H. Holmström Olsson (Malmö University, Sweden)
3. **Emerging Computing Technologies** (ECT): R. Abreu (University of Porto and Meta Inc., Portugal), A. Janes (Free University of Bozen-Bolzano, Italy), V. Lenarduzzi (University of Oulu, Finland), and S. Ali (Simula Research Laboratory, Oslo, Norway)
4. **Model-Driven Engineering and Modeling Languages** (MDEML): A. Bucaioni (Mälardalen University, Sweden), F. Ciccozzi (Mälardalen University, Sweden), and A. Wortmann (Stuttgart University, Germany)

5. **Software Management: Measurement, Peopleware, and Innovation** (SM): O. Demirors (Izmir Institute of Technology, Turkey), and V. Pontillo (Vrije Universiteit Brussel, Belgium)
6. **Systematic Literature Reviews and Mapping Studies in Software Engineering** (SMSE): S. Swift (Brunel University London, UK), and Mahir Arzoky (Brunel University London, UK)
7. **Software Process and Product Improvement** (SPPI): S. Biffl (Vienna University of Technology, Austria), R. Rabiser (Johannes Kepler University Linz, Austria), and D. Winkler (Vienna University of Technology, Austria)
8. **Software Analytics: Mining Software Open Datasets and Repositories** (STREAM): A. Ampatzoglou (University of Macedonia, Greece), and E.M. Arvanitou (University of Macedonia, Greece)
9. **Practical Aspects of Software Engineering** (KKIO): L. Madeyski, (Wrocław University of Science and Technology, Poland), M. Ochodek (Poznań University of Technology, Poland), M. Staron (University of Gothenburg, Sweden), and A. Zalewski (Warsaw University of Technology, Poland)

We extend our gratitude to the SEAA 2025 keynote speakers—Henry Muccini from FrAmeLab, University of L'Aquila, and Alberto Brandolini from Avanscoperta—for sharing their thought-provoking insights and helping to spark discussions throughout the event. Their talks on LLM-Agent Architectures and the Pitfalls of Remote Work were true highlights of the program.

Finally, we would also like to thank SEAA Steering Committee members for their continued guidance and valuable advice throughout the organization of the conference.

We hope you thoroughly enjoyed Euromicro SEAA 2025 and found it inspiring, insightful, and engaging.

July 2025                                                                 Davide Taibi
                                                                         Darja Šmite

# Organization

## Program Committee Chairs

Davide Taibi                 University of Oulu, Finland
Darja Šmite                Blekinge Institute of Technology, Sweden

## General Chairs

Gemma Catolino          University of Salerno, Italy
Carmine Gravino         University of Salerno, Italy

## Publicity Chair

Matteo Esposito         University of Oulu, Finland

## Proceedings Chairs

Ashley van Can          Utrecht University, Netherlands
Julian Frattini           Chalmers University of Technology and
                                   University of Gothenburg, Sweden

## Finance Chair

Francesco Leporati       University of Pavia, Italy

## Steering Committee

Stefan Biffl                 Technische Universität Wien, Austria
Michel Chaudron        Eindhoven University of Technology, Netherlands
Onur Demirors          IzTech, Turkey
Carmine Gravino         University of Salerno, Italy

| Helena Holmström Olsson | Malmö University, Sweden |
|---|---|
| Andreas Wortmann | Stuttgart University, Germany |

## Program Committee

| | |
|---|---|
| Alain Abran | École de Technologie Supérieure, Canada |
| Shaukat Ali | Simula Research Laboratory, Norway |
| Rami Almwari | Brunel University London, UK |
| Mohammad Alshayeb | King Fahd University of PetroleumMinerals, Saudi Arabia |
| Ahmad Altarawneh | Brunel University London, UK |
| Sousuke Amasaki | Nanzan University, Japan |
| Apostolos Ampatzoglou | University of Macedonia, Greece |
| Areti Ampatzoglou | Aristotle University of Thessaloniki, Greece |
| Vasilios Andrikopoulos | University of Groningen, the Netherlands |
| Lefteris Angelis | Aristotle University of Thessaloniki, Greece |
| Paolo Arcaini | National Institute of Informatics, Japan |
| Ove Armbrust | Apple, USA |
| Elvira-Maria Arvanitou | University of Macedonia, Greece |
| Mahir Arzoky | Brunel University London, UK |
| Vaibhav Kumar Bajpai | Microsoft, USA |
| Francesco Basciani | Gran Sasso Science Institute, Italy |
| Steffen Becker | University of Stuttgart, Germany |
| Christian Berger | University of Gothenburg, Sweden |
| Stamatia Bibi | University of Western Macedonia, Greece |
| Stefan Biffl | TU Wien, Austria |
| Ilona Bluemke | Warsaw University of Technology, Poland |
| Florian Bock | Friedrich-Alexander Universität Erlangen, Germany |
| Marek Bolanowski | Rzeszów University of Technology, Poland |
| Matthias Book | University of Iceland, Iceland |
| Jan Bosch | Chalmers University of Technology, Sweden |
| Ruth Breu | University of Innsbruck, Austria |
| Alessio Bucaioni | Mälardalen University, Sweden |
| Alena Buchalcevova | Prague University of Economics and Business, Czechia |
| Daniel Bujosa | Mälardalen University, Sweden |
| Piotr Błaszyński | West Pomeranian University of Technology, Poland |
| Matteo Camilli | Politecnico di Milano, Italy |
| Jose Campos | University of Porto, Portugal |

| | |
|---|---|
| Volker Gruhn | University of Duisburg-Essen, Germany |
| Rong Gu | Mälardalen University, Sweden |
| Sebastian Götz | Dresden University of Technology, Germany |
| Tuna Hacaloglu | Atilim University, Turkey and École de Technologie Superieure, Canada |
| Simon Hacks | Stockholm University, Sweden |
| Philipp Haindl | St. Pölten University of Applied Sciences, Austria |
| David Halasz | Microsoft, Czechia |
| Rachel Harrison | Oxford Brookes University, UK |
| Sara Hassan | Birmingham City University, UK |
| Petra Heck | Fontys University of Applied Sciences, The Netherlands |
| Jens Heidrich | Fraunhofer IESE, Germany |
| Paula Herber | University of Münster, Germany |
| Sebastian Herold | Karlstad University, Sweden |
| Hans-Martin Heyn | Chalmers University of Technology, Sweden and University of Gothenburg, Sweden |
| Bogumila Hnatkowska | Wrocław University of Technology, Poland |
| Petr Hnetynka | Charles University, Czechia |
| Helena Holmström Olsson | Malmö University, Sweden |
| Frank Houdek | Mercedes-Benz AG, Germany |
| Zbigniew Huzar | Wrocław University of Technology, Poland |
| Sami Hyrynsalmi | LUT University, Finland |
| Martin Höst | Malmö University, Sweden |
| Zear Ibrahim | Brunel University London, UK |
| Andrea Janes | Free University of Bozen-Bolzano, Italy |
| Aleksander Jarzebowicz | Gdańsk University of Technology, Poland |
| Frank Johnsen | Norwegian Defence Research Establishment (FFI), Norway |
| Robbert Jongeling | Mälardalen University, Sweden |
| Marija Katic | University of London, UK |
| Wiem Khlif | University of Sfax, Tunisia |
| Michael Klaes | Fraunhofer IESE, Germany |
| Verena Klös | Universität Oldenburg, Germany |
| Ayça Kolukısa Tarhan | Hacettepe University, Turkey |
| Sylwia Kopczynska | Poznań University of Technology, Poland |
| Piotr Kosiuczenko | Military University of Technology, Poland |
| Marek Kretowski | Bialystok University of Technology, Poland |
| Marco Kuhrmann | Reutlingen University, Germany |
| Supriya Lal | Yelp Inc., USA |
| Malvina Latifaj | Mälardalen University, Sweden |
| Valentina Lenarduzzi | University of Oulu, Finland |

| | |
|---|---|
| Zengyang Li | Central China Normal University, China |
| Peng Liang | Wuhan University, China |
| Sherlock Licorish | University of Otago, New Zealand |
| Lech Madeyski | Wrocław University of Science and Technology, Poland |
| Nazim Madhavji | University of Western Ontario, Canada |
| Ashley Mann | Brunel University of London, UK |
| Faisal Maramazi | Brunel University of London, UK |
| Rui Maranhao | University of Porto, Portugal |
| Bartosz Marcinkowski | University of Gdansk, Poland |
| Antonio Martini | University of Oslo, Norway |
| Jacopo Mauro | University of Southern Denmark, Denmark |
| Alistair Mcewan | University of Derby, UK |
| Jorge Melegati | Free University of Bozen-Bolzano, Italy |
| Emilia Mendes | Aarhus University, Denmark |
| Andreas Metzger | Paluno and University of Duisburg-Essen, Germany |
| Judith Michael | RWTH Aachen University, Germany |
| Jakub Miler | Gdansk University of Technology, Poland |
| Yoshiki Mitani | SEC and IPA, Japan |
| Milko Monecke | Technische Universität Berlin, Germany |
| Maurizio Morisio | Politecnico di Torino, Italy |
| Saad Mubeen | Mälardalens University, Sweden |
| Henry Muccini | University of L'Aquila, Italy |
| Tomi Männistö | University of Helsinki, Finland |
| Jürgen Münch | Reutlingen University, Germany |
| Elisa Yumi Nakagawa | University of São Paulo, Brazil |
| Jerzy Nawrocki | Poznań University of Technology, Poland |
| Erika Nazaruka | Riga Technical University, Latvia |
| Michael Neumann | Hochschule Hannover, Germany |
| Yen Ying Ng | Nicolaus Copernicus University, Poland |
| Arne Noyer | Ostfalia University of Applied Sciences, Germany |
| Mirosław Ochodek | Poznań University of Technology, Poland |
| Marco Ortu | University of Cagliari, Italy |
| Necmettin Ozkan | Gebze Technical University, Turkey |
| Claus Pahl | Free University of Bozen-Bolzano, Italy |
| Oscar Pastor | Universidad Politécnica de Valencia, Spain |
| Andrzej Paszkiewicz | Rzeszów University of Technology, Poland |
| Fabiano Pecorelli | Pegaso University, Italy |
| Rui Humberto Pereira | Instituto Superior de Contabilidade e Administração do Porto, Portugal |
| Manuela Petrescu | Babeş-Bolyai University Cluj-Napoca, Romania |

| | |
|---|---|
| Aneta Poniszewska-Maranda | Lodz University of Technology, Poland |
| Valeria Pontillo | Vrije Universiteit Brussel, Belgium |
| Adam Przybylek | University of Galway, Ireland |
| Fethi Rabhi | The University of New South Wales, Australia |
| Rick Rabiser | Software Science at Software Competence Center Hagenberg GmbH and Johannes Kepler University Linz, Austria |
| Łukasz Radliński | West Pomeranian University of Technology, Poland |
| Rudolf Ramler | Software Science at Software Competence Center Hagenberg GmbH and Johannes Kepler University Linz, Austria |
| Adam Roman | Jagiellonian University, Poland |
| Simone Romano | University of Salerno, Italy |
| Bruno Rossi | Masaryk University, Czech Republic |
| Gabriele Rotoloni | Università degli Studi dell'Insubria, Italy |
| Daniela S. Cruzes | Norwegian University of Science and Technology and Visma, Norway |
| Mika Saari | Tampere University of Technology, Finland |
| Małgorzata Sadowska | Politechnika Wrocławska, Poland |
| Norsaremah Salleh | International Islamic University Malaysia, Malaysia |
| Slawomir Samolej | Rzeszów University of Technology, Poland |
| Gleison Santos | Federal University of the State of Rio de Janeiro, Brazil |
| Zenepe Satka | Mälardalen University, Sweden |
| Klaus Schmid | University of Hildesheim, Germany |
| Sibylle Schupp | Hamburg University of Technology, Germany |
| Asma Sellami | Higher Institute of Computer Science and Multimedia of Sfax, Tunis |
| Gheorghe Cosmin Silaghi | Babeş-Bolyai University Cluj-Napoca, Romania |
| Samira Silva | Gran Sasso Science Institute, Italy |
| Michal Smialek | Warsaw University of Technology, Poland |
| Michel Soares | Federal University of Sergipe, Brazil |
| Janusz Sosnowski | Warsaw University of Technology, Poland |
| Zenon A. Sosnowski | Bialystok University of Technology, Poland |
| Hassan Soubra | ECE Paris, France |
| Érica Souza | Federal Technological University of Paraná, Brazil |
| Luigi Libero Lucio Starace | Università degli Studi di Napoli Federico II, Italy |
| Miroslaw Staron | Chalmers University of Technology, Sweden |
| Krzysztof Stencel | University of Warsaw, Poland |

Daniel Strüber            Chalmers University of Technology and
                          University of Gothenburg, Sweden, and
                          Radboud University Nijmegen, Netherlands
Jacek Stój                Silesian University of Technology, Poland
Dan Mircea Suciu          Babeş-Bolyai University Cluj-Napoca, Romania
Jakub Swacha              University of Szczecin, Poland
Stephen Swift             Brunel University of London, UK
Kari Systä                Tampere University of Technology, Finland
Tomasz Szmuc              AGH University of Science and Technology,
                          Poland
Marcin Szpyrka            AGH University of Science and Technology,
                          Poland
Davide Taibi              University of Oulu, Finland
Matthias Tichy            Ulm University, Germany
Juha-Pekka Tolvanen       MetaCase, Finland, and University of Jyväskylä,
                          Finland
Adam Trendowicz           Fraunhofer IESE, Germany
Dimitri Van Landuyt       Katholieke Universiteit Leuven, Belgium
Anita Walkowiak           Wrocław University of Science and Technology,
                          Poland
Bartosz Walter            Poznań University of Technology, Poland
Jörg Walter               OFFIS Institute for Information Technology,
                          Germany
Xiaofeng Wang             Free University of Bozen-Bolzano, Italy
Bianca Wiesmayr           Johannes Kepler University Linz, Austria
Dietmar Winkler           Vienna University of Technology, Austria
Emily Winter              Lancaster University, UK
Andreas Wortmann          University of Stuttgart, Germany
Konrad Wrona              NATO Communications and Information Agency,
                          The Netherlands
Włodzimierz Wysocki       West Pomeranian University of Technology,
                          Poland
Andrzej Zalewski          Warsaw University of Technology, Poland
Janusz Zalewski           Florida Gulf Coast University, USA
Jianjun Zhao              Kyushu University, Japan
Zbigniew Zielinski        Military University of Technology, Poland
Darja Šmite               Blekinge Institute of Technology, Sweden

# Sponsors

# Contents – Part III

**Software Management: Measurement, Peopleware, and Innovation**

An Empirical Study on Learning Paths and Gender Dynamics in Scrum
Master Roles .......................................................... 3
  *Manuela Petrescu and Paul Razvan Petrescu*

Measuring the Size of Change Requests in Microservice-Based Software
Projects .............................................................. 14
  *Melih Yenel, Huseyin Unlu, and Onur Demirors*

Aligning Experimentation with Product Operations: A Taxonomy
for Structuring Experimentation Teams ................................. 23
  *Nils Stotz, Ben Labay, Lukas Vermeer, and Paul Drews*

Socio-Technical Well-Being of Quantum Software Communities:
An Overview on Community Smells ...................................... 39
  *Stefano Lambiase, Manuel De Stefano, Fabio Palomba,*
  *Filomena Ferrucci, and Andrea De Lucia*

Differences Between Neurodivergent and Neurotypical Software
Engineers: Analyzing the 2022 Stack Overflow Survey ................... 57
  *Pragya Verma, Marcos Vinicius Cruz, and Grischa Liebel*

"Good" and "Bad" Failures in Industrial CI/CD–Balancing Cost
and Quality Assurance ................................................ 75
  *Simin Sun, David Friberg, and Miroslaw Staron*

Exploring Software Fairness Debt in Gray Literature ................... 85
  *Rodrigo Sotolani, Sávio Freire, Felipe Fronchetti,*
  *Ronnie de Souza Santos, and Rodrigo Spinola*

An Evidence-Based Study on the Relationship of Software Engineering
Practices on Code Smells in Python ML Projects ....................... 105
  *Giammaria Giordano, Antonio Della Porta, Filomena Ferrucci,*
  *and Fabio Palomba*

H-TURF: Detecting Optimal Green Software Engineering Skillsets Using
TURF Analysis and Hierarchical Cumulative Voting ..................... 121
  *Vasileios Ntaoulas, Konstantinos Georgiou, Nikolaos Mittas,*
  *and Lefteris Angelis*

Rookie Mistakes: Measuring Software Quality in Student Projects
to Guide Educational Enhancement ..................................... 137
    *Marco De Luca, Sergio Di Martino, Sergio Di Meglio,*
    *Anna Rita Fasolino, Luigi Libero Lucio Starace, and Porfirio Tramontana*

*"The Candle is Burning Out on its Own.."*: Modeling Fatigue and Empathy
Among Chinese Developers ........................................... 155
    *Damian A. Tamburri, Haotian Zhang, Kelly Blincoe, Rick Kazman,*
    *Giammaria Giordano, Valeria Pontillo, and Fabio Palomba*

From Diverse Origins to a DEI Crisis: The Pushback Against Equity,
Diversity, and Inclusion in Software Engineering ......................... 174
    *Ronnie de Souza Santos, Cleyton Magalhaes, Ann Barcomb,*
    *and Mairieli Wessel*

REST in Pieces: RESTful Design Rule Violations in Student-Built Web
Apps ............................................................... 191
    *Sergio Di Meglio, Valeria Pontillo, and Luigi Libero Lucio Starace*

DevScholar: A Reuse-Based Approach for Evaluating Developer
Contribution ....................................................... 201
    *Yahya Elnouby, Selen Uysal, Umut Cihan, Hakan Erdogmus,*
    *and Eray Tüzün*

Teaching Software Engineering for Artificial Intelligence: An Experience
Report ............................................................. 214
    *Fabio Palomba, Gianmario Voria, Alessandra Parziale,*
    *Viviana Pentangelo, Antonio Della Porta, Vincenzo De Martino,*
    *Gilberto Recupito, and Giammaria Giordano*

A Reasoning Framework for Architecting Carbon-Aware
Software-as-a-Service Applications ................................... 231
    *Samuele Giussani, Mauro Caporuscio, and Diego Perez-Palacin*

**Software Process and Product Improvement**

Prompt Engineering Guidelines for Using Large Language Models
in Requirements Engineering ......................................... 245
    *Krishna Ronanki, Simon Arvidsson, and Johan Axell*

Navigating Uncertainty and Adaptability: A Survey on the Role of Kanban
and Scrum in Software Startups ...................................... 263
    *Omid Mojabi, Mikael Svahnberg, and Michael Unterkalmsteiner*

Towards AI-Driven Organizations ...................................... 280
  *Jan Bosch and Helena Holmström Olsson*

BEWT: A Benchmark for End-to-End Web Testing ....................... 296
  *Dario Olianas, Maurizio Leotta, and Filippo Ricca*

**Software Analytics: Mining Software Open Datasets and Repositories**

The Ground Truth Effect: Investigating SZZ Variants in Just-in-Time
Vulnerability Prediction ............................................. 317
  *Alfonso Cannavale, Emanuele Iannone, Gianluca Di Lillo,*
  *Fabio Palomba, and Andrea De Lucia*

Generate with CodeXHug: A Dataset to Enhance Model Cards with Code
Usage Patterns ...................................................... 327
  *Stefano Palombo, Claudio Di Sipio, Juri Di Rocco, and Davide Di Ruscio*

Investigating the Relationship Between Churning and Code Smells .......... 345
  *Kevin Cerqueira Gomes, Elivelton Ramos Cerqueira, Gabriel Moraes,*
  *Lidiany Cerqueira, Glauco Carneiro, Rodrigo Spínola,*
  *Manoel Mendonça, and José Amancio Macedo Santos*

An Empirical Analysis on the Use of Third-Party HTTP Clients
in Open-Source Java Projects ......................................... 361
  *Leif Bonorden*

Lessons from Visualizing Software Architecture Structure Conformance
at Thermo Fisher Scientific .......................................... 372
  *Filip Zamfirov, Andrei Radulescu, Jacob Krüger,*
  *and Michel R. V. Chaudron*

Does Context Matter? An Exploratory Study on God Class Distribution
Based on Contextual Attributes ....................................... 390
  *Elivelton Ramos Cerqueira, Gabriel Moraes, Lidiany Cerqueira,*
  *Glauco Carneiro, Rodrigo Spínola, Manoel Mendonça,*
  *and José Amancio Macedo Santos*

**Emerging Computing Technologies**

Towards a Defense-in-Depth Approach for Securing Collaborative Cloud
Infrastructures ...................................................... 409
  *Dimosthenis Natsos and Andreas L. Symeonidis*

QuTiP-MRL: A Library for Multiple-Valued Reversible Logic Simulations  .... 419
*Fabio Pievani, Asma Taheri Monfared, Andrea Bombarda,*
*and Angelo Gargantini*

Design Decisions for Architecting Digital Twins of Microservices-Based
Systems ......................................................... 428
*Aurora Macías, Evangelos Ntentos, Uwe Zdun, and Elena Navarro*

**Author Index** ...................................................... 447

# Software Management: Measurement, Peopleware, and Innovation

# An Empirical Study on Learning Paths and Gender Dynamics in Scrum Master Roles

Manuela Petrescu$^{(\boxtimes)}$ ⓘ and Paul Razvan Petrescu ⓘ

Department of Computer Science, Babes Bolyai University, Cluj-Napoca, Romania
manuela.petrescu@ubbcluj.ro, rpetrescu@gmail.com

**Abstract.** **Context**: Agile development methodology has been widely adopted by industry and the demand for experienced professionals in Agile-related roles is persistently high.**Objectives**: We focus on the learning path for a Scrum Master role in multicultural software companies and investigate the role in relation to team size, together with the learning process for a career path, and how companies monitor soft skills development.**Method**: We conducted our study in two phases, two qualitative surveys (interview studies) and performed a qualitative and quantitative data analysis of the results.**Conclusions**: Our results identified that the need for a Scrum Master (SM) depends on the size of the team, with our study indicating a six-member limit. There is no overall standardized process for soft skills learning or metrics to measure progress. Some companies measure soft skills based on feedback received from the client or from the team, and other companies are taking both types of feedback into consideration. Many learning initiatives, especially on soft skills for an SM role, were based on employees' actions.

**Keywords:** Scrum Master learning · career path · Agile · software

## 1 Introduction

The Software Product Development Lifecycle (SDLC) has experienced an ongoing evolution over time to address the requirements of contemporary projects. There are different methodologies based on Agile framework such as Scrum, KanBan, Extreme Programming. Scrum framework was widely adopted, offering benefits such as team planning, continuous iterations, and consistent testing [17]. According to the Scrum Guide (2020), a Scrum team consists of three key roles: the Scrum Master, the Product Owner, and the developers. The role of the Scrum Master includes acting as a facilitator who has the ability to motivate and understand the team.

© The Author(s), under exclusive license to Springer Nature Switzerland AG 2026
D. Taibi and D. Smite (Eds.): SEAA 2025, LNCS 16083, pp. 3–13, 2026.
https://doi.org/10.1007/978-3-032-04207-1_1

In response to a growing demand in the market, certain companies have successfully facilitated the inclusion of people lacking technical experience in the engineering industry, particularly in roles related to computer science such as Scrum Master (SM) or Business Analyst (BA) [1]. There are studies on how to create systems using Scrum [16], others are related to the importance of the Scrum Master position, [18,20], gender diversity in this role [7,19], soft skills for the role of SM are investigated in [8,18] but studies that address the learning path for the position of Scrum Master are relatively few. This is the main reason we focus on the Scrum Master role. We focus on gender, as the study [9] has indicated that there is a tendency for men to occupy more technical roles within the field of computer science, while women tend to be more prevalent in positions that require greater emphasis on soft skills and fewer technical competencies.

Skills can be categorized into hard/technical - specialized knowledge and soft skills. Soft skills refer to a set of personal attributes, behaviours, and characteristics of an individual. This research paper examines the learning path for a Scrum Master from an empirical perspective, completing studies by [4] and [14] which have explored the crucial hard and soft skills required in Scrum. The following articles are related to our work in terms of methodology, using interviews [4,11] and focus groups [4] to acquire qualitative data, and in terms of results when verifying the necessary skills [3,4] for the Scrum Master position and exploring a potential career path in this field.

This study serves as an extended continuation of the research presented in [12], which focused on identifying the necessary competencies, responsibilities, and gender balance for the role of SM. The main research questions in the preliminary paper were related to finding the technical and soft skills essentially linked to the SM role and to finding out if 'the Scrum Master role was doubled by managerial or technical duties'. The objective of this study was to determine the learning path for a Scrum Master role within the context of Agile development methodology, as well as to examine career-related facts of women in relation to Scrum Master positions. To achieve this goal, we have formulated the objectives **1:** Understand and identify the relationship between the size of the team and the need for an SM in a team. **2:** Comprehend the learning process for a career path for women in SM positions. **3:** Examine how companies monitor the skills development associated with Scrum Master positions.

## 2   Study Design

This section describes the design of the study and information on data collection. The structure of this study conforms to established community standards for Qualitative Surveys [13]. For this study, we used qualitative approaches, more specifically, to conduct two phases of interviews using Teams to record them. Having interviews enabled us to follow a structure but at the same time let the respondents answer in free text about their own opinion around the subject. We intended to position the need for a SM role in different teams, depending on their size, and to discover the learning path for this position in different software companies. The current paper is an extension of [12], where we explored the skills necessary to perform the SM role.

For each phase, we had different sets of questions for the interviews, some of the questions were specifically designed to focus on women's roles. The first set consisted of questions related to the company's specificity, personal information such as current role, overall IT experience, company type: [multinational, outsourcing], size of the team, and also questions related to Agile, questions 1 to 5. The interviewees were asked to describe the Agile process used, to specify learning processes related to the SM roles. The second set was specific for women who perform Scrum Master roles in IT development teams. The second set of questions was divided into two sections: The first section was used for group selection and data processing, including details such as the interviewer's name and interview status. The second section focused on how women perform the Scrum Master role within specific project contexts. The second set of questions (except for the specificity questions) is listed in Table 1.

**Table 1.** Interview Questions

| |
|---|
| What type of background do you have (technical/nontechnical). |
| Please describe previous positions. |
| Please describe the career path to the SM role. |
| Did you have SM specific preparation (workshops, courses, conferences, tutorials)? |
| Did you have mentors for the SM career path? |
| Please describe the support received from your organization. |

## 2.1 Participants

For each phase, we had different participant selection criteria. In the first phase, we had individual discussions with 32 people from 14 companies, to be included in our study they had to have significant prior experience in Agile methodology and/or in fulfilling the role of an SM, to hold for at least 5 years a leadership or managerial position that involves leading, supervising, or overseeing a development team, to guarantee representation across various company sizes. We tried to promote gender diversity (when feasible, we prioritized interviews with women over men, since the majority of eligible candidates for interviews were men), we had 14 women and 18 men. In the second phase, for the second round of interviews, we searched for women who have experience and worked in SM positions; the selection criteria did not take into account the size of the company or the size of the team. The average experience for the set of participants was 13.64 years in the computer science field. In terms of company size, the participants worked in six small companies and eight large companies (company size was determined using the criteria outlined in EUROSTAT (2022)). There were no biases in establishing the participant set, as we initiated the study participation invitation to all our collaborators and encouraged them to extend invitations to other persons who met the eligibility criteria.

## 2.2 Methodology

**Data collection** process followed the standard procedures outlined in [13] for the interviews, and for the focus group. The interviews were conducted online and recorded with the consent of the interviewee. We paid attention to ethical concerns and communicated the study objectives, used anonymization, and obtained consent for the final transcript. Two project members were responsible for conducting the interviews and writing the interview transcripts. An independent third project member, uninvolved in both the interview and transcript creation processes, reviewed the transcript by cross-referencing it with the recorded interview. During the first phase (32 interviews), more than 33 h were dedicated to conducting interviews and an additional 52 h were invested in reviewing the data and generating transcripts for the first set of interviews; at the end of that period, the discussion in the focus group with SM professionals lasted more than three hours. The second phase consisted of a series of 12 interviews with women who performed Scrum master roles in IT teams. For the second phase, we dedicated around 8 h to conducting interviews and another 17 h to review data and generate the transcripts. We have adopted a reflexive methodology for data analysis, taking into account the subsequent steps based on [6]. Consequently, for free-text responses, we selected thematic analysis as recommended by [6], described in [12] and previously used in other research studies in software engineering [2,11].

The focus group was organized according to existing standard procedures and good practices recommended by [13,15]. The focus group meeting was led by two of the co-authors, one acting as a moderator and another as an assistant. The focus group participants, already familiar with the study's topic from interviews, shifted the three-hour discussion from project-specific details to a broader exploration of their experiences and learning in the SM role.

## 3 Empirical Investigation Into Scrum Master Learning Path Results

### 3.1 RQ1: What is the Need for a Scrum Master Role Depending on the Size of the Team?

To find the answer to RQ1, we analysed the data from the first set in interviews to see if there is a correlation between the size of the team and the need for a SM role and the gender of the person who performs this role. We discussed the responses received for the questions: *"Please specify the team size"*, *"Specify if there was a person having SM position"*, *"Please specify the gender"*.

We found that the largest software development team had 70 members (a multicultural team of Romanians, Indians, and others), and the smallest had only four members. More than half of the teams had less than 10 members. With one exception, all teams having more than six members had a person in the SM position, even if, for some teams, the person having this role performed other tasks and/or roles. Teams that worked using Agile and did not have an SM role had 6 or less than 6 members. In conclusion, the need for an SM correlates with the size of the software team; in our case, the size limit was six. In our study, the role of SM was performed by 29.41% women and 57.14% men. So, even if women are a good fit based on the skills required for an SM role [10], in our study, most of the time, this role was carried out by men.

### 3.2 RQ2. How is the Learning Process for a Career Path for Women in Scrum Master Roles?

To find the answer to this question, we focused on the women in our study who were performing in Scrum Master roles. The distribution of our respondents from technical background point of view is: 7 have technical background in terms of traditional academic degree, 3 come from business/economics background, one from engineering field (other than computer), and one from European studies background. Although all of them acquired some kind of experience in technical concepts through previous positions or internships as students. In some cases (3 persons) they possess relatively simple programming skills (testing, business analyst). In one case, the respondent declared that she considers business skills essential and more important than technology (programming).

Different forms of learning have been identified during interviews, such as courses, finalized with/without certification (either on site or online), community learning (forum, local meetups) and self-learning. A complete map of these forms can be seen in Fig. 1(a).

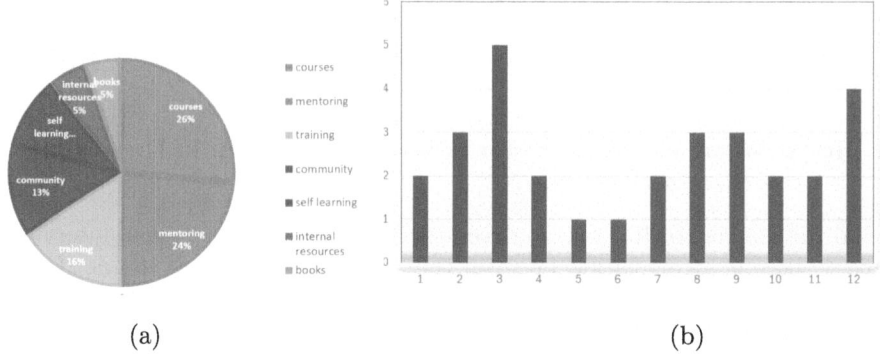

(a)                                                        (b)

**Fig. 1.** (a) Map of learning forms and (b) Support offered by company: number of distinct supporting activities for each respondent

We might notice the diverse forms of learning, in which courses, including online courses, and mentoring represent 50% of them. It is also worth remarking that 53% of learning methods, mentoring, trainings, and community learning are interactive, which is important as experience and communication are some essential characteristics of the SM role. We found that the learning forms are very different and that the abilities for such a role are gathered from different learning experiences, as described by the respondents: *"we had a mentor/coach for one to one discussion; we had daily syncs to make sure we get results"*, *"It helped me to coach other colleagues about event adoption, other Scrum issues"*, *"Community learning: Reddit, local meetups"*. As a notice, we did not correct, modify, or edit the participant's responses, and we cited them as they were, so possible English language issues or short forms of the verbs might appear. Obtaining a certification might not be of high importance, as only 4 out of 11 interviewed persons mention that after course completion they went to the certification process.

The support offered by the organization was also very diverse, from very low offered (*"No support from the company except the opportunity to follow this path"*, *"No official program for the learning and development part (except Udemy and PMP)"*, *"time to learn"*), to continuous support in different forms: courses, certification, funding to follow courses, training programs, mentoring, shadowing programs. Without differentiating between different supporting actions, if we simply count these actions, the distribution is shown in Fig. 1 (b), with the remark that company support can, in most cases, be more consistent.

Conclusion: The interactive learning forms are prevailing, providing means to gain facilitation abilities; Support of organization, even present in more cases, can be more consistent and can be provided in more forms, thus up-skilling own human resources to Scrum Master role, rather than searching for external ones and many learning initiatives came from employees.

### 3.3   RQ3. How Do Companies Monitor the Skills Development for a Scrum Master Role?

According to the results of [12], soft skills are a must for a Scrum Master role, as having technical skills is a plus. Because of this, we focused on the responses for soft skills improvement. We noticed that most of the software companies have defined metrics for technical skills measurement such as number of bugs resolved, number of implemented features, team velocity; they formalized technical evaluations for teams and for individuals, also using code review, certifications, etc. We believed there was little innovation in measuring technical skills, so we did not pay attention to this topic. However, companies did not define metrics to measure soft skills, and thus the subject is worthy of investigation.

According to our data, soft skills are measured using feedback: in 53.12% of the responses. Sometimes feedback comes from the client, sometimes from the team: *"Soft skills in one to one to manager and based on the client's feedback"*, *"Peer review: questionnaire completed by everyone who worked with"*. The next largest category of answers (31.25%) mentioned that nothing is standardized for the evaluation of soft skills, it is more an informal process: *"For soft skills we have intuitive measures, nothing standardized"*, *"We don't have KPIs for soft skills; for soft skills we do it intuitively and punctual"*. Evaluations are performed twice a year (18.75%), once a year (15.65%) or every month (9.37%). Other responses stated that developing soft skills is *"each one's responsibility"*, and other stated that certifications are taken into account. There were two answers that stated how soft skills development is encouraged, but nothing is mandatory: *"There is no formal tracking for soft skills development, but there is encouragement within the company to participate in internal soft skills training programs, especially for junior to mid levels (as there are multiple in each bracket), and there are more advanced programs for leadership and management designed for mid and higher levels"*, *"Additionally, within the team we also encourage initiatives in communication with the client, preparing demo presentations, providing internal trainings and constant feedback for these activities on the project"*. We also got answers such as *"not measured"* and one answer stating *"No idea"*.

Conclusion: There is no overall standardized process for soft skills; for some companies, everything is based on feedback received from the client or from the developing team; other companies are taking both types of feedback into consideration. None of the companies have defined metrics for "how well someone communicates, chairs a meeting, negotiates or solves a conflict", everything is in one big bucket, general feedback from the client and/or team.

# 4   Discussion

Soft skills have a longer life span, but it is harder to quantity them and define specific metrics. Technical skills acquirement and progress are easier to measure compared to soft skills, and software companies invest in up-skilling their employees technical skills by different methods: courses, pair-programming, mentoring, etc.

As indicated in the RQ1 findings, the necessity of a Scrum Master (SM) depends on the size of the team, our study indicating a threshold of six members. Although women possess the necessary skills for the Scrum Master (SM) role [10], our study found that men predominantly filled this position. This suggests potential gender imbalances in Agile leadership, highlighting the need for more research on organizational biases, cultural factors, and opportunities to encourage more women in SM roles. The process of acquiring Scrum Master skills varies widely and is influenced by the company culture, personal motivation, and available resources. Some organizations emphasize structured training programs, while others rely on mentorship and hands-on experience. Interactive learning methods, such as workshops, simulations, and peer discussions, are particularly effective in developing facilitation abilities.Companies do not have a standardized method to evaluate soft skills, employees often take the initiative in their learning journey, seeking training, certifications, and practical experiences to improve their skills.

There is no universal standard for assessing soft skills in the SM role. Some companies rely solely on feedback from clients and teams, while others consider both perspectives. However, none have established concrete metrics to evaluate communication, facilitation of meetings, negotiation, or conflict resolution. The absence of standardized evaluation methods makes it challenging to measure and improve these critical skills systematically. A more structured approach, including defined benchmarks and assessment tools, could help organizations better develop and refine these competencies. Establishing clear evaluation criteria would enhance leadership effectiveness and contribute to a more consistent and efficient Agile environment.

# 5    Threats to Validity

As an empirical investigation, the study has taken measures to address threats to validity. The authors adhered to established guidelines [13] and took into account the following factors: construct validity, internal validity, and external validity. We took steps to anonymize the data by removing identification information about the individuals and companies involved. Construct validity refers to the pertinence and coherence of the interview. Before conducting the interviews, two persons with expertise as SM and Product Manager validated the proposed set of questions. Their feedback was used to calibrate the questions.

Internal validity refers to the various factors that exert an influence on the results of a study. To address the potential risks posed by the participant pool, we implemented a strategy aimed at diversifying the composition by deliberately selecting individuals who occupied various roles and positions and ensuring a balanced gender representation, taking into account the size of the company.

External validity: We examined how the results of this study can be generalized to a wider range of companies and how can they be replicated in different settings and different types of projects [20]. The key to answer to this question lies in the selection of the participants (from 14 multinational or outsourcing companies) plus 7 additional companies from the focus group. Because of this, we consider the results can be generalized to Romanian IT companies. Generalizing the results for IT companies in general can only be done with some caution, since Romania exports around 80% of the ITC products (Information Technology and Cybersecurity) according to the CEIC report [21]. However, Romanian companies can have some specificity related to internal processes and learning methodologies.

# 6    Conclusions and Future Work

Throughout this study, we have investigated the learning path for a Scrum Master to thrive in the technological industry, to comprehend the support offered by software companies, and to analyze women's' training for a Scrum Master position. In order to do this, we have organized two sets of interviews and a focus group. The data collected showed that the acquisition of Scrum Master skills varies according to the company culture, personal motivation, and availability of resources. Although organizational support is prevalent, there is potential to improve its consistency and diversity, as many learning initiatives were created by employees. Our findings indicate that software companies monitor technical skills development, as soft skills for an SM role are difficult to monitor and evaluate, as most companies based their evaluation on the feedback received, without having defined any metrics.

In conclusion, it is our contention that this study has significance in determining the learning path in software companies for the position of Scrum Master. In future work, we intend to extend our investigation on the learning process to other roles within Agile teams.

# References

1. Chau, T., Maurer, F.: Tool support for inter-team learning in agile software organizations. In: International Workshop on Learning Software Organizations, pp. 98–109. Springer (2004)
2. Cruzes, D.S., Dyba, T.: Recommended steps for thematic synthesis in software engineering. In: 2011 International Symposium on Empirical Software Engineering and Measurement, pp. 275–284 (2011)
3. Hemon-Hildgen, A., Lyonnet, B., Rowe, F., Fitzgerald, B.: From agile to DevOps: smart skills and collaborations. Inf. Syst. Front. **22** (2020)
4. Hidayati, A., Budiardjo, E.K., Purwandari, B.: Hard and soft skills for scrum global software development teams. In: Proceedings of the 3rd International Conference on Software Engineering and Information Management, ICSIM '20, pp. 110–114, New York, Association for Computing Machinery (2020)
5. Paasivaara, M.: Teaching the scrum master role using professional agile coaches and communities of practice. In: 2021 IEEE/ACM 43rd International Conference on Software Engineering: Software Engineering Education and Training (ICSE-SEET), pp. 30–39 (2021)
6. b14, M.E., Varpio, L.: Thematic analysis of qualitative data: AMEE guide no. 131. Medical Teacher **42**(8), 846–854 (2020)
7. Marsden, N., Ahmadi, M., Wulf, V., Holtzblatt, K.: Surfacing challenges in scrum for women in tech. IEEE Softw. **39**(6), 80–87 (2022)
8. Matturro, G., Fontán, C., Raschetti, F.: Soft skills in scrum teams. In: the 27th International Conference on Software Engineering and Knowledge Engineering, SEKE 2015, pp. 6–8 (2015)
9. McKinsey and Co, L.: Women in the workplace (2019)
10. Motogna, S., Alboaie, L., Todericiu, I.A., Zaharia, C.: Retaining women in computer science: the good, the bad and the ugly sides. In: Proceedings of the Third Workshop on Gender Equality, Diversity, and Inclusion in Software Engineering, b21@ICSE '22, pp. 35–42. Association for Computing Machinery (2022)
11. Petrescu, M.A., Motogna, S., Berciu, L. (2023). Women in scrum master role: challenges and opportunities. In: 2023 IEEE/ACM 4th Workshop on Gender Equity, Diversity, and Inclusion in Software Engineering (b21ICSE), pp. 49–55. IEEE
12. Ralph, Paul (ed.) ACM Sigsoft Empirical Standards for Software Engineering Research, version 0.2.0 (2021)
13. Ramin, F., Matthies, C., Teusner, R.: More than code: contributions in scrum software engineering teams. In: Proceedings of the IEEE/ACM 42nd International Conference on Software Engineering Workshops, ICSEW'20, pp. 137–140, New York. Association for Computing Machinery (2020)
14. Ruokonen, M., Saarenketo, S.: The strategic orientations of rapidly internationalizing software companies. Eur. Bus. Rev. **21**(1), 17–41 (2009)
15. Schwaber, K. and Beedle, M.: Agile software development with Scrum. Prentice Hall PTR (2001)

16. Schwaber, K., Sutherland, J.: The scrum guide (2020). https://scrumguides.org/docs/scrumguide/v2020/2020-Scrum-Guide-US.pdf. Accessed 20 Oct 2023
17. Shastri, Y., Hoda, R., Amor, R.: Spearheading agile: the role of the scrum master in agile projects. Empir. Softw. Eng. **26**(1), 1–31 (2021)
18. Spichkova, M., Schmidt, H.H., Trubiani, C.: Role of women in software architecture: an attempt at a systematic literature review. pp. 31–34 (2017)
19. Spiegler, S.V., Heinecke, C., Wagner, S.: Leadership gap in agile teams: how teams and scrum masters mature. In: International Conference on Agile Software Development, pp. 37–52. Springer, Cham (2019)
20. Wieringa, R., Daneva, M.: Six strategies for generalizing software engineering theories. In Sci. Comput. Program. **101**,(2015). https://doi.org/10.1016/j.scico.2014.11.013
21. CEIC DATA, Romania Exports: ICT Goods In https://www.ceicdata.com/en/indicator/romania/exports-ict-goods, Accessed 02 July 2024

# Measuring the Size of Change Requests in Microservice-Based Software Projects

Melih Yenel[ID], Huseyin Unlu[(✉)][ID], and Onur Demirors[ID]

Izmir Institute of Technology, 35430 Izmir, Turkey
{melihyenel,huseyinunlu,onurdemirors}@iyte.edu.tr

**Abstract.** Accurately estimating the effort required for implementing change requests remains a critical challenge in software engineering, especially in microservice-based software architectures (MSSA). Traditional functional size measurement methods often fail to capture the distinct characteristics of MSSAs. To address this limitation, we propose a change size measurement method based on MicroM, a size measurement approach specifically developed for MSSAs. The proposed method counts added, deleted, and modified events across functional, architectural, and algorithmic levels, and includes the number of affected initial requirements. We conducted an exploratory case study with 18 change requests and built four regression-based effort estimation models. The results show that combining event counts with the number of affected requirements improves estimation accuracy. Our method provides a more precise and context-aware way to estimate change-related effort in MSSA projects.

**Keywords:** Software Size Measurement · Effort Estimation · Change · MicroM · Case Study

## 1 Introduction

Delivering high-quality software that satisfies stakeholder requirements within the constraints of time and budget is a fundamental objective in software engineering [1]. Yet, the dynamic and evolving nature of software projects renders change an unavoidable reality. Since the introduction of the Agile Manifesto [2], the ability to accommodate change has been embraced as a core principle of modern development methodologies, thereby establishing change management as an essential discipline. Changes may arise during development—such as through evolving customer needs or quality assurance processes—or during the maintenance phase after deployment. Regardless of when they occur, managing and estimating the impact of these changes is critical. Accurate estimation hinges on effective measurement of software size, which remains one of the most influential factors in project planning and control [3].

This challenge becomes even more prominent in microservice-based software architectures (MSSA), which offer modularity, scalability, and agility through independently deployable services [4, 5]. While MSSA aligns well with Agile practices [6], it complicates traditional effort estimation methods [7]. Subjective techniques like Story Points

© The Author(s), under exclusive license to Springer Nature Switzerland AG 2026
D. Taibi and D. Smite (Eds.): SEAA 2025, LNCS 16083, pp. 14–22, 2026.
https://doi.org/10.1007/978-3-032-04207-1_2

are commonly used but often criticized for inconsistency and lack of objectivity [8–12]. On the other hand, Functional Size Measurement (FSM) methods provide standardized and objective estimations, yet were originally designed for monolithic, data-centric systems [3]. As MSSA moves toward decentralized, event-driven, and behavior-oriented designs, existing FSM methods—such as COSMIC [13]—fall short in representing its complexity [14–16]. This underscored the need for new, context-specific size measurement approaches tailored to modern microservice environments, particularly those that can effectively support change estimation.

While previous research highlights the importance of measuring software change size—especially for effort estimation—most studies focus on maintenance tasks and monolithic systems, overlooking the unique characteristics of modern architectural paradigms such as MSSA [17]. Moreover, current approaches often lack rigor in data analysis and fail to provide tailored solutions for Agile environments or systems undergoing architectural shifts.

We previously proposed a size measurement method called MicroM, specifically developed for MSSAs, which utilizes events—the fundamental components of MSSAs— for size measurement [18]. MicroM takes into account the unique characteristics of MSSAs and overcomes the limitations of existing FSM methods. However, the effectiveness of MicroM has been evaluated in different case studies involving new project development but has not yet been assessed in the context of change request requirements.

To address this gap, our study proposes a change size measurement method specifically designed for microservice-based software projects. By introducing a novel approach grounded in counting added, deleted, and modified events, and incorporating the number of affected initial requirements, we aim to support more accurate effort estimation of change requests in MSSA settings. To evaluate the proposed methods, we performed an exploratory case study. This method is intended to better accommodate the complexities of MSSAs, offering a more precise and relevant approach for measuring changes within this architectural paradigm.

The remainder of this paper is structured as follows. Section 2 describes the measurement method. Section 3 summarizes the followed research methodology in this study. Section 4 presents the results. Section 5 concludes the by stating further studies.

## 2    Measurement Method

In this study, we use the MicroM method to measure the size of change requests. MicroM is an objective size measurement method specifically designed for MSSAs [18]. It focuses on the events that form the foundation of microservices, categorizing these events into different abstraction levels of software representations based on architectural characteristics: (1) Functional Level, (2) Architectural Level, and (3) Algorithmic Level (see Fig. 1).

The Functional Level captures events related to user and database interactions. User interaction events include user inputs and outputs, while database interaction events consist of database inputs and outputs. This level abstracts the system behavior between the functional user and the persistent storage.

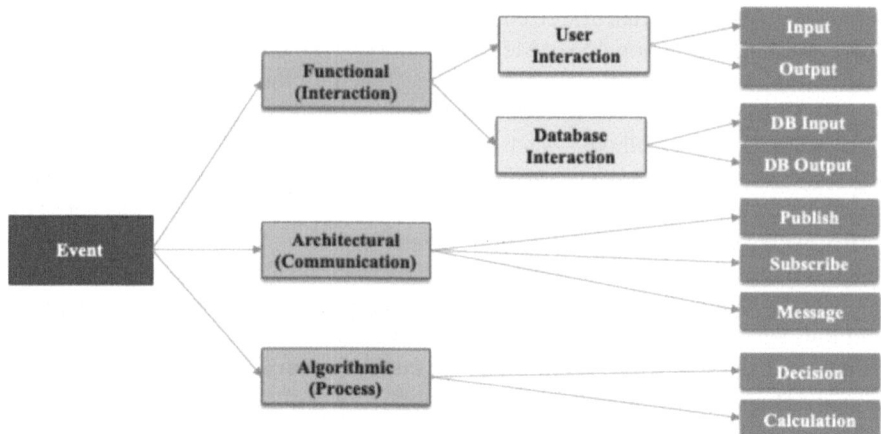

**Fig. 1.** MicroM size measurement method.

The Architectural Level encompasses events related to communication within the system. These include message exchanges between microservices as well as events triggered by publish/subscribe mechanisms in event-driven systems. As this level reflects system design, it assumes that architectural decisions have already been made. It is a distinct abstraction level introduced by MicroM to address the specific communication patterns of MSSAs.

The Algorithmic Level captures processing-related events such as decisions and calculations. This level, introduced by MicroM to address gaps in functional size measurement methods like COSMIC, plays a critical role in representing algorithmic complexity in software systems. Decision events are associated with logic constructs such as "OR", "XOR", and "AND", while calculation events involve tasks like arithmetic operations, filtering, reporting, and file generation.

The MicroM method is designed to measure the size of newly developed MSSA projects. The size of a requirement is determined by the total number of events. Alternatively, the size can be expressed as the sum of events across different abstraction levels.

In the change size measurement method developed in this study, it is assumed that a change can occur in three forms: addition, deletion, or modification. The events affected by the change (added, deleted, or modified) are counted separately within three levels: functional, architectural, and algorithmic (see Fig. 2). The data obtained in this way can be utilized in various forms. The size of a change can be represented by the total number of affected events, or, assuming that changes in each event category have different impacts on effort, effort estimation models can be developed using multiple regression techniques. We also believe that the number of initial requirements affected by the change influences the effort required for a change request. Therefore, in this study, we considered not only the number of added, deleted, and modified events but also the number of affected initial requirements when performing effort estimation. Accordingly, we evaluated the performance of four different regression models in estimating the effort of change requests:

1. Linear regression with total number of events
2. Multiple linear regression with functional, architectural, and algorithmic level events
3. Multiple linear regression with added, deleted, and modified events
4. Multiple linear regression with the number of affected initial requirements, and added, deleted, and modified events

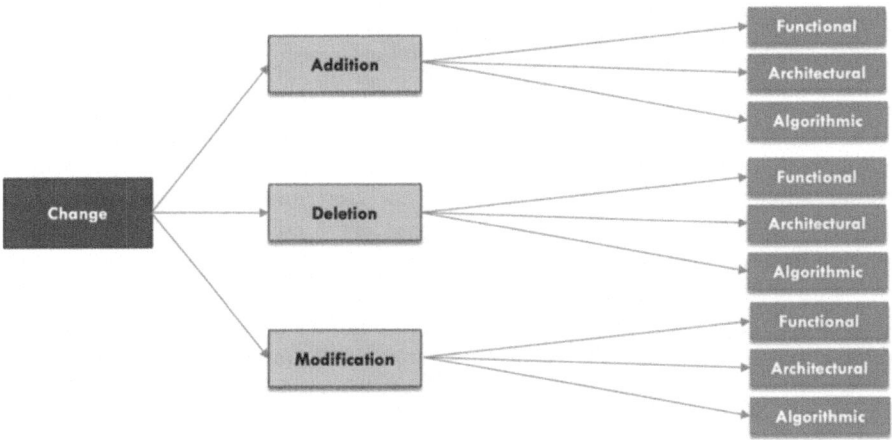

**Fig. 2.** MicroM change measurement method.

## 3   Research Methodology

In this study, we adopted the exploratory case study approach [19]. The design of the case study, along with a description of the case and relevant details, is presented in the following subsections.

### 3.1   Case Study Design

In this study, we conducted an exploratory case study with the aim of developing a method to measure the size of change requests in microservice-based projects. Accordingly, we formulated our research question as follows:

• How can the size of change requests be measured in microservice-based projects?

To answer our research question, we evaluated the success of effort estimation using four different methods that we proposed.

**Case Selection Criteria.** The criteria for selecting a project include that it has been developed using a microservice-based architecture, is completed, contains change requests, has defined requirements, and has recorded effort data for these requirements.

**Data Gathering Technique.** Measurers aimed to keep records of the following project-related data gathered during the case study: (1) the total MicroM size, (2) MicroM size in terms of functional, architectural, and algorithmic levels, (3) MicroM size in terms of addition, deletion, and modification events, (4) the number of initial requirements affected by the change request, and (5) change request effort in person-hours.

**Measurement Plan.** The MicroM size is planned to be measured by two measurers. One of them is from the organization that developed the project, and the other is the researcher who developed the MicroM size measurement method as part of a Ph.D. thesis and evaluated it in various projects. First, the representative from the organization received training on the MicroM method. Then, the measurements were conducted jointly by both measurers. This approach ensured that no assumptions were made about the requirements and that the method was applied correctly.

During the measurement process, the initial requirements affected by the change requests with a determined MicroM size, along with the effort in person-hours, were recorded. After the measurements were completed, effort estimation models were developed using 23 change requests. In the initial models, 5 outlier change requests were identified and excluded from the dataset. These outliers typically involved tasks that were being performed for the first time within the organization and, as a result, exhibited unusually high effort values. It was assumed that the elevated effort in these cases reflected organizational learning curves rather than the intrinsic size of the change, and therefore they were excluded from the modeling. The models were then rebuilt using the remaining 18 change requests.

## 3.2 Case Description

The project in this study is a custom software solution developed for a company engaged in the production and sale of trucks, equipment, and spare parts. The software was designed to manage the company's entire sales process and address challenges caused by fluctuating exchange rates, variable costs, and complex pricing structures. Due to the company's unique operational needs, off-the-shelf products were deemed insufficient, leading to the development of a tailored system. Project requirements were identified using the Event Storming technique, and all tasks were tracked in Notion with detailed descriptions, assignments, and time records.

Following a two-month infrastructure phase, development proceeded through biweekly progress meetings and a structured task workflow: Planning, Development, Review, Merge, and Presentation. Change requests were recorded separately—both during development and after delivery—and linked to original requirements, allowing comparison of initial vs. change-related effort. The project was carried out by a team of one senior and two mid-level developers over five months and remains under active development. The software company, founded in 2013, has over 10 years of experience delivering custom solutions to more than 20 universities, educational institutions, and large enterprises, benefiting from its agile structure and ability to quickly adapt to client needs.

# 4   Results

We developed effort estimation models using four different methods based on 18 non-outlier change requests. These effort estimation models are constructed as follows:

1. Linear regression with total number of events
2. Multiple linear regression with functional, architectural, and algorithmic level events
3. Multiple linear regression with added, deleted, and modified events
4. Multiple linear regression with the number of affected initial requirements, and added, deleted, and modified events

We used Magnitude of Relative Error (MRE), Mean Magnitude of Relative Error (MMRE), and PRED(30) metrics to evaluate the success of the effort estimation models. These results are presented in Table 1.

According to Hastings and Sajeev [20], the models with MMRE less than 0.20 can be considered predictive, while MMRE between 0.20 and 0.50 is acceptable and MMRE greater than 0.50 is not acceptable. In this case, the results indicate that when the MicroM method was applied on its own, it did not achieve acceptable effort estimation—based on the MMRE metric—in either (1) linear or (2) multiple linear regression models. Similarly, based on the PRED(30) results, MicroM also failed to provide good estimations [21]. This is an expected outcome, as the MicroM method was originally developed for use in new development projects based on MSSA.

In this study, we improved effort estimation by applying the proposed principle of counting (3) added, deleted, and modified events. With an MMRE value of 0.35, the model achieved acceptable effort estimation. Although the PRED(30) value also showed improvement, it unfortunately did not indicate a good model.

Finally, in addition to counting added, deleted, and modified events, we proposed (4) including the number of initial requirements affected by the change as an input in the multiple linear regression model. This method yielded the best results. An MMRE of 0.23 indicates a nearly predictive estimation, while a PRED(30) value of 0.78 demonstrates that a good prediction model was achieved. These results suggest that in microservice-based projects, beyond counting added, edited, and deleted events, the number of affected initial requirements is also a significant predictor in regression-based effort estimation. In fact, this is an expected outcome—the more initial requirements a change request affects, the higher its complexity, and consequently, the more effort it requires.

**Table 1.** Analysis results.

| No | Act. Eff. | Total Size | # of Initial Req. | Change-based Size | | | MicroM Size | | | (1) | | (2) | | (3) | | (4) | |
|---|---|---|---|---|---|---|---|---|---|---|---|---|---|---|---|---|---|
| | | | | Add | Modify | Delete | Func | Arch | Alg | Pr. Eff. | MRE | Pr. Eff. | MRE | Pr. Eff. | MRE | Pr. Eff. | MRE |
| C1 | 6 | 13 | 5 | 5 | 4 | 4 | 3 | 8 | 2 | 13.45 | 1.24 | 9.89 | 0.65 | 6.58 | 0.10 | 6.14 | 0.02 |
| C2 | 9 | 13 | 4 | 8 | 5 | 0 | 7 | 4 | 2 | 13.45 | 0.49 | 11.73 | 0.30 | 16.57 | 0.84 | 15.88 | 0.76 |
| C3 | 14 | 8 | 5 | 4 | 4 | 0 | 6 | 0 | 2 | 10.18 | 0.27 | 10.32 | 0.26 | 11.91 | 0.15 | 16.91 | 0.21 |
| C4 | 12.25 | 9 | 1 | 7 | 2 | 0 | 4 | 3 | 2 | 10.83 | 0.12 | 9.59 | 0.22 | 13.04 | 0.06 | 11.00 | 0.10 |
| C5 | 21 | 10 | 5 | 4 | 6 | 0 | 3 | 2 | 5 | 11.49 | 0.45 | 13.58 | 0.35 | 13.63 | 0.35 | 12.87 | 0.39 |
| C6 | 7 | 6 | 1 | 4 | 1 | 1 | 4 | 2 | 0 | 8.87 | 0.27 | 6.18 | 0.12 | 7.76 | 0.11 | 6.85 | 0.02 |
| C7 | 26 | 11 | 3 | 9 | 1 | 1 | 6 | 1 | 4 | 12.14 | 0.53 | 13.73 | 0.47 | 12.51 | 0.52 | 18.78 | 0.28 |
| C8 | 21 | 17 | 2 | 14 | 3 | 0 | 14 | 1 | 2 | 16.06 | 0.24 | 15.71 | 0.25 | 20.55 | 0.02 | 19.76 | 0.06 |
| C9 | 14 | 7 | 5 | 3 | 4 | 0 | 5 | 0 | 2 | 9.53 | 0.32 | 9.67 | 0.31 | 10.96 | 0.22 | 15.84 | 0.13 |
| C10 | 5 | 3 | 1 | 1 | 2 | 0 | 1 | 0 | 2 | 6.91 | 0.38 | 7.07 | 0.41 | 7.34 | 0.47 | 4.58 | 0.08 |
| C11 | 5 | 5 | 1 | 2 | 3 | 0 | 1 | 0 | 4 | 8.22 | 0.64 | 10.29 | 1.06 | 9.15 | 0.83 | 3.63 | 0.27 |
| C12 | 10.5 | 11 | 4 | 6 | 2 | 3 | 11 | 0 | 0 | 12.14 | 0.16 | 10.35 | 0.01 | 7.38 | 0.30 | 10.92 | 0.04 |
| C13 | 9 | 10 | 2 | 8 | 2 | 0 | 7 | 0 | 3 | 11.49 | 0.28 | 12.58 | 0.40 | 13.99 | 0.55 | 15.36 | 0.71 |
| C14 | 3 | 3 | 1 | 1 | 1 | 1 | 0 | 0 | 3 | 6.91 | 1.30 | 8.03 | 1.68 | 4.91 | 0.64 | 3.64 | 0.21 |
| C15 | 8 | 19 | 2 | 13 | 2 | 4 | 15 | 0 | 4 | 17.37 | 1.17 | 19.39 | 1.42 | 12.46 | 0.56 | 8.87 | 0.11 |
| C16 | 16 | 11 | 2 | 8 | 3 | 0 | 8 | 1 | 2 | 12.14 | 0.24 | 11.81 | 0.26 | 14.85 | 0.07 | 13.34 | 0.17 |
| C17 | 10.5 | 10 | 2 | 7 | 3 | 0 | 6 | 0 | 4 | 11.49 | 0.09 | 13.54 | 0.29 | 13.90 | 0.32 | 12.27 | 0.17 |
| C18 | 3 | 4 | 2 | 1 | 1 | 2 | 2 | 1 | 1 | 7.57 | 1.52 | 6.30 | 1.10 | 3.34 | 1.10 | 3.97 | 0.32 |
| MMRE | | | | | | | | | | 0.54 | | 0.53 | | 0.35 | | 0.23 | |
| MdMRE | | | | | | | | | | 0.35 | | 0.33 | | 0.31 | | 0.17 | |
| PRED(30) | | | | | | | | | | 0.44 | | 0.39 | | 0.50 | | 0.78 | |

# 5   Conclusion

In this study, we proposed a method for measuring the size of change requests in MSSAs, building on the MicroM size measurement approach. While MicroM was initially designed for new project development, we extended it to account for change-specific elements such as added, modified, and deleted events across multiple abstraction levels. Additionally, we incorporated the number of affected initial requirements to capture the broader scope of change requests.

Our exploratory case study evaluated four different effort estimation models using regression techniques. The results revealed that models based solely on MicroM size—without further contextualization—did not yield acceptable estimation accuracy. However, when the types of changes (additions, deletions, and modifications) were individually counted, estimation performance improved. The most accurate and predictive model was achieved when the number of affected initial requirements was included alongside change-type event counts, resulting in a model with an MMRE of 0.23 and a PRED(30) value of 0.78.

These findings demonstrate that the effort associated with change requests in MSSA projects is influenced not only by the number of changes but also the extent of their impact on existing requirements. This result is expected. When a change request affects a larger number of initial requirements, it introduces additional complexity in terms of traceability, consistency, and coordination across multiple components. As a result, the effort required to implement such changes increases accordingly.

Practitioners can use this method to make more informed planning decisions by analyzing the specific characteristics of each change request. The approach helps project teams identify which changes are likely to require more effort and adjust their resource allocation accordingly. By focusing on measurable aspects of change, such as events and affected requirements, teams can reduce uncertainty in effort estimation and improve predictability in MSSA environments.

Given the exploratory nature of this study, the findings—though promising—are limited in scope and not suitable for generalization. As the results are based on a single case study with a small dataset, they do not provide sufficient evidence to support broad conclusions. The limited number of data points, a common challenge in empirical software engineering, further restricts the strength of the inferences. To mitigate potential biases, we ensured that the analyzed change tasks were performed by developers with comparable roles and experience levels. To validate and refine the proposed method, future studies should involve larger datasets and multiple case studies conducted in diverse organizational and project contexts.

**Disclosure of Interests.**   The authors have no competing interests to declare that are relevant to the content of this article.

# References

1. Standish Group Chaos Report. T.S.G. International (2020)
2. Beck, K., et al.: Manifesto for Agile Software Development. https://agilemanifesto.org/. Accessed 08 Jul 2023

3. Gencel, C., Demirors, O.: Functional size measurement revisited. ACM Trans. Softw. Eng. Methodol. **17**, 15:1–15:36 (2008). https://doi.org/10.1145/1363102.1363106
4. Ünlü, H., Bilgin, B., Demirors, O.: A survey on organizational choices for microservice-based software architectures. Turk. J. Electr. Eng. Comput. Sci. (2022). https://doi.org/10.3906/elk-2109-84
5. Ünlü, H., Kennouche, D.E., Soylu, G.K., Demirörs, O.: Microservice-based projects in agile world: A structured interview. Inf. Softw. Technol. **165**, 107334 (2024). https://doi.org/10.1016/j.infsof.2023.107334
6. Newman, S.: Building Microservices. O'Reilly Media, Inc. (2021)
7. Ünlü, H., Hacaloglu, T., Küçükateş Ömüral, N., Çalışkanel, N., Leblebici, O., Demirors, O.: An exploratory case study on effort estimation in microservices. In: 2023 49th Euromicro Conference on Software Engineering and Advanced Applications (SEAA) (2023)
8. Hacaloğlu, T., Demirörs, O.: Challenges of using software size in agile software development: a systematic literature review. In: Academic Papers at IWSM Mensura 2018. (2018)
9. Kang, S., Choi, O., Baik, J.: Model-based dynamic cost estimation and tracking method for agile software development. In: 2010 IEEE/ACIS 9th International Conference on Computer and Information Science, pp. 743–748 (2010). https://doi.org/10.1109/ICIS.2010.126
10. Hohman, M.M.: Estimating in actual time [extreme programming]. In: Agile Development Conference (ADC'05), pp. 132–138 (2005). https://doi.org/10.1109/ADC.2005.22
11. Huijgens, H., van Solingen, R.: A replicated study on correlating agile team velocity measured in function and story points. In: Proceedings of the 5th International Workshop on Emerging Trends in Software Metrics, New York, NY, USA, pp. 30–36. Association for Computing Machinery (2014). https://doi.org/10.1145/2593868.2593874
12. Buglione, L., Trudel, S.: Guideline for sizing agile projects with COSMIC. In: Proceedings of the IWSM/MetriKon/Mensura, Stuttgart, Germany (2010)
13. ISO/IEC 19761:2017 - Software Engineering – COSMIC: A Functional Size Measurement Method. International Organization for Standardization (2017)
14. Bonér, J.: Reactive Microservices Architecture. O'Reilly Media, Inc. (2016)
15. Bonér, J.: Reactive Microsystems. O'Reilly Media, Inc. (2017)
16. Unlu, H., Tenekeci, S., Yıldız, A., Demirors, O.: Event oriented vs object oriented analysis for microservice architecture: an exploratory case study. In: 2021 47th Euromicro Conference on Software Engineering and Advanced Applications (SEAA), pp. 244–251 (2021). https://doi.org/10.1109/SEAA53835.2021.00038
17. Hacaloglu, T., Küçükateş Ömüral, N., Kilinc Soylu, G., Demirors, O.: software change size measurement: an exploratory systematic mapping study. In: The 33rd International Workshop on Software Measurement and the 18th International Conference on Software Process and Product Measurement (IWSM-MENSURA 2024) (2024)
18. Ünlü, H.: Microm: a size measurement method for microservice-based architectures (2024)
19. Yin, R.K.: Case Study Research and Applications. Sage (2018)
20. Hastings, T.E., Sajeev, A.S.M.: A vector-based approach to software size measurement and effort estimation. IEEE Trans. Software Eng. **27**, 337–350 (2001). https://doi.org/10.1109/32.917523
21. MacDonell, S.G., Gray, A.R.: A comparison of modeling techniques for software development effort prediction (1998)

# Aligning Experimentation with Product Operations: A Taxonomy for Structuring Experimentation Teams

Nils Stotz[1]([⊠]), Ben Labay[2], Lukas Vermeer[3], and Paul Drews[1]

[1] Institute of Information Systems, Leuphana University, Lüneburg, Germany
nils.stotz@stud.leuphana.de, paul.drews@leuphana.de
[2] Speero, Austin, TX, USA
ben@speero.com
[3] Vista, Delft, The Netherlands
lukas@lukasvermeer.nl

**Abstract.** Organizations increasingly rely on experimentation to drive data-informed decision-making and innovation. While models like the Flywheel offer guidance on scaling, they often assume a fixed operational context without addressing its impact on experimentation practices. This study examines how experimentation team structures interact with an organization's operating model. Based on semi-structured interviews with 19 industry experts, we identified recurring organizational patterns and developed a multi-dimensional taxonomy. Our findings reveal four quadrants defined by team structures (centralized, decentralized, Center of Excellence) and operational models (Product vs. Feature-Management Operating Models). Each quadrant presents distinct challenges and trade-offs. By clarifying these interactions, our results support organizations in evaluating their experimentation maturity and applying targeted changes—such as introducing a Center of Excellence or adjusting operating models—to enhance scalability and alignment.

**Keywords:** Continuous Experimentation · Product Operating Model · Experimentation Program · Center of Excellence

## 1 Introduction

In today's fast-paced and data-rich environment, organizations are increasingly striving to become more data-driven. The ability to make informed decisions based on empirical evidence rather than intuition is a key competitive advantage. However, achieving this transformation is far from straightforward. Many organizations struggle with bridging the gap between aspiration and execution, as the complexity of modern software development often renders requirements unclear in advance [17]. Instead of following a rigid, upfront planning approach, organizations must adopt more flexible and iterative ways to validate their decisions [18].

D. Taibi and D. Smite (Eds.): SEAA 2025, LNCS 16083, pp. 23–38, 2026.
https://doi.org/10.1007/978-3-032-04207-1_3

One of the most promising approaches to addressing this challenge is Continuous Experimentation, where assumptions are tested systematically throughout all stages of the development cycle [12,18]. This method shifts organizations away from reliance on gut feeling and towards an evidence-based decision-making process. By validating hypotheses early and often, companies can mitigate risk, reduce costly missteps, and foster an experiment-driven development culture [17].

The success of companies like Microsoft [19], Google [20] and Booking.com [21] suggests that a well-structured experimentation process can drive innovation, improve customer satisfaction, and enhance business performance. However, despite these success stories, organizations attempting to implement such a model face a set of recurring challenges [6,22].

A significant barrier to widespread adoption lies in the cultural and organizational aspects of experimentation [2]. Beyond the technical and methodological considerations, fostering a culture where teams feel empowered to experiment, learn from failures, and iterate rapidly is crucial. Research has identified that structural aspects—such as team setup, leadership buy-in, and incentives—play a pivotal role in determining the effectiveness of an organization's experimentation efforts [4,6,22].

While prior work has focused on how to structure teams to support experimentation [7,10], there has been comparatively little emphasis on how the operating model influences the ability to experiment at scale. The shift from traditional feature-based models to product operating models, as discussed by contemporary product management thought leaders, represents a fundamental shift in how teams execute [1]. Recent signals indicate that organizations with a product operating model instead of a feature-management operating model experience increased business performance, improved customer engagement, accelerated innovation and higher customer satisfaction [16].

This paper aims to explore the intersection of organizational structures and product operating models in experimentation-driven companies. Specifically, we investigate how different organizational setups interact with operating models and what characteristics define companies at different stages of this journey. This leads us to our core research question:

**RQ 1: How do the organizational structures of an experimentation team interact with the operating model of an organization?**

By addressing this question, we aim to contribute to the understanding of how organizations can effectively integrate experimentation into their strategic and operational frameworks, paving the way for more informed and effective decision-making.

Our research makes two key contributions to the literature on experimentation organizations by addressing limitations in existing frameworks and providing a more comprehensive approach to understanding organizational experimentation.

First, we expose implicit assumptions within established models, such as the Flywheel model [10], which primarily conceptualizes experimentation maturity as a linear progression toward scale. This model, while influential, presumes that organizations follow a standardized trajectory, largely overlooking the diversity of operational conditions and organizational structures that shape experimentation practices. Implicitly, it suggests that companies face similar challenges and evolve through comparable stages, regardless of their strategic goals, technological capabilities, or structural configurations. Our findings challenge this assumption by revealing that organizations encounter unique structural and operational trade-offs that significantly influence their experimentation practices. Rather than progressing along a uniform path, companies must navigate distinct barriers and opportunities shaped by their specific contexts. Making these assumptions explicit enables a more nuanced and context-aware understanding of how organizations embed and scale experimentation.

Second, we introduce a taxonomy that extends existing frameworks by integrating experimentation team structures (centralized, decentralized, Center of Excellence) with operational models (Product Operating Model vs. Feature-Management Operating Model). Previous models primarily focus on the evolution of experimentation capabilities without considering how these capabilities interact with broader organizational structures and operational models. Our dual-axis framework addresses this gap by systematically categorizing organizations into distinct quadrants that highlight the specific challenges and trade-offs inherent to different structural and operational combinations. This classification is essential because it reveals how scalability, effectiveness, and alignment of experimentation practices vary significantly depending on the organizational setup. Additionally, we provide preliminary insights into how companies transition within this framework, offering pathways for improvement that are tailored to their technological maturity, strategic objectives, and cultural readiness. This taxonomy not only advances theoretical understanding but also provides practical guidance for organizations aiming to enhance their experimentation programs in alignment with their broader operational strategies.

## 2  Background

This section outlines the foundational concepts and streams of literature that underpin the study of experimentation in organizations. To understand how companies successfully embed experimentation into their decision-making and innovation processes, it is essential to examine both the structural setup of experimentation teams and the processes through which experiments are conducted and scaled. These two dimensions determine not only how experimentation is integrated into an organization's operating model but also how effectively insights from experiments translate into strategic decisions. This paper focuses on two key streams of literature: experimentation team structures and experimentation processes. The first stream examines how organizations organize their experimentation functions, from centralized teams to decentralized approaches and hybrid models such as Centers of Excellence. The second stream explores the methodologies and frameworks that govern how experiments are designed, executed, and leveraged for decision-making. Together, these streams provide the theoretical grounding necessary to analyze how organizations build sustainable experimentation capabilities, ensuring that teams have both the right structural support and well-defined processes to drive continuous learning and innovation.

## 2.1 Experimentation Team Structure

In modern digital organizations, experimentation is increasingly recognized as a fundamental driver of product innovation and business growth [12]. However, the effectiveness of experimentation is affected by the structure of the teams responsible for running and scaling experiments. Different organizational models influence how experimentation teams function, ranging from centralized to decentralized structures, as well as hybrid models such as Centers of Excellence (CoE) [7]. These structures interact with a company's Operating Model, which defines how teams make decisions, prioritize work, and integrate experimentation into their broader strategy [1]. The Product Operating Model is introduced as a foundational framework for structuring experimentation teams within modern product organizations [1]. In a company driven by a Product Operating Model, product teams are empowered to make data-driven decisions, requiring seamless integration between experimentation capabilities and product development [1]. Organizations transitioning from feature-based structures to product-centric models often restructure their experimentation teams to ensure that experimentation is not an afterthought but a core function of product teams [1]. The Experimentation Growth Model describes how companies mature their experimentation capabilities [5]. At early stages, experimentation is typically ad hoc or managed by a small, centralized team [5]. As organizations scale, they often move toward decentralized structures, where product teams own their experiments but rely on a central platform team for tooling and best practices [5]. The most advanced stage integrates experimentation directly into product development workflows, ensuring rapid iteration and evidence-based decision-making across the company [5]. Leading organizations such as Amazon, Booking.com, and Microsoft have successfully embedded experimentation within their operational frameworks by ensuring that teams have both technical infrastructure and organizational autonomy [7]. The challenges are also described and include cultural resistance, governance complexity, and ensuring the validity of results across multiple teams [6,15]. A critical factor influencing experimentation team structures is whether the company follows a Centralized, Decentralized, or Hybrid (CoE) Model [7]. Centralized teams ensure rigor and governance but may create bottlenecks. Decentralized models empower product teams but risk inconsistent methodologies. Hybrid models, often used in large tech companies, strike a balance by providing central guidance while enabling distributed teams to execute experiments independently [8].

## 2.2   Experimentation Process

The experimentation process in organizations plays a crucial role in ensuring that product development is supported by empirical evidence rather than untested assumptions. A well-structured experimentation process enables companies to systematically test hypotheses, measure their impact, and iteratively improve their products [17]. A model for embedding experimentation at scale is the A/B Testing Flywheel [10], which describes a reinforcing cycle that organizations must establish to sustain and grow their experimentation capabilities. The Flywheel model argues that experimentation success does not come from a single initiative but from a continuous investment in infrastructure, education, and cultural change [10]. As teams conduct more A/B tests and demonstrate measurable business impact, interest in experimentation increases across the organization. This growing interest leads to further investments in tooling and processes, making it easier to run experiments efficiently [10]. Over time, the organization builds momentum, with experimentation becoming an integral part of decision-making rather than an occasional activity [10].

The development of systematic experimentation processes has been explored in other models that provide structured methodologies for organizations at different stages of maturity. The HYPEX Model introduces a hypothesis-driven approach to product development, where new ideas are treated as experiments rather than pre-defined feature requirements [11]. This model is designed to close the feedback loop between product teams and customers by ensuring that every development effort is validated through real-world data [11]. Instead of relying on opinions or intuition, teams implement Minimum Viable Features (MVFs) to test hypotheses, collect data on actual user behavior, and refine their product strategy accordingly. This approach aligns with the RIGHT Model, which emphasizes rapid iteration and high-frequency testing as key principles of continuous experimentation [12]. This model suggests a structured process for integrating experimentation results into decision-making, ensuring that insights from tests directly inform product development cycles [12].

Beyond digital-first companies, structured experimentation must be adapted to more complex environments, such as business-to-business (B2B) and mission-critical systems. The HURRIER Model addresses the specific challenges of experimentation in industries where reliability, compliance, and operational stability are critical [13]. This model ensures that experimentation is conducted in a controlled manner, allowing for iterative learning while mitigating risks associated with large-scale deployments [13]. Similarly, the importance of continuous validation of customer value is highlighted, advocating for an experimentation process that systematically prioritizes features based on real-world impact rather than assumptions [14]. By embedding these structured approaches into their experimentation frameworks, organizations can ensure that A/B testing and other experimental methods evolve from isolated practices into a core capability for driving innovation and strategic decision-making.

# 3  Method

This study employs a qualitative research design, using semi-structured interviews to explore the organizational structures of experimentation teams and their interaction with different operating models. The research follows an inductive approach, aiming to derive insights based on empirical data rather than testing pre-existing hypotheses. Given the complexity of experimentation practices across organizations and the lack of a standardized framework for structuring experimentation teams, a qualitative methodology was chosen to capture diverse perspectives and contextual differences. The study follows best practices in qualitative research, ensuring methodological rigor in data collection, analysis, and interpretation [23].

## 3.1  Data Collection

This study draws on semi-structured interviews with 19 experimentation experts who hold key roles in designing, leading, or scaling experimentation programs within their organizations.[1] To ensure a broad range of perspectives, participants were selected based on their influence over experimentation strategies, with an emphasis on including individuals from various industries, company sizes, and stages of experimentation maturity. This selection approach was aimed at capturing insights from organizations ranging from early-stage adoption to those with fully embedded experimentation programs, providing a comprehensive view of different operational models and team structures. The participant selection process followed a purposeful sampling strategy to enhance the theoretical relevance of the findings. Specifically, we sought to include experts who could provide insights into how organizational structures and operating models interact with experimentation practices. While convenience sampling from existing networks played a role, efforts were made to diversify the sample by including participants from industries such as e-commerce, SaaS, financial services, and consultancy. This approach aimed to achieve theoretical saturation—where new interviews did not yield substantially new insights—rather than numerical representativeness.

The interviews were designed to explore the interaction between experimentation team structures and operational models, focusing on aspects such as organizational characteristics, governance mechanisms, decision-making processes, and challenges in scaling experimentation. A core set of guiding questions was used to ensure consistency while allowing flexibility for participants to elaborate on areas most relevant to their expertise. The semi-structured format facilitated comparability across interviews while allowing for spontaneous insights, particularly regarding unforeseen challenges and organizational trade-offs. The interviews were conducted remotely using platforms such as Zoom and Riverside, typically lasting around 45 min. Following each interview, transcripts were generated using automated transcription tools and manually refined for accuracy.

---

[1] A supplemental file with the interview questions and additional material can be viewed here: https://zenodo.org/records/15824272.

Additionally, two of the authors are recognized subject matter experts in the field of experimentation, contributing approximately 20 years of combined experience. Ben Labay, CEO of Speero, has been consulting companies on scaling experimentation since 2016, while Lukas Vermeer previously served as Director of Experimentation at both Booking.com and now as Senior Director of Product Vista. Their expertise provided valuable context during the data collection process, enhancing the depth of the interviews.

## 3.2   Data Analysis

The collected data was analyzed through an iterative pattern identification process aimed at uncovering recurring themes and developing a structured taxonomy that accurately reflects how experimentation teams interact with broader operational frameworks. The analysis involved several collaborative online sessions where we collectively refined concepts through discussion and validation. The process began with an initial review of all interview transcripts, during which we independently noted recurring themes related to team structures, operational alignment, decision-making processes, and challenges in scaling experimentation. Early in the process, participants frequently described their organizational setup not only by how teams were formally arranged but also by how their ways of working aligned with broader strategic objectives. This observation prompted a closer investigation into how experimentation team structures (centralized, decentralized, Center of Excellence) intersect with operational models (Product Operating Model, Feature-Management Operating Model). Through iterative discussion sessions, we systematically identified patterns across interviews and progressively mapped them to a conceptual framework. This process revealed two critical dimensions influencing experimentation maturity: organizational structure and operating model. The identification of these dimensions was driven by participants' descriptions of how they structured their experimentation programs and aligned them with broader operational models. Participants often described shifts from centralized teams to more decentralized models to enhance agility and responsiveness, or efforts to embed experimentation capabilities within product teams for closer alignment with strategic objectives. Such descriptions clarified that structural and operational alignment were fundamental factors shaping experimentation practices. The construction of the four-quadrant taxonomy resulted from a deliberate process of categorization and comparison. As themes related to structure and operational alignment became increasingly consistent across interviews, we refined our framework by examining how participants described their evolution along these dimensions. The quadrants were not predetermined; rather, they were constructed through a careful process of pattern recognition and categorization, reflecting how companies navigated structural and operational trade-offs. To enhance validity and consistency, we revisited the transcripts with the evolving framework in mind, verifying that the identified themes were adequately supported by the data. This iterative process involved cross-referencing insights from multiple interviews to ensure coherence across participants' descriptions. Additionally, the resulting taxonomy was compared with existing literature to identify similarities, differences, and potential extensions to prior models. As participants often described desired transitions between quadrants to improve their setups, these insights were incorporated into the framework, guiding the inclusion of suggested movements in the findings. The collaborative nature of the analysis, involving repeated discussion and refinement, enhanced the robustness of the findings.

## 4    Findings

### 4.1    Introduction of the Taxonomy

The taxonomy developed in this study provides a structured framework for classifying how organizations structure their experimentation teams and integrate them into their operational frameworks. It is built on two primary dimensions: the structural model of experimentation teams (x-axis) and the operational model governing decision-making (y-axis). The resulting taxonomy is visualized in Fig. 1. These dimensions define how experimentation is executed, governed, and scaled across different organizational contexts. The first dimension, the structural model of experimentation teams, describes how organizations distribute responsibility for experimentation. Three structures are identified. **The centralized model** relies on a dedicated team responsible for executing and analyzing experiments across the organization. This approach ensures methodological rigor and consistency but can create bottlenecks that hinder scalability and speed. **The decentralized model** distributes responsibility across multiple teams, allowing product teams to autonomously design, execute, and analyze experiments. While fostering agility and embedding experimentation into development workflows, this model can face challenges related to governance, knowledge sharing, and maintaining consistency. **The Center of Excellence (CoE) model** offers a hybrid approach where a central team provides best practices, infrastructure, and governance while allowing execution to be distributed. While CoEs are included as one of the three structural models, they are not shown as a distinct quadrant, as they often act as a hybrid or transitional configuration that supports scalability during structural change. The second dimension, the operational model governing decision-making, defines how experimentation is integrated into organizational processes. Two dominant approaches are identified. **The product operating model** emphasizes iterative, continuous development, where teams operate autonomously with experimentation embedded into decision-making processes. Closely aligned with agile methodologies, this approach prioritizes rapid iteration, decentralized ownership, and data-driven learning. **The feature management operating model**, by contrast, relies on structured, milestone-driven projects with predefined objectives. Experimentation here often serves as a validation tool rather than a continuous driver of decision-making, constrained by rigid frameworks and upfront planning. These two dimensions interact to define distinct approaches to experimentation governance and execution, providing a framework to assess current practices and consider improvements. Understanding how experimentation team structures align with operational models allows organizations to evaluate their experimentation maturity, identify inefficiencies, and explore strategies for enhancing innovation and business outcomes.

## 4.2   The Four Quadrants

The taxonomy yields four quadrants that represent distinct ways in which organizations structure and integrate experimentation within their broader operational models. Each quadrant is defined by the interaction between the structural model of the experimentation team and the overarching operating model that governs how work is organized and decisions are made. The quadrants reflect different levels of centralization or decentralization in experimentation execution, as well as differences in how embedded experimentation is within the broader operational workflows of the organization.

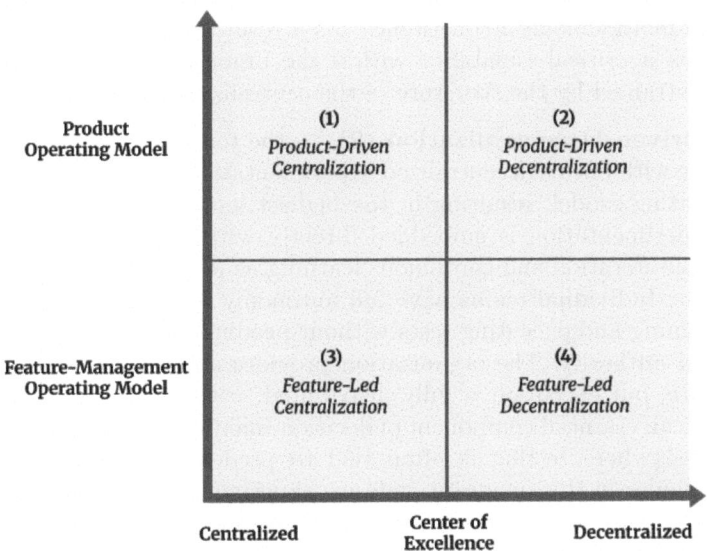

**Fig. 1.** Multi-dimensional taxonomy of experimentation configurations. The x-axis reflects team structures and the y-axis shows operational models. The Center of Excellence represents a hybrid or transitional structure across the configurations.

**Product-Driven Centralization (1):** In the top-left quadrant, organizations also maintain a centralized experimentation function, but in contrast to the third quadrant, they operate under a product-driven model that emphasizes iterative learning and continuous product evolution. Here, the centralized experimentation team plays a key role in supporting data-driven decision-making across multiple product teams, ensuring that experimentation insights are systematically incorporated into ongoing development efforts. Unlike in feature-driven organizations, where experimentation serves primarily as a validation mechanism, companies in this quadrant use experimentation more proactively as a way to shape product direction. The centralized team provides expertise, governance, and tooling, but product teams actively seek to leverage experimentation to inform their decisions at various stages of the development process. Experimentation is deeply embedded in workflows, with product teams frequently collaborating with the centralized function to test hypotheses, refine product features, and optimize customer experiences. However, despite the product-driven approach, the dependence on a single, centralized experimentation function creates operational bottlenecks, as teams must rely on limited resources to execute their tests. While experimentation is positioned as a key enabler of product success, the constraint of centralization means that not all teams can run as many experiments as they would like, leading to prioritization challenges. The experimentation team itself often becomes an internal consultant to multiple stakeholders, working to balance the needs of different product teams while maintaining governance and methodological consistency. As a result, experimentation is widely recognized as a critical capability within the organization, but its execution remains constrained by the structure of the centralized model.

**Product-Driven Decentralization (2):** In the top-right quadrant, organizations operate with both a decentralized experimentation structure and a product-driven operating model, resulting in the highest level of experimentation integration. Experimentation is embedded directly within cross-functional teams, enabling rapid iteration and continuous learning as part of the product development process. Individual teams have full autonomy over their experimentation efforts, designing and executing tests without needing approval or support from a centralized authority. The organization provides a common experimentation infrastructure, but execution is fully distributed, with teams leveraging experimentation as an essential component of decision-making. Unlike in feature-driven organizations, where testing is often tied to predefined milestones, product-driven companies in this quadrant embrace experimentation as an ongoing process, using data to refine and optimize products continuously. Experimentation is not a separate function but rather an intrinsic part of how the organization operates, with product managers, designers, and engineers all playing an active role in formulating and testing hypotheses. The decentralized model ensures that teams can move quickly, running experiments at scale without bottlenecks or resource constraints. However, to prevent methodological inconsistencies, organizations in this quadrant often invest heavily in shared best practices, training programs, and internal governance structures that provide guidance without enforcing rigid controls. The widespread adoption of experimentation fosters a strong culture of data-driven decision-making, where teams rely on empirical evidence to guide product evolution rather than intuition or hierarchical decision-making. This quadrant represents the most mature state of experimentation within an organization, where experimentation is not just a tool but a fundamental driver of innovation and competitive advantage.

**Feature-Led Centralization (3):** In the bottom-left quadrant experimentation is centralized within a single team while the broader organization operates under a feature-management-driven approach. This configuration results in an experimentation function that primarily serves as a support entity rather than a fully integrated part of the product development lifecycle. The centralized experimentation team is responsible for designing, executing, and analyzing experiments across multiple business units, acting as a methodological gatekeeper that ensures statistical rigor and consistency. Since the organization follows a structured feature-management model, experimentation is typically introduced at predefined stages within the development cycle, often as a means of validating key decisions before major launches or investments. This model leads to a highly structured experimentation process where tests are scoped according to specific business questions, rather than being an ongoing driver of iterative product development. Experimentation requests generally come from other teams and must be prioritized within a backlog, with execution dependent on the availability of the centralized team. As a result, experimentation tends to be constrained by project timelines, meaning that tests must align with pre-planned initiatives rather than being used as an exploratory mechanism. This setup often results in experimentation being used more for risk mitigation than for continuous innovation, as the feature-based nature of the organization dictates that most initiatives move forward regardless of the insights generated by experimentation.

**Feature-Led Decentralization (4):** In the bottom-right quadrant, organizations adopt a decentralized approach to experimentation but continue to operate within a feature-management framework. In this configuration, experimentation capabilities are distributed across multiple teams, allowing individual business units or product teams to run their own experiments independently. However, despite the decentralized execution of experimentation, the overarching operating model remains feature-driven, meaning that teams conduct tests within predefined project scopes rather than engaging in continuous, strategic experimentation. Each team has its own experimentation resources, either in the form of dedicated analysts or embedded experimentation specialists, who design and run tests tailored to the needs of their specific projects. Unlike in organizations where experimentation is centralized, there is no single governing body overseeing methodological consistency, leading to variation in experimentation maturity across teams. Some teams may have well-developed experimentation practices, while others may lack the necessary expertise to conduct rigorous testing, resulting in inconsistent methodologies and varying levels of confidence in results. Since the organization follows a feature-management approach, the role of experimentation remains somewhat constrained, as testing efforts are often planned around major launches or initiatives rather than being a continuous and strategic practice. While the decentralized structure allows for greater autonomy in running experiments, the absence of centralized oversight means that knowledge sharing is limited, and best practices may not be systematically enforced. The lack of a unifying experimentation infrastructure can also create inefficiencies, as different teams may use different tools, methodologies, or success criteria, leading to fragmentation in how experimentation insights are leveraged across the organization.

## 4.3   Potential Movement

The taxonomy presented in this study illustrates how companies operate within different configurations, but these structures are not static. While the **Product-Driven Decentralization Quadrant (2)** is the most mature and effective model for embedding experimentation as a strategic function, companies do not always follow the same path to reach this state. Organizations transition between quadrants depending on their starting point, growth stage, and strategic objectives. These movements are often shaped by leadership philosophy, organizational complexity, and the degree to which experimentation is integrated as a strategic function. Many companies start their experimentation journey in the **Product-Driven Centralization Quadrant (1)** due to their centralized structures and reliance on a Product Operating Model. Organizations in this quadrant have a strong product-centric mindset, and when they decide to decentralize experimentation capabilities across teams, they often progress directly to the **Product-Driven Decentralization Quadrant (2)**. This horizontal movement is facilitated by maintaining the product-centric model while distributing decision-making power and embedding experimentation into autonomous teams. In such cases, companies benefit from their initial alignment with iterative product development practices, making the transition to decentralized experimentation smoother and more effective. However, not all companies manage to progress horizontally. Some move downward from the **Product-Driven Centralization Quadrant (1)** to the **Feature-Led Centralization Quadrant (3)** as they grow and encounter scaling challenges. This descent often results from efforts to introduce structure and governance through a feature-management-driven operational model. While this approach provides standardization, it shifts experimentation away from continuous learning toward validation, making further progress more challenging. Once in the **Feature-Led Centralization Quadrant (3)**, organizations frequently struggle to achieve the ideal state of the **Product-Driven Decentralization Quadrant (2)**. Instead, they often attempt to decentralize experimentation within a feature-management framework, moving to the **Feature-Led Decentralization Quadrant (4)**. The **Feature-Led Decentralization Quadrant (4)** was rarely mentioned, as it represents a decentralized setup constrained by a feature-management-driven operational model. Organizations in this quadrant often find their experimentation efforts fragmented and lacking strategic alignment. Moving from this state to the **Product-Driven Decentralization Quadrant (2)** is particularly difficult because the underlying operational model does not prioritize experimentation as a strategic function. Without shifting to a product-centric mindset, companies in this quadrant face significant obstacles in embedding experimentation within broader decision-making processes. Organizations do not always transition directly from centralized to fully decentralized structures. In many cases, the Center of Excellence (CoE) model serves as an important transitional configuration, especially for organizations seeking to scale experimentation while maintaining governance and methodological consistency. For example, companies moving from **Product-Driven Centralization (1)** toward **Product-Driven Decentralization (2)** often adopt a CoE to facilitate capability-building, tooling standardization, and internal education before full decentralization. Similarly, organizations in the **Feature-Led Centralization Quadrant (3)** may introduce a CoE as a step toward enabling decentralized execution while retaining quality control. While the CoE is not depicted as a separate quadrant in our taxonomy, it operates as a structural overlay—supporting transitions by bridging centralized governance with distributed execution. The **Product-Driven Decentralization Quadrant (2)** represents the most mature state, where companies operate with decentralized experimentation within a Product Operating Model. Organizations that reach this state have typically achieved a delicate balance between autonomy and governance, where experimentation is integrated deeply into strategic decision-making. Maintaining coherence across decentralized teams requires continuous investment in frameworks, knowledge sharing, and leadership development. However, the transition to this state is often complex and varies significantly depending on the starting point. Effective transitions are those where experimentation is not only redistributed across teams but also embedded within the organization's strategic decision-making processes.

## 5  Discussion and Conclusion

### 5.1  Contributions to Research

This study advances prior research on the organizational setup of experimentation programs by challenging foundational assumptions within existing frameworks and introducing a novel taxonomy that addresses the interplay between experimentation team structures and operational models.

First, we critically examine implicit assumptions within established frameworks such as the A/B Testing Flywheel Model [10]. While the Flywheel Model offers a robust framework for scaling experimentation through increased volume, investment, and reduced execution costs, it implicitly assumes that experimentation becomes more integrated into decision-making processes as volume scales. Our findings challenge this assumption by demonstrating that without structured team configurations, governance mechanisms, and alignment with overarching product development processes, increased experimentation volume alone does not yield meaningful improvements in decision-making. This insight highlights a crucial oversight: frameworks like the Flywheel Model are most applicable to organizations operating under a Product Operating Model [1], where continuous and autonomous product development aligns well with scaling experimentation which corresponds to the Product-Driven Decentralization Quadrant (2) in our framework. However, many organizations operate under alternative models, such as Feature-Management Models or hybrid approaches, where centralized experimentation efforts can conflict with broader strategic objectives. Our work reveals that the Flywheel Model's recommendations are often less applicable to companies whose organizational structures differ significantly from the idealized Product Operating Model, underscoring a critical gap in its applicability.

Second, we contribute to the literature by introducing a multi-dimensional taxonomy that systematically integrates experimentation team structures (centralized, decentralized, Center of Excellence) with operational models (Product Operating Model vs. Feature-Management Model). Unlike prior frameworks that focus narrowly on team configuration or process maturity, our taxonomy categorizes organizations across two intersecting dimensions, highlighting the specific challenges and trade-offs associated with different structural and operational combinations. This structured framework addresses a significant gap in the literature by acknowledging that scalability and effectiveness in experimentation are contingent upon alignment between organizational structure and operational model. By mapping organizations into distinct quadrants, our approach offers practical guidance for companies aiming to refine and scale their experimentation practices according to their specific needs and readiness for experimentation. Our findings also underscore persistent barriers to effective experimentation adoption, including structural misalignment, governance bottlenecks, and leadership incentives. Recognizing these obstacles highlights the need for experimentation to be embedded within empowered product teams rather than isolated optimization or analytics units. This research emphasizes that organizations transitioning from Feature-Management Models to Product Operating Models often encounter friction when experimentation remains centralized, further validating the need for distributed ownership of experimentation.

Overall, our work contributes to a deeper understanding of how organizational structures and operational models influence experimentation maturity.

## 5.2   Practical Contributions

This research provides a structured taxonomy that enables organizations to assess and refine their experimentation capabilities by understanding how different team structures interact with operational models. By categorizing experimentation teams as centralized, decentralized, or operating within a Center of Excellence, and linking them to either a product-led or feature-driven operating model, organizations can identify their current state and make informed strategic decisions to optimize their experimentation practices.

The findings offer practical guidance for companies aiming to scale experimentation while maintaining methodological rigor. Organizations with centralized models can use these insights to gradually decentralize and empower product teams, whereas those with decentralized models can implement governance mechanisms to ensure consistency and reliability. The taxonomy serves as a diagnostic tool for leaders to align experimentation efforts with broader business goals, ensuring that experimentation is not just a validation step but a core driver of product innovation. Additionally, this research provides actionable insights for experimentation platform teams, consultants, and decision-makers, helping them establish best practices, design scalable infrastructures, and embed experimentation as an integral part of the product development lifecycle.

## 5.3   Limitations and Future Research

The exploratory nature of this study required a flexible, qualitative approach aimed at developing a taxonomy reflecting how experimentation teams interact with broader operational models. While well-suited for uncovering complex relationships, this approach introduces several limitations. First, the reliance on semi-structured interviews means findings are based on self-reported data, which may not fully reflect actual practices. To mitigate this, we used collaborative analysis through repeated discussions to enhance consistency, though the absence of formal triangulation remains a limitation. Future research could strengthen validity through independent coding, validation workshops, or triangulation with additional data sources. The taxonomy was developed through iterative theme identification without formal coding or inter-rater reliability checks. Although discussion-based refinement and comparison with existing literature supported internal consistency, the lack of structured analysis may limit replicability. Future studies could apply formal qualitative techniques, such as thematic coding with inter-rater reliability. Additionally, the authors' domain expertise may have influenced interpretation. While collaboration helped minimize bias, involving external researchers or using blinded analysis could improve objectivity. This study focused primarily on enterprise-level organizations with mature experimentation practices. Its applicability to startups, regulated sectors, or non-tech industries remains uncertain. Future research could expand the sample scope to improve generalizability. Finally, our findings reflect a specific moment in time, whereas operating models continue to evolve. Longitudinal or quantitative follow-up studies could provide insights into how organizations transition across quadrants over time. Despite these limitations, the taxonomy provides a valuable foundation for understanding and optimizing experimentation structures, offering practical insights and directions for further research.

# References

1. Cagan, M.: Transformed: Moving to the Product Operating Model. Wiley (2024)
2. Anderson, K., Visser, D., Mannen, J.-W., Jiang, Y., van Deursen, A.: Challenges in applying continuous experimentation: a practitioners' perspective. In: 44th International Conference on Software Engineering: Software Engineering in Practice (ICSE-SEIP), Pittsburgh, PA, USA, 21–29 May 2022 (2022)
3. Fabijan, A., Dmitriev, P., Holmström Olsson, H., Bosch, J.: Online controlled experimentation at scale: an empirical survey on the current state of A/B testing. In: Proceedings of the 44th Euromicro Conference on Software Engineering and Advanced Applications (SEAA), pp. 68–77 (2018)
4. Quin, F., Weyns, D., Galster, M., Silva, C.C.: A/B testing: a systematic literature review (2023). arXiv preprint arXiv:2308.04929
5. Fabijan, A., et al.: Experimentation growth: evolving trustworthy A/B testing capabilities in online software companies. J. Softw. Evol. Process (2018)
6. Gupta, S., Kohavi, R., Tang, D., Vermeer, L.: Top challenges from the first practical online controlled experiments summit. ACM SIGKDD Explor. Newsl. (2019)

7. Thomke, S.: Experimentation Works: The Surprising Power of Business Experiments. Harvard Business Review Press (2020)
8. Yaman, S.G., Munezero, M., Münch, J., Fagerholm, F., Syd, O.: Introducing continuous experimentation in large software-intensive product and service organizations. J. Syst. Softw. (2017)
9. Gioia, D.A., Corley, K.G., Hamilton A.L.: Seeking qualitative rigor in inductive research. Org. Res. Methods **16**(1), 15–31 (2013)
10. Fabijan, A., Dmitriev, P., Arai, B., Vermeer, L.: It takes a flywheel to Fly: kick-starting and growing the A/B testing momentum at scale. In: SEAA Conference (2021)
11. Olsson, H.H., Bosch, J.: The HYPEX model: from opinions to data-driven software development (2014)
12. Fagerholm, F., Mäenpää, H., Münch, J., Sanchez Guinea, A.: The RIGHT model for continuous experimentation. J. Syst. Softw. (2017)
13. Mattos, D.I., Dakkak, A., Bosch, J., Holmström Olsson, H.: The HURRIER process for experimentation in business-to-business mission-critical systems (2021)
14. Olsson, H.H., Bosch, J.: Towards continuous validation of customer value (2015)
15. Bojinov, I., Gupta, S.: Online experimentation: benefits, operational and methodological challenges, and scaling guide. Harvard Data Sci. Rev. (2022)
16. Chawla, A., Harrysson, M., Mayer, H., Sinha, M.: The bottom-line benefit of the product operating model. McKinsey and Company (2023). https://www.mckinsey.com/capabilities/mckinsey-digital/our-insights/the-bottom-line-benefit-of-the-product-operating-model
17. Münch, J., Lindgren, E.: Raising the odds of success: the current state of experimentation in product development. Inf. Softw. Technol. (2016)
18. Fagerholm, F., Guinea, A.S., Mäenpää, H., Münch, J.: Building blocks for continuous experimentation. In: Proceedings of the 1st International Workshop on Rapid Continuous Software Engineering (RCoSE 2014), Hyderabad, India, 3 June 2014, pp. 26–35 (2014)
19. Li, L., Kim, J.Y., Zitouni, I.: Toward predicting the outcome of an A/B experiment for search relevance. In: Proceedings of the Eighth ACM International Conference on Web Search and Data Mining (WSDM 2015), pp. 37–46. Association for Computing Machinery, New York (2015)
20. Tang, D., Agarwal, A., O'Brien, D., Meyer, M.: Overlapping experiment infrastructure: more, better, faster experimentation. In: Proceedings 16th Conference on Knowledge Discovery and Data Mining, pp. 17–26 (2010)
21. Kaufman, R.L., Pitchforth, J., Vermeer, L.: Democratizing online controlled experiments at Booking.com, arXiv Preprint. arXiv:1710.08217, pp. 1–7 (2017)
22. Auer, F., Ros, R., Kaltenbrunner, L., Runeson, P., Felderer, M.: Controlled experimentation in continuous experimentation: knowledge and challenges. Inf. Softw. Technol. **134**, 106551 (2021)
23. Runeson, P., Höst, M.: Guidelines for conducting and reporting case study research in software engineering. Empir. Softw. Eng. **14**(2), 131–164 (2008)

# Socio-Technical Well-Being of Quantum Software Communities: An Overview on Community Smells

Stefano Lambiase$^{(\boxtimes)}$ (iD), Manuel De Stefano (iD), Fabio Palomba (iD),
Filomena Ferrucci (iD), and Andrea De Lucia (iD)

University of Salerno, Fisciano, SA, Italy
`{slambiase,madestefano,fpalomba,fferrucci,adelucia}@unisa.it`

**Abstract.** Quantum computing has gained significant attention due to its potential to solve computational problems beyond the capabilities of classical computers. With major corporations and academic institutions investing in quantum hardware and software, there has been a rise in the development of quantum-enabled systems, particularly within open-source communities. However, despite the promising nature of quantum technologies, these communities face critical socio-technical challenges, including the emergence of socio-technical anti-patterns known as community smells. These anti-patterns, prevalent in open-source environments, have the potential to negatively impact both product quality and community health by introducing technical debt and amplifying architectural and code smells. Despite the importance of these socio-technical factors, there remains a scarcity of research investigating their influence within quantum open-source communities. This work aims to address this gap by providing a first step in analyzing the socio-technical well-being of quantum communities through a cross-sectional study. By understanding the socio-technical dynamics at play, it is expected that foundational knowledge can be established to mitigate the risks associated with community smells and ensure the long-term sustainability of open-source quantum initiatives.

**Keywords:** Quantum Software Enginering · Socio-Technical Aspects · Community Smells · Open Source Communities

## 1 Introduction

In recent years, *quantum computing*, a field of computer science based on quantum theory, has gained significant attention in both research and industry. Quantum software technologies are increasingly adopted for their potential to solve computational problems beyond the capabilities of classical computers [13,16]. As a result, major companies like IBM and Google have invested heavily in quantum hardware, offering users access to resources for experimentation and development. This has enabled the creation of *quantum-enabled systems* that

D. Taibi and D. Smite (Eds.): SEAA 2025, LNCS 16083, pp. 39–56, 2026.
https://doi.org/10.1007/978-3-032-04207-1_4

integrate quantum software into their operations, offering significant benefits for software development. For example, the exponential increase in processing power from quantum computing [43] could lead to higher-quality software products, while *quantum machine learning (QML)* supports deeper analysis of large, complex datasets, advancing both machine learning and scientific research.

To democratize access to this transformative technology, the field of *quantum software engineering (QSE)* has emerged [19, 23–25]. Since the publication of the Talavera Manifesto, researchers have been actively designing and implementing advanced quantum software applications that leverage the computational capabilities of quantum computers [42]. In parallel, significant efforts have been made to keep quantum software development largely an open-source practice [26, 27, 31, 39]. This approach is reinforced by academic studies that explore this phenomenon from different perspectives [7, 31]. An important observation is that today, it can be observed that the majority of the community involved in quantum software development operates within open-source contexts, as evidenced by the numerous repositories and contributors across various collaboration platforms [26, 27, 31, 39].

However, the advantages of open-source activities come with significant socio-technical challenges. Extensive research has examined the socio-technical dynamics within open-source communities, resulting in the identification and classification of various socio-technical anti-patterns, which highlight problems in the organizational and collaborative structures of these communities [5, 20, 33, 35]. These issues can have serious consequences, potentially leading to critical project failures and, in the worst scenarios, the death of the community. Indeed, software development, by its nature, is a socio-technical activity [4, 14, 28], involving stakeholders from diverse backgrounds who collaborate on innovative technologies. Poor management of this diversity can lead to subtle, often unnoticed social problems, eventually contributing to what is termed *social debt*, the hidden costs of maintaining a development community with suboptimal dynamics [35]. Researchers' work on identifying and addressing these problems has led to the concept of *community smells*, socio-technical anti-patterns (e.g., excessive formality) and behavioral patterns (e.g., repeated condescension or sudden departures) that can exacerbate social debt [34, 36]. These anti-patterns should not be underestimated. Research has demonstrated that community smells, particularly in open-source environments, have the potential to significantly harm both the community and the product. For instance, they can negatively impact product quality and introduce technical debt through the amplification of both architectural [32] and code smells [20, 35].

Given that quantum software development is primarily conducted as an open-source activity, it can be argued that quantum communities are not immune to socio-technical anti-patterns like community smells. As a result, these communities may face socio-technical challenges that could impede their progress, which is particularly crucial during this pivotal phase of technological innovation that quantum computing and development are experiencing. Despite the relevance of these concerns, also reported by relevant literature [10, 31], **studies specifically**

**investigating the socio-technical dimensions of quantum open-source communities are entirely absent.** This lack of research is problematic for several reasons. First, without socio-technical insights, it becomes difficult to identify and address challenges that could slow the development and adoption of quantum technologies, which are heavily dependent on collaborative efficiency. Second, the absence of research in this area limits the ability of community leaders to foster inclusive and sustainable environments, potentially leading to the exclusion of diverse talents that are vital for innovation. Finally, as quantum technologies continue to grow rapidly, unresolved community smells risk accumulating into social debt, which could increase long-term project costs and hinder the scalability of open-source quantum initiatives.

To address the limitations mentioned above, we aimed to provide a first step into the investigation of the socio-technical well-being of quantum software communities by means of a statistical overview. By doing so, we aimed to depict the current situation of open-source communities developing quantum-enabled projects to put foundational knowledge and reasons for ulterior works in such a context. It is reasonable that this knowledge is essential: as highlighted earlier, the presence of socio-technical anti-patterns (like community smells) has been correlated with, and shown to influence, the emergence of other issues not only of a social nature but also strictly technological (such as architectural and code smells [20,32,35]). These issues have the potential to undermine a software community, significantly limiting, and in some cases completely nullifying its impact.

To achieve our goal, we carried out a *cross-sectional study* [11,38], which is a type of research designed to assess and illustrate essential traits of a population at a particular moment in time. Such studies offer a snapshot of the occurrence of a disease or condition (community smells) and the spread of various factors among a population (communities developing quantum-enabled systems).

## 2   Background and Related Work

This section describes the background and related work that is the foundation for our contributions.

### 2.1   Quantum Computing and Quantum Software Communities

Quantum computing is a field within computer science that leverages the principles of quantum theory, specifically applying quantum mechanics to perform computations [13,16]. Unlike classical computing, which relies on bits that take binary values (zero or one), quantum computing uses qubits, which can exist in a superposition of both zero and one states simultaneously. Quantum gates, which perform unitary transformations, are used to manipulate quantum information. Quantum programming languages manage both classical and quantum data using registers, and quantum programs are represented as quantum circuits, where gates are applied in a specific sequence. These circuits are executed on either real quantum hardware or simulators, with the results measured and stored in classical registers.

Quantum Software Engineering (QSE) is an emerging research field that has been formalized through the *Talavera Manifesto* [24], which established the foundational principles for this discipline. In extending this contribution, Piattini et al. [25] focused on defining specific research domains within QSE. They identified four areas: the design of quantum-hybrid systems, testing methodologies, assessing the quality of quantum programs, and re-engineering classical-quantum information systems. A key point raised in their work is the need to bridge the knowledge gap between quantum computer scientists and traditional software engineers, as collaboration between these fields is essential for advancing QSE.

Building on this work, De Stefano et al. [9] conducted a systematic mapping study to reveal the current state of research in QSE. Their study [9] found that the primary focus of QSE research has been on software testing, highlighting a concentration of efforts in this area. However, their findings also suggest the need for a more balanced distribution of research efforts across other QSE domains. In particular, socio-technical aspects within quantum software development communities and software engineering management have received less attention, despite growing recognition of their importance. Both contributors [39] and researchers [10,31] have called for increased research in these areas to address the unique challenges posed by the interdisciplinary nature of quantum software development.

## 2.2 Socio-Technical Well-Being—Community Smells

Software development and its engineering are inherently socio-technical activities. To assess the influence of social dynamics on software development, researchers—drawing on the well-established notion of Technical Debt [20,21]—introduced the concept of *Social Debt*, which refers to the unforeseen costs associated with sub-optimal decisions in collaboration, communication, and team management [5,35]. Additionally, in an effort to further characterize and identify the sources of Social Debt, researchers proposed the concept of *Community Smell*, defined as socio-technical anti-patterns that may negatively impact the socio-technical well-being of a software development team, potentially leading to the accumulation of Social Debt [5].

The research explored the relationship between community smells and various aspects of software development. Notably, Palomba et al. [20] examined the connection between community smells and code smells, their product-oriented counterpart, demonstrating that community smells are among the primary factors influencing the emergence of code smells. Tamburri et al. [33] conducted a large-scale study across 60 open-source ecosystems to assess (1) the diffusion of community smells and (2) their perceived impact by developers, revealing that community smells are both widespread and perceived to affect the evolution and sustainability of software communities. These findings indicate that socio-technical antipatterns can influence maintenance and evolution in two ways: by directly increasing social debt (i.e., increasing costs related to socio-technical problems) and by affecting product-related factors, thereby increasing techni-cal debt. Furthermore, two mining studies conducted by Catolino et al. [6] and Lambiase et al. [17] revealed correlations between the emergence of community smells and gender diversity (in the former) and cultural heterogeneity (in the latter).

Regarding detection methods, Palomba and Tamburri [37] proposed a machine learning approach for predicting community smells based on socio-technical metrics, achieving promising results with an F-measure of 78%. Addi-tionally, Almarimi et al. [2] introduced a multi-label learning model using genetic algorithms to detect ten community smells and developed the community smells detection tool CSDETECTOR [1]. Building on Almarimi et al.'s work [1,2], Voria et al. [40] developed CADOCS, a conversational agent capable of detecting ten community smells from a software repository and proposing refactoring strate-gies for some of them. Moreover, Advanced network models, such as the MOGen higher-order network model, have been developed to detect community smells by analyzing complex relationships and interaction patterns within software teams [12].

**☰ Related Work: Summary and Research Gap.**

The effort to keep quantum computing tied to open source has not been matched by efforts to understand the socio-technical challenges of these com-munities. This gap limits contributors' ability to assess community health and restricts QSE researchers from exploring a well-established area of soft-ware engineering.

# 3    Cross-Sectional Study—An Overview

This section provides the reader with basic knowledge of observational stud-ies [38,41]. For space limitations, we suggest reading the work of Saarimäki et al. [29,30] to gain a better understanding of the method.

## 3.1    Cross-Sectional Studies

*Observational studies*, including *cross-sectional studies*, are widely used in epi-demiology to examine associations between exposures and outcomes without intervention [38,41]. The main types include *cohort, case-control*, and *cross-sectional* designs [38,41].

*Cross-sectional studies* capture population characteristics at a single time point, providing a snapshot of prevalence and exposure distribution [41]. Data are collected simultaneously from all participants, enabling efficient assessment of existing conditions. *Prevalence*—the proportion of individuals with a given condition—is central to these studies [41]. The *Prevalence Odds Ratio (POR)* quantifies the association between an exposure and a condition by comparing the odds of exposure in affected versus unaffected individuals [38,41].

Cross-sectional studies are time- and cost-efficient and useful for estimating prevalence and generating hypotheses [38,41]. However, they cannot determine causality or temporal order and may be affected by biases from self-reported data.

**Table 1.** Community Smells investigated in our study.

| Community Smell | Definition |
| --- | --- |
| Organizational Silo (OSE) | Siloed areas of the community that do not communicate, except through one or two of their members. |
| Black Cloud (BCE) | Information overload due to a lack of structured communications or cooperation governance. |
| Radio Silence (RS) | One interposes herself into every formal interaction across more sub-communities with little flexibility to introduce other channels. |
| Prima Donnas (PDE) | A team member is unwilling to respect external changes from other team members. |
| Sharing Villainy (SV) | Cause of a lack of information exchange, team members share essential knowledge such as outdated, wrong, and unconfirmed information. |
| Organizational Skirmish (OS) | A eisalignment between different expertise levels of individuals involved in the project leads to dropped productivity and affects the project's timeline and cost. |
| Solution Defiance (SD) | The development community presents different levels of cultural and experience background, leading to the division of the community into similar subgroups with completely conflicting opinions. |
| Truck Factor Smell (TF) | Risk of significant knowledge loss due to the turnover of developers resulting from the fact that project information and knowledge are concentrated in a minority of the developers. |
| Unhealthy Interaction (UI) | Long delays in stakeholder communications cause slow, light and brief conversations and discussions. |
| Toxic Communication (TC) | Communications between developers are subject to toxic conversations and negative sentiments containing unpleasant, anger or even conflicting opinions towards various issues that people discuss. |

## 3.2   Mining Software Repositories as Observational Studies

The Software Engineering research community has seen a significant increase in studies that use mining software repositories (MSR), with the rise in popularity of online code repository platforms like GitHub. This has led to the introduction of rules of thumb, highlighting common pitfalls [15] to improve the quality of these studies and their outcomes.

However, it is important to note that these studies cannot provide causal explanations for observed phenomena, despite their usefulness and straightforward execution. To address this limitation, Saarimäki et al. [29,30] recommended the adoption of observational studies, particularly cohort studies, which offer the highest level of scientific evidence.

In the context of QSE, a relatively emerging discipline with limited guidelines and tools for investigating socio-technical issues, a cross-sectional study is justified for several reasons. Firstly, guidelines for MSR studies are somewhat limited [29], and pitfalls abound [15]. Secondly, in the field of QSE, socio-technical aspects have not been extensively explored [9]. A cross-sectional study hence represents a pragmatic and cost-effective initial step to spark the investigation of socio-technical aspects in QSE, which in this context are represented by community smells and the relationships among them.

Research on socio-technical aspects of QSE is a new area that has not been explored yet [9]. Cross-sectional studies can provide valuable insights into this field's current conditions and associations. These studies are especially helpful in generating hypotheses and exploring potential connections. Despite the limitations, cross-sectional studies provide a practical starting point for further research.

## 4   Research Design

The *goal* of this research was to examine the socio-technical well-being of open-source software communities developing quantum software enabled-systems. The *purpose* was to uncover foundational knowledge able to (1) inform open-source contributors' future choices and (2) shed light on future research agenda on socio-technical aspects in the field of QSE.

In order to reach our objective, we operationalized the socio-technical well-being of open-source communities using community smells. At first, we wanted to understand the current situation of such communities, aiming to depict the current diffusion of community smells. Identifying how widespread community smells are in quantum computing projects helps to highlight socio-technical challenges that can impact the productivity and health of these open-source communities. Thus, we formulated the following research question:

> ⓘ **RQ₁**: *What is the prevalence of community smells in quantum projects?*

After assessing the diffusion of smells, in order to better characterize the socio-technical well-being of open-source quantum software communities and the phenomenon of community smells inside them, we investigated the correlation between the different smells in the same community. Exploring relationships between different community smells can reveal deeper socio-technical issues, helping us understand how these problems interact and impact community dynamics. Thus, we formulated the following second research question:

> ⓘ **RQ₂**: *Is there any relationship between different community smells in the context of quantum projects?*

To answer the research questions, we conducted a cross-sectional study. First, we selected a set of quantum-enabled software projects on GitHub and extracted community smells from them. Then, to answer $RQ_1$, we computed the *prevalence* of the community smells, while, to answer $RQ_2$, we computed the *Prevalence Odds Ratio* to assess the correlations between community smells. Further details about our research process are in the following sections and in our online appendix [18].

**Table 2.** Metrics for the 17 analyzed repositories.

| Repository | Contributors | Commits | Stars | Start Date |
|---|---|---|---|---|
| qrand | 3 | 287 | 22 | 2020-10-14 |
| bloch_sphere | 3 | 27 | 76 | 2020-06-01 |
| tweedledum | 6 | 263 | 86 | 2018-07-13 |
| xacc | 21 | 2546 | 138 | 2017-09-19 |
| tequila | 35 | 1313 | 305 | 2020-04-28 |
| qsearch | 3 | 895 | 29 | 2019-05-29 |
| quantpy | 3 | 20 | 13 | 2017-09-28 |
| QTensor | 6 | 453 | 40 | 2018-07-23 |
| quantum_decomp | 2 | 77 | 21 | 2019-05-06 |
| node-red-contrib-quantum | 7 | 148 | 13 | 2021-06-16 |
| nanite | 11 | 667 | 14 | 2012-01-24 |
| scikit-quant | 3 | 220 | 34 | 2019-01-10 |
| dc-qiskit-qml | 2 | 85 | 10 | 2019-01-13 |
| quantum-robot | 3 | 199 | 4 | 2020-06-22 |
| OpenFermion-FQE | 10 | 404 | 42 | 2020-04-01 |
| shor | 4 | 80 | 8 | 2020-02-19 |
| OpenFermion-Cirq | 15 | 254 | 267 | 2018-03-20 |

### 4.1   Population and Data Collection

To answer our research questions, we investigated the contributors of communities that actively participate in the development of open-source quantum-related software. Thus, we chose to focus on a representative subset of the target population due to logistical limitations in collecting information across all quantum open-source projects on GitHub.

We took advantage of a previous dataset of 115 repositories published in a paper by De Stefano et al. [8]. The number of contributors per repository ranges from just 1 to a maximum of 10. This indicates that most repositories have a small core team, while a few involve slightly larger groups. The number of commits varies widely, with a median value of 65, indicating significant differences in development activities across repositories. The number of stars, used as an indicator of popularity, also shows considerable variability, with a median of 10 stars per repository, suggesting a generally modest level of community recognition.

After selecting the communities for analysis, community smells were computed for each one project. The augmented version of CSDETECTOR [1],[1] available in the main repository of CADOCS [40], was used for this task. It is important to note that the tool can detect ten types of community smells, reported in Table 1. Specifically, the tool was applied with its default parameters to each repository in the selected dataset of quantum open-source repositories. To work properly, CSDETECTOR requires the URL of the repository and that certain criteria are met.[2]

Ultimately, 17 repositories (described in Table 2) out of the original 115 were successfully analyzed.[3] These repositories have varying numbers of contributors, ranging from 2 to 35, reflecting different scales of community involvement. The number of commits ranges from 20 to 2546, indicating diverse levels of development activity. The repositories also have different levels of community recognition, as shown by their stars, which range from 4 to 305. The opening and last commit dates provide insights into the lifecycle of each repository, showcasing both long-standing and more recent projects.

## 4.2 Data Analysis

To determine the prevalence of each community smell (thus, to answer the first research question), we computed the prevalence denoted as $P(X)$ [41], which represents the ratio of repositories where a specific smell was identified to the total number of repositories analyzed: $P(X) = \frac{\text{Repositories with Smell X}}{\text{Total Repositories}}$

To assess correlations among community smells (thus, to answer $RQ_2$), we employed the POR as a statistical tool [41]. It evaluates how the presence of one condition ($X_1$) correlates with the presence or absence of another condition ($X_2$)—community smells, in our context. The formula for POR is $POR = \frac{AD}{BC}$ [41], where: $A$ is the number of cases where both conditions ($X_1$ and $X_2$) are present, $B$ is the number of cases where condition $X_1$ is present, but condition $X_2$ is absent, $C$ is the number of cases where condition $X_1$ is absent, but condition $X_2$ is present, and $D$ is the number of cases where both conditions ($X_1$ and $X_2$) are absent.

To further interpret the POR results, values significantly above 1 suggest a strong positive association between the community smells. For example, a POR of 2 would indicate that community smell $X_1$ is twice as likely to occur in communities where community smell $X_2$ is present, compared to those where it is absent. On the other hand, a POR less than 1 indicates a negative correlation,

---

[1] CSDETECTOR augmented: https://github.com/gianwario/csDetector.

[2] CSDETECTOR criteria include (1) the presence of commits, (2) the existence of multiple authors, (3) the availability of a main branch, (4) at least one pull request (or more), (5) ensuring that the messages associated with these pull requests are not empty, and (6) at least one issues (or more).

[3] It is important to note that various state-of-the-art tools were tested to detect community smells [22,37], but CSDETECTOR was the only one capable of analyzing a subset of the original dataset.

meaning the presence of smell $X_2$ decreases the likelihood of smell $X_1$. For instance, a POR of 0.5 would imply that community smell $X_1$ is half as likely to occur in the presence of smell $X_2$, suggesting that smell B may play a mitigating role.

### 4.3   Threat to Validity

The study acknowledges the presence of threats to validity that could impact the integrity of the findings.

Regarding *construct validity*, the study's scope is limited to a subset of known community smells due to tool limitations, which could potentially overlook certain socio-technical challenges within quantum developer communities. However, despite this limitation, the study highlights the importance of considering community smells in software development. It is worth noting that every component in a repository may be affected by community smells, and while the assumption made in the study may not be entirely accurate, it serves as a useful starting point. Furthermore, the technical limitations of the employed tools should be taken into account when interpreting the study's results. Overall, this study provides valuable insights into the impact of community smells on software development while also highlighting the need for further research in this area.

Concerning *conclusion validity*, the cross-sectional nature of the study design poses a threat to drawing causal conclusions between exposure factors (community smells) and outcomes. The absence of longitudinal data precludes establishing temporal relationships or causal links.

Regarding *internal validity*, a potential selection bias arises from the reliance on repositories analyzed in a previous study, limiting the generalizability of results to the entire quantum open-source landscape. Additionally, the application of the CSDETECTOR tool introduces the possibility of measurement bias, as not all community smells may be detected.

Concerning *external validity*, the study's findings cannot be universally generalized to all quantum open-source repositories, as the sample was selected based on a previous study and analyzed using a specific tool. Therefore, the broader quantum developer community may not be fully represented.

## 5   Results

In this section, we present the results of our analysis that we conducted and described in Sect. 4.

Figure 1 depicts the prevalence of community smells that we found in the sample. What is most evident is that more than half of the considered smells—i.e., Black Cloud Effect (BCE), Power Distance Effect (PDE), Sharing Villainy (SV), Toxic Communication (TC), and Truck Factor (TF)—have a prevalence of more than 50%. This implies that these particular smells are pervasive within the analyzed repositories, with more than half of the repositories exhibiting them. The most extreme values are shown by PDE and TF, which occur in 94% of

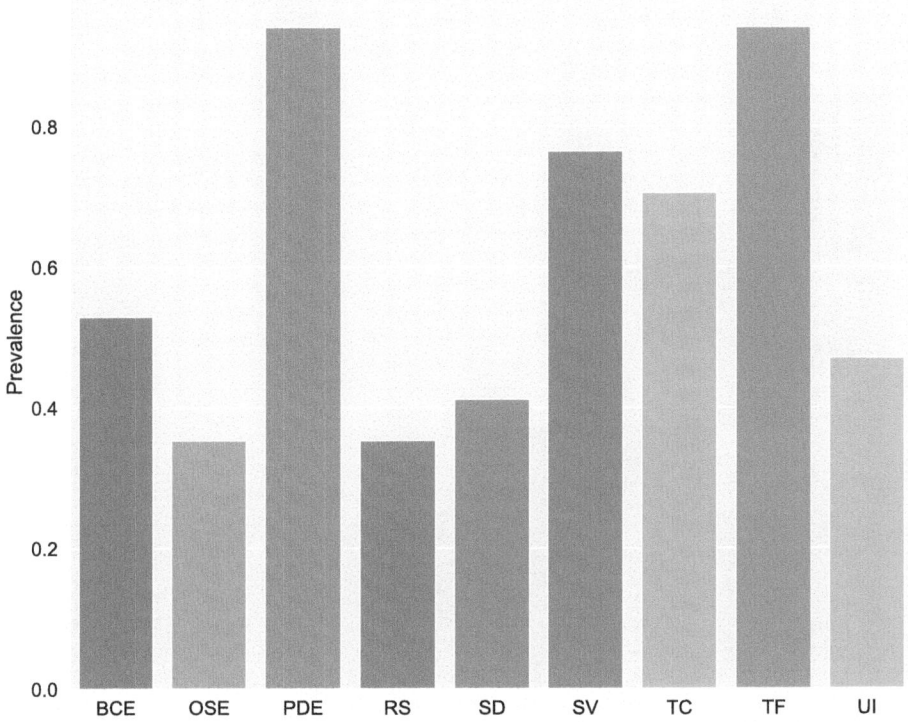

**Fig. 1.** Prevalence of community smells affecting the sampled repositories.

the cases. On the flipped side, Radio Silence (RS) and Organizational Silo Effect (OSE) are the least occurring smells, both exhibiting a prevalence of 35%, while Solution Defiance (SD) exhibits a prevalence of 40%. What is also interesting is that Organizational Skirmish (OS) is the only smell that never occurs in any of the considered repositories.

These findings provide a direct answer to $RQ_1$, showing that several community smells—most notably PDE and TF—are highly prevalent in quantum projects, with over half of the repositories affected by at least five different smells.

In Fig. 2, we can see the matrix of the POR that affects the considered repositories. What can be immediately seen is that there is no smell that has only positive correlations with the other smells. On the contrary, there are some smells that have only negative correlations. Starting from the positive correlations, we discovered some interesting patterns from our analysis. For instance, if RS is present in a repository, it is highly likely to encounter BCE, as they have a strong association (POR 8.750). Similarly, if a repository has SD, it is more likely to feature OSE, as they have an association (POR 5.333). We also found moderate positive correlations between several other community smells: RS and OSE have a POR of 2.667, SV and SD have a POR of 2.571, OSE and BCE have a POR of 2.400, and TC and BCE have a POR of 2.100. The presence of

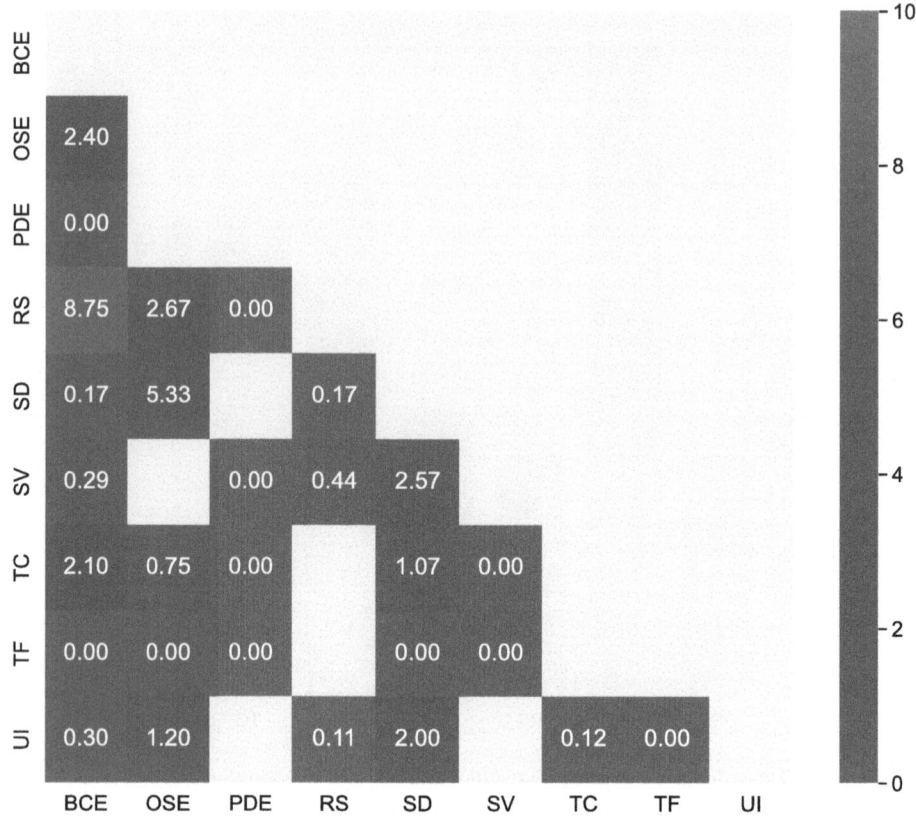

**Fig. 2.** Prevalence Odds Ratio among the community smells affecting the sampled repositories.

UI moderately associates with the presence of SD (POR 2.000) but only weakly associates with OSE (POR 1.200). Lastly, we observed no correlation between TC and SD (POR 1.07).

The observations where the POR is below 1 clearly indicate a significantly lower likelihood of co-occurrence. For example, we noted a POR of 0.75 which indicates a negative correlation between TC and OSE. This means that repositories containing TC are less likely to have OSE. Similarly, when compared to RS, SV exhibited a POR of 0.444, which indicates a reduced likelihood of finding RS in repositories featuring SV. We also discovered additional negative correlations. Notably, SD and BCE exhibit a POR of 0.171, signifying a strong negative correlation. This indicates that when SD is present, repositories are significantly less likely to exhibit BCE. Similar negative correlations were identified between SD and RS, as well as UI and BCE, TC, and RS. Interestingly, a few pairs exhibited a POR of 0.0, suggesting a complete absence of correlation between these community smells. These pairs included various combinations, such as PDE and

BCE, TF and PDE, TF and SV, TF and SD, TC and SV, TF and OSE, TF and BCE, RS and PDE, TC and PDE, SV and PDE, and UI and TF.

In summary, these findings address $RQ_2$ by confirming that community smells in quantum projects exhibit both strong positive and negative relationships, with some pairs frequently co-occurring and others rarely appearing together.

# 6  Discussions and Implications

This section reports some discussion points and implications that better contextualize our findings and could open up future work in the context of quantum software communities.

## 6.1  $RQ_1$: On the Prevalence of Community Smells

The results demonstrate that community smells, particularly Black Cloud (BCE), Prima Donnas (PDE), Sharing Villainy (SV), Toxic Communication (TC), and Truck Factor (TF), are highly prevalent within quantum software projects. With over half of the repositories exhibiting these smells, the data suggest that these issues are embedded in the fabric of quantum open-source communities. Notably, the extreme prevalence of PDE and TF, at 94%, indicates structural problems in collaboration and knowledge retention.

Compared to classical open-source communities, as explored by Tamburri et al. [33] and reported by Caballero-Espinosa et al. [5], quantum repositories exhibit a distinct pattern of smell manifestation. While classical settings often report Bottleneck, Lone Wolf, and Organizational Silo, such smells rarely reach similar extremity. These differences likely stem from the relative immaturity of quantum ecosystems, which are shaped by niche expertise, smaller contributor bases, and tightly coupled development workflows. A cross-domain comparison with ML-enabled systems further supports this interpretation. Building on the work by Annunziata et al. [3], which shares the same detection strategy as ours, both PDE and TF again emerged as dominant, confirming that knowledge concentration and authority imbalance are recurring issues in high-tech domains. However, quantum repositories exhibited higher prevalence of TC, possibly reflecting the greater communicative friction introduced by the abstract and rapidly evolving nature of quantum computing. These patterns underscore the necessity of domain-aware socio-technical strategies when managing emerging software ecosystems.

Our findings have significant implications both for researchers and contributors to these projects:

- For *researchers*, the results highlight the need for targeted studies on the role of community smells—particularly PDE and TF—in shaping the sustainability of quantum software projects. These smells were not only highly prevalent but more extreme than in classical or ML-enabled systems, suggesting domain-specific coordination challenges. Future work should investigate whether such smells hinder innovation or community growth and explore interventions like improved governance or communication structures to mitigate them. This would extend socio-technical theory into the context of emerging, expertise-driven ecosystems.

- For *open-source contributors*, the prevalence of PDE and TF indicates risks related to centralization and knowledge retention. While smaller teams and uniform expertise—reflected in the absence of OS—may ease collaboration, they also require proactive practices to prevent silos and ensure continuity. Lightweight mentoring, onboarding strategies, and documentation can help reduce these risks and support healthier project evolution.

### 6.2  RQ$_2$: On the Relationship Between Community Smells

The results reveal a complex network of both positive and negative correlations between community smells in quantum software projects, providing valuable insights for both researchers and open-source contributors. The significant positive correlations, such as those between Radio Silence (RS) and Black Cloud (BCE) (POR 8.750), as well as Solution Defiance (SD) and Organizational Skirmish (OSE) (POR 5.333), suggest that these particular smells often co-occur. This may indicate systemic issues in communication and collaboration, which reinforce each other. For instance, the strong link between RS and BCE highlights the potential for communication breakdowns leading to information overload, while the connection between SD and OSE points to the misalignment of expertise exacerbating silos within the community.

On the other hand, the negative correlations, such as that between TC and OSE (POR 0.75), suggest that certain smells are less likely to appear together. This could imply that when one issue is present, it mitigates or prevents the formation of others, possibly due to counterbalancing effects in community dynamics. The negative correlation between SD and BCE (POR 0.171) supports this idea, suggesting that repositories struggling with conflicting opinions and expertise may paradoxically avoid issues related to unstructured communication.

Unlike classical open-source systems, for which—to the best of our knowledge—no existing studies analyze correlations between community smells, ML-enabled projects provide a useful comparison always in the work by Annunziata et al. [3]. The co-occurrence patterns observed in quantum repositories—such as RS–BCE (POR 8.750) and SD–OSE (POR 5.333)—were notably stronger than those found in ML projects, suggesting tighter coupling between specific communication and coordination issues in the quantum domain. While ML repositories also exhibit elevated PORs for pairs like OSE–PDE or BCE–OSE, these associations tend to be more evenly distributed and of lower magnitude. Moreover, the greater number of smell pairs with POR equal to zero in quantum repositories—e.g., PDE–BCE, TF–PDE, and TC–SV—points to a more fragmented or modular manifestation of smells, in contrast to the more interconnected landscape of ML systems. Finally, negative associations were more frequent in quantum projects, indicating divergent team dynamics or counterbalancing patterns that are less apparent in ML contexts. These differences likely reflect the early-stage and specialized nature of quantum software development.

Also here we can provide some implications:

- For *researchers*, the results highlight the need to explore how specific smells interact and whether they trigger or reinforce one another. Strong associations—such as RS–BCE—may indicate cascading coordination failures, while the absence of overlap between smells like PDE–BCE suggests contextual or structural separation. Compared to ML-enabled systems, the sharper and more polarized correlations in quantum repositories call for domain-sensitive models that move beyond treating smells in isolation and toward understanding their interdependencies.
- For *open-source contributors*, these patterns suggest that addressing certain high-risk combinations—such as RS and BCE—may reduce the impact of multiple smells simultaneously. The presence of negative correlations, such as TC–OSE, implies that mitigating one issue may lower the risk of others. Unlike the more entangled smell networks in ML projects, quantum repositories may benefit from focused interventions targeting the most disruptive pairs.

## 7  Conclusion

The findings of our study revealed not only the widespread presence of community smells but also significant correlations between different smells. As called for in the introduction, this research represents a preliminary yet foundational step toward a more comprehensive investigation of socio-technical issues in the QSE domain. In terms of contributions, we provided:

1. an empirical investigation of the presence of ten community smells in open-source quantum communities;
2. a statistical analysis of the correlations between pairs of these ten smells within the same communities; and
3. a publicly available online appendix [18], provided to ensure replicability and reliability of the findings.

This study opens promising avenues for future research. A more detailed investigation into the specific socio-technical dynamics that lead to the emergence of these community smells is necessary. Such studies could employ qualitative methods to further explore the circumstances surrounding these smells and to identify effective mitigation strategies. Moreover, understanding these socio-technical issues can inform the technical side of software development. Previous research has suggested a link between community smells and technical debt, and future work should aim to confirm this relationship within the quantum software context.

**Acknowledgments.** This work has been partially supported by the project 'QUASAR: QUAntum software engineering for Secure, Affordable, and Reliable systems', grant 2022T2E39C, under the PRIN 2022 MUR program funded by the EU NextGenerationEU.

**Disclosure of Interests.** The authors have no competing interests to declare that are relevant to the content of this article.

# References

1. Almarimi, N., Ouni, A., Chouchen, M., Mkaouer, M.W.: csDetector: an open source tool for community smells detection. In: Proceedings of the 29th ACM Joint Meeting on European Software Engineering Conference and Symposium on the Foundations of Software Engineering, ESEC/FSE 2021, pp. 1560–1564. Association for Computing Machinery, New York (2021). https://doi.org/10.1145/3468264.3473121

2. Almarimi, N., Ouni, A., Mkaouer, M.W.: Learning to detect community smells in open source software projects. Knowl.-Based Syst. **204**, 106201 (2020). https://doi.org/10.1016/j.knosys.2020.106201

3. Annunziata, G., Lambiase, S., Palomba, F., Catolino, G., Ferrucci, F.: How do communities of ML-enabled systems smell? a cross-sectional study on the prevalence of community smells. In: Proceedings of the 29th International Conference on Evaluation and Assessment in Software Engineering (2025)

4. Brooks Jr, F.P.: The Mythical Man-month: Essays on Software Engineering. Pearson Education (1995)

5. Caballero-Espinosa, E., Carver, J.C., Stowers, K.: Community smells–the sources of social debt: a systematic literature review. Inf. Softw. Technol. **153**, 107078 (2023)

6. Catolino, G., Palomba, F., Tamburri, D.A., Serebrenik, A., Ferrucci, F.: Gender diversity and women in software teams: how do they affect community smells? In: 2019 IEEE/ACM 41st International Conference on Software Engineering: Software Engineering in Society (ICSE-SEIS), pp. 11–20. IEEE (2019)

7. De Stefano, M.: An empirical study on the current adoption of quantum programming In: Proceedings of the ACM/IEEE 44th International Conference on Software Engineering: Companion Proceedings

8. De Stefano, M., Pecorelli, F., Di Nucci, D., Palomba, F., De Lucia, A.: Software engineering for quantum programming: how far are we? J. Syst. Softw. **190**, 111326 (2022). https://doi.org/10.1016/j.jss.2022.111326

9. De Stefano, M., Pecorelli, F., Di Nucci, D., Palomba, F., De Lucia, A.: The quantum frontier of software engineering: a systematic mapping study. Inf. Softw. Technol., 107525 (2024)

10. De Stefano, M., Pecorelli, F., Palomba, F., Taibi, D., Di Nucci, D., De Lucia, A.: Quantum software engineering issues and challenges: insights from practitioners. In: Exman, I., Pérez-Castillo, R., Piattini, M., Felderer, M. (eds.) Quantum Software, pp. 337–355. Springer, Cham (2024). https://doi.org/10.1007/978-3-031-64136-7_13

11. Gordis, L.: Epidemiology E-Book. Elsevier Health Sciences (2013)

12. Gote, C., et al.: Locating community smells in software development processes using higher-order network centralities. Soc. Netw. Anal. Min. **13**(1), 129 (2023)

13. Hoare, T., Milner, R.: Grand challenges for computing research. Comput. J. **48**(1), 49–52 (2005)

14. Hoda, R.: Socio-technical grounded theory for software engineering. IEEE Trans. Software Eng. **48**(10), 3808–3832 (2021)

15. Kalliamvakou, E., Gousios, G., Blincoe, K., Singer, L., German, D.M., Damian, D.: The promises and perils of mining GitHub. In: Proceedings of the 11th Working Conference on Mining Software Repositories, MSR 2014, pp. 92–101. Association for Computing Machinery, New York (2014). https://doi.org/10.1145/2597073. 2597074
16. Knight, W.: Serious quantum computers are finally here. what are we going to do with them. MIT Technol. Rev. **30**, 2018 (2018)
17. Lambiase, S., Catolino, G., Tamburri, D.A., Serebrenik, A., Palomba, F., Ferrucci, F.: Good fences make good neighbours? On the impact of cultural and geographical dispersion on community smells. In: Proceedings of the 2022 ACM/IEEE 44th International Conference on Software Engineering: Software Engineering in Society, ICSE-SEIS 2022, pp. 67–78. Association for Computing Machinery, New York (2022). https://doi.org/10.1145/3510458.3513015
18. Lambiase, S., De Stefano, M., Palomba, F., Ferrucci, F., De Lucia, A.: Socio-technical well-being of quantum software communities: a preliminary overview—online appendix. https://doi.org/10.6084/m9.figshare.28307573
19. Moguel, E., Berrocal, J., García-Alonso, J., Murillo, J.M.: A roadmap for quantum software engineering: applying the lessons learned from the classics. In: Q-SET@ QCE, pp. 5–13 (2020)
20. Palomba, F., Andrew Tamburri, D., Arcelli Fontana, F., Oliveto, R., Zaidman, A., Serebrenik, A.: Beyond technical aspects: how do community smells influence the intensity of code smells? IEEE Trans. Software Eng. **47**(1), 108–129 (2021). https://doi.org/10.1109/TSE.2018.2883603
21. Palomba, F., Tamburri, D.A.: Predicting the emergence of community smells using socio-technical metrics: a machine-learning approach. J. Syst. Softw. **171**, 110847 (2021). https://doi.org/10.1016/j.jss.2020.110847
22. Paradis, C., Kazman, R., Tamburri, D.: Analyzing the tower of babel with Kaiaulu. J. Syst. Softw. **210**, 111967 (2024)
23. Piattini, M., Peterssen, G., Pérez-Castillo, R.: Quantum computing: a new software engineering golden age. ACM SIGSOFT Softw. Eng. Notes **45**(3), 12–14 (2021)
24. Piattini, M., et al.: The talavera manifesto for quantum software engineering and programming. In: QANSWER, pp. 1–5 (2020)
25. Piattini, M., Serrano, M., Perez-Castillo, R., Petersen, G., Hevia, J.L.: Toward a quantum software engineering. IT Prof. **23**(1), 62–66 (2021)
26. Quantum Open Software Foundation: awesome quantum software (2024). https:// github.com/qosf/awesome-quantum-software. Accessed 14 Oct 2024
27. Quantum Open Software Foundation: quantum open software foundation (QOSF) (2024). https://qosf.org. Accessed 14 Oct 2024
28. Ralph, P., Chiasson, M., Kelley, H.: Social theory for software engineering research. In: Proceedings of the 20th International Conference on Evaluation and Assessment in Software Engineering, EASE 2016. Association for Computing Machinery, New York (2016). https://doi.org/10.1145/2915970.2915998
29. Saarimäki, N., Lenarduzzi, V., Vegas, S., Juristo, N., Taibi, D.: Cohort Studies in Software Engineering: A Vision of the Future (2020). https://doi.org/10.1145/ 3382494.3422160
30. Saarimäki, N., Moreschini, S., Lomio, F., Penaloza, R., Lenarduzzi, V.: Towards a robust approach to analyze time-dependent data in software engineering. In: 2022 IEEE International Conference on Software Analysis, Evolution and Reengineering (SANER), pp. 36–40 (2022). https://doi.org/10.1109/SANER53432.2022.00015

31. Shaydulin, R., Thomas, C., Rodeghero, P.: Making quantum computing open: lessons from open source projects. In: Proceedings of the IEEE/ACM 42nd International Conference on Software Engineering Workshops, pp. 451–455 (2020)
32. Tamburri, D.A.: Software architecture social debt: managing the incommunicability factor. IEEE Trans. Comput. Soc. Syst. **6**(1), 20–37 (2019)
33. Tamburri, D.A., Palomba, F., Kazman, R.: Exploring community smells in open-source: an automated approach. IEEE Trans. Software Eng. **47**(3), 630–652 (2021). https://doi.org/10.1109/TSE.2019.2901490
34. Tamburri, D.A., Kazman, R., Fahimi, H.: The architect's role in community shepherding. IEEE Softw. **33**(6), 70–79 (2016)
35. Tamburri, D.A., Kruchten, P., Lago, P., Vliet, H.: Social debt in software engineering: insights from industry. J. Int. Serv. Appl. **6**(1), 1–17 (2015). https://doi.org/10.1186/s13174-015-0024-6
36. Tamburri, D.A., Lago, P., Vliet, H.v.: Organizational social structures for software engineering. ACM Comput. Surv. (CSUR) **46**(1), 1–35 (2013)
37. Tamburri, D.A., Palomba, F., Kazman, R.: Exploring community smells in open-source: an automated approach. IEEE Trans. Softw. Eng. (2019)
38. Tillman, R.E., Eberhardt, F.: Learning causal structure from multiple datasets with similar variable sets. Behaviormetrika **41**(1), 41–64 (2014). https://doi.org/10.2333/bhmk.41.41
39. Unitary Fund: quantum open source software survey (2024). https://unitaryfund.github.io/survey-website/. Accessed 14 Oct 2024
40. Voria, G., et al.: Community smell detection and refactoring in SLACK: the CADOCS project. In: 2022 IEEE International Conference on Software Maintenance and Evolution (ICSME), pp. 469–473. IEEE (2022)
41. Wang, X., Cheng, Z.: Cross-sectional studies: strengths, weaknesses, and recommendations. Chest **158**(1), S65–S71 (2020). https://doi.org/10.1016/j.chest.2020.03.012
42. Yarkoni, S., Raponi, E., Bäck, T., Schmitt, S.: Quantum annealing for industry applications: introduction and review. Rep. Prog. Phys. **85**(10), 104001 (2022)
43. Zhang, Y., Ni, Q.: Recent advances in quantum machine learning. Quantum Eng. **2**(1), e34 (2020)

# Differences Between Neurodivergent and Neurotypical Software Engineers: Analyzing the 2022 Stack Overflow Survey

Pragya Verma$^{(\boxtimes)}$ [ID], Marcos Vinicius Cruz [ID], and Grischa Liebel [ID]

Reykjavik University, Reykjavik, Iceland
{pragyav,marcosc,grischal}@ru.is

**Abstract.** Neurodiversity describes variation in brain function among people, including common conditions such as Autism spectrum disorder (ASD), Attention deficit hyperactivity disorder (ADHD), and dyslexia. While Software Engineering (SE) literature has started to explore the experiences of neurodivergent software engineers, there is a lack of research that compares their challenges to those of neurotypical software engineers. To address this gap, we analyze existing data from the 2022 Stack Overflow Developer survey that collected data on neurodiversity. We quantitatively compare the answers of professional engineers with ASD (n = 374), ADHD (n = 1305), and dyslexia (n = 363) with neurotypical engineers. Our findings indicate that neurodivergent engineers face more difficulties than neurotypical engineers. Specifically, engineers with ADHD report that they face more interruptions caused by waiting for answers, and that they less frequently interact with individuals outside their team. This study provides a baseline for future research comparing neurodivergent engineers with neurotypical ones. Several factors in the Stack Overflow survey and in our analysis are likely to lead to conservative estimates of the actual effects between neurodivergent and neurotypical engineers, e.g., the effects of the COVID-19 pandemic and our focus on employed professionals.

**Keywords:** neurodiversity · software engineering · diversity and inclusion · survey · stack overflow

## 1 Introduction

Neurodiversity describes variation in brain function among people [9], including conditions such as Autism spectrum disorder (ASD), Attention deficit hyperactivity disorder (ADHD), and dyslexia. The neurodiversity movement argues that this variation should be seen as natural diversity among individuals and that society should accommodate this diversity, instead of focusing on finding a "cure" for people with disorders in the medical sense [25]. Including approximately 15% to 20% of the world population [8], neurodivergent (ND) individuals represent a major part of the actual and potential work force.

D. Taibi and D. Smite (Eds.): SEAA 2025, LNCS 16083, pp. 57–74, 2026.
https://doi.org/10.1007/978-3-032-04207-1_5

Software Engineering (SE) literature has started to explore the experiences of ND engineers for various conditions, e.g., for ADHD [17], ASD [18], dyslexia [19], and combinations of these conditions [12, 21]. However, there are only few studies in SE providing comparisons to neurotypical (NT) engineers, i.e., those that have what is considered 'normal' cognitive function. As challenges and strengths of ND engineers overlap with those of NT engineers, and as most conditions included in ND exhibit large variation in symptoms, it is therefore unclear if and to what extent ND engineers differ from the general SE population.

To address this gap, we analyze existing data from the 2022 Stack Overflow Developer survey[1]. This survey has been conducted every year since 2011 by Stack Overflow among thousands of software developers, and collected data on neurodiversity for the first and last time in 2022. We quantitatively compare the answers of professional developers with ASD ($n = 374$), ADHD ($n = 1305$), and dyslexia ($n = 363$) with NT professionals. We aim to answer the following research question (RQ):

**RQ:** What differences exist between professional developers with dyslexia, ADHD, and ASD and their neurotypical peers?

Specifically, we compare the answers with respect to knowledge sharing, interaction, and finding information of each of these three groups with the same amount of NT developers, sampled randomly as well as sampled based on the work mode and the work experience distributions.

We find that ND developers, especially those with ADHD working in a hybrid work mode, face more difficulties in obtaining and sharing knowledge within their organization. However, we find only few significant differences, and with small effect sizes. Our findings indicate that difficulties with respect to the analyzed factors exist among ND professionals, but are not substantially different to NT professionals. Various aspects are not considered in the Stack Overflow survey and might confound the results, e.g., the impact of accommodations at the workplace and tailoring of remote or hybrid work environments. As such, our study likely provides a conservative baseline that can be used in future studies to further explore the challenges of ND professionals in SE, as well as how to address them.

The filtered and preprocessed data, as well as the corresponding scripts are available on Zenodo [3].

## 2    Related Work

Neurodiversity has emerged as a studied topic in SE literature in the last years, e.g., [17–21].

Morris et al. [21] investigate challenges faced by ND engineers in SE by conducting interviews with 10 ND engineers, followed by a survey among 846 engineers. The authors find that ND engineers face various challenges related

---

[1] https://survey.stackoverflow.co/2022.

to their work and to interpersonal aspects, and that they fear stigmatization. Their survey reveals some differences of ND engineers compared to their NT colleagues, namely that they find it comparably more challenging to work in shared offices, or deciding when to seek help for tasks.

In a series of qualitative studies based on interviews, Gama et al. [12,17] investigate the experiences of engineers with ASD and ADHD in SE. The studies find that the interviewed individuals face various challenges related to cognitive and emotional dysfunctions and to social interaction and communication. In turn, these challenges lead to stress that affects their work performance. They suggest various accommodations that can help addressing the challenges and the resulting stress. However, these studies provide little insights in how the reported challenges, stressors, and accommodations compare to experiences by NT colleagues.

Focusing on dyslexia, a series of experiments by McChesney and Bond [19,20] use eye tracking to study how developers with dyslexia read software code. They find that the studied individuals, in reading code, are not affected in the same way as when reading text.

Marquez et al. [18] conduct a systematic literature review on the inclusion of individuals with ASD in SE. They find that barriers are commonly reported, but potential interventions are not studied empirically. The articles included in the review are primarily studies focused on education or secondary studies.

Beyond SE, there are various studies on the practices and performance of ND individuals at the workplace, e.g., [1,6,26] Das et al. [6] investigate the remote work practices of ND individuals during COVID-19, including also software developers. The authors report that ND individuals tailor their home environments, successfully negotiate their communication practices with team members, and balance various tensions related to productivity and fatigue.

Zolyomi et al. [26] investigate the needs of individuals with ASD related to video calls. The authors find their interviewees develop various coping mechanisms, such as adopting NT behavior.

Based on a community and a clinical sample, Fuermaier et al. [11] analyze the work performance of individuals with ADHD. They find that individuals with ADHD especially struggle with not meeting their own expectations and potential, but that this does not commonly result in low evaluations. Similarly, symptoms of inattention are strongly associated with work performance.

Rogers et al. [23] conduct a cross-sectional between-subjects study of individuals with and without ADHD, finding that individuals with ADHD are significantly more fatigued than the control. In a similar direction, based on perceived stress data collected from 983 individuals, Combs et al. [5] find that ADHD symptoms are positively associated with stress. Finally, a cross-sectional study based on over 15.000 participants finds that ADHD symptoms are positively associated with workaholism [2].

Summarizing work on employment and employment-related challenges of individuals with ASD, Hendricks [13] reports that interaction-related challenges are most common among this group, as well as difficulties in attention or working memory, and high levels of stress and anxiety.

Finally, in a literature review on employment of individuals with Dyslexia, De Beer et al. [7] summarize 33 qualitative and quantitative studies according to the two-level classification of the International Classification of Functioning, Disability and Health[2] (ICF). The study finds that 318 of the ICF factors are covered in existing studies, with the most common ones related to mental functions (e.g., anxiety or frustration), activities (e.g., difficulties in reading and writing, but also strengths in problem solving and speaking), working conditions (e.g., positive and negative experiences with accommodations at work), and personal factors (e.g., stress).

In terms of method, Silveira et al. [16] analyzed how gender relates to confidence in programming in the 2018 SO survey. They find that women and non-binary respondents believe they are not as good as their peers.

## 3    Methodology

Stack Overflow is an online Question and Answer (Q&A) platform that provides individuals with an opportunity to discuss a wide range of topics [4]. Starting 2011, Stack Overflow has been conducting an annual survey[3] to understand the user demographics and their practices. The results and the raw data of the annual developer surveys are available publicly and can be analyzed to gain deeper insights. We took this survey as a starting point for our study, as we describe in the following.

### 3.1    Data Collection: The 2022 Stack Overflow Developer Survey

The 2022 annual Stack Overflow Developer Survey[4] was conducted from May 11, 2022 to June 1, 2022. A total of 73,268 respondents participated in this developer survey, of whom 70.03% were developers by profession. According to the information available on the Stack Overflow website, the survey respondents were recruited with the help of channels owned by Stack Overflow such as blog posts, onsite messaging, or email lists. While Stack Overflow does not define what their target population is, they name the survey the "Developer" survey, and talk about "software developers" in their methodology.

The survey questions can be categorized into different blocks, e.g., asking about demographics (e.g., age, company size, country), used tools and technologies, use of Stack Overflow, and productivity at work. In addition, for the first and last time since 2011, the 2022 survey collected information about mental health, including a question about neurodiversity and/or any emotional or anxiety disorder.

---

[2] https://www.who.int/standards/classifications/international-classification-of-functioning-disability-and-health.

[3] https://survey.stackoverflow.co/.

[4] https://survey.stackoverflow.co/2022.

The 2022 survey also included seven knowledge questions (K1–K7) and three frequency questions (F1–F3). The knowledge questions focused on the respondents' ability to find knowledge and information within their organization. The respondents had to answer these knowledge questions on a five-point Likert scale ranging from 'strongly disagree' to 'strongly agree'. The frequency questions focused on how frequently the respondents experienced situations in which they had to interact with others in their organization and encountered productivity difficulties. The responses to these three frequency questions were also obtained on a five-point Likert scale, ranging from 'never' to '10+ times a week'. The questions are as follows.

- K1: 'I have interactions with people outside of my immediate team'
- K2: 'Knowledge silos prevent me from getting ideas across the organization (i.e., one individual or team has information that isn't shared with others)'
- K3: 'I can find up-to-date information within my organization to help me do my job.'
- K4: 'I am able to quickly find answers to my questions with existing tools and resources.'
- K5: 'I know which system or resource to use to find information and answers to questions I have.'
- K6: 'I often find myself answering questions that I've already answered before'
- K7: 'Waiting on answers to questions often causes interruptions and disrupts my workflow'
- F1: 'Needing help from people outside of your immediate team?'
- F2: 'Interacting with people outside of your immediate team?'
- F3: 'Encountering knowledge silos (where one individual or team has information that's not shared or distributed with other individuals or teams) at work'

Since existing work in SE and in general workplace studies indicates that ND and NT individuals might differ in their ability to find information at work and their interaction with others, we chose to analyze the differences between the responses of ND and NT respondents to these ten questions. Thus, in this work, we (i) descriptively analyze the respondent demographics and the time spent answering/searching for questions and (ii) investigate whether there exist statistical differences between the responses to the seven knowledge questions and the three frequency questions between ND and NT individuals.

**Filtering the 2022 Stack Overflow Developer Survey.** We only considered respondents who were full-time employed and over 18 years of age. Since we were interested in investigating the differences (if any) between the group of ND individuals and the group of NT individuals, we further filtered the data into different groups, i.e., those having (i) dyslexia without any co-morbidity (i.e., having learning differences), (ii) ADHD without any co-morbidity, (iii) ASD without any co-morbidity and (iv) no neurodiversity (none of the specified conditions). We removed responses where the first knowledge question (K1) and the first frequency question (F1) were not answered, as most of these answers had skipped this part of the survey altogether. This resulted in 363 individuals in the dyslexic group, 1305 individuals in the ADHD group and 374 individuals in the ASD group. For each of these three groups, we randomly selected an equal number of NT individuals. We then removed these individuals from the pool of NT individuals for the remaining sampling steps, ensuring that no NT individual is present in more than one sample.

Since the responses to the 7 knowledge questions and 3 frequency questions can be impacted by the work mode as well as the number of years of work experience one has, we additionally adopted a paired sampling approach based on (a) work mode and (b) number of years of work experience. We filtered the data to include datasets of dyslexic, ADHD and ASD individuals working (i) fully remote, (ii) full in-person and (iii) hybrid. This resulted in 148 dyslexic, 664 ADHD and 176 ASD individuals working fully remote; 34 dyslexic, 133 ADHD and 41 ASD individuals working full in-person; and 181 dyslexic, 507 ADHD and 157 ASD individuals working hybrid. For each of the ND groups belonging to the three different work modes, we randomly selected an equal number of NT individuals, still ensuring that no NT individual is present in more than one sample. We performed the same kind of sampling for work experience, by grouping participants into 0–5 years of work experience, 6–10 years of work experience, and 10+ years of work experience.

## 3.2   Data Analysis

We started our analysis by calculating descriptive statistics for questions addressing time spent for answering questions and for searching for solutions to problems. To analyze the various countries reported by survey participants, we grouped them by continent. To do so, we use the division of National Geographic[5] into seven continents, i.e., Asia, Africa, North America, South America, Antarctica, Europe, and Australia, as well as "Other" and "Nomadic".

To answer our RQ ("What differences exist between professional developers with dyslexia, ADHD, and ASD and their neurotypical peers?"), we test whether there exist statistically significant differences in the responses to K1–K7 and F1–F3 between the ND and NT groups. To do so, we carried out non-parametric Mann-Whitney U tests. Since the individual participants in the Stack Overflow survey are independent, the key assumption of the Mann-Whitney U test regarding independence is given. We used an alpha level of 5% for all tests. While we ensured unique NT groups for each comparison, there is an overlap within the groups each condition (i.e., Dyslexic, ADHD and ASD) for different conditions. For instance, a dyslexic individual working fully remote is also present in the overall sample of dyslexic individuals and in one of the work experience samples. Thus, due to multiple Mann-Whitney U tests being conducted on data groups that might have common instances, the probability of making Type I errors (family-wise errors) increases [10]. To control for this probability, we applied the

---

[5] https://education.nationalgeographic.org/resource/Continent/.

Bonferroni-Holm correction [15] on all tests within one condition (i.e., dyslexia, ADHD, and ASD).

### 3.3  Validity Threats

In the following, we will discuss potential threats to the validity of our study in terms of internal, external, and construct validity, as well as reliability.

**Internal Validity.** While pairing the ND and NT groups based on number of years of work experience, we consider range in the years of work experience and do not match based on same mean years of experience. To adjust for inflated Type I errors, we used the Bonferroni-Holm correction for each of the ND groups. This might lead to overly conservative results, i.e., there might be more differences between the ND and NT groups.

The Stack Overflow developer survey was conducted during COVID-19, which could affect the effect of remote work. However, we argue that it might indeed be the most suitable timing for this survey, as software developers might have been working according to their preferred work mode, not restricted by either remote work or return-to-office mandates.

We selected ND individuals who had no other ND or mental health condition. Apart from filtering out individuals with multiple ND conditions, such as a combination of ASD and ADHD, this also included filtering out people with mental health issues such as anxiety or depression. While this strengthens the chance that observed differences are in fact due to the ND condition, it might also exclude more severe cases, e.g., where a ND condition has already led to developing anxiety or depression, or where the symptoms of multiple ND conditions cause more challenges.

**External Validity.** It is likely that respondents who took part in this survey are not representative of the ND and NT developers worldwide. While this poses a threat to external validity, we also observe that there is a relatively broad representation across different continents in comparison to many surveys in SE. This is further discussed in Sect. 4.1. Additionally, the focus of the Stack Overflow survey is on developers and might limit the generalizability to other SE-related roles.

**Construct Validity.** Our aim is to understand the differences and/or similarity in the experiences of ND developers from that of NT developers in the SE domain. Though knowledge sharing, interaction, and finding information play a key role in determining one's experience at the workplace, there can be other factors that can contribute to the overall work experience and satisfaction.

It is possible that the questions used in the survey are worded in an ambiguous way. Additionally, they might not measure valid constructs, thereby influencing the responses obtained. Since we did not design the survey, we do not have much information about its theoretical framework and had no influence on the design and wording of the questions.

**Reliability.** The dataset of the 2022 Stack Overflow developer survey as well as the questionnaire are publicly available under https://survey.stackoverflow.co/ 2022. In addition, we published the filtered data we used, our final samples, as well as the scripts for sampling and analysis [3], so that others can replicate our work or use it as an inspiration for future work.

## 4    Results

In the following, we describe our results. We start with an overview of descriptive statistics of the demographic data of our unpaired samples (i.e., all ND individuals and the random corresponding samples of NT individuals). Similar descriptive statistics can be obtained for the paired samples using the scripts published as a part of our dataset. Then, we present the results of the statistical tests, answering **RQ**.

### 4.1    Demographics and Descriptive Statistics

We observed that, for all three conditions, there is a clear difference between the origins of the survey respondents. For individuals with Dyslexia and the corresponding NT group, the majority of the respondents were from Europe (63.36% and 37.74% respectively). A similar trend was observed for individuals with ASD and the corresponding NT group, with the majority of the respondents being from Europe (52.94% and 42.51% respectively). For individuals with ADHD, the majority of the respondents were from North America (45.67%) with majority of the respondents in the corresponding NT group being from Europe (40.08%).

In terms of education, all three samples are relatively similar to their NT counterparts, with the majority in all samples having Bachelor degrees (51.49% of individuals with ADHD, compared to 51.84% in the NT sample; 44.65% of individuals with ASD, compared to 47.33% in the NT sample; 44.35% of individuals with dyslexia, compared to 48.21% in the NT sample). It is noteworthy that fewer ND individuals have a Master degree (15.71% of individuals with ADHD, compared to 25.46% in the NT sample; 25.40% of individuals with ASD, compared to 28.88% in the NT sample; 25.34% of individuals with dyslexia, compared to 26.72% in the NT sample) and more have attended college/university without earning a degree (17.24% of individuals with ADHD, compared to 11.04% in the NT sample; 15.24% of individuals with ASD, compared to 10.43% in the NT sample; 13.77% of individuals with dyslexia, compared to 12.12% in the NT sample).

In terms of coding experience, individuals with ADHD indicated an average of 12 years of coding experience, with their NT peers reporting an average of 13 years.

The majority of respondents were within the 25–34 age range. Among individuals with dyslexia, 51.24% (N = 186) were in this category, compared to 51.52% (N = 187) of NT. For individuals with ASD, 45.72% (N = 171) were within this age range, lower than the 52.94% (N = 198) of their NT counterparts. In the ADHD group, 52.57% (N = 686) were aged 25–34, compared to 49.66% (N = 648) among NT.

Figures 1, 2, and 3 show the comparisons of time spent in answering work-related questions by individuals with dyslexia, ADHD, and ASD. Most individuals across all groups spent between 15–60 min per day. Interestingly, the time individuals with ADHD spent on answering questions is almost identical to their NT counterparts, while there are more differences observable in the other two groups.

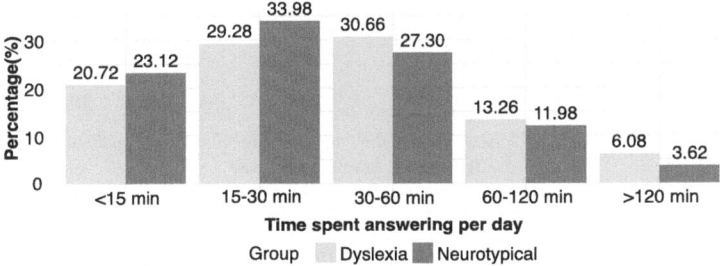

**Fig. 1.** Daily time answering questions in the Dyslexia sample and the corresponding neurotypical sample.

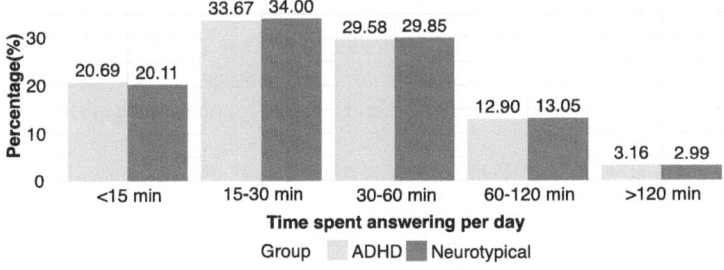

**Fig. 2.** Daily time answering questions in the ADHD sample and the corresponding neurotypical sample.

Figures 4, 5, and 6 show the comparisons of time spent searching for answers or solutions to work-related problems by individuals with dyslexia, ADHD, and ASD. For all three conditions, there seems to be a difference to NT peers in terms of individuals spending more than 120 min per day.

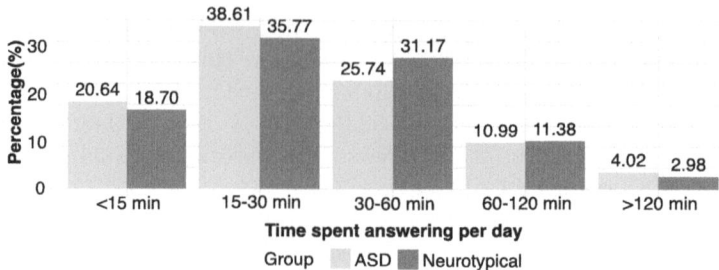

**Fig. 3.** Daily time answering questions in the ASD sample and the corresponding neurotypical sample.

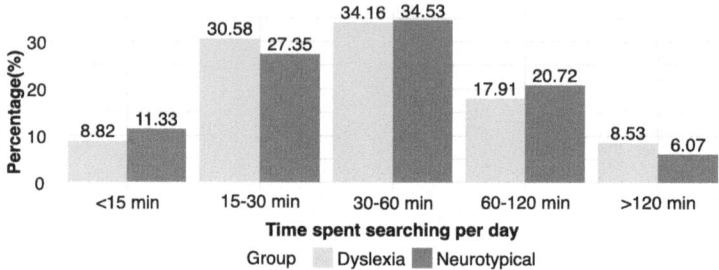

**Fig. 4.** Daily time searching in the Dyslexia sample and the corresponding neurotypical sample.

### 4.2 Inter-group Comparison for Unpaired Sampling

We first compare the responses to K1–K7 and F1–F3 using an unpaired sampling approach. We then check for differences in these 10 questions using a paired sampling approach where we pair ND and NT individuals based on (i) work mode and (ii) number of years of experience. Table 1 summarizes the results of Mann-Whitney U Test with Bonferroni-Holm correction for the 10 questions (K1–K7 and F1–F3) for the ND groups and the corresponding randomly selected NT group.

For individuals with ADHD and the randomly selected NT group, we observe statistically significant differences (with a small effect size) for K7 and F2 respectively, i.e., the ADHD group faces interruptions in their workflow while waiting for answers more often, and they have fewer interactions outside their team. For individuals with ASD, we observe a statistically significant difference in K4 (with a small effect size). That is, individuals with ASD have a harder time finding answers to their questions with existing tools and resources.

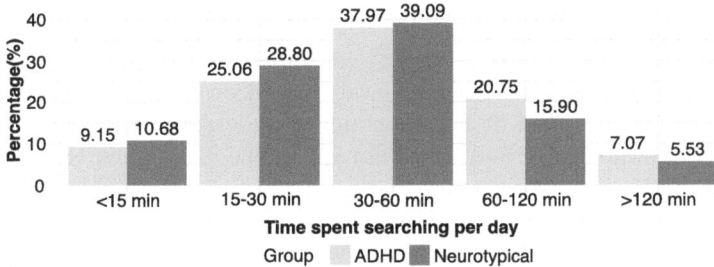

**Fig. 5.** Daily time searching in the ADHD sample and the corresponding neurotypical sample.

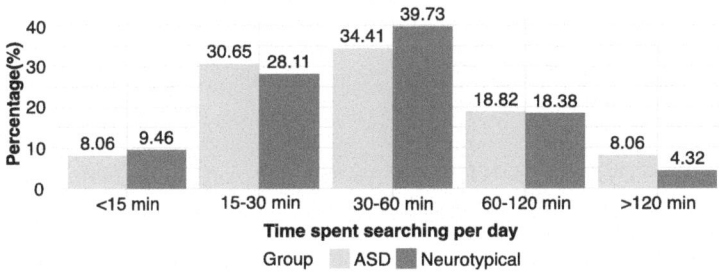

**Fig. 6.** Daily time searching in the ASD sample and the corresponding neurotypical sample.

**Table 1.** Corrected p-value for neurodivergent vs. randomly sampled neurotypical groups

|    | Dyslexia vs. NT | ADHD vs. NT | Autism vs. NT |
|----|------|------|------|
| K1 | 1.00 | 1.00 | 1.00 |
| K2 | 1.00 | 1.00 | 1.00 |
| K3 | 1.00 | 1.00 | 1.00 |
| K4 | 1.00 | 0.989 | **0.003**\*\* $(-0.148)$ |
| K5 | 1.00 | 0.076 | 1.00 |
| K6 | 1.00 | 1.00 | 0.285 |
| K7 | 1.00 | **0.0006**\*\* $(-0.086)$ | 1.00 |
| F1 | 1.00 | 1.00 | 1.00 |
| F2 | 1.00 | **0.020**\* $(-0.070)$ | 1.00 |
| F3 | 1.00 | 0.254 | 1.00 |

Note: * indicates significant difference at p-value < 0.05
** indicates significant difference at p-value < 0.01
value in () indicates the effect size
NT represents randomly selected Neurotypical group

## 4.3   Inter-group Comparison for Paired Sampling Based on Work Mode

Since it is possible that experience can vary based on whether they work fully remote, in-person or hybrid, it is important to understand if differences in the responses to the knowledge and frequency questions exist when the groups are matched on the basis of work mode.

The results of Mann-Whitney U Test with Bonferroni-Holm correction for the ND versus NT groups working fully remote and fully in person resulted in no statistically significant differences for any of the ten questions (K1–K7 and F1–F3).

Table 2 summarizes the results of Mann-Whitney U Test with Bonferroni-Holm correction for the 10 questions (K1–K7 and F1–F3) for the ND versus NT groups working in hybrid mode.

**Table 2.** Corrected p-value for Neurodivergent vs. Neurotypical groups working in hybrid mode

|     | Dyslexia vs. NT | ADHD vs. NT | Autism vs. NT |
| --- | --- | --- | --- |
| K1 | 1.00 | 1.00 | 0.417 |
| K2 | 1.00 | 1.00 | 1.00 |
| K3 | 1.00 | 1.00 | 0.051 |
| K4 | 0.565 | 0.474 | 0.055 |
| K5 | 0.569 | 1.00 | 0.979 |
| K6 | 1.00 | 1.00 | 1.00 |
| K7 | 1.00 | 0.0001** $(-0.147)$ | 1.00 |
| F1 | 1.00 | 1.00 | 1.00 |
| F2 | 1.00 | 0.0003** $(-0.142)$ | 1.00 |
| F3 | 1.00 | 1.00 | 1.00 |

Note: ** indicates significant difference at p-value < 0.01
value in () indicates the effect size
NT represents randomly selected Neurotypical group

Our results indicate that there are no significant differences between the responses for individuals with dyslexia and their NT counterparts and between individuals with ASD and the corresponding NT individuals working in hybrid mode. However, similar to our finding for the unpaired samples, we found statistically significant differences (with small effect size) for individuals with ADHD in questions K7 and F2. Hence, individuals with ADHD working in hybrid mode face interruptions in their workflow while waiting for answers more commonly than their NT peers. Similarly, they have fewer interactions outside their team.

## 4.4  Inter-group Comparison for Paired Sampling Based on Number of Years of Work Experience

In addition to work mode, work experience could have an effect on the answers. Thus, we tested differences in the responses to the knowledge and frequency questions (K1–K7 and F1–F3) when pairing groups on the basis of number of years of work experience. For this, we conducted inter-group comparisons using Mann-Whitney U tests along with the Bonferroni-Holm correction while matching the ND and NT groups based on their number of years of work experience.

**0–5 Years.** Table 3 summarizes the results of the Mann-Whitney U tests with Bonferroni-Holm correction for the 10 questions (K1–K7 and F1–F3) for the ND versus NT groups with 0 to 5 years of work experience.

**Table 3.** Corrected p-value for Neurodivergent vs. Neurotypical groups having 0–5 years of work experience

|      | Dyslexia vs. NT       | ADHD vs. NT | Autism vs. NT |
|------|-----------------------|-------------|---------------|
| K1   | 1.00                  | 1.00        | 1.00          |
| K2   | 1.00                  | 1.00        | 1.00          |
| K3   | 1.00                  | 1.00        | 1.00          |
| K4   | 1.00                  | 1.00        | 1.00          |
| K5   | 0.008** (−0.219)      | 1.00        | 1.00          |
| K6   | 1.00                  | 1.00        | 1.00          |
| K7   | 1.00                  | 1.00        | 1.00          |
| F1   | 1.00                  | 1.00        | 1.00          |
| F2   | 1.00                  | 1.00        | 1.00          |
| F3   | 1.00                  | 1.00        | 1.00          |

Note: ** indicates significant difference at p-value
< 0.01
value in () indicates the effect size
NT represents randomly selected Neurotypical group

We found a statistically significant difference for K5 (with medium effect size) between responses from individuals with dyslexia and the randomly selected NT individuals. None of the other comparisons between the three ND groups and their corresponding NT groups was significant.

**6-10 Years.** The results of the Mann-Whitney U tests with Bonferroni-Holm correction for the ND versus NT groups with 6 to 10 years of work experience indicated no statistical significance for the 10 questions (K1–K7 and F1–F3).

**10+ Years.** Similar to our comparison for 6–10 years of work experience, we observed no statistical significance for the 10 questions (K1–K7 and F1–F3) for the ND versus NT groups with 10+ years of work experience.

## 5   Discussion

Our results show few significant differences between ND and NT developers. This could indicate that other factors, e.g., the type of work they do or their seniority, have a larger influence on knowledge sharing, interaction, and finding information. Similarly, the severity of ND conditions, as well as potentially undisclosed or undiagnosed conditions in our NT sample could affect the results. This is particularly noteworthy given the differences in the ND paradigm across cultures. Hirota et al. [14] report that, in many cultures, uniqueness due to ND could be interpreted negatively thereby affecting interpersonal relations. This could lead to individuals in such cultures not seeking diagnosis due to fear of discrimination or stigmatization, as also highlighted in the SE context in [17]. To study this in more depth, and to allow for generalizable results, replication studies are needed with more systematic sampling.

Our results show differences in responses to two questions (i.e., K7 and F2) between developers with ADHD and NT developers working in hybrid mode. However, we did not observe any difference in any of the questions between the three groups of ND developers and the corresponding NT groups working fully remote or fully in-person. As mentioned previously, the survey was conducted towards the end of COVID-19, at a time when developers could likely work in their preferred work mode and not as restricted by their organizations. Ralph et al. [22] find that the COVID-19 pandemic had negative effects on most developers, especially on well-being and productivity. While the authors note that people with disabilities are disproportionally affected, they do not specifically mention ND developers. Furthermore, this disproportionate effect could manifest in unexpected ways. For instance, while ND developers might have been affected stronger with respect to well-being, working from home could indeed have helped them in other ways, e.g., in reducing distractions or allowing for more suitable interaction and communication styles with their teams. Indeed, existing qualitative study highlight that ND software engineers often like to work from home, in an environment tailored to their specific needs [17,21]. Similarly, ND developers choosing to work fully in person may be those with less severe conditions, or NT developers working from home may be those with challenges similar to ND peers, including with undiagnosed ND conditions. Further investigations that take into account such information might reveal meaningful insights about the differences in the workplace experiences of ND and NT engineers working in different work modes and can be helpful in creating more inclusive workplace environments.

Since we did not conduct the survey ourselves, we had no influence on the questions asked. As a result, there are several questions that might suffer from low validity, and aspects of ND challenges that remain unexplored in this study.

Regarding the first point, it is for example unclear whether the concept of "interaction" used in two questions (i.e., K1 and F2) relates only to work-related interaction or also describes social interaction. Further, cultural differences can affect workplace interaction. For instance, Sanchez-Burks et al. [24] report that individuals from different cultural backgrounds often use "different relational schemas to navigate their workplace interactions". Thus, differences in the cultural background of the respondents might have had an impact on their interpretation of questions K1, F1 and F2.

A third limitation of this study is that we included only employed and retired developers. However, studies on neurodiversity at the workplace show large percentages of unemployment among ND individuals, e.g., up to 50–75% of individuals with ASD [13]. As these individuals are likely to face more challenges than employed individuals, considering the perspective of unemployed ND software engineers could show more pronounced patterns.

Despite the limitations of the Stack Overflow survey and our analysis, this study provides a good baseline for future work. For instance, as hybrid work is common in SE, the findings that developers with ADHD working in hybrid mode experience more interruptions when waiting on answers compared to their NT peers warrants further investigation of this setting. Similarly, while it is expected that the demographics of our comparison groups differ, we observe similar patterns in many of the demographic questions, as reported in Sect. 4.1. For instance, organization sizes and the time spent answering questions and searching for information are similar in the ND groups and the unpaired random NT samples. One exception is the global distribution, where the continents differ clearly.

Our findings support that ND conditions affect the individuals to some extent, even in environments that they might tailor to their needs (e.g., remote or hybrid). This connects well to existing work, e.g., by Gama et al. [12,17] and Morris et al. [21]. However, the survey lacks details on important aspects that could affect their challenges. Specifically, both Gama et al. [12] and Morris et al. [21] highlight the important effect of accommodations and awareness, and the role that the environment plays for ND individuals - both aspects that are not visible in the Stack Overflow survey.

While differences are small, there is a larger percentage of ND developers spending more than 120 min per day answering questions and searching for information than NT individuals. This could relate to common symptoms in all conditions related to attention, memory, and reading and writing skills.

## 6   Implications

Our findings have implications on how to create more inclusive workspace for ND professionals in SE. As symptoms of both ADHD and ASD are on a spectrum, inclusive practices will also benefit practitioners without an ADHD or ASD diagnosis and, therefore, SE practice as a whole. Since our results indicate that developers with ADHD interact less frequently with individuals outside their team, SE companies can provide communication training to ND and NT developers to ensure easy communication between ND developers and those within and outside their teams. This will facilitate ND developers to obtain and share their knowledge with others. Further, as engineers with ADHD face more interruptions caused by waiting for answers, we recommend that project managers provide explicit instructions for task completion and highlight the important todos. To support the strengths and address the challenges faced by ND SE practitioners, we recommend developing and using tools that can offer personalized suggestions to improve communication and performance, help prioritize and schedule tasks, and allow users to anonymously raise concerns to other team members. This will be helpful for both ND and NT SE practitioners. We believe that incorporation of such a tool in the workflow can improve practices and support within teams, thereby creating a more inclusive SE workplace. Finally, our recommendations are also suitable for SE courses and can help SE teachers create a more inclusive learning environment for ND students.

## 7  Conclusion

In this paper, we present an analysis of the 2022 Stack Overflow developer survey with respect to neurodiversity, answering the research question "What differences exist between professional developers with dyslexia, ADHD, and ASD and their neurotypical peers?". We quantitatively compare the answers of professional developers with dyslexia (n = 363), ADHD (n = 1305), and ASD (n = 374) with randomly sampled neurotypical professionals in terms of knowledge sharing, interaction, and finding information. We also compare the responses of the neurodivergent developers with neurotypical developers paired on the basis of work mode and number of years of work experience.

Our findings show few significant differences between the groups. Among the observed differences, we find that developers working with ADHD working in a hybrid work mode face more difficulties in obtaining and sharing knowledge within their organization. Despite these few differences, our current work lays a strong foundation for future research in this domain to understand the needs and experiences of neurodivergent software engineers with an overall aim of creating more inclusive workplace environment.

Various aspects are not considered or potentially invalid in the Stack Overflow survey, and might influence the results, e.g., the impact of accommodations at the workplace and tailoring of remote or hybrid work environments. On the one hand, this means there exist various threats to validity in our findings. On the other hand, this also means there is ample potential for follow-up work in the future. For instance, taking a closer look at cultural differences is an important next step, as our samples differ in the reported continents. Similar, many of the strengths and difficulties of neurodivergent software engineers reported in existing SE work, such as creativity, systems thinking, or difficulties in keeping up attention, are not covered by the Stack Overflow Developer Surveys. These points should therefore be investigated in the future.

As such, our study likely provides a conservative baseline that can be used in future studies to further explore the challenges of ND professionals in SE, as well as how to address them.

# References

1. Alqahtani, Y., McGuire, M., Chakraborty, J., Feng, J.H.: Understanding how ADHD affects visual information processing. In: Antona, M., Stephanidis, C. (eds.) HCII 2019. LNCS, vol. 11573, pp. 23–31. Springer, Cham (2019). https://doi.org/10.1007/978-3-030-23563-5_3
2. Andreassen, C.S., Griffiths, M.D., Sinha, R., Hetland, J., Pallesen, S.: The relationships between workaholism and symptoms of psychiatric disorders: a large-scale cross-sectional study. PLoS ONE **11**(5), e0152978 (2016)
3. Anonymous: Dataset: differences between neurodivergent and neurotypical software engineers: analyzing the 2022 stack overflow survey (2025). https://doi.org/10.5281/zenodo.14779344
4. Barua, A., Thomas, S.W., Hassan, A.E.: What are developers talking about? An analysis of topics and trends in stack overflow. Empir. Softw. Eng. **19**, 619–654 (2014)
5. Combs, M.A., Canu, W.H., Broman-Fulks, J.J., Rocheleau, C.A., Nieman, D.C.: Perceived stress and ADHD symptoms in adults. J. Atten. Disord. **19**(5), 425–434 (2015). https://doi.org/10.1177/1087054712459558
6. Das, M., Tang, J., Ringland, K.E., Piper, A.M.: Towards accessible remote work: Understanding work-from-home practices of neurodivergent professionals. Proc. ACM Human-Comput. Interact. **5**(CSCW1), 1–30 (2021)
7. De Beer, J., Engels, J., Heerkens, Y., van der Klink, J.: Factors influencing work participation of adults with developmental dyslexia: a systematic review. BMC Public Health **14**, 1–22 (2014)
8. Doyle, N.: Neurodiversity at work: a biopsychosocial model and the impact on working adults. Br. Med. Bull. **135**(1), 108–125 (2020)
9. Doyle, N., McDowall, A.: Diamond in the rough? An "empty review" of research into "neurodiversity" and a road map for developing the inclusion agenda. Equality Divers. Incl. Int. J. **41**(3), 352–382 (2021)
10. Field, A., Miles, J., Field, Z.: Discovering statistics using R. Sage (2012)
11. Fuermaier, A.B., Tucha, L., Butzbach, M., Weisbrod, M., Aschenbrenner, S., Tucha, O.: ADHD at the workplace: ADHD symptoms, diagnostic status, and work-related functioning. J. Neural Transm. **128**, 1021–1031 (2021)
12. Gama, K., Liebel, G., Goulão, M., Lacerda, A., Lacerda, C.: A socio-technical grounded theory on the effect of cognitive dysfunctions in the performance of software developers with ADHD and autism. In: Proceedings of the 47th International Conference on Software Engineering: Software Engineering in Society, ICSE-SEIS 2025. Association for Computing Machinery, New York (2025)
13. Hendricks, D.: Employment and adults with autism spectrum disorders: challenges and strategies for success. J. Vocat. Rehabil. **32**(2), 125–134 (2010)
14. Hirota, T., Cheon, K.A., Lai, M.C.: Neurodiversity paradigms and their development across cultures: some reflections in east Asian contexts. Autism **28**(11), 2685–2689 (2024)
15. Holm, S.: A simple sequentially rejective multiple test procedure. Scand. J. Stat., 65–70 (1979)

16. Kohl Silveira, K., Musse, S., Manssour, I.H., Vieira, R., Prikladnicki, R.: Confidence in programming skills: gender insights from stackoverflow developers survey. In: 2019 IEEE/ACM 41st International Conference on Software Engineering: Companion Proceedings (ICSE-Companion), pp. 234–235 (2019)
17. Liebel, G., Langlois, N., Gama, K.: Challenges, strengths, and strategies of software engineers with ADHD: a case study. In: Proceedings of the 46th International Conference on Software Engineering: Software Engineering in Society, ICSE-SEIS 2024, pp. 57–68. Association for Computing Machinery, New York (2024). https://doi.org/10.1145/3639475.3640107
18. Márquez, G., Pacheco, M., Astudillo, H., Taramasco, C., Calvo, E.: Inclusion of individuals with autism spectrum disorder in software engineering. Inf. Softw. Technol., 107434 (2024)
19. McChesney, I., Bond, R.: Eye tracking analysis of computer program comprehension in programmers with dyslexia. Empir. Softw. Eng. **24**(3), 1109–1154 (2019)
20. McChesney, I., Bond, R.: Observations on the linear order of program code reading patterns in programmers with dyslexia. In: Proceedings of the Evaluation and Assessment in Software Engineering, pp. 81–89 (2020)
21. Morris, M.R., Begel, A., Wiedermann, B.: Understanding the challenges faced by neurodiverse software engineering employees: towards a more inclusive and productive technical workforce. In: Proceedings of the 17th International ACM SIGACCESS Conference on Computers and Accessibility, pp. 173–184 (2015)
22. Ralph, P., et al.: Pandemic programming: how COVID-19 affects software developers and how their organizations can help. Empir. Softw. Eng. **25**, 4927–4961 (2020)
23. Rogers, D.C., Dittner, A.J., Rimes, K.A., Chalder, T.: Fatigue in an adult attention deficit hyperactivity disorder population: a trans-diagnostic approach. Br. J. Clin. Psychol. **56**(1), 33–52 (2017)
24. Sanchez-Burks, J., Bartel, C.A., Blount, S.: Performance in intercultural interactions at work: cross-cultural differences in response to behavioral mirroring. J. Appl. Psychol. **94**(1), 216 (2009)
25. Singer, J.: Odd people in: the birth of community amongst people on the "autistic spectrum" (1998)
26. Zolyomi, A., et al.: Managing stress: the needs of autistic adults in video calling. Proc. ACM Human-Comput. Int. **3**(CSCW), 1–29 (2019)

# "Good" and "Bad" Failures in Industrial CI/CD–Balancing Cost and Quality Assurance

Simin Sun[1]([✉])[iD], David Friberg[2][iD], and Miroslaw Staron[1][iD]

[1] Chalmers University of Technology and University of Gothenburg,
417 56 Gothenburg, Sweden
{simin.su,miroslaw.staron}@gu.se
[2] Zenseact, Lindholmspiren 2, 417 56 Gothenburg, Sweden
david.friberg@zenseact.com

**Abstract.** Continuous Integration and Continuous Deployment (CI/CD) pipeline automates software development to speed up and enhance the efficiency of engineering software. These workflows consist of various jobs, such as code validation and testing, which developers must wait to complete before receiving feedback. The jobs can fail, which leads to unnecessary delays in build times, decreasing productivity for developers, and increasing costs for companies.

To explore how companies adopt CI/CD workflows and balance cost with quality assurance during optimization, we conducted a qualitative study based on discussions with representatives from four companies, reporting their industry experiences with CI/CD practices."

Our findings reveal that organizations can confuse the distinction between CI and CD, whereas code merge and product release serve as more effective milestones for process optimization and risk control. While numerous tools and research efforts target the post-merge phase to enhance productivity, limited attention has been given to the pre-merge phase, where early failure prevention brings more impacts and less risks.

**Keywords:** CI/CD · Software Management · Quality Assurance

## 1 Introduction

In modern software development, Continuous Integration and Continuous Delivery (CI/CD) pipelines are essential for improving development efficiency and maintaining software quality. Since the introduction of these concepts by Fowler and Foemmel in 2006 [11], a wide range of CI/CD tools—such as Jenkins, Travis CI, GitLab CI, and GitHub Actions—have emerged to automate the process [1–5]. A typical pipeline involves committing code, triggering builds via a CI server, receiving automated feedback, and updating the repository [13].

CI/CD pipelines execute numerous jobs to enforce testing, security, and compliance standards. However, developers frequently face long build times and delayed feedback, which reduce productivity and increase operational costs. To address this, researchers have proposed a variety of optimization techniques, including job prioritization [6,14], selective execution [15], and prediction-based methods for anticipating job outcomes [8,9,21]. Despite these advances, challenges remain in balancing efficiency with risk—early failures that are missed can lead to larger issues downstream [13].

While the adoption of CI/CD research has evolved in the last decade, the ways in which pipelines are viewed and implemented in practice have also evolved. In particular, organizations are increasingly recognizing the need to optimize pipelines not only for performance but also for reliability and maintainability. In this paper, we explore how contemporary software teams manage their CI/CD workflows, with a focus on how they balance cost and quality considerations. By engaging directly with developers and CI/CD practitioners across different organizational contexts, we examine the coexistence, migration, and optimization of CI/CD tools in real-world environments.

Our empirical investigation is grounded in a year-long qualitative study involving eight participants from four software companies, ranging from large-scale enterprises to small startups. These collaborators provided in-depth insights into their development practices, tooling architectures, and strategic decisions around CI/CD adoption and evolution. Their contributions were instrumental not only in shaping the direction of our research but also in identifying key challenges and opportunities. This study aims to answer the following two research questions:

- RQ1: What are the current CI/CD architectures used by the surveyed companies, and what factors influence their architectural choices?
- RQ2: How can CI/CD jobs be categorized to balance the trade-off between higher productivity and lower risk?

Our findings show that modern CI/CD pipelines can be divided into three distinct phases, separated by two critical milestones: code merge and product release. The dynamics of the CI/CD pipelines change significantly in these parts and reflect a shift in ownership, responsibility, and impact. While the product release has long been recognized as a transition in the pipeline, our results highlight the growing significance of the code merge phase as a pivotal transition. In the pre-merge phase, developers hold primary responsibility, and issues tend to affect individuals, often leading to personal frustration. In the post-merge phase, responsibility shifts toward the organization, and while more developers may be impacted by failures, individual accountability becomes diffuse. We find that the pre-merge phase presents a unique opportunity for low-risk, high-impact improvements.

## 2    Methodology

We aimed to identify industrial practitioners with experience in CI/CD workflows, DevOps, or familiarity with these processes. To achieve this, we contacted our collaborating companies and asked them to shortlist potential candidates who met the criteria. We then contacted the shortlisted participants to assess their expertise and willingness to participate in the research. Eventually, we had discussions with eight experts from four different companies. The sample represents professional software engineering in the embedded software domain, covering a variety of organization contexts and sizes and practitioner roles.

## 2.1 Data Collection and Analysis

We conducted this research by a series of discussions, either in person, via Microsoft Teams or by E-mail. Each time began with a brief introduction to our study, followed by obtaining participants' consent to use the content of our conversation for research purposes.

The discussions followed a structured set of open-ended questions categorized into three main areas: (1) CI/CD pipeline, and (2) Optimization strategy. To better understand CI/CD practices, we inquired about tool usage, existing jobs, migration history, tool coexistence, and participants' motivations for these choices. We also explored the cost of their current CI/CD pipeline in terms of time and effort, as well as strategies for cost reduction, including build time optimization, skip/non-skip strategies, and test case prioritization. Participants were asked about the advantages and disadvantages of these strategies.

All participants were anonymized, and no personal data were collected or stored. Some participants provided real-world design representations under confidentiality agreements. Our analysis followed an inductive approach, with an initial classification based on CI/CD tools. To validate our findings, we presented the categorized data and analysis to an experienced software developer and a professor of software engineering for independent review. To analyze the qualitative data, we followed established guidelines [19].

# 3 Results

## 3.1 RQ1

The first finding about the architectures of CI/CD in all participators' companies is that tool coexistence and migration are prevalent across all companies, often functioning as both a cause and a consequence of workflow changes. This observation aligns with prior research on tool migration [18] and the adoption of GitHub Actions [10]. GitHub Actions has gained popularity due to increasing industry demands for automation and its scalability in large-scale development. However, Jenkins remains widely used across all participated companies, primarily due to its flexibility, extensive plugin ecosystem, and ease of integration into existing workflows. We also noticed that all recent research done in the participated companies did their trail test using the Jenkins instead of the real CI/CD tool.

The second finding comes from the discussion about different phases of CI/CD pipelines, all participants noted the difficulty of defining a clear milestone that marks the transition from CI to CD, particularly in companies providing software for larger systems. Additionally, they emphasized that CI activities may continue even after software release, as integration with other systems may be necessary. Unlike traditional CI/CD pipelines, where CI and CD are sequential, these processes often occur in parallel. However, we found the code merge and product release are clear milestones during the software development process, and we demonstrate it in Fig. 1.

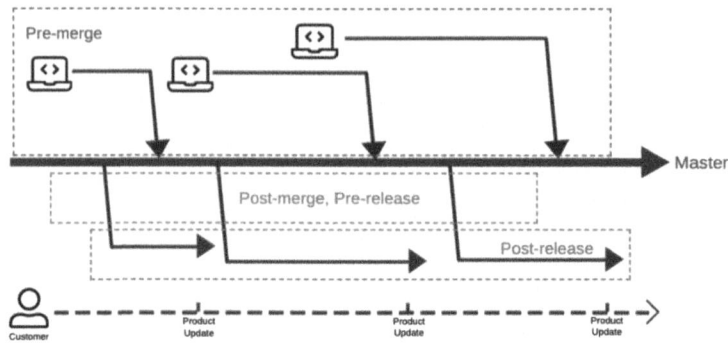

**Fig. 1.** Phases in the CI/CD Pipeline

Lastly, based on their descriptions, we aim to develop a general framework applicable to all participated companies, regardless of their domain or size. The common architectures we identified, which are widely used across these companies, are summarized in Fig. 2.

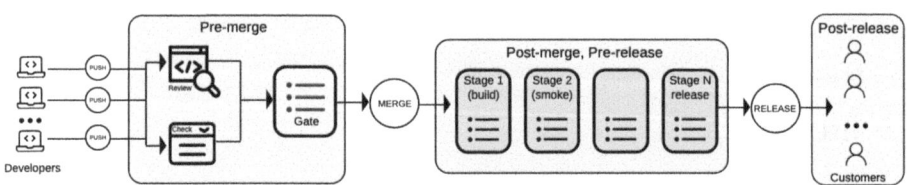

**Fig. 2.** Standard Pipeline Structure Observed Across Multiple Companies

## 3.2 RQ2

While CI/CD pipelines include a variety of jobs that differ across companies, some are widely adopted. According to our participants, these jobs can generally be categorized as follows:

- Code Quality: Includes tasks such as static code analysis and functional test cases.
- Security: Includes security vulnerability checks.

- Dependency and Compliance: Involves verifying dependency versions and compliance verification across different software versions and system architectures
- License Management: Ensures the proper licensing of all packages used.
- Infrastructure and Configuration: Focuses on validating the configuration and related infrastructure.
- Deployment and Release: Includes mock installations and software deployment simulations.

The ideal or safest scenario is to run all jobs at the pre-merge phase to ensure software security and reliability. However, this approach can lead to inefficiencies and increased costs, as developers must wait longer for the pipeline to complete, ultimately lowering productivity and raising operational expenses.

To better understand the trade-offs, we analyzed CI/CD job execution data from 2024 at one company. We found a notable discrepancy in failure rates—the failure rate of pre-merge checks compared to post-merge is 5:3. Moreover, this does not take into account that many post-merge failures are sticky, meaning they are counted repeatedly until a fix is applied and has propagated downstream. As a result, the ratio may understate the true discrepancy, since it conservatively overestimates the number of unique post-merge failures. We also found that the overall ratio of checks run in pre-merge versus post-merge is approximately 15:1. This highlights not only the imbalance in the total number of check runs between the pre-merge and post-merge phases, but also that pre-merge runs—already far more numerous—are more prone to failure. A key contributor to this higher failure rate is the significantly greater number of jobs per check in the pre-merge phase, compared to the number of jobs that are unique to post-merge—that is, jobs which have not already succeeded in pre-merge.

When considering the higher job count per check in pre-merge, the scale of check volume—with millions of runs annually—and the constrained resources within organizations, these findings suggest that optimizing the pre-merge phase—whether by reducing failures or improving efficiency—could drive more immediate and meaningful improvements to the developer experience than equivalent efforts focused on post-merge.

Another key observation is that, in addition to the commonly reported causes of long build times and job failures—such as test failures, build misconfigurations, and dependency issues, as noted in prior research [12,17]—two of the participants highlighted flaky tests and intermittent failures as major contributors to CI/CD job failures in their companies. Notably, recent research [7] has begun to focus on these types of failures, underscoring their growing significance in the field. Additionally, for one company, software configuration management (SWM) and product configuration management (PCM) were identified as key failure points, particularly in infrastructure- and configuration-related jobs. For their release process, ensuring compatibility between all system components, including both hardware and software, was crucial.

While long build times pose challenges for both developers and organizations, there is hesitation in adopting early-phase build optimization techniques, especially those involving skipped builds or test cases. Participants preferred exposing failures earlier rather than later, aiming to detect as many issues as possible in the early phases. By contrast, failures in later phases – particularly during integration into a more extensive architecture or product release – should be minimal or nonexistent. As a result, unless skipping techniques provide trustworthy and explainable justifications, they are used with caution.

Currently, job prioritization is done using cache-based and code comparison techniques. Our analysis showed that teams rely on these tools to analyze diffs and dependencies in code to validate new commits efficiently and schedule the execution of jobs. However, they primarily operate in the post-merge and pre-release phases.

While post-merge optimization remains a widely studied area in CI/CD research, there is growing interest in pre-merge optimizations. Since code at this phase has not yet been merged into the main branch, any issues identified can be addressed with minimal cost and no risk to the overall system architecture. Three of the four companies expressed interest in solutions for predicting build outcomes at runtime or during the pre-merge phase, as these approaches could significantly reduce resource consumption and prevent failures. Participants from two different companies mentioned that they had done research on exploring this direction using generative artificial intelligence models to enhance prediction accuracy and streamline CI/CD workflows.

## 4  Discussion

The findings of this study highlight two critical milestones: code merge and product release, in the software development lifecycle that are widely recognized across companies and developers. The implications of our research include the following:

**For Company:** A key insight from this study is the distinction between "good" failures, which occur early in the development process (e.g., pre-merge), and "bad" failures, which arise at later phases (e.g., post-merge). The cost of addressing issues at these phases varies significantly. While companies aim to enhance developer productivity by reducing build frequency and optimizing build time in the early phases, they must also consider the risks associated with such strategies. A balance must be struck to prevent critical failures in later phases, which can be far more costly.

A widely adopted approach is history-based analysis [16], which leverages failure and test execution history to detect faults in submitted code. This remains an active research area. In industry, tools like Bazel have gained popularity for their ability to track history and perform comparisons. Another strategy is scheduling automated build jobs during off-peak hours, such as evenings or weekends, to minimize developer wait times and reduce computational load. These methods are generally safe, with skipping and auto-run mechanisms remaining under manual control.

While some companies have observed that postponing rarely failing jobs to later phases can improve overall efficiency, they approach this with caution. Post-merge failures could result in pre-merge effect such as merge stop, which impacts the entire team. In such cases, resolving issues after the merge can be significantly more time-consuming and complex, potentially outweighing the benefits of deferred execution.

**For Individual Developers:** Our findings suggest that while pipeline bottlenecks occur in both the pre-merge and post-merge stages, individual developers often feel the impact more acutely during the pre-merge phase. This is the phase they interact with most frequently and where they encounter productivity barriers such as job failures, extended wait times, and time-consuming debugging. These challenges are align with prior research [13,22]. The productivity bottleneck is very much present in pre-merge, particularly as a) many jobs fails (and not always "good"), and b) the majority of load on the CI machinery comes from pre-merge.

Current research primarily focuses on test case prioritization [15,16], build-skipping techniques [6,14,20], and build prediction [8,21]. However, these approaches operate at a higher level, optimizing overall efficiency rather than directly addressing developers' pain points. Developers still experience delays while waiting for builds to complete and must debug issues themselves.

While existing tools and optimization strategies primarily target post-merge and pre-release phases, there is a lack of support for the pre-merge phase—an area where improvements could further enhance developer efficiency and software quality. In practice, the dominant approach in most companies remains manual error resolution, with developers fixing CI/CD issues independently or seeking help from colleagues via group chats or in-person discussions.

**For Researchers:** Based on Shahin's systematic review [23], most current research aimed at facilitating the CI/CD process focuses on six key areas, namely shorten the build time, visibility and awareness of the results, automated testing, detecting the faults, security and scalability, and dependability and reliability in CD. However, all six areas primarily address the post-merge and pre-release phases, with limited attention given to predicting failures or resolving issues before developers commit their code. Notably, none of these areas directly enhance developer efficiency, as companies tend to prioritize quality assurance over efficiency.

However, there is an underexplored opportunity that could benefit both companies and developers: the pre-merge phase. By predicting build outcomes and assisting developers in debugging before code is merged or even committed, we could strike a balance between quality and efficiency, addressing a long-standing dilemma in CI/CD.

Furthermore, despite the diverse architectures of CI/CD workflows in practice, there is a pressing need for a universal framework that can address these challenges across different development environments. Future research should explore predictive models and proactive solutions to enhance early-phase error detection and resolution.

## 5    Validity Evaluation

We discussed the internal, external, construct and external validity thereat that could affect our results used the framework by Wohlin [24]. A threat to **internal validity** arises from participant selection, as their experiences and perspectives shape the conclusions of this study, making them indicative rather than definitive. To mitigate this, we selected participants with substantial experience in CI/CD and DevOps. Additionally, we asked participants to provide concrete examples when making strong claims to ensure the reliability of their insights. A threat to **external validity** stems from the limited scope of our study and the specific settings of our discussions. Categorizing and evaluating CI/CD practices across four companies may affect the generalizability of our findings. To address these concerns, we selected companies of varying sizes and domains to enhance the diversity and applicability of our findings. A threat to **construct validity** arises if participants do not fully understand the questions or if the questions are not entirely applicable to their company. If a participant is not entirely familiar with certain aspects, we invite an additional participant from the same company to ensure all questions can be properly understood and answered. A threat to **conclusion validity** arises from potential researcher bias in data analysis. Since this is a qualitative study, all conclusions are drawn from conversations with participants and analyzed based on meeting notes, which may introduce bias or lead to the omission of key insights. To mitigate this risk, we implemented an expert review process involving professionals from both industry and academia to ensure a more objective and comprehensive analysis.

## 6    Conclusion

This empirical study highlights the critical role of CI/CD in modern software development and release processes. Practitioners take a broad view of the boundary between CI and CD, yet they consistently recognize two key milestones: code merge and product release. These milestones are frequently used to separate different phases of development, suggesting their potential application in CI/CD workflows to balance efficiency and risk management.

Our findings provide clear evidence that practitioners prefer "good" failures—those occurring early in the development process (e.g., pre-release)—over "bad" failures that emerge later (e.g., post-release). When considering optimization strategies, companies must weigh the trade-offs between efficiency gains and potential risks. While techniques such as build skipping and test case prioritization can enhance productivity, many companies hesitate to adopt them due to concerns about undetected failures. Instead, they favor strategies that provide clear explanations and traceability.

Additionally, our study identifies a significant gap in existing CI/CD tooling: pre-merge support. Current research primarily focuses on reducing build time after code submission and job execution, yet few tools help developers detect issues before merging code. Companies are actively seeking solutions that minimize waiting time while mitigating risks in early development phases or at runtime. Addressing this gap presents an opportunity for future research and tool development in CI/CD optimization.

In future studies, we aim to investigate developers' perspectives on pre-merge support in CI/CD, focusing on the specific tasks or areas where they seek assistance. Additionally, we plan to explore the potential of large language models in supporting these tasks and examine developers' opinions regarding their adoption in real-world practice.

**Acknowledgments.** We sincerely thank all industry participants for their valuable insights and contributions, which have been instrumental in shaping this work.

This work has also been partially funded by Software Center, a collaboration between University of Gothenburg, Chalmers and 18 universities and companies – www.software-center.se.

# References

1. Cruisecontrol (2001). https://cruisecontrol.sourceforge.net/. Accessed 13 Oct 2024
2. Jenkins (2011). https://www.jenkins.io/. Accessed 13 Oct 2024
3. Travis ci (2011). https://travis-ci.org/. Accessed 13 Oct 2024
4. Gitlab ci (2014). https://about.gitlab.com/features/continuous-integration/. Accessed 13 Oct 2024
5. Github actions (2019). https://github.com/features/actions. Accessed 13 Oct 2024
6. Abdalkareem, R., Mujahid, S., Shihab, E., Rilling, J.: Which commits can be ci skipped? IEEE Trans. Software Eng. **47**(3), 448–463 (2019)
7. Aïdasso, H., Bordeleau, F., Tizghadam, A.: On the diagnosis of flaky job failures: understanding and prioritizing failure categories. arXiv preprint arXiv:2501.04976 (2025)
8. Al-Sabbagh, K., Staron, M., Hebig, R.: Predicting build outcomes in continuous integration using textual analysis of source code commits. In: Proceedings of the 18th International Conference on Predictive Models and Data Analytics in Software Engineering, pp. 42–51 (2022)
9. Bisong, E., Tran, E., Baysal, O.: Built to last or built too fast? Evaluating prediction models for build times. In: 2017 IEEE/ACM 14th International Conference on Mining Software Repositories (MSR), pp. 487–490. IEEE (2017)
10. Decan, A., Mens, T., Mazrae, P.R., Golzadeh, M.: On the use of github actions in software development repositories. In: 2022 IEEE International Conference on Software Maintenance and Evolution (ICSME), pp. 235–245. IEEE (2022)
11. Fowler, M., Foemmel, M.: Continuous integration (2006)
12. Ghaleb, T.A., da Costa, D.A., Zou, Y.: An empirical study of the long duration of continuous integration builds. Empir. Softw. Eng. **24**(4), 2102–2139 (2019). https://doi.org/10.1007/s10664-019-09695-9
13. Hilton, M., Nelson, N., Tunnell, T., Marinov, D., Dig, D.: Trade-offs in continuous integration: assurance, security, and flexibility. In: Proceedings of the 2017 11th Joint Meeting on Foundations of Software Engineering, pp. 197–207 (2017)
14. Jin, X., Servant, F.: Which builds are really safe to skip? Maximizing failure observation for build selection in continuous integration. J. Syst. Softw. **188**, 111292 (2022)

15. Jin, X., Servant, F.: Hybridcisave: a combined build and test selection approach in continuous integration. ACM Trans. Softw. Eng. Methodol. **32**(4), 1–39 (2023)
16. Lima, J.A.P., Vergilio, S.R.: Test case prioritization in continuous integration environments: a systematic mapping study. Inf. Softw. Technol. **121**, 106268 (2020)
17. Rausch, T., Hummer, W., Leitner, P., Schulte, S.: An empirical analysis of build failures in the continuous integration workflows of java-based open-source software. In: 2017 IEEE/ACM 14th International Conference on Mining Software Repositories (MSR), pp. 345–355. IEEE (2017)
18. Rostami Mazrae, P., Mens, T., Golzadeh, M., Decan, A.: On the usage, co-usage and migration of CI/CD tools: a qualitative analysis. Empir. Softw. Eng. **28**(2), 52 (2023)
19. Runeson, P., Höst, M.: Guidelines for conducting and reporting case study research in software engineering. Empir. Softw. Eng. **14**, 131–164 (2009)
20. Saidani, I., Ouni, A., Mkaouer, M.W.: Detecting continuous integration skip commits using multi-objective evolutionary search. IEEE Trans. Software Eng. **48**(12), 4873–4891 (2021)
21. Saidani, I., Ouni, A., Mkaouer, M.W.: Improving the prediction of continuous integration build failures using deep learning. Autom. Softw. Eng. **29**(1), 1–61 (2022). https://doi.org/10.1007/s10515-021-00319-5
22. Saroar, S.G., Nayebi, M.: Developers' perception of github actions: a survey analysis. In: Proceedings of the 27th International Conference on Evaluation and Assessment in Software Engineering, pp. 121–130 (2023)
23. Shahin, M., Babar, M.A., Zhu, L.: Continuous integration, delivery and deployment: a systematic review on approaches, tools, challenges and practices. IEEE Access **5**, 3909–3943 (2017)
24. Wohlin, C., Runeson, P., Höst, M., Ohlsson, M.C., Regnell, B., Wesslén, A.: Experimentation in Software Engineering. Springer (2012)

# Exploring Software Fairness Debt in Gray Literature

Rodrigo Sotolani[1]([✉])⬤, Sávio Freire[2]⬤, Felipe Fronchetti[3]⬤,
Ronnie de Souza Santos[4]⬤, and Rodrigo Spinola[1]⬤

[1] Department of Computer Science, Virginia Commonwealth University,
Richmond, VA, USA
`{silvasotolr,spinolaro}@vcu.edu`
[2] Federal Institute of Ceará, Morada Nova, Ceará, Brazil
`savio.freire@ifce.edu.br`
[3] Department of Computer Science, Louisiana State University,
Baton Rouge, LA, USA
`ffronchetti@lsu.edu`
[4] Schulich School of Engineering, University of Calgary, Calgary, Canada
`ronnie.desouzasantos@ucalgary.ca`

**Abstract.** *Context:* Bias in AI and software systems has raised
widespread concern due to its role in perpetuating discrimination,
prompting the emergence of the concept of software fairness debt. *Objective:* This study explores how fairness debt in software is portrayed in
gray literature, aiming to identify real-world examples, root causes, and
effects. *Method:* Using a query-based approach, we retrieved and analyzed 79 articles from gray literature, applying content analysis guided
by an established fairness debt conceptual model. *Results:* We identified 23 examples of fairness debt (e.g., racism, sexism), 32 causes (e.g.,
training, societal, and historical bias), and 14 primary effects (e.g., proliferation of discrimination, reinforcement of stereotypes). *Conclusion:*
Our findings extend the fairness debt framework with empirical insights
from nonacademic sources, offering a broader understanding of software
fairness and guiding future research and mitigation strategies.

**Keywords:** software fairness · fairness debt · gray literature

## 1 Introduction

As digital technologies become increasingly integrated into daily life, growing
evidence shows that software and AI/ML systems often inherit biases that lead to
discriminatory outcomes [8,34,37]. For instance, algorithmic decisions in hiring
and credit can reinforce existing inequalities [5], and facial recognition systems
have been shown to misclassify darker-skinned women at significantly higher
rates than lighter-skinned men [7]. These issues underscore the importance of
fairness as a crucial dimension of software quality, particularly in high-stakes
domains such as law enforcement, healthcare, and finance [14].

© The Author(s), under exclusive license to Springer Nature Switzerland AG 2026
D. Taibi and D. Smite (Eds.): SEAA 2025, LNCS 16083, pp. 85–104, 2026.
https://doi.org/10.1007/978-3-032-04207-1_7

Software fairness is the principle of ensuring that systems and algorithms produce just and unbiased outcomes across diverse groups, regardless of race, gender, ethnicity, or socioeconomic status [14]. Bias—manifesting as racial, gender, socioeconomic, or geographic disparities—is a major source of fairness violations [21]. Notable examples include biased hiring algorithms [1,18], predictive policing systems targeting specific communities [22], and medical AI models with lower accuracy for underrepresented groups [10,21]. These issues highlight the need for bias detection [10], fairness-aware models [4,23,35], and regulatory oversight [2].

The concept of software fairness debt captures the accumulation of unresolved biases and ethical shortcomings in software systems. Introduced by de Souza Santos et al. [34], it frames fairness issues as a form of technical debt, highlighting the societal costs of deploying biased systems without mitigating their root causes. Similarly, Petrozzino [28] described AI ethical debt as the hidden cost of neglecting fairness, often revealed only after deployment, with harmful consequences. These studies stress the importance of proactive bias mitigation throughout the software lifecycle [5,7,28,34].

Gray literature (GL) includes non-peer-reviewed documents from government, academia, industry, and other sectors—such as policy reports and public commentary—that offer valuable insights into emerging issues [30]. In software engineering, GL has been utilized to examine topics such as technical debt [16,17,29], human aspects [3], and requirements engineering [12,13]. For example, Baltes et al. [3] and Freire et al. [13] used public discourse—a form of GL involving open societal discussions—to explore age bias and requirements debt. While GL has proven valuable in examining software engineering issues, the perspectives of practitioners, policymakers, and affected communities—often captured in GL—remain underrepresented in efforts to understand the real-world implications of software fairness debt.

This work aims to investigate examples of software fairness debt, their causes, and main effects. To this end, we elicited gray literature using a query-based approach to identify web addresses related to fairness debt via Google. From these sources, we selected relevant articles and conducted a content analysis [24] to extract and examine the discussed examples, causes, and effects.

We analyzed 79 articles related to fairness and algorithmic discrimination. We identified 23 categories of fairness debt examples, 32 root causes, and 14 main effects, expanding the conceptual map on fairness debt [34]. The most frequently cited forms of fairness debt were racism, sexism, and classism, while training bias, societal bias, and historical bias were the most common root causes. The leading reported effects included the proliferation of discrimination, the reinforcement of stereotypes, and the exacerbation of social inequality, with the first being the most emphasized outcome. These findings underscore the value of insights from GL. They both validate and extend the previous framework by introducing a broader set of fairness debt categories, causes, and effects. For practitioners, this offers a new lens on software quality informed by real-world concerns, while researchers gain a foundation for comparison with existing academic literature.

The remainder of this article is ordered as follows: Sect. 2 gives background on software fairness debt. Section 3 describes the methodology for analyzing gray literature. Section 4 presents key findings. Section 5 discusses the results. Section 6 concludes with recommendations for future research and practice.

## 2   Background

Software fairness arises when systems embed biases that disproportionately affect specific groups, resulting in ethically and socially harmful outcomes [36]. It reflects the consequences of neglecting fairness in software design and implementation. Notable cases include facial recognition systems misclassifying darker-skinned individuals [7], racially biased health prediction algorithms [27], and recidivism risk tools used by U.S. judges that show racial bias [9].

Software fairness extends beyond ethical considerations. Unfair software systems can cause legal liability, reputational damage, and loss of user trust [15, 20]. Moreover, regulatory frameworks such as the General Data Protection Regulation and the Algorithmic Accountability Act are increasing pressure on organizations to mitigate algorithmic biases [19]. The complexity of fairness assessment and mitigation requires a collaborative approach that integrates software engineering, data science, ethics, law, and social sciences expertise.

According to Brun and Meliou [6], software fairness is analogous to software quality and security: while good design and appropriate algorithms are essential, so are quality control practices such as testing and formal verification. Addressing fairness challenges requires robust methodologies, transparent decision-making, and a commitment to continuous evaluation and improvement.

In software systems, as discussed in de Souza Santos et al. [34], fairness debt refers to a set of design, implementation, or management practices that may provide immediate benefits when developing AI solutions. However, these practices create long-term challenges with significant societal implications. They introduce biases that are often complex and costly to identify or correct over time. This results in liabilities that affect not only the internal quality of the system but also have broader societal consequences, as the biases embedded in AI can lead to harmful or unjust outcomes for users and communities. In Fig. 1, the conceptual map inside the bold rectangle defines the software fairness debt and its elements and relationships, as proposed by de Souza Santos et al. [34]. It simplifies the understanding of software fairness. It highlights the causes that lead development teams to accumulate software fairness debt (shown in blue), provides a definition of fairness debt, lists instances where it can occur (marked in yellow), and outlines the consequences of its occurrence (depicted in orange). The elements presented outside the bold rectangle are contributions of this work, and they will be described in Sect. 5.

By integrating software fairness debt with insights from gray literature, this study offers a new perspective grounded in broader technical and public discussions in software engineering. Exploring these dynamics provides researchers and practitioners with an additional lens to better understand, assess, and address fairness-related challenges in software systems. The following section presents the research method.

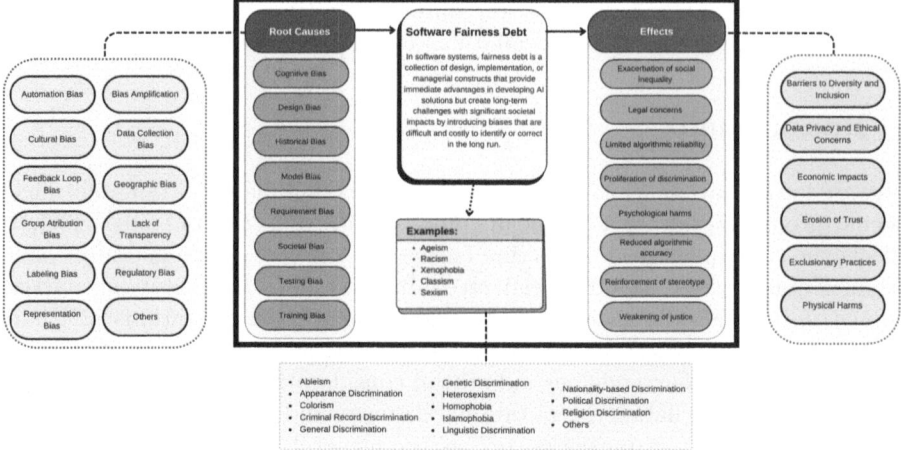

**Fig. 1.** Software Fairness Debt Conceptual Map. Adapted from [34]. (Color figure online)

## 3 Research Method

This section outlines the research questions and the data collection and analysis procedures employed in this study.

### 3.1 Research Questions

This study aims to investigate examples, causes, and effects of fairness debt as reflected in gray literature. To achieve this goal, we formulated the following research questions (RQs):

- *RQ1*: **What examples of fairness debt in software systems are reflected in gray literature?** We seek to identify specific instances of fairness debt in software systems. The goal is to uncover real-world cases where fairness issues have been raised regarding software systems, notably those related to race, gender, socioeconomic status, and other protected categories.
- *RQ2*: **What are the causes of fairness debt in software systems as reported in gray literature?** This question aims to explore the underlying causes or drivers of unfairness within software systems. The focus is on identifying systemic issues that lead to biased outcomes, from a technical and social perspective.
- *RQ3*: **What are the effects of fairness debt in software systems as described in gray literature?** This research question focuses on understanding the consequences of fairness issues in software systems. It aims to map how biased or discriminatory systems affect individuals, organizations, and society as a whole. By analyzing how these effects are discussed in gray literature, the question highlights the real-world harms and adverse outcomes associated with fairness debt.

## 3.2   Data Collection

To collect data from gray literature, we adopted a query-based approach similar to Baltes et al. [3] and Freire et al. [13]. Using the Google API, we initially retrieved the top 100 results for the query `fairness AND (software OR system)`, but found that many focused on legal rather than software contexts. To refine the search, we (1) adjusted the query to `fairness AND software` and (2) generated additional keywords based on the software fairness debt conceptual model [34]. Table 1 presents the complete list of keywords we used in our study. We retrieved the top 25 results for each of the 22 search strings, yielding a total of 650 web addresses (550 + 100 from the initial search). All searches were performed in July 2024. All metadata and extracted data are available in our replication package [33].

**Table 1.** Software Fairness Debt Keywords

| #  | Element  | Keywords |
|----|----------|----------|
| 0  | Main     | `fairness AND software` |
| 1  | Examples | `software ageism` |
| 2  | Examples | `software racism` |
| 3  | Examples | `software xenophobia` |
| 4  | Examples | `software classism` |
| 5  | Examples | `software sexism` |
| 6  | Effects  | `software fairness AND social inequality` |
| 7  | Effects  | `software fairness AND legal concerns` |
| 8  | Effects  | `software fairness AND algorithm reliability` |
| 9  | Effects  | `software fairness AND discrimination` |
| 10 | Effects  | `software fairness AND psychological harms` |
| 11 | Effects  | `software fairness AND algorithm accuracy` |
| 12 | Effects  | `software fairness AND stereotype` |
| 13 | Effects  | `software fairness AND justice` |
| 14 | Causes   | `software fairness AND bias` |
| 15 | Causes   | `software fairness AND cognitive bias` |
| 16 | Causes   | `software fairness AND design bias` |
| 17 | Causes   | `software fairness AND historical bias` |
| 18 | Causes   | `software fairness AND model bias` |
| 19 | Causes   | `software fairness AND requirement bias` |
| 20 | Causes   | `software fairness AND societal bias` |
| 21 | Causes   | `software fairness AND testing bias` |
| 22 | Causes   | `software fairness AND training bias` |

We limited retrieval to the top 25 results per query based on pilot tests showing that lower-ranked results were often less relevant and more repetitive. Given our 22 keyword combinations, this cap balanced data volume with quality. We acknowledge this may introduce bias due to Google's ranking algorithm and address this in the threats to validity section.

After collecting the web addresses, we found that most were articles—well-structured, non-peer-reviewed documents discussing fairness debt. To ensure relevance, we applied the inclusion and exclusion criteria shown in Table 2. Two researchers independently reviewed all addresses using scanning and skimming techniques, followed by full reading when appropriate. Each article was marked as "included" or "excluded," with exclusion reasons documented. A third researcher resolved any disagreements. After consensus, 113 web addresses were selected for data extraction.

**Table 2.** Inclusion (IC) and Exclusion (EC) Criteria

| Criteria | Description |
| --- | --- |
| IC1 | **Gray literature about software fairness**. The source must be gray literature on software fairness. |
| EC1 | **Article not available online**. Not available for online reading or downloading. We also excluded articles with access restrictions, such as subscriptions or limited access. |
| EC2 | **Incomplete texts**. Texts not completed, drafts, summaries, slides, partial access, and other non-full access or content were excluded. |
| EC3 | **Articles not written in English**. Results found in languages other than English were excluded. |
| EC4 | **Articles duplicated**. Since we retrieved articles from many keywords, some works were found to be duplicates. The first article found was kept, while the others were excluded. |
| EC5 | **Not a gray literature (it is a paper)**. White literature, papers, books, chapters, and other academic works were excluded. |

### 3.3  Data Extraction

To extract the data, one researcher reviewed all 113 web addresses and identified record units—short text segments containing information relevant to each research question [24, 38]. These units were documented in an Excel spreadsheet (see Table 3). Articles were considered relevant if they addressed at least one research question, resulting in 34 articles being excluded, leaving 79 articles for analysis. A second researcher reviewed all record units during the analysis phase.

**Table 3.** Data extraction table definition

| Data collection variable | Purpose |
| --- | --- |
| Title | Demographics |
| Author Source | Demographics |
| Source link (publication media) | Demographics |
| Full text | Demographics |
| Year of publication | Demographics |
| Search string | Demographics |
| Search date | Demographics |
| Examples of fairness debt in software | RQ1 |
| Primary causes of fairness debt in software systems | RQ2 |
| Leading effects of fairness debt in software systems | RQ3 |

## 3.4   Data Analysis

A total of 815 recorded units were initially extracted from the 79 articles. Each recorded unit addressed one of the research questions (RQs). For example, "word embeddings trained on Google News articles exhibit and perpetuate gender-based stereotypes in society" represents an instance of fairness debt (RQ1). The unit "AI fairness and bias can arise from various sources, such as data, algorithms, design, or deployment" corresponds to a cause (RQ2). Meanwhile, "a machine learning system that is unfair to people of color might also be unfair to the elderly or the young," illustrates an effect (RQ3).

We conducted a content analysis [24] in three iterations, using manual coding [31] to identify examples, causes, and effects in the recorded units. The first iteration was a pilot involving two randomly selected articles. Two annotators independently coded the units and met to consolidate their findings. They observed that a single unit could reference multiple elements—for example, "Amazon's Rekognition, which also showed racial bias against darker-skinned women (31% error in gender classification)" reflects both racism and sexism.

In the second iteration, the annotators conducted a calibration round with 20 articles (137 recorded units). They found that the conceptual map [34] lacked some causes and effects, so the lists were expanded with support from ChatGPT-4o. This tool was employed as a brainstorming aid to surface additional terminology and dimensions not initially covered in the academic model. The generated outputs were carefully reviewed and validated by the researchers before integration. Each proposed item was examined for conceptual alignment with the study objectives, clarity, and potential redundancy with existing categories. This iterative process ensured traceability and consistency in the integration of LLM-generated suggestions. While we did not implement full LLM self-refinement cycles [25], we acknowledge this as a promising avenue for improving LLM-supported taxonomy construction in future work. Table 4 shows the prompt used, and Table 5 presents the updated lists that guided the remaining coding.

**Table 4.** Prompt used on ChatGPT to expand the categories

| RQ | Source | Prompt |
|---|---|---|
| 1 | List of examples | Considering the source attached, which contains a list of examples of fairness debt in software systems, expand it comprehensively. Include an explanation for each category. |
| 2 | List of causes | Considering the source attached, which contains a list of categories of causes of lack of fairness in software systems, expand it comprehensively. Include an explanation for each category. |
| 3 | List of effects | Considering the source attached, which contains a list of categories of effects of lack of fairness in software systems, expand it comprehensively. Include an explanation for each category. |

**Table 5.** Extended elements of software fairness debt (* original elements from [34])

| Example of Fairness Debt | Cause | Effects |
|---|---|---|
| Racism* | Cognitive Bias* | Exacerbation of Social Inequality* |
| Xenophobia* | Design Bias* | Legal Concerns* |
| Classism* | Historical Bias* | Limited Algorithmic Reliability* |
| Sexism* | Model Bias* | Proliferation of Discrimination* |
| Ageism* | Requirements Bias* | Psychological Harms* |
| Ableism | Societal Bias* | Reduced Algorithmic Accuracy* |
| Homophobia | Testing Bias* | Reinforcement of Stereotypes* |
| Transphobia | Training Bias* | Weakening of Justice* |
| Religious Discrimination | Lack of Transparency | Erosion of Trust |
| Anti-Semitism | Regulatory Bias | Economic Impacts |
| Islamophobia | Feedback Loop Bias | Exclusionary Practices |
| Sizeism | Cultural Bias | Barriers to Diversity and Inclusion |
| Colorism | Data Collection Bias | Data Privacy and Ethical Concerns |
| Heterosexism | Labeling Bias | Hindered Innovation |
| Linguistic Discrimination | Contextual Bias | Adverse Effects on Education |
| Neurodiversity Discrimination | Geographic Bias | |
| Casteism | Algorithmic Complexity Bias | |
| Relational Discrimination | User Interaction Bias | |
| Nationality-Based Discrimination | Bias Amplification | |
| Occupational Discrimination | Temporal Bias | |
| Speciesism | Representation Bias | |
| Political Discrimination | Interaction Bias | |
| Genetic Discrimination | Group Attribution Bias | |
| Parental Status Discrimination | Automation Bias | |
| Pregnancy Discrimination | Post-Processing Bias | |
| Mental Health Discrimination | Economic Bias | |
| Criminal Record Discrimination | Infrastructure Bias | |
| Appearance Discrimination | Normative Bias | |
| Gender Identity Discrimination | Interpretability Bias | |
| | Bias in Preprocessing | |
| | Bias in Benchmarking | |
| | Network Bias | |

In the final iteration, one annotator coded all 591 remaining units using the updated lists, and a second annotator reviewed the coding. Disagreements were resolved in a consensus meeting. For example, the unit "If you make a technology that can classify people by an ethnicity, someone will use it to repress that ethnicity" was initially coded as Data Privacy and Ethical Concerns and Proliferation of Discrimination, but the annotators ultimately agreed on the latter.

To identify the relationships between fairness debt examples (RQ1) and their root causes (RQ2), we analyzed the co-occurrence of these examples within the same recorded unit. Each unit was reviewed to determine whether it mentioned both an example (e.g., racism) and a cause (e.g., training bias). These co-occurrence relationships were recorded in a mapping table and aggregated across all 79 articles. The resulting frequency counts were then visualized in Fig. 3. Similar logic was applied for the example–effect mapping (RQ1 and RQ3) shown in Fig. 4.

To assess inter-rater reliability, we calculated Cohen's Kappa coefficient ($\kappa$) [26], which ranges from $-1$ (complete disagreement) to $+1$ (perfect agreement). We used the ReCal2 tool [11] to compute $\kappa$ after all three iterations. For examples of discrimination (RQ1), we obtained $\kappa = 0.88$, indicating strong agreement. For both root causes (RQ2) and leading effects (RQ3), the coefficient was $\kappa = 0.72$, reflecting fair to good agreement between the annotators.

## 4 Results

We analyzed 79 articles (676 recorded units) on fairness debt. Figure 2 shows their yearly distribution, revealing a rising trend. The following subsections present our results by research question.

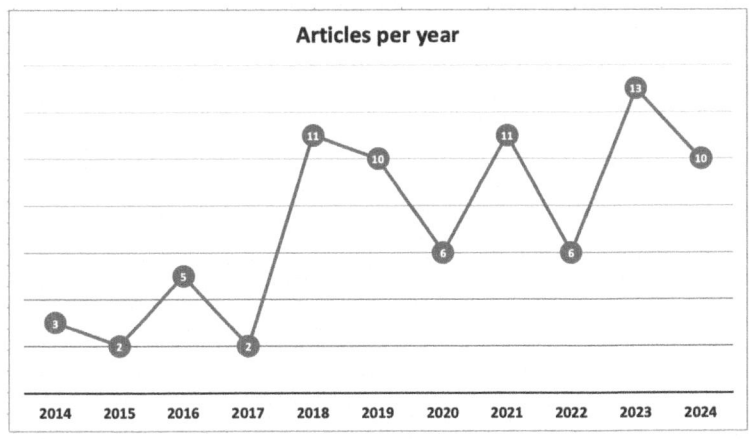

**Fig. 2.** Identified articles from gray literature, per year. (*) Until July 2024.

## 4.1    RQ1: What Examples of Fairness Debt in Software Systems Are Reflected in Gray Literature?

Table 6 presents the top five discrimination examples out of the 23 identified in this study. The full list is available in [33]. Racism was the most frequently cited (53), followed by sexism (39), classism (24), xenophobia (18), and colorism (13). Racism refers to discrimination based on race or ethnicity, while sexism is based on gender, typically targeting women. Classism involves bias based on social or economic class; xenophobia is prejudice against individuals from other countries or cultures; and colorism is discrimination based on skin tone, usually within the same racial or ethnic group. For example, the recorded unit "AI image tools tend to spin up disturbing clichés: Asian women are hypersexual. Africans are primitive. Europeans are worldly. Leaders are men. Prisoners are Black" simultaneously reflects racism, sexism, classism, and xenophobia. Another recorded unit, "Algorithmic bias against people of color, however, is a persistent and pervasive issue across industries," illustrates colorism.

Unlike the source model [34], the gray literature reveals a wider range of discrimination types, expanding from 5 to 23 categories. While academic work focuses on common cases like racism and sexism, nonacademic sources address broader issues like ableism and political bias. Still, both align on the top discrimination categories.

**Table 6.** Top 5 examples of fairness debt

| Discrimination Example | # | Recorded Units |
|---|---|---|
| Racism | 53 | A010, A017, A027, A034, A059, A070, A087, A152, A154, A155, A156, A159, A160, A162, A164, A165, A166, A169, A170, A173, A175, A177, A186, A188, A189, A190, A195, A196, A207, A212, A219, A238, A252, A260, A267, A272, A280, A294, A312, A320, A324, A380, A416, A448, A450, A455, A471, A472, A505, A508, A521, A542, A598 |
| Sexism | 39 | A017, A034, A087, A115, A152, A154, A159, A164, A166, A170, A186, A188, A190, A196, A207, A211, A212, A219, A225, A238, A252, A267, A272, A280, A312, A320, A324, A335, A361, A380, A450, A455, A485, A505, A508, A520, A521, A523, A542 |
| Classism | 24 | A010, A035, A063, A086, A087, A135, A155, A156, A170, A173, A186, A189, A238, A267, A294, A320, A380, A450, A455, A508, A520, A521, A542, A598 |
| Xenophobia | 18 | A017, A156, A159, A169, A170, A177, A186, A195, A196, A238, A267, A294, A324, A416, A448, A450, A505, A520 |
| Colorism | 13 | A017, A160, A166, A170, A175, A188, A189, A196, A252, A320, A380, A455, A525 |

**Finding #1:** Racism, sexism, and classism are the most frequently cited examples of unfairness, indicating that the articles primarily focus on traditional forms of discrimination. In contrast, less attention is given to other types of bias, such as those related to neurodivergence, appearance, or language.

## 4.2   RQ2: What Are the Causes of Fairness Debt in Software Systems as Reported in Gray Literature?

We identified 32 causes contributing to fairness debt. Table 7 presents the five most frequently mentioned. The full list is available in [33]. The most commonly cited causes were training bias, societal bias, historical bias, cognitive bias, and model bias.

Training bias arises from the data or labels used during the model training process, where particular groups may be underrepresented or misrepresented. Historical bias reflects longstanding societal inequalities embedded in the data used to train models. For instance, the recorded unit "Another problem with the algorithms is that many were trained on white populations outside the US" illustrates both training and historical bias.

Societal bias stems from broader social norms, structures, and inequalities that influence how software is developed and deployed. Cognitive bias is introduced by developers, data scientists, or users through inherent flaws in human judgment and decision-making. These biases are exemplified in the statement: "Someone—a human—has to first decide where the 'high risk' threshold should lie, whether by using Blackstone's ratio or something else. That depends on all kinds of considerations—political, economic, and social."

Finally, model bias refers to biases inherent in the algorithm itself, often due to simplifications, flawed assumptions, or overfitting. An example is found in the recorded unit: "Several errors in the algorithm—errors in how it characterized the medical needs of people with certain disabilities."

While the gray literature adds 24 new cause categories to the original eight from [34], including labeling and regulatory bias, the top causes—cognitive, design, and historical bias—remain consistent across both studies.

**Table 7.** Top 5 causes of fairness debt

| Causes | # | Recorded Units |
|---|---|---|
| Training Bias | 49 | A155, A156, A010, A017, A027, A028, A034, A035, A051, A070, A087, A115, A152, A159, A162, A164, A165, A166, A170, A173, A186, A188, A195, A207, A211, A212, A225, A238, A262, A267, A280, A294, A299, A319, A320, A324, A335, A380, A416, A448, A450, A455, A456, A468, A471, A472, A485, A508, A523 |
| Societal Bias | 34 | A155, A010, A017, A027, A051, A056, A086, A087, A152, A154, A162, A170, A173, A175, A188, A189, A190, A195, A225, A262, A267, A280, A294, A319, A324, A380, A416, A456, A468, A485, A505, A521, A523, A542 |
| Historical Bias | 31 | A155, A156, A010, A034, A051, A056, A070, A082, A087, A152, A162, A164, A170, A186, A196, A225, A280, A294, A312, A319, A324, A450, A456, A468, A471, A472, A508, A520, A521, A523, A598 |
| Cognitive Bias | 27 | A010, A035, A051, A056, A059, A087, A115, A162, A170, A186, A212, A267, A320, A324, A335, A380, A416, A455, A456, A468, A472, A474, A505, A508, A520, A542, A598 |
| Model Bias | 25 | A156, A010, A017, A027, A034, A051, A086, A115, A159, A170, A186, A190, A238, A267, A280, A380, A448, A450, A455, A456, A472, A508, A520, A523, A598 |

**Finding #2:** Training, societal, and historical bias are the most referred to root causes of lack of fairness, illustrating the multiple sources of unfairness.

We further examined the co-occurrence between fairness debt and its underlying causes. Figure 3 illustrates the most significant connections between these elements. This analysis focuses on the five most frequently cited examples of fairness debt. As shown, each of these is linked to at least six different causes, while most causes are associated with at least four examples, except for colorism, regulatory bias, and design bias. Notably, racism is connected to all identified causes, and training bias is linked to every example of fairness debt.

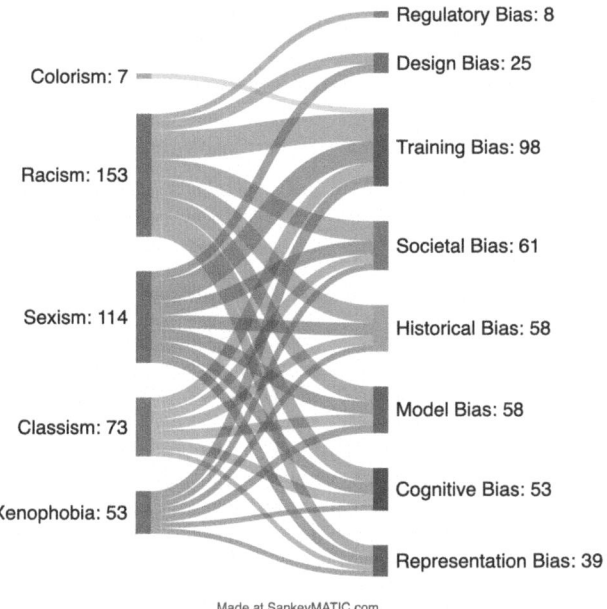

**Fig. 3.** Relation between fairness debt examples (RQ1) and causes (RQ2)

**Finding #3:** Racism is linked to all identified causes, and training bias is associated with every major example of fairness violation, which demonstrates their central role in software unfairness.

### 4.3  RQ3: What are the Effects of Fairness Debt in Software Systems as Described in Gray Literature?

We identified 14 effects of fairness debt. Table 8 shows the five most frequently reported, with the full list available in [33]. The most commonly cited effects were the proliferation of discrimination, the reinforcement of stereotypes, the exacerbation of social inequality, limited algorithmic reliability, and limited algorithmic accuracy.

The proliferation of discrimination refers to how biased algorithms can exacerbate unfair practices across various sectors, including hiring, finance, and policing. Reinforcement of stereotypes refers to algorithms perpetuating societal biases and normalizing prejudiced views—for example: "predictive policing tools and the abuse of data by police forces... perpetuate systemic racism." Exacerbation of social inequality highlights how unfair systems disproportionately impact marginalized groups, as in: "identifying certain areas as hot spots primes officers to expect trouble... leading to arrests based on prejudice rather than need."

Lastly, limited algorithmic reliability and accuracy refer to reduced trust and performance of algorithms, especially for diverse users. One example noted: "AI systems were consistently better at identifying pedestrians with lighter skin tones than darker."

As with previous questions, the gray literature expanded the effect categories from 8 to 14, adding topics like economic impacts, exclusionary practices, and data privacy. Still, the top effects align with those in [34].

**Table 8.** Top 5 effects of fairness debt

| Effects | # | Recorded Units |
|---|---|---|
| Proliferation of Discrimination | 56 | A155, A156, A010, A017, A027, A034, A051, A056, A059, A087, A118, A135, A152, A154, A162, A164, A165, A166, A169, A170, A173, A175, A186, A188, A189, A190, A195, A212, A219, A252, A262, A267, A272, A294, A299, A312, A319, A320, A324, A335, A380, A416, A448, A450, A455, A468, A471, A472, A485, A505, A508, A521, A523, A525, A542, A598 |
| Reinforcement of Stereotypes | 41 | A155, A156, A010, A017, A035, A082, A087, A118, A135, A152, A154, A162, A170, A175, A186, A188, A189, A195, A207, A210, A211, A212, A219, A225, A238, A267, A272, A299, A319, A324, A335, A380, A416, A448, A450, A455, A471, A485, A505, A523, A542 |
| Exacerbation of Social Inequality | 36 | A155, A156, A010, A017, A027, A034, A051, A057, A059, A135, A152, A154, A162, A170, A175, A177, A186, A195, A212, A238, A262, A267, A280, A294, A320, A324, A335, A380, A450, A455, A471, A505, A508, A525, A542, A598 |
| Limited Algorithmic Reliability | 31 | A057, A087, A159, A160, A165, A170, A188, A190, A195, A207, A212, A238, A262, A267, A272, A280, A294, A319, A320, A324, A361, A380, A416, A448, A450, A471, A472, A474, A523, A525, A542 |
| Reduced Algorithmic Accuracy | 28 | A027, A051, A152, A160, A166, A170, A177, A188, A190, A212, A219, A225, A238, A267, A272, A294, A299, A319, A320, A335, A416, A448, A455, A468, A471, A485, A542, A598 |

**Finding #4:** Proliferation of discrimination is the most frequently reported effect of fairness debt, highlighting how biased software systems can amplify inequality across multiple domains.

We also examined the co-occurrence between fairness debt examples and their effects. Figure 4 illustrates the connections among the five most frequently cited fairness debt examples, highlighting that racism is linked to all identified impacts, while the effect proliferation of discrimination is associated with all examples of fairness debt.

> **Finding #5:** Racism is linked to all identified effects of fairness debt, while the proliferation of discrimination emerges as a universal consequence across all major examples.

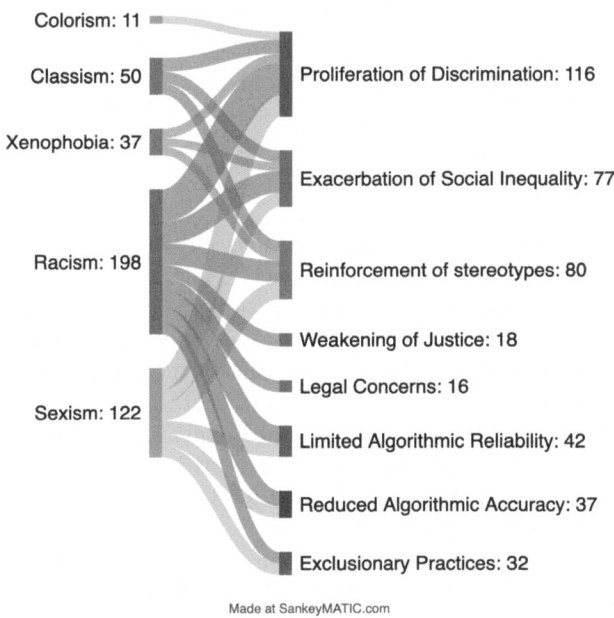

**Fig. 4.** Fairness debt examples (RQ1) and their effects (RQ3)

## 5   Discussion

This section introduces an updated version of the conceptual map proposed initially by de Souza Santos et al. [34], incorporating insights from our analysis. We also discuss the implications of our study and the threats to validity.

### 5.1   Updated Version of the Conceptual Map

Figure 1 presents the updated conceptual map, which extends the original proposed conceptual framework of fairness debt [34] by incorporating additional examples, causes, and effects of software fairness debt identified in gray literature. The elements shown outside the bold rectangle labeled Software Fairness Debt represent new elements revealed through this study.

These additions reflect the specific contributions of our analysis to each research question. For example, beyond the five examples of fairness debt found in academic literature, the gray literature highlights new instances such as criminal record discrimination, ableism, and political discrimination. Similarly, we identified new causes, including underrepresentation, regulatory bias, and cultural bias. Regarding effects, additional categories emerged, including exclusionary practices and the erosion of public trust.

Given the nature of the sources—nonacademic, publicly accessible documents—our results represent societal perceptions of software fairness debt. While they reaffirm findings from academic literature, they also offer a broader, practice-oriented perspective that enriches the current understanding of the topic.

## 5.2    Implications

Considering the increasing integration of AI and software systems, this study has implications for researchers and practitioners. The implications for academia include an expanded empirical foundation for fairness research that incorporates nonacademic perspectives such as practitioner accounts, organizational reports, and public discourse. By extending the conceptual framework of fairness debt [34], our work reinforces the understanding of fairness as a socio-technical concern shaped by historical, societal, and cognitive influences, encouraging researchers to adopt interdisciplinary approaches that engage not only with technical dimensions but also with ethical, legal, and social contexts when studying fairness in software engineering.

Regarding implications for industrial practice, our study offers practical insights into the presence of fairness debt in real-world systems, highlighting common patterns of discrimination and linking them to underlying causes, such as training and societal bias. By drawing on gray literature, the findings reflect ongoing discussions within the practitioner community, making them immediately relevant for software engineers and decision-makers responsible for AI system development.

## 5.3    Threats to Validity

The study ensures **trustworthiness** by aligning with the Empirical Standards for Software Engineering [32]. To establish **credibility**, the methodology was grounded in a previously developed conceptual map from a scoping study [34], which informed the choice of search keywords. One researcher systematically identified relevant web addresses via Google, applying well-defined inclusion and exclusion criteria focused on fairness debt. A second researcher independently reviewed this selection to verify the process. Similarly, the initial extraction of recorded units from gray literature was conducted by one researcher and checked by another for consistency. During analysis, the team conducted multiple annotation rounds to align their understanding and ensure consistent identification of fairness debt elements such as examples, causes, and effects.

A potential **search engine ranking bias risk** stems from the ranking algorithm used by Google Search, which determines the order of results. Because we limited our retrieval to the top 25 results per query, relevant sources in lower positions—due to factors like search engine optimization (SEO), popularity metrics, or recency—may have been excluded. However, this risk is reduced by the broad and diverse search strategy. Specifically, we created 22 distinct keyword combinations based on the conceptual model of software fairness debt. Each query targeted different linguistic and conceptual aspects of the phenomenon being studied.

While ChatGPT-4o was used to assist in expanding the lists of categories, we recognize the limitations inherent to large language models. These tools can sometimes generate non-factual or biased content, and their outputs lack direct source attribution. To mitigate this, all AI-generated suggestions were cross-checked for conceptual validity and consistency with the research goals. Future work may explore more systematic validation of such AI-assisted expansions, possibly involving expert review or triangulation with additional datasets.

To mitigate the risk of **interpretation bias**, we conducted a co-occurrence analysis that identified frequent associations between fairness-related concepts (e.g., examples, contributing factors, and outcomes). However, these associations do not imply causation. Accordingly, we have carefully described them as correlations or associations rather than causal relationships.

To support **transferability**, the analysis drew from a broad range of web-based sources that discuss fairness debt, without restricting the findings to a specific software process or organizational setting. This design allows the results to be applicable across various domains with appropriate contextual adjustments. **Dependability** was reinforced through a detailed and transparent description of all data collection and analysis procedures, including concrete examples, which supports **reproducibility**. Finally, **confirmability** was addressed by cross-referencing the study's findings with the original conceptual map [34], extending it by integrating evidence from both gray literature and peer-reviewed publications cited in de Souza Santos et al. [34].

# 6    Conclusion

We investigated how fairness debt is portrayed in gray literature, providing a complementary view to academic research. Through a query-based analysis of 79 articles, we identified 23 examples, 32 causes, and 14 effects of fairness debt in software systems. These findings validate and expand the conceptual map by de Souza Santos et al. [34], offering a richer understanding of fairness challenges grounded in real-world contexts. Key patterns include recurring forms of discrimination—such as racism, sexism, and classism—driven by training, societal, and historical bias. The most cited effects were the proliferation of discrimination, reinforcement of stereotypes, and increased social inequality.

By bridging gray literature and empirical research, the study broadens the discourse on software fairness. It highlights the value of practitioner perspectives and emphasizes the need for mitigation strategies that go beyond technical fixes. Future work may build on these results by exploring other gray literature sources and mapping proposed solutions to the examples, causes, and effects identified here, guiding efforts toward more responsible and fairness-aware software development.

**Disclosure of Interests.** The authors have no competing interests to declare that are relevant to the content of this article.

# References

1. Alexander, L., III., Song, Q.C., Hickman, L., Shin, H.J.: Sourcing algorithms: rethinking fairness in hiring in the era of algorithmic recruitment. Int. J. Sel. Assess. **33**(1), e12499 (2025)
2. Bahangulu, J.K., Owusu-Berko, L.: Algorithmic bias, data ethics, and governance: ensuring fairness, transparency, and compliance in AI-powered business analytics applications. World J. Adv. Res. Rev., 1746–1763 (2025)
3. Baltes, S., Park, G., Serebrenik, A.: Is 40 the new 60? How popular media portrays the employability of older software developers. IEEE Softw. **37**(6), 26–31 (2020). https://doi.org/10.1109/MS.2020.3014178
4. Bansal, C., Pandey, K.K., Goel, R., Sharma, A., Jangirala, S.: Artificial intelligence (AI) bias impacts: classification framework for effective mitigation. Issues Inf. Syst. **24**(4), 367–389 (2023)
5. Barocas, S., Selbst, A.D.: Big data's disparate impact. Calif. L. Rev. **104**, 671 (2016)
6. Brun, Y., Meliou, A.: Software fairness. In: Proceedings of the 2018 26th ACM Joint Meeting on European Software Engineering Conference and Symposium on the Foundations of Software Engineering, pp. 754–759 (2018)
7. Buolamwini, J., Gebru, T.: Gender shades: intersectional accuracy disparities in commercial gender classification. In: Friedler, S.A., Wilson, C. (eds.) Proceedings of the 1st Conference on Fairness, Accountability and Transparency. Proceeings of Machine Learning Research, vol. 81, pp. 77–91. PMLR (2018)
8. Chen, Z.: Ethics and discrimination in artificial intelligence-enabled recruitment practices. Humanit. Soc. Sci. Commun. **10**(1), 1–12 (2023)
9. Engel, C., Linhardt, L., Schubert, M.: Code is law: how COMPAS affects the way the judiciary handles the risk of recidivism. Artif. Intell. Law **33**, 1–22 (2024)
10. Ferrara, E.: Fairness and bias in artificial intelligence: a brief survey of sources, impacts, and mitigation strategies. Science **6**(1), 3 (2023)
11. Freelon, D.G.: ReCal: intercoder reliability calculation as a web service. Int. J. Internet Sci. **5**(1), 20–33 (2010)
12. Freire, S., et al.: Requirements engineering issues experienced by software practitioners: a study on stack exchange. In: Ferrari, A., Penzenstadler, B. (eds.) REFSQ 2023. Lecture Notes in Computer Science, vol. 13975, pp. 3–20. Springer, Cham (2023). https://doi.org/10.1007/978-3-031-29786-1_1
13. Freire, S., Maciel, R.S.P., Mendonça, M., Leite, J.C.: Eliciting public discourse of se tool providers in a study on requirements process debt - a different shade of gray. In: Proceeding of the XXIII Brazilian Symposium on Software Quality, pp. 189–198. ACM (2024)

14. Galhotra, S., Brun, Y., Meliou, A.: Fairness testing: testing software for discrimination. In: Proceedings of the 2017 11th Joint Meeting on Foundations of Software Engineering, pp. 498–510 (2017)
15. Goertzel, K.M.: Legal liability for bad software. CrossTalk **23** (2016)
16. Gomes, F., Santos, E., Freire, S., Mendes, T.S., Mendonça, M., Spínola, R.: Investigating the point of view of project management practitioners on technical debt - a study on stack exchange. J. Softw. Eng. Res. Dev. **11**(1), 12:1 – 12:15 (2023). https://doi.org/10.5753/jserd.2023.3191
17. Gomes, F., dos Santos, E.P., Freire, S., Mendonça, M., Mendes, T.S., Spínola, R.: Investigating the point of view of project management practitioners on technical debt - a preliminary study on stack exchange. In: 2022 IEEE/ACM International Conference on Technical Debt (TechDebt), pp. 31–40 (2022)
18. Hunkenschroer, A.L., Luetge, C.: Ethics of AI-enabled recruiting and selection: a review and research agenda. J. Bus. Ethics **178**(4), 977–1007 (2022)
19. Kaminski, M.E.: Binary governance: Lessons from the GDPR's approach to algorithmic accountability. S. Cal. L. Rev. **92**, 1529 (2018)
20. Kaminski, M.E., Malgieri, G.: Algorithmic impact assessments under the GDPR: producing multi-layered explanations. Int. data privacy law **11**(2), 125–144 (2021)
21. Kasy, M.: Algorithmic bias and racial inequality: a critical review. Oxf. Rev. Econ. Policy **40**(3), 530–546 (2024)
22. Kaufmann, M., Egbert, S., Leese, M.: Predictive policing and the politics of patterns. Br. J. Criminol. **59**(3), 674–692 (2019)
23. Kheya, T.A., Bouadjenek, M.R., Aryal, S.: The pursuit of fairness in artificial intelligence models: a survey. arXiv preprint arXiv:2403.17333 (2024)
24. Krippendorff, K.: Content analysis: An introduction to its methodology (2019)
25. Madaan, A., et al.: Self-refine: iterative refinement with self-feedback. Adv. Neural. Inf. Process. Syst. **36**, 46534–46594 (2023)
26. McHugh, M.L.: Interrater reliability: the kappa statistic. Biochem. Med. (Zagreb) **22**(3), 276–282 (2012)
27. Obermeyer, Z., Powers, B., Vogeli, C., Mullainathan, S.: Dissecting racial bias in an algorithm used to manage the health of populations. Science **366**(6464), 447–453 (2019)
28. Petrozzino, C.: Who pays for ethical debt in AI? AI Ethics **1**(3), 205–208 (2021)
29. Santos, E.P., Gomes, F., Freire, S., Mendonça, M., Mendes, T.S., Spínola, R.: Technical debt on agile projects: managers' point of view at stack exchange. In: Proceedings of the XXI Brazilian Symposium on Software Quality. Association for Computing Machinery (2023). https://doi.org/10.1145/3571473.3571500
30. Schöpfel, J.: Towards a Prague definition of grey literature. Grey J. **7**(1), 5–18 (2011)
31. Seaman, C.: Qualitative methods in empirical studies of software engineering. IEEE Trans. Softw. Eng. **25**(4), 557–572 (1999)
32. The ACM SIGSOFT Empirical Standards: ACM SIGSOFT empirical standards for software engineering. https://github.com/acmsigsoft/EmpiricalStandards
33. Sotolani, R., Freire, S., de Souza Santos, R., Fronchetti Dias, L.F., Spínola, R.: Results for software fairness debt on gray literature (2025). https://doi.org/10.5281/zenodo.15844175
34. de Souza Santos, R., Fronchetti, F., Freire, S., Spinola, R.: Software fairness debt: building a research agenda for addressing bias in AI systems. ACM Trans. Softw. Eng. Methodol. (2025). https://doi.org/10.1145/3709357

35. Srivastava, S., Sinha, K.: From bias to fairness: a review of ethical considerations and mitigation strategies in artificial intelligence. Int. J. Res. Appl. Sci. Eng. Technol. **11**, 2247–2251 (2023)
36. Suresh, H., Guttag, J.V.: A framework for understanding unintended consequences of machine learning. arXiv preprint arXiv:1901.10002 **2**(8), 73 (2019)
37. Venkatasubbu, S., Krishnamoorthy, G.: Ethical considerations in AI addressing bias and fairness in machine learning models. J. Knowl. Learn. Sci. Tech., 130–138 (2022). ISSN 2959-6386
38. Weber, R.: Basic content analysis (1990). https://doi.org/10.4135/9781412983488

# An Evidence-Based Study on the Relationship of Software Engineering Practices on Code Smells in Python ML Projects

Giammaria Giordano(✉) [iD], Antonio Della Porta[iD], Filomena Ferrucci[iD], and Fabio Palomba[iD]

Software Engineering (SeSa) Lab—University of Salerno, Fisciano, Italy
{giagiordano,adellaporta,fferrucci,fpalomba}@unisa.it

**Abstract.** The rapid adoption of Machine Learning (ML) technologies has introduced new challenges for code quality. Code smells, i.e., suboptimal design and implementation choices applied when developing source code, represent a particularly prevalent problem. While software engineering (SE) practices are often recommended to improve maintainability, their actual impact on code smells in ML projects remains unclear. In this paper, we present an evidence-based empirical study of 566 real-world Python ML projects from the NICHE dataset, labeled according to adherence to eight established SE practices. Using static analysis and statistical testing, we assess the relationship between these practices and the presence of ten Python-specific code smells. Our results show that projects adopting SE practices exhibit significantly fewer code smells. In particular, Continuous Integration is negatively correlated with the *Complex Container Comprehension* smell. These findings highlight the importance of engineering discipline in managing code quality in ML development.

**Keywords:** Quality Metrics · Software Maintenance Effort · Empirical Software Engineering

## 1 Introduction

The adoption of Machine Learning (ML) technologies has grown rapidly across industries, enabling data-driven automation and decision-making. While this growth has led to major technological advancements, it has also introduced new challenges in software quality assurance. In particular, ML projects often exhibit maintainability and evolvability issues, due to a combination of fast-paced prototyping, experimentation-driven development, and limited use of mature software engineering (SE) practices. Among these issues, *code smells*, i.e., suboptimal design and implementation choices that complicate maintenance and evolution, are notably prevalent [9]. Sculley *et al.* [21] highlighted that ML systems are

© The Author(s), under exclusive license to Springer Nature Switzerland AG 2026
D. Taibi and D. Smite (Eds.): SEAA 2025, LNCS 16083, pp. 105–120, 2026.
https://doi.org/10.1007/978-3-032-04207-1_8

susceptible to technical debt, including code smells, due to their inherent complexity and lack of traditional software safeguards. This observation has since been echoed in studies emphasizing the scarcity of quality assurance tools tailored to the peculiarities of ML pipelines [14].

To help assess and guide the engineering rigor of software repositories, Munaiah *et al.* [17] introduced a framework consisting of eight SE practices, ranging from the use of Continuous Integration and Unit Testing to the presence of documentation and licensing information. This framework, designed to be agnostic of specific programming languages or application domains, serves as a proxy to characterize a project's engineering quality. Although originally proposed for general software, a natural yet underexplored question arises: *to what extent are these practices related to the emergence (or mitigation) of code smells in ML projects?*

In this paper, we apply *evidence-based* research to investigate the impact that these software engineering practices may have on the presence and distribution of code smells in real-world ML projects. Drawing from 566 real-world ML repositories in the NICHE dataset [28], we quantitatively analyze the relationship between the presence of code smells and adherence to the SE practices identified by Munaiah *et al.* We use the PySmell tool [4] to detect ten Python-specific code smells and investigate their distribution across three project size strata (*Small, Medium, Large*) defined by Lines of Code percentiles. Our analysis combines descriptive statistics, non-parametric tests, and correlation analysis to uncover statistically significant associations.

Our findings report that projects adhering to the SE practices in Munaiah's framework exhibit significantly fewer code smells. Among the practices, the adoption of Continuous Integration tools is negatively correlated with the presence of the *Complex Container Comprehension* smell. These results suggest actionable implications for both researchers and practitioners. For practitioners, especially ML developers, the evidence supports the adoption of SE practices as a way to mitigate code quality issues. For researchers, our study provides a validated methodology for operationalizing engineering quality in ML projects and opens new directions for quality-focused tooling in data-centric development workflows.

## 2   Related Work

This section summarizes the most relevant literature regarding code smell in traditional and ML Projects.

Over the years, numerous studies have examined code smells, primarily focusing on Java from various perspectives [2,8,13,25,30]. Tufano et al. [24] investigated the introduction and removal of code smells in Java projects, discovering that code smells are usually introduced during the initial stages of development and are often removed when files are deleted. Giordano *et al.* [12] explored the relationship between reusability mechanisms and code smells over time, finding a statistical relation between adopting reusability mechanisms and the reduction of code smell severity.

A study that bridges the gap between code smells in Java and other programming languages was conducted by Vavrová and Zaytsev [27], who statistically compared smells between Java and Python projects. Their findings revealed Python methods are generally longer than Java methods, and code smells related to sub-optimal use of classes are rarely detected. Giordano *et al.* [10] corroborated these results by examining ML projects from the NICHE dataset, noting the infrequent detection of code smells related to object-oriented practices.

Similarly, Tang *et al.* [23] inspected 26 ML projects written in Python, highlighting that *duplicated code* is one of the most frequent smells. Van Oort *et al.* [18] extended the previous study by examining 74 ML projects, reaching similar conclusions. Cardozo et al. [3] further confirmed these findings by investigating 29 Reinforcement Learning (RL) projects, emphasizing the emergence of code smells for these systems.

Our study complements the existing body of literature. While previous work analyzes the diffusion of code smells in ML projects, we statistically investigated whether the software engineering practices proposed by Munaiah [17] are related to code smells.

## 3  Study Design

The *goal* of this evidence-based study is to quantitatively assess the extent to which software engineering practices, as defined by the framework of Munaiah *et al.* [17], correlate with the presence and distribution of code smells in real-world Python-based ML projects. The *purpose* is to statistically investigate the correlation between such practices and the presence of code smells. The *quality focus* of this study is on the software engineering practices of Munaiah *et al.* as measurable indicators of project quality. The *perspective* is for both practitioners and researchers: From the practitioners' standpoint, particularly ML developers, the study provides actionable evidence on how adopting certain software engineering practices is related to structural code issues in ML projects. From the researchers, the study contributes to the empirical software engineering community by validating and operationalizing the framework of Munaiah *et al.* [17] in a large-scale setting.

Based on our goal, we formulated the following research questions:

> **Q RQ₁.** *To what extent software engineering practices impact code smells distribution in ML projects?*

**RQ₁** aims to analyze the relation from a statistical viewpoint in terms of distribution between projects "not-well-engineered" and "well-engineered".

> **Q RQ₂.** *Are software engineering practices correlated to code smell presence in ML projects?*

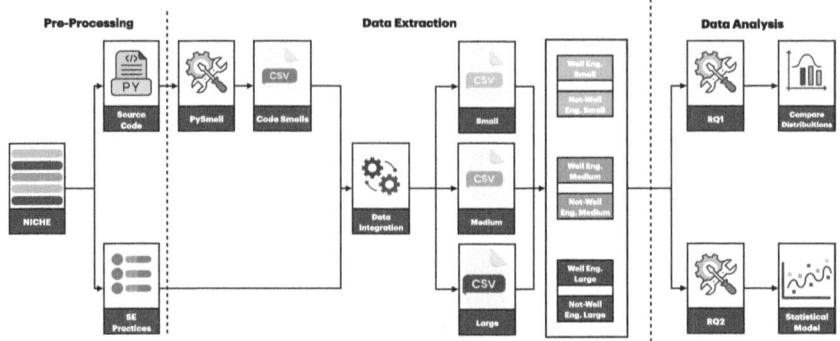

**Fig. 1.** Overview of the Research Method.

**Table 1.** Descriptive statistics of the NICHE projects.

|          | Stars   | LOC     | Commits |
|----------|---------|---------|---------|
| Min      | 100     | 234     | 100     |
| 1st Q.   | 211.2   | 4,022   | 218.2   |
| Median   | 538.5   | 9,303   | 419.5   |
| Mean     | 1991.3  | 24,672  | 1,241.3 |
| 3rd Qu.  | 1,641.0 | 22,308  | 1,065.8 |
| Max      | 76,838  | 699,513 | 90,927  |

**RQ$_2$** aims to statistically analyze whether and how software engineering practices are related to code smell variations in ML projects.

Our empirical research had statistical connotations *i.e.* we approached our research questions using statistical tests. The research method follows the guidelines of Wohlin *et al.* [29] and the ACM/SIGSOFT *Empirical Standards.*[1] Specifically, we used "General Standard", "Data Science", and "Repository Mining" guidelines. First, we cloned projects from NICHE [28], a dataset composed of 572 ML projects labeled as "well-engineered" and "not-well-engineered" according to eight software engineering practices; second, we identified code smells instances by running PySmell [4] *i.e.* a static smell analyzer; then, we combined smell-related information with data provided from NICHE and split dataset calculating the LOC percentile, and lastly, we divided projects "well-engineered" and "not-well-engineered" and applied statistical tests to respond of our research questions. Figure 1 describes the research method applied. All data, materials, and scripts are publicly available in our online appendix [11].

---

[1] Available at: https://github.com/acmsigsoft/EmpiricalStandards.

## 3.1   Dataset Description and Pre-processing

The careful selection of a representative and reliable dataset is essential to ensure the validity and generalizability of empirical findings. In this study, we rely on the *NICHE* dataset [28], which offers a curated collection of machine learning projects. This dataset was selected based on two primary considerations.

First, *NICHE* comprises only active and widely-used repositories, thereby minimizing the inclusion of personal or abandoned projects. Specifically, it includes 572 open-source projects, collectively accounting for 13,964,565 commits. Each project satisfies a set of inclusion criteria: a minimum of 100 GitHub stars, at least 100 commits, and a last commit date later than May 1$^{\text{st}}$, 2020. To further refine the dataset and eliminate potential toy projects, we excluded six repositories containing fewer than 100 lines of code.

Second, all projects in *NICHE* have been manually classified as either "well-engineered" or "not-well-engineered", based on the framework defined by Munaiah *et al.* [17] *i.e. Unit Testing, Architecture, Documentation, Issues, Continuous Integration, History, Community*, and *License*. A project is considered "well-engineered" when the majority of these practices are observed. This manual labeling process enables a principled comparison of engineering quality across projects, grounded in clearly defined dimensions.

**Table 2.** Description of the Software Engineering Practices Proposed by Munaiah *et al.*

| Attribute | Description |
|---|---|
| Architecture | Defines the internal structure of the project by outlining its components and how they interact with other parts of the system. |
| Community | Indicates the presence of a broad and active group of contributors responsible for maintaining and evolving the repository. |
| Continuous Integration | Refers to the adoption of CI mechanisms to ensure a stable and reliable codebase throughout development and release. |
| Documentation | Includes technical documentation and supplementary resources that support understanding and maintenance activities. |
| History | Reflects the continuity of maintenance over time, highlighting frequent developer contributions and long-term viability. |
| Issues | Describes how requirement tracking and project management are handled directly through GitHub Issues, improving traceability. |
| License | Specifies the terms and conditions for reuse by explicitly declaring a software license in the repository. |
| Unit Testing | Indicates the presence of unit tests aimed at verifying the correctness of individual software components. |

Table 2 presents the eight-dimensional metrics defined by the Munaiah framework *et al.* [17]. As shown, the framework encompasses attributes that pertain to both the product and the development process. Within the scope of the NICHE dataset [28], the authors manually assessed the presence of these attributes. However, in most instances, they did not provide quantitative values. Instead, the attributes were often represented using descriptive string values. For example, for the attribute "Issues", rather than reporting a specific number of issues, the authors used qualitative descriptors such as *"Do reply to issues last time but not recently"*.

Considering this, as will be discussed in the following sections, it was not feasible to incorporate all metrics proposed by Munaiah *et al.* in our analysis.

**Table 3.** Statistics of Projects Well Engineered.

|        |         | Stars   | LOC     | Commits |
|--------|---------|---------|---------|---------|
| Small  | Min     | 100     | 234     | 102     |
|        | 1st Q.  | 166.5   | 1,704   | 171     |
|        | Median  | 336     | 2,724   | 276     |
|        | Mean    | 978.2   | 2,679   | 635     |
|        | 3rd Q.  | 875     | 3,583   | 517     |
|        | Max     | 12,388  | 4,683   | 13,542  |
| Medium | Min     | 100     | 4,689   | 102     |
|        | 1st Q.  | 175     | 6,560   | 252.5   |
|        | Median  | 352     | 8,192   | 424     |
|        | Mean    | 1,203   | 8,230   | 701.9   |
|        | 3rd Q.  | 911     | 9,726   | 861.5   |
|        | Max     | 18,087  | 11,685  | 3,938   |
| Large  | Min     | 105     | 11,711  | 105     |
|        | 1st Q.  | 373.5   | 17,509  | 439.8   |
|        | Median  | 1,133   | 25,618  | 959     |
|        | Mean    | 3,204.5 | 51,952  | 2,442.6 |
|        | 3rd Q.  | 3,702   | 45,550  | 1,905.8 |
|        | Max     | 76,838  | 699,513 | 90,927  |

Table 1 provides the statistical description of the attributes "Stars", "LOC", and "Commits" of the remaining 566 projects. As it is possible to see from the table, the distribution of the dataset shows a median of 538 Stars, 9,303 LOC, and 419 Commits. The statistical analysis reveals significant variability in project metrics, suggesting a high level of development activity. Furthermore, we observed substantial variation in LOCs. According to Zhou *et al.* [15], this aspect is a confounding factor in analyzing code-related metrics. To enhance our understanding of the NICHE dataset, we first segmented it into three groups—small, medium, and large—based on percentile calculations. Subsequently, we divided these groups further by sorting each according to the values in the "Engineered" column.

**Table 4.** Statistics of Projects Not Well Engineered.

|        |         | Stars   | LOC     | Commits |
|--------|---------|---------|---------|---------|
| Small  | Min     | 111     | 238     | 100     |
|        | 1st Q.  | 210     | 1,259   | 118.5   |
|        | Median  | 443     | 1,652   | 162     |
|        | Mean    | 1,348   | 2,080   | 247.2   |
|        | 3rd Q.  | 897     | 2,913   | 276     |
|        | Max     | 16,987  | 4,647   | 1,681   |
| Medium | Min     | 100     | 4,687   | 105     |
|        | 1st Q.  | 177.5   | 5,614   | 178.5   |
|        | Median  | 318     | 7,481   | 327     |
|        | Mean    | 895.4   | 7,708   | 375.6   |
|        | 3rd Q.  | 1,496.8 | 9,369   | 420.2   |
|        | Max     | 3,944   | 11,672  | 1479    |
| Large  | Min     | 136     | 12,756  | 133     |
|        | 1st Q.  | 251.5   | 19,040  | 222.5   |
|        | Median  | 596     | 27,017  | 365     |
|        | Mean    | 3,831.3 | 62,085  | 776     |
|        | 3rd Q.  | 1,793.5 | 73,721  | 915     |
|        | Max     | 64,439  | 268,628 | 4,914   |

**Small:** This group consists of projects where the number of lines of code falls below the $30^{th}$ percentile. It includes 107 "well-engineered" projects and 59 "not-well-engineered", each less than 4,683 LOCs.

**Medium:** The second group includes projects whose LOCs fall between the $30^{th}$ and $60^{th}$ percentiles. This category includes 127 "well-engineered" projects and 44 projects "not-well-engineered" with LOCs between 4,683 and 11,685.

**Large:** The final group comprises projects that exceed the $60th$ percentile in terms of LOCs. It includes 202 "well-engineered" projects and 27 "not-well-engineered" projects. This group includes projects with more than 11,685 LOCs.

Table 3 and Table 4 provide a statistical description for projects labeled "well-engineered" and "not-well-engineered", respectively.

As the final step, we select from the practices proposed by Munaiah *et al.* [17] the most closely related to production code *i.e.* we considered for this study the adoption of CI practices. It is important to note that we neglected the other factors due to their influential impact on the source code. However, to give more robustness to our analysis, we also extracted the exact number of members of the Community (a.k.a. Contributors) using PyDriller [22]. Lastly, we decided to discard the "History" attribute and instead use the number of commits, as the former offers only a string value (*e.g.* "*Evidence of sustained commit activity*").

In contrast, the latter provides a precise, quantitative measure of the project's development activity.

## 3.2   Data Extraction

After cloning projects, we ran a static analyzer, namely PYSMELL [4], to identify smells. We selected this tool for two reasons. First, PySmell can detect ten instances of smells, some of which are derived from Fowler's original catalog [9] (*e.g. God Class*), while others are specifically tailored for Python projects (*e.g. Complex Container Comprehension*). Second, PySmell is considered state-of-the-art in detecting code smells in PYTHON projects, showing an average of 87%, 92%, and 89% of precision, recall, and F-Measure, respectively, and it was used in previous studies for similar purposes [4,10,26]. We first divided projects according to Sect. 3.1; second, we ran PySmell over the experimental objects, calculating the smell distribution.

## 3.3   RQ$_1$. Analyzing Code Smell Distribution

To address **RQ$_1$**, we examined the distribution of code smells in projects classified as "not-well-engineered" and "well-engineered" based on their specific percentiles. We utilized non-parametric statistical tests to determine if the distribution of each smell varied significantly between these two groups. Specifically, we employed the MANN-WHITNEY test [16], a non-parametric version of the Wilcoxon rank-sum test. We chose it due to the sample size and the non-normal distribution of the data [7]. We also applied CLIFF'S DELTA ($\delta$) [5] to measure the effect size of the observed differences. This test is particularly useful for evaluating the extent to which the distribution of smells differs between groups according to their percentile. Before conducting these statistical tests, we normalized the frequency of detected smells using the MIN-MAX strategy in the range [0–1] [20], ensuring a uniform scale for analysis.

The results were considered statistically significant at $\alpha = 0.05$. We formulated the following null hypothesis:

**H0:** *There are no statistically significant differences in terms of frequencies of Smell $S_i$ of the Group $_j$ between projects "well-engineered" and "not-well-engineered"*

Where $S_i \in$ {list of smells detectable by PySmell} and j $\in$ {Small, Medium, Large}.

## 3.4   RQ$_2$. Analyzing Correlation Between Software Engineering Practices and Code Smells

To address **RQ$_2$**, we built a statistical model to analyze if and how software engineering practices are related to the emergence of smell. In the following, we reported this study's interesting independent, dependent, and control variables and the statistical test applied.

**Independent Variables.** Our goal is to understand how software engineering practices relate to the emergence of code smells. To this end, we focused on the software engineering practices that characterize a "well-engineered" project according to Munaiah *et al.* [17]. It is important to note that these dimensions are already included in the NICHE dataset [28]. As discussed in Sect. 3.1, we excluded Architecture, Documentation, History, Issues, License, and Unit Testing from our analysis. As a result, our set of independent variables includes Continuous Integration and Number of Contributors.

**Response Variable.** We considered the set of code smells detectable by PySmell as a response variable *i.e. Large Class, Long Parameter List, Long Method, Long Scope Chaining, Long Base Class List, Long Lambda Function, Long Ternary Conditional Expression, Long Message Chain, Complex Container Comprehension, Multiply-Nested*.

Table 5 shows the smells detectable by PySmell with their description.

**Control Variable.** Code smells can depend on variables unrelated to the independent variables. To mitigate potential threats to conclusions, we selected three control variables recognized as reliable estimators of code quality: Lines of Code (LOC), Number of Commits, and Number of Stars [19]. These control variables are already available in the NICHE dataset [28]. We limited our analysis to these metrics because there are no validated tools in the literature for extracting additional metrics. To ensure the validity of our findings, we manually assessed the potential for multi-collinearity between the variables in our study, and did not identify any multi-collinearity between variables.

**Statistical Model.** To assess possible correlation between independent, control, and the dependent variables, we employed the KENDALL TAU ($\tau$) rank correlation coefficient [1]. Compared to other correlation metrics such as Spearman or Pearson, the Kendall tau coefficient provides several benefits: 1) It does not presume any particular type of relationship between variables, meaning a linear relationship is not required; 2) It does not necessitate that the data adhere to a normal distribution; 3) It does not require that values be equidistant; 4) It is highly robust against outliers; 5) The test can be used for a small sample size. It is important to note that Kendall's tau values are generally lower than other rank correlation coefficients, such as Spearman's, and cannot be directly compared. Given the lack of standardized interpretation, we followed Cohen's guidelines [6]: values between 0.1 and 0.3 indicate a weak correlation, 0.3 to 0.5 moderate, and above 0.5 high correlation. Statistical significance was assessed using two-sided p-values.

**Table 5.** List of Code Smells Detectable by PySmell and the Related Description

| Smell | Description |
|---|---|
| Large Class | A class that is excessively large |
| Long Parameter List | A method or function with an extensive parameter list |
| Long Method | A method that is excessively long |
| Long Scope Chaining | A method or function with multiple levels of nesting |
| Long Base Class List | A class definition with an excessive number of base classes |
| Long Lambda Function | A lambda function that is excessively long in terms of character count |
| Long Ternary Conditional Expression | A ternary conditional expression that is excessively long |
| Long Message Chain | An expression that accesses an object through an extensive chain of attributes or methods using the dot operator |
| Complex Container Comprehension | A container comprehension that is too complex is one that includes multiple nested comprehensions or conditions |
| Multiply-Nested | A container, such as a dictionary or list, with multiple levels of nesting. |

## 4    Analysis and Discussion of the Results

In this section, we report the results of our study and discuss the implications of our findings.

### 4.1    On the Distribution of Code Smells in ML Projects

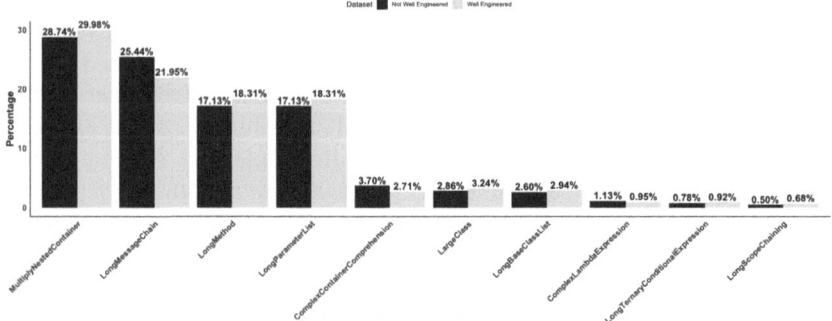

**Fig. 2.** Diffusion of Smells in Well and Not Well Engineered Projects.

In addressing the first research question, we first analyzed smell diffusion in absolute terms. Figure 2 illustrates the smell diffusion for "not-well-engineered" and "well-engineered" projects. From this figure, two key observations can be made. First, both groups exhibit the same top four smell frequencies. Second, we observed that "well-engineered" projects have a slightly higher propensity to

**Table 6.** Results of The Mann-Whitney-Wilcoxon and Cliff Delta Tests

| Code Smell | Small | | Medium | | Large | |
|---|---|---|---|---|---|---|
| | Mann-Whitney-Wilcoxon | Cliff Delta | Mann-Whitney-Wilcoxon | Cliff Delta | Mann-Whitney-Wilcoxon | Cliff Delta |
| Complex Container Comprehension | 1.538e-08 | -0.50 Large | 3.031e-10 | -0.63 Large | 8.385e-07 | -0.58 Large |
| Complex Lambda Expression | 2.704e-05 | -0.36 Medium | 1.616e-07 | -0.51 Large | 2.386e-10 | -0.74 Large |
| Large Class | 7.225e-09 | -0.52 Large | 7.615e-13 | -0.71 Large | 9.542e-09 | -0.68 Large |
| Long Base Class List | 4.386e-08 | -0.49 Large | 2.535e-13 | -0.73 Large | 1.016e-08 | -0.68 Large |
| Long Message Chain | 3.965e-11 | -0.60 Large | 4.313e-12 | -0.70 Large | 4.462e-09 | -0.69 Large |
| Long Method | 2.773e-11 | -0.60 Large | 3.571e-12 | -0.70 Large | 4.298e-09 | -0.70 Large |
| Long Parameter List | 2.773e-11 | -0.60 Large | 3.571e-12 | -0.70 Large | 4.298e-09 | -0.69 Large |
| Long Scope Chaining | 0.0001423 | -0.32 Small | 4.805e-08 | -0.53 Large | 1.862e-09 | -0.71 Large |
| Long Ternary Conditional Expression | 0.0005 | -0.29 Small | 1.197e-10 | -0.64 Large | 1.981e-09 | -0.71 Large |
| Multiply Nested Container | 3.664e-12 | -0.63 Large | 1.602e-12 | -0.71 Large | 5.079e-08 | -0.64 Large |

be affected by the *Multiply Nested Container* smell (30% for "well-engineered" projects and 29% for "not-well-engineered projects"). These results align with previous findings by Zhang *et al.* [31], which identified Multiply Nested Container smell as the most frequent in Python code. This result could suggest that the framework of Muniah *et al.* [17] is not enough to capture the complexity of ML systems, and, in turn, suggests that other factors (*e.g.* the number of stars or LOC) could be more relevant indicators for code smells.

Table 6 presents the results of the Mann-Whitney and Cliff's Delta tests. This comparison examines the distributions of "not-well-engineered" projects and "well-engineered" projects. Additionally, the results were organized based on their percentiles. The comparison shows significant differences in code smell distribution between the two categories. In many cases (*e.g.* Complex Container Comprehension), extremely low p-values confirm strong statistical significance. Cliff's Delta also indicates a large effect size across all project sizes, suggesting a link between software engineering practices and reduced code smells. To conclude, we rejected the null hypothesis **H0**, *i.e.* we identified statistical differences between code smell distributions between "well-engineered" and "not-well-engineered" projects.

---

🔍 **Key findings of RQ$_1$.**

**RQ$_1$** indicates that code smell diffusion is broadly similar across "well-engineered" and "not-well-engineered" projects, with *Multiply Nested Container* being the most frequent in both groups. However, projects following SE practices are statistically associated with a lower overall presence of code smells.

**Table 7.** Results of the Kendall Correlation Coefficients for Projects Well-Engineered.

| Dependent Variable | Continuous Integration | Community | Stars | Lines of Code | Commits |
|---|---|---|---|---|---|
| Complex Container Comprehension | -0.137** | 0.076 | 0.051 | 0.306*** | 0.048 |
| Complex Lambda Expression | 0.047 | 0.066 | 0.106* | 0.276* | 0.068 |
| Large Class | -0.062 | 0.136* | 0.136* | 0.331*** | 0.103* |
| Long Base Class List | -0.079 | 0.115* | 0.135* | 0.289** | 0.077 |
| Long Message Chain | -0.071 | 0.079 | 0.113* | 0.360*** | 0.105* |
| Long Method | -0.078 | 0.104* | 0.120* | 0.368*** | 0.109* |
| Long Parameter List | -0.078 | 0.104* | 0.120* | 0.368*** | 0.109* |
| Long Scope Chaining | -0.037 | 0.056 | 0.098 | 0.303*** | 0.039 |
| Long Ternary Conditional Expression | -0.040 | 0.020 | 0.104* | 0.244* | 0.005 |
| Multiply Nested Container | -0.087 | 0.030 | 0.025 | 0.330*** | 0.050 |

## 4.2   On the Correlation Between Software Engineering Practices and Code Smells

Table 7 presents the results of the Kendall Correlation test for "well-engineered", large-sized projects. Due to space constraints, the other analyses can be found in our replication package [11].

Looking at the table, several key observations can be made. Firstly, there is a strong correlation between LOCs and all code smells. This result is expected, as an increase in LOC aligns with the definitions of code smells related to the LOC, such as *Large Class* and *Long Method*. The results indicate that as LOCs increase, the likelihood of code smells also increases significantly.

Examining the independent variables, our findings indicate a statistically significant negative correlation between CI tools and the *Complex Container Comprehension smell*. This suggests that CI tools could help maintain code quality by reducing the incidence of certain code smells. Community is positively related to *Large Class*, *Long Base Class List*, *Long Method*, and *Long Parameters List*, suggesting that the probability of certain code smells increases when the number of contributors increases.

Control variables such as stars, LOC, and commits exhibit a positive correlation with code smells. For example, projects with more stars tend to show smells like *Large Class* and *Long Message Chain*, possibly due to their larger size and more extensive evolution. This trend is reinforced by the positive correlation with commits, suggesting that frequent maintenance activities may contribute to smell proliferation over time.

---

**⚲ Key findings of RQ$_2$.**

RQ$_2$ results show a positive correlation between control variables (Stars, LOCs, Commits) and code smells, suggesting that larger or more active projects are more prone to smell accumulation. We also found that a larger contributor base correlates with certain smells (*e.g. Large Class*), while CI tool usage is negatively associated with smells like *Complex Container Comprehension*.

# 5   Take-Away Messages

Our results allowed us to formulate multiple reflections and implications.

**CI Tools as Health Monitors.** Our findings show a statistically significant negative correlation between the use of CI tools and the *Complex Container Comprehension* smell. This suggests that CI pipelines—especially when augmented with static analysis or quality gates—can play a role in proactively detecting and limiting code smells. Rather than merely automating builds and tests, CI may act as a structural safeguard, promoting consistent coding practices and early detection of complexity issues.

  ☞ *CI tools can serve as real-time health monitors of code structure, helping prevent the accumulation of code smells during development.*

**More Contributors, More Complexity.** We observed a consistent positive correlation between the number of contributors and several code smells, including *Large Class, Long Method*, and *Long Parameter List*. While community involvement is crucial in open-source ML projects, it can inadvertently increase structural complexity when coordination and coding conventions are lacking. Onboarding new developers without sufficient architectural guidance or automated checks may lead to divergence in coding styles and design decisions, amplifying the risk of technical debt.

  ☞ *Increasing the number of contributors can elevate structural complexity; scalable contributor strategies must include quality safeguards.*

**Engineering Practices and Quality.** Beyond CI and community size, our results show that ML projects labeled as "well-engineered" exhibit significantly fewer code smells across all size strata. This reinforces the value of applying general software engineering practices even in data-driven or experimental ML environments. Although not all individual practices could be quantitatively analyzed, the aggregate evidence supports their collective importance.

  ☞ *A disciplined engineering approach contributes to better code quality in ML projects, even in fast-paced or research-oriented contexts.*

**Other Risk Factors.** Control variables like LOC, number of stars, and number of commits were all positively correlated with smell presence. This is expected—larger and more active projects have more opportunity for smells to emerge—but it also implies that code quality monitoring should scale with project growth. Popularity (e.g., GitHub stars) does not imply structural cleanliness and may even mask accumulating technical debt.

  ☞ *Highly active or popular projects require proportionate investment in quality assurance to prevent degradation over time.*

Overall, our findings highlight the value of integrating software engineering practices into ML development. For practitioners, they offer evidence-based motivation to adopt CI and manage contributors effectively. For researchers and tool builders, they suggest directions for developing quality assurance solutions tailored to ML workflows. Future work may extend these insights across languages and domains to better align ML development with engineering discipline.

## 6    Threats to Validity

Some factors may have influenced our results. To address potential *construct validity* threats, we relied on the NICHE dataset, which includes only active and popular ML projects hosted on GitHub and provides a classification of engineering practices. While our use of PySmell for code smell detection introduces some limitations in terms of precision and recall, it remains a state-of-the-art tool for analyzing Python code and has been validated in prior work. In addition, still referring to the NICHE dataset, we used a binary classification where a project is considered well-engineered if the majority of the software engineering practices defined by Munaiah et al. [17] are fulfilled. While this approach is consistent with previous work, we acknowledge that it introduces a simplification: a project meeting just over half the criteria is treated the same as one meeting all, and differently from one falling just below the threshold. We highlight this as a limitation and an opportunity for future work to explore more granular scoring. Regarding *internal validity*, we mitigated the influence of confounding variables by controlling for project size (LOC), popularity (stars), and development activity (commits), which are known to correlate with code quality. In terms of *external validity*, our results are based on Python-based ML projects and may not generalize to other ecosystems. However, the dataset includes a wide range of projects in terms of size and complexity, and we plan to extend the analysis to other programming languages. Lastly, to preserve *conclusion validity*, we adopted robust statistical techniques, including non-parametric testing and Kendall's tau correlation, and verified the absence of multicollinearity among variables to ensure reliable interpretations.

## 7    Conclusion and Future Work

We investigated the relationship between software engineering practices and code smells in 566 Python-based ML projects from the *NICHE* dataset. Our analysis shows that projects adhering to established engineering practices, particularly Continuous Integration, tend to exhibit fewer code smells. Conversely, a higher number of contributors is associated with increased smell presence.

These findings highlight the importance of disciplined engineering and contributor management in maintaining code quality in ML projects. As future work, we aim to extend our analysis to other programming languages and explore practitioners' perceptions of code smells.

**Acknowledgment.** This work was partially supported by project FAIR (PE0000013), funded under the Italian NRRP (National Recovery and Resilience Plan), MUR program, and co-financed by the European Union – NextGenerationEU, and

Project PRIN 2022 "QualAI: Continuous Quality Improvement of AI-based Systems" (grant n. 2022B3BP5S, CUP: H53D23003510006).

# References

1. Abdi, H.: The kendall rank correlation coefficient. Encyclopedia Meas. Stat. **2**, 508–510 (2007)
2. Beck, K., Fowler, M., Beck, G.: Bad smells in code. In: Refactoring: Improving the Design of existing code, vol. 1
3. Cardozo, N., Dusparic, I., Cabrera, C.: Prevalence of code smells in reinforcement learning projects. In: 2023 IEEE/ACM 2nd International Conference on AI Engineering–Software Engineering for AI (CAIN), pp. 37–42. IEEE (2023)
4. Chen, Z., Chen, L., Ma, W., Zhou, X., Zhou, Y., Xu, B.: Understanding metric-based detectable smells in python software: a comparative study. Inf. Softw. Technol. **94**, 14–29 (2018). https://doi.org/10.1016/j.infsof.2017.09.011, https://www.sciencedirect.com/science/article/pii/S0950584916301690
5. Cliff, N.: Dominance statistics: ordinal analyses to answer ordinal questions. Psychol. Bull. **114**(3), 494 (1993)
6. Cohen, J.: Statistical Power Analysis for the Behavioral Sciences. Routledge (2013)
7. Conover, W.J.: Practical Nonparametric Statistics, vol. 350. Wiley (1999)
8. Fontana, F.A., Braione, P., Zanoni, M.: Automatic detection of bad smells in code: an experimental assessment. J. Object Technol. **11**, 5–1 (2012)
9. Fowler, M.: Refactoring: Improving the Design of Existing Code. Addison-Wesley Professional (2018)
10. Giordano, G., Annunziata, G., De Lucia, A., Palomba, F., et al.: Understanding developer practices and code smells diffusion in AI-enabled software: a preliminary study (2021)
11. Giordano, G., Della Porta, A., Palomba, F., Ferrucci, F.: The yin and yang of software quality: on the relationship between design patterns and code smells – online appendix. https://figshare.com/s/bb51da5b17872e473d53
12. Giordano, G., Fasulo, A., Catolino, G., Palomba, F., Ferrucci, F., Gravino, C.: On the evolution of inheritance and delegation mechanisms and their impact on code quality. In: 2022 IEEE International Conference on Software Analysis, Evolution and Reengineering (SANER), pp. 947–958. IEEE (2022)
13. Gupta, A., Suri, B., Misra, S.: A systematic literature review: code bad smells in java source code. In: Gervasi, O., et al. (eds.) ICCSA 2017, Part V. LNCS, vol. 10408, pp. 665–682. Springer, Cham (2017). https://doi.org/10.1007/978-3-319-62404-4_49
14. Lenarduzzi, V., Lomio, F., Moreschini, S., Taibi, D., Tamburri, D.A.: Software quality for AI: where we are now? In: Winkler, D., Biffl, S., Mendez, D., Wimmer, M., Bergsmann, J. (eds.) SWQD 2021. LNBIP, vol. 404, pp. 43–53. Springer, Cham (2021). https://doi.org/10.1007/978-3-030-65854-0_4
15. Lu, H.M., Zhou, Y.M., Xu, B.W.: The potentially confounding effect of class size on the ability of object-oriented metrics to predict change-proneness: a meta-analysis. Jisuanji Xuebao/Chinese J. Comput. **38**, 1069–1081 (2015). https://doi.org/10.3724/SP.J.1016.2015.01069
16. McKnight, P.E., Najab, J.: Mann-Whitney U test. The Corsini Encyclopedia of Psychology, pp. 1–1 (2010)

17. Munaiah, N., Kroh, S., Cabrey, C., Nagappan, M.: Curating github for engineered software projects. Empir. Softw. Engg. **22**(6), 3219–3253 (2017). https://doi.org/10.1007/s10664-017-9512-6

18. van Oort, B., Cruz, L., Aniche, M., van Deursen, A.: The prevalence of code smells in machine learning projects (2021)

19. Palomba, F., Tamburri, D.A., Serebrenik, A., Zaidman, A., Arcelli Fontana, F., Oliveto, R.: How do community smells influence the intensity of code smells? In: 2018 IEEE/ACM 40th International Conference on Software Engineering (ICSE), pp. 1064–1074. IEEE (2018)

20. Patro, S.G., Sahu, D.K.K.: Normalization: a preprocessing stage. In: IARJSET (2015). https://doi.org/10.17148/IARJSET.2015.2305

21. Sculley, D., et al.: Hidden technical debt in machine learning systems. In: Advances in Neural Information Processing Systems, vol. 28 (2015)

22. Spadini, D., Aniche, M., Bacchelli, A.: Pydriller: Python framework for mining software repositories. In: Proceedings of the 2018 26th ACM Joint Meeting on European Software Engineering Conference and Symposium on the Foundations of Software Engineering, pp. 908–911 (2018)

23. Tang, Y., Khatchadourian, R., Bagherzadeh, M., Singh, R., Stewart, A., Raja, A.: An empirical study of refactorings and technical debt in machine learning systems. In: 2021 IEEE/ACM 43rd International Conference on Software Engineering (ICSE)

24. Tufano, M., et al.: When and why your code starts to smell bad (and whether the smells go away). IEEE Trans. Softw. Eng. https://doi.org/10.1109/TSE.2017.2653105, https://www.scopus.com/inward/record.uri?eid=2-s2.0-85040307811&doi=10.1109%2fTSE.2017.2653105&partnerID=40&md5=d2b0c8b235fdd2cfb1fa8d1ec2b401ea

25. Van Emden, E., Moonen, L.: Java quality assurance by detecting code smells. In: Ninth Working Conference on Reverse Engineering, 2002. Proceedings, pp. 97–106. IEEE (2002)

26. Vatanapakorn, N., Soomlek, C., Seresangtakul, P.: Python code smell detection using machine learning. In: 2022 26th International Computer Science and Engineering Conference (ICSEC), pp. 128–133 (2022). https://doi.org/10.1109/ICSEC56337.2022.10049330

27. Vavrová, N., Zaytsev, V.: Does Python smell like Java? Tool support for design defect discovery in Python. Art Sci. Eng. Program. **1**(2) (2017). https://doi.org/10.22152/programming-journal.org/2017/1/11

28. Widyasari, R., et al.: Niche: a curated dataset of engineered machine learning projects in python. In: 2023 IEEE/ACM 20th International Conference on Mining Software Repositories (MSR), pp. 62–66 (2023). https://doi.org/10.1109/MSR59073.2023.00022

29. Wohlin, C., Runeson, P., Höst, M., Ohlsson, M.C., Regnell, B., Wesslén, A.: Experimentation in Software Engineering. Springer, Cham (2012)

30. Yamashita, A., Moonen, L.: Do code smells reflect important maintainability aspects? In: 2012 28th IEEE International Conference on Software Maintenance (ICSM). IEEE (2012)

31. Zhang, B., Liang, P., Feng, Q., Fu, Y., Li, Z.: Copilot refinement: addressing code smells in copilot-generated Python code (2024)

# H-TURF: Detecting Optimal Green Software Engineering Skillsets Using TURF Analysis and Hierarchical Cumulative Voting

Vasileios Ntaoulas[1] , Konstantinos Georgiou[1]([⊠]) , Nikolaos Mittas[2] ,
and Lefteris Angelis[1]

[1] School of Informatics, Aristotle University of Thessaloniki, Thessaloniki, Greece
{ntaoulasv,konsgeor,lef}@csd.auth.gr
[2] Department of Chemistry, Democritus University of Thrace, Kavala, Greece
nmittas@chem.duth.gr

**Abstract.** As technological advancements reshape employment patterns in IT, real-time job market monitoring is essential to address emerging skills demands and shifts in workforce trends. Amid growing global efforts toward environmental sustainability, Green Software Engineering has gained significant importance. The principles of GSE suggest the use of sustainable technologies and acquiring relevant knowledge. Hence, identifying key green skills and skillsets is critical for shaping education, labour policies and industry strategies, ensuring an equitable and sustainable future in software. In this paper, to identify important green skills and skillsets, we introduce H-TURF, an expansion of the Total Unduplicated Reach and Frequency Analysis algorithm using Hierarchical Cumulative Voting. The suggested algorithm is employed in a dataset of Software Engineering job postings. Our findings reveal the growing integration of green skills with software development, emphasizing their significance in shaping the future workforce. These insights can guide policymakers, educators, and industry leaders in adapting curricula, designing targeted training programs, and refining recruitment strategies to meet evolving market needs.

**Keywords:** skills prioritization · TURF analysis · Hierarchical Cumulative Voting · green software engineering · skillsets

## 1 Introduction

As digitalization accelerates, the environmental impact of software systems has emerged as a significant concern. [1] Green Software Engineering (GSE) [18] aims to develop energy-efficient software solutions by incorporating sustainability principles into software design, development, and deployment. [17] Traditional Software Engineering (SE) has primarily focused on performance, scalability and security, often overlooking energy consumption and carbon emissions.

D. Taibi and D. Smite (Eds.): SEAA 2025, LNCS 16083, pp. 121–136, 2026.
https://doi.org/10.1007/978-3-032-04207-1_9

However, with increasing awareness of climate change and the urgent need to reduce global energy consumption, integrating sustainable practices into SE has become imperative. [19] Energy-intensive computing processes, inefficient algorithms, and excessive hardware utilization contribute to a growing carbon footprint [20, 21]. By adopting energy-efficient programming techniques and optimizing software architectures, developers can mitigate these effects and contribute to more sustainable technological ecosystems. [2]

Beyond technical improvements, green skills—the specialized knowledge and competencies required to build sustainable software—are becoming essential in modern software development [22]. These skills encompass energy-aware coding, resource-efficient system design, and the ability to leverage renewable energy sources in cloud computing environments. As governments and organizations implement stricter environmental policies, companies must invest in upskilling their workforce to align with sustainability goals. Additionally, fostering collaboration between software engineers, environmental scientists, and policymakers can drive innovation in eco-friendly computing [23]. Advancing green skills in SE will not only help reduce the environmental impact of software systems but also ensure that sustainability becomes an integral part of future technological advancements.

Driven by the aforementioned principles of digital transformation, sustainability and GSE, the European Union (EU) makes considerable efforts not only on standardizing skills in established taxonomies such as the European Skills, Competences, Qualifications and Occupations (ESCO) taxonomy[1], but also on promoting sustainability as a concept that requires specific skills to be achieved. It is thus evident that upskilling and reskilling, even in the sector of GSE, are crucial for the future of SE in order to secure the well-being of the planet while producing actionable software solutions. However, in order to upskill effectively, there needs to be meticulous detection of skills that hold higher importance than others and are most in demand in job postings. Simultaneously, the discovery of green skillsets (i.e. combinations of green skills) that characterize SE jobs would constitute a valuable pathway for upskilling strategies and learning outcomes.

In this work, which is part of the SKILLAB HORIZON Europe project[2] [17] for skills identification and mapping, the general goals are twofold:

- **g1** - Identification of GSE skills that hold higher importance in relevant job postings: Via the use of Hierarchical Cumulative Voting (HCV) [16], the detected skills are prioritized and weighted based on their appearance in the job postings. This in turn allows employers to produce clear and structured job postings that capture the real needs of the labour market. In turn, job seekers are able to identify the truly necessary competences and skills required by specific job positions and act accordingly.
- **g2** - Detection of GSE skill combinations which provide ground for learning outcomes: While the previous goal explores individual skill importance, in

---

[1] https://ec.europa.eu/esco.
[2] https://cordis.europa.eu/project/id/101132663.

this research objective the focus shifts in detecting skillsets that effectively capture the landscape of GSE and can provide viable learning strategies and outcomes for job seekers. This objective is achieved using Total Unduplicated Reach and Frequency (TURF) Analysis [14] on prioritized GSE skills, with the goal of showcasing the most important skillsets.

To achieve the aforementioned objectives, we introduce a modified version of TURF analysis in labor market data, in order to assess the potential of detecting GSE skillsets that characterize SE jobs. Thus, the primary contribution of this paper is the introduction of *Hierarchical TURF* (H-TURF), an enhancement of the classical TURF Analysis, which uses the HCV algorithm for skill prioritization and produces skillsets with optimal labour market coverage.

The introduced method is validated via an applied case study of the SE labour landscape. For our purposes, we leverage a large-scale dataset of SE job postings from several job portals, extracting green skills from the ESCO taxonomy, and evaluating whether the extracted skills and skillsets truly capture the requirements of the GSE market.

The remainder of this paper is structured as follows: Sect. 2 reviews related work on GSE and its core principles. Section 3 presents the methodological framework, analyzing the leveraged algorithms. Section 4 illustrates the results and provides answers to the research goals. Section 5 discusses the insights, while Sect. 6 provides closing remarks, relevant threats to validity and proposes directions for future research.

## 2  Related Work

GSE has gained significant attention in recent years as the environmental impact of software systems becomes more apparent. Prior studies emphasize strategies such as energy-efficient coding, cloud and serverless computing, optimized data management, and lifecycle-aware design as key enablers of environmentally sustainable software [4].

Microsoft has incorporated green design into its development processes to meet carbon reduction targets, while Accenture has trained over 70,000 engineers in GSE and transitioned a majority of its applications to the public cloud [5]. Similarly, Thoughtworks supports GSE through green cloud strategies and sustainable architecture, and GitHub has maintained carbon neutrality since 2019 [5].

At infrastructure level, advances such as edge and parallel computing have enhanced energy efficiency by enabling local data processing and parallel task execution [6].

GSE principles have also been applied beyond traditional software domains. In environmental monitoring, IoT-based systems leveraging low-power wireless networks and edge-cloud integration offer energy-efficient solutions for real-time ecosystem tracking [7]. These technologies benefit from miniaturized sensors and advanced connectivity.

The disconnect between academic training and industry needs is also high-lighted [8]. Drawing insights from professionals across 28 organizations in nine countries, it identifies gaps in competencies required for sustainable software development. Challenges include conceptual ambiguity, financial barriers, and the absence of structured educational programs aligned with real-world demands.

GSE is also positioned as a response to the rising energy consumption of software systems [9]. The need for a paradigm shift among developers and organizations toward energy-aware practices is emphasized, including code refactoring, sustainable design, and the use of renewable energy. Notably, GSE is framed as a core element of broader Green Systems Engineering, especially in sectors like automotive manufacturing.

Energy efficiency in data centers has likewise been a key focus. [10]. A comprehensive analysis of green computing methods includes core power-consuming components such as central processing units (CPU), dynamic random access memory (DRAM), storage systems, and networking infrastructure. Among the investigated techniques virtualization, dynamic scaling, workload scheduling, and virtual machine migration are discussed [10].

Further contributing to the GSE discourse, the Green-Based Model was introduced for Sustainable Software Engineering (GMSSE) [11], which monitors power, memory usage, and $CO_2$ emissions across the Software Development Life Cycle (SDLC). Unlike previous models limited to specific phases, GMSSE incorporates green principles throughout the entire lifecycle, offering a holistic and iterative framework.

Moreover, with the growing adoption of IoT and big data analytics, energy consumption in cloud infrastructures has become increasingly problematic. [12], The evaluation of virtual machine (VM) consolidation techniques on real-world cloud infrastructure using OpenStack NEAT and Apache Spark is proposed as a viable alternative [12].

Lastly, in their study on sustainable digital infrastructure [13], the authors project that data centers could consume 10% of global electricity by 2030, with the broader IT sector potentially accounting for up to one-third. To address this, they advocate for Green IT and GSE, emphasizing energy-efficient development practices. The Lower Energy Acceleration Program (LEAP) outlines solutions across three horizons that include cloud-native and serverless applications, intelligent server idling, federated learning, and long-term innovations such as integrated photonics and neuromorphic computing.

## 3    Methodology

Relevant literature reveals the growing importance of GSE for the benefit of the planet and the production of sustainable software solutions. Given the growing role of green skills, the discovery of truly important GSE skills that characterize the labour market could provide pathways for effective upskilling. The introduced H-TURF methodology serves as a viable option for discovering prioritized green skills and green skillsets and is comprised of four separate stages, while at its

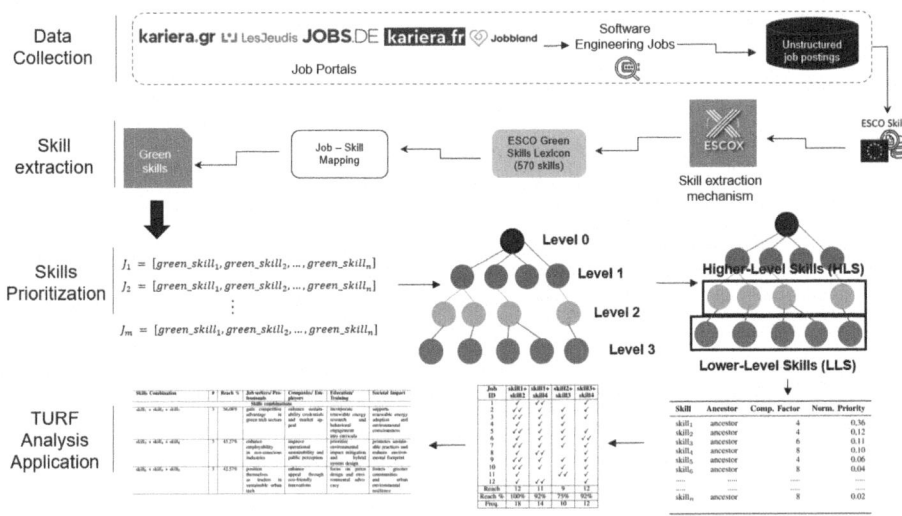

**Fig. 1.** H-TURF Framework Methodology

core involves the application of HCV on job postings and the subsequent use of TURF analysis on prioritized skills. In this section we provide a brief overview of the ESCO taxonomy and leveraged algorithms while also presenting, in detail, the employed framework.

## 3.1 The ESCO Taxonomy

ESCO is the official classification of skills and competences across the EU. It is translated into 27 languages, and used to describe the required skills, competences and qualifications of the EU labour market in a standardized, cross-country manner. The classification is updated to keep track of labour market trajectories and requirements. The ESCO taxonomy serves as the official EU classification of skills, occupations, and qualifications, enabling the structured portrayal of skills that are required in job postings in different EU countries. It currently has more than 13500 different skills, ranging from generic to more specific. For example, under "environmental protection," ESCO may list skills like "advise on sustainability solutions" or "implement sustainable procurement."

The ESCO taxonomy includes two main types of concepts (also known as **pillars**) which serve as separate ways of grouping skills: the Knowledge pillar, i.e., theoretical subjects related to a field of study, and the Skills pillar, i.e., the ability to apply knowledge and capabilities in a given working task. The skills included in the ESCO taxonomy are structured in an hierarchical manner, with general skills leading to more refined and specific skills. The described hierarchy is expressed in four levels (or layers) of depth for both pillars, from Level 1, which is more abstract (e.g., management skills, communication skills), to Level 4, which is more specific (e.g., promote sustainable practices, collect biological data).

## 3.2 TURF Analysis

TURF analysis [14] is a robust statistical methodology employed to optimize selection decisions among multiple alternatives within resource constraints. Initially developed for media planning, TURF analysis has evolved into a versatile analytical framework applicable to product portfolio optimization, market segmentation, and strategic resource allocation [15]. TURF analysis systematically evaluates all possible combinations of options to identify the optimal subset that maximizes unique consumer engagement while adhering to implementation constraints [3,14]. This approach enables organizations to make evidence-based decisions regarding product assortments, communication strategies, and resource allocation, thereby enhancing market penetration efficiency within finite resources. As a marketing analysis technique, TURF can be used to identify the smallest set of features (in this case, skills) that maximally cover a target population (job ads). In our context, it highlights combinations of skills that appear in the highest number of job postings.

The methodology quantifies two critical metrics: **reach**, defined (in the context of this study) as the number of job advertisements that include at least one skill from a given combination; and **frequency**, representing the total number of skill mentions across all job advertisements for a given combination. TURF prioritizes maximizing the reach metrix, ensuring that the produced skill combinations cover the highest percentage of job postings. A high reach value means that at least one skill from a produced skill combination is present in the majority of job postings and thus can effectively describe the skill requirements of the examined jobs.

*TURF Analysis Example*: To illustrate the practical application of TURF analysis in human resources, consider that in the context of this study, we have avail-

**Table 1.** Skills Featured in Job Advertisements

| Job ID | Python | JS | SQL | Cloud | DevOps | UI/UX |
|--------|--------|----|-----|-------|--------|-------|
| 1 | ✓ | | | | | ✓ |
| 2 | ✓ | | | | ✓ | |
| 3 | ✓ | | | | ✓ | |
| 4 | ✓ | | | ✓ | | |
| 5 | ✓ | | | | ✓ | |
| 6 | | | | | ✓ | ✓ |
| 7 | ✓ | | | | ✓ | |
| 8 | ✓ | | | | | ✓ |
| 9 | ✓ | | | | ✓ | |
| 10 | ✓ | | | | ✓ | |
| 11 | | | | ✓ | ✓ | |
| 12 | ✓ | | | | | ✓ |

**Table 2.** TURF Analysis Results for Two-Skill Combinations

| Job ID | Python+ DevOps | Python+ UI/UX | Cloud+ DevOps | DevOps+ UI/UX |
|---|---|---|---|---|
| 1 | ✓ | ✓✓ | | ✓ |
| 2 | ✓✓ | ✓ | ✓ | ✓ |
| 3 | ✓✓ | ✓ | ✓ | ✓ |
| 4 | ✓ | ✓ | ✓ | |
| 5 | ✓✓ | ✓ | ✓ | ✓ |
| 6 | ✓ | ✓ | ✓ | ✓✓ |
| 7 | ✓✓ | ✓ | ✓ | ✓ |
| 8 | ✓ | ✓✓ | | ✓ |
| 9 | ✓✓ | ✓ | ✓ | ✓ |
| 10 | ✓✓ | ✓ | ✓ | ✓ |
| 11 | ✓ | | ✓✓ | ✓ |
| 12 | ✓ | ✓✓ | | ✓ |
| Reach | 12 | 11 | 9 | 12 |
| Reach % | 100% | 92% | 75% | 92% |
| Freq. | 18 | 14 | 10 | 12 |

able data on 12 job postings, each featuring some combination of six technical skills (Python, JavaScript, SQL, Cloud, DevOps, and UI/UX). Table 1 presents the distribution of skills across the job advertisements, while Table 2 presents the reach and frequency of 2-skill combinations across the dataset.

The TURF analysis shows that "Python + DevOps" has the highest reach (100%) and frequency (18), making it the most in-demand and widely required combination across job ads. "DevOps + UI/UX" also demonstrates high reach (92%) with a solid frequency (12), indicating strong relevance. Although "Cloud + DevOps" has a lower reach (75%), its presence across multiple ads highlights a niche but notable demand. While frequency reflects how often combinations appear, reach is more insightful for identifying skill sets that cover the widest range of job opportunities. Focusing on high-reach combinations allows candidates to meet the needs of more employers with fewer, more targeted skills.

### 3.3   Hierarchical Cumulative Voting

The HCV algorithm extends standard frequency-based ranking by considering the position of a skill within a hierarchy. For example, a skill that appears frequently and belongs to an important skill family gets higher priority than one that is isolated or overly specific. The HCV algorithm [16], is the primary methodology used in our analysis to assign priorities to the detected green skills. Originally developed for SE requirement prioritization, HCV was designed to overcome the limitations of traditional voting methods (e.g., AHP, cumulative voting), which are often time-consuming or unsuitable for hierarchical data structures. As an illustrative example in Fig. 1, skills are expressed in levels of a tree, with higher-level skills (HLSs) and lower-level skills (LLSs). Each skill carries an initial weight (called the *assigned priority*), expressed by its *relative frequency*, i.e. the number of job postings that a skill appears in divided by the total number of job postings. Executed in a level-wise manner, the HCV algorithm then calculates *intermediate priorities* for each LLS using the formula:

$$p_{i,\mathrm{LLS}_u} = c_{\mathrm{HLS}_u} \cdot p_{a,\mathrm{LLS}_u} \cdot p_{a,\mathrm{HLS}_u} \tag{1}$$

where $c_{\mathrm{HLR}_u}$ (or *compensation factor*) is the number of HHS under a LLs and the $p_a$ terms are the assigned priorities (the relative frequencies). In the final stage, the intermediate priorities are *normalized* using:

$$p_{f,\mathrm{LLS}_u} = \frac{p_{i,\mathrm{LLS}_u}}{\sum_k p_{i,\mathrm{LLS}_k}} \tag{2}$$

so that the final priorities sum to 1 across each level. As mentioned before, in our adaptation of the HCV algorithm for ESCO skill prioritization, assigned priorities are based on the relative frequency of skills in job advertisements, rather than expert judgment, enabling data-driven evaluation across the four-level ESCO tree.

## 3.4    Methodological Framework

The methodological framework that was applied is divided into four distinct stages, each comprising a crucial part of the approach. These are (i) data collection, (ii) skill extraction & data preprocessing, (iii) skill prioritization and (iv) TURF analysis application. In this section we analyze each stage separately, highlighting the novel approach that we introduce.

**Data Collection:** In the data collection process, we employed web scraping techniques across five European job portals: https://www.kariera.gr, https://www.lesjeudis.com, https://jobs.de, https://kariera.fr, and https://jobbland.se. The web scraper was designed to systematically navigate these platforms, extract all available job postings, and store the retrieved information in a structured format within an SQLite database.

As this study focused on the software engineering (SE) domain, a structured search strategy was implemented using carefully formulated queries. The authors experimented with various keyword combinations to ensure sufficient data coverage and optimize information retrieval. The final query used was:

```
(Softwar* Develop*) OR (Softwar* Engin*)
```

This resulted in a collection of 3,579 job advertisements, which were stored for subsequent analysis.

**Data Preprocessing and Skill Extraction:** In the preprocessing phase, multiple steps were undertaken to ensure consistency, completeness, and quality of the job advertisements before proceeding to skill extraction. Job advertisements that lacked a job description were removed, while excessive whitespaces were eliminated from all textual fields to maintain data consistency and avoid processing errors. Finally, all extracted textual information was automatically translated into English to standardize the dataset, using the DeepL translator[3].

Following data preprocessing, a skill extraction mechanism was employed to identify relevant skills from job descriptions. To extract relevant skills, we utilized the **ESCO Skill Extractor** [24], a specialized tool designed for identifying skills and occupations based on the ESCO taxonomy. The ESCO Skill Extractor employs a transformer-based model that processes text embeddings and performs skill matching using cosine similarity. The extraction process consists of the following steps:

1. Generating embeddings for ESCO skills and ISCO occupations.
2. Extracting skills from job descriptions using the SkillNER[4] framework.
3. Creating embeddings for the extracted skills to enable effective similarity computation.
4. Comparing the embeddings of ESCO skills or ISCO occupations with those of the extracted skills. A match is established if the cosine similarity exceeds a predefined threshold.

**Table 3.** Prioritized GSE skills for ESCO Skills Pillar

| Skill | Ancestor | Comp. Factor | Norm. Priority |
|---|---|---|---|
| collaborate on international energy projects | advising on environmental issues | 6 | 0.30 |
| promote the use of sustainable transport | promoting products, services, or programs | 5 | 0.15 |
| promote sustainability | promoting products, services, or programs | 5 | 0.14 |
| promote sustainable energy | promoting products, services, or programs | 5 | 0.11 |
| advise on sustainability solutions | advising on environmental issues | 6 | 0.11 |
| select sustainable technologies in design | advising on products and services | 2 | 0.06 |
| inform customers environmental protection | advising on environmental issues | 6 | 0.03 |
| implement sustainable procurement | promoting products, services, or programs | 5 | 0.03 |
| promote innovative infrastructure design | designing structures or facilities | 1 | 0.02 |
| promote responsible consumer behaviour | promoting products, services, or programs | 5 | 0.02 |

The extracted skills are stored in a structured format, with their respective Uniform Resource Identifiers (URIs) for further analysis. Additionally, API calls are utilized to retrieve the corresponding skill labels based on the extracted URIs. This systematic skill extraction approach enables a structured representation of competencies required for various occupations, facilitating downstream analytical tasks such as labor market trend analysis and job-to-skill mapping. The produced data structure for each job posting is a list $J$, where all the identified skills are portrayed as $J = \{\text{skill}_1, \text{skill}_2, \text{skill}_3, \ldots, \text{skill}_n\}$.

---

[3] https://www.deepl.com/en/translator.

[4] https://huggingface.co/nestauk/en_skillner.

**Table 4.** Prioritized GSE skills for ESCO Knowledge Pillar

| Skill | Ancestor | Comp. Factor | Norm. Priority |
|---|---|---|---|
| sustainable finance | finance, banking and insurance | 4 | 0,36 |
| impact investing | finance, banking and insurance | 4 | 0,12 |
| green computing | environmental protection technology | 6 | 0.11 |
| offshore renewable energy technologies | electricity and energy | 8 | 0.10 |
| global standards for sustainability reporting | finance, banking and insurance | 4 | 0.06 |
| district heating and cooling | electricity and energy | 8 | 0.04 |
| corporate social responsibility | management and administration | 1 | 0.04 |
| types of heat pumps | electricity and energy | 8 | 0.03 |
| artificial lighting systems | electricity and energy | 8 | 0.02 |
| combined heat and power generation | electricity and energy | 8 | 0.02 |

In the final stage, using a predefined list of green skills from the ESCO taxonomy, the structured skill lists are reduced, keeping only job postings that include at least one recorded green skill. The final dataset that was used for further analysis consisted of 1901 SE jobs.

**Skills Prioritization.** Having reduced each job advertisement in a list of green skills derived from the ESCO taxonomy, the analysis shifts into discovering the green skills that hold higher importance in the overall set of job advertisements. This allows us to filter the collective mapping of jobs to skills, keeping only the top skills of each ESCO layer, ensuring that the subsequent TURF analysis subsets capture essential skillsets and information.

To achieve the skills prioritization procedure, the HCV algorithm was applied in the jobs, as an effective way of mapping skill importance for each ESCO layer. Hence, the outcome of the algorithm was, for each level a table that contained the identified skills, along with several useful information such as the compensation factor, the normalized priority and the respective skill level.

The table reveals the structure of the HCV algorithm output, mapping the prioritized skills across ESCO levels. For each skill, the algorithm reports its name, id, level and ancestor as well as the compensation factor, normalized priority and rank. Given that all the identified green skills belonged to the final layer of the ESCO taxonomy, the TURF analysis was conducted only for this level.

**TURF Analysis Application.** Following the skills prioritization process via the HCV algorithm, the top twenty skills for the two ESCO pillars were selected and the TURF analysis was employed for combinations of two, three, four and five skills respectively. Via this process, the introduced methodological framework leveraged skills with higher importance to identify skillsets that are expressed in a high number of retrieved job advertisements.

# 4    Results

In this section, the insights from the conducted analysis are presented, providing separate answers for each research goal. Overall, the results highlight the GSE skills that are considered more important in published job postings while also shedding light into skills combinations that can effectively capture the demands of the labour market and lead to proper learning outcomes.

**Goal 1: Identification of Prioritized GSE Skills.** In the first research goal, the aim was to discover, leveraging the HCV algorithm, highly prioritized skills across the dataset of GSE postings. The analysis was conducted for two ESCO pillars (Skills, Knowledge). In Tables 3 and 4, the top ten green skills for skills and knowledge are presented, while the transversal pillar only had four skills. It should be noted that all identified green skills belonged to the last ESCO layer, hence the remaining layers were omitted from the results presentation.

Based on the prioritized skills, we can infer the primary directions and demands for green skills of SE job postings published on the portals that were used for retrieval. Most notably, regarding necessary and prioritized skills (Skills Pillar - Table 3), related postings involve producing software solutions for projects related to the energy sector *collaborate on international energy projects* as well as software relevant to sustainable transport (*promote the use of sustainable transport*). In addition, some skills relevant to the production of SE itself emerge, such as the selection of appropriate green technologies (*select sustainable technologies*), providing customer support for environmental solutions (*inform customers environmental protection*) as well as the design of sustainable infrastructure to ensure that the produced software does not violate the GSE principles (*promote innovative infrastructure design*).

In terms of knowledge (Knowledge Pillar - Table 4), the focus shifts into designing sustainable software for the financial sector (*sustainable finance,impact investing*) while other notable skills include the adoption of sustainable computing and corporate principles (*green computing,corporate social responsibility*) and the procurement of software and systems targeted towards heating and energy (*district heating and cooling,types of heat pumps,combined heat and power generation*).

**Goal 2: Skill Combinations.** Due to space limitations, in Fig. 2, some indicative 3-skills, 4-skills and 5-skills extracted from the TURF analysis are presented. Separate tables for the Skills and Knowledge pillars and combinations from all skills can be found in a dedicated Google Drive[5], for further inspection.

As summarized in Fig. 2, various combinations of green skills contribute uniquely to the development of sustainable software systems and the advancement of GSE. Among the combinations evaluated, one representative from each

---

[5] https://drive.google.com/drive/folders/15brQUMab185_
LSrmOqrtQBMv1gbmzYPo?usp=drive_link.

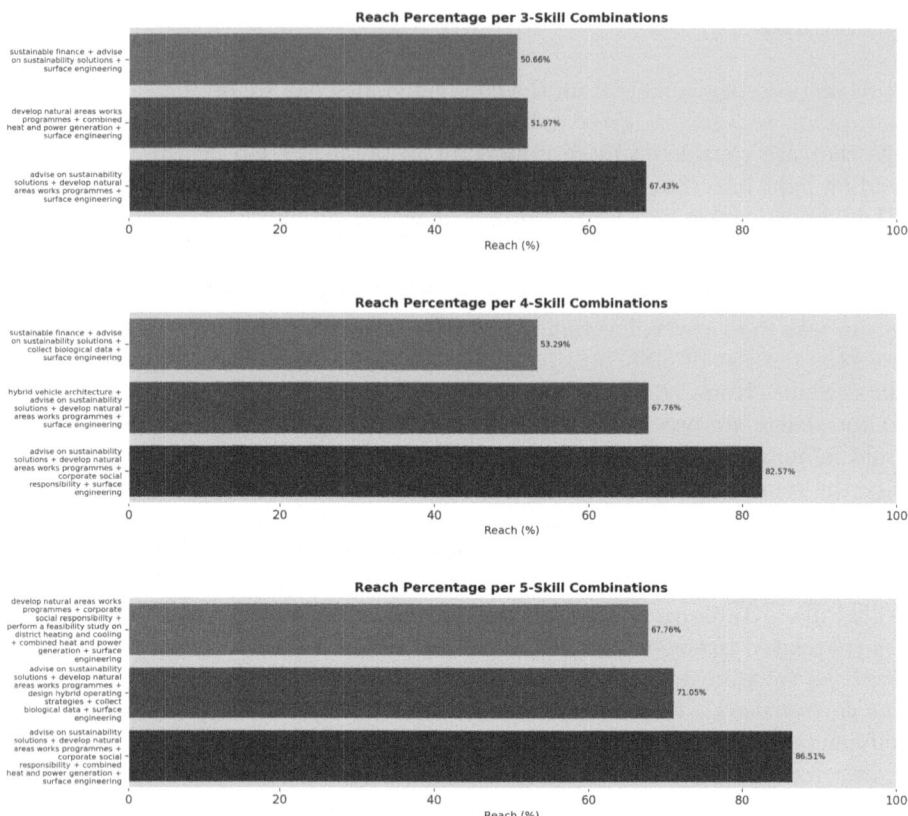

**Fig. 2.** Reach percentages of high-coverage GSE skill combinations, grouped by number of skills.

skill category is outlined below to illustrate their practical significance and stake-holder impact.

Among the 3-skill combinations, one of the most impactful includes *advise on sustainability solutions*, *develop natural areas works programmes*, and *surface engineering*, covering 67.43% of the job postings. This trio highlights the synergy between environmental planning, sustainability consulting, and applied engineering. Expanding to a 4-skill combinations by adding *corporate social responsibility* raises the reach to 82.57%, reflecting how ethical and social considerations enhance the appeal of technical sustainability profiles. The most effective 5-skill combination—incorporating *combined heat and power generation* alongside the previous four—achieves 86.51% reach, showcasing the added value of energy efficiency integration and multi-dimensional sustainability. These results emphasize that green skillsets blending technical innovation, environmental awareness, and social accountability are best aligned with stakeholder needs and sustainable market evolution, as indicated in Table 5

**Table 5.** Stakeholder Contributions by Skill Combination

| Job Seekers/Professionals | Companies/Employers | Education/Training | Societal Impact |
|---|---|---|---|
| **3-skills combinations** | | | |
| build careers in environmental planning and engineering | improve eco-innovation in infrastructure projects | blend ecological design and sustainable tech education | enhances green spaces and environmental resilience |
| access hybrid energy and green infrastructure roles | advance integrated energy-efficiency initiatives | teach applied sustainability in energy systems | reduces carbon footprint and supports green energy adoption |
| enter green finance and sustainable development fields | align investment with eco-conscious innovation | combine environmental economics with engineering | supports sustainable investment and infrastructure |
| **4-skills combinations** | | | |
| position for roles linking CSR and environmental design | boost brand with integrated sustainability practices | merge ethics, sustainability, and engineering training | strengthens social and environmental accountability |
| prepare for eco-transport and urban design careers | innovate in sustainable mobility solutions | teach clean energy and land-use planning | encourages low-emission transport and eco-urbanism |
| enter sustainability analytics and green investment | leverage data for eco-financial strategy | combine environmental data science with green finance | promotes data-driven sustainability policies |
| **5-skills combinations** | | | |
| pursue leadership in sustainable infrastructure | implement energy-smart and socially responsible systems | integrate CSR, energy systems, and sustainability design | accelerates climate action and corporate responsibility |
| target complex roles in environmental risk and planning | improve compliance and eco-strategy in energy sectors | teach integrated project design with sustainability focus | minimizes environmental disruption and promotes awareness |
| qualify for energy transition and urban development jobs | design efficient and socially responsible energy systems | focus on feasibility studies and clean energy planning | enables climate-friendly urban infrastructure |

GSE is becoming increasingly vital as organizations aim to reduce the environmental impact of digital technologies. The impact in stakeholders is effectivelt showcased in Table 5, for the four identified dimensions. By optimizing code efficiency, minimizing energy consumption, and improving data center performance, developers play a key role in promoting sustainability within the tech sector. This shift creates value across multiple dimensions: businesses can align with environmental goals, reduce operational costs, and meet regulatory requirements; policymakers can support sustainable innovation through targeted initiatives; and educators, including universities and training providers, can prepare students for emerging roles in green technology. Incorporating GSE into academic and professional development frameworks helps build a future-ready workforce that is both technologically skilled and environmentally conscious.

# 5    Discussion

The extracted results indicate that having environmental conscience along with promoting sustainability principles and opting for sustainable technologies and design are highly demanded by employers. This extends to many sectors, including finance, energy and heating as well as horizontal corporate responsibility towards the environment. Overall, across the three primary ESCO pillars, prioritized skills appear to be diverse in their objectives and characteristics, spanning multiple facets of GSE and focusing on different areas.

The skill combinations extracted from the table reveal a clear emphasis on developing sustainable operating strategies, conducting feasibility studies, and integrating energy-efficient systems. This suggests that designing green infrastructure—whether physical or digital—requires deliberate planning, technical assessment, and strategic implementation. The most impactful combinations highlight the importance of minimizing energy consumption and carbon emissions while ensuring systems remain functional, efficient, and aligned with broader sustainability objectives.

Overall, both in the prioritized skills and the produced green skillsets a heavy focus on the finance, energy and transport sectors, while the corporate social policies seem to play a major role. Thus, the deployment of software solutions that adhere to social principles around sustainability is crucial for the future of GSE, the promotion of sustainability and the benefit of the supporting of ecological well-being.

# 6    Conclusions

Software is an important and inextricable part of the modern digitalized world. However, as computational demands increase, so does the environmental burden of cloud infrastructures, data centers and deployment of software solutions, among other aspects of IT. In this work, based on a modification of the TURF analysis algorithm, augmented by prioritized skills derived from the HCV algorithm, the goal was to introduce not only vital green skills that are required in modern SE job positions but also to highlight skill combinations that can lead to tangible benefits for multiple interested parties.

Some potential threats to the validity of this study include the need for testing the methodology to other sectors (e.g. healthcare, marketing etc.) in order to validate the findings and provided insights. In addition, the study serves as a baseline analysis of European job postings and does not reflect the general landscape of the labour market. While the leveraged dataset offers valuable insights into the European labour market, it cannot reflect the global landscape, particularly in regions such as North America or Asia, where other skills and skillsets might be prioritized. Future work could expand the scope of analysis to assess cross-regional trends in GSE demand. In terms of internal validity, it should be noted that based on different executions of the algorithms on different pillars, the number of jobs differed, particularly if some jobs had no pillar-specific skills present in their extracted skills. Large-scale experimentation is required to further test the algorithm, both in terms of accuracy but also in terms of computational times and space requirements. Also, external validation and feedback of the extracted skillsets could greatly enhance interpretability and reproducibility.

As future work, we plan to expand the algorithm to include additional job postings from other portals, along with including a portal of experts in the process, who will verify and interpret the findings in a clearer manner. In addition, more robust course and learning outcomes suggestions can be provided using a recommendation system that integrates the H-TURF algorithm to prioritize skills from different sectors, timeframes and regions and provide a holistic overview of the current and future labour market.

**Acknowledgment.** The work was supported by European Unionn's Horizon Europe Framework Programme SKILLAB under grant agreement No. 101132663.

# References

1. Vona, F., Marin, G., Consoli, D., Popp, D.: Environmental regulation and green skills: an empirical exploration. J. Assoc. Environ. Resour. Econ. **5**,(2018). https://doi.org/10.1086/698859
2. Ardito, L., Procaccianti, G., Torchiano, M., Vetrò, A.: Understanding green software development: a conceptual framework. In: IT Professional, vol. 17, no. 1, pp. 44–50 (2015). https://doi.org/10.1109/MITP.2015.16
3. Kuesten, C., Bi, J.: TURF analysis for CATA data using R package 'turfR'. Food Qual. Prefer. **91** (2021). https://doi.org/10.1016/j.foodqual.2021.104201
4. Matthew, U.O., Asuni, O., Fatai, L.O.: Green software engineering development paradigm: an approach to a sustainable renewable energy future. In: Sharma, A., Chanderwal, N., Prajapati, A., Singh, P., Kansal, M., (eds.), Advancing Software Engineering Through AI, Federated Learning, and Large Language Models, pp. 281–294. IGI Global Scientific Publishing (2024). https://doi.org/10.4018/979-8-3693-3502-4.ch018
5. Buyya, R., Ilager, S., Arroba, P.: Energy-efficiency and sustainability in new generation cloud computing: a vision and directions for integrated management of data centre resources and workloads. Softw. Pract. Exp. **54**(1), 24–38 (2024). https://doi.org/10.1002/spe.3248
6. Gupta, A., Singh, P., Jain, D., Sharma, A.K., Vats, P., Sharma, V.P.: A sustainable green approach to the virtualized environment in cloud computing. In: Zhang, Y.D., Senjyu, T., So-In, C., Joshi, A. (eds.) Smart Trends in Computing and Communications. LNNS, vol. 396, pp. 751–760. Springer, Singapore (2022). https://doi.org/10.1007/978-981-16-9967-2_71
7. Khanh, Q.V., Nguyen, V.-H., Minh, Q.N., Van, A.D., Le Anh, N., Chehri, A.: An efficient edge computing management mechanism for sustainable smart cities. Sustain. Comput. Inf. Syst. **38**, 100867 (2023). https://doi.org/10.1016/j.suscom.2023.100867
8. Heldal, R., et al.: Sustainability competencies and skills in software engineering: an industry perspective, J. Syst. Softw. **211**, 111978 (2024). ISSN 0164-1212, https://doi.org/10.1016/j.jss.2024.111978

9. Freed, M., et al.: An investigation of green software engineering. In: 30th European Conference on Software Process Improvement (EuroSPI 2023), 30 Aug–1 Sept 2023, Grenoble, France (2023). ISBN 978-3-031-42306-2

10. Katal, A., Dahiya, S., Choudhury, T.: Energy efficiency in cloud computing data center: a survey on hardware technologies. Clust. Comput. **25**, 1–31 (2022). https://doi.org/10.1007/s10586-021-03431-z

11. Verma, N., Jotwani, V.: Green based software engineering approach for sustainable protocol. Int. J. Res. Appl. Sci. Eng. Technol. (2022)

12. Ganesan, M., Kor, A.-L., Pattinson, C., Rondeau, E.: Green cloud software engineering for big data processing. Sustainability **12**(21), 9255 (2020). https://doi.org/10.3390/su12219255

13. Verdecchia, R., Lago, P., Ebert, C., de Vries, C.: Green IT and green software. IEEE Softw. **38**(6), 7–15 (2021). https://doi.org/10.1109/MS.2021.3102254

14. Miaoulis, G., Parsons, H., Free, V.: Turf: a new planning approach for product line extensions. Mark. Res. **2**(1) (1990)

15. Conklin, W.M., Lipovetsky, S.: Marketing decision analysis by TURF and Shapley value. Int. J. Inf. Technol. Decis. Making **4**(01), 5–19 (2005)

16. Berander, P., Jönsson, P.: Hierarchical cumulative voting (hcv)–prioritization of requirements in hierarchies. Int. J. Softw. Eng. Knowl. Eng. **16**(06), 819–849 (2006)

17. Aluas, M., et al.: SKILLAB: skills matter. In 2024 50th Euromicro Conference on Software Engineering and Advanced Applications (SEAA), pp. 491–498. IEEE (2024)

18. Manotas, I., et al.: An empirical study of practitioners' perspectives on green software engineering. In: Proceedings of the 38th International Conference on Software Engineering, pp. 237–248 (2016)

19. Calero, C., Piattini, M.: Introduction to Green in Software Engineering, pp. 3–27. Springer, Cham (2015)

20. Kern, E., Dick, M., Naumann, S., Hiller, T.: Impacts of software and its engineering on the carbon footprint of ICT. Environ. Impact Assess. Rev. **52**, 53–61 (2015)

21. Matthew, U.O., Asuni, O., Fatai, L.O.: Green software engineering development paradigm: an approach to a sustainable renewable energy future. In: Advancing Software Engineering Through AI, Federated Learning, and Large Language Models, pp. 281–294. IGI Global (2024)

22. Sern, L.C., Zaime, A.F., Foong, L.M.: Green skills for green industry: a review of literature. J. Phys. Conf. Ser. **1019**(1), 012030. IOP Publishing (2018)

23. Zubir, M.Z.M., Lai, C.S., Zaime, A.F., Lee, M.F., Ibrahim, B., Ismail, A.: Dimension of green skills: perspectives from the industry experts. J. Tech. EducTrain. **13**(1), 159–166 (2021)

24. Kavargyris, D.C., Georgiou, K., Papaioannou, E., Petrakis, K., Mittas, N., Angelis, L.: ESCOX: a tool for skill and occupation extraction using LLMs from unstructured text. Softw. Impacts **100772** (2025). https://doi.org/10.1016/j.simpa.2025.100772

# Rookie Mistakes: Measuring Software Quality in Student Projects to Guide Educational Enhancement

Marco De Luca⬤, Sergio Di Martino⬤, Sergio Di Meglio⁽✉⁾⬤,
Anna Rita Fasolino⬤, Luigi Libero Lucio Starace⬤,
and Porfirio Tramontana⬤

University of Naples "Federico II", Naples, Italy
{marco.deluca2,fasolinosergio.dimartino,sergio.dimeglio,
annarita.fasolino,luigiliberolucio.starace,ptramon}@unina.it

**Abstract.** When teaching Programming and Software Engineering in Bachelor's Degree programs, the emphasis on creating functional software projects often overshadows the focus on software quality, a trend that aligns with ACM curricula recommendations. Software Engineering courses are typically introduced later in the curriculum, and can generally allocate only limited time to quality-related topics, leaving educators with the challenge of deciding which quality aspects to prioritize. In this decision, the literature offers limited guidance, as most existing studies focus on code written by novice students and small code units, making it unclear whether those findings extend to intermediate-level students with foundational object-oriented programming skills working on more complex software projects. To address this gap, we analyze 83 object-oriented team projects developed by 172 university students across 4 different editions of the Object-Oriented Programming course. We apply a static analysis pipeline used in prior research to assess software quality, combining SONARQUBE and ARCHUNIT to detect code smells and architectural anti-patterns. Our findings highlight recurring quality issues and offer concrete evidence of the challenges students face at this stage, providing valuable guidance for educators aiming to continuously improve Software Engineering curricula and promote quality-oriented development practices.

**Keywords:** oop courses · code quality · quality criteria · architectural anti-patterns

## 1 Introduction

In Bachelor's Degree programs, such as Computer Science and Computer Engineering, the focus of programming and software engineering education often leans more towards the ability to develop functional projects rather than emphasizing software quality. This aligns with the ACM Computer Science and Computer Engineering curriculum recommendations for undergraduate degrees [7].

D. Taibi and D. Smite (Eds.): SEAA 2025, LNCS 16083, pp. 137–154, 2026.
https://doi.org/10.1007/978-3-032-04207-1_10

According to these guidelines, software quality is typically only lightly addressed in three-year Bachelor's programs. In these programs, introductory CS1 courses concentrate primarily on programming skills, with basic concepts of software quality introduced later, primarily in Software Engineering courses.

However, even within Software Engineering courses, the time dedicated to software quality teaching is limited. Educators face the challenge of determining which aspects of software quality to prioritize within these constraints. Furthermore, there is a significant gap in the literature regarding research into the foundational software quality challenges specifically faced by intermediate-level students when developing software projects. This lack of insight leaves instructors of more advanced Software Engineering courses with little direction on how to prioritize quality aspects in their curricula.

In this study, we present an empirical investigation of software quality in a set of 83 projects developed by 172 Computer Science students involved in an Object-Oriented Programming (OOP) course taken in two consecutive academic years. Our study leverages a static code analysis pipeline validated in prior research [9], applying state-of-the-art tools such as SONARQUBE[1] and ARCHU-NIT[2] to detect code smells and architectural anti-patterns, two indicators of structural degradation and design compromise often referred to as social debt when accumulated in collaborative environments. By identifying recurring quality problems in student code, this work provides concrete evidence to support iterative course improvements aligned with real-world development standards [33], as shown in Fig. 1. The insights gained from this analysis can guide educators in refining both introductory programming courses and more advanced Software Engineering modules, ultimately fostering a culture of quality awareness and reflective development practices in future software engineers.

The remainder of the paper is structured as follows. Section 2 presents background information on software quality and related work. Section 3 describes the study we conducted, including detailed information about the OOP courses and the topics covered, allowing readers to compare them with their own teaching contexts. Section 4 presents the results, highlighting the most relevant findings, which are then discussed in Sect. 5, with a focus on their implications for educators. Last, Sect. 6 outlines the threats to the validity of our findings, while Sect. 7 presents final remarks and directions for future work.

## 2     Background and Related Works

In the following, we introduce key concepts related to software quality, focusing on both code-level and architectural aspects. We also review existing tools used for quality assessment and summarize prior research on software quality issues in student-developed code.

---

[1] SonarQube, available at https://www.sonarsource.com/products/sonarqube/.
[2] ArchUnit, available at https://www.archunit.org/.

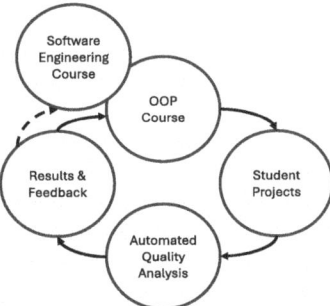

**Fig. 1.** Cyclical evaluation process: the analysis of the quality of OOP students projects brings feedback useful to improve this course and also Software Engineering courses.

## 2.1   Software Quality

Software quality captures how effectively a system satisfies its specified requirements and fulfills user expectations [12]. The ISO 25010 standard [16] provides a widely adopted model for assessing software quality, defining key attributes such as modularity, reusability, and testability [14]. These quality attributes are primarily shaped by two fundamental aspects: the clarity and maintainability of the source code, and the soundness of the software's architectural design. Both play a critical role in ensuring the system remains robust, adaptable, and easy to evolve over time. To ensure and maintain these properties, various Software Quality Management (SQM) practices are employed throughout the development process. These include code reviews, automated testing, static code analysis, and architecture conformance checks [4,18,29], often supported by tools such as SONARQUBE, CHECKSTYLE, and similar analyzers. In recent years, SQM has also extended to the social dimension of software development. Community detection techniques have been used on software dependency graphs to identify architectural issues, and on developer collaboration networks to uncover coordination problems, knowledge silos, or uneven code ownership [5,10,27,28]. These analyses provide complementary insights to technical evaluations, enabling a more comprehensive understanding of software quality.

**Source Code Quality.** The notion of source code quality lacks a single, universally accepted definition and is often interpreted in various ways. One of the most well-known and widely used interpretations is the notion of *Clean Code*, as introduced by Martin et al. [23]. According to this perspective, clean code is characterized by its readability, clarity of intent, ease of writing, and maintainability. It is designed not only to be understood by compilers, but also to be easily interpreted by other developers.

To support the development of such code, a variety of static analysis tools have been introduced and are commonly adopted in both industry and education. These tools are intended to automatically detect violations of clean code principles. A comparative study by Lenarduzzi et al. [21] evaluated several popular tools, including BETTER CODE HUB, CHECKSTYLE, COVERITY SCAN, FIND-BUGS, PMD, and SONARQUBE. Their findings highlighted SONARQUBE as the most effective tool for detecting a broad range of code quality issues.

**Software Architectural Design.** The architecture of a software system, defined as its structural organization into components, their relationships, and the rules governing their interactions, plays a critical role in determining overall system quality [2,24]. A well-structured architecture contributes to building systems that are robust, scalable, and maintainable, while inadequate architectural decisions can lead to technical debt, reduced performance, and decreased reliability. To address recurring challenges in system design, software architectural patterns have been proposed as standardized, reusable solutions to common design problems [32]. These patterns serve as high-level design strategies that promote important architectural qualities such as modularity, reusability, and scalability [8,30]. By guiding the organization of system components, they help ensure that software systems are easier to evolve and maintain over time. To verify that the implemented architecture adheres to the intended design, developers can perform Architecture Conformance Checks (ACC) [34]. These checks can be automated using dedicated tools and libraries, such as ARCHUNIT, which allow developers to define and enforce architectural rules directly within the codebase.

## 2.2    Software Quality Issues in Student Code

Prior research has extensively examined the quality of code produced by university students, particularly those at the introductory level or with limited programming experience. Several studies (e.g., [3,19,22]) have explored the use of automated analysis tools to monitor and improve the quality of student code throughout a course, providing continuous feedback as a means of supporting the learning process. While these approaches have demonstrated a positive influence on student outcomes, their primary focus has been on measuring quality improvements over time, rather than uncovering the underlying challenges faced by novice programmers. Other studies have sought to identify recurring quality issues in student-written code by analyzing large sets of code submissions after completion. For instance, Keuning et al. [20] examined over 2.6 million code snapshots created using the BlueJ environment to uncover frequent problems encountered by beginners. Similarly, Effenberger and Pelánek [15] analyzed more than 114,000 Python solutions to small-scale programming tasks—typically no longer than 20 lines of code—to construct a taxonomy of common code defects among students in CS1-level courses. A more recent study by Sun et al. [31] focused on the performance of students in OOP courses, assessing both the quality of their code and the tests they wrote. However, this study also centered on relatively small assignments that did not involve substantial architectural design decisions. In a different educational context, Chren et al. [6] evaluated how a course explicitly focused on software quality impacted the code developed by students. Their evaluation considered 54 student projects using a combination of manual inspection and automated tools (e.g., SONARQUBE and CHECKSTYLE), assessing multiple metrics such as code size, duplication, bugs, and code smells.

Despite the breadth of these studies, most are limited in two important ways. First, they typically examine simple, self-contained tasks, often solvable in just a few lines of code. This raises questions about whether their conclusions hold when students are tasked with more complex, OOP projects that integrate components such as graphical user interfaces (GUIs) and relational databases. Second, due to the simplicity of the programming problems under consideration, prior work has rarely addressed architectural quality issues, such as violations of design patterns or the emergence of architectural anti-patterns. To our knowledge, these limitations reduce the applicability of existing research to intermediate-level students working on structured, multi-component software systems, as found in typical OOP courses. In such contexts, the scope and architectural complexity of student projects differ significantly from those studied in most prior work.

A first exploratory study based on some projects from a single course was previously presented by the same authors [9] as a proof-of-concept of the idea of mining projects made by students of an OOP course for finding the presence of anti-patterns and code smells.

## 3   Study Design

### 3.1   Goal and Research Questions

The goal of this study is to assess the software quality of Java projects developed by students attending an OOP course. These courses typically mark the students' first exposure to the principles of designing and implementing software systems using the object-oriented paradigm. By examining the students' code, we aim to identify recurring design flaws and code smells and better understand the foundational quality issues they face at this stage of their learning.

To this end, we conducted an empirical study involving two different editions of an OOP course taught by two of the authors as part of a Computer Science bachelor's degree program. We applied a static analysis pipeline grounded in prior research to investigate the presence of structural and design issues, as illustrated in Fig. 1.

This study addresses the following research questions:

**RQ₁.** *How common are architectural pattern violations found in students' projects?*

**RQ₂.** *How common are code quality issues in students' projects?*

The research questions aim to identify the most common shortcomings in student-developed projects, both from an architectural and a programming perspective. The findings are intended to provide actionable insights that can help educators improve both introductory OOP courses and more advanced courses, such as Software Engineering, by guiding them on which quality aspects to prioritize in their teaching.

## 3.2    Object-Oriented Programming Course

The objects of this study are the software projects developed by students as the final examination assignment for an OOP course.

We considered two editions of two OOP courses offered within the same Bachelor's degree program in Computer Science at the same university. These two courses share the same teaching materials, structure, and learning objectives, and are delivered during the same semester. Due to the large number of enrolled students, the cohort is divided into two groups based on students' surnames. Each group is assigned to a different teacher, both of whom are coauthors of this study. To account for possible variation over time, we included projects from two consecutive academic years, namely 2021/2022 and 2022/2023. For clarity, we refer to the courses taught by the two teachers as Group 1 and Group 2 throughout the paper.

The OOP courses included 48 h of lectures, corresponding to 6 ECTS, in the standard European Credit Transfer and Accumulation System (ECTS) way of defining the academic characteristics of courses. The prerequisites for these courses include successful completion of prior CS1 programming courses included in the bachelor's degree program, which entail 72 and 24 lecture hours, respectively. In these courses, students learned the fundamentals of procedural programming using the C language. Moreover, an additional prerequisite was completing the Database course, which is provided in the same year as the OOP course. The OOP courses introduce students to the Java programming language, OOP principles, the UML modeling language, and basic software quality and architecture concepts. The official reference textbooks for the course are *"Java How to Program"* [11], and *"UML Distilled: A Brief Guide to the Standard Object Modeling Language"* [17]. The teachers did not require the use of a specific IDE to support development, but Eclipse was the most used by these classes of students. As part of the course, students are also introduced to a reference architectural pattern designed for GUI-based applications. This pattern organizes the system into four main packages: (1) a GUI package (2) a Controller package, (3) a Model package, (4) a Data Access Object (DAO) package, with, possibly, another package with utility classes. The proposed reference architecture is sketched in Fig. 2.

The GUI Package includes GUI classes representing the user entry point to the application. These classes should depend on Controller classes, implementing the application logic. Controller classes, on the other hand, depend on Model classes that are responsible for the transient storage of the information domain data and on DAO classes for accessing the persistent data stored in the database. Controller classes are allowed to open GUI instances. The teachers recommended to follow this architectural pattern and to avoid the introduction of too much dependencies between packages. In particular, they recommended that the GUI should remain independent from data management components. Although this

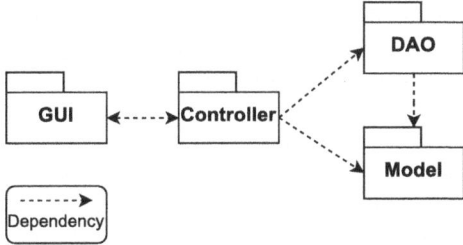

**Fig. 2.** UML Package diagram representing the project architecture according to the proposed pattern.

pattern may not be representative of other patterns adopted in complex software systems (e.g. MVC), they adopted it as a didactic introduction to the principle of separation of concerns and to avoid an excessive coupling between the application's components.

To pass the course, students have to submit a final assignment consisting of developing a GUI-based desktop application, representing a typical information system, relying on a relational database for data persistence. In this final assignment, students have to self-organize in teams of two or three students and use the Java programming language and the reference architecture presented during the course. The project requirements are assigned by the teacher to each team. In each course edition, three different sets of project requirements, each with comparable complexity, were defined and randomly assigned to each team. The teachers graded the submitted projects based on their completeness and correctness w.r.t. the assigned requirements, and overall software quality. Each student was also subjected to a final oral exam during which the project was discussed. This final moment of evaluation was useful to obtain feedback from the students regarding their choices and the mistakes they had made.

In these editions of the Object Orientation course the teachers did not explicitly present the concept of code smell, nor did they present analysis tools such as ArchUnit and SonarQube so the primary goal of the experiments presented in this paper is to show the issues that students most frequently introduce without an explicit education on software quality assessment.

In total, as objects of our study, we collected 83 projects developed by 172 students. Table 1 and Fig. 3 summarize, for each course edition, the number of considered projects, the number of involved students, and some statistics about project size (mean number of classes and non-commenting lines of code - NCLOC, along with the standard deviation). Note that these projects are remarkably more complex than the simple assignments employed in related works investigating software quality in student-developed code, with an average number of classes per project ranging from 36 to 51, depending on the edition of the course, and 3,000 or more NCLOC on average.

**Table 1.** Characteristics of the considered projects

| Course | Year | Num. Proj. | Num. Stud. | Num. of classes | | NCLOC | |
|--------|------|-----------|-----------|------|------|------|------|
| | | | | Mean | St.d. | Mean | St.d. |
| Gr. 1 | 21/22 | 23 | 46 | 51 | 26 | 5797 | 3099 |
| | 22/23 | 20 | 47 | 40 | 24 | 3887 | 2610 |
| Gr. 2 | 21/22 | 26 | 50 | 41 | 13 | 4647 | 1616 |
| | 22/23 | 14 | 29 | 36 | 11 | 3011 | 1171 |

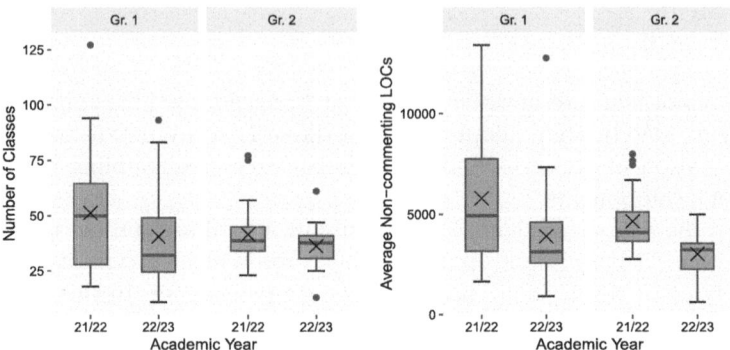

**Fig. 3.** Project Statistics. From left to right, boxplots represent the distribution of the number of classes and the number of non-commenting lines of code per project. The cross, in each boxplot, represents the average value.

## 3.3 Automated Quality Analysis

To evaluate the student submissions, we adopted an automated quality analysis pipeline inspired by the approach proposed in [9]. The pipeline performs two distinct but complementary analyses: *Architecture Conformity Check* and *Static Code Quality Analysis*. The Architecture Conformity Check leverages ARCHU-NIT, a Java library that allows developers to encode architectural rules as JUnit tests. A suite of ARCHUNIT test cases was created by two of the authors to verify compliance with the architectural patterns taught during the course. These tests systematically check for disallowed dependencies between packages and flag any violations. For each type of violation, we recorded the number of student projects where it occurred at least once, and we qualitatively examined frequent violations to understand their underlying causes. For the Code Quality Analysis, we relied on SONARQUBE, a widely used static analysis platform. We configured a dedicated SONARQUBE instance to analyze the codebases against the full set of 677 default Java rules. SONARQUBE classifies issues into Bugs (reliability), Vulnerabilities (security), and Code Smells (maintainability), and assigns a severity level ranging from Info to Blocker. For each rule, we recorded the number of student projects in which at least one violation was detected.

## 4   Results

***RQ₁: How common are architectural pattern violations found in students' projects?***

Table 2 reports the number and percentage of projects from each considered group that presented at least one occurrence of a disallowed type of coupling (respectively from GUI to Model, from Model to GUI, from GUI to DAO, from DAO to GUI, from Model to Controller, from DAO to Controller and from Model to DAO).

**Table 2.** Overview of package dependencies across projects. Disallowed dependencies are highlighted in red. Legend: G = GUI, C = Controller, M = Model, D = DAO.

| | | | Couplings | | | | | | | | | | | |
|---|---|---|---|---|---|---|---|---|---|---|---|---|---|---|
| Gr | Year | #Proj | M→G | C→G | D→G | G→M | C→M | D→M | G→C | M→C | D→C | G→D | M→D | C→D |
| 1 | 21/22 | 23 | 9% | 100% | 0% | 65% | 91% | 91% | 96% | 13% | 35% | 22% | 4% | 96% |
| 1 | 22/23 | 20 | 0% | 95% | 15% | 75% | 90% | 85% | 95% | 10% | 45% | 35% | 10% | 100% |
| 2 | 21/22 | 26 | 0% | 15% | 4% | 88% | 96% | 96% | 100% | 4% | 4% | 31% | 0% | 88% |
| 2 | 22/23 | 21 | 0% | 50% | 7% | 64% | 100% | 57% | 93% | 0% | 0% | 7% | 0% | 93% |
| **Overall** | | **83** | **2%** | **64%** | **6%** | **75%** | **94%** | **86%** | **96%** | **7%** | **22%** | **25%** | **4%** | **94%** |

The most common violations of the expected architectural pattern were due to the existence of dependencies from the GUI package to the Model package (G→M) (75%). The direct dependencies from GUI to Model (G→M) were not allowed because in these courses the teachers recommended that Model classes and objects should be managed only by Controllers and not directly by GUI classes to make the GUI implementation independent from the information modelling. We observed this architectural issue very often, in all the courses (in 75% of projects). *These dependencies usually represented a shortcut adopted by students to avoid the need to serialize data from model classes in data structures for the GUI.* On the other hand, we observed that the inverse coupling (M→G), due to model classes that request data from the GUI, was correctly avoided in almost all the projects, except 5 of them (2%).

The direct interactions between classes of the GUI package and DAO classes (G→D and D→G) were sometimes observed: on average, 25% of projects included calls from GUI to DAO, whereas only 6% of projects included calls from DAO to GUI. These interactions are violations causing the GUI to depend on the database and on its data representation, or vice versa. *Also these interactions were introduced by students as shortcuts but they caused unneeded couplings between packages that should remain unlinked between them.*

The unallowed interaction between DAO and Controller (D→C) was observed in a significant set of projects, almost all belonging to Group 1 (22% on average). The DAO object should only return data to the Controller, without other calls. *We observed that some student teams included part of the business logic into the methods of the DAO classes, maybe confusing those methods with database triggers.*

We observed a few cases (only in 7% of projects) in which classes of the Model package interacted with the Controller (M→C). Also in that case, these interactions corresponded to methods of the Model that carried out part of the business logic that should be an exclusive responsibility of Controllers.

Finally, we observed some cases in which objects of the Model package directly queried the database by calling items from the DAO package. Although this interaction is allowed in some simple architectural patterns (i.e. Boundary-Control-Entity-Database, BCED), it represents a disallowed interaction in the suggested pattern. These interactions were observed in few projects (only 3 projects from the Group 1, consisting in 4% of the total number of projects).

> **RQ$_1$.** Overall, the students' projects presented 7 different types of violations of the prescribed architectural pattern. The frequencies of these violations ranged between 2% (Model→GUI) and 75% (GUI→Model). Most of the violations were essentially due to (1) bad practices (e.g. shortcuts) adopted by the students to avoid serialization and deserialization operations for passing data between classes of different packages, and (2) inadequate understanding of the principles for correctly assigning responsibilities to classes and for sharing them between specialized packages.

*RQ$_2$: How common are code quality issues in students' projects?*
Table 3 reports, for each course group and edition, the number of analysed projects and the average number of different types of code issues detected in all the projects belonging to that specific group and edition.

**Table 3.** Overall number of different code issues typologies observed in student's projects

| Course | Year | Number of Projects | Average Number Issue types |
|--------|------|--------------------|-----------------------------|
| Gr. 1 | 21/22 | 23 | 33.1 |
|        | 22/23 | 20 | 30.8 |
| Gr. 2 | 21/22 | 26 | 36.8 |
|        | 22/23 | 14 | 27.9 |

The average number of typologies of detected issues varied from 33.1 and 36.8, measured in blended course editions (21/22) and 30.8 and 27.9, measured in the 22/23 editions of the courses. A possible cause for these slight reductions in the number of detected code smells per project might be due to the increased effectiveness of teaching in person. In addition, in the second editions of the courses, both the teachers presented in more detail the "Good Programming Practice" and the "Common Programming Error" boxes present in the textbook "Java: How to Program" [11] in order to better focus on these aspects.

Complete tables, including the entire list of smell typologies observed in all the student projects, are included in the anonymized replication package [1]. To have a summary view of the most common issues in the selected student projects, we limited the scope of our analysis to the ones occurring in the majority (more than 50%) of the projects. We have filtered out from this set some issues that were explicitly related to topics outside the scope of the course (e.g., the lack of use of lambda expressions, which are introduced in advanced programming courses). As a result of this filtering step, 17 types of issues were selected. With respect to their severity, one of them is classified as Blocker, 3 as Critical, 7 as Major, and the remaining 6 as Minor. Only one of them is considered a Bug, whereas all the other ones are classified as Code Smells. Moreover, no issues labeled with the Vulnerability tag were found in the majority of projects. 16 out of 17 issues affect the maintainability of the project, whereas the remaining one (i.e., the Bug) affects its reliability.

Table 4 reports the list of the 17 issue types found in the majority of the examined student projects. For each issue type, the table reports its description as provided by SONARQUBE. In the other columns, we reported the classification of the issue (Bug or Code Smell) and its severity (Blocker, Critical, Major, or Minor). The last columns of the table report the number (and percentage) of students' projects of each group in which the issue type was detected.

The Blocker category issue is concerned with Resources that were not properly closed. It was found in 76% of projects. The issues were generally due to student inexperience: leaving open a stream or connection to an external resource can cause concurrency problems or memory leaks, but these topics are usually explained in third year courses.

The three Critical issues found in the majority of student projects are classified as Code Smells and are respectively "*String literals should not be duplicated*", "*Cognitive Complexity of methods should not be too high*", and "*Methods should not be empty*", respectively found in 96%, 71% and 52% of projects. All of them negatively affected the maintainability of the projects. In particular, the first one may cause inconsistencies when string literals have to be modified (e.g. translated into another language), while the second one may make hard the comprehension of methods behaviour. The third one may be a symptom of project incompleteness.

The 7 most common issues categorized by SONARQUBE as Major issues correspond to other Code Smells negatively affecting the understandability and modifiability of the source code. For example, the use of System.out for logging purposes (found in 86% of the projects) is not recommended because log outputs may mix with standard outputs and error outputs. Other frequent issues are related to unused assignments (71%) or private fields (62%), methods with too many parameters (65%), old sections of code commented out (64%), local variables with the same name of class fields (56%), branches of the same conditional

**Table 4.** List of the most common code issues found in student projects

| Sonar Rule Description | Issue Type | Severity | Group 1 | | Group 2 | | Overall (%) |
|---|---|---|---|---|---|---|---|
| | | | 21/22 | 22/23 | 21/22 | 22/23 | |
| Resources should be closed | BUG | BLOCKER | 16 (70%) | 17 (77%) | 22 (85%) | 10 (71%) | 76% |
| String literals should not be duplicated | SMELL | CRITICAL | 23 (100%) | 21 (95%) | 26 (100%) | 12 (86%) | 96% |
| Cognitive Complexity of methods should not be too high | SMELL | CRITICAL | 18 (78%) | 7 (32%) | 25 (96%) | 10 (71%) | 71% |
| Methods should not be empty | SMELL | CRITICAL | 9 (39%) | 15 (68%) | 14 (54%) | 6 (43%) | 52% |
| Standard outputs should not be used directly to log anything | SMELL | MAJOR | 18 (78%) | 18 (82%) | 24 (92%) | 13 (93%) | 86% |
| Unused assignments should be removed | SMELL | MAJOR | 17 (74%) | 16 (73%) | 21 (81%) | 6 (43%) | 71% |
| Methods should not have too many parameters | SMELL | MAJOR | 12 (52%) | 15 (68%) | 17 (65%) | 11 (79%) | 65% |
| Sections of code should not be commented out | SMELL | MAJOR | 15 (65%) | 12 (55%) | 17 (65%) | 10 (71%) | 64% |
| Unused "private" fields should be removed | SMELL | MAJOR | 15 (65%) | 12 (55%) | 17 (65%) | 9 (64%) | 62% |
| Local variables should not shadow class fields | SMELL | MAJOR | 12 (52%) | 14 (64%) | 17 (65%) | 5 (36%) | 56% |
| Branches in a conditional structure should not have the same implementation | SMELL | MAJOR | 6 (26%) | 2 (9%) | 23 (88%) | 12 (86%) | 51% |
| Variables and method parameters should comply with naming conventions | SMELL | MINOR | 21 (91%) | 22 (100%) | 25 (96%) | 12 (86%) | 94% |
| Field names should comply with a naming convention | SMELL | MINOR | 19 (83%) | 20 (91%) | 23 (88%) | 9 (64%) | 84% |
| Unnecessary imports should be removed | SMELL | MINOR | 17 (74%) | 8 (36%) | 25 (96%) | 14 (100%) | 75% |
| Method names should comply with a naming convention | SMELL | MINOR | 14 (61%) | 19 (86%) | 18 (69%) | 5 (36%) | 66% |
| Unused local variables should be removed | SMELL | MINOR | 18 (78%) | 15 (68%) | 16 (62%) | 6 (43%) | 65% |
| Class variable fields should not have public accessibility | SMELL | MINOR | 6 (26%) | 15 (68%) | 16 (62%) | 9 (64%) | 54% |

structure with the same implementation (51%). All these bad practices appeared to be due to programmers' lack of attention to the quality of their code. Similarly, the 6 most common Minor issues corresponded to Code Smells. Many of them were due to a lack of coherence in the use of naming conventions about local variables, method parameters, and field and method names (e.g., starting with a capital letter). In addition, in 75% of the projects, unused imports were found, and in 54% of the projects, fields with public accessibility were used instead of private fields with possible public getter or setter methods. All these smells denoted a lack of knowledge about naming conventions and best practices that were explicitly presented during lectures.

It is worth noting that, even though not appearing in the majority of the projects, we observed that a security vulnerability was quite common. This vulnerability (classified as Blocker by SONARQUBE) was the hard-coding of database credentials in the source code of the projects (found in 39% of projects). This issue is also due to student inexperience (most of the students developed the code locally, thus they did not consider the risks in sharing the source code, including private credentials).

> **RQ$_2$.** The analysis of students' projects revealed common code issues, mainly related to poor resource handling (unclosed resources in 76% of projects) and programming bad practices. Frequent problems included duplicated string literals (96%), excessive cognitive complexity (71%), and empty methods (52%). Naming convention violations were also widespread (up to 94%), along with issues like unused assignments (71%) and inappropriate public field accessibility (54%).

## 5   Discussion and Implications

Building on the insights from our study, the following discusses the implications of these findings and suggests strategies to mitigate the issues observed, with the goal of improving both the courses and the quality of students' software engineering skills.

Regarding architectural violations, many were the result of students' limited experience, especially as they tackled their first substantial software projects. At this early stage, students often lack an understanding of how shortcuts or suboptimal decisions can negatively affect the long-term structure of a project. To address this, educators should place greater emphasis on explaining the *why* behind architectural decisions, rather than just the *what*. By providing clear examples and counterexamples that illustrate the consequences of poor architectural choices, educators can significantly help students make more informed and effective design decisions [26,34]. Most of the code smells observed in students' projects were linked to fundamental issues, such as unused code (e.g., redundant imports, fields, method parameters, and empty methods) and improper naming conventions for variables, fields, methods, and classes. These issues are typically the first encountered by students and can be effectively addressed with a stronger focus on clean code practices. At the introductory level, particularly in Object-Oriented Programming (OOP) courses, it would be beneficial to emphasize the most common and straightforward code smells, such as poor naming conventions, redundant variables, and unnecessary methods. Educators should encourage students to prioritize these foundational practices, as they directly improve code maintainability and readability. Teachers should stress the importance of writing clean, concise, and understandable code, illustrating how small adjustments can significantly enhance software quality.

As students progress to more advanced courses, such as Software Engineering, the curriculum should evolve to address a broader range of code smells, including more subtle and intricate issues that arise in larger-scale software projects. In these advanced courses, educators can introduce static analysis tools and more sophisticated techniques for identifying deeper code quality issues. One such tool, SONARQUBE, offers automated code quality checks and can help students integrate these tools into their development workflows.

Many code smells also stem from improper resource management, particularly with files, databases, and streams. This issue may be further compounded by students' prior experience with C, where resource management requires explicit handling of file streams and memory allocation. Having learned to manually close resources in C, students may mistakenly believe that Java, with its automatic garbage collector, eliminates the need for explicit resource management.

This misunderstanding can lead to resource leaks when students neglect to close resources like file streams, resulting in inefficient resource usage and potential application crashes. To address this, educators should clarify the differences between C and Java in terms of resource management, emphasizing the importance of explicit resource handling in Java despite the presence of garbage collection. Introducing concepts such as the try-with-resources statement in Java can help students understand the necessity of managing resources properly.

## 6   Threats to Validity

Several factors may have influenced the conclusions drawn in this study. Below, we discuss the main limitations and mitigation strategies applied.

**Threats to Internal Validity.** While this study investigates software quality in student projects, the results may be influenced by the detection capabilities of the tools employed, namely SONARQUBE and ARCHUNIT. Although these tools are the most widely adopted in the industry for static code analysis and are considered the state of the practice, they still have limitations in detecting certain types of code smells and architectural anti-patterns. We have attempted to mitigate this limitation by ensuring that SONARQUBE was configured according to best practices and that ARCHUNIT was specifically tuned and validated to detect violations in a way that closely aligns with industry standards.

**Threats to External Validity.** The study's findings are based on projects developed by Computer Science students in two different OOP courses at a single university. As a result, the generalizability of the results to other contexts, such as different educational institutions, programming languages, or course structures, may be limited. To mitigate this, we have provided extensive details about the courses, including the curriculum, student demographics, and project scope. This allows other researchers to compare their own courses with ours and assess the extent to which our findings may apply to other settings. Additionally, while our study focused on detecting code smells and architectural anti-patterns, we acknowledge that these may not encompass all aspects of software quality.

## 7   Conclusions and Future Work

This study investigates the prevalence of architectural and code smells in Java projects developed by students in OOP courses. By analyzing 83 student projects, we identified recurring architectural violations and code quality issues, revealing the most common bad practices and their causes. Our findings suggest that both early programming courses (CS1) and advanced software engineering courses must address these issues to foster better design and coding practices. The results also highlight the importance of focusing on clean code principles and architectural decisions throughout the curriculum to improve software quality awareness.

Future work will focus on: (1) replicating this study in similar courses across different universities or degree programs (e.g., Software Engineering) to broaden the applicability of our findings; (2) extending the study to other Object Orientation classes that will be instead previously instructed about code smells, architectural anti-patterns and their automatic assessment, to evaluate the possible improvements of the quality of the projects; (3) extending the evaluation to more complex student projects that integrate both front- and back-end components [13,25], allowing a deeper investigation of architectural decisions, division of responsibilities, and the practical application of design principles in full-stack development scenarios. This will help assess the effectiveness of these improvements in fostering better design practices and enhancing the overall quality of student projects.

**Acknowledgments.** This work has been partially supported by the Italian PNRR MUR project PE0000013-FAIR and by the project GATT (GAmification in Testing Teaching), funded by the University of Naples Federico II Research Funding Program (FRA).

# References

1. GitHub repo. https://github.com/SergioDME/SEAA2025
2. Aldrich, J., Chambers, C., Notkin, D.: ArchJava: connecting software architecture to implementation. In: Proceedings of the 24th International Conference on Software Engineering, ICSE 2002, pp. 187–197. Association for Computing Machinery, New York (2002). https://doi.org/10.1145/581339.581365
3. de Andrade Gomes, P.H., Garcia, R.E., Spadon, G., Eler, D.M., Olivete, C., Messias Correia, R.C.: Teaching software quality via source code inspection tool. In: 2017 IEEE Frontiers in Education Conference (FIE), pp. 1–8 (2017). https://doi.org/10.1109/FIE.2017.8190658
4. Cassee, N., Vasilescu, B., Serebrenik, A.: The silent helper: the impact of continuous integration on code reviews. In: 2020 IEEE 27th International Conference on Software Analysis, Evolution and Reengineering (SANER), pp. 423–434 (2020). https://doi.org/10.1109/SANER48275.2020.9054818
5. Chantian, B., Muenchaisri, P.: A refactoring approach for too large packages using community detection and dependency-based impacts, pp. 27–31 (2019). https://doi.org/10.1145/3362125.3362132
6. Chren, S., Macák, M., Rossi, B., Buhnova, B.: Evaluating code improvements in software quality course projects. In: Proceedings of the 26th International Conference on Evaluation and Assessment in Software Engineering, EASE 2022, pp. 160–169. Association for Computing Machinery, New York (2022). https://doi.org/10.1145/3530019.3530036
7. Clear, A., Parrish, A.S., Impagliazzo, J., Zhang, M.: Computing curricula 2020: introduction and community engagement. In: Proceedings of the 50th ACM Technical Symposium on Computer Science Education, pp. 653–654 (2019)
8. Clements, P., Garlan, D., Little, R., Nord, R., Stafford, J.: Documenting software architectures: views and beyond. In: 2003 Proceedings of the 25th International Conference on Software Engineering, pp. 740–741 (2003). https://doi.org/10.1109/ICSE.2003.1201264
9. De Luca, M., Di Meglio, S., Fasolino, A.R., Starace, L.L.L., Tramontana, P.: Automatic assessment of architectural anti-patterns and code smells in student software projects. In: Proceedings of the 28th International Conference on Evaluation and Assessment in Software Engineering, pp. 565–569 (2024)
10. De Luca, M., Fasolino, A., Ferraro, A., Moscato, V., Sperlì, G., Tramontana, P.: A community detection approach based on network representation learning for repository mining. Expert Syst. Appl. **231**, 120597 (2023). https://doi.org/10.1016/j.eswa.2023.120597
11. Deitel, P.J., Deitel, H.: Java How to Program, Early Objects, Student Value Edition, 11th edn. Pearson (2017)
12. Denning, P.J.: What is software quality? Commun. ACM **35**(1), 13–15 (1992)
13. Di Meglio, S., Libero Lucio Starace, L., Di Martino, S.: E2E-loader: a tool to generate performance tests from end-to-end GUI-level tests. In: 2025 IEEE Conference on Software Testing, Verification and Validation (ICST), pp. 747–751 (2025). https://doi.org/10.1109/ICST62969.2025.10989035
14. Di Meglio, S., Starace, L.L.L., Di Martino, S.: Starting a new rest API project? A performance benchmark of frameworks and execution environments. In: IWSM-Mensura (2023)
15. Effenberger, T., Pelánek, R.: Code quality defects across introductory programming topics. In: Proceedings of the 53rd ACM Technical Symposium on Computer

Science Education, SIGCSE 2022, vol. 1, pp. 941–947. Association for Computing Machinery, New York (2022). https://doi.org/10.1145/3478431.3499415

16. Estdale, J., Georgiadou, E.: Applying the ISO/IEC 25010 quality models to software product. In: Larrucea, X., Santamaria, I., O'Connor, R.V., Messnarz, R. (eds.) EuroSPI 2018. CCIS, vol. 896, pp. 492–503. Springer, Cham (2018). https://doi.org/10.1007/978-3-319-97925-0_42

17. Fowler, M.: UML Distilled: A Brief Guide to the Standard Object Modeling Language, 3rd edn. Addison-Wesley Longman Publishing Co., Inc., USA (2003)

18. Grambow, G., Oberhauser, R.: Towards automated context-aware software quality management. In: 2010 Fifth International Conference on Software Engineering Advances, pp. 347–352 (2010). https://doi.org/10.1109/ICSEA.2010.59

19. Jansen, J., Oprescu, A., Bruntink, M.: The impact of automated code quality feedback in programming education. In: Proceedings of the Software Engineering Education and Training (SEET) Workshop at ICSE, vol. 2070 (2017)

20. Keuning, H., Heeren, B., Jeuring, J.: Code quality issues in student programs. In: Proceedings of the 2017 ACM Conference on Innovation and Technology in Computer Science Education, ITiCSE 2017, pp. 110–115. Association for Computing Machinery, New York (2017). https://doi.org/10.1145/3059009.3059061

21. Lenarduzzi, V., Pecorelli, F., Saarimaki, N., Lujan, S., Palomba, F.: A critical comparison on six static analysis tools: detection, agreement, and precision. J. Syst. Softw. **198**, 111575 (2023). https://doi.org/10.1016/j.jss.2022.111575

22. Lu, Y., Mao, X., Wang, T., Yin, G., Li, Z.: Improving students' programming quality with the continuous inspection process: a social coding perspective. Front. Comput. Sci. **14**(5) (2019). https://doi.org/10.1007/s11704-019-9023-2

23. Martin, R.C.: Clean Code: A Handbook of Agile Software Craftsmanship. Pearson Education (2009)

24. Meglio, S.D., Libero Lucio Starace, L.: Evaluating performance and resource consumption of rest frameworks and execution environments: insights and guidelines for developers and companies. IEEE Access **12**, 161649–161669 (2024). https://doi.org/10.1109/ACCESS.2024.3489892

25. Meglio, S.D., Starace, L.L.L., Pontillo, V., Opdebeeck, R., Roover, C.D., Martino, S.D.: E2EGit: a dataset of end-to-end web tests in open source projects. In: 2025 IEEE/ACM 22nd International Conference on Mining Software Repositories (MSR), pp. 836–840 (2025). https://doi.org/10.1109/MSR66628.2025.00121

26. Mo, R., Cai, Y., Kazman, R., Xiao, L., Feng, Q.: Architecture anti-patterns: automatically detectable violations of design principles. IEEE Trans. Softw. Eng. **47**(5), 1008–1028 (2021). https://doi.org/10.1109/TSE.2019.2910856

27. Oliveira, G.P., Moura, A.F.C., Batista, N.A., Brandão, M.A., Hora, A., Moro, M.M.: How do developers collaborate? Investigating github heterogeneous networks. Softw. Qual. J. **31**(1), 211–241 (2022). https://doi.org/10.1007/s11219-022-09598-x

28. Pan, W.F., Jiang, B., Li, B.: Refactoring software packages via community detection in complex software networks. Int. J. Autom. Comput. **10**(2), 157–166 (2013). https://doi.org/10.1007/s11633-013-0708-y

29. Poth, A., Heimann, C.: How to innovate software quality assurance and testing in large enterprises? In: Larrucea, X., Santamaria, I., O'Connor, R.V., Messnarz, R. (eds.) EuroSPI 2018. CCIS, vol. 896, pp. 437–442. Springer, Cham (2018). https://doi.org/10.1007/978-3-319-97925-0_37

30. Shaw, M., Garlan, D.: Software Architecture: Perspectives on an Emerging Discipline. Prentice-Hall, Inc. (1996)

31. Sun, Q., Wu, J., Liu, K.: Toward understanding students' learning performance in an object-oriented programming course: the perspective of program quality. IEEE Access **8**, 37505–37517 (2020)
32. Taylor, R.N., Medvidovic, N., Dashofy, E.M.: Software Architecture: Foundations, Theory, and Practice. Wiley (2010)
33. Yurkofsky, M.M., Peterson, A.J., Mehta, J.D., Horwitz-Willis, R., Frumin, K.M.: Research on continuous improvement: exploring the complexities of managing educational change. Rev. Res. Educ. **44**(1), 403–433 (2020)
34. Zakurdaeva, A., Weiss, M., Muegge, S.: Detecting architectural integrity violation patterns using machine learning. In: Proceedings of the 35th Annual ACM Symposium on Applied Computing, SAC 2020, pp. 1480–1487. Association for Computing Machinery, New York (2020). https://doi.org/10.1145/3341105.3374008

# "*The Candle is Burning Out on its Own..*": Modeling Fatigue and Empathy Among Chinese Developers

Damian A. Tamburri[1]([✉])(iD), Haotian Zhang[2], Kelly Blincoe[3](iD),
Rick Kazman[4](iD), Giammaria Giordano[5](iD), Valeria Pontillo[6,7](iD),
and Fabio Palomba[5](iD)

[1] University of Sannio, Benevento, Italy
datamburri@unisannio.it
[2] Politecnico di Milano, Milan, Italy
haotian.zhang@studenti.polimi.it
[3] HASEL, University of Auckland, Auckland, New Zealand
k.blincoe@auckland.ac.nz
[4] University of Hawaii, Honolulu, USA
kazman@hawaii.edu
[5] Software Engineering (SeSa) Lab, University of Salerno, Fisciano, Italy
{giagiordano,fpalomba}@unisa.it
[6] Software Languages (SOFT) Lab, Vrije Universiteit Brussel, Brussel, Belgium
valeria.pontillo@gssi.it
[7] Gran Sasso Science Institute (GSSI), L'Aquila, Italy

**Abstract.** Developer turnover and layoffs are at a historical peak, contributing to increased stress, fatigue, and declining morale among software developers. To investigate this issue, in this paper, we surveyed 178 developers in China and found that over half reported experiencing psychological distress, which is significantly higher than the national average. Using factor analysis and regression modeling, we identified key psychological dimensions of fatigue and empathy and examined their relationship to workplace conditions. We complemented the survey with 17 behavioral metrics from *Azure DevOps* and *Microsoft Viva Insight*, enabling a data-driven assessment of developers' work context. Finally, we developed the *Empathy Catalogues Analysis Model*, a statistical model linking work context metrics to empathy scores, revealing a significant negative correlation between workload burden and perceived empathy. Our findings provide a foundation for scalable, automated monitoring of psychological well-being in teams.

**Keywords:** Social Software Engineering · Application Lifecycle Management · Organisational Structures

## 1 Introduction

As software systems grow increasingly complex and interconnected [17], software developers are facing ever-intensifying demands on their morale and energy.

D. Taibi and D. Smite (Eds.): SEAA 2025, LNCS 16083, pp. 155–173, 2026.
https://doi.org/10.1007/978-3-032-04207-1_11

These demands stem from the intricate balancing act between technical problem-solving, team collaboration, and tight delivery schedules leading to persistently high levels of stress, burnout[1] [34], and reduced empathy among developers and their teams [5]. A recent *Stack Overflow* survey[2] confirms the severity of this issue, with 58.3% of developers reporting burnout, and over a quarter experiencing it "sometimes" or "often". These figures highlight the urgent need for solutions that can support the well-being and productivity of software teams through measurable and manageable; hence, potentially data-driven—approaches. We call this research effort *PsyOps*: an initiative to embed psychological operational capacities into DevOps pipelines, aimed at quantifying team morale and developer fatigue[3] through dedicated, automated metrics.

One of the key challenges in developing such analytics lies in assessing the anthropometric [10] and psychological characteristics associated with developer fatigue, with the aim of supporting both well-being and team productivity. Although work-related data can be automatically collected via widely used collaboration and development tools, e.g., *Microsoft Viva Insight*, *Azure DevOps*, and *Jira*, the integration and comprehensive analysis of these data sources remains limited. In particular, current approaches often fall short in capturing indicators of software developers' fatigue, as well as the empathy exercised by Application Lifecycle Management governors, e.g., product owners [31], toward their teams.

In this paper, we develop a data-driven approach to analyse developer fatigue and empathy, focusing on key anthropometric and psychological factors such as stress levels, emotional turmoil, work engagement, and perceived empathy. Building on the need for measurable indicators of well-being in software teams, our mixed-methods study combines survey responses with work context data. As summarized in Fig. 1, we first conducted a large-scale questionnaire with 178 software developers in China, focusing on those with 3+ years of experience to represent a typical workforce. We then complemented the survey findings with work context data extracted from *Microsoft Viva Insight* and *Azure DevOps*. Our study addresses the following research questions:

- **RQ₁:** What are the key anthropometric characteristics of software developers' fatigue?
- **RQ₂:** To what extent can work context data be used to evaluate these characteristics?
- **RQ₃:** How effective is this data in identifying mitigating factors towards fatigue?

Our results show that developer fatigue and empathy levels are strongly influenced by work context factors such as workload intensity, overtime, and meeting overload. Through factor and regression analyses, we find that increased work context burden, as measured by metrics like meeting frequency, overtime hours,

---

[1] https://crackedlabs.org/dl/CrackedLabs_Christl_MobileWork.pdf.

[2] https://www.theregister.com/2022/05/11/stack_overflow_stress/.

[3] https://betterprogramming.pub/development-fatigue-fe092f036d4f.

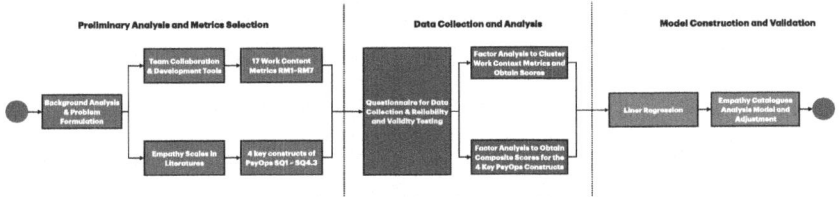

**Fig. 1.** Overview of Research Framework for *PsyOps*.

and defect resolution pressure, is significantly associated with higher psychological strain and reduced empathy. As part of our *PsyOps* initiative, we developed the *Empathy Catalogues Analysis Model*, which quantifies the relationship between work context and psychological well-being. This model confirms a negative correlation between work burden and empathy, suggesting that intensified workloads contribute to empathy fatigue and elevated stress. Our findings highlight the importance of monitoring and managing work context factors to support developers' mental health. The *PsyOps* framework demonstrates how workplace data, collected from tools like *Microsoft Viva Insight* and *Azure DevOps* platforms, can be used to assess and predict psychological strain. This data-driven approach offers a scalable path for organizations to proactively identify mental health risks and foster a more empathetic and sustainable work environment.

## 2 Related Work

In software development, empathy refers to developers' ability to understand and relate to the thoughts, feelings, and perspectives of others, including users, team members, and stakeholders [5,25]. It involves emotional awareness, sensitivity to others' needs, and supportive behaviour.

Empathy spans several dimensions. *User* empathy helps developers design with user needs in mind. *Team* empathy fosters collaboration through communication and mutual support [1]. *Ethical* empathy concerns socially responsible design decisions. *Contextual* empathy reflects awareness of organizational and project constraints. *Self*-empathy involves recognizing and managing one's own stress and emotions [22,36]. As the reader may see, analysing empathy in development is complex, involving emotional states, expressions, and interactions, often supported by technological tools [37]. Gathering input from team members can improve emotional insight and enhance problem-solving [15]. Previous studies showed that empathy contributes to project success [19,26] and can be implemented through behaviours like active listening and emotional support [21,30]. High stress levels, linked to long hours and pressure, can impair empathy, with symptoms such as anxiety and fatigue [18,20,24,35].

Compared to the current body of knowledge on developer well-being and empathy in software engineering—which lacks integrated, operationalizable models—*our paper contributes a novel, data-driven framework* for quantifying developer empathy and fatigue using subjective survey responses and objective workplace metrics, along with an *Empathy Catalogues Analysis Model* that reveals a significant negative correlation between work context burden and empathy.

## 3    Empirical Study Design

To address our **RQs**, we gathered developers' perceptions of empathy and fatigue through an online questionnaire and complemented this with work habit data from *Microsoft Viva Insight* and *Azure DevOps*. We then applied factor analysis and linear regression to examine the relationships between the two data sources. The following sections detail our methods.

### 3.1    Part I: Questionnaire

**Design of the Study.** Based on prior literature in psychology and software engineering [6,8,27], we identified four key constructs to explore in our questionnaire: (1) *empathy*, (2) *stress levels*, (3) *personal or emotional turmoil*, and (4) *work engagement*. These constructs were selected for their strong theoretical and empirical links to developer well-being and team dynamics. Each was operationalized through validated indicators drawn from established scales and mapped to specific questions in our instrument. Table 1 presents the full list of items, which participants answered using a five-point Likert scale.

*Empathy.* In software teams, empathy plays a critical role in fostering collaboration and responsiveness to the emotional and cognitive needs of colleagues and users [8,33]. It captures the degree to which developers perceive, express, and respond to others' emotions.

*Stress Level.* Stress reflects physiological and behavioural signs of psychological strain. Measuring stress helps identify whether developers experience chronic pressure or burnout due to high job demands [6,35,38].

*Work Engagement.* This construct assesses how motivated, committed, and energized developers feel in their work. It is a key predictor of productivity and job satisfaction [14,15,27].

*Personal or Emotional Turmoil.* This dimension includes major life events, mental health conditions, and interpersonal conflicts that may negatively affect well-being. It captures the broader emotional landscape in which developers operate [20,40].

**Participants Selection and Recruitment.** We focused our study on software developers based in mainland China for both theoretical and practical reasons. China hosts one of the world's fastest-growing software industries, marked by rapid digital transformation, intense work cultures, and concentrated

**Table 1.** Scale items for the main constructs: empathy, stress level, work engagement, and personal or emotional turmoil.

| ID | Item |
|---|---|
| *Empathy* [9,33] | |
| SQ1.1 | How well do you think you understand the needs and emotions of your colleagues and users? |
| SQ1.2 | How often do you communicate with your colleagues and users about their emotions and concerns? |
| SQ1.3 | How often do you provide emotional support or encouragement to your colleagues and users? |
| SQ1.4 | How well do you feel supported and understood by your colleagues and superiors? |
| *Stress level* [6,35,38] | |
| SQ2.1 † | Have you ever experienced burnout or mental health issues related to your work as a software developer? |
| SQ2.2 † | How often do you experience symptoms of stress (e.g., anxiety, insomnia, fatigue, irritability)? |
| SQ2.3 † | How well does the stress in your professional life affect your personal life? |
| *Work engagement* [14,15,27] | |
| SQ3.1 | How satisfied are you with working as a software developer? |
| SQ3.2 | How motivated are you to perform well in your job? |
| SQ3.3 | How often do you feel engaged and energized by your work? |
| *Personal or emotional turmoil* [20,40] | |
| SQ4.1 † | Have you experienced any significant life events (e.g., divorce, bereavement, illness) in the past year that have impacted your well-being? |
| SQ4.2 † | Do you have some mental health conditions (e.g., depression, anxiety) that impact your work as a software developer? |
| SQ4.3 † | Have you noticed some physical symptoms or changes that may be related to stress or emotional turmoil (e.g., headaches, fatigue, muscle tension, changes in appetite or weight)? |

urban tech hubs.[4] Yet, the psychological well-being of developers in this context remains largely understudied [12]. These conditions make Chinese developers a particularly relevant population for examining stress, fatigue, and empathy in high-pressure environments. Additionally, we had direct access to this population through professional and social platforms in the Chinese IT sector, which enabled efficient recruitment. Participants were indeed selected through *convenience sampling* by distributing the questionnaire via WENJUANXING[TM] (https://www.wjx.cn), a popular online survey tool in China. The 10-minute questionnaire, consisting of 12 open and closed questions, was disseminated without incentives to minimize selection bias. In total, we received 178 complete responses. As shown in Fig. 2, most respondents were based in major software development regions, including Shanghai, Jiangsu Province, Beijing, and Fujian

---

[4] https://www.globenewswire.com/news-release/2024/12/27/3002160/28124/en/
The-Digital-Transformation-Market-in-China-Forecast-to-2029-Trends-Demand-Drivers-Challenges-and-Emerging-Opportunities.html.

Province. While the focus on a single national context may limit generalizability, it provides valuable insights into a high-intensity and globally significant segment of the software workforce.

**Fig. 2.** Distribution of completed questionnaires.

**Data Analysis.** Prior to performing analysis, the negatively worded items, as indicated by † in Table 1, were reverse-scored. Cronbach's alpha was used to check scale reliability. Scores range from 0 to 1, with higher scores being indicative of greater consistency in the scale items [7]. A score of 0.9 or higher is excellent, 0.8 or higher is good, and 0.7 or higher is acceptable. The result of Cronbach's alpha coefficient was 0.829, which is greater than 0.8, thus indicating good reliability of the questionnaire data.

## 3.2   Part II: Data Pipeline

As the second part of the study, we aimed to complement self-reported perceptions with objective behavioural data from workplace tools. *Microsoft Viva Insight* collects and analyses data from email, calendars, and collaboration platforms to generate metrics on productivity (e.g., focus hours, meeting load) and collaboration (e.g., interaction frequency, team engagement, network centrality). In addition, we considered data from *Azure DevOps*, which offers process-level metrics like code commits, build activity, deployment frequency, lead time, and

**Table 2.** Representative metrics of work context data.

|  | Metric | Note |
|---|---|---|
| VIVA INSIGHT | RM1 | Work overtime in a month (%) |
|  | RM2 | Meeting arranged at least one day in advance (%) |
|  | RM3 | Meeting no overlap (%) |
|  | RM4 | Meeting Ended on time (%) |
|  | RM5 | Collaboration time within work hours (hours) |
|  | RM6 | Collaboration time outside work hours (hours) |
|  | RM7 | Available to focus time (%) |
|  | RM8 | Meeting time out of collaboration time (%) |
|  | RM9 | Emails time out of collaboration time (%) |
|  | RM10 | Chats time out of collaboration time (%) |
| DEVOPS | RM11 | Number of builds per week (times) |
|  | RM12 | Number of commits per week (times) |
|  | RM13 | Number of tasks assigned per week (pieces) |
|  | RM14 | Number of tasks completed per week (pieces) |
|  | RM15 | Failed test cases out of planned test cases per week (%) |
|  | RM16 | Number of defects reported per week (pieces) |
|  | RM17 | Defects resolved out of the total number of defects (%) |

defect reports. Together, these sources allowed us to examine how work context factors relate to developers' psychological well-being in a data-driven manner.

We collected the 17 metrics listed in Table 2 from *Microsoft Viva Insight* and *Azure DevOps* platforms using standard log mining tools in Python (PM4Py[5]). After removing outliers, we normalized each metric to a 0–1 scale to account for differences in magnitude across indicators. The normalization was performed using min–max scaling, as shown in Eq. (1), where $X_{ij}$ is the original value of the $j$-th metric for the $i$-th participant, and $X_{jmin}$ and $X_{jmax}$ are the minimum and maximum values of that metric across all participants:

$$\hat{X_{ij}} = \frac{X_{ij} - X_{jmin}}{X_{jmax} - X_{jmin}} \tag{1}$$

We developed data pipeline integrations to automatically collect and transfer relevant metrics from *Microsoft Viva Insight* and *Azure DevOps* platforms into a centralized data repository. This repository supports further analysis of patterns and correlations between work context metrics and the anthropometric indicators described above.

---

[5] https://pypi.org/project/pm4py/.

### 3.3    Part III: Developer Fatigue Indicator Model

Next, we explore the relationship between work context metrics and developers' self-reported perceptions. We apply factor analysis to identify latent constructs and use multivariate linear regression to model their associations. An overview of the combined data sources is shown in Fig. 3.

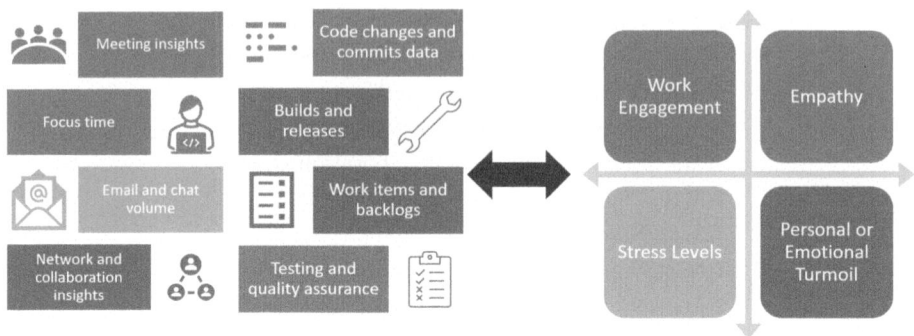

**Fig. 3.** Overview of data from both sources.

**Factor Analysis.** We sought to identify the underlying relationships in both sources of data. To do this, we employed an *Explanatory Factor Analysis* with the maximum variance rotation method (varimax), which is the most common rotation that maximizes the differences between the factors [11,13].

*Factorability.* We assessed factorability using the Kaiser-Meyer-Olkin (KMO) metric and Bartlett's test of sphericity [29]. For both data sources, the KMO exceeds the 0.5 threshold and Bartlett's test is significant ($p < 0.01$), confirming the analysis's suitability (Table 3).

**Table 3.** Factorability and Factor Analysis Model Fit.

|  | KMO | Bartlett | RMSR | RMSEA | TLI |
|---|---|---|---|---|---|
| Questionnaire Cata | 0.821 | $\chi^2 = 1300.798$; $df = 78$; $p < 0.001$ | 0.17 | 0.198 | 0.672 |
| Work Context Data | 0.937 | $\chi^2 = 1179.26$; $df = 136$; $p < 0.001$ | 0.171 | 0.041 | 0.96 |

*Number of Factors.* To identify the number of factors, we retained those with eigenvalues greater than 1. This commonly used criterion ensures that each retained factor explains a significant portion of the variance, thereby representing the underlying structure of the data effectively [16].

*Model Fit.* Model fit was assessed using RMSR, RMSEA, and TLI, with standard thresholds: lower is better for RMSR (0 is ideal), RMSEA $< 0.06$, and TLI $>$ 0.90 (adequate), $> 0.95$ (good) [3] [28]. As shown in Table 3, the work context model meets these criteria (RMSEA $= 0.041$, TLI $= 0.960$), though RMSR is relatively high. In contrast, the questionnaire model shows poor fit across all metrics (RMSR $= 0.170$, RMSEA $= 0.198$, TLI $= 0.672$), suggesting it does not adequately capture the data's structure.

*Factor Loading.* We used a 0.3 cutoff for factor loading [16, 32]. Variables below this threshold have been excluded.

*Factor Scores.* Finally, to obtain the overall factor score for each dimension of empathy, we compute the weighted sum of the individual factor scores. **E** represents the vector of factor scores for empathy dimensions, with dimensions corresponding to the identified empathy dimensions. The calculation of the overall factor score **p** for each dimension is expressed as:

$$\mathrm{p} = \sum_{j=1}^{n}(E_j \times w_j) \tag{2}$$

where $E_j$ represents the factor score for the survey samples on principal component j, and $w_j$ represents the weight assigned to principal component j. The weights reflect the importance of each principal component in contributing to the respective empathy dimension.

*Correlations Between Items.* Figure 4 shows the correlation matrix of the questionnaire responses. A strong correlation is observed among items within each construct. Notably, SQ1.2 and SQ1.4 are negatively correlated with the other variables and were therefore positively normalized.

We also performed a correlation analysis of the work context data (RM1–17). As shown in Fig. 5, these metrics likewise exhibit strong correlations.

**Linear Regression Model.** To examine the relationship between empathy levels and work context burden, we used a linear regression model estimated via Ordinary Least Squares (OLS). This approach identifies how changes in work context factors predict variations in empathy, with coefficients representing the effect of each factor while holding others constant.

The *Empathy Catalogues Analysis Model* combines factor analysis and linear regression to quantify empathy dimensions from questionnaire responses and link them to work context metrics. This enables the identification of significant predictors and the estimation of their impact on empathy levels.

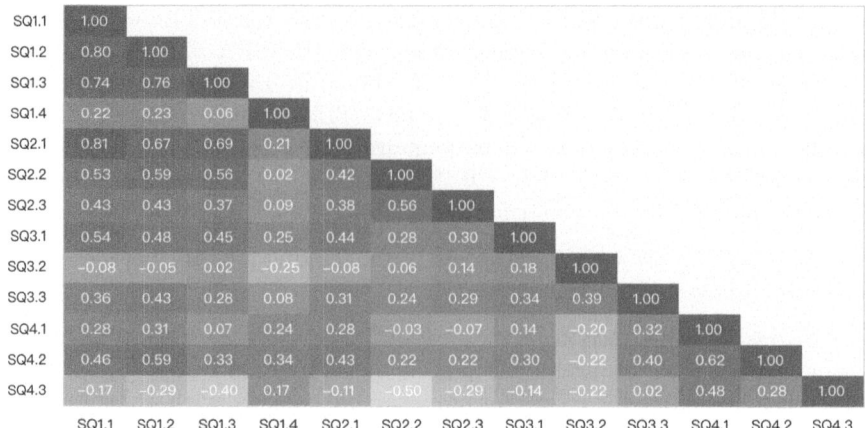

**Fig. 4.** Correlation matrix of SQ1.1–SQ4.3.

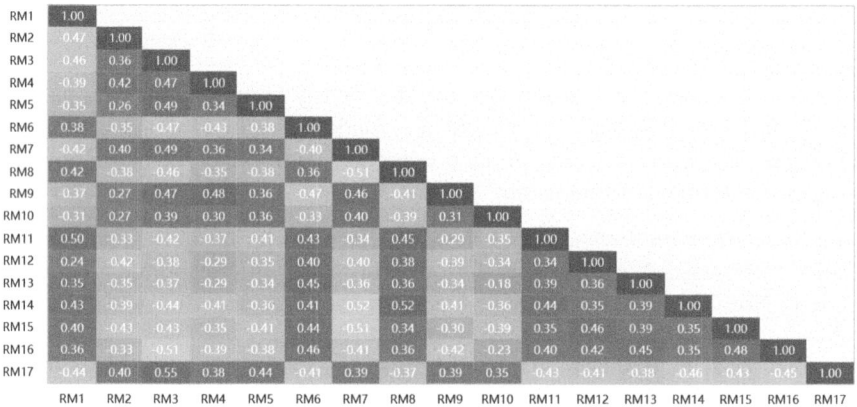

**Fig. 5.** Correlation matrix of RM1–RM17.

## 4   Analysis of the Results

In this section, we first analyse and observe the frequency counts and descriptive statistics reflective of the data to understand the empathy and workload of the software practitioners. Then, we analyse the data with factor analysis and regression analysis to exercise our proposed fatigue indicator model.

### 4.1   Frequency Analysis

**Empathy Analytics Data.** Figure 6 shows the frequency distribution of SQ1.1–SQ4.3. It is noteworthy that 57% of the respondents chose 4 and 5 for SQ1.3, 50% of the respondents chose 1 and 2 for SQ1.4, which suggests that **software developers feel that they provide considerable emotional support**

to their colleagues and users, but they are supported and understood by the colleagues and superiors not so well.

Unit: times

| | 1 | 2 | 3 | 4 | 5 |
|---|---|---|---|---|---|
| SQ4.3 | 10 | 23 | 55 | 75 | 15 |
| SQ4.2 | 19 | 27 | 32 | 79 | 21 |
| SQ4.1 | 2 | 42 | 52 | 52 | 30 |
| SQ3.3 | 15 | 52 | 79 | 28 | 4 |
| SQ3.2 | 2 | 23 | 85 | 57 | 11 |
| SQ3.1 | 28 | 41 | 52 | 50 | 7 |
| SQ2.3 | 17 | 93 | 29 | 26 | 15 |
| SQ2.2 | 6 | 44 | 75 | 37 | 16 |
| SQ2.1 | 2 | 17 | 63 | 44 | 52 |
| SQ1.4 | 3 | 84 | 67 | 20 | 4 |
| SQ1.3 | 12 | 39 | 24 | 60 | 43 |
| SQ1.2 | 20 | 28 | 41 | 30 | 59 |
| SQ1.1 | 32 | 42 | 52 | 46 | 6 |

**Fig. 6.** Answer distribution of SQ1.1–SQ4.3, in which 1 and 5 refer respectively to the least frequent or compliant and the most frequent or compliant.

Only 10% of the respondents chose 1 and 2 in SQ2.1, but 50% of the respondents chose 3 and 4, indicating that **most software developers have experienced burnout or mental health issues related to their work**. Moreover, 62% of the respondents chose 1 and 2 in SQ2.3, indicating that **most software developers believe that the stress of their professional life significantly affects their personal life**.

For the work engagement, i.e., questions SQ3.1, SQ3.2, and SQ3.3, most of the respondents gave neutral choices, **suggesting uncertainty about their connection to the work**.

For SQ4.2, and SQ4.3, 55% and 50% of the respondents chose 4 and 5, which **proves that more respondents believe that they have some mental health conditions** (e.g., depression, anxiety), and that **their mental health has caused some physical symptoms** (e.g., headaches, fatigue, muscle tension, changes in appetite or weight). This percentage is much higher than that reported in the *China National Mental Health Development Report (2021–2022)* published by the Institute of Psychology of the Chinese Academy of Sciences and the Social Science Literature Publishing House, where only 13.9% of the respondents chose a high level [39].

**Work Context Data.** Figure 7 shows the distribution of the answers for the metrics related to the work context. On the one hand, we can observe that for RM2, 3, 4, 5, 7, most of the respondents filled in larger values, proving **that software practitioners in China have better meeting arrangements (scheduled in advance, no overlap, end on time, collaborate during working hours, have more focus time)**. Additionally, the answers received for RM8,

9, and 10 prove that **most software developers spend more collaboration time on email and chat than on meetings.**

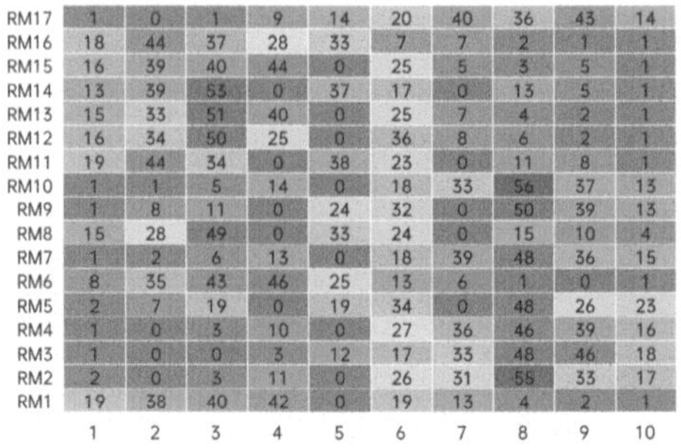

**Fig. 7.** Answer distribution of RM1–RM17.

On the other hand, the comparison of RM11, 12, 13, 14, 15, 16 with RM17, proves that the number of defects resolved still falls in the larger range when most of the people are at the workload, which suggests that **software developers are facing a greater challenge to resolve the defects.**

**Table 4.** Total Variance Explained for SQ1.1-SQ4.3.

| Component | Initial Eigenvalues | | | Extraction Sums of Squared Loadings | | |
|---|---|---|---|---|---|---|
| | Total | % of Variance | Cumulative % | Total | % of Variance | Cumulative % |
| 1 | 5.021 | 38.620 | 38.620 | 5.021 | 38.620 | 39.006 |
| 2 | 2.350 | 18.074 | 56.694 | 2.350 | 18.074 | 56.694 |
| 3 | 1.370 | 10.540 | 67.234 | 1.370 | 10.540 | 67.234 |
| 4 | .897 | 6.898 | 74.132 | | | |
| 5 | .816 | 6.277 | 80.410 | | | |
| 6 | .571 | 4.391 | 84.801 | | | |
| 7 | .479 | 3.681 | 88.482 | | | |
| 8 | .367 | 2.820 | 91.302 | | | |
| 9 | .321 | 2.471 | 93.773 | | | |
| 10 | .286 | 2.199 | 95.972 | | | |
| 11 | .222 | 1.704 | 97.676 | | | |
| 12 | .189 | 1.452 | 99.128 | | | |
| 13 | .113 | .872 | 100.000 | | | |

## 4.2 Factor Analysis

**Empathy Analytics Data.** Table 4 presents the results of the factor extraction, including the amount of information captured by the extracted factors. A total of three factors were extracted, each with an eigenvalue greater than 1. After rotation, these three factors explained 38.6%, 18%, 10.5%, respectively. The cumulative variance explained after rotation is 67.2%, denoted as $w_j$.

**Table 5.** Rotated Component Matrices

(a) Matrix for SQ1.1–SQ4.3

| Item | Comp. 1 | Comp. 2 | Comp. 3 |
|------|---------|---------|---------|
| SQ1.3 | .862 | | |
| SQ1.2 | .857 | | |
| SQ1.1 | .851 | | |
| SQ2.2 | .777 | | |
| SQ2.1 | .766 | | |
| SQ2.3 | .623 | | |
| SQ4.1 | | .846 | |
| SQ4.2 | | .760 | |
| SQ4.3 | | .698 | |
| SQ3.2 | | | .855 |
| SQ3.3 | | | .744 |
| SQ1.4 | | | |
| SQ3.1 | | | |

(b) Matrix for RM1–RM17

| Item | Component |
|------|----------|
| RM3 | −.740 |
| RM7 | −.700 |
| RM17 | −.693 |
| RM14 | .686 |
| RM6 | .681 |
| RM15 | .671 |
| RM8 | .670 |
| RM16 | .668 |
| RM1 | .658 |
| RM11 | .651 |
| RM9 | −.645 |
| RM4 | −.630 |
| RM5 | −.624 |
| RM12 | .621 |
| RM2 | −.610 |
| RM13 | .604 |
| RM10 | |

Table 5(a) shows the information extraction of the factors for the questions and the correspondence between the factors and the questions—we sorted the coefficients of the questions in order of magnitude. SQ1.4 and SQ3.1 are empty because the value is less than 0.3. Items originally designed to capture empathy (SQ1.1, SQ1.2, and SQ1.3) and stress levels (SQ2.1, SQ2.2, and SQ2.3) loaded strongly on the same factor. This suggests that respondents perceive emotional support and psychological strain as closely linked rather than distinct dimensions. We interpret this as a unified **Empathy–Stress Levels** factor. The second factor, formed by SQ4.1 to SQ4.3, corresponds to **Personal or Emotional Turmoil**, in line with prior literature [20, 40]. The third factor, derived from SQ3.2 and SQ3.3, captures **Work Engagement**, which also aligns with previous literature [14, 15, 27].

Although the questionnaire was designed around four constructs, the analysis revealed a three-factor structure. Based on the rotation variance, we constructed Fig. 8 to illustrate the contribution of each factor, where empathy and stress levels had the strongest influence, and work engagement the weakest. These factor scores were then used to compute the overall composite score $p$.

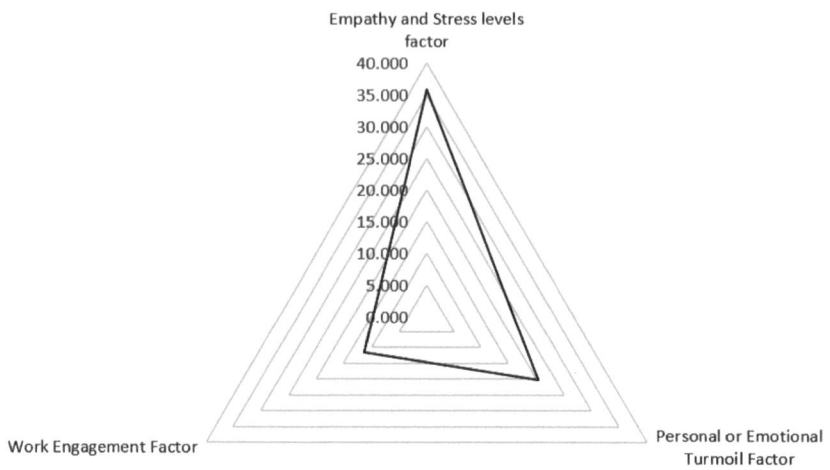

**Fig. 8.** Anthropometric Factor Contribution Model.

**Work Context Data.** For the RM1–RM17 metrics, only one factor was extracted, as shown in Table 5(b). Based on the Rotated Component Matrix and the correlation matrix, we developed a data correlation model describing the relationships between key aspects of the work context. The analysis reveals several meaningful groupings.

RM2, RM3, and RM4 form the **Meeting on Time** cluster, which negatively contributes to the work context burden score—indicating that more timely meetings are associated with reduced perceived burden. Similarly, RM5, RM7, and RM9 define the **Available to Focus** cluster, which also shows a negative contribution, suggesting that increased focus time alleviates burden.

In contrast, RM1, RM6, and RM8 belong to the **Work Overtime** cluster, which contributes positively, reflecting that extended working hours increase perceived workload. RM12, RM13, and RM14 form the **Development Load** cluster, also with a positive contribution, indicating that heavier development workloads correlate with greater burden.

Additionally, RM11, RM15, and RM16 compose the **Failed & Defect** cluster, which further increases the burden score, emphasizing the impact of defects and failures on developers. Finally, RM10 and RM17 define the **Defect Resolved** cluster, which negatively affects the burden score, suggesting that resolving defects helps reduce the overall burden.

The relationship between these matrices and their respective contributions to the work context burden score is illustrated in Fig. 9. Based on these patterns, we derive a comprehensive score $z$ to represent overall work context burden.

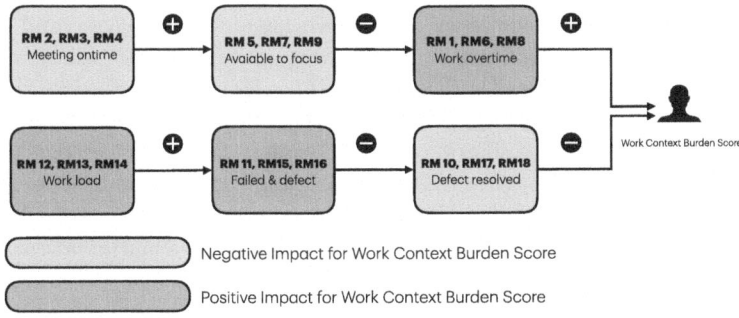

**Fig. 9.** Developer fatigue indicator model.

## 4.3 Linear Regression

To build the *Empathy Catalogues Analysis Model* and examine the relationship between the overall factor score **p** (developer empathy) and the work context burden score **z**, we applied linear regression.

As shown in Table 6, the $R^2$ value is 0.540, indicating that the RM final score accounts for 54.0% of the variance in the composite empathy score. The F-test confirms the model's significance ($F = 206.679$, $p = 0.000 < 0.05$), demonstrating that the RM score has a statistically significant impact. The regression coefficient for the RM final score is $-0.371$ ($t = -14.376$, $p = 0.000 < 0.01$), indicating a significant negative linear relationship. In other words, **the greater the burden of the work context, the lower the empathy score**.

**Table 6.** Linear Regression Analysis Results.

| | Regr. Coefficient | 95% CI | Cov. Diagnostic | |
|---|---|---|---|---|
| | | | VIF | Tolerance |
| Constant | 0.000 (0.000) | $-0.136 \sim -0.136$ | – | – |
| Z | $-0.371^{**}$ ($-14.376$) | $-0.422 \sim -0.321$ | 1 | 1 |
| Sample Size | 178 | | | |
| $R^2$ | 0.540 | | | |
| *Adjusted* $R^2$ | 0.537 | | | |
| *F value* | *F (1,176) = 206.679, p = 0.000* | | | |

## 5   Discussion and Lessons Learned

This research addresses our three research questions by identifying and quantifying key work context factors that influence developers' psychological well-being and empathy. Regarding **RQ₁**, we found that over half of surveyed developers report psychological distress—far above national averages—underscoring the urgency of addressing fatigue in software development, where cognitive demands elevate mental health risks. For **RQ₂**, factor analysis identified four key matrices—Meeting on Time, Available to Focus, Work Overtime, and Development Load—forming the *Work Context Burden Score*. While overtime and workload increase burden, structured meetings and focus time alleviate it. These constructs, integrated in our model, offer an empirical basis for assessing work-related strain. In response to **RQ₃**, regression analysis via the *Empathy Catalogues Analysis Model* confirms a strong negative correlation between burden and empathy, indicating that heavier workloads reduce empathetic capacity.

Empathy emerges as context-sensitive rather than fixed. Among the three related constructs—Empathy and Stress Levels, Personal or Emotional Turmoil, and Work Engagement—the first most strongly shapes overall empathy. This suggests that improving work context can directly benefit developers' psychological and interpersonal functioning. Our findings carry implications for both practitioners and researchers. Organizations can reduce burnout and enhance team cohesion by minimizing overtime, managing workloads, and promoting time for structured focus. Since the metrics used are available in common development and collaboration tools, they can support automated monitoring and timely managerial action. For researchers, our results support treating empathy and mental health as operationalizable constructs in software engineering. The *PsyOps* framework opens avenues for longitudinal studies and predictive tools for developer well-being based on passively collected behavioral data.

## 6   Threats to Validity

This study is subject to several limitations that may affect the generalizability and robustness of its findings. First, the sample was restricted to a specific demographic and geographic region within China, which may limit the applicability of results to other cultural or organizational contexts [2,4]. Cultural nuances unique to the Chinese setting might have influenced the observed correlations between empathy and work context, suggesting the need for cross-cultural studies to validate these results.

Second, reliance on self-reported data for empathy and psychological measures may introduce biases such as social desirability [23], potentially affecting data accuracy. While objective work context data was obtained from *Microsoft Viva Insight* and *Azure DevOps*, these sources may miss interpersonal or unquantified environmental factors relevant to developers' psychological well-being.

Finally, the use of linear regression in the *Empathy Catalogues Analysis Model* may not fully capture the complex or non-linear relationships between empathy and work context burden. Future research could apply advanced models, including machine learning, to identify subtler patterns. Longitudinal data could also provide insights into the temporal dynamics of work conditions and mental health, enhancing both the precision and predictive power of the model.

# 7 Conclusion and Future Work

In this paper, we investigated the mental health and empathy of Chinese software developers through a questionnaire combining 17 work context items and 13 empathy-related questions. Over half of the participants reported psychological distress, far exceeding the national average of 13.9%, highlighting the urgency of the issue. We identified four key empathy-related dimensions and analyzed 17 objective workplace metrics collected from tools like *Microsoft Viva Insights* and *Azure DevOps*. Our *Empathy Catalogues Analysis Model* revealed a significant negative correlation between work context burden and empathy, enabling automated, data-driven assessments of developers' psychological well-being. This study offers a novel, scalable approach for monitoring empathy and mental health in software teams using workplace data. Future work will aim to refine the model and validate it in broader organizational and cultural contexts.

# References

1. Akgün, A.E., Keskin, H., Cebecioglu, A.Y., Dogan, D.: Antecedents and consequences of collective empathy in software development project teams. Inf. Manage. **52**(2), 247–259 (2015)
2. Beaton, D.E., Bombardier, C., Guillemin, F., Ferraz, M.B.: Guidelines for the process of cross-cultural adaptation of self-report measures. Spine **25**(24) (2000)
3. Bentler, P.M.: Comparative fit indexes in structural models. Psychol. Bull. **107**(2), 238 (1990)
4. Borsa, J.C., Damásio, B.F., Bandeira, D.R.: Cross-cultural adaptation and validation of psychological instruments: Some considerations. Paidéia (Ribeirão Preto) **22**, 423–432 (2012)
5. Cerqueira, L., et al.: Empathy and its effects on software practitioners' well-being and mental health. IEEE Softw. (2024)
6. Cohen, S., Kamarck, T., Mermelstein, R.: A global measure of perceived stress. J. Health Soc. Behav. 385–396 (1983)
7. Cronbach, L.J.: Coefficient alpha and the internal structure of tests. Psychometrika **16**(3), 297–334 (1951). https://doi.org/10.1007/BF02310555
8. Davis, M.H.: Measuring individual differences in empathy: evidence for a multidimensional approach. J. Pers. Soc. Psychol. **44**(1), 113 (1983)
9. Diener, E., et al.: New well-being measures: Short scales to assess flourishing and positive and negative feelings. Soc. Indicators Res. **97**, 143–156 (2010)
10. Espitia-Contreras, A., Sanchez-Caiman, P., Uribe-Quevedo, A.: Development of a kinect-based anthropometric measurement application. In: 2014 IEEE Virtual Reality (VR), pp. 71–72 (2014). https://doi.org/10.1109/VR.2014.6802056
11. Forina, M., Armanino, C., Lanteri, S., Leardi, R.: Methods of varimax rotation in factor analysis with applications in clinical and food chemistry. J. Chemom. **3**(S1), 115–125 (1989)

12. Godliauskas, P., Šmite, D.: The well-being of software engineers: a systematic literature review and a theory. Empir. Softw. Eng. **30**(1), 1–42 (2025)
13. Finch, W.H.: Exploratory factor analysis. In: Teo, T. (ed.) Handbook of Quantitative Methods for Educational Research, pp. 167–186. SensePublishers, Rotterdam (2013). https://doi.org/10.1007/978-94-6209-404-8_8
14. Graziotin, D., Fagerholm, F.: Happiness and the productivity of software engineers. In: Sadowski, C., Zimmermann, T. (eds.) Rethinking Productivity in Software Engineering, pp. 109–124. Springer, Heidelberg (2019). https://doi.org/10.1007/978-1-4842-4221-6_10
15. Graziotin, D., Wang, X., Abrahamsson, P.: Happy software developers solve problems better: psychological measurements in empirical software engineering. PeerJ (2014)
16. Hair, J.F., Jr., Anderson, R.E., Tatham, R.L.: Multivariate Data Analysis with Readings. Macmillan Publishing Co., Inc. (1986)
17. Hou, X., et al.: Large language models for software engineering: a systematic literature review (2024). http://arxiv.org/abs/2308.10620
18. van der Hulst, M.: Long workhours and health. Scand. J. Work Environ. Health **29**(3), 171–88 (2003)
19. Judge, T.A., Heller, D.K., Mount, M.K.: Five-factor model of personality and job satisfaction: a meta-analysis. J. Appl. Psychol. (2002)
20. Kawakami, N., Haratani, T.: Epidemiology of job stress and health in japan: review of current evidence and future direction. Ind. Health **37**(2), 174–186 (1999)
21. King, S., Jr., Holosko, M.J.: The development and initial validation of the empathy scale for social workers. Res. Soc. Work. Pract. **22**(2), 174–185 (2012)
22. Levy, M.: Educating for empathy in software engineering course. In: REFSQ (2018)
23. Van de Mortel, T.F.: Faking it: social desirability response bias in self-report research. Aust. J. Adv. Nurs. **25**(4), 40–48 (2008)
24. Noboru, I., Norito, K., Takashi, H., Katsuyuki, M., Shunichi, A.: Job stressor-mental of Japanese working negative questions? Health adults associations in a sample: artifacts of positive and (2007)
25. Pérez-Acosta, A.M.: Vandenbos, gr (ed.)(2007). apa dictionary of psychology. Rev. Latinoamericana Psicol. **40**(2), 381–384 (2008)
26. Saleh, H.G.A., Hu, W., Hassan, H.M.A., Khudaykulova, M.: Dark leadership impact on psychological well-being and work-family conflict: implications for project success of bahrain companies. J. Int. Bus. Res. **3**, 32–39 (2018)
27. Schaufeli, W.: Work engagement: What do we know and where do we go? Roman. J. Appl. Psychol. **14**(1), 3–10 (2012)
28. Schreiber, J.B., Nora, A., Stage, F.K., Barlow, E.A., King, J.: Reporting structural equation modeling and confirmatory factor analysis results: a review. J. Educ. Res. **99**(6), 323–338 (2006). https://doi.org/10.3200/JOER.99.6.323-338
29. Shrestha, N.: Factor analysis as a tool for survey analysis. Am. J. Appl. Math. Stat. **9**(1), 4–11 (2021)
30. Skovholt, T.M.: The cycle of caring: a model of expertise in the helping professions. J. Ment. Health Couns. **27**(1), 82–93 (2005)
31. de Ste-Croix, A., Easton, A.: Proceedings of the agile development conference 2008. In: AGILE. IEEE, Washington, DC (2008)
32. Stevens, J.P.: Applied Multivariate Statistics for the Social Sciences. Routledge
33. Tian, Q., Robertson, J.L.: How and when does perceived CSR affect employees' engagement in voluntary pro-environmental behavior? J. Bus. Ethics (2019)

34. Tulili, T.R., Capiluppi, A., Rastogi, A.: Burnout in software engineering: a systematic mapping study. Inf. Softw. Technol. **155**, 107116 (2023). https://doi.org/10.1016/j.infsof.2022.107116, https://www.sciencedirect.com/science/article/pii/S0950584922002257

35. Virtanen, M., et al.: Long working hours and symptoms of anxiety and depression: a 5-year follow-up of the whitehall II study. Psychol. Med. **41**, 2485–2494 (2011)

36. Wallin, A., Nokelainen, P., Kira, M.: From thriving developers to stagnant self-doubters: an identity-centered approach to exploring the relationship between digitalization and professional development. Vocat. Learn. (2022)

37. Werder, K.: The evolution of emotional displays in open source software development teams: an individual growth curve analysis. 2018 IEEE/ACM 3rd International Workshop on Emotion Awareness in Software Engineering (SEmotion), pp. 1–6 (2018). https://api.semanticscholar.org/CorpusID:49864772

38. Wong, N., Jackson, V., Van Der Hoek, A., Ahmed, I., Schueller, S.M., Reddy, M.: Mental wellbeing at work: perspectives of software engineers. In: Proceedings of the 2023 CHI Conference on Human Factors in Computing Systems, pp. 1–15 (2023)

39. Xiaolan, F., Kan, Z., Xuefeng, C., Zhiyan, C.: China National Mental Health Development Report (2021-2022). Institute of Psychology of the Chinese Academy of Sciences and the Social Science Literature Publishing House (2022)

40. Zapf, D., Seifert, C., Schmutte, B., Mertini, H., Holz, M.: Emotion work and job stressors and their effects on burnout. Psychol. Health **16**(5), 527–545 (2001)

# From Diverse Origins to a DEI Crisis: The Pushback Against Equity, Diversity, and Inclusion in Software Engineering

Ronnie de Souza Santos[1]([⊠]), Cleyton Magalhaes[2], Ann Barcomb[1], and Mairieli Wessel[3]

[1] University of Calgary, Calgary, AB, Canada
{ronnie.desouzasantos,ann.barcomb}@ucalgary.ca
[2] Universidade Federal Rural de Pernambuco, Recife, PE, Brazil
cleyton.vanut@ufrpe.br
[3] Radboud University, Nijmegen, Netherlands
mairieli.wessel@ru.nl

**Abstract.** Diversity, equity, and inclusion (DEI) are rooted in the very origins of software engineering and are shaped by the contributions of many individuals from underrepresented groups to the field. Yet today, DEI efforts in the industry face growing resistance, with companies retreating from visible commitments and pushing back on initiatives started only a few years ago. *Aims:* This study explores how the DEI backlash is unfolding in the software industry by investigating institutional changes, lived experiences, and the strategies used to sustain DEI practices. *Method:* We conducted an exploratory qualitative study using 59 publicly available Reddit posts authored by self-identified software professionals. Data were analyzed using reflexive thematic analysis. *Results:* Our findings show that software companies are responding to the DEI backlash in varied ways, including re-structuring programs, scaling back investments, or quietly continuing efforts under new labels. Professionals reported a wide range of emotional responses, from anxiety and frustration to relief and happiness, shaped by identity, role, and organizational culture. Yet, despite the backlash, multiple forms of resistance and adaptation have emerged to protect inclusive practices in software engineering. *Conclusions:* The DEI backlash is reshaping DEI in software engineering. While public messaging may soften or disappear, core DEI values persist in adapted forms. This study offers a new perspective on how inclusion is evolving under pressure and highlights the resilience of DEI in software environments.

**Keywords:** EDI in software engineering · equity · diversity · inclusion

## 1 Introduction

Diversity, equity, and inclusion (DEI), sometimes referred to as EDI, are interrelated concepts that aim to foster fair, respectful, and supportive environments

D. Taibi and D. Smite (Eds.): SEAA 2025, LNCS 16083, pp. 174–190, 2026.
https://doi.org/10.1007/978-3-032-04207-1_12

for individuals from all backgrounds [1]. Diversity refers to the presence of differences (e.g., race, gender, age), equity focuses on fairness by addressing unequal starting points, and inclusion emphasizes creating environments where everyone feels valued and heard [1]. In software engineering, DEI plays a significant role in shaping team dynamics and the success of software systems [2–5].

Recent studies have demonstrated that DEI can lead to tangible benefits such as increased creativity, improved team effectiveness, stronger morale, greater engagement, and higher retention of developers [2,5–8]. At the same time, DEI can also introduce challenges that must be carefully managed, including the potential for relational conflict when inclusion and psychological safety are lacking, and the persistent emphasis on diversity over equity and inclusion, which limits the development of comprehensive strategies [2,5,6,8].

Even with the benefits of diversity, equity, and inclusion increasingly recognized across various domains, including software engineering, these principles have encountered growing resistance. This backlash has emerged in response to shifting public narratives, critiques of implementation, and debates about the scope and focus of DEI programs [9–11]. Critics argue that some initiatives are symbolic or unevenly applied, while others fear that DEI efforts may inadvertently create new forms of exclusion or division [9]. Still, others are motivated simply by political positioning or a lack of understanding about the historical and structural purposes of DEI work [10]. In the field of software engineering, this shifting landscape is prompting companies to adjust their internal policies, hiring practices, and training efforts, ultimately affecting how software professionals, particularly those from underrepresented groups, experience their workplace and their role within development teams [12–14].

With diversity, equity, and inclusion efforts coming under increasing pressure, there is a growing need to understand how these shifts unfold within the software industry, particularly how they are being perceived and experienced by software professionals navigating this crisis. This study aims to investigate this problem through the following research questions:

- **RQ1.** *What changes caused by the DEI backlash have been observed and experienced in the software industry?*
- **RQ2.** *How is the backlash against DEI affecting software professionals within the software industry?*
- **RQ3.** *What strategies are currently being used in the software industry to protect and sustain DEI efforts in response to the backlash?*

From this introduction, this study is organized as follows. In Sect. 2, we present a literature review on the subject. Section 3 describes our methodology. In Sect. 4, we present our findings, which are discussed in Sect. 5, along with the implications and limitations of this study. Finally, Sect. 6 summarizes our contributions and final considerations.

## 2   The DEI Backlash in the Software Industry

Software engineering has always been shaped by individuals from diverse backgrounds, including many who broke ground despite being part of underrepresented groups. Ada Lovelace, considered the first computer programmer, Alan Turing, a gay mathematician whose work was foundational to AI, and Grace Hopper, who developed the first compiler, exemplify this legacy. Others, like Clarence "Skip" Ellis, the first African American with a PhD in computer science who made essential contributions to real-time collaborative systems, Peter Landin, an openly bisexual pioneer in programming language theory, and Christopher Strachey, who advanced formal methods, show that diversity is not a new goal in the field, but it is part of its foundation [17, 18, 20, 21].

Despite these historical roots, diversity remains a persistent challenge in software engineering. Systemic barriers continue to shape access and success, starting in academic settings and extending into industry. Underrepresented groups (including women, racialized individuals, LGBTQ+ people, and those with disabilities) face unequal access to support, mentorship, and advancement opportunities [19, 22, 25, 27]. These inequities result in a narrowing pipeline from the university to the software industry, resulting in a lack of diverse perspectives in system design, impacting not only fairness but also innovation, usability, and security [2, 7, 24, 28, 30, 31].

It is not enough that diversity in software engineering has remained a persistent challenge for decades, and the field is now facing a new and compounding crisis: a growing pushback against diversity, equity, and inclusion efforts. While attention to DEI gained momentum in the early 2020s, the scenario began to shift in 2023, when a wave of legal and political challenges started raising conflicts about the legitimacy and perceived fairness of diversity and inclusion initiatives. By 2024, several significant rollbacks were underway, and by 2025, these actions had escalated into a broader trend of retrenchment across the tech sector [12, 13, 15, 16].

This shift is not only organizational but cultural. Internal communications and public statements reveal a move away from explicitly equity-focused strategies toward more generic expressions of inclusion and strategies aimed at minimizing controversy or legal exposure [14, 15]. Roles and departments specifically dedicated to DEI have been downsized or eliminated, and public commitments are increasingly being replaced by less targeted initiatives [10]. These changes have introduced uncertainty within software teams, particularly for professionals engaged in or benefited from earlier DEI initiatives.

Researchers caution that this backlash, while cyclical in nature, poses unique risks in the current landscape. Rather than signaling the resolution of equity challenges, the pullback may undermine long-term efforts to create more inclusive technical environments [9, 11]. In software engineering, the effects might be far-reaching, as it threatens the development of technologies that account for the needs of diverse users, weakens trust in design decisions, and narrows the perspectives contributing to critical systems [2, 7, 30].

# 3  Method

This work adopts an exploratory qualitative study design to investigate how software professionals experience and respond to the growing backlash against diversity, equity, and inclusion initiatives in the software industry [32,33].

## 3.1  Research Design and Rationale

Qualitative studies are appropriate when studying contemporary phenomena in complex, real-world contexts, where boundaries between the phenomenon and its setting are unclear [32,33]. In our case, the DEI backlash cannot be easily separated from industry shifts, global political dynamics, and evolving workplace cultures.

This topic is also sensitive and politically charged. Software professionals may feel discouraged or even afraid to discuss their employers' DEI policies, especially given recent layoffs. Consequently, conducting interviews or identifying a specific organization as a case would have posed ethical and logistical challenges. Additionally, while survey-based methods can be used to assess broader populations, they are limited in their ability to capture rich personal narratives, and defining a representative sample of affected individuals across demographic groups is particularly difficult in this context.

Given these constraints, we selected Reddit as our data source. Our objective is not to generalize to all software professionals, but to explore how those participating in public discourse perceive and articulate their experiences with the DEI backlash by treating the Reddit posts as archival records of discourse, repurposed for qualitative analysis [34,35].

## 3.2  The Site

Reddit is a popular social media platform organized into user-moderated communities called subreddits, each dedicated to specific topics, professions, or identity groups. These communities facilitate semi-anonymous, many-to-many conversations, where users post questions, share experiences, and comment in threaded discussions. Reddit is widely used among software professionals [36,37], and its public nature makes it well-suited for archival internet research [35].

For this study, we defined our case site as a cluster of six subreddits: *r/softwaredevelopment*, *r/SoftwareEngineering*, *r/womenintech*, *r/AskLGBT*, *r/Neurodivergent*, and *r/cptsd_bipoc*. We began by selecting subreddits focused on software development and engineering that demonstrated *high activity levels and consistent engagement* (e.g., *r/softwaredevelopment*, *r/SoftwareEngineering*, and *r/womenintech*). However, in order to reach a broader range of perspectives, particularly from professionals belonging to underrepresented groups, we expanded our selection to include identity-based subreddits where members often discuss work-related issues from lived experiences (e.g., *r/AskLGBT*, *r/Neurodivergent*, and *r/cptsd_bipoc*).

To investigate how software professionals were experiencing the DEI backlash, our initial plan was to identify and analyze existing posts on Reddit that already discussed the phenomenon. While we found general conversations about the DEI backlash across several subreddits, none addressed it in the context of the software industry, or offered detailed, experience-based accounts from software professionals themselves. Given this lack of contextual evidence, we opted to seed the discussion ourselves. To do so, we created an open-ended post in each subreddit to prompt voluntary narratives directly tied to our research questions:

> **Any Other Software Devs Here? How Are You Handling the Anti-DEI Wave?** Hey everyone, just curious—are there other software developers here? Lately, there's been a lot of backlash against DEI efforts, and I've been wondering how others in the software industry are experiencing it, especially with big tech companies scaling back DEI initiatives.

This strategy allowed us to directly reach software professionals and underrepresented individuals in tech communities while avoiding intrusive methods, aligning with qualitative study conventions [32] and indirect observation approaches, allowing participants to articulate their experiences in their own words and on their own terms.

### 3.3   Data Collection

Data were collected during March 2025. After seeding the post in each subreddit, we manually screened all responses to identify relevant data. We included posts that:

- Were made by individuals who claimed to work in the software industry;
- Addressed an experience, observation, or concern explicitly related to DEI practices or their rollback in the software industry;
- Demonstrated evidentiary value, meaning the post described a situation, reaction, or institutional change that could be interpreted within the broader theme of the DEI backlash.

Posts that were off-topic, vague, purely opinion-based without anchoring in experience, or unrelated to software contexts were excluded. The final dataset consisted of 59 unique comments and responses from the six subreddits. Each post was assigned an anonymized identifier for analysis (e.g., comment_01, comment_02). No usernames, timestamps, or metadata were retained.

### 3.4   Data Analysis

We conducted a reflexive thematic analysis [38, 39] to identify how participants constructed meaning around the DEI backlash and to trace recurring patterns in their narratives. Two researchers worked independently on this task, and we did not use automated tools, e.g., all coding was conducted manually in shared documents to preserve the contextuality of each comment. The analysis involved the following steps:

- **Initial familiarization**: Both researchers independently read the full dataset multiple times to identify early patterns and note potential codes.
- **Open coding**: Each researcher manually coded the dataset line by line, assigning descriptive labels to meaningful narrative segments. Coding was inductive, allowing for bottom-up construction of themes.
- **Code reconciliation**: Researchers met to review their codes, resolve discrepancies through discussion, and refine the themes collaboratively. A third researcher was available to adjudicate if needed.
- **Theme development**: Once the coding stabilized, we organized codes into candidate themes, reviewing for internal coherence and distinctiveness. Final themes were named and defined through iterative discussion.

Finally, saturation is a key principle in qualitative research, indicating that enough data has been collected to capture the main patterns in participants' experiences [32]. In our study, the amount of data depended on the willingness of participants on the platform to engage in the discussion, and although our dataset is small, it was rich in detail. Considering this limitation, we assessed saturation throughout the coding process and determined it had been reached when no new codes or meaningful themes were emerging from the data we obtained.

### 3.5   Ethical Considerations

This study involved an archival analysis of publicly available data from Reddit. Although user accounts were required to make the original posts, we only collected data after logging out, ensuring that we only accessed content available to the general public. Posts were collected without usernames, profile links, or any identifying information. Quotes used in reporting have been lightly edited for clarity and de-identified to protect anonymity. Finally, because the data were public, non-interactive, and presented minimal risk to participants, the study was reviewed and deemed exempt by the Research Ethics Board.

## 4   Results

Our dataset consists of 59 posts collected from five Reddit communities where members discussed the current backlash against diversity, equity, and inclusion in the software industry. The majority of the posts came from the subreddit *r/womenintech*, accounting for 66.1% (39/59) of the dataset. This was followed by *r/SoftwareEngineering* with 16.9% (10/59), *r/softwaredevelopment* with 8.5% (5/59), and *r/AskLGBT* with 6.8% (4/59). One post (1.7%) was contributed from the community *r/cptsd_bipoc*. These varied sources offer insights into how the DEI backlash is perceived and experienced across different groups within the software development ecosystem.

Additionally, we observed notable differences in the tone and dynamics of the conversations depending on the community in which the posts appeared. In forums centered on underrepresented groups, such as *r/womenintech*, *r/AskL-GBT*, and *r/cptsd_bipoc*, discussions were generally more progressive and approached the topic of DEI with empathy and openness. Even when users expressed disagreement, their exchanges tended to remain respectful and constructive, reflecting a shared commitment to thoughtful engagement with DEI-related issues. In contrast, the two general software engineering communities (*r/SoftwareEngineering* and *r/softwaredevelopment*) presented a different atmosphere.

Several posts in these forums included negative views and attacks toward DEI and people from underrepresented groups, sometimes accompanied by discriminatory remarks or dismissive language. During the data collection process, we observed that many of these comments were deleted by the users shortly after posting, which could mean that users regretted engaging. As the posts were deleted, we were unable to identify their content or include them in the analysis. Eventually, moderators locked both threads in the general software engineering communities within six hours of their creation, effectively ending further engagement. By contrast, all threads in the communities centered on underrepresented groups remained open for discussion, although no new interactions were observed after the end of the collection period.

## 4.1 Observed Changes in the Software Industry Due to the DEI Backlash

Our first set of findings reflected the observed or experienced changes in the software industry resulting from the DEI backlash. Out of the 59 collected posts, 21 described changes occurring within software organizations. Based on our thematic analysis we grouped them into four distinct categories that reflect how companies are responding to external pressures regarding DEI. The most frequently observed change was *DEI Revisions* (18.6%, 11 posts), followed by *Job Cuts or Layoffs* (6.8%, 4 posts), *DEI Initiatives Cancelation* (5.1%, 3 posts), and *Reduction in DEI Investment* (5.1%, 3 posts). The remaining 38 posts either stated that no changes had occurred so far or focused on other perspectives related to DEI. Below, we describe each category in detail.

- **DEI Revisions**: The evidence obtained from the posts demonstrates that some companies continued to support inclusive practices but removed explicit references to DEI, often rebranding programs to avoid criticism. In one specific example, the company replaced the acronym "DEI" with alternatives such as "IDEA" (Inclusion, Diversity, Equity, and Accessibility), or chose more neutral terms to maintain their programs. One user commented: *"During a meeting for leaders across our various groups (queer folks, people of color, etc.), we were asked about 'rebranding' the term DEI externally since it had gotten a bad rep, while still pursuing the same mission of inclusiveness internally"* (Comment_01). Another participant shared: *"We still have inclusivity* *training and sensitivity training, but they are just called that and not DEI. Simple. Easy. Done"* (Comment_30).

– **Job Cuts or Layoffs**: In this theme, users reported job losses or reduced hiring prospects in environments where DEI was being challenged or deprioritized. Although not all layoffs were directly attributed to DEI backlash, some users linked job loss to DEI-related decisions, such as facing hiring freezes in environments that deprioritized diversity. One user wrote: *"They created the bootcamp's first ever group applications made entirely by women. I got a PIP [Personal Improvement Plan] for doing this and was eventually fired"* (Comment_21), referring to their decision to support an all-women project group. Another user reflected: *"For me, I feel like the chances of me getting a job after my layoff 1.5 years ago is getting worse and worse"* (Comment_07).

– **DEI Initiatives Cancelation**: Another observed change includes more direct and comprehensive eliminations of DEI programs, including the disbanding of employee resource groups, removal of DEI-related language from public platforms, and elimination of minority groups' celebrations. These cancellations were sometimes tied to contracts or political pressure. One user noted: *"They were required to sign something stating they didn't practice DEI in order to keep the contracts. So they did and disbanded all the groups they had (women, lgbt, etc.)"* (Comment_14). Another wrote: *"We had to remove all DEI keywords and phrases from our organization's websites and apps"* (Comment_40).

– **Reduction in DEI Investment**: We also identified that some companies did not cancel DEI programs outright but scaled back their visibility, funding, or external communications. Reductions often targeted advocacy efforts, marketing campaigns, or internal communication budgets. One user shared: *"The internal advocate groups still exist but don't get marketing money"* (Comment_58). Another noted: *"Our company released an internal news article about striking DEI programs"* (Comment_53).

Taken together, these changes suggest a complex response to the DEI backlash in the software industry. While some companies have responded by scaling back, removing, or canceling their DEI-related efforts, others appear to be engaged in a form of quiet resistance, e.g., using rebranding to preserve the underlying goals of inclusion while adjusting the visibility of such programs, considering external and internal interaction.

## 4.2 Emotional Responses and Lived Experiences of Software Professionals

Our second set of findings focused on how professionals in the software industry are feeling in response to the ongoing DEI backlash. Out of the 59 collected posts, 24 described personal emotional responses or workplace experiences associated with the current climate. We grouped these responses into seven distinct categories that reflect a range of emotions and experiential states: *Anxiety* (20.8%, 5 posts), *Frustration* (20.8%, 5 posts), *Relief* (20.8%, 5 posts), *Hopelessness*

(12.5%, 3 posts), *Happiness* (12.5%, 3 posts), *Fear* (4.2%, 1 post), and *Uncertainty* (4.2%, 1 post). These categories are not mutually exclusive and represent the dominant affective tone of each post. Below, we define each category and illustrate it with selected narratives.

- **Anxiety**: This category includes posts where participants explicitly mentioned being nervous, tense, or worried, particularly about the possibility of future discrimination or loss of job security. The anxiety expressed often stemmed from anticipation rather than concrete events. One participant explained: *"So far I haven't had any adverse action, but I'm tense and anxious"* (Comment_34). Another user shared concerns about how DEI backlash might affect hiring practices: *"I'm worried about interviewing now... I'm going to be interviewing as a woman in her 40s which is definitely a double whammy"* (Comment_17).
- **Frustration**: Posts about frustration often describe a disconnect between organizational values and the personal or professional identity of the participant. Frustration was also expressed when DEI efforts were perceived as shallow or when the culture no longer felt inclusive. One user described emotional exhaustion: *"Feeling extremely burnt out and like nobody has my back at work"* (Comment_23). Another shared: *"It makes me want to quit tbh. It's hard to feel like tech aligns with my values anymore"* (Comment_11).
- **Relief**: This emotion was expressed by participants whose companies reaffirmed their DEI commitments or did not show signs of retreat. Relief emerged when participants felt protected by strong internal values or proactive leadership. One participant shared: *"Our company did make it a point to emphasize that DEI efforts weren't going anywhere, so that's cool"* (Comment_13). Another expressed satisfaction with recent messaging from leadership: *"In the quarterly meeting, he talked about the importance of diversity and inclusion in our culture and mission statement (...) I feel a lot better about my company now"* (Comment_16).
- **Hopelessness**: This category captures emotional fatigue and resignation in response to repeated rejections, job insecurity, or emotional distress. These narratives often included language about giving up or feeling that things will be harder without DEI efforts. One user wrote: *"I don't even think it's worth applying to anything because getting hit with 5-ish rejections a day is just miserable"* (Comment_07). Another, after crying in front of their manager, summarized: *"Badly.... Cried in front of my manager. Had a conversation with HR.... Shit's hard right now"* (Comment_45).
- **Happiness**: Some participants expressed happiness or satisfaction, because they disagreed with previous DEI practices. In these cases, the backlash was not experienced negatively, but rather as a return to something that the professionals felt more comfortable. One user shared: *"I actually love it. Was so sick of being made to join female-focused affinity groups. Now I can just go to work and... work."* (Comment_29). Another expressed a desire for change against DEI: *"It's a good thing, maybe finally we can return to the days of excellence"* (Comment_47).

- **Fear**: This post captured a sudden shift in the workplace environment following visible actions to erase DEI. The language used by the participant conveyed a sense of loss of safety and fear of retaliation: *"For us they've gutted everything perceived as DEI related: from the office to people's personal affects and scrubbed any digital footprint. Full on panic mode"* (Comment_24). Fear in this context was closely tied to the speed and severity of the backlash.
- **Uncertainty**: Finally, one post expressed vague apprehension about the future without reporting any concrete consequences. The participant noted: *"I don't know how long it'll fly under their radar"* (Comment_54), referring to their company's keeping DEI initiatives amid pressure. This response reflected a sense of waiting and watching in a volatile environment.

These findings reveal that the DEI backlash is not only a matter of institutional policy but a lived and deeply personal experience for many software professionals. While some find reassurance in strong leadership and consistency, others face growing emotional strain as they attempt to navigate ambiguous organizational climates. The feelings expressed, ranging from anxiety and frustration to relief and hopelessness, reflect a broad emotional spectrum shaped by individual roles, identities, and software development environments.

### 4.3 Strategies to Protect or Sustain DEI Efforts in the Software Industry

To complement our analysis of organizational changes and individual emotional responses, we also explored how software companies are responding to the DEI backlash through strategies of resistance and adaptation. Out of the 59 posts, 29 described some form of resistance or adaptation strategy. These were grouped into four categories: *Organizational Resistance* (22.0%, 13 posts), *Rebranding* (20.3%, 12 posts), *Strategic Framing* (11.9%, 7 posts), and *Quiet Continuity* (10.2%, 6 posts). These forms of adaptation reflect various ways that DEI efforts are being sustained or reshaped without being completely dismantled. Below, we define and describe each category with examples.

- **Organizational Resistance**: Posts in this category described companies that explicitly reaffirmed their DEI values and continued their programs despite the broader backlash. This form of resistance involved visible and verbal commitments from leadership, maintenance of resource groups, and continued celebration of cultural events. One user noted: *"ERGs [Employee Resource Groups] are if anything a bit more active than they used to be, plenty of pronouns in Slack and email signatures"* (Comment_27). Another shared: *"The big gigantic wall mural that says, 'Diversity, Equity, Inclusion' in 2-foot-high letters is still up. ERGs still meet"* (Comment_26).
- **Rebranding**: Rebranding refers to changing the terminology used to describe DEI efforts while continuing to implement them. This was the most tactical form of adaptation, aimed at appeasing critics without abandoning core practices. One user explained: *"As someone who's been in branding for years, I can*

*understand this move. It's at least better than completely abandoning the values"* (Comment_02). Another shared: *"I think the rebranding just gets [name removed] off your back and you can keep doing the same things. I would try to rebrand it as increasing team performance because it's been proven that diversity does that"* (Comment_06). Importantly, rebranding kept the structure of DEI initiatives intact but distanced them from politicized language.

- **Strategic Framing**: This form involved adjusting both the language and presentation of DEI initiatives, sometimes in combination with operational changes, to align them with broader corporate goals or legal compliance. While rebranding changes only the terms, strategic framing includes modifying how the initiative is justified or implemented. One user described this process: *"So they did and disbanded all the groups they had (women, lgbt, etc.) and are 'working on a solution.'"* (Comment_14). Another noted: *"The internal advocate groups still exist but dont get marketing money."* (Comment_58), reflecting a situation where DEI was paused or scaled back while the company looked for alternative approaches.

- **Quiet Continuity**: Some users reported that DEI practices remained intact, but were not prominently advertised or labeled under the DEI banner. This subtle form of continuity often relied on geographic, organizational, or political positioning to avoid visibility. One user explained: *"Nothing has changed. I moved to a blue city because I figured it would be better, and it really is"* (Comment_28). Another shared: *"We are continuing to hire a diverse workforce ("the right thing"), because we are too small for the anti-DEI witch-hunters to notice us"* (Comment_59).

These findings demonstrate that while the DEI backlash has changed the public visibility of diversity initiatives in the software industry, it has also given rise to a diverse set of responses aimed at sustaining inclusive practices. Whether through explicit resistance, quiet continuity, rebranding, or strategic repositioning, these strategies illustrate that, to some extent, support for DEI has not disappeared; it has adapted.

## 5    Discussion

We organize our discussion in three parts. First, we answer the research questions that guided our study. Second, we compare our results to related literature. Finally, we discuss the broader implications of our findings.

### 5.1    Answering the Research Questions

Each of our research questions offers a different perspective to understand the DEI backlash in the software industry. Hence, rather than treating the phenomenon a single issue, we explored it from three angles: institutional change, personal experience, and strategic adaptation. We can answer the questions as follows.

**RQ1. What changes caused by the DEI backlash have been observed and experienced in the software industry?** The changes reported by participants are not limited to outright elimination of DEI programs; rather, they reflect a spectrum of responses, from visible dismantling to strategic adaptations. These organizational shifts reveal that the backlash in the software industry is less about ending DEI altogether and more about renegotiating how it is expressed and operationalized. In some cases, companies are making calculated moves to retain the spirit of DEI while minimizing exposure to avoid political and public controversies. In others, however, symbolic gestures give way to substantive rollbacks, leaving software engineers uncertain about the values their organizations uphold.

**RQ2. How is the backlash against DEI affecting software professionals within the software industry?** While organizational changes are often described in neutral or strategic terms, their impact on people is profoundly personal. The range of emotions that we captured in the posts shows that professionals interpret these shifts through the lens of their own identities, histories, and expectations. The emotional diversity observed reflects deeper tensions about their role as software professionals, belonging, recognition, and the fragility of diversity practices. As software companies recalibrate, software professionals are left to navigate a climate marked by ambiguity and uneven signals about what is safe, supported, or valued.

**RQ3. What strategies are currently being used in the software industry to protect and sustain DEI efforts in response to the backlash?** Across the dataset, we identified forms of resilience that demonstrate how software organizations are attempting to preserve DEI values. Rebranding, strategic framing, and quiet continuity are not just coping mechanisms; they are calculated responses that reveal the complexity of doing DEI work in a contested environment. These strategies suggest that DEI is evolving, not disappearing. By adapting its vocabulary and operational modes, DEI will remain a presence in many software development environments, albeit one that is increasingly shaped by the need to balance principle with pragmatism.

## 5.2   Comparing Findings with the Literature

Recent studies have shown DEI efforts are undergoing significant changes across various sectors, with many organizations reducing the visibility or scope of their initiatives [10,12,13,15,16]. These changes include rebranding programs, downsizing DEI-specific roles, and shifting toward broader, less targeted terms like "belonging" or "team culture" [14,40,41]. While much of the current literature has focused on fields like business administration and management, our study extends this work by identifying similar patterns in the software industry and exploring how they align with broader organizational strategies.

Our findings confirm that software companies are undergoing comparable structural transformations. Participants reported the elimination of DEI-specific roles, the withdrawal of public-facing commitments in software products, and a shift in internal messaging within teams. These organizational changes reflect trends already discussed in the literature [10, 41], but our study adds a distinct contribution by centering the experiences of software engineers. While prior work has largely investigated institutional shifts or executive strategies, we focused on how these changes are felt by those working directly in software development, discussing the day-to-day impact of these changes on communication, motivation, and perceived support for inclusion.

Another key contribution of our study is the focus on emotional responses. While some supported the changes, many engineers described feelings of anxiety, discouragement, disappointment, and uncertainty as DEI efforts were scaled back. This emotional dimension has received limited attention in earlier work, which tends to analyze DEI at the structural or organizational level. Our findings complement recent discussions that the retreat from DEI can have lasting consequences for individual well-being and organizational climate, which may be detrimental to software development environments where collaboration and trust are essential [9, 11]. Additionally, while prior literature has documented compliance-oriented adaptations and legal reframing of diversity goals [40, 42], we observed that informal networks and peer-driven practices are continuing to support inclusive values in more discreet ways.

### 5.3   Implications for Research and Practice in Software Engineering

Our findings have important implications for both research and practice in software engineering. By focusing on how software professionals experience changes in DEI efforts, our study moves the conversation beyond institutional policies and toward the everyday realities of software development. We show that inclusion (or its absence) directly shapes how software engineers engage with their work, their teams, and their organizations. This perspective is essential for understanding the full impact of ongoing shifts in DEI across the software industry.

For researchers, our study suggests the need to move beyond broad discussions of representation and instead explore the lived impacts of DEI changes. This includes how software engineers interpret organizational messaging, navigate uncertainty, and adjust their behaviors in response to shifting norms. We also encourage academics to explore new lines of research, such as how DEI changes affect team collaboration, trust, software quality, and even financial outcomes in projects.

For practitioners, our findings highlight the gap between formal DEI programs and the values held by many software professionals. Even as organizations scale back public commitments, many engineers continue to care about fairness, representation, and belonging. Without support, however, these values can become difficult to act on, leading to silence, discomfort, and reduced psychological safety. For software companies, rather than abandoning DEI, this moment offers an opportunity to strengthen it through everyday practices, for instance by embedding inclusion into team culture through mentoring, onboarding, informal networks, and space for reflection.

## 5.4    Threats to Validity

Following qualitative research standards [32], we identified and addressed several threats to validity. **Credibility** was a concern due to the reliance on self-reported experiences, which may be incomplete or selectively recalled. To mitigate this, we included only posts from individuals who clearly identified as software professionals and used direct quotations to ensure that our interpretations were grounded in participants' own words. **Transferability** is limited by the non-representative nature of the dataset, which does not allow for statistical generalization. Instead, we expect that our findings can be re-interpreted in other contexts based on the rich contextual descriptions provided. **Reflexivity** posed a risk given the authors' personal and academic commitments to inclusion. Regarding this, we explicitly acknowledge that all authors belong to underrepresented groups, but we ensured that our analysis was grounded by consistently returning to the raw data to verify interpretations, including also narratives from participants that are against DEI practices. Finally, regarding **rigor**, we did not have access to other sources of data to conduct external data triangulation; instead, we relied on a systematic open coding process, comparing patterns across multiple posts and user perspectives.

## 6    Conclusions

This study investigated how software professionals are experiencing the ongoing backlash against DEI in the software industry. Our findings highlight three central aspects of this moment: organizational changes affecting DEI programs, the emotional responses of software professionals, and the strategies being developed to support inclusive values. Our findings suggest that the current moment should not be interpreted as a complete abandonment of DEI within the software industry but as an ongoing recalibration of how inclusion is pursued.

While formal programs may be changing or being reduced, most software professionals in our study demonstrated a strong commitment to DEI values and viewed these principles as important to their work. Looking at software companies, rather than disengaging, several of them are adjusting their approaches, finding new ways to maintain DEI values present in their environments. This ongoing engagement signals that equity, diversity, and inclusion continue to matter within software teams and are being sustained through creativity, resilience, and different forms of resistance.

For future research, we plan to develop a large-scale survey to explore how software professionals across regions and roles perceive DEI in their organizations. We also aim to analyze public statements and corporate communication materials to trace how company-level DEI commitments are evolving. Together, these efforts will deepen our understanding of how the DEI backlash is unfolding and how inclusion is being sustained, transformed, or contested over time.

**Data Availability.** The replication package for this study is available at: https:// figshare.com/s/b03efc273fd5be2b9227

# References

1. Russen, M., Dawson, M.: Which should come first? Examining diversity, equity and inclusion. Int. J. Contemp. Hosp. Manag. **36**(1), 25–40 (2023)
2. Rodríguez-Pérez, G., Nadri, R., Nagappan, M.: Perceived diversity in software engineering: a systematic literature review. Empir. Softw. Eng. **26**, 1–38 (2021)
3. Menezes, Á., Prikladnicki, R.: Diversity in software engineering. In: Proceedings of the 11th International Workshop on Cooperative and Human Aspects of Software Engineering, pp. 45–48 (2018)
4. Kohl, K., Prikladnicki, R.: Benefits and difficulties of gender diversity on software development teams: a qualitative study. In: Proceedings of the XXXVI Brazilian Symposium on Software Engineering, pp. 21–30 (2022)
5. Aleem, S., Ahmed, F.: Practicing equity diversity inclusion (EDI) in software development teams: a systematic literature survey. IEEE Access **11**, 98977–98987 (2023)
6. Verwijs, C., Russo, D.: The double-edged sword of diversity: how diversity, conflict, and psychological safety impact software teams. IEEE Trans. Software Eng. **50**(1), 141–157 (2023)
7. Albusays, K., et al.: The diversity crisis in software development. IEEE Softw. **38**(2), 19–25 (2021)
8. Mason, S.A., Kuttal, S.K.: Diversity's double-edged sword: analyzing race's effect on remote pair programming interactions. ACM Trans. Softw. Eng. Methodol. **34**(1), 1–45 (2024)
9. Finn, M.G., Kamerlin, S.C.L.: Representation matters: responding to the current campaign against DEI efforts. EMBO Rep. **24**(9), e57850 (2023)
10. McGowan, B.L., Hopson, R., Epperson, L., Leopold, M.: Navigating the backlash and reimagining diversity, equity, and inclusion in a changing sociopolitical and legal landscape. J. Coll. Char. **26**(1), 1–11 (2025)
11. Sitzmann, T., Bassani, G., Stansifer, M.L.: Don't get bogged down by the backlash. Ind. Organ. Psychol. **17**(4), 525–529 (2024)
12. Palmer, A.: Amazon to halt some of its DEI programs: Internal memo. CNBC. https://perma.cc/Y4UP-ZX5W. Accessed 19 Apr 2025
13. Alfonseca, K., Zahn, M.: How corporate America is slashing DEI workers amid backlash to diversity programs. ABC News. https://perma.cc/MCG7-U2JQ. Accessed 19 Apr 2025
14. Dave, P., Elliot, V.: Meta Is Dismantling DEI Programs but Tells Investors It Still Wants 'Cognitive Diversity'. Wired. https://perma.cc/VNW9-HECN. Accessed 19 Apr 2025
15. Wong, Q., Lee, W.: Google and Meta used to champion DEI efforts. Why Big Tech is pulling back. Los Angeles Times. https://perma.cc/8WZ6-649G. Accessed 20 Apr 2025
16. Bryan, C., Lyons, B.: Understanding the backlash against corporate DEI — and how to move forward. The Conversation. https://perma.cc/2W8Q-YM27. Accessed 20 Apr 2025
17. de Souza Santos, R., Stuart-Verner, B., de Magalhaes, C.V.C.: Diversity in software engineering: a survey about scientists from underrepresented groups. In: 2023 IEEE/ACM 16th International Conference on Cooperative and Human Aspects of Software Engineering (CHASE), pp. 161–166. IEEE (2023)
18. de Souza Santos, R., Santos, I., Santos, R., Magalhaes, C.: Hidden figures in software engineering: a replication study exploring undergraduate software students'

awareness of distinguished scientists from underrepresented groups. In: IEEE International Conference on Software Analysis, Evolution and Reengineering (SANER 2025), pp. 1–12 (2025)

19. de Souza Santos, R., Santos, I., Santos, R., Magalhaes, C.: Diversity in software engineering education: exploring motivations, influences, and role models among undergraduate students. In: IEEE Conference on Software Engineering Education and Training (CSEE&T 2025), pp. 1–12 (2025)
20. Dodig-Crnkovic, G.: History of computer science. https://perma.cc/79R4-ZN5H. Accessed 30 Dec 2023
21. Mijwel, M.M.: History of Artificial Intelligence Yapay Zekânın Tarihi, vol. 2018 (2015)
22. Ibe, N.A., Howsmon, R., Penney, L., Granor, N., DeLyser, L.A., Wang, K.: Reflections of a diversity, equity, and inclusion working group based on data from a national CS education program. In: Proceedings of the 49th ACM Technical Symposium on Computer Science Education, pp. 711–716 (2018)
23. Ouhbi, S., Pombo, N.: Software engineering education: challenges and perspectives. In: 2020 IEEE Global Engineering Education Conference (EDUCON), pp. 202–209. IEEE (2020)
24. Zolduoarrati, E., Licorish, S.A.: On the value of encouraging gender tolerance and inclusiveness in software engineering communities. Inf. Softw. Technol. **139**, 106667 (2021)
25. de Souza Santos, R., Stuart-Verner, B., de Magalhaes, C.V.C.: LGBTQIA+ (In) visibility in computer science and software engineering education. In: 2023 IEEE/ACM 16th International Conference on Cooperative and Human Aspects of Software Engineering (CHASE), pp. 167–172. IEEE Computer Society (2023)
26. Sax, L.J., Zimmerman, H.B., Blaney, J.M., Toven-Lindsey, B., Lehman, K.: Diversifying undergraduate computer science: the role of department chairs in promoting gender and racial diversity. J. Women Minor. Sci. Eng. **23**(2) (2017)
27. Hyrynsalmi, S.M.: How diversity and inclusion are approached in software engineering university-level teaching. In: 2023 IEEE/ACM 4th Workshop on Gender Equity, Diversity, and Inclusion in Software Engineering (GEICSE), pp. 17–24. IEEE (2023)
28. Oliveira, T., Barcomb, A., de Souza Santos, R., Barros, H., Baldassarre, M.T., França, C.: Navigating the path of women in software engineering: from academia to industry. In: Proceedings of the 46th International Conference on Software Engineering: Software Engineering in Society, pp. 154–165 (2024)
29. Gama, K., Santos, R.: It's not all about gender: a multi-dimensional course perspective on diversity and inclusion in software engineering education. In: Simpósio Brasileiro de Engenharia de Software (SBES), pp. 487–498. SBC (2024)
30. Adams, B., Khomh, F.: The diversity crisis of software engineering for artificial intelligence. IEEE Softw. **37**(5), 104–108 (2020)
31. de Souza Santos, R., de Magalhaes, C.V.C., Ralph, P.: Benefits and limitations of remote work to LGBTQIA+ software professionals. In: 2023 IEEE/ACM 45th International Conference on Software Engineering: Software Engineering in Society (ICSE-SEIS), pp. 48–57. IEEE (2023)
32. Ralph, P., et al.: Empirical standards for software engineering research. arXiv preprint arXiv:2010.03525 (2020)
33. Runeson, P., Höst, M.: Guidelines for conducting and reporting case study research in software engineering. Empir. Softw. Eng. **14**, 131–164 (2009)
34. Fisher, G.G., Chaffee, D.S.: Research using archival data. In: Advanced Research Methods for Applied Psychology, pp. 76–84. Routledge (2018)

35. Nguyen, H., Weber, M.S.: Internet archives as a tool for research: decay in large scale archival records. In: 2015 IEEE International Congress on Big Data, pp. 724–727. IEEE (2015)

36. Li, T., Louie, E., Dabbish, L., Hong, J.I.: How developers talk about personal data and what it means for user privacy: a case study of a developer forum on Reddit. Proc. ACM Hum.-Comput. Interact. **4**(CSCW3), 1–28 (2021)

37. Fang, H., Vasilescu, B., Herbsleb, J.: Understanding information diffusion about open-source projects on Twitter, HackerNews, and Reddit. In: 2023 IEEE/ACM 16th International Conference on Cooperative and Human Aspects of Software Engineering (CHASE), pp. 56–67. IEEE (2023)

38. Cruzes, D.S., Dybå, T.: Recommended steps for thematic synthesis in software engineering. In: 2011 International Symposium on Empirical Software Engineering and Measurement, pp. 275–284. IEEE (2011)

39. Clarke, V., Braun, V.: Thematic analysis. J. Posit. Psychol. **12**(3), 297–298 (2017)

40. Douglas, M., et al.: Returning to our values: how to continue DEIA efforts in an ever-changing landscape. Ann. Fam. Med. **23**(1), 85 (2025)

41. Einwiller, S.A., Wolfgruber, D., Leitner, A.K.: Addressing backlash? Corporate DEI communication and user complaints on social media. J. Market. Commun., 1–19 (2025)

42. Maizel, C.D., Maizel, E.B.: DEI as cultural commitment in an era of backlash. Am. Bankruptcy Inst. J. **43**(7), 26–53 (2024)

# REST in Pieces: RESTful Design Rule Violations in Student-Built Web Apps

Sergio Di Meglio[1(✉)], Valeria Pontillo[2,3], and Luigi Libero Lucio Starace[1]

[1] Department of Electrical Engineering and Information Technology, University of Naples Federico II, Naples, Italy
sergio.dimeglio@unina.it, luigiliberolucio.starace@unina.it
[2] Software Languages (SOFT) Lab, Vrije Universiteit Brussel, Ixelles, Belgium
valeria.pontillo@gssi.it
[3] Gran Sasso Science Institute (GSSI), L'Aquila, Italy

**Abstract.** In Computer Science Bachelor's programs, software quality is often underemphasized due to limited time and a focus on foundational skills, leaving many students unprepared for industry expectations. To better understand the typical quality of student code and inform both education and hiring practices, we analyze 40 full-stack web applications developed in a third-year Web Technologies course. Using an automated static analysis pipeline, we assess adherence to REST API design rules. Results reveal frequent violations of foundational conventions, such as missing hyphens in endpoint paths (98%), incorrect pluralization (88%), and misuse of HTTP methods (83%). These findings highlight the need for more focused instruction on API design and support the adoption of automated tools to improve code quality in student projects.

**Keywords:** Web Applications · Software Quality · Static Analysis · REST

## 1 Introduction

In Computer Science Bachelor's programs, software development education often emphasizes functional application building over software quality, consistent with ACM guidelines recommending limited early focus on quality aspects [4]. Time constraints and difficult pedagogical trade-offs further limit the comprehensive teaching of software quality principles [5]. Moreover, empirical data on the structural and architectural quality of realistic student projects—especially full-stack applications—are scarce, hindering informed curriculum decisions and impacting industry readiness [21].

This gap has significant industry implications: graduates lacking solid skills in clean, maintainable code shift the retraining burden to employers, who must

This work has been partially supported by the Italian PNRR MUR project PE0000013-FAIR.

invest resources to bring junior developers up to production standards [16]. Bridging this academia-industry divide requires a better understanding of student software quality.

To address this gap, we conducted an empirical investigation on 40 full-stack web applications developed by students enrolled in a third-year Web Technologies course within a Computer Science Bachelor's program. This course, typically taken in the final semester before graduation, requires students to design and implement complete web systems that integrate both front-end and back-end components. To this end, we designed a semi-automated analysis pipeline that leverages RESTRULER, a tool to identify REST API design rule violations, an indicator of structural degradation and design decay, commonly associated with the accumulation of social debt in collaborative software projects. Our findings indicate that while students delivered functional full-stack applications, they frequently violated key REST design conventions—most notably the use of hyphens in endpoint paths (98% of projects), plural nouns for collections (88%), and correct use of GET methods (83%).

These insights can inform teaching strategies to better prepare students for professional development. A replication package with all analysis artifacts is available to support further research and validation [14].

## 2    Background and Related Works

In the following, we introduce key concepts related to software quality, with a focus on design-level aspects specific to RESTful APIs. We also review existing tools for assessing REST API design rule violations and summarize prior research on the quality of student-developed software systems.

Software quality refers not only to the absence of defects but also to architectural and structural design, which supports maintainability, usability, and long-term sustainability [13]. In web applications, where systems interact through Web APIs, API design plays a crucial role: poor design can lead to misuse and increase maintenance costs [7,13].

The Representational State Transfer (REST) architectural style, introduced by Fielding [9], has become the dominant paradigm for designing modern Web APIs. REST is not a protocol or a standard, but an architectural style defined by a set of constraints: statelessness, client-server separation, cacheability, a uniform interface, a layered system, and optional code-on-demand. APIs that fully adhere to these constraints are called REST APIs, and services that implement them are often referred to as RESTful [12].

A REST API is composed of interlinked resources, and this assembly of resources forms the REST API resource model. Each resource is uniquely addressable via URIs and manipulated through a set of well-defined operations using standard HTTP methods (e.g., GET, POST, PUT, DELETE). In a RESTful system, the structure and semantics of URIs, HTTP methods, response codes, and payload formats should follow clear and consistent patterns [19].

Designing a REST API, however, is not always straightforward. Although some guidelines are implied by the HTTP standard itself, others have emerged

**Table 1.** The 14 rules implemented to RESTRULER [2].

| Rule Description | Identifier | Category |
|---|---|---|
| `401 ("Unauthorized")` must be used when there is a problem with the client's credential | RC401 | HTTP Status Codes |
| A plural noun should be used for collection or store names | PluralNoun | URI Design |
| A singular noun should be used for document names | SingularNoun | URI Design |
| A trailing forward slash (/) should not be included in URIs | NoTrailingSlash | URI Design |
| A verb or verb phrase should be used for controller names | VerbController | URI Design |
| CRUD function names should not be used in URIs | NoCRUDNames | URI Design |
| Content-Type must be used | ContentType | Metadata Design |
| Description of request should match with the type of the request | DescriptionType | Metadata Design |
| Forward slash separator (/) must be used to indicate a hierarchical relationship | ForwardSlash | URI Design |
| `GET` and `POST` must not be used to tunnel other request methods | NoTunnel | Request Methods |
| `GET` must be used to retrieve a representation of a resource | GETRetrieve | Request Methods |
| Hyphens (-) should be used to improve the readability of URIs | Hyphens | URI Design |
| Lowercase letters should be preferred in URI paths | Lowercase | URI Design |
| Underscores (\_) should not be used in URI | NoUnserscores | URI Design |

as best practices adopted by the community over time. These range from URI naming conventions to error handling and response formatting. Examples include placing verbs in URIs (e.g., `/createUser` instead of `/users`), misusing HTTP methods (e.g., using `GET` to delete a resource), or inconsistently applying status codes. As a result, REST API design is often viewed as a craft—balancing technical correctness, developer ergonomics, and consistency [3].

To reduce ambiguity and promote consistency in RESTful API design, numerous studies have attempted to formalize the abstract principles of REST into standardized design rules and best practices. These include both academic contributions, such as those by Petrillo et al. [20], Palma et al. [18], and Massè et al. [12]. These works provide actionable guidance on resource naming, proper use of HTTP methods, status codes, and error handling, serving as foundational references for REST API design.

Building on foundational guidelines, several works have focused on automatically detecting REST API design rule violations that reduce usability and maintainability. Tools like SARA [17] and SOFA [15] use rule-based and semantic analysis to uncover issues in URI structure, HTTP verb usage, and resource modeling. More recently, Bogner et al. introduced RESTRULER [2], a Java-based open-source tool that leverages static analysis to detect violations of 14 REST design rules, as shown in Table 1. Other empirical studies have analyzed open-source APIs to assess real-world adherence to REST principles, revealing frequent deviations despite claims of RESTfulness [3,11].

Despite the importance of adhering to REST design principles, little attention has been paid to how these guidelines are understood and applied in educational settings. To date, no comprehensive studies have investigated the extent to which students are aware of these rules, nor how frequently they violate them when designing Web APIs. This lack of insight limits our ability to improve REST education and address misunderstandings at their root.

## 3   Study Design

The *goal* of this study is to evaluate the quality of RESTful back-end components in full-stack web applications developed by students enrolled in a third-year Web Technologies course within a Computer Science Bachelor's Degree program. As one of the final courses before graduation, it requires students to build complete web systems that integrate both front-end and back-end components.

This setting offers an opportunity to assess the technical competencies students acquire by the end of their academic journey. In particular, we focus on the design of REST APIs to identify recurring violations of established design principles. To this end, we pose the following research question:

> **RQ$_1$.** *What are the most frequent REST API design rule violations in student-developed web applications?*

The results of this study are intended to help educators refine course content by highlighting specific design aspects that require greater emphasis. Furthermore, the findings offer insight into the level of API design maturity that companies can expect from recent graduates entering the job market.

### 3.1   Web Technologies Course

The projects analyzed in this study were developed as part of Web Technologies, a 6 ECTS third-year course in the B.Sc. in Computer Science at the University of Naples Federico II, taught by the last author of the paper. The course builds on prior knowledge of object-oriented programming, software engineering and computer networks, and covers the basis of modern web development. Involved students are expected to be familiar with object-oriented programming and core software engineering concepts such as the software development lifecycle, software architecture and design, and code quality.

The course covers both client- and server-side web development, starting with foundational topics such as HTTP, modern HTML and CSS (including Flexbox, Grid, and responsive design), and advanced JavaScript (ES6+), focusing on DOM manipulation and asynchronous programming patterns. Server-side development progresses from traditional approaches like CGI and PHP to modern Node.js applications using Express, middleware, templating, and ORMs like Sequelize. REST APIs are a key focus, with dedicated lectures on authentication via JWT and design best practices [12].

The course further explores modern front-end development with tooling, SPA architecture, TypeScript, and detailed coverage of the Angular framework, emphasizing components, dependency injection, and HTTP interceptors. Security and web testing are strongly emphasized, addressing vulnerabilities such as XSS, CSRF, and SQL injection, alongside testing strategies including end-to-end tests with tools like Playwright [6,8].

Assessment combines a written exam and a practical project requiring students to design and develop an SPA with a RESTful backend supporting authentication and CRUD operations. The students were instructed that the project work would be graded primarily based on its functional correctness, but also taking into account overall software quality and adherence to established REST guidelines. Students may select technologies from the course or alternative frameworks, provided they respect SPA architectural principles.

## 3.2  Collected Projects

The web applications analyzed in this study were developed by students enrolled in the Spring 2024 edition of the Web Technologies course. From the initial submission of 52 projects, we conducted a manual validation process in which the first and third authors verified the satisfaction of dependencies, compilation, and execution capabilities. This quality control phase resulted in the exclusion of 12 projects, yielding a final dataset of 40 functionally complete and manually verified applications.

The technological composition of these projects demonstrates consistency in backend implementation; specifically, 39 projects (97.5%) adopted JavaScript with the Express framework (consistent with the examples shown during the course), while one project (2.5%) used Java with the Spring framework. Front-end implementations exhibited greater diversity, with Angular, which was also discussed in detail during the course, dominating as the framework of choice (33 projects, 82.5%), followed by React (6 projects, 15%), and a single instance using Vue (2.5%). We have also observed notable differences between front-end and backend modules. The front-end modules demonstrate substantially larger codebases, averaging 2,099 lines of code (NCLOC) (Standard Deviation = 727) compared to 847 NCLOC (Standard Deviation = 603) for backend modules. A similar disparity can be observed for file organization, with front-end comprising an average of 66 files (Standard Deviation = 19), while the average for back-ends is 20 files (Standard Deviation = 11).

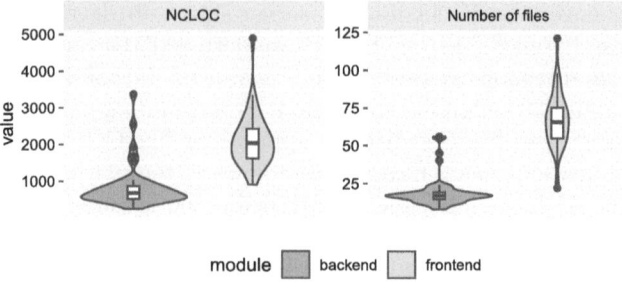

**Fig. 1.** Project Statistics.

The distribution of these metrics is reported in Fig. 1. The Figure shows that while backend sizes cluster relatively tightly around the mean, front-end sizes exhibit greater variability, particularly in NCLOC. This pattern likely reflects both the inherent complexity of client-side development and the varying approaches students take in developing the front-end architecture.

### 3.3  Automated Pipeline

To evaluate the student submissions, we adopted an automated quality analysis pipeline inspired by the approach proposed by De Luca et al. [5]. The pipeline starts by extracting OpenAPI specifications from the back-end components of each project. For Express-based applications, we used `express-oas-generator` [1], while for Spring Boot projects, we employed `springdoc-openapi` [10]. These tools automatically inspect routing and controller logic to generate OpenAPI-compliant specifications. Once generated, the OpenAPI files were analyzed using RESTRULER [2], a tool that detects violations of widely accepted REST API design rules. We executed RESTRULER via its standalone JAR interface, producing a structured report for each project detailing the types and frequency of rule violations identified.

## 4  Results for RQ₁: What are the Most Frequent REST API Design Rule Violations in the Student-Developed Web Applications?

The aggregated results on the detected REST design rule violations are reported in Table 2. These results show that notable patterns exist in how frequently certain best practices and design rules were overlooked across student projects.

The most widespread issue was the *missed use of hyphens to enhance readability* in endpoint paths, with the *Hyphens* rule violated in 98% of projects (39 out of 40). Similarly, pluralized nouns were not used for collection resource paths (*PluralNoun*) in 88% of projects (35 out of 40), while the *GETRetrieve* rule, which ensured GET methods are used only for retrieval of resource representations, was violated in 83% of projects (33 out of 40). These high percentages

**Table 2.** Overview of rule violations in REST APIs, including occurrence count, affected projects, and percentage.

| Rule Identifier | Occurrences | #Projects | (%) |
|---|---|---|---|
| RC401 | 52 | 5 | 13 |
| PluralNoun | 179 | 35 | 88 |
| SingularNoun | 48 | 12 | 30 |
| NoTrailingSlash | 5 | 5 | 13 |
| VerbController | 1 | 1 | 3 |
| NoCRUDNames | 61 | 11 | 28 |
| ContentType | 322 | 14 | 35 |
| DescriptionType | 10 | 9 | 23 |
| ForwardSlash | 3 | 3 | 8 |
| NoTunnel | 28 | 4 | 10 |
| GETRetrieve | 201 | 33 | 83 |
| Hyphens | 170 | 39 | 98 |
| Lowercase | 35 | 5 | 13 |
| NoUnderscores | 5 | 3 | 8 |

suggest that foundational REST conventions related to URI structure and HTTP method semantics were either not fully internalized or deliberately disregarded by the majority of students.

Other rules exhibited moderate prevalence. The *ContentType* rule, which mandates explicit content-type headers, was violated in 35% of projects (14 out of 40), indicating that a significant subset of students overlooked this aspect of API communication. Similarly, *NoCRUDNames* (avoiding CRUD terms in URIs) and *SingularNoun* (using singular nouns for document names) were violated in 28% and 30% of projects, respectively. These findings suggest that while some students adhered to these conventions, a substantial minority did not, potentially reflecting inconsistent emphasis during instruction or varying interpretations of REST guidelines.

Less common but still noteworthy were violations of rules like *VerbController* (3% of projects) and *ForwardSlash* (8% of projects). Their low prevalence implies that these were either more intuitive for students or less prone to ambiguity in teaching materials. However, even minor violations, such as *NoTrailingSlash* and *Lowercase* (each appearing in 13% of projects), highlight areas where targeted instruction could further improve adherence.

Collectively, these results underscore that while students generally grasped high-level REST concepts, specific design principles, particularly those related to URI formatting and HTTP method usage, were frequently misapplied. The prevalence of violations in these areas suggests opportunities to refine pedagogical focus, perhaps through more explicit examples or automated linting tools during development.

# 5    Threats to Validity

## 5.1    Construct Validity

RESTRULER's rule violations are based on a predefined set of REST design principles that may not encompass all real-world API design considerations. Additionally, since some projects required manual instrumentation to generate OpenAPI specifications for RESTRULER, inconsistencies in this process could introduce bias in the REST violation analysis.

## 5.2    Internal Validity

Manual steps involved in preparing projects for analysis—such as configuring or correcting OpenAPI generation—may have introduced variability in how RESTRULER was applied. Incomplete or improperly generated OpenAPI specifications might have caused some violations to be missed, affecting the completeness and comparability of results across projects.

## 5.3    External Validity

Our findings are based on a single cohort of students from a single university who followed a Web Technologies course. As such, the generalizability of the results to other educational contexts or professional settings may be limited. Additionally, the projects were developed under academic constraints (e.g., deadlines, grading criteria), which may not reflect real-world development practices.

# 6    Conclusion and Future Work

Our comprehensive analysis of 40 student-developed full-stack web applications revealed several patterns in REST API design violations that have important implications for computer science education. The findings demonstrate that while students generally master the functional aspects of web development, they struggle with quality-related concerns. These findings suggest that architectural design rules deserve more explicit attention in undergraduate computer science curricula. Specifically, educators should consider integrating automated quality checks into course projects, providing targeted feedback on REST API design, and emphasizing the industrial relevance of these quality aspects.

For future works, we plan to extend our analysis to include software quality aspects such as code smells and maintainability issues by integrating tools like SonarQube into the evaluation process. Furthermore, we intend to investigate the effectiveness of various pedagogical interventions in improving students' software quality. This will involve comparing project quality before and after introducing dedicated lectures on software quality, incorporating continuous static analysis during development, and providing REST API design templates or checklists.

# References

1. express-oas-generator — npmjs.com. https://www.npmjs.com/package/express-oas-generator. Accessed 04 May 2025
2. Bogner, J., Kotstein, S., Abajirov, D., Ernst, T., Merkel, M.: RESTRuler: towards automatically identifying violations of restful design rules in web APIs. In: 2024 IEEE 21st International Conference on Software Architecture (ICSA), pp. 123–134 (2024)
3. Bogner, J., Kotstein, S., Pfaff, T.: Do restful API design rules have an impact on the understandability of web APIs? Empir. Softw. Eng. **28**(6), 132 (2023)
4. Clear, A., Parrish, A.S., Impagliazzo, J., Zhang, M.: Computing curricula 2020: introduction and community engagement. In: Proceedings of the 50th ACM Technical Symposium on Computer Science Education, pp. 653–654 (2019)
5. De Luca, M., Di Meglio, S., Fasolino, A.R., Starace, L.L.L., Tramontana, P.: Automatic assessment of architectural anti-patterns and code smells in student software projects. In: Proceedings of the 28th International Conference on Evaluation and Assessment in Software Engineering, pp. 565–569 (2024)
6. Di Meglio, S., Starace, L.L.L., Di Martino, S.: E2E-loader: a tool to generate performance tests from end-to-end GUI-level tests. In: 2025 IEEE Conference on Software Testing, Verification and Validation (ICST), pp. 747–751 (2025)
7. Di Meglio, S., Starace, L.L.L., Di Martino, S.: Starting a new rest API project? A performance benchmark of frameworks and execution environments. In: IWSM-Mensura (2023)
8. Di Meglio, S., Starace, L.L.L., Pontillo, V., Opdebeeck, R., De Roover, C., Di Martino, S.: E2EGit: a dataset of end-to-end web tests in open source projects. In: Proceedings of the 22nd International Conference on Mining Software Repositories, pp. 836–840 (2025)
9. Roy Thomas Fielding: Architectural Styles and the Design of Network-Based Software Architectures. University of California, Irvine (2000)
10. Library for OpenAPI 3 with spring-boot By Badr NASS LAHSEN. OpenAPI 3 Library for spring-boot — springdoc.org. https://springdoc.org/. Accessed 04 May 2025
11. Kotstein, S., Bogner, J.: Which RESTful API design rules are important and how do they improve software quality? A Delphi study with industry experts. In: Barzen, J. (ed.) SummerSOC 2021. CCIS, vol. 1429, pp. 154–173. Springer, Cham (2021). https://doi.org/10.1007/978-3-030-87568-8_10
12. Masse, M.: REST API Design Rulebook: Designing Consistent RESTful Web Service Interfaces. O'Reilly Media, Inc. (2011)
13. Di Meglio, S., Starace, L.L.L.: Evaluating performance and resource consumption of rest frameworks and execution environments: insights and guidelines for developers and companies. IEEE Access **12**, 161649–161669 (2024)
14. Di Meglio, S., Pontillo, V., Starace, L.L.L.: Rest in pieces: code quality issues and restful design rule violations in student-built web apps — online appendix (2025). https://zenodo.org/records/15492462
15. Moha, N., et al.: Specification and detection of SOA antipatterns. In: Liu, C., Ludwig, H., Toumani, F., Yu, Q. (eds.) ICSOC 2012. LNCS, vol. 7636, pp. 1–16. Springer, Heidelberg (2012). https://doi.org/10.1007/978-3-642-34321-6_1
16. Molnar, A.-J., Motogna, S., Cristea, D., Sotropa, D.-F.: Exploring complexity issues in junior developer code using static analysis and FCA. In: 2024 50th Euromicro Conference on Software Engineering and Advanced Applications (SEAA), pp. 407–414 (2024)

17. Palma, F., Gonzalez-Huerta, J., Founi, M., Moha, N., Tremblay, G., Guéhéneuc, Y.-G.: Semantic analysis of restful APIs for the detection of linguistic patterns and antipatterns. Int. J. Coop. Inf. Syst. **26**(02), 1742001 (2017)
18. Palma, F., Olsson, T., Wingkvist, A., Gonzalez-Huerta, J.: Assessing the linguistic quality of rest APIs for IoT applications. J. Syst. Softw. **191**, 111369 (2022)
19. Pautasso, C., Zimmermann, O., Leymann, F.: Restful web services vs. "big" web services: making the right architectural decision. In: Proceedings of the 17th International Conference on World Wide Web, pp. 805–814 (2008)
20. Petrillo, F., Merle, P., Moha, N., Guéhéneuc, Y.-G.: Are REST APIs for cloud computing well-designed? An exploratory study. In: Sheng, Q.Z., Stroulia, E., Tata, S., Bhiri, S. (eds.) ICSOC 2016. LNCS, vol. 9936, pp. 157–170. Springer, Cham (2016). https://doi.org/10.1007/978-3-319-46295-0_10
21. Włodarski, R., Falleri, J.-R., Parvéry, C.: Assessment of a hybrid software development process for student projects: a controlled experiment. In: 2021 IEEE/ACM 43rd International Conference on Software Engineering: Software Engineering Education and Training (ICSE-SEET), pp. 289–299. IEEE (2021)

# DevScholar: A Reuse-Based Approach for Evaluating Developer Contribution

Yahya Elnouby[1] , Selen Uysal[2], Umut Cihan[1], Hakan Erdogmus[3],
and Eray Tüzün[1(✉)]

[1] Bilkent University, Ankara, Turkey
{yahya.elnouby,umut.cihan}@bilkent.edu.tr, eraytuzun@cs.bilkent.edu.tr
[2] ASELSAN, Ankara, Turkey
selenuysal@aselsan.com
[3] Carnegie Mellon University, Pittsburgh, USA
hakan.erdogmus@sv.cmu.edu

**Abstract.** Evaluating each developer's contributions within collaborative software projects is essential for effective resource allocation, recognition of expertise, and identifying training needs. Traditional metrics such as lines of code (LOCs) or the number of commits fail to provide a comprehensive context since code varies in importance and complexity. On the other hand, writing reusable code is an essential coding practice that can serve as a metric for measuring the quality of the developers' contributions. Our goal is to develop a methodology and a practical tool for evaluating developers' reusable code contributions within a software project. Drawing inspiration from Hirsch's H-Index, a benchmark metric in academia, we constructed the Developer H-Index (DH-Index). It tracks each method's usage throughout the project identified via call graphs akin to citations in academic research and links these references to the respective developer contributions. We also created a variation of the DH-Index that weighs method usage with the Lines-of-Code-Weighted Developer H-Index (LWDH-Index). We developed DevScholar, a publicly available prototype that extracts and analyzes method-based contributions from software developers of a Java project. We compared our tool's capabilities with GitHub Insights on four Open Source Software (OSS) projects, Apollo, Spring Boot, Retrofit, and Dubbo but only presenting the results of Apollo project. LWDH-Index resulted in a stronger metric, as it smoothed out the effect of the disproportionate contribution of frequently called methods that are too simple and of rarely called methods that are too long. In conclusion, compared to simple metrics based only on LOC or the number of commits, the DH-Index and LWDH-Index offer additional perspectives for evaluating developers' contributions to reusable code within a software project team.

**Keywords:** Developer Contribution · Key Developers · Core developers · H-Index · Call Graphs · Lines of Code · Reusable Code

D. Taibi and D. Smite (Eds.): SEAA 2025, LNCS 16083, pp. 201–213, 2026.
https://doi.org/10.1007/978-3-032-04207-1_14

# 1    Introduction

Software projects typically involve the collaboration of multiple developers. Determining each developer's contribution to software projects is intricate due to the software's intangible and changing nature. Moreover, a development team's effectiveness is gauged by its collective output, including both software and other assets such as documentation. These factors make accurately evaluating the quality of each individual's input within the team a complicated task.

Platforms such as GitHub [2] rank repository contributors based on the number of commits and lines of code (LOCs) added or deleted. Although commits serve as contribution indicators, they are of different lengths and importance, rendering them incomparable and potentially misleading. This approach can encourage a higher quantity of commits, but not necessarily of better quality. Ranking developer contributions based on the number of added or deleted LOC can lead to the same issue.

Existing methodologies propose commit-based and LOC-based approaches [3,8,17,19,21,23,24] pull request and issue-based approach [4], and bugfix-based approaches [12,20]. This study was motivated by the absence of a metric capable of evaluating the reusability of the developer's contribution. The following research question guides our study:

**RQ:** How can we assess individual developers' contributions within a software project from the perspective of contributions' reusability?

Similar efforts have been made in academia to quantify and measure the author's contributions. Academic indexes such as the Hirsch's Index (H-Index) are used to evaluate individuals' cumulative academic work. H-Index is based on the idea that a researcher's work cannot be measured solely by the number of publications or citations they have. The H-Index is defined as the largest $h$ number of publications with at least $h$ citations, which estimate the cumulative impact of a researcher's work [15].

Our motivation is to develop a metric aligned with the notion of the H-Index. To that end, we investigated whether the principles of the H-Index can help us evaluate the quality of the developers' contributions to a software project in terms of code reusability. In software development, method references/usages can be a valuable synonym for citations as they reveal the interdependence and reusability of the code authored by individual developers. When a method is referenced many times, the developer's work is utilized throughout the project. Simply counting a developer's total method references can be problematic, similar to citation counts in academic work, where the frequency of citations varies greatly. Some methods are referenced extensively, while others are seldom used. To address this variability, we applied the H-Index concept, commonly used in academia, to identify and rank critical methods, thus providing a more meaningful metric.

## 2    Methodology

### 2.1    Generation of DH-Index and LOC-Weighted DH-Index

For applying the H-Index concept to software development, we generate the DH-Index to evaluate the quality of the developers' contributions in terms of reusability. DH-Index is represented as the largest number $h$ such that $h$ methods have at least $h$ usages, which is calculated as follows,

$$DH\text{-}Index \ (Usage) = \max\{h \in \mathbb{N} : Usage(h) \geq h\} \qquad (1)$$

**Table 1.** Mapping H-Index Analogy to Software Development

| Comparison Criteria | H-Index Concept | DH-Index Concept |
|---|---|---|
| Artifact | Publication | Method |
| Artifact Contributor | Publication's Author(s) | Method's Developer(s) |
| Ranking of Artifact Authors | Author Order | Developer Ranking |
| Level of Contribution to the Artifact | Order of Authors Listed On the Publication | Comparative LOC Contribution |
| Stability of Contributor Rankings over Time | Stable | Changeable |
| Importance Determinant of Artifact | Number of Citations to the Publication | Number of Usages of the Method |
| Artifact Scope | All Recognized Publication Venues | Project |
| Self Citation | Not Preferred | Accepted (Recursive Methods or Same Author's Methods) |
| Lifetime of an Artifact | Infinite | Finite |
| Acceptance of an Artifact | Publication in Conference/Journal | Approved through a Merge/Pull Request |
| Artifact Contents | Stable | Changeable |
| Editability of the Artifact | None | Rewriting/Refactoring the Method |

To further elaborate, we draw an analogy and comparison of the H-Index in academia and the DH-Index in software development, as shown in Table 1. For the H-Index, the primary artifact under consideration is the academic publication, while in software development, the principal artifact becomes the method implemented by the developers. While the publication is written by the author(s), a method is written by the developer(s), and the key difference is that the authors of a publication do not change over time. In contrast, developers of a method are dynamic; as new developers contribute to an implemented method, we consider them to be one of the developers of that method. The publication's authors are ordered according to who contributed more to the publication. In a software project, the developers' ranking is dynamic as the developers are ranked according to their methods' number of usage, which evolves. H-Index concept covers all recognized publication venues. However, the DH-Index is computed only for a specific project. A conceptual difference between citations and code usage is that, in academia, self-citation is believed to inflate an author's H-Index value, but in software projects, a developer reusing code, whether their own or another developer's, is natural, so differentiating self-use is not necessary. The lifetime of a publication is infinite since a publication cannot be deleted, while in a software project, code fragments, including methods, can be deleted. Another difference concerns how contributions are legitimized: publications are legitimized by their acceptance to a recognized publication venue, after which citations to that publication are counted. In software projects, there is no standard vetting of contributed code, even when projects are required to use pull requests (PR) with quality checks. If that is the case, we could think of a PR as analogous to a contributed code fragment. Other differences relate to the artifact content and editability of the artifact. A publication's content is stable once published, but code is ever-changing: in a software project, a method written by a contributor can be deprecated, rewritten, or refactored at any point.

When experimenting with the DH-Index, some deficiencies came to light, which prompted us to create a variation. For example, we noticed that methods such as getters and setters could disproportionately inflate a developer's ranking. Since these methods tend to be called more frequently than other methods, their inclusion without any adjustment can create a bias. In the academic version, H-Index, citations are the single contribution factor, but this does not need to be the case in DH-Index: more nuanced and fair variations are possible by incorporating code length into the index through LOC.

We decided to use LOCs to adjust the DH-Index. We first multiply the method usage with LOC to generate a new count, the LOC-Weighted Usage (LWUsage). We add one to the usage before weighting to prevent a possible discontinuity when usage equals zero so that the volume of the contributed code in a method is counted even when the method is not called from somewhere else. This may happen, for example, in API-level methods that are not meant to be called anywhere else from the codebase but can still be important: the LOC weighting scheme thus allows such methods to be included. Finally, we adjust the result by the percentage of the total contributed LOC to the method attributed to the particular developer for whom the index is calculated. The resulting adjusted counts are given by the following equations:

$$LWUsage = \lceil \text{Method's LOC} \cdot (Usage + 1) \cdot \%of Contribution \rceil \qquad (2)$$

where

$$\%of\ Contribution = \left( \frac{\text{Developer's LOC Contribution}}{\text{Total Method LOC Contribution By Contributors}} \right) \qquad (3)$$

Then, the variation of the DH-Index, the LWDH-Index, can be defined based on LWUsage. LWDH-Index is calculated as the largest number $h$ such that $h$ methods have at least $h$ LWUsage as shown below:

$$LWDH\text{-}Index\ (LWUsage) = \max\{h \in \mathbb{N} : LWUsage(h) \geq h\} \qquad (4)$$

The analogy between the H-Index and the LWDH-Index is the same as the analogy with the DH-Index, with only one difference, which is citations being represented as LWUsage in the LWDH-Index.

## 2.2   Implementation of DevScholar

We implemented a web application named DevScholar that analyzes Java software projects by extracting developers' contributions and calculating metrics for the developers and methods. Due to the use of CodeShovel [13], which focuses on

Java projects, we limited our scope to Java projects. CodeShovel is a tool that navigates through the entire history of a method while categorizing the method changes in each commit. The workflow of how DevScholar works is shown in Fig. 1.

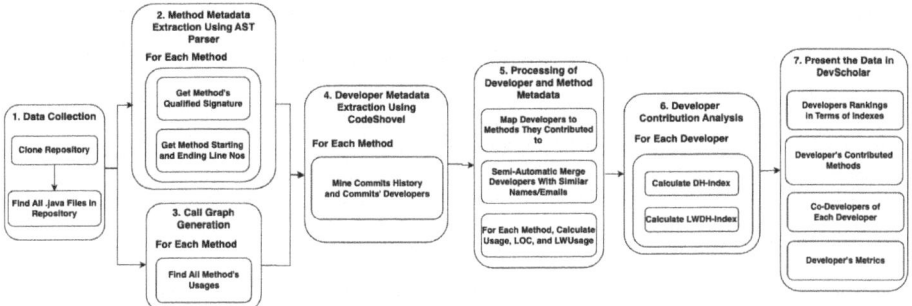

**Fig. 1.** Workflow of DevScholar

**Data Collection.** The selected project is cloned as a first step of the project analysis, and all the Java files' paths are extracted.

**Method Metadata Extraction Using AST Parser.** In the next step, using Java's Abstract Syntax Tree (AST) parser[1], the metadata of the methods, including the starting and ending lines and the method's signature, are extracted.

**Call-Graph Generation.** In parallel, using a call-graph generation tool for each method, we obtain all its references throughout the project. The tool generates a graph where the nodes correspond to the methods and the edges indicate the caller-callee relationships between the methods. This graph is extracted from the call information provided by tracing the AST of each file.

**Developer Metadata Extraction Using CodeShovel.** Next, for each method, we use CodeShovel [13] to extract the related method's commit history. These commits include changes to the method, such as to its signature, body, name, location, or the name of the file containing the method. The commit data are composed of the developer's name and email, the date of the commit, and the changes made.

---

[1] https://github.com/javaparser/javaparser.

**Processing of Developer and Method Metadata.** Using the data extracted in the previous steps, we first process the method's data. This includes calculating the method's LOC (Current LOC), number of references (Usage), and LWUsage. We then remove the bots from the developer's list if the developer's email or username contains '[bot]', as this is an indicator for bots in the project. Then, we map the developers to the methods to which they have contributed. In addition, when mapping, we merge authors using different commit identities into a single developer if a similarity is detected using the fuzzy string matching algorithm [1], which is an algorithm for finding a string that matches a given pattern. A sample result of this step is shown in Tables 2 and 3. Dev/Total (Contributed LOC) represents all the additions and deletions made by the method contributor, including changed LOCs divided by all the contributions to the method. The additions or deletions of empty LOCs or comments are excluded from the contribution calculation.

**Table 2.** Methods to Which Developer X Has Contributed

| Method Name | Usage | LWUsage | Current LOC | % Contributed | Dev/Total (Contributed LOC) |
|---|---|---|---|---|---|
| assignAndNotify() | 5 | 36 | 10 | 60% | 12/20 |
| sendMessage() | 2 | 9 | 15 | 20% | 6/30 |
| getUser() | 5 | 12 | 5 | 40% | 4/10 |

**Table 3.** Methods to Which Developer Y Has Contributed

| Method Name | Usage | LWUsage | Current LOC | % Contributed | Dev/Total (Contributed LOC) |
|---|---|---|---|---|---|
| assignAndNotify() | 5 | 24 | 10 | 40% | 8/20 |
| sendMessage() | 2 | 36 | 15 | 80% | 24/30 |
| deleteMessage() | 1 | 20 | 10 | 100% | 20/20 |

**Developer Contribution Analysis.** After the data is processed, we calculate the metrics for each developer. The calculated metrics include the LWDH-Index, DH-Index, and Total Contributed LOC, as shown in Table 4. The Total Contributed LOC is calculated as the total number of LOCs that the developer has contributed to the methods.

**Table 4.** Developers Indexes Calculation Result

| Developer | LWDH-Index | DH-Index | Total Contributed LOC |
|---|---|---|---|
| X | 3 | 2 | 22 |
| Y | 3 | 2 | 52 |

**Present the Data in DevScholar.** Finally, the processed data are displayed to the user. In the application, the user can select a developer to see their processed data. Developer data, such as their associated names and emails, the number of methods attributed to them, co-developers, the calculated indexes, and the methods attributed to them. On the same page, the top developers of the project, with their calculated indexes, are shown in an ordered manner based on the LWDH-Index by default. The developers can be sorted according to any of the other metrics. After clicking on a method, the method's developers and the number of LOCs they contributed are displayed. With these features of our application, we provide a user-friendly interface to navigate through the methods and developers of the methods in the history of the project.

## 3    Validation

We started our validation approach in the absence of a definitive ground truth, which prevented us from using conventional validation techniques. Validating the developer contribution metrics that embrace a method that deviates from conventional norms has been a point of contention [21]. Therefore, we conducted a comparative case analysis by contrasting the capabilities and top developers identified by GitHub Insights with those identified by our tool for four OSS projects. Our goal was to generate illustrative examples to highlight the differences and discuss the advantages and disadvantages. In the following subsections, we discuss the selection of sample projects and provide a comparison with GitHub Insight.

### 3.1    Selection of OSS Projects

We first determined relevant criteria to select the projects for our analysis from GitHub [2]. The first criterion was the programming language, where we focused on Java, as DevScholar relies on CodeShovel, which is Java-based. We aimed to include projects with a substantial history of changes to ensure rich data on method modifications. Thus, our second and third criteria required projects to have (>2000) commits and (>1000) pull requests. The fourth criterion was a contributor count (>100), as a larger, more diverse contributor base increases the likelihood of encountering edge cases for further analysis. Lastly, we ensured project popularity, selecting those with (>25000) stars on GitHub. Using these criteria, we employed the GitHub search tool by Dabic et al. [9] to filter and select suitable projects. There were 64 projects that fit the criteria we mentioned above, due to page limitations, we selected four representative projects at random from the filtered set as shown in Table 5, and ran DevScholar on them.

Due to the similarity of the results of the analyzed projects and the page limitation, only the results of one OSS project, Apollo, are discussed. Data extraction was completed on 8 October 2024. The results of this project are discussed in the following subsection.

**Table 5.** Selected Projects

| Project | Stars | Contributors | Commits | Pull Requests |
|---------|-------|--------------|---------|---------------|
| Apollo | 29.3k | 162 | 2925 | 1734 |
| Spring Boot | 76k | 1137 | 52691 | 6656 |
| Retrofit | 43.3k | 160 | 2453 | 1459 |
| Dubbo | 40.7k | 592 | 8291 | 7673 |

## 3.2 Comparison of DevScholar Results with GitHub's Insights (Number of Commits)

In Table 6, the GitHub Insights ranking of developers, their total commits, the DH-Index ranking and value, the LWDH-Index ranking, the value, and the total contributed LOC and methods of developers are given. Looking at the GitHub Insights and the DevScholar results of the Apollo project in Table 6, we find that the rankings are similar but display several notable differences. For example, although dev1 has the highest number of commits, it comes second in both the DH-Index and LWDH-Index rankings. This is an interesting case, as the commits dev1 has made are four times dev2's commits, so dev1 could be expected to be ranked first in all metrics. We can also see from DevScholar that dev2 has contributed to 1437 methods with a total LOC of 13882, while dev1 has contributed to 1146 methods with a total LOC of 11624. DevScholar metrics include usage as a proxy of contributions' reusability, which puts dev2 above dev1 in Table 6. Also, DevScholar disregards empty LOCs and comments, avoiding their potentially disproportionate inflationary effect.

**Table 6.** Comparison of GitHub Insights, DH-Index and LWDH-Index Ranking of Developers for Apollo Project

| GitHub Insights | | DH-Index | | LWDH-Index | | | |
|---------|---------------|---------|-------|---------|-------|-----------|---------|
| Ranking | No of Commits | Ranking | Value | Ranking | Value | Total LOC | Methods |
| dev1 | 1140 | dev2 | 18 | dev2 | 62 | 13882 | 1437 |
| dev2 | 252 | dev1 | 13 | dev1 | 48 | 11624 | 1146 |
| dev3 | 135 | dev3 | 10 | dev5 | 32 | 2541 | 341 |
| dev4 | 47 | dev4 | 8 | dev4 | 28 | 1992 | 316 |
| dev5 | 47 | dev5 | 7 | dev3 | 24 | 2674 | 228 |
| dev6 | 37 | dev8 | 7 | dev11 | 18 | 691 | 94 |
| dev7 | 33 | dev6 | 5 | dev12 | 17 | 751 | 99 |
| dev8 | 30 | dev11 | 4 | dev8 | 16 | 1015 | 252 |
| dev9 | 24 | dev12 | 4 | dev14 | 13 | 235 | 27 |
| dev10 | 12 | dev13 | 4 | dev6 | 12 | 425 | 75 |

We noticed that dev7, dev9, and dev10 are not in the top 10 developers in the DevScholar ranking system. dev7 is ranked $34^{th}$ in the DH-Index and $32^{nd}$ in the LWDH-Index ranking. The differences between these rankings are much higher. When we go through dev7's contributed methods, we see that dev7 has contributed to one method with a usage of four, while the usage of other methods is zero. We can argue that dev7's method contribution is minimal concerning their usage in the code, so dev7 does not appear in DevScholar's top 10 listing. In addition, dev9 is $19^{th}$ in the DH-Index and $12^{th}$ in the LWDH-Index ranking, while dev10 is $29^{th}$ in the DH-Index and also $22^{nd}$ in the LWDH-Index ranking. Neither developer is in the top 10 in DevScholar, although they are in GitHub Insights. This difference again stems from the same phenomenon: both dev9 and dev10's contributed methods have few or zero usages.

Our last observation is about dev1: the most used method of dev1 is a getter method with a usage of 71 and LOC of three. The seventh most used method is not a getter/setter method; its usage is 15, and LOC is 13. The LWUsages of these methods are 124 and 208, respectively. While getter/setter methods are easier to write and tend to have higher usage, their significant impact on rankings is questionable. LWDH-Index compensates for the effect trivial methods can have on the rankings by equalizing long methods' contributions relative to those of short methods: this can, in turn, prevent many short methods with plenty of usage from assigning higher scores to one developer and fewer methods with significant content but less usage from assigning lower scores to another developer.

## 4 Related Work

### 4.1 H-Index in Software Development

Capiluppi et al. [5], to our knowledge, was the first to apply the concept of H-Index in software development. They formulated three different H-Index-based indexes to evaluate the developer contributions over multiple OSS projects as discussed in the introduction. However, our aim throughout this study is to quantify and evaluate the contributions within a single project. Ding et al. [11] proposed four H-Index-based metrics to identify key classes in a weighted class network of software such that the nodes represent the classes, the edges imply the dependency between classes, and the weights are given based on the number of dependencies between classes. While this study focuses on identifying key classes, our study focuses on the developers themselves and their contributions.

### 4.2 Identifying Key Developers

Orrei et al. [21] identified key developers in software projects using the *Pony Factor* metric, which defines core contributors as those responsible for more than 50% of total commits, calculated across parameters such as total changed LOCs, recent contributions, and file types. Similarly, Yamashita et al. [24] used commit-based, LOC-based, and access-based heuristics, identifying core developers as those responsible for 80% of total commits or LOC changes, or as developers with write access and contributions. Joblin et al. [17] took a relational approach, analyzing both frequency-based metrics (commit and LOC counts) and network-based metrics, like centrality and connectivity, to distinguish core and peripheral developers. Çetin et al. [6,7] identify key developers by constructing an artifact graph with nodes representing developers, change sets, files, and issues, and edges based on commits, reviews, issue links, and file inclusions. While these studies focus on identifying core developers, we aim to quantify and evaluate developer contributions in terms of code reusability.

### 4.3    Assessing Developer Contributions

Previous work on evaluating developer contributions has employed diverse metrics and methodologies. Ren et al. [22] developed DevRank, utilizing PageRank based on method usage and applying NLP and ML techniques to commit messages to detect non-code contributions. De Bassi et al. [10] used software quality metrics, while Curry et al. [8] highlighted First Authorship and Recency of Modification as key indicators by correlating development history metrics. Other approaches, such as those by Nagwani and Verma [20] and Gousios et al. [12], assessed contributions using combined metrics like bug-fix frequency, comment volume, and repository activities. In contrast, our approach focuses solely on direct codebase contributions. Lima et al. [19] assessed developer contributions using metrics such as LOC, method complexity, and bug-fixing activities, finding code contribution and complexity metrics positively received, while bug-related metrics were viewed negatively.

Another notable research stream addresses the bus factor—the minimum number of developers whose loss would stall a project. Avelino et al. [3] first operationalised this risk by mining commit history and file ownership; in a survey of 67 systems, 84% of practitioners agreed that their tool correctly identified the main authors. Jabrayilzade et al. [16] broadened the metric by incorporating code-review activity and meeting participation, and an industry survey confirmed that engineers regard bus-factor tracking as critical for project health. Complementing these algorithmic advances, Klimov et al. [18] released Bus Factor Explorer, a web tool that computes the metric and offers interactive treemap visualisations and "what-if" simulations to pinpoint at-risk components. Haratian et al. [14] introduced BFSig, which weights files by structural importance in the dependency graph and cuts estimation error by up to 18% while reducing false-negative risk cases. In contrast, our study evaluates contributions at the granularity of individual methods—tracking who implemented each method, how those methods are reused, and the exact lines of code each developer added—yielding a finer-grained perspective on knowledge concentration and bus-factor risk.

### 4.4 Comparison Against Existing Methodologies

This study addresses the complex challenge of quantifying developer contributions, where no universally accepted baseline exists. GitHub Insights offers metrics based on commits and LOC changes but lacks quality considerations, treating all LOCs equally. DevScholar, by contrast, introduces nuanced metrics that differentiate high- and low-quality contributions based on reusability. Orrei et al. [21] introduced Pony Factor metrics to identify key developers; we compared their "Ponies onLines" factors with our LWDH-Index, finding alignment in identifying top developers in the Apollo and Spring Boot projects. Unlike Orrei et al. [21], who only identify key developers, DevScholar evaluates all contributors, resolves aliasing issues for accurate rankings, and provides detailed breakdowns of LWDH-Index scores with method-level granularity. It also offers visualization options, enabling in-depth exploration of contributions across GitHub projects.

## 5 Conclusion

In this study, we introduced two indexes to evaluate the quality of the developers' contributions from a reusability perspective. The first metric, called the DH-Index, applies the H-Index concept by treating method usage similarly to publication citations. While beneficial, it has some limitations as a result of only considering usage to quantify method-level contributions. The second metric developed within this study is the LWDH-Index, which considers the LOC of a method, the usage of the method, and the percentage of the developer's contribution to the method. We also implemented "DevScholar"[2], designed to calculate metrics and present results in a user-friendly interface. The replication package[3] contains the datasets, scripts, and documentation needed to reproduce our results and adapt the tool to new contexts.

## References

1. Fuzzywuzzy, fuzzy string matching in python. https://pypi.org/project/fuzzywuzzy/. Accessed 6 Oct 2024
2. Github. https://github.com/. Accessed 01 July 2023
3. Avelino, G., Passos, L., Hora, A., Valente, M.T.: A novel approach for estimating truck factors. In: 2016 IEEE 24th International Conference on Program Comprehension (ICPC), pp. 1–10. IEEE (2016)
4. Bock, T., Alznauer, N., Joblin, M., Apel, S.: Automatic core-developer identification on github: a validation study. ACM Trans. Softw. Eng. Methodol. (2023)
5. Capiluppi, A., Serebrenik, A., Youssef, A.: Developing an h-index for OSS developers. In: 2012 9th IEEE Working Conference on Mining Software Repositories (MSR), pp. 251–254 (2012)
6. Çetin, H.A., Tüzün, E.: Analyzing developer contributions using artifact traceability graphs. Empirical Softw. Engg. **27**(3) (2022)

---

[2] https://devscholar.netlify.app/.
[3] https://zenodo.org/records/15501808.

7. Çetin, H.A., Tüzün, E.: Identifying key developers using artifact traceability graphs. In: Proceedings of the 16th ACM International Conference on Predictive Models and Data Analytics in Software Engineering, pp. 51–60 (2020)

8. Cury, O., Avelino, G., Santos Neto, P., Britto, R., Túlio Valente, M.: Identifying source code file experts. In: Proceedings of the 16th ACM / IEEE International Symposium on Empirical Software Engineering and Measurement, ESEM 2022, pp. 125–136. Association for Computing Machinery, New York (2022)

9. Dabic, O., Aghajani, E., Bavota, G.: Sampling projects in github for MSR studies. In: 18th IEEE/ACM International Conference on Mining Software Repositories, MSR 2021, pp. 560–564. IEEE (2021)

10. de Bassi, P.R., Wanderley, G.M.P., Banali, P.H., Paraiso, E.C.: Measuring developers' contribution in source code using quality metrics. In: 2018 IEEE 22nd International Conference on Computer Supported Cooperative Work in Design ((CSCWD)), pp. 39–44 (2018)

11. Ding, Y., Li, B., He, P.: An improved approach to identifying key classes in weighted software network. Math. Probl. Eng. **1–9**, 2016 (2016)

12. Gousios, G., Kalliamvakou, E., Spinellis, D.: Measuring developer contribution from software repository data. In: Proceedings of the 2008 International Working Conference on Mining Software Repositories, MSR 2008, pp. 129–132. Association for Computing Machinery, New York (2008)

13. Grund, F., Chowdhury, S.A., Bradley, N., Hall, B., Holmes, R.: CodeShovel: constructing method-level source code histories. In: Proceedings of the International Conference on Software Engineering (ICSE) (2021)

14. Haratian, V., Evtikhiev, M., Derakhshanfar, P., Tüzün, E., Kovalenko, V.: BFSig: leveraging file significance in bus factor estimation. In: Proceedings of the 31st ACM Joint European Software Engineering Conference and Symposium on the Foundations of Software Engineering, ESEC/FSE 2023, pp. 1926–1936. Association for Computing Machinery, New York (2023)

15. Hirsch, J.: An index to quantify an individual's scientific research output. Proc. Natl. Acad. Sci. U.S.A. **102**, 16569–165672 (2005)

16. Jabrayilzade, E., Evtikhiev, M., Tüzün, E., Kovalenko, V.: Bus factor in practice. In: Proceedings of the 44th International Conference on Software Engineering: Software Engineering in Practice, ICSE-SEIP 2022, pp. 97–106. Association for Computing Machinery, New York (2022)

17. Joblin, M., Apel, S., Hunsen, C., Mauerer, W.: Classifying developers into core and peripheral: an empirical study on count and network metrics. In: 2017 IEEE/ACM 39th International Conference on Software Engineering (ICSE), pp. 164–174. IEEE (2017)

18. Klimov, E., Ahmed, M.U., Sviridov, N., Derakhshanfar, P., Tüzün, E., Kovalenko, V.: Bus factor explorer. In: 2023 38th IEEE/ACM International Conference on Automated Software Engineering (ASE), pp. 2018–2021 (2023)

19. Lima, J., Treude, C., Figueira Filho, F., Kulesza, U.: Assessing developer contribution with repository mining-based metrics. In: 2015 IEEE International Conference on Software Maintenance and Evolution (ICSME) (2015)

20. Nagwani, N., Verma, S.: Rank-me: a Java tool for ranking team members in software bug repositories. J. Softw. Eng. Appl. **05**, 255–261 (2012)

21. Orrei, V., Raglianti, M., Nagy, C., Lanza, M.: Contribution-based firing of developers? In: ESEC/FSE 2023 Ideas, Visions and Reflections (2023)

22. Ren, J., Yin, H., Hu, Q., Fox, A., Koszek, W.: Towards quantifying the development value of code contributions. In: Proceedings of the 2018 26th ACM Joint Meeting

on European Software Engineering Conference and Symposium on the Foundations of Software Engineering, ESEC/FSE 2018, pp. 775–779. Association for Computing Machinery, New York (2018)

23. Sun, Y., Xu, Z., Liu, C., Zhang, Y., Liu, Y.: Who is the real hero? Measuring developer contribution via multi-dimensional data integration. In: 2023 38th IEEE/ACM International Conference on Automated Software Engineering (ASE), pp. 825–836. IEEE Computer Society, Los Alamitos (2023)

24. Yamashita, K., McIntosh, S., Kamei, Y., Hassan, A.E., Ubayashi, N.: Revisiting the applicability of the pareto principle to core development teams in open source software projects. In: Proceedings of the 14th International Workshop on Principles of Software Evolution, IWPSE 2015, pp. 46–55. Association for Computing Machinery, New York (2015)

# Teaching Software Engineering for Artificial Intelligence: An Experience Report

Fabio Palomba⑩, Gianmario Voria⑩, Alessandra Parziale⑩,
Viviana Pentangelo⑩, Antonio Della Porta⑩, Vincenzo De Martino⑩,
Gilberto Recupito⑩, and Giammaria Giordano(✉)⑩

Software Engineering Lab, Department Of Computer Science—University Of Salerno,
Salerno, Italy
{fpalomba,gvoria,alparziale,vpentangelo,adellaporta,
vdemartino,grecupito,giagiordano}@unisa.it

**Abstract.** As Artificial Intelligence (AI) becomes integral to modern software systems, the software engineering (SE) research community has been actively developing methods, tools, and frameworks to address software quality assurance of AI-enabled systems across critical dimensions such as robustness, ethics, security, and sustainability. These contributions are designed to tackle the complexity of AI systems, such as their probabilistic nature, data dependencies, and societal impact, ensuring they meet the standards of modern software engineering. These advances have, in turn, inspired educators to introduce Software Engineering for Artificial Intelligence (SE4AI) courses aimed at preparing the next generation of software engineers, with notable success examples already reported in the literature. In this *experience report*, we contribute to the field of SE4AI education by sharing lessons learned in designing and teaching a course that addresses the unique characteristics of AI-enabled systems. Drawing on insights gathered over four iterations of the course, we discuss how students perceive and apply key software engineering concepts, the challenges they encounter with tools and techniques, and how project-based learning bridges the gap between theoretical knowledge and real-world application. Furthermore, we address the broader educational challenges, such as interdisciplinary barriers and the integration of rapidly evolving AI technologies, and provide recommendations to enhance SE4AI education. By reflecting on these experiences, we aim to offer insights and strategies for improving the teaching of SE4AI topics.

**Keywords:** Software Engineering for Artificial Intelligence ·
Experience Report · Software Engineering Education

## 1 Introduction

The rapid growth of Artificial Intelligence (AI) has transformed industries and everyday applications, becoming integral to sectors like healthcare and finance by enhancing efficiency, decision-making, and innovation [27,29,38,41].

D. Taibi and D. Smite (Eds.): SEAA 2025, LNCS 16083, pp. 214–230, 2026.
https://doi.org/10.1007/978-3-032-04207-1_15

This widespread adoption of AI has introduced unique challenges for software engineering, prompting the Software Engineering (SE) research community to establish a dedicated field known as Software Engineering for Artificial Intelligence (SE4AI). SE4AI focuses on extending traditional SE practices to meet the demands of AI-driven systems. Bosch et al. [8] described AI engineering as integrating specialized technologies and processes essential for building AI-enabled systems, while Martínez-Fernández et al. [24] characterized these systems as architectures combining both traditional software components and AI-specific elements. Sculley et al. [34] noted that AI components often constitute only a small part of such systems, which are supported by conventional software that enables and manages AI functionalities.

AI-enabled systems face challenges beyond those of traditional software projects, particularly in ensuring quality across dimensions such as robustness, scalability, ethics, and risk management [8]. These challenges arise from the inherent characteristics of AI-enabled systems, including their probabilistic behavior, reliance on large-scale data, and significant societal impact [25]. Systematic processes and practices are essential for addressing these issues and for ensuring that software meets predefined quality standards. These standards cover both functional attributes, such as correctness, and non-functional ones, such as security, fairness, transparency, and environmental sustainability.

The growing need for advanced practices in AI-enabled systems has motivated educators to develop SE4AI courses that prepare the next generation of software engineers. These courses aim to equip students with the skills to develop, evaluate, and maintain systems integrating AI, while tackling the distinct challenges these systems present. Inspired by notable examples in the literature [20, 22], this *experience report* contributes to the field of SE4AI education by sharing preliminary insights from designing and teaching a course focused on the attributes of AI-enabled systems. We discuss how students perceive and apply key concepts, the challenges they encounter with tools and techniques, and how project-based learning bridges the gap between theoretical understanding and real-world application. Furthermore, we address broader educational challenges, such as interdisciplinary barriers and the need to integrate rapidly evolving AI technologies. By reflecting on these experiences, we aim at offering recommendations for advancing SE4AI education and supporting future research and practice in preparing software engineers for the complexities of AI-enabled systems.

## 2   Related Works

For decades, the primary focus of software engineering research and education related to artificial intelligence has been on leveraging AI techniques to address SE challenges, often referred to as *Artificial Intelligence for Software Engineering* (AI4SE) [26]. This area includes, for instance, the use of AI approaches to predict and manage software defects [7, 18], generate test cases [3, 4, 9], detect and refactor source code design flaws [2, 5, 23], or optimize software development processes [37, 39, 40]. Educational courses aligned with this focus are now widely diffused, with many examples discussed in experience reports and educational articles describing how to emphasize the application of AI methods in traditional software engineering contexts [14, 15, 36].

In recent years, there has been a notable shift toward studying the application of software engineering principles and practices in the development of Artificial Intelligence-enabled systems, often termed *Software Engineering for Artificial Intelligence* (SE4AI) [24]. This paradigm has the opposite goal of AI4SE, namely that of addressing the engineering challenges posed by AI components, such as managing data and model quality, handling model evolution, and ensuring scalability and robustness in production systems. The SE4AI research community has grown rapidly, producing significant contributions to software quality assurance aspects of AI-enabled systems. A notable example is represented by the technical debt research field, where researchers attempted to study solutions to deal with AI debt, i.e., issues arising from the peculiar component and activities of AI-enabled systems, such as data dependencies, model versioning, and the maintenance of continuously evolving pipelines, making them harder to scale and manage over time. The seminal work by Sculley et al. [34] highlighted how these challenges differ from traditional software engineering debt, emphasizing risks like entanglement, undeclared consumers, and system-level anti-patterns that may impact other non-functional attributes of AI-enabled systems, including security and privacy [32]. Other rapidly growing research areas include ethics & fairness [13] and verification & validation [33]. In these areas, researchers have developed methodologies and tools to (i) detect and mitigate biases in AI models [12, 17, 31], (ii) support the robustness of AI-enabled systems to deal with non-deterministic nature of AI models [1, 11, 21].

The challenges of engineering AI-enabled systems have led to an even more pressing need to educate the next generation of software engineers with specialized knowledge and skills to address these complexities. In response to this need, many institutions have begun offering courses specifically focused on SE4AI—this was also fostered by the availability of books and teaching resources that emphasize the intersection of SE and AI engineering, like Smith's *"Machine Learning Systems"* [35], Hulten's *"Building Intelligent Systems"* [19], and Burkov's *"Machine Learning Engineering"* [10]. Among the most well-established courses on the matter, a notable case if the one of the *"Software Engineering for AI-enabled Systems"* course taught by Prof. Kästner at Carnegie Mellon University (CMU) [20]. The course combines theoretical foundations with practical assignments, leveraging real-world scenarios to teach students about AI system requirements, testing, deployment, and quality assurance practices. Similarly, Lanubile et al. [22] reported on teaching MLOps through project-based learning, emphasizing the importance of hands-on approaches to teach the complexities of AI system development and operations.

The course object of this experience report is inspired by the Kästner's course and indeed shares similar learning objectives. Specifically, it aims to (1) illustrate the engineering challenges in building production systems with machine learning (ML) components, beyond model creation; and (2) compare the roles, goals, and challenges faced by software engineers and data scientists in developing AI-enabled systems. While grounded in the foundational structure of the CMU's course, our course varies some aspects to (i) address the rapidly changing landscape of AI and (ii) adapt itself to the structure of our Master's degree:

**Teaching Material.** The topics of the course have been evolved to reflect recent advances in AI engineering. For instance, the course includes topics such as the analysis of Large Language Models, advances in fairness engineering, and considerations for ML sustainability. These additions are informed by the latest research in SE4AI, including insights from our own research projects on these themes, and periodically updated to provide students with a fresh research perspectives on the fast-growing topics of the course.

**Hands-on Education.** While the CMU course emphasizes assignments to build hands-on experience, our course adopts a semester-long team project to stimulate practical learning. This divergence was mainly due to the need of adopting a similar educational approach as other courses available in our Master's degree—the recommended guidelines are to let students engage with real-world challenges which, in our case, implies the application of SE4AI methods across the lifecycle of a project, from conception to evaluation, thereby fostering collaboration and problem-solving skills.

**Industry Integration.** Guest lectures from partner companies provide students with practical insights into SE4AI challenges. These lectures are complemented by case studies and experience reports. For instance, one of the case studies discussed in the course is the one by Beede et al. [6], who evaluated the deployment of a deep learning system for diabetic retinopathy detection in clinical settings, showing issues and challenges that motivate the need for software engineering instruments in AI-enabled system development.

## 3    The Software Engineering for Artificial Intelligence Course

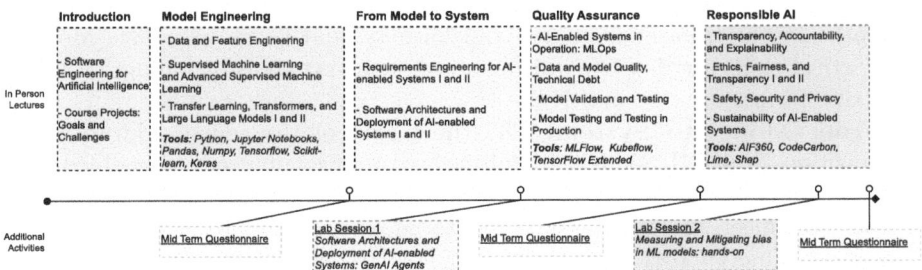

**Fig. 1.** Design and Timeline of the *"Software Engineering for Artificial Intelligence"* Course.

The course we base our experience on is entitled *"Software Engineering for Artificial Intelligence"* and is taught at the University of *Salerno*. It is designed for Master's students who have prior knowledge in functional and object-oriented programming, software engineering, and the fundamentals of artificial intelligence, obtained during their Bachelor's studies.

The course is part of the *"Software Engineering and IT Management"* curriculum within the Master's Degree in Computer Science, and provides 48 h of instruction (6 ECTS). The course aims to introduce students to end-to-end ML engineering, encompassing key phases from requirements gathering to verification, validation, and deployment. Now, in its fourth edition, the course is taught in English by a main lecturer and supported by multiple teaching assistants.

The teaching methods include: (1) *in-person lectures*, delivered by the main lecturer; (2) *laboratory sessions*, supervised by teaching assistants, focusing on hands-on practical work; (3) *individual study assignments*, where students independently explore specific topics and participate in discussions through a flipped-classroom approach; and (4) *classwork activities*, where students analyze case studies and reason about the application of SE practices introduced during lectures. Figure 1 provides a summary of the course design, including a timeline that illustrates how the course topics are delivered over time and how they interweave with the course's additional activities.

More specifically, the course is structured into five main parts: (1) *'Introduction to SE4AI'*; (2) *'Model Engineering'*, (3) *'From Model to System Engineering'*, (4) *'Quality Assurance'*, and (5) *'Responsible AI'*.

(1) **Introduction to SE4AI.** Students are introduced to the foundational concepts of SE4AI. Frontal lectures focus on comparing AI-enabled systems to traditional software systems. Additionally, this part provides an overview of key AI techniques underlying contemporary software systems, including data and feature engineering, search-based algorithms, and supervised learning.

(2) **Model Engineering.** The second part of the course focuses on building robust AI systems through model engineering. It begins with an overview of ML pipelines, emphasizing the critical roles of data preparation and feature engineering. Students then explore supervised ML, covering key concepts in model training, validation, and testing. The module progresses to advanced techniques such as deep learning and ensemble methods, followed by an in-depth look at transfer learning, transformers, and Large Language Models. Practical skills are developed using state-of-the-art tools including TENSOR-FLOW, SCIKIT-LEARN, and KERAS.

(3) **From Model to System.** The third part of the course addresses the transition from ML models to full-fledged and engineered AI-enabled systems, exploring the diverse shapes of SE4AI practices. It begins with requirements engineering, focusing on when to adopt ML, how to define functional and non-functional requirements, and how to set meaningful measurement goals. Students also learn techniques for gathering requirements. The module then explores the architectural design of AI-enabled systems, discussing common patterns like client-server, multi-tier, service-oriented, microservices,

and data-flow architectures. A laboratory session on Generative AI agents further enriches this part by examining current trends and system integration challenges in modern AI applications.

**(4) Quality Assurance** The fourth part of the course centers on the quality of AI-enabled systems. Students are first introduced to MLOps practices, covering essential topics such as model versioning, pipeline management, and infrastructure deployment. Tools such as MLFLOW, KUBEFLOW, and TENSORFLOW EXTENDED are introduced to facilitate these practices. The module covers data and model quality, as well as challenges like concept and data drift. Topics also include managing technical debt, validating and testing models, and strategies for testing in production. A case study offers students hands-on insight into cutting-edge research and practices in production-level AI system testing.

**(5) Responsible AI** The final module focuses on the ethical, legal, and societal implications of AI. It begins with an overview of transparency, accountability, and regulatory considerations, concluding with methods for achieving explainability in AI models. Students are introduced to fairness in ML, including techniques for detecting and mitigating bias through pre-processing, in-processing, and post-processing approaches, through a laboratory session. The section draws on recent research and real-world applications. Topics also include safety, security, and privacy, highlighting threats like adversarial attacks and techniques for robust system design. The module concludes with a discussion on the sustainability of AI-enabled systems, covering environmental impact and long-term maintainability insights from current research. Students use tools such as AIF360, LIME, SHAP, and CODECARBON to assess, monitor, and improve these quality attributes over time.

The course includes three individual mid-term questionnaires designed to assess students' comprehension of the material covered up to that point, as illustrated in Fig. 1. Each questionnaire consists of closed-ended questions focused on specific concepts discussed during the lectures. These assessments serve both as a tool to gauge students' understanding and as a component in determining their final evaluation.

In addition to the lectures and individual mid-term questionnaires, students are required to work on a team project, choosing between two project types. The first option involves developing a prototype of an AI-enabled system using the methods introduced in the course. The second option focuses on conducting a quality assurance analysis of an existing AI-enabled system, emphasizing specific properties such as fairness, robustness, or explainability. Student groups can range from 1 to 4 participants, depending on the scope of the project, which is preliminarily validated by the lecturer.

Finally, students are assessed through two components. At first, a project discussion, lasting 30 min: students present their team project (10 min) and engage in a discussion with the lecturer and teaching assistants (20 min) about the validity, limitations, and challenges encountered. The project discussion aims to evaluate students' abilities in engineering AI-enabled systems, as well as their capacity to effectively communicate the key methodological approaches and results achieved in their projects. Secondly, an oral examination, typically lasting from 45 to 60 min: students are tested on the theoretical and practical topics covered during the course.

The course attracts approximately 50 students every year. Over the four editions, we collected data on participants' background knowledge across various topics in AI and SE. Participation in the questionnaire was voluntary, and up to today, we have collected 91 answers to the background survey. This data was used to inform and fine-tune the course content, addressing gaps in knowledge where needed or adapting to students' advanced understanding in specific areas. During these years, 56% of participants had a Software Engineering background, while 22% of students came from the Data Science and Machine Learning domain. A small number of participants came from the Security or Cloud Computing domain, while the others were enrolled in the course through other types of university programs (e.g., Ph.D. students). The survey's design, along with the anonymized aggregated responses, can be found in our online appendix [30].

## 4    Experience Design and Report

This section presents the lessons learned from our four-year experience delivering the *"Software Engineering for Artificial Intelligence"* course at the University of *Salerno, Italy*. We outline the primary focus areas of our analysis and provide an account of the insights gained over the years.

### 4.1    Primary Focus Areas of Our Experience Report

This experience report is centered on the aspects of AI-enabled systems, as taught and applied in our course. The following focus areas highlight the key dimensions of our report, emphasizing the lessons learned in addressing specific challenges of AI-enabled systems.

**F1. Students' Perception of Course Topics.** We analyze students' perceptions of the topics covered in the course, focusing on their relevance to real-world AI engineering tasks. In particular, we concentrate on how students value the introduction of concepts such as technical debt, security, fairness, explainability, and verification & validation in the context of AI-enabled systems and whether they find these concepts practically useful in their projects. Through the analysis of feedback and project outcomes, we identify areas where students feel confident and areas where additional support or alternative teaching methods may be required.

**F2. Challenges in Understanding Concepts and Tools.** As further discussed in this paper, certain topics and tools introduced during the course posed significant challenges for students. These include advanced testing techniques for AI-enabled systems, methods to identify and mitigate AI debt, and tools for monitoring fairness and robustness. This focus area examines these difficulties and discusses approaches to help students overcome them. This focus area also explores the role of hands-on activities, case studies, and real-world examples in helping students bridge the gap between theoretical knowledge and practical application.

**F3. Challenges in SE4AI Projects.** The project component of the course serves as a testing ground for applying the methods taught to AI-enabled systems. We discuss the obstacles students encountered, such as integrating best practices into iterative ML development cycles, managing trade-offs between quality attributes (e.g., accuracy vs fairness), and using tools for monitoring and maintaining model attributes over time. In addition, we explore the socio-technical dynamics that arise during team-based projects, including how students collaborate to address conflicting priorities between software quality attributes and AI-specific goals.

**F4. Educational Challenges in Teaching AI-enabled Systems.** According to our experience, teaching on aspects as quality, robustness, ethics, security, and sustainability for AI-enabled systems introduces unique challenges, particularly given the rapidly evolving nature of AI technologies. This section explores issues such as keeping course content aligned with state-of-the-art practices, providing practical examples for abstract concepts, and ensuring students understand how traditional software practices apply in the context of AI.

To address these four focus areas, we systematically collected and analyzed student data across the four years the course has been offered. Specifically, we gathered demographic and academic background information for each cohort. In addition, at the end of each course edition, we conducted a survey to capture students' perceptions of the course, with a particular emphasis on the practical applicability of the topics, tools, and methods covered. The survey included both closed-ended and open-ended questions, and participation was not mandatory. Closed-ended questions use Likert-scale responses [28] to assess various aspects, such as (1) the complexity of the course, (2) the usefulness of the tools and methods taught, (3) the satisfaction with specific themes, (4) the usefulness of the hands-on and case study activities, and (5) the perceived practical applicability of the tools and methods studied in the course. Open-ended questions provide students the opportunity to elaborate on areas for improvement and share detailed reflections on their learning experiences, challenges encountered, and overall perception of the practicality of the course. The survey structure is accessible in our online appendix [30].

We analyzed the collected data using established research methods, treating our experience similarly to other survey-based studies conducted in the field [16]. Likert-scale responses from closed-ended questions were analyzed through descriptive statistics to identify patterns and trends in students' feedback. Responses to open-ended questions were examined using content analysis research methods, enabling the identification of recurring themes and insights into students' experiences. The most significant open-ended student sentences were extracted and represented through the symbol ✎ . In total, we collected 59 survey participants over the years. For the sake of space limitations, our experience report treats the four course's editions in an aggregated manner (as opposed to reporting year-by-year trends); nonetheless, we plan to further elaborate on the evolution of the course as part of our future research agenda. The results of these data analysis procedures informed our discussion of focus areas **F1**, **F2**, and **F3**. As for **F4**, insights were derived from periodic retrospective meetings between the main lecturer and the teaching assistants, complemented by direct feedback collected from students who previously completed the course.

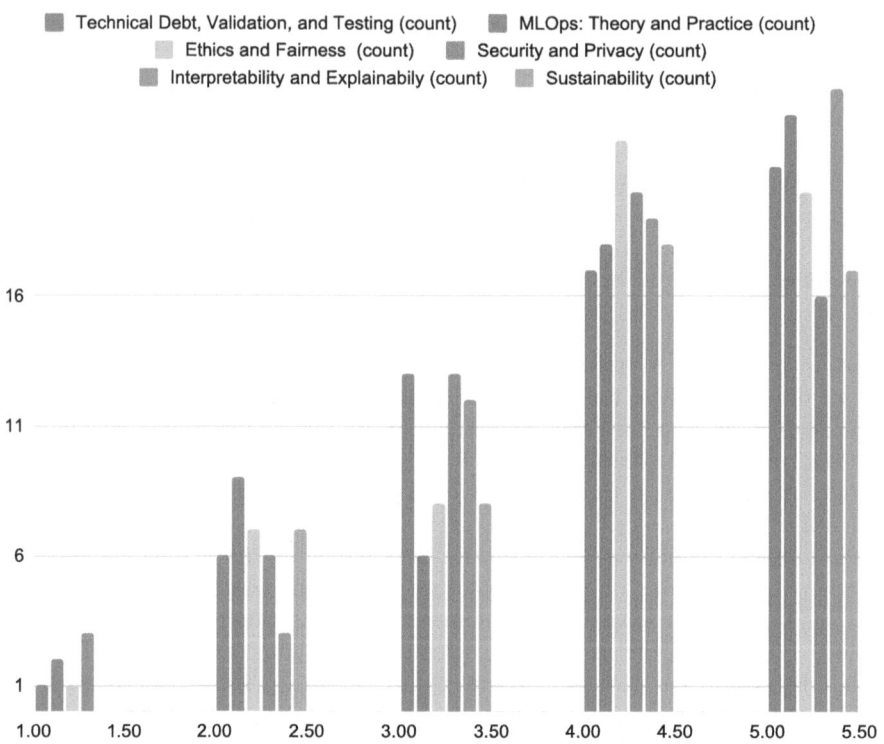

**Fig. 2.** Students' perceived usefulness of topics during the course.

### 4.2   Insights and Implications from Our Experience

According to the data acquired over the four editions of the course and our own retrospective, this section discusses the main lessons learned for each of the primary focus area.

**F1 - Students' Perception of the Topics.** Figure 2 shows students' perceived usefulness of topics discussed during the course, rated on a scale from

1 (least useful) to 5 (most useful). Many participants valued the introduction of non-functional quality aspects such as fairness and explainability while also pushing for greater concreteness and connections to real-world applications. For instance, one participant emphasized the importance of approaching the subject matter from a highly practical perspective. Several students highlighted that a sense of concreteness in how the subject is presented is essential for fully understanding its concepts and usefulness. This feedback suggests a potential shift in teaching topics, moving toward in-person lectures that focus less on standalone theoretical definitions and more on integrating these definitions into concrete, practical examples.

### F1.1 - Lesson Learned

Non-functional requirements such as fairness, explainability, and sustainability are essential in AI-enabled system development but often challenging for students to grasp in isolation. Embedding these topics in practical, real-world scenarios—through case studies or applied assignments—can improve student engagement and conceptual retention across diverse SE4AI contexts.

Concerning less appreciated topics, our analysis revealed that *technical debt* and *MLOps* emerged as areas with significant room for improvement, with MLOps being particularly variable in students' perceptions. This variability did not derive from a lack of interest; on the contrary, MLOps was among the most frequently discussed topics in open-ended questions. The feedback indicated that students considered it one of the *most interesting and promising* areas but felt that more time is needed to understand its relevance and applicability fully. In particular, advanced topics like technical debt and MLOps require an understanding of the long-term evolution of AI-enabled systems, which may not be fully conveyed within the constraints of a two-month course. This likely highlights the need for alternative teaching strategies, e.g., longitudinal case studies or follow-up courses, to provide deeper engagement with these advanced topics.

### F1.2 - Lesson Learned

Topics like MLOps and technical debt demand systems-level thinking and familiarity with long-term software evolution. Educators should consider spreading these concepts across multiple modules or courses, or supporting them with longitudinal case studies, to reinforce their practical relevance and complexity.

### F2 - Bridging Conceptual Gaps with Practical Tools.

Students emphasized difficulties with some advanced topics and tools introduced during the course. They specifically highlighted the need for a more gradual introduction and additional focus on complex concepts or tools, such as generative adversarial networks (GANs), MLOps, or TensorFlow. This may stem from the diverse range of technologies introduced, which often assume a technical machine learning background that should not be taken for granted. As one student commented: 💬 *"...furthermore, I would dedicate more time and effort to recent topics such as MLOps, GANs, etc., as these are interesting but need more laboratory sessions..."*, which confirms the importance of hands-on practice in the teaching process and highlights the potential for implementing active learning approaches, such as flipped classrooms and lab sessions, to address the more challenging aspects and enhance students' understanding and application of these concepts.

---

**💡 F2 - Lesson Learned**

Advanced tools common in AI engineering—such as TensorFlow or SHAP—can pose a steep learning curve, especially for students without strong ML backgrounds. Gradually introducing tools in problem-driven contexts, supported by hands-on labs, helps reduce overload and builds practical confidence.

---

**F3 - Challenges in SE4AI Projects.** One of the challenges revealed was the course's project-based nature. The feedback analysis revealed that integrating specific practices into a software project can be challenging and not easily intuitive in interactive machine learning development cycles. This may indicate that there is a need to give particular space to the project activity so that each student can learn and transpose the concepts to what they are working on, whose contexts were disparate, from medical applications to smart agriculture models. Concerning technical tools and methods, students' comments align with discussions in the other focus areas, as these tools are frequently revealed to be challenging for students to understand and apply in a short time. Despite this, students perceived their tutors as highly actively supporting them during the project and did not deem it too complex. This indicates that certain technical tools pose specific challenges, compensated by easier challenges in other SE4AI areas.

---

**💡 F3.1 - Lesson Learned**

Integrating SE practices into AI-enabled systems is not always intuitive for students, particularly in iterative ML workflows. SE4AI educators should allocate dedicated space within project work for students to contextualize concepts and explore quality trade-offs relevant to their domain.

---

As highlighted in Sect. 3, the SE4AI course brings together participants from diverse knowledge areas, such as Software Engineering, Security, or Data Science and Machine Learning. This diversity has revealed broader socio-technical challenges, including differing team dynamics stemming from varied perspectives on project needs. These insights highlight the importance of providing both technical and organizational support to help students navigate the complexities of collaborative activities in AI engineering. More importantly, it seems that project-based education may effectively simulate real-world conditions, offering students a valuable experience that prepares them for interdisciplinary collaboration in professional environments.

> **♀ F3.2 - Lesson Learned**
>
> SE4AI projects often bring together students from diverse backgrounds (e.g., software engineering, ML, cloud). These perspectives can lead to valuable, real-world-style team dynamics, but may also cause misalignments. Educators should actively support interdisciplinary collaboration with coaching or reflective checkpoints.

**F4 - Educational Challenges in Teaching SE4AI.** Upon collection of the students' feedback and our retrospective, we could identify several challenges for educators related to the teaching of engineering practices for AI-enabled systems.

*Keeping the Course Up to Date.* One of the primary challenges encountered in our experience is maintaining course content that reflects state-of-the-art practices. The rapid advances in AI, especially given by the rise of Large Language Models and Foundation Models, require continuous updates to the course design. While regular updates are a common requirement for most courses, this challenge is especially pronounced in the context of SE4AI. This applies not only to the topics themselves but also to the training required for teaching novel tools and frameworks effectively.

In our case, we implemented a collaborative approach by creating a shared channel where the lecturer and teaching assistants could exchange research articles, tutorials, and other resources. These materials are then analyzed during multiple ad-hoc meetings held prior to the course's start. The objective of these sessions is to evaluate how disruptive techniques and tools can be seamlessly integrated into the course. While this strategy has been sometimes effective, it also highlights a significant challenge: *finding the right balance between breadth and depth in course content.* Covering too many topics superficially risks overwhelming students and diluting their understanding, while focusing too deeply on a few areas can leave critical knowledge gaps.

Our experience suggests that the core lectures should focus on well-established and widely applicable methods, avoiding the frequent introduction of topics that are still rapidly evolving. Simultaneously, the exploration of the latest technologies can be reserved for classwork sessions or industry talks, where students can engage with cutting-edge topics through practical case studies. This approach allows students to cultivate curiosity and deepen their knowledge independently, without disrupting the overall course structure.

At the same time, we really see the potential added value of *collaborative efforts among educators* in sharing teaching materials and best practices. Such collaboration could significantly reduce the burden on individual instructors to independently track every development in this fast-evolving field. We hope this experience report may open a broader discussion among SE4AI educators, encouraging the development of shared resources to support the community.

> **♥ F4.1 - Lesson Learned**
>
> SE4AI content evolves rapidly, making it difficult to maintain both breadth and depth. A recommended strategy is to focus core lectures on foundational methods, while reserving rapidly evolving topics for exploratory sessions (e.g., case studies, guest lectures, or flipped classrooms).

***Accounting for Domain Specificity.*** The diversity of domains where AI is applied introduces additional complexities, as the quality assurance requirements of systems like medical diagnostics, recommendation engines, and autonomous vehicles vary significantly. Understanding these differences is essential for students to grasp how engineering practices must be adapted to meet domain-specific challenges. In our case, we incorporated diverse case studies and industry talks to provide students with real-world examples of how such practices are applied in different contexts. For instance, classwork sessions might explore fairness in medical AI applications or robustness in autonomous systems. While generally satisfactory, the results of these sessions revealed a key limitation: *students often understood the general idea of tailoring practices based on context but struggled to provide concrete, tailored solutions for engineering AI-enabled systems.* This gap suggests a need for more immersive and interactive learning methods to bridge the divide between theoretical understanding and real-world application.

In this respect, we are considering enhancing learning by integrating *game-based strategies.* For instance, by designing interactive scenarios or simulations, students could actively experiment with applying SE practices across various domains, exploring trade-offs, and crafting solutions themselves. Such an approach could not only foster active learning and critical thinking but also allow students to engage directly with diverse challenges in a controlled yet dynamic environment. We see this as an opportunity for further research and innovation in SE4AI education. The design and evaluation of effective game-based learning tools tailored to SE4AI could significantly enhance students' ability to connect theory to practice.

> **♥ F4.2 - Lesson Learned**
>
> Quality assurance challenges vary significantly across AI domains (e.g., healthcare vs. recommendation systems). Using varied case studies is helpful, but immersive techniques such as domain simulations or game-based learning can deepen student understanding of domain-specific trade-offs.

***Cultural Barriers and Educational Boundaries.*** Teaching SE4AI presents unique challenges due to its interdisciplinary nature, the cognitive shift required for students, and the incorporation of ethical and societal considerations. A key difficulty lies in the inherent interdisciplinarity: many topics, such as MLOps, rely on foundational knowledge from areas like software architecture, cloud infrastructure, and data engineering. A single course cannot comprehensively cover these domains, requiring a *coordinated educational effort across multiple courses and disciplines.* For example, a software architecture course might address containerization and microservices, while a data engineering course could cover pipeline design and data quality, both crucial for MLOps. Viewing SE4AI education as part of a broader learning network allows each course to contribute to building the necessary skills. In our case, coordination across different research groups posed a challenge, though improved collaboration among SE4AI educators may help address this issue. Another major barrier involves guiding students through the shift from traditional software engineering principles to those needed for AI-enabled systems. Unlike conventional systems, AI-enabled systems are probabilistic, data-driven, and less deterministic, which often creates a *cognitive gap* for students. Bridging this gap requires emphasizing AI-specific characteristics while showing how traditional practices, such as modularity and monitoring, remain relevant. Explicitly contrasting these paradigms and using hands-on activities can help ease the transition.

Finally, integrating ethical and societal dimensions adds further complexity. Topics like fairness, transparency, and environmental impact push students *to think beyond technical implementation and consider broader consequences.* Real-world failures and their repercussions can make these themes more relatable and impactful. We have observed increasing interest among students in pursuing ethical SE practices in their thesis work, reflecting the engaging nature of this educational approach.

> **♀ F4.3 - Lesson Learned**
>
> The interdisciplinary nature of SE4AI—spanning software engineering, ethics, ML, and systems design—creates both pedagogical and curricular challenges. Coordination across courses, combined with contrastive examples and societal case studies, can help students bridge conceptual gaps and recognize the broader impact of AI-enabled systems.

## 5   Conclusion

This experience report presents preliminary insights from our four-year Master's course, *"Software Engineering for Artificial Intelligence"*. The course introduces students to end-to-end ML engineering, covering key phases from requirements to verification, validation, and deployment, with a focus on the challenges and practices relevant to AI-enabled systems.

We discuss lessons learned across four focus areas, highlighting key challenges in teaching software engineering for AI. These initial findings offer insights for future research and educational efforts, which we plan to further refine and extend to better support the next generation of SE/AI engineers.

**Acknowledgment.** We acknowledge the use of ChatGPT-4 to ensure linguistic accuracy and enhance the readability of this article.

We acknowledge the support of the European Union - NextGenerationEU through the Italian Ministry of University and Research, Project PRIN 2022 PNRR "FRINGE: context-aware FaiRness engineerING in complex software systEms" (grant n. P2022553SL, CUP: D53D23017340001), Project FAIR (PE0000013) under the NRRP MUR program funded by the EU - NGEU.

# References

1. Abdessalem, R.B., Nejati, S., Briand, L.C., Stifter, T.: Testing vision-based control systems using learnable evolutionary algorithms. In: Proceedings of the 40th International Conference on Software Engineering, pp. 1016–1026 (2018)
2. Albuquerque, D., et al.: Managing technical debt using intelligent techniques-a systematic mapping study. IEEE Trans. Software Eng. **49**(4), 2202–2220 (2022)
3. Ali, S., Briand, L.C., Hemmati, H., Panesar-Walawege, R.K.: A systematic review of the application and empirical investigation of search-based test case generation. IEEE Trans. Software Eng. **36**(6), 742–762 (2009)
4. Anand, S., et al.: An orchestrated survey of methodologies for automated software test case generation. J. Syst. Softw. **86**(8), 1978–2001 (2013)
5. Azeem, M.I., Palomba, F., Shi, L., Wang, Q.: Machine learning techniques for code smell detection: a systematic literature review and meta-analysis. Inf. Softw. Technol. **108**, 115–138 (2019)
6. Beede, E., et al.: A human-centered evaluation of a deep learning system deployed in clinics for the detection of diabetic retinopathy. In: Proceedings of the 2020 CHI Conference on Human Factors in Computing Systems, pp. 1–12 (2020)
7. Bocu, R., Baicoianu, A., Kerestely, A.: An extended survey concerning the significance of artificial intelligence and machine learning techniques for bug triage and management. IEEE Access (2023)
8. Bosch, J., Olsson, H.H., Crnkovic, I.: Engineering ai systems: a research agenda. Artificial Intelligence Paradigms for Smart Cyber-Physical Systems, pp. 1–19 (2021)
9. Brunetto, M., Denaro, G., Mariani, L., Pezzè, M.: On introducing automatic test case generation in practice: a success story and lessons learned. J. Syst. Softw. **176**, 110933 (2021)
10. Burkov, A.: Machine learning engineering, vol. 1. True Positive Incorporated Montreal, QC, Canada (2020)
11. Byun, T., Sharma, V., Vijayakumar, A., Rayadurgam, S., Cofer, D.: Input prioritization for testing neural networks. In: 2019 IEEE International Conference On Artificial Intelligence Testing (AITest), pp. 63–70. IEEE (2019)
12. Chakraborty, J., Majumder, S., Menzies, T.: Bias in machine learning software: Why? how? what to do? In: Proceedings of the 29th ACM Joint Meeting on European Software Engineering Conference and Symposium on the Foundations of Software Engineering, pp. 429–440 (2021)

13. Chen, Z., Zhang, J.M., Sarro, F., Harman, M.: A comprehensive empirical study of bias mitigation methods for machine learning classifiers. ACM Trans. Softw. Eng. Methodol. **32**(4), 1–30 (2023)
14. Chenoweth, S., Linos, P.K.: Teaching machine learning as part of agile software engineering. IEEE Trans. Educ. (2023)
15. Diosan, L., Motogna, S.: Artificial intelligence meets software engineering in the classroom. In: Proceedings of the 1st ACM SIGSOFT International Workshop on Education through Advanced Software Engineering and Artificial Intelligence, pp. 35–38 (2019)
16. Fioravanti, M.L., Sena, B., Paschoal, L.N., Silva, L.R., Allian, A.P., Nakagawa, E.Y., Souza, S.R., Isotani, S., Barbosa, E.F.: Integrating project based learning and project management for software engineering teaching: An experience report. In: Proceedings of the 49th ACM Technical Symposium on Computer Science Education, pp. 806–811. SIGCSE '18. Association for Computing Machinery, New York (2018). https://doi.org/10.1145/3159450.3159599
17. Galhotra, S., Brun, Y., Meliou, A.: Fairness testing: testing software for discrimination. In: Proceedings of the 2017 11th Joint Meeting on Foundations of Software Engineering, pp. 498–510 (2017)
18. Hall, T., Beecham, S., Bowes, D., Gray, D., Counsell, S.: A systematic literature review on fault prediction performance in software engineering. IEEE Trans. Software Eng. **38**(6), 1276–1304 (2011)
19. Hulten, G.: Building intelligent systems: a guide to machine learning engineering. Apress (2018)
20. Kästner, C., Kang, E.: Teaching software engineering for ai-enabled systems. In: Proceedings of the ACM/IEEE 42nd International Conference on Software Engineering: Software Engineering Education and Training, pp. 45–48 (2020)
21. Kim, J., Feldt, R., Yoo, S.: Guiding deep learning system testing using surprise adequacy. In: 2019 IEEE/ACM 41st International Conference on Software Engineering (ICSE). pp. 1039–1049. IEEE (2019)
22. Lanubile, F., Martínez-Fernández, S., Quaranta, L.: Teaching mlops in higher education through project-based learning. In: 2023 IEEE/ACM 45th International Conference on Software Engineering: Software Engineering Education and Training (ICSE-SEET). pp. 95–100. IEEE (2023)
23. Mariani, T., Vergilio, S.R.: A systematic review on search-based refactoring. Inf. Softw. Technol. **83**, 14–34 (2017)
24. Martínez-Fernández, S., Bogner, J., Franch, X., Oriol, M., Siebert, J., Trendowicz, A., Vollmer, A.M., Wagner, S.: Software engineering for ai-based systems: a survey. ACM Trans. Softw. Eng. Methodol. (TOSEM) **31**(2), 1–59 (2022)
25. Menzies, T.: The five laws of se for ai. IEEE Softw. **37**(1), 81–85 (2020). https://doi.org/10.1109/MS.2019.2954841
26. Menzies, T., Zimmermann, T.: Software analytics: What's next? IEEE Softw. **35**(5), 64–70 (2018)
27. Miller, C.C.: Can an algorithm hire better than a human. The New York Times **25** (2015)
28. Nemoto, T., Beglar, D.: Likert-scale questionnaires. In: JALT 2013 Conference Proceedings, pp. 1–8 (2014)
29. Ni, J., Chen, Y., Chen, Y., Zhu, J., Ali, D., Cao, W.: A survey on theories and applications for self-driving cars based on deep learning methods. Appl. Sci. **10**(8), 2749 (2020)

30. Palomba, F., Voria, G., Parziale, A., Pentangelo, V., Della Porta, A., De Martino, V., Recupito, G., Giammaria, G.: Online appendix - teaching software quality assurance for artificial intelligence: An experience report https://figshare.com/s/c0797c1cd4569ce3d285

31. Peng, K., Chakraborty, J., Menzies, T.: Fairmask: better fairness via model-based rebalancing of protected attributes. IEEE Trans. Software Eng. **49**(4), 2426–2439 (2022)

32. Recupito, G., et al.: Technical debt in ai-enabled systems: on the prevalence, severity, impact, and management strategies for code and architecture. J. Syst. Softw. (2024). https://doi.org/10.1016/j.jss.2024.112151

33. Riccio, V., Jahangirova, G., Stocco, A., Humbatova, N., Weiss, M., Tonella, P.: Testing machine learning based systems: a systematic mapping. Empir. Softw. Eng. **25**(6), 5193–5254 (2020). https://doi.org/10.1007/s10664-020-09881-0

34. Sculley, D., et al.: Hidden technical debt in machine learning systems. Advances in neural information processing systems 28 (2015)

35. Smith, J.: Machine Learning Systems: Designs that Scale. Simon and Schuster (2018)

36. Sperling, A., Lickerman, D.: Integrating ai and machine learning in software engineering course for high school students. In: Proceedings of the 17th ACM Annual Conference on Innovation and Technology in Computer Science Education, pp. 244–249 (2012)

37. Wan, Z., Xia, X., Lo, D., Murphy, G.C.: How does machine learning change software development practices? IEEE Trans. Software Eng. **47**(9), 1857–1871 (2019)

38. Wang, P., Fan, E., Wang, P.: Comparative analysis of image classification algorithms based on traditional machine learning and deep learning. Pattern Recogn. Lett. **141**, 61–67 (2021)

39. Yang, Y., Xia, X., Lo, D., Bi, T., Grundy, J., Yang, X.: Predictive models in software engineering: challenges and opportunities. ACM Trans. Softw. Eng. Methodol. (TOSEM) **31**(3), 1–72 (2022)

40. Yang, Y., Xia, X., Lo, D., Grundy, J.: A survey on deep learning for software engineering. ACM Comput. Surv. (CSUR) **54**(10s), 1–73 (2022)

41. Zhou, J., Chen, F.: Human and Machine Learning. Springer (2018)

# A Reasoning Framework for Architecting Carbon-Aware Software-as-a-Service Applications

Samuele Giussani[1](✉), Mauro Caporuscio[1], and Diego Perez-Palacin[1,2]

[1] Linnaeus University, Växjö, Sweden
{samuele.giussani,mauro.caporuscio,diego.perez}@lnu.se
[2] Karlsruhe Institute of Technology (KIT), Karlsruhe, Germany

**Abstract.** Software-as-a-Service solutions are increasingly being adopted when developing software applications, as they are scalable, cost-effective, and facilitate rapid deployment while providing high availability and flexibility. However, the impact of Software-as-a-Service in terms of carbon emissions is not yet adequately addressed as a design concern, and most of the existing efforts revolve around measuring and containing the carbon impact after the deployment. Our work proposes a model-driven reasoning framework that integrates UML-based software architecture modeling with carbon-aware concerns. Architectural elements are supplemented with sustainability and performance properties of interest through a dedicated Domain Specific Language; then, a model-driven transformation generates a simulation model to evaluate multiple architectural designs according to their Software Carbon Intensity and performance metrics. The results guide decision-making by assessing and comparing the trade-offs between performance and carbon intensity for the analyzed designs. In this way, the reasoning framework provides an automated, tool-supported approach to designing environmentally responsible Software-as-a-Service applications.

## 1 Introduction

Software-as-a-Service (SaaS) has become the dominant software delivery model across industries, including (but not limited to) AI assistants, audio/video streaming, and games [25]. SaaS applications are deployed on cloud infrastructure and provided to end-users via the Internet [12].

The Information and Communication Technology (ICT) industry, which includes cloud infrastructure that hosts SaaS applications, is responsible for a significant amount of greenhouse gas emissions into the atmosphere, heavily contributing to the generation of global warming pollutants [6]. It is of the utmost importance to reduce the environmental impact of computing systems by adopting sustainable practices that can limit carbon emissions throughout the software life cycle, from design to waste disposal [21]. At the same time, carbon intensity, which indicates the ratio between carbon emissions and energy

D. Taibi and D. Smite (Eds.): SEAA 2025, LNCS 16083, pp. 231–241, 2026.
https://doi.org/10.1007/978-3-032-04207-1_16

usage, must be kept as low as possible. Despite numerous research efforts focused on optimizing the performance indices associated with cloud applications [3, 27], little attention is being given to reducing their carbon intensity, with most sustainability efforts primarily directed toward the optimization of the electricity usage [14]. Although this focus is crucial, given the substantial and growing contribution of cloud computing to global energy consumption [7], a software application's carbon impact is not always proportional to its energy efficiency. The *operational emissions*—defined as the $CO_2$ equivalents produced during the operations of the software infrastructure—are, in fact, dependent on the power source of the electrical grid: if powered by electricity obtained from fossil fuels, highly energy-efficient implementations may have poor carbon efficiency; conversely, solutions that are not optimized to use as little energy as possible but that primarily rely on renewable energy may outperform the former in carbon efficiency [29]. Moreover, software's *embodied emissions* should also be considered to obtain the full extent of the carbon impact. This category of emissions represents the $CO_2$ equivalents associated with the construction of the software infrastructure and all the fabrication stages (procurement of material, manufacturing, assembly, and transportation) of its components. Therefore, reducing operational emissions may not be sufficient to improve a software system's overall environmental sustainability: manufacturing overheads and shorter hardware lifetimes contribute to higher embodied emissions, possibly neutralizing or even exceeding a potential operational footprint decrease [15]. For this reason, even though energy consumption remains one of the factors that influence the carbon footprint of software, carbon awareness should be considered distinct from energy awareness [15, 29].

The optimization of carbon emissions in software is often seen merely as a challenge to be addressed through measurements and adjustments, rather than being treated as an essential concern of software architecture. Additionally, the relation between carbon footprint and other performance indicators, such as throughput and response times, is seldom considered. Companies still struggle to efficiently incorporate sustainability-oriented practices into their everyday operations, often considering them irrelevant to their business or simply being unaware of their value [18]. However, given the significant threat that environmental pollution poses to the future of our planet, the carbon impact of software should be regarded with the same importance as other non-functional requirements and evaluated from the early stages of development. In fact, the later in the development process this concern is raised, the more challenging and expensive it is to address it properly [19].

In this paper, we introduce a software architecture-oriented methodology for estimating the carbon intensity of cloud-based SaaS applications, supported by a reasoning framework for evaluating different deployment strategies in search of an optimal balance between performance and carbon intensity. Reasoning frameworks are versatile and structured approaches employed in several domains for assessing a system's behavior in relation to one or more quality attributes [2, 16]. They specialize in interpreting architectural descriptions through well-defined theories and are suitable for model-driven engineering techniques [2]. In our contribution, the reasoning framework processes a UML model enclosing the cloud application software design and generates a simulation model to evaluate the system's performance and carbon impact. The iteration of the framework's capabilities on various architectural designs ultimately allows for a responsible choice toward a better trade-off between these two factors and effectively addresses carbon awareness concerns before the software implementation.

## 2    Related Work

The pursuit of carbon awareness and sustainability is a central topic in the modern technological landscape. Aside from the contributions targeting energy efficiency, most of the proposed carbon-aware approaches aim to increase the ratio of clean energy drawn from the electrical grids during the software runtime [8]. Radovanović et al. [23] proposed a carbon-intelligent management system to delay flexible workloads in data centers until grid energy is less carbon-intensive. An analogous scheduling approach was presented by Claßen et al. [8], while Saboor et al. [24] developed a ranking system for microservices to favor their carbon-optimal distribution in the cloud. All these approaches, however, are centered on reducing the operational emissions of software but do not consider the impact of the hardware's embodied emissions on the total carbon computation.

Acun et al. [1] adopted a holistic approach for carbon-aware data centers. They combined workload scheduling with energy storage and complementary sources in search of optimal settings for 24/7 carbon-free operations. Their research highlighted the existing challenges in developing runtime strategies that effectively reduce operational and embodied emissions at the same time. Patel et al. [22] proposed an agile framework as a set of guidelines and best practices for cloud data center operations to tackle the existing carbon awareness challenges. One of the framework's purposes is to improve the visibility of emissions in cloud applications, emphasizing the limitations of measurement-based assessment techniques and discussing the adoption of model-based techniques.

In contrast, Schmidt et al. [26] discussed awareness of the carbon footprint in software by focusing on factors beyond the application level. Their contribution recognized the accuracy of Software Carbon Intensity as a carbon footprint score and aimed at implementing its mathematical foundation as an operating-system service. Forti et al. [11] used known behavioral patterns to address carbon intensity concerns since the design stages of interactive software services, registering promising results in the reduction of carbon emissions. Despite not covering the aspects related to embodied emissions, their conceptual approach is the closest to the one presented in this paper, albeit focusing on carbon optimization of code rather than architectural design.

While most existing solutions prioritize runtime optimizations, our method addresses carbon awareness at an earlier stage by integrating the Software Carbon Intensity estimation into the design phase of SaaS applications. By adopting a reasoning framework and model-driven engineering, it aims to expand the previous limited research efforts on carbon awareness in SaaS design by reasoning on the software architecture description.

## 3    Software Carbon Intensity

The Software Carbon Intensity (SCI) score was defined by the Standard Working Group of the Green Software Foundation[1] and is meant to be a support to users and developers of any software application in calculating the rate of carbon emissions. This indicator was specified to support carbon-related decisions from the early system design and was designed as a relative indicator, scaled on a functional unit $R$ of interest, to be compatible with several aggregation scenarios. These properties align with the purpose of this paper. The formula adopted in our methodology, derived by refining the score's specification [17] with the calculation steps used in the Impact Framework[2], is the following:

$$O = I \cdot \left( E_N + \frac{res_R}{res_T} \cdot \frac{\Delta t \cdot tdp \cdot ACW(U)}{3.6 \cdot 10^6} \right) \qquad M = e_e \cdot \frac{\Delta t}{ls_{exp}} \cdot \frac{res_R}{res_T}$$

$$SCI = (O + M) \ per \ R$$

The operational emissions attributable to the software are indicated as $O$. They are calculated by multiplying the grid carbon intensity $I$, i.e., how many grams of $CO_2$ are produced for every $kWh$ of consumed electricity, by the total amount of used energy. This amount is composed of the energy dissipated for network communications, $E_N$, and the energy required by the reserved hardware to execute the software. In particular, the thermal design power $tdp$ of the CPUs involved in the computation is scaled with a factor resulting from the interpolation of the Average Consumption per Watt (ACW) curve[2] with the CPUs utilization $U$ and multiplied by the duration $\Delta t$ of the execution adjusted by a factor of $3.6 \cdot 10^6$ so that it is expressed in $kWh$. A further scaling with the resource-share of processing units, that is, the ratio of reserved resources $res_R$ over their total number $res_T$, ensures that the $SCI$ calculation considers only the energy dissipation caused by the software under analysis.

$M$ indicates, instead, the portion of embodied carbon in the creation and disposal of the hardware devices that are allocated to the software execution. The embodied emissions $e_e$ represent the sum of Life Cycle Assessment (LCA) emissions for all the components used by the software, and a fraction of them is used to derive the value of embodied carbon depending on the software's resource-share and time-share. In this case, the time-share is the time reserved for the software execution over the expected life span $ls_{exp}$ of the physical components. The sum of embodied carbon and operational emissions results in the $SCI$ value for the functional unit $R$ of interest.

## 4    The Reasoning Framework

The proposed reasoning framework adheres to the definition by Bass et al. [5] and includes six main elements. The *Problem Description* individuates one or

---

[1] https://greensoftware.foundation.
[2] https://if.greensoftware.foundation.

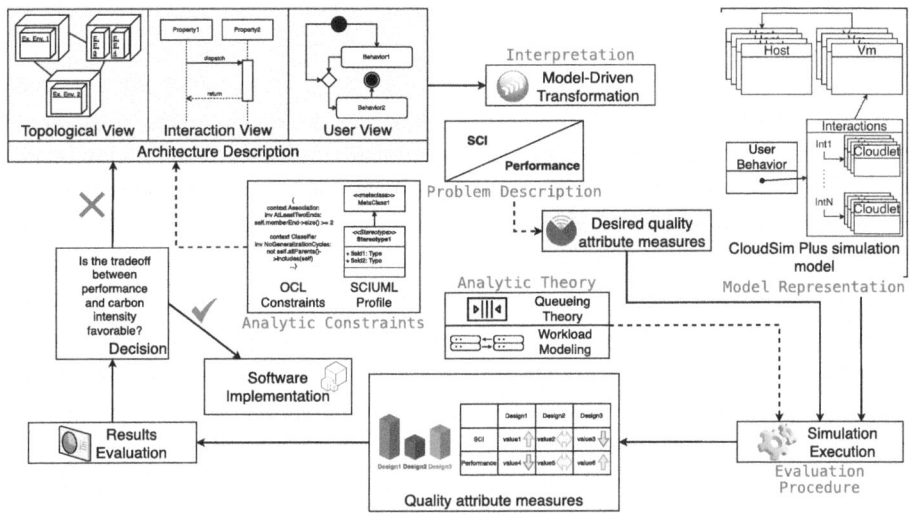

**Fig. 1.** The Reasoning Framework

more quality measures to be assessed for the class of behaviors targeted by the framework. These desired quality attribute measures represent the input for the reasoning framework alongside the architecture description employed for their evaluation. It is fundamental for the framework's analysis to be based on a solid *Analytic Theory*, paired with a set of *Analytic Constraints* to restrict the design space to the required extent. The provided architecture description is processed through an *Interpretation* procedure and results in the generation of a *Model Representation*, in a format that is ready for the *Evaluation Procedure*. The latter should derive the desired attributes passed as input using the knowledge and the algorithms provided in the *Analytic Theory*.

The implementation of our reasoning framework is detailed in Fig. 1. The desired quality attribute measures are defined by the framework's *Problem Description*, which, in our case, involves identifying an optimal tradeoff between SCI and average service time across various functional units. The framework's soundness is supported by its foundational *Analytic Theory*, which consists of queueing theory and workload modeling. Queueing theory is used to define the stochastic processes that represent users connecting to the cloud application [13]. Meanwhile, workload modeling is utilized to simulate resource allocation and calculate the utilization of each instantiated component in terms of CPU, bandwidth, and memory. The architecture description of the cloud-based SaaS application under analysis is provided as input using the standard UML language, adhering to the specifications provided by the Object Management Group (OMG) [9]. In particular, the framework's assessment requires the instantiation of *Analytic Constraints* to ensure that the provided architecture description is indeed compatible with the reasoning process. To achieve this goal, we introduce a Domain-Specific Language (DSL) in the form of a UML profile called SCIUML. This language enables the architecture description to include the necessary information, such as the embodied emissions of servers and the geographic region where they are located, for the framework to calculate the required quality attributes. In particular, the framework needs the geographic position to derive the correct grid carbon intensity to apply in its calculations. The DSL also defines Object Constraint Language (OCL) invariant rules to specify additional characteristics that the architecture description must provide to be compatible with SCIUML.

The architecture description is composed of three perspectives: Topological View, Interaction View, and User View. The Topological View is depicted through a Deployment Diagram and outlines the assignments of software artifacts to hardware nodes in the cloud application. The Interaction View is provided as a set of Sequence Diagrams, each one describing how the atomic services communicate to perform the functionalities offered by the application. The User View consists of multiple activity diagrams illustrating the various expected behaviors while using the application. The perspectives are linked together in a single UML model through OCL-compliant relationships and serve as input for the framework's *Interpretation*, consisting of a model-driven transformation.

The framework's *Interpretation* is responsible for transitioning the reasoning process from the modeling domain to the simulation domain. It generates a simulation model, i.e., the framework's *Model Representation*, by mapping the relevant UML classes and SCIUML applied stereotypes to the simulation engine's components (i.e., CloudSim Plus [28]).

The Topological View is connected to the Interaction View in the given UML structure. In fact, interactions need to be traceable back to the physical and virtual components of the systems that are designed to execute them. Thanks to this connection, the transformation can instruct the simulation engine to bind the on-demand tasks generated during the simulation runtime to the correct computational resource. More in detail, every interaction designed as a sequence diagram in the modeling domain is translated into a task scheduler in the simulation domain. This functional interface contains the instructions for instantiating a new set of workloads at runtime that symbolize a user's interaction with the system and sets its parameters through the stereotypes provided in the DSL.

The User View is necessary for the model transformation to reproduce user behavior during the simulation. Each of its elements in the modeling domain defines a user category interacting with the application and corresponds to the conditional flow of interactions that a specific class of users would perform with the system. In particular, every stage of the modeled behavior is linked to the Interaction View by using UML relationships, and the behavioral pattern of each user is supported by the DSL through a weight function for randomly choosing each simulated user's workflow. All this information is translated into the simulation domain by constructing an oriented graph for each class of users. During the simulation execution, each new user connection to the application will trigger the sequential execution of the task schedulers referenced in the generated graph belonging to the user category of interest.

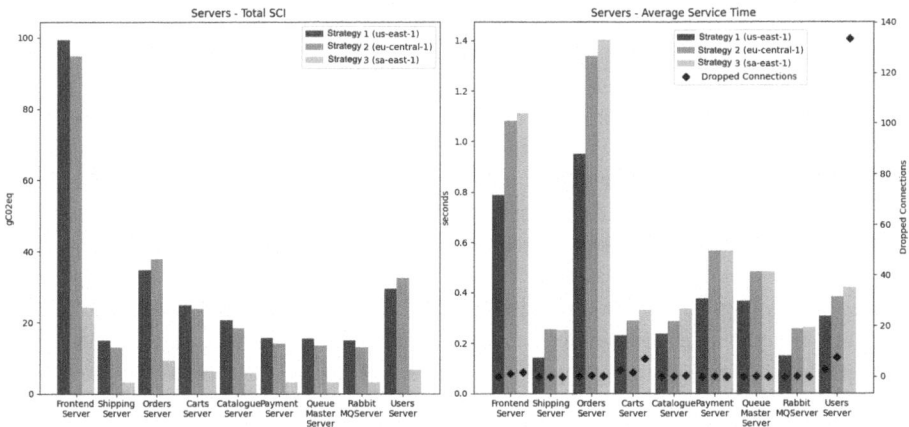

**Fig. 2.** Simulation Results adopting the servers as functional unit

As shown in Fig. 1, once the framework's *Model Representation* is generated, the *Evaluation Procedure* can be initiated. The procedure is carried out by performing several independent replications of the cloud application's simulation to increase the confidence level of the results [4] and returns an assessment of the desired quality attribute measures input in the reasoning framework, composed of the SCI score and the service time estimates for the interactions and physical machines in the system.

The presentation of the evaluation results usually represents the final step of a reasoning framework [5]. However, the measured SCI is returned as a score, making it easier to compare to a baseline case or between multiple designs rather than being elicited as a non-functional requirement [17]. For this reason, the proposed framework is made iterative through the addition of a decision node: the Software Implementation phase can start only when multiple architecture descriptions have been analyzed by the reasoning framework and one architectural design's tradeoff between SCI and performance is chosen among the others.

## 5    Preliminary Results and Future Directions

As SaaS applications are increasingly being implemented using microservices architecture [12], to evaluate the proposed Reasoning Framework, we performed a trade-off analysis between SCI and performance across three deployment strategies[3]. To this end, we use Sock Shop[4], a well-known microservice benchmark application [20]. We aim to identify the most carbon-aware deployment strategy that meets the application's requirements.

---

[3] The replication package is available at https://github.com/eres-lnu/Carbon-Aware-Reasoning-Framework/.

[4] https://github.com/ocp-power-demos/sock-shop-demo.

Through the framework's *Interpretation*, the deployment strategies are transformed into *Model Representations* in the simulation domain and executed through the *Evaluation Procedure*. The simulation outcome is shown in Fig. 2. Given that the optimality of both quality attributes of interest is found in lower values, the second strategy is Pareto-dominated by the first, as all the attributes of the former consistently perform worse than those of the latter [10]. Therefore, the second strategy does not represent an optimal candidate for implementation. The first deployment strategy is the best in terms of performance but has a higher carbon impact, while the third is the most carbon-aware but does not satisfy the application's performance requirements. Moreover, dropped connections may represent a severe performance issue, revealing the non-optimality of the chosen topology for the given setup. Following these results, the software engineers will determine whether to analyze additional deployment strategies—potentially adopting the third strategy as a starting point—to pursue a more sustainable design within performance requirements, or to proceed with the implementation of the first strategy.

The reasoning framework applied to various deployment strategies of a SaaS application provides a structured and tool-supported method for increasing carbon awareness in SaaS design. Indeed, the obtained results show how the SCI indicator gains relevance as a relative score, helping to understand the carbon impact by comparing several design options for the same functional unit.

However, the proposed approach has some limitations that should be considered. The reasoning framework's *Interpretation* is implemented with a focus on architecture descriptions that utilize a limited subset of UML classes, which were enforced through the framework's *Analytic Constraints*. This tightness in defining the constraints was necessary to thoroughly apply the *Analytic Theory* to the given problem and to reach the desired analytic capabilities as a part of a co-refinement process [5]. It is, in fact, standard practice in engineering reasoning frameworks to target architecture descriptions presenting simplified elements from the generic case, aiming at successfully achieving a significant *Evaluation Procedure* before expanding the supported set of inputs to more complex designs. For instance, the current implementation requires the available interactions to always have a definite sequence of microservice executions without conditional structures or optional flows, as `uml::CombinedFragment`s in the modeling domain do not yet possess a mapping in the model-driven transformation.

In the simulation domain, instead, the effects of dynamic scaling of microservices on the output quality measures are not examined, allowing for the moment only static resource and computational units' allocation derived from the modeling domain. The outlined limitations, all requiring refinements achievable within the expressive power of UML and the simulation capabilities of CloudSim Plus, represent a driving factor towards the progressive relaxation of *Analytic Constraints* envisioned for the co-refinement process of the proposed framework.

Future work will prioritize the progression of the co-refinement process to overcome the known approach's limitations and extend the compatibility range of supported architecture designs. Architecture scaling, both horizontal and vertical, is also planned for implementation in the simulation logic. Finally, we look forward to applying the framework in a real-life SaaS application case study.

# References

1. Acun, B., et al.: Carbon explorer: A holistic framework for designing carbon aware datacenters. In: Proceedings of the 28th ACM International Conference on Architectural Support for Programming Languages and Operating Systems, vol. 2, pp. 118–132. ASPLOS 2023. Association for Computing Machinery, New York (2023). https://doi.org/10.1145/3575693.3575754

2. Andersson, J., Caporuscio, M., D'Angelo, M., Napolitano, A.: Architecting decentralized control in large-scale self-adaptive systems. Computing **105**(9), 1849–1882 (2023). https://doi.org/10.1007/s00607-023-01167-9

3. Aslanpour, M.S., Gill, S.S., Toosi, A.N.: Performance evaluation metrics for cloud, fog and edge computing: A review, taxonomy, benchmarks and standards for future research. Internet Things **12**, 100273 (2020). https://doi.org/10.1016/j.iot.2020.100273

4. Banks, J., Carson, J.S., Nelson, B.L., Nicol, D.M.: Discrete-Event System Simulation (5th Edition). Pearson Education (2010)

5. Bass, L., Ivers, J., Klein, M.H., Merson, P.F.: Reasoning Frameworks. Tech. rep., Carnegie Mellon University, July 2005. https://doi.org/10.1184/R1/6582911.v1

6. Belkhir, L., Elmeligi, A.: Assessing ict global emissions footprint: Trends to 2040 & recommendations. J. Clean. Prod. **177** (2018). https://doi.org/10.1016/j.jclepro.2017.12.239

7. Centofanti, C., Santos, J., Gudepu, V., Kondepu, K.: Impact of power consumption in containerized clouds: a comprehensive analysis of open-source power measurement tools. Comput. Netw. **245**, 110371 (2024). https://doi.org/10.1016/j.comnet.2024.110371

8. Claßen, H., Thierfeldt, J., Tochman-Szewc, J., Wiesner, P., Kao, O.: Carbon-Awareness in CI/CD. In: Monti, F., et al. (eds.) Service-Oriented Computing – ICSOC 2023 Workshops, pp. 213–224. Springer Nature Singapore, Singapore (2024). https://doi.org/10.1007/978-981-97-0989-2_17

9. Cook, S., et al.: Unified modeling language (UML) version 2.5.1. Standard, Object Management Group (OMG), December 2017. https://www.omg.org/spec/UML/2.5.1

10. Emmerich, M.T.M., Deutz, A.H.: A tutorial on multiobjective optimization: fundamentals and evolutionary methods. Nat. Comput. **17**(3), 585–609 (2018). https://doi.org/10.1007/s11047-018-9685-y

11. Forti, S., Soldani, J., Brogi, A.: Carbon-aware software services. In: Pahl, C., Janes, A., Cerny, T., Lenarduzzi, V., Esposito, M. (eds.) Service-Oriented and Cloud Computing, pp. 65–80. Springer Nature Switzerland, Cham (2025). https://doi.org/10.1007/978-3-031-84617-5_6

12. Golding, T.: Building Multi-Tenant SaaS Architectures. Inc, O'Reilly Media (2024)

13. Gross, D., Shortle, J.F., Thompson, J.M., Harris, C.M.: Fundamentals of Queueing Theory, 4th edn. Wiley-Interscience, USA (2008)

14. Guldner, A., et al.: Development and evaluation of a reference measurement model for assessing the resource and energy efficiency of software products and components–green software measurement model (gsmm). Futur. Gener. Comput. Syst. **155**, 402–418 (2024). https://doi.org/10.1016/j.future.2024.01.033

15. Gupta, U., Kim, Y.G., Lee, S., Tse, J., Lee, H.H.S., Wei, G.Y., Brooks, D., Wu, C.J.: Chasing carbon: The elusive environmental footprint of computing. IEEE Micro **42**(4), 37–47 (2022). https://doi.org/10.1109/MM.2022.3163226

16. Im, T., Vullam, S., McGregor, J.D.: Reasoning about safety during software architecture design. In: Rahal, I., Zalila-Wenkstern, R. (eds.) ISCA 19th International Conference on Software Engineering and Data Engineering (SEDE-2010) June 16-18, 2010, San Francisco, CA, USA, pp. 1–8. ISCA (2010)

17. ISO/IEC 21031:2024: Information technology – Software Carbon Intensity (SCI) specification. Standard, International Organization for Standardization, Geneva, CH (Mar 2024). https://www.iso.org/standard/86612.html

18. Karita, L., Mourão, B.C., Machado, I.: Software industry awareness on green and sustainable software engineering: a state-of-the-practice survey. In: Proceedings of the XXXIII Brazilian Symposium on Software Engineering, pp. 501–510. SBES '19. Association for Computing Machinery, New York(2019). https://doi.org/10.1145/3350768.3350770

19. Kern, E., Dick, M., Naumann, S., Hiller, T.: Impacts of software and its engineering on the carbon footprint of ict. Environ. Impact Assess. Rev. **52**, 53–61 (2015). https://doi.org/10.1016/j.eiar.2014.07.003

20. von Kistowski, J., et al.: Microservice Benchmark Applications, pp. 305–321. Springer Nature Switzerland (2025)

21. Nazaré, T., Gadelha, J., Nepomuceno, E., Lozi, R.: Green computing for energy transition: a survey. IEEE Lat. Am. Trans. **21**(9), 937–948 (2023). https://doi.org/10.1109/TLA.2023.10251799

22. Patel, P., Gregersen, T., Anderson, T.: An agile pathway towards carbon-aware clouds. SIGENERGY Energy Inform. Rev. **4**(3), 10–17 (2024). https://doi.org/10.1145/3698365.3698368

23. Radovanović, A., et al.: Carbon-aware computing for datacenters. IEEE Trans. Power Syst. **38**(2), 1270–1280 (2023). https://doi.org/10.1109/TPWRS.2022.3173250

24. Saboor, A., Mahmood, A.K., Omar, A.H., Hassan, M.F., Shah, S.N.M., Ahmadian, A.: Enabling rank-based distribution of microservices among containers for green cloud computing environment. Peer-to-Peer Networking Appl. **15**(1), 77–91 (2021). https://doi.org/10.1007/s12083-021-01218-y

25. Saltan, A., Smolander, K.: Towards a saas pricing cookbook: a multi-vocal literature review. In: International Conference on Software Business (2019). https://api.semanticscholar.org/CorpusID:207946350

26. Schmidt, A., et al.: carbond: an operating-system daemon for carbon awareness. SIGENERGY Energy Inform. Rev. **4**(3), 52–57 (2024). https://doi.org/10.1145/3698365.3698374

27. Shen, Z., et al.: X-Containers: Breaking Down Barriers to Improve Performance and Isolation of Cloud-Native Containers. In: Proceedings of the Twenty-Fourth International Conference on Architectural Support for Programming Languages and Operating Systems, pp. 121–135. ASPLOS '19. Association for Computing Machinery, New York (2019). https://doi.org/10.1145/3297858.3304016

28. Silva Filho, M.C., Oliveira, R.L., Monteiro, C.C., Inácio, P.R.M., Freire, M.M.: Cloudsim plus: A cloud computing simulation framework pursuing software engineering principles for improved modularity, extensibility and correctness. In: 2017 IFIP/IEEE Symposium on Integrated Network and Service Management (IM), pp. 400–406 (2017). https://doi.org/10.23919/INM.2017.7987304

29. Souza, A., et al.: Ecovisor: A Virtual Energy System for Carbon-Efficient Applications. In: Proceedings of the 28th ACM International Conference on Architectural Support for Programming Languages and Operating Systems, vol. 2, pp. 252–265. ASPLOS 2023. Association for Computing Machinery, New York (2023). https://doi.org/10.1145/3575693.3575709

# Software Process and Product Improvement

# Prompt Engineering Guidelines for Using Large Language Models in Requirements Engineering

Krishna Ronanki[1,2(✉)] 📧, Simon Arvidsson[1,2], and Johan Axell[1,2]

[1] Chalmers University of Technology, Gothenburg, Sweden
krishna.ronanki@gu.se
[2] University of Gothenburg, Gothenburg, Sweden

**Abstract.** The rapid emergence of generative AI models like Large Language Models (LLMs) has demonstrated its utility across various activities, including within Requirements Engineering (RE). Ensuring the quality and accuracy of LLM-generated output is critical, with prompt engineering serving as a key technique to guide model responses. However, existing literature provides limited guidance on how prompt engineering can be leveraged, specifically for RE activities. The objective of this study is to explore the applicability of existing prompt engineering guidelines for the effective usage of LLMs within RE. To achieve this goal, we began by conducting a systematic review of primary literature to compile a non-exhaustive list of prompt engineering guidelines. Then, we conducted interviews with RE experts to present the extracted guidelines and gain insights on the advantages and limitations of their application within RE. Our literature review indicates a shortage of prompt engineering guidelines for domain-specific activities, specifically for RE. Our proposed mapping contributes to addressing this shortage. We conclude our study by identifying an important future line of research within this field.

**Keywords:** Requirements Engineering · Generative AI · Large Language Models · Prompt Engineering · Guidelines

## 1 Introduction

The development of Artificial Intelligence (AI) techniques such as Natural Language Processing (NLP), Machine Learning (ML) and Deep Learning (DL) methods for various requirements engineering (RE) activities, including requirements classification, prioritisation, tracing, ambiguity detection, and modelling has been increasing Alhoshan et al. (2023a), Zhao, Liping and Alhoshan, Waad and Ferrari, Alessio and Letsholo, Keletso J and Ajagbe, Muideen A and Chioasca, Erol-Valeriu and Batista-Navarro, Riza T 2021. It has been empirically observed

---

S. Arvidsson and J. Axell—Contributed equally to this work.

D. Taibi and D. Smite (Eds.): SEAA 2025, LNCS 16083, pp. 245–262, 2026.
https://doi.org/10.1007/978-3-032-04207-1_17

that natural language is the most commonly used medium for drafting requirements in the industrial context. This significant synergy between natural language and requirements has led to the emergence of NLP in the field of RE Zhao, Liping and Alhoshan, Waad and Ferrari, Alessio and Letsholo, Keletso J and Ajagbe, Muideen A and Chioasca, Erol-Valeriu and Batista-Navarro, Riza T (2021). Despite the advancements in NLP for RE, there is a noticeable lack in the application of natural language generation (NLG)-based method in support of RE activities Zhao, Liping and Alhoshan, Waad and Ferrari, Alessio and Letsholo, Keletso J and Ajagbe, Muideen A and Chioasca, Erol-Valeriu and Batista-Navarro, Riza T (2021). Moreover, the majority of existing state-of-the-art approaches for supporting RE activities and processes rely on ML/DL. These methods necessitate substantial amounts of task-specific labelled training data.

One potential solution to overcome the need of large quantities of high quality labelled training data and advance NLG within RE is using pre-trained generative AI models like Large Language Models (LLM). Utilising LLMs for performing RE activities can potentially remove the need for large amounts of labelled data. Recent LLMs are demonstrating increasingly impressive capabilities when performing a wide range of tasks Brown, Tom and Mann, Benjamin and Ryder, Nick and Subbiah, Melanie and Kaplan, Jared D and Dhariwal, Prafulla and Neelakantan, Arvind and Shyam, Pranav and Sastry, Girish and Askell, Amanda and others (2020), including their significant enhancements in NLP tasks Haque, Mubin Ul and Dharmadasa, Isuru and Sworna, Zarrin Tasnim and Rajapakse, Roshan Namal and Ahmad, Hussain (2022). The GPT-3.5 LLM has demonstrated a surprising proficiency in specific technical tasks Choi, Jonathan H and Hickman, Kristin E and Monahan, Amy and Schwarcz, Daniel 2023, including RE Alhoshan et al. (2023a).

However, the input prompts to the LLM are observed to significantly impact the quality of the LLM's output Vogelsang (2024). The emerging practice of utilising carefully selected and composed natural language instructions to achieve a desirable output from an LLM is called *prompt engineering* Liu and Chilton (2022a). Prompt engineering plays a crucial role as the selection of prompts can have a significant impact on downstream tasks Perez et al. (2021). However, there are no guidelines or strategies that RE practitioners can leverage to utilise LLM effectively.

To address this research gap, we conducted a systematic review of primary studies to identify and analyse existing prompt engineering guidelines for LLMs and explore their applicability within RE. By mapping these guidelines to RE activities, we aim to bridge a gap in the literature and provide a structured approach for both researchers and practitioners. In order for us to realise these objectives, the following research questions were formed:

**RQ1:** What are the existing prompt engineering guidelines for effective use of LLMs?

**RQ2:** What are the advantages and the limitations of using these guidelines for the effective usage of LLMs within RE?

**RQ3:** What are the relevant prompt engineering guidelines for the effective usage of LLMs within RE?

Section 2 present the relevant background literature that motivates our research goals. Section 3 describes our research design and execution. Section 4 presents the results of the our study and answer the **RQ1**, **RQ2** and **RQ3**. We discuss the implications of the gathered results along with the threats to validity of our study in Sect. 5. Finally, in Sect. 6, we conclude our study and present potential areas for further research based on the discussed implications.

## 2  Background and Related Work

Recent research in prompt engineering has proposed guidelines for effective prompt engineering of generative AI models, particularly LLMs and large vision models Liu and Chilton (2022b). The existing research on the development of prompting techniques for domain-specific tasks such as RE, however, remains sparse with some generally applicable outcomes provided by White et al. White et al. (2023a). The literature on prompt engineering guidelines and approaches tied specifically to RE remains limited at the time of this study, with only a few papers partially covering guidelines for tasks and prompt learning within RE activities.

Rodriguez et al. (2023) explore the process of prompt engineering to extract link predictions from an LLM. They provide detailed insights into their approach for constructing effective prompts and propose multiple strategies for leveraging LLMs. Their key takeaways include the impact of minor changes to prompts on the quality of the outputs, the effect of chain-of-thought reasoning, and the importance of specifying targeted usage to get desired outcomes. However, this study's biggest drawback is its limitation to only one task.

Ronanki et al. (2024b) evaluate the effectiveness of 5 of the prompt patterns' White et al. (2023c) ability to make GPT-3.5 turbo perform binary requirements classification and requirements traceability tasks. They also offer recommendations on which prompt pattern to use for a specific RE task and provide an evaluation framework as a reference for researchers and practitioners who want to evaluate different prompt patterns for different RE tasks. The results of this study are limited to only the two mentioned RE tasks and the five prompt patterns that were used in the experiments.

Sasaki et al. (2024) present a systematic literature review focusing on practical applications of prompt engineering in SE. They identified and classified prompt engineering patterns, showcasing their application across different SE tasks. They also provide a taxonomy of prompt engineering techniques for SE that has five categories, eleven sub-categories and twenty one patterns along with the problems they can applied to and the solution you receive. However, the prompt engineering patterns covered within the study are from various SE tasks like code generation, testing, debugging, etc.

The reviewed studies broadly agree that the "context" and "structure" of prompts significantly impact the quality of generated outputs. However, there is considerable variation in the recommended approaches for achieving high-quality results. "Few-shot prompting" has been observed to improve the LLM output quality compared to alternative methods Chen et al. (2023), West et al. (2021). Conversely, other studies highlight cases where few-shot prompting falls short, suggesting that its effectiveness depends on specific conditions Yu et al. (2022), Clavié et al. (2023).

Furthermore, research on models like GPT-3, GPT-3.5, and ChatGPT indicates persistent challenges in tasks requiring emotional understanding or mathematical reasoning, regardless of the prompting approach used Yang et al. (2023). Additionally, these models are prone to confidently generating incorrect facts, a phenomenon known as hallucinations. Various studies propose mitigation strategies to address these inaccuracies Koralus and Wang-Maścianica (2023). Recent studies have also explored applying prompt engineering guidelines to new domains, including SE. These studies often propose domain-specific adaptations of existing guidelines, expanding the applicability of prompt engineering techniques White et al. (2023a), Yu et al. (2022), Clavié et al. (2023), Chen et al. (2023), Yang et al. (2023). These sources, while crucial for shaping and enhancing our understanding of prompt engineering for LLMs, fail to address the gap of lack of standard prompt engineering guidelines applicable for RE activities, further strengthening the motivation of our study.

Through the works of Pressman, R.S. Pressman (2005) and Sommerville, I. Sommerville and Sawyer (1997), the five main RE activities identified in the literature are elicitation, analysis, specification, validation, and management. These activities are crucial for successful product development and face various challenges. Our mapping of prompt engineering guidelines to RE was done while focusing primarily on these five activities.

## 3 Methodology

We conducted a systematic review of primary studies to identify prompt engineering guidelines for LLMs to answer **RQ1**. Then, we conducted interviews with three RE experts to gain insights into how the extracted guidelines can be used to leverage LLMs more effectively during RE activities. These interviews helped us gain insight into the advantages and limitations of the prompt engineering guidelines, answering **RQ2**. Based on the expert's insights, a mapping of relevant prompt engineering guidelines to different RE activities was performed following the thematic synthesis approach Cruzes and Dybå (2011). This mapping, has the potential to help RE practitioners leverage LLMs more effectively, and answers **RQ3**.

## 3.1   Systematic Review of Primary Studies

We based our systematic review process partially on the guidelines for conducting a systematic literature review Kitchenham and Charters (2007). To construct a comprehensive search strategy, we identified relevant keywords through prior research in related domains and a snowballing approach. Based on our research objectives and questions, we formulated the following search string: ("Prompt Engineering" OR "Prompt Patterns" OR "Prompt Design" OR "Prompt Catalog" OR "Prompt Guidelines") AND ("Large Language Models" OR "Generative AI"). During the initial exploration, we observed inconsistencies in terminology across studies. Consequently, we expanded the search string to improve coverage. The string was then adapted to match the interface requirements of each database while preserving the original keywords.

We restricted our search to papers published from 2018 onward, as this marks the introduction of transformer architectures with OpenAI's Generative Pre-trained Transformer (GPT) and Google's Bidirectional Encoder Representations from Transformers (BERT) Vaswani et al. (2017), Devlin et al. (2018), Radford et al. (2018). This time frame constraint also helps ensure relevancy and state-of-the-art within the field of prompt engineering to match the rapid development of large generative models.

Our review covered five databases: ACM, Scopus, IEEE Xplore, ScienceDirect, and arXiv. The first four were selected due to their extensive coverage and credibility in computer science and software engineering research. arXiv was later included to capture emerging studies, given the field's fast-paced development.

To identify relevant primary studies for this systematic review, we applied inclusion and exclusion criteria, as detailed in Table 1. Each study was initially assessed based on its title, abstract, introduction, conclusion, and keywords. If ambiguity remained after this stage, a full-text review was conducted to determine its relevance. Applying the search string to the selected databases yielded 271 studies for initial screening. After evaluating them against the inclusion and exclusion criteria presented in Table 1 and removing duplicates, 28 studies (10.3%) were identified as primary studies.

**Table 1.** Inclusion and exclusion criteria for the review.

| Inclusion criteria | Exclusion criteria |
| --- | --- |
| Written in English language | Papers with sections or content in languages other than English |
| Date of publication from 2018 | Published prior to 2018 |
| Emphasises generative AI models | Unrelated to generative AI models |
| Focus on Natural language prompts | Emphasis on model tuning |
| Relevant to RQ1 | Does not contain prompt engineering guidelines |

In order to conduct extraction of relevant data, the form depicted in Table 2 was used. This form was established in order to ensure an organised as well as standardised data collection process. It also facilitated the process of distinguishing relevant data for our research question.

**Table 2.** Data extraction form

| Data | Description | Relevant RQ |
|------|-------------|-------------|
| Year | To ensure temporal relevance of the extracted prompt engineering guidelines | General |
| Model Type | Text-to-image and text-to-text. | RQ1 |
| Prompt Method | What prompt engineering techniques were studied? | RQ1 |
| Guidelines | What guidelines are presented? | RQ1 |
| Findings | Strengths or limitations of the guidelines presented | RQ1 |

### 3.2 Interviews: Data Collection and Analysis

To assess the advantages and limitations of the identified prompt engineering guidelines and gain insights on which guidelines are relevant for the activities involved within the selected RE phases, we conducted semi-structured interviews Robson, Colin (1993) with three experts from different academic institutions, each specialising in distinct areas of RE. The primary selection criterion was expertise in RE, with additional consideration given to knowledge in AI4RE and related fields. Experts were identified based on their academic background and publication history. While our study focuses on RE, the selected experts provided diverse perspectives, spanning fields such as RE4AI and NLP4RE as well. Experts were contacted via email with an introduction to the study and details on the interview process. All interviews were conducted online via Zoom, each lasting approximately 30 min. We ensured all the interviews were conducted by following the ethical interview checklist presented by P.E. Strandberg Strandberg, Per Erik (2019).

We chose qualitative content analysis Drisko and Maschi (2016) to extract insights from the qualitative data collected from the interviews. The transcripts of the interviews were edited, validated through member checking [Seaman, C.B., 1999), and anonymised before we performed content analysis. We then conducted a thematic synthesis to map the relevant prompt engineering guidelines to different activities within the selected RE phases. Our thematic synthesis approach was inspired by Cruzes and Dybå Cruzes and Dybå (2011), involved summarising, integrating, and comparing findings on a specific topic to generate new insights, such as theories, frameworks, or conclusions. The final mapping was developed by integrating the insights provided by the RE experts for mapping of the guidelines to the RE activities.

## 4   Results

The results of this study are presented in three subsections, each corresponding to an **RQ**. Subsection 4.1 addresses **RQ1**, presenting a non-exhaustive list of prompt engineering guidelines. These guidelines are categorised into the nine most frequently occurring themes identified in our review. Subsection 4.2 explores the advantages and limitations of applying the identified prompt engineering guidelines in RE based on expert interviews, providing insights necessary for answering **RQ2**. Subsection 4.3 answers **RQ3** by mapping the identified guidelines to relevant RE activities.

## 4.1  Prompt Engineering Guidelines

From the 28 included primary studies, we identified and extracted 36 prompt engineering guidelines. These guidelines were categorised into nine distinct themes based on their defining characteristics. Each theme was defined to capture the underlying concepts and group similar guidelines, providing a clearer overview of their overall intent and purpose.

**Context.** The "Context" theme revolves around guidelines that relate to contextual information in any manner for prompts.

**Persona.** The "Persona" theme is a high-level abstraction of guidelines that revolves around strategies for LLMs to take on specific or different perspectives on specified tasks by using prompts. Persona in this instance can be compared to perspectives or points of view.

**Templates.** The "Templates" theme encapsulates guidelines that only provide an explicit structure of prompts, known as a template.

**Disambiguation.** The "Disambiguation" theme refers to guidelines that aim to address ambiguity, clarification, or understanding of intent.

**Reasoning.** The "Reasoning" theme captures guidelines that aim to affect reasoning capabilities or the ability to think through complex problems or tasks in a generated output.

**Analysis.** The theme "Analysis" revolve around guidelines examining, evaluating, or analysing information or tasks.

**Keywords.** The theme "Keywords" represent guidelines that involve any use of single-word modifiers to prompts.

**Wording.** The theme "Wording" refers to guidelines that relate to choices of words, text formatting, writing styles, or inclusion and exclusion of text.

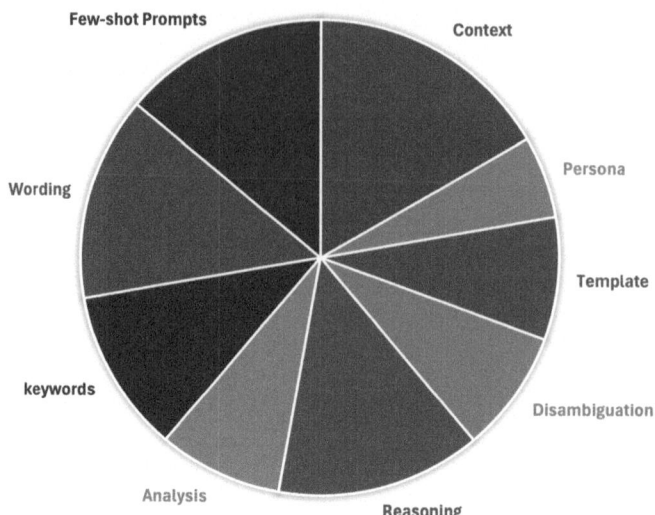

**Fig. 1.** Theme distribution of the extracted guidelines from the studies in the review.

**Few-Shot Prompts.** The theme "Few-shot Prompts" categorises guidelines that are intended for any form of few-shot prompting.

Each guideline was assigned to one of the nine themes and given a unique identifier, as listed in Table 3. This categorisation provides insight into the most common types of guidelines found in the literature. As shown in Fig. 1, the "Context" theme consists of the highest number of guidelines, followed by "Reasoning", "Wording", and "Few-shot Prompts" themes. The "Persona" theme had the lowest number of guidelines, with only 2. To reference specific guidelines in this paper, we use a combination of the theme's initial letter and the guideline's identifier. For example, C1 refers to the first guideline within the "Context" theme.

## 4.2   Expert Insights: Interview Analysis

Interviews were conducted with three different RE experts, enquiring about their views on the advantages and the limitations of guidelines from our review and their possible usage for LLMs within RE activities.

**Requirements Elicitation.** Each of the experts interviewed emphasised the importance of context in prompts, especially for requirement elicitation. Regarding the advantages, Expert 2 discussed the potential of leveraging contextual prompts for LLMs in this process, noting that they could encourage creative requirements exploration. They stated, "It may be creative requirements, like [for the LLM] to say, hey, have you thought of this? And then a person says, oh, that's a good idea, or no, that's a bad idea." Expert 3 emphasised that templates could be beneficial across various prompt-related activities and RE

**Table 3.** Thematic Classification of Prompt Engineering Guidelines

| Theme | Description |
|---|---|
| Context (C) | 1. Adding context to examples in prompts produce more efficient and informative output. Reynolds and McDonell (2021)<br>2. Provide context to all prompts to avoid output hallucinations. Kumar (2023)<br>3. Provide context of the prompt to ensure a closely related output. Lubiana et al. (2023), Zhou et al. (2022a)<br>4. The more context tokens pre-appended to prompts, the more fine-grained output.Zhou et al. (2022a)<br>5. The Context Manager Pattern enables users to specify or remove context for a conversation with an LLM White et al. (2023b)<br>6. Providing more context and instructions is an effective strategy to increase the semantic quality of the output Vogelsang (2024) |
| Persona (P) | 1. Improves the generation quality by conditioning the prompt with an identity, such as "Python programmer" or "Math tutor" Wei et al. (2023)<br>2. To explore the requirements of a software-reliant system, include:<br>- "I want you to act as the system",<br>- "Use the requirements to guide your behaviour"White et al. (2023c) |
| Templates (T) | 1. To improve reasoning and common sense in output, follow a template such as:<br>- "Reason step-by-step for the following problem. [Original prompt inserted here]" Koralus and Wang-Maścianica (2023)<br>2. The following prompt template has shown an impressive quality of AI art:<br>- "[Medium] [Subject] [Artist(s)] [Details] [Image repository support]"Oppenlaender et al. (2023)<br>3. I am going to provide a template for your output; This is the template: PATTERN with PLACEHOLDERS White et al. (2023b) |
| Disambi-guation (D) | 1. Ensure any areas of potential miscommunication or ambiguity are caught, by providing a detailed scope:<br>- "Within this scope",<br>- "Consider these requirements or specifications" White et al. (2023c)<br>2. To find points of weakness in a requirements specification, consider including:<br>- "Point out any areas of ambiguity or potentially unintended outcomes" White et al. (2023c)<br>3. The persona prompt method can be used to consider potential ambiguities from different perspectives. White et al. (2023a) |
| Reasoning (R) | 1. Prepending "Let's think step by step" improves zero-shot performance. Zhou et al. (2022b)<br>2. Extending the previously known "Let's think step by step", with "to reach the right conclusion," to highlight decision-making in the prompt. Clavié et al. (2023)<br>3. Chain Of Thought (CoT) prompting improves LLM performance and factual inconsistency evaluation compared to Zero-shot.Chen et al. (2023), Luo et al. (2023)<br>4. Tree of thought (ToT) allows LLMs to perform deliberate decision making by considering multiple different reasoning paths and self-evaluating choices to decide the next course of action Yao et al. (2024)<br>5. The intent of the Cognitive Verifier pattern is to force the LLM to always subdivide questions into additional questions that can be used to provide a better answer to the original question White et al. (2023b) |
| Analysis (A) | 1. self-consistency boosts the performance of chain-of-thought prompting Wang et al. (2022a)<br>2. The best of three strategy improves the LLM output stability and detecting hallucinations Ronanki et al. (2024a)<br>3. Emotion-enhanced CoT prompting is an effective method to leverage emotional cues to enhance the ability of ChatGPT on mental health analysis. Yang et al. (2023) |

(continued)

**Table 1.** (*continued*)

| Theme | Description |
|---|---|
| Keywords (K) | 1. When picking the prompt, focus on the subject and style keywords instead of connecting words. Liu and Chilton (2022b)<br>2. Pre-appending keywords to prompts are shown to greatly improve performance by providing the language model with appropriate context. Gero et al. (2022)<br>3. Modifiers/Keywords can be added to the details or image repository sections of a template such as:<br>- "[Medium] [Subject] [Artist(s)] [Details] [Image repository support]" Oppenlaender et al. (2023)<br>4. The inclusion of multiple descriptive keywords tends to align results closer to expectations. Hao et al. (2022) |
| Wording (W) | 1. In translation tasks, adding a newline before the phrase in a new language increases the odds that the output sentence is still English. Reynolds and McDonell (2021)<br>2. A complete sentence definition with stop words performs better as a prompt than a set of core terms that were extracted from the complete sentence definition after removing the stop words. Yong et al. (2022)<br>3. Words such as "well-known" and "often used to explain" are successful for analogy generation. Bhavya et al. (2022)<br>4. Modifying prompts to resemble pseudocode tend to be the most successful in coding tasks. Denny et al. (2023), White et al. (2023c)<br>5. Prompts to contain explicit algorithmic hints in engineering tasks perform better. Denny et al. (2023) |
| Few-shot Prompts (F) | 1. Inclusion of "Question:" and "Answer:" improves the response, but rarely gives a binary answer. Trautmann et al. (2022)<br>2. For easier understanding, number examples in few-shot prompting. West et al. (2021)<br>3. The format of [INPUT] and [OUTPUT] should linguistically imply the relationship between them. West et al. (2021)<br>4. Specifications can be added to each [INPUT] and [OUTPUT] pair to give extra insight into complicated problems. West et al. (2021)<br>5. In Few-shot prompting include a rationale in each shot (Input-rationale-output). Wang et al. (2022b) |

activities where LLMs provide value, specifically mentioning requirements elicitation as a key application. They suggested that keyword-based guidelines can be appropriate for requirements elicitation.

However, the experts also had concerns regarding the effectiveness of term "context" included in the guidelines, arguing how it could be ambiguous as it is a quite general word. Expert 3 stated "I would say that context may need to be decomposed in somehow because otherwise, the guideline may be too generic." Expert 1 mentioned that the context that the guidelines refer to may vary depending on assumptions made by different stakeholders. Expert 2 brought up another limitation, on how the context may not fully cover what the stakeholders want, stating "So you can use it to elicit requirements, but they're not necessarily requirements that anyone wants to implement."

**Requirements Analysis.** Expert 2 acknowledged a potential advantage in using LLMs to assess key qualities of requirements, stating, "If you're asking [the LLM], 'Is this maintainable? Is this verifiable? Is this unambiguous?' then you could come back and say yes or no, and that might be useful." They 2 also suggested that templates could be useful for analysing completeness of requirements.

However, they ultimately emphasised the limitations, explaining that the uncertainty surrounding the output, coupled with a lack of confidence in the feedback provided by LLMs, would make the results unreliable and of limited practical value. Expert 1 highlighted a key limitation, noting a lack of confidence in the feedback generated and the inherent uncertainty surrounding it. They raised concerns about the inconsistencies in LLM-generated outputs, particularly the variability in responses even when identical prompts are used. They cautioned against over-reliance on templates in requirements analysis.

Expert 1 also pointed out the difficulty in understanding how an LLM interprets reasoning steps. Similarly, Expert 2 stated, "It is only capturing one very narrow type of reasoning. If you are trying to get it to reason in a process view, like step one, step two, step three, I am not even sure that is reasoning." They further questioned whether LLMs could effectively support the type of reasoning required in RE.

Despite these concerns, Expert 3 noted potential advantages, stating, "It could be useful for the analysis of requirements towards the generation of system architecture" They also suggested that embedding prompting guidelines within LLMs could support automated sub-tasks that aid in requirements analysis, referencing implementation approaches such as AutoGPT AutoGPT (2025). Overall, experts agreed that requirements analysis is likely too complex for current LLMs to handle effectively. They expressed scepticism about the capability of existing LLMs to fully support this task given their current state of development.

**Requirements Specification.** Expert 1 emphasised the potential to iteratively explore unclear aspects of requirements, stating, "You can explore, maybe even iteratively, any unclear aspects of your requirements and, as I say, any ambiguities where there could be potential misunderstanding" They further suggested that integrating persona-based guidelines could enhance this process by enabling ambiguity exploration from multiple perspectives. They stressed the importance of justifications, explaining that there is a need for reasoning behind why a requirement is deemed ambiguous or weak.

Expert 2 identified a key advantage, noting that "it [LLM] could help to point out weaknesses in a requirement specification" and that "prompt engineering could help point out ambiguity." However, they also acknowledged that ambiguity might not always be a concern, referencing prior studies on smaller teams where such issues had minimal impact.

Expert 3 exclusively highlighted advantages, emphasising that these guidelines could be beneficial not only for requirement specification but also for requirements review. They provided an example related to guideline D2, stating, "So this is a useful prompt for sure, it's going to change the way we make requirements reviews." They further elaborated on the critical role of requirements reviews, particularly in safety-critical contexts.

**Requirements Validation** Experts 1 and 3 acknowledged potential advantages of using LLMs for requirements validation. Expert 3 suggested that the use of LLMs in validation could be a promising area for further research. They proposed that LLMs could assist in validating requirements against the needs of specific user types, rather than solely acting as the system itself, stating,"Validating requirements based on the needs of a specific user could be beneficial, instead of simply acting as the system." However, they emphasised the necessity of providing extensive descriptions of the system to the LLM within the prompts as a potential limitation.

Expert 1 also noted a potential advantage in using LLMs to explore the validity of specific goals or targets from multiple perspectives. However, they raised concerns regarding the role of context among different personas. In this context, context refers to what the personas know about the system, and a key limitation is determining the appropriate scope of this knowledge. Expert 1 cautioned that restricting the LLM's perspective to a specific dimension of the problem could significantly narrow the scope of validation, making it applicable only to the predefined perspective. They stated, "If you limit the LLM only to look from a certain dimension or certain perspective on the problem, then you scope down your validation a lot to be only valid for that certain perspective that you define beforehand." They also acknowledged a key advantage of templates, explaining that templates are always nice because you can validate that templates actually work nicely beforehand, and then people can just use it without having to analyse if the template is good.

Expert 2 expressed scepticism regarding the use of LLMs for requirements validation, stating, "I think it's a bad idea to use the prompt engineering for validation." They argued that LLMs lack the capability to determine whether a system is correct, making them unsuitable for requirements validation. Additionally, Expert 3 highlighted a fundamental challenge in using LLMs for validation, noting that validation is the final stage of the requirements process. They expressed uncertainty about whether current LLMs possess the necessary accuracy to process the substantial amount of technical information that systems typically require at this stage of development.

**Requirements Management.** Experts 2 and 3 identified potential advantages of keyword-based guidelines, particularly in their ability to assist with sorting and classifying requirements into categories. Expert 3 further suggested that these guidelines could support additional requirements management tasks, such as similarity analysis and traceability.

Expert 1 focused on the role of keywords in providing context, explaining that they could help establish assumptions and enhance the precision of LLM-generated outputs. However, they also highlighted a key limitation, noting that increased precision could "limit the scope out of which the output can come" potentially excluding important aspects from consideration. They also pointed to a broader advantage of structured reasoning within LLMs, emphasising that "you get much better traceability or track why a certain decision has been made by the LLM or why a certain output was generated." This suggests that structured guidelines could enhance transparency in LLM-driven requirements analysis. Expert 3 questioned whether keywords alone would be sufficient for requirements management tasks, as these tasks often require in-depth project and domain knowledge.

## 4.3    RE Activities and Applicable Guidelines

The proposed mapping between RE activities and the identified guideline themes, along with the corresponding justifications, is outlined in this section. A detailed representation of this mapping is provided in Table 2.

**Table 2.** Mapping of Guidelines and RE

| RE Phase | Applicable Guidelines |
|---|---|
| Elicitation | Context, Template, Keyword |
| Analysis | Template, Analysis, Reasoning |
| Specification | Persona, Disambiguation |
| Validation | Persona, Template |
| Management | Keyword, Reasoning |

We believe the users performing requirements elicitation using LLMs can benefit from employing guidelines categorised under the "context", "template" and "keyword" themes, presented in Table 3. This mapping was done based on the experts' insights presented in detail within Subsect. 4.2.

For requirements analysis, the "template", "analysis" and "reasoning" guidelines can be useful. Guidelines such as "self-consistency" Wang et al. (2022a) and "best of three strategy" Ronanki et al. (2024a) can help in improving the consistency of the LLM output, which was a major limitation mentioned by the experts related to requirements analysis. The reasoning guidelines such as chain-of-thought and tree-of-thought can help in improving the reasoning capabilities of the LLMs, which is another limitation emphasised by the experts within this phase.

For users performing requirements specification using LLMs can benefit from using "Persona" and "Disambiguation" templates. The primary reason is eliminate and reduce ambiguities present within requirements specifications as per the experts' opinions.

For requirements validation using LLMs, "persona" guidelines can be helpful for validating requirements against the needs of specific user types. The "template" guidelines can help in having some predefined approaches which saves time by reducing the need for experimenting with finding optimal prompts for particular use cases.

Finally, for users performing requirements management tasks using LLMs, "keyword" and "reasoning" guidelines can be most helpful. Keyword guidelines can help put the task being performed into appropriate contexts by establishing the right assumptions. The need for traceability and reasoning can be addressed by following "reasoning" guidelines while prompting LLMs.

## 5   Discussion

One of the main objectives of this study was to explore how existing prompt engineering guidelines can help users in leveraging LLMs in RE activities. Our findings indicate that while various guidelines exist, they originate from a diverse range of models, including text-to-text models such as GPT-3.5 and BERT, as well as text-to-image and multi-modal models like DALL-E and the combination of CLIP and VQGAN. Although some guidelines exhibit overlap, our analysis reveals notable differences, suggesting that the role of prompt engineering will continue to grow in importance. Notably, the majority of guidelines identified through our literature review were mentioned only once across studies. This shows that, while there is much interest in improving the performance of the LLM through coming up various prompt based approaches, this field of study is still in its early stages and needs to mature before this becomes an established discipline of study. The guidelines and techniques need to be validated across broader range of use cases to reach a generalisable conclusion on which techniques work reliably enough for which tasks and use cases and what are the constraints and limitations of them.

We also examined how these guidelines apply to different RE activities by mapping them to guideline themes. Our interviews confirmed that while multiple interpretations of these mappings exist, there was general agreement on the value of the guideline themes. The template theme guidelines seems to the most relevant ones, as they are mapped to three of the five RE activities. The keyword, persona and reasoning theme guidelines were mapped to two activities each while the context, analysis and disambiguation themes were only mapped to one activity. However, based on the experts' insights, while the context and disambiguation guidelines are applicable to fewer use cases, they bring more value to the use cases they are applicable to compared to the rest of the guideline themes. This indicates that the prompt engineering guidelines can serve two major purposes: broadly apply to various RE activities and bring value to the tasks they are used within.

Another interesting observation is that these seven themes of prompt engineering guidelines make up 72% of the all the prompt engineering guidelines we found. Some guidelines, such as those focused on few-shot prompting and wording which make up 28% of all the prompt engineering guidelines we found in our literature, were deemed irrelevant to RE and were not part of the mapping. This indicates that, while existing prompt engineering guidelines are fairly applicable to RE activities, there is also a risk that a good chunk of them are not. This points to the need for either developing new prompt engineering guidelines, specific to RE or fine-tuning existing guidelines to make them more applicable and effective for RE. Overall, our findings show both the potential and limitations of prompt engineering guidelines for using LLMs in RE. Providing context is key to improving LLM performance, but more research is needed to refine these guidelines and explore their use in more advanced RE activities.

### 5.1  Threats to Validity

While we followed established methods and techniques for the collection and analysis of the data to ensure methodological rigour and soundness, it is essential to acknowledge and address potential threats to the validity of the findings.

**Internal Validity:** Despite selecting a review period from 2018 to the present, there is a risk of omitting relevant studies. However, as large language models (LLMs) largely emerged after 2017, and prompt-related guidelines first appeared in 2021, this risk is likely minimal. Limited available literature and inconsistencies in terminology pose risks. Selection bias may arise from reviewing a restricted set of studies. Open discussions among researchers aimed to minimise misinterpretations.

**External Validity:** The study's findings may have limited generalisability due to its specific focus and the rapidly evolving field. Including unpublished preprints from arXiv introduces potential bias but helps capture cutting-edge research. Interviewed experts may have personal biases influencing their responses, potentially introducing confirmation bias.

**Construct Validity:** The study's inclusion and exclusion criteria may affect the construct validity. Also, the interviewed RE experts' varying understanding of the terminology within the guidelines is another threat.

## 6  Conclusion

The primary motivation to conduct and present this study was to address the lack of domain specific prompt engineering guidelines for using LLMs, especially within RE. To that extent, our study provided an overview of existing prompt engineering guidelines. We examined the benefits and limitations of these guidelines through interviews with three RE experts. Our interviews highlighted the usefulness of the identified guidelines, especially for the context, template, keywords, analysis, reasoning, persona, and disambiguation guidelines for various RE activities. Based on the insights gathered from these interviews, we proposed a mapping for prompt engineering guidelines for different RE activities.

We believe that as LLMs become more reliable in RE activities, they could help reduce errors, detect issues earlier in the process, and prevent costly corrections later in development. This, in turn, could lower project failure rates and improve overall efficiency in RE workflows. Our findings contribute to the improvement of RE practices by supporting the development of tailored prompt engineering guidelines. Future work should explore how general prompt guidelines can be adapted for specific domains like RE and whether additional fine-tuning of these guidelines is required to make them more effective.

# References

Alhoshan, W., Ferrari, A., Zhao, L.: Zero-shot learning for requirements classification: An exploratory study. Inf. Softw. Technol. **159**, 107202 (2023)

AutoGPT. Empower your digital tasks with AutoGPT (2025). https://agpt.co/. Accessed: 19/02/2025

Bhavya, B., Xiong, J., Zhai, C.: Analogy generation by prompting large language models: A case study of instructgpt. arXiv preprint arXiv:2210.04186 (2022)

Brown, T., et al.: Language Models are Few-shot Learners. Adv. Neural. Inf. Process. Syst. **33**, 1877–1901 (2020)

Chen, S., Li, Y., Lu, S., Van, H., Aerts, H.J.W.L., Savova, G.K., Bitterman, D.S.: Evaluation of chatgpt family of models for biomedical reasoning and classification. arXiv preprint arXiv:2304.02496 (2023)

Choi, J.H., Hickman, K.E., Monahan, A., Schwarcz, D.: ChatGPT Goes to Law School. Available at SSRN (2023)

Clavié, B., Ciceu, A., Naylor, F., Soulié, G., Brightwell, T.: Large language models in the workplace: a case study on prompt engineering for job type classification. arXiv preprint arXiv:2303.07142 (2023)

Cruzes, D.S., Dybå, T.: Research synthesis in software engineering: a tertiary study. Inf. Softw. Technol. **53**(5), 440–455 (2011). ISSN 0950-5849. https://doi.org/10.1016/j.infsof.2011.01.004. https://www.sciencedirect.com/science/article/pii/S095058491100005X. Special Section on Best Papers from XP2010

Denny, P., Kumar, V., Giacaman, N.: Conversing with copilot: Exploring prompt engineering for solving cs1 problems using natural language. In: Proceedings of the 54th ACM Technical Symposium on Computer Science Education V. 1, pp. 1136–1142 (2023)

Devlin, J., Chang, M.-W., Lee, K., Toutanova, K.: Bert: pre-training of deep bidirectional transformers for language understanding. arXiv preprint arXiv:1810.04805 (2018)

Drisko, J.W., Maschi, T.: Content analysis. Oxford university press (2016)

Gero, K.I., Liu, V., Chilton, L.: Sparks: inspiration for science writing using language models. In: Designing Interactive Systems Conference, pp. 1002–1019 (2022)

Hao, Y., Chi, Z., Dong, L., Wei, F.: Optimizing prompts for text-to-image generation. arXiv preprint arXiv:2212.09611 (2022)

Haque, M.U.l., Dharmadasa, I., Sworna, Z.T., Rajapakse, R.N., Ahmad, H.: "I think this is the most disruptive technology": Exploring Sentiments of ChatGPT Early Adopters using Twitter Data. arXiv preprint arXiv:2212.05856 (2022)

Kitchenham, B., Charters, S.: Guidelines for performing systematic literature reviews in software engineering. **2**, 01 (2007)

Koralus, P., Wang-Maścianica, V.: Humans in humans out: On gpt converging toward common sense in both success and failure. arXiv preprint arXiv:2303.17276 (2023)

Kumar, K.: Geotechnical parrot tales (gpt): Harnessing large language models in geotechnical engineering. arXiv e-prints, pages arXiv–2304 (2023)

Liu, V., Chilton, L.B.: Design guidelines for prompt engineering text-to-image genera-tive models. In: Proceedings of the 2022 CHI Conference on Human Factors in Com-puting Systems, CHI '22. Association for Computing Machinery, New York (2022a). ISBN 9781450391573. https://doi.org/10.1145/3491102.3501825. URL https://doi.org/10.1145/3491102.3501825

Liu, V., Chilton, L.B.: Design guidelines for prompt engineering text-to-image gen-erative models. In: Proceedings of the 2022 CHI Conference on Human Factors in Computing Systems, pp. 1–23 (2022b)

Lubiana, T., et al.: Ten quick tips for harnessing the power of chatgpt/gpt-4 in com-putational biology. arXiv preprint arXiv:2303.16429 (2023)

Luo, Z., Xie, Q., Ananiadou, S.: Chatgpt as a factual inconsistency evaluator for abstractive text summarization. arXiv preprint arXiv:2303.15621 (2023)

Oppenlaender, J., Linder, R., Silvennoinen, J.: Prompting ai art: an investigation into the creative skill of prompt engineering. arXiv preprint arXiv:2303.13534 (2023)

Perez, E., Kiela, D., Cho, K.: True Few-shot Learning with Language Models. Adv. Neural. Inf. Process. Syst. **34**, 11054–11070 (2021)

Pressman, R.S.: Software engineering: a practitioner's approach. Pressman and Asso-ciates (2005)

Radford, A., Narasimhan, K., Salimans, T., Sutskever, I., et al.: Improving language understanding by generative pre-training (2018)

Reynolds, L., McDonell, K.: Prompt programming for large language models: Beyond the few-shot paradigm. In: Extended Abstracts of the 2021 CHI Conference on Human Factors in Computing Systems, pp. 1–7 (2021)

Robson, C.: Real World Research: A Resource for Social Scientists and Practitioner-Researchers. Blackwell (1993). https://cir.nii.ac.jp/crid/1130282271686871424

Rodriguez, A.D., Dearstyne, K.R., Cleland-Huang, J.: Prompts matter: Insights and strategies for prompt engineering in automated software traceability. In: 2023 IEEE 31st International Requirements Engineering Conference Workshops (REW), pp. 455–464 (2023). https://doi.org/10.1109/REW57809.2023.00087

Ronanki, K., Cabrero-Daniel, B., Berger, C.: Chatgpt as a tool for user story quality evaluation: trustworthy out of the box? In: Agile Processes in Software Engineering and Extreme Programming – Workshops, pp. 173–181. Springer (2024a). ISBN 978-3-031-48550-3

Ronanki, K., Cabrero-Daniel, B., Horkoff, J., Berger, C.: Requirements Engineering Using Generative AI: Prompts and Prompting Patterns, pp. 109–127. Springer, Cham (2024b). https://doi.org/10.1007/978-3-031-55642-5_5

Sasaki, Y., Washizaki, H., Li, J., Sander, D., Yoshioka, N., Fukazawa, Y.: Systematic literature review of prompt engineering patterns in software engineering. In: 2024 IEEE 48th Annual Computers, Software, and Applications Conference (COMPSAC), pp. 670–675 (2024).https://doi.org/10.1109/COMPSAC61105.2024.00096

Seaman, C.B.: Qualitative methods in empirical studies of software engineering. IEEE Trans. Software Eng. **25**(4), 557–572 (1999). https://doi.org/10.1109/32.799955

Sommerville, I., Sawyer, P.: Requirements Engineering: A Good Practice Guide, 1st edn. John Wiley & Sons Inc, USA (1997). 0471974447

Strandberg, P.E.: Ethical Interviews in Software Engineering. In: 2019 ACM/IEEE International Symposium on Empirical Software Engineering and Measurement (ESEM), pp. 1–11 (2019). https://doi.org/10.1109/ESEM.2019.8870192

Trautmann, D., Petrova, A., Schilder, F.: Legal prompt engineering for multilingual legal judgement prediction. arXiv preprint arXiv:2212.02199 (2022)

Vaswani, A., et al.: Attention is all you need. Advances in neural information processing systems, 30 (2017)

Vogelsang, A.: From specifications to prompts: On the future of generative large language models in requirements engineering. IEEE Softw. **41**(5), 9–13 (2024). https://doi.org/10.1109/MS.2024.3410712

Wang, X., et al.: Self-consistency improves chain of thought reasoning in language models. arXiv preprint arXiv:2203.11171 (2022a)

Wang, X., Wei, J., Schuurmans, D., Le, Q., Chi, E., Zhou, D.: Rationale-augmented ensembles in language models. arXiv preprint arXiv:2207.00747 (2022b)

Wei, J., Kim, S., Jung, H., Kim, Y.-H.: Leveraging large language models to power chatbots for collecting user self-reported data. arXiv preprint arXiv:2301.05843 (2023)

West, P., et al.: Symbolic knowledge distillation: from general language models to commonsense models (2021). arXiv preprint arXiv:2110.07178

White, J., et al.: A prompt pattern catalog to enhance prompt engineering with chatgpt (2023a). arXiv preprint arXiv:2302.11382

White, J., et al.: A Prompt Pattern Catalog to Enhance Prompt Engineering with ChatGPT (2023b)

White, J., Hays, S., Fu, Q., Spencer-Smith, J., Schmidt, D.C.: Chatgpt prompt patterns for improving code quality, refactoring, requirements elicitation, and software design (2023c). arXiv preprint arXiv:2303.07839

Yang, K., Ji, S., Zhang, T., Xie, Q., Ananiadou, S.: On the evaluations of chatgpt and emotion-enhanced prompting for mental health analysis (2023). arXiv preprint arXiv:2304.03347

Yao, S., et al.: Tree of thoughts: Deliberate problem solving with large language models. Advances in Neural Information Processing Systems, 36 (2024)

Yong, G., Jeon, K., Gil, D., Lee, G.: Prompt engineering for zero-shot and few-shot defect detection and classification using a visual-language pretrained model. Computer-Aided Civil and Infrastructure Engineering (2022)

Yu, F., Quartey, L., Schilder, F.: Legal prompting: teaching a language model to think like a lawyer. arXiv preprint arXiv:2212.01326 (2022)

Zhao, L., et al.: Natural Language Processing for Requirements Engineering: A Systematic Mapping Study. ACM Comput. Surv. (CSUR) **54**(3), 1–41 (2021)

Zhou, K., Yang, J., Loy, C.C., Liu, Z.: Learning to prompt for vision-language models. Int. J. Comput. Vis. **130**(9), 2337–2348 (2022)

Zhou, Y., et al.: Large language models are human-level prompt engineers (2022b). arXiv preprint arXiv:2211.01910

# Navigating Uncertainty and Adaptability: A Survey on the Role of Kanban and Scrum in Software Startups

Omid Mojabi(✉) ⓘ, Mikael Svahnberg ⓘ, and Michael Unterkalmsteiner ⓘ

Software Engineering Research Lab (SERL), Blekinge Institute of Technology, Valhallavägen 1, 37179 Karlskrona, Sweden
ommo22@student.bth.se,
{mikael.svahnberg,michael.unterkalmsteiner}@bth.se

**Abstract.** Software startups operate in uncertain environments that require agile methodologies that support adaptability. Although Scrum and Kanban are widely adopted in software startups, their contributions to managing uncertainty and adaptability remain underexplored. This study investigates which aspects of Scrum and Kanban are the most effective in addressing uncertainty and volatility to improve adaptability in software startups. The goal is to identify key practices that improve agility and examine how startups tailor agile methodologies, particularly where they face limitations. To achieve this, a mixed methods approach was used, combining a literature review with a survey. The survey collected responses from 121 startup professionals to assess their experiences with Scrum and Kanban in handling uncertainty, workload management, workflow visualization, iteration planning, risk management, and testing. The results show that iterative development and a sustainable pace in it, prioritization, and visualization improve agility and productivity. Scrum supports structured iteration and events, while Kanban enhances workflow transparency and flow management. However, limitations in risk management, team structure, collaboration between business and technical people, and testing suggest agile frameworks require further adaptation in startups. In general, the study reinforces the need for context-specific adaptations of agile methods, as no single approach fully addresses the adaptability and uncertainty of startup environments. It highlights pivotal aspects of Scrum and Kanban to construct hybrid or customized approaches for complex, fast-paced software environments.

**Keywords:** Uncertainty · Adaptability · Software Startups · Scrum · Kanban

## 1 Introduction

Software startups are new organizations that create innovative high-tech products and have no prior operating history [7,41]. According to Giardino et al. [15],

D. Taibi and D. Smite (Eds.): SEAA 2025, LNCS 16083, pp. 263–279, 2026.
https://doi.org/10.1007/978-3-032-04207-1_18

there is no unique definition in the literature of what constitutes a startup; however, some of the characteristics that define startups are innovation in product development, market-driven development, small size in terms of employees, short time to market, and web-based development. Software startups play a notable role in the industry, distinguished by their focus on innovation and rapid adoption of emerging technologies [15,39,46] and their dependence on external investments in uncertain markets [10,53]. Despite the crucial role of innovative products and the need for external funding, the startup context suffers from a notable lack of comprehensive support for established software engineering practices [21,32,57]. The existing gap is compounded by the absence of development methods that address the distinctive features of startups [19], including their flexible [50] and dynamic nature, the emphasis on speed [39] and the reliance on customer feedback [51]. Software startups often exhibit a pragmatic approach to the adoption of methodologies, tailoring practices to their specific needs in the early stages of their growth period [19,22,51]. However, the factors that influence the selection or adaptation of agile methods in this context remain poorly studied. Challenges such as lack of competence in business administration, uncertainty in choosing technologies, and inadequate startup support in development methods further hinder the seamless integration of agile practices [17]. Existing software engineering methods, not tuned to the business intricacies of startups [19,36], may fail to address their unique requirements, although some of these methods (e.g. [15,31,45,58]) The limited literature on agile development practices in software startups hinders a complete understanding of the dynamics involved [32].

Agile software development (ASD) has brought a variety of benefits to the software industry, including enhanced "team capacity", "increased customer involvement" [49], and the delivery of high-quality products to customers [18], among others. Agile development has gained widespread adoption in the software industry since the early 21st century, as evidenced by the increasing number of publications on Agile practices between 2001 and 2010 [11]. However, startups have faced various challenges in implementing these methodologies. Research on agility and software processes is widely focused on frameworks, methods, and practices [25]. Popular Agile methods like Scrum and Kanban offer efficient frameworks for delivering high-quality software. Scrum, founded on empiricism and lean principles, emphasizes incremental and iterative development [44]. Kanban, focusing on the design and continuous improvement of the flow system, promotes collaboration and transparency [4]. Both methods prioritize customer satisfaction and value delivery, making them suitable approaches for software startups. According to Abrantes and Furtado [1], Kemell et al. [19] and Tegegne et al. [51], software startups face unique challenges when adopting agile methodologies, as these frameworks offer distinct advantages but also inherent constraints. Evaluating their effectiveness in achieving startup objectives is crucial. However, inconsistencies can arise when methodologies are customized or key features are omitted, potentially hindering their successful and consistent implementation. Although hybrid agile methods have been developed and utilized (for example, see [9, 18, 29, 42]), understanding their aspects and capabilities in different contexts is crucial to avoid the potential pitfalls of customizing agile methods in software startups. This study investigates which components of Scrum and Kanban are the most effective in managing uncertainty and ambiguity in fast-paced environments. To address this, we examine the key attributes of both methods, providing a foundation for understanding their practical applicability. This research makes the following key contributions:

1. **Empirical insights** into how Scrum and Kanban are applied in startups, providing a deeper understanding of their role in managing uncertainty.
2. **Identification of critical agile practices** that improve adaptability and sustainable development, forming agile adoption strategies.
3. **Hybrid agile guidance**, offering practical tips for startups seeking to balance structure with flexibility.

These contributions impact both research and practice. For researchers, the study fills a gap in understanding how startups tailor agile methodologies to their needs, paving the way for future research into hybrid agile frameworks. For practitioners, the findings provide actionable insights into the selection and adaptation of Scrum and Kanban elements, helping startups optimize their workflows, improve responsiveness, and maintain agility in a competitive landscape. The remainder of this paper is structured as follows. Section 2 reviews related academic work. Section 3 details the research method, Sect. 4 considers threats to the validity of the investigation, Sect. 5 presents the survey results, Sect. 6 contains the discussion and implications, and Sect. 7 concludes the study and suggests future research directions.

## 2    Related Work

Several studies have explored the adoption and effectiveness of agile methodologies in software startups. A systematic mapping study by Paternoster et al. [39] analyzed 213 software development practices in 43 primary studies, revealing that only 16 practices explicitly focused on software development methods in startups, with only 9 studies demonstrating high scientific rigor. This highlights the limited empirical evidence on how agile methodologies are applied in startup environments. Further research by Giardino et al. [14] introduced the Greenfield Startup Model (GSM) based on interviews with 13 startups, showing that startups prefer iterative prototyping over formalized processes to rapidly release a minimum viable product (MVP).

Similarly, a study of Brazilian startups [45] found that in the early stages, teams select impromptu practices and tools, based on prior experience, while in the later stages, they move towards structured processes for scalability. Agile methodologies, particularly Scrum and Kanban, have been identified as widely used approaches in software development teams. The HELENA study [26], a two-year global investigation involving 1,500 teams, confirmed that Scrum and Kanban are among the most widely adopted agile methods. Further studies have examined specific agile practices in different contexts. A survey of 1,526 software startups [38] found that teams prioritize agile practices related to speed (e.g. frequent releases and agile planning) over quality-focused practices (e.g. refactoring and test-first development). Furthermore, a statistical study [27] examined project management factors in Scrum and Kanban-based projects, indicating that both methodologies contribute to successful outcomes, but require adaptation.

A systematic mapping study [51] in 14 startups in Finland, Italy and Norway revealed that startups tend to tailor methodologies to their specific needs, removing and modifying existing practices rather than strictly following predefined frameworks. Another study on motivations for agile adoption [32] identified rapid product delivery, adaptability to changing priorities, maintainability, process simplification, and predictability as the main drivers of agile use in startups. However, the lack of empirical data on how these motivations influence the selection and adaptation of methods creates uncertainty for researchers and practitioners. Identifying which aspects of Scrum and Kanban benefit startups requires evaluating their use across teams, projects, and organizations [1,51].

Existing studies suggest that startups frequently customize agile frameworks, but our research reveals that there is insufficient research on how these adaptations impact their ability to manage uncertainty and maintain agility. Additionally, while past studies provide insight into agile adoption, there is a need for a deeper understanding of how specific Scrum and Kanban practices directly contribute to managing uncertainty and adaptability in startup environments. This study builds on previous findings by focusing on transferable elements of Scrum and Kanban that support startup sustainability and success.

## 3    Research Method

### 3.1    Research Objectives and Research Question

This study aims to explore which components of Kanban and Scrum are best suited to navigate uncertainty and ambiguity in a fast-paced environment. To achieve this objective, our research question explores and identifies these aspects in Scrum and Kanban methods, laying the groundwork for our investigation.

**Research Question (RQ):** What specific aspects of Kanban and Scrum effectively address uncertainty and adaptability within the dynamic and fast-paced environment characteristic of software startups?

### 3.2    Research Survey

We aimed to comprehensively address the research question by seeking the impact of Scrum and Kanban on development approaches within software startups. In software-oriented enterprises, the widespread adoption of agile and lean methods requires a systematic approach to elucidate similarities and differences in the implementation of Scrum and Kanban. According to Unterkalmsteiner et al. [53], these criteria are placed among engineering activities, human aspects, and startup ecosystems. However, theoretical knowledge alone isn't sufficient for enterprise-level applications in software startups. Hence, we designed an online survey (available as a Google form[1]) to collect adequate data on practical experiences. Given the diversity of software startups, our research approach helps identify common patterns and key differences in how Scrum and Kanban are implemented across various startup environments.

**Questionnaire Objectives and Structure.** The survey aims to gain insight into the motivations and evolving practices surrounding the adoption of Kanban, Scrum, or hybrid approaches. We ensured the comprehensiveness of our survey by refining the questionnaire through multiple iterations. We reduced bias, adjusted the clarity of the questions, and piloted them with both a general respondent and an agile practitioner. The final version features 23 questions. The first part of the questionnaire is introductory, providing a definition and motivation for the research. The second part includes screening questions, focusing on demographics, before the main questionnaire to ensure respondent eligibility, maintaining data quality and relevance. The third part contains seventeen core questions in multiple choice format, designed to capture practical insights into how Scrum and Kanban address uncertainty and adaptability in software startups. We designed questions based on key differences and similarities between Scrum and Kanban identified in the literature, covering aspects such as compatibility with Lean and Agile principles, sustainable pace, fostering self-organization, requirement prioritization, Work In Progress (WIP) limits [2,23,56], feedback loop, scope management  [2,28], team structure [2,27], iterative development, frequent delivery [23,44], workload visualization [4] and responding to change [44,56]. These questions assess key aspects that contribute to managing rapid change and unpredictability. By analyzing the responses, we identify patterns in how teams apply these agile practices, providing a structured approach to answering the research question. Table 1 shows the questions used in this survey. In particular, the questionnaire used a well-established method to capture nuanced perceptions and reduce response bias in research [8,48,54]. This scale allowed participants to provide responses at seven points, ranging from "Strongly Disagree" to "Strongly Agree".

**Target Population and Sampling.** To execute the questionnaire, we needed to create a repository of people considered software startup practitioners. According to various studies in the context of software startup (such as [6,35,39,46,52]), software engineers with varying levels of experience and skills are essential for startups of all types and sizes. Furthermore, research on agile transformation in software startups (such as [1,13,47,52]) highlights agile practitioners as key players in this fast-paced and innovative environment. Consequently, we considered these two main groups to ensure that our sample

---

[1] https://forms.gle/HVA4j2sqiRN4mbTM7.

**Table 1.** Survey Questions used in this study

| Topics/Principles/Practices | Statements for participants to express their views or agreement |
|---|---|
| Demographic and Screening Questions | D1-Participant Age/ Profession/ Skills/ Job |
| | D2-Software Startup Experience (Yes/No) |
| | D3-The option that best describes your experience (Screening Question) |
| | D4-Software Startup Size Worked for |
| | D5-The phase of Startup Company Formation |
| | D6-Duration of Collaboration |
| Iterative Requirement Engineering and Software Development | Q1-The company allowed teams to iteratively refine/develop their product/project requirements and deliverables. |
| Sustainable Pace in Software Development Life Cycle (SDLC) | Q2-The team achieved an enhanced sustainable pace in releasing work during the iterations |
| | Q3-The team(s) effectively managed workloads and established a sustainable pace of workflow |
| Iteration Size Effects | Q4-Implementing shorter iterations reduced the delay in the team's delivery |
| Visualization of Flow | Q5-Visual task boards clarified work for the team and facilitated a quicker completion |
| | Q6-Visualizing the work facilitated prioritization for our team regarding their tasks |
| Limited Work In Progress | Q7-There was an opportunity for the team to manage and limit work in progress |
| Estimation and Prioritization | Q8-Estimating tasks aided the team in identifying better prioritization |
| | Q9-An ordered backlog of tasks let the team choose the next task promptly after completing the current one |
| Testing first approach or testing during the development | Q10-There was an opportunity for the team to test during the development |
| | Q11-Testing first caused a tangible decrease in the time needed to complete tasks |
| Pair Working/Programming | Q12-Pair working on tasks helped the team to resolve them more accurately and quickly |
| Daily Events/Team Structure | Q13-Short Daily Meetings reduced the need for other unplanned ad hoc meetings during workdays |
| | Q14-Business and technical teams collaborated daily toward the goals of the product/project |
| Goal Setting/Risk Management/Team Structure | Q15-Business owners recognize and assess risks and effectively communicate them to the dev team |
| | Q16-The team formulated actionable plans for delivering their goal during planning events |
| Customizing Method | Q17-Removed certain elements from Scrum/Kanban implementation |

accurately represents any software startup. These groups are chosen because they best represent the perspectives of those working in startups at different stages of their life cycles. We further divided each group into different strata to cover all roles responsible for the Software Development Lifecycle (SDLC) in startups. These subgroups form our pool for "Quota Sampling" (see [16, 34] for more information). To reach a diverse audience for the survey, we used email lists, online forums and communities, and social media platforms (such as LinkedIn, Instagram, etc.). Quotas are set for different demographic groups within the target population to ensure a balanced sample, minimize bias, and accurately reflect population diversity. According to Yang and Banamah [55], quota sampling cannot be considered an acceptable alternative to probability sampling methods. To enhance randomness in sampling, we used open-survey platforms and encouraged participants to redistribute the questionnaire within their networks. By avoiding industry-specific targeting and sharing across diverse online platforms, we aimed to minimize bias and reach a broader audience.

**Survey Data Cleaning Policy.** To maintain the quality and validity of the survey data, we undergo thorough data cleaning and validation procedures. Initial attention directed toward respondents' responses to demographic questions is crucial for filtering out inadequate samples. The demographic questions are designed to determine the eligibility of the participants, focusing on their experiences within software startup environments. Participants who lack such experience as software engineers within this ecosystem are excluded from the study. Furthermore, we established a minimum threshold of 15 answered questions (out of 23 survey questions) for each data entry. Entries that do not meet this criterion are removed from the dataset. Additionally, duplicate columns introduced during the data exporting process are eliminated. Lastly, we addressed various evident errors that affected data integrity and accuracy, such as the data export process and incomplete responses. For example, some participants, in answering the screening question, stated "Please select the option that best describes your experience", selected "I have worked for at least one software startup in my career" but left the startup size question unanswered. Such incomplete responses were removed to ensure consistency and reliability in the analysis.

## 4    Validity Threats

This section outlines the potential validity threats in this study, in order to ensure the credibility and reliability of the findings.

### 4.1    Construct Validity

Throughout this investigation, we conducted three iterations of questionnaire design and piloting. The initial 86-question survey encountered several challenges, including an overwhelming volume of questions, participant comprehension, and interpretation issues regarding Scrum/Kanban methods, as well as biases such as acquiescence and social desirability. To address these issues, we gradually refined the questionnaire, reducing it to 23 questions. Although this reduction risked losing some depth in covering the subject, it was necessary to balance completeness with response rate, as longer surveys tend to decrease participant engagement. In addition, each iteration included an evaluation phase, in which feedback on clarity and completion time was collected from an experienced agile practitioner and a bilingual English speaker.

## 4.2   Internal Validity

One threat to internal validity comes from self-selection bias, where people who are more interested in Agile methods may be more likely to respond to the survey. Another issue is the order or timing of questions can affect answers because people might get tired or be influenced by earlier questions. To reduce these risks, we used random selection in selecting a part of the respondents and reduced the number of topic questions to 17, which can be answered in less than 15 min.

## 4.3   External Validity

The next potential threat lies in the selection of practitioners, as responses may not fully reflect the diversity of software startup professionals, posing a risk to internal validity. To mitigate this, we intentionally sampled professionals from diverse domains using a quota strategy to ensure balanced representation across specialization, age, and experience levels, aiming for a dataset that better reflects the broader population. The generalizability of our findings may be limited by the sample's coverage of startup software practitioners, potentially affecting external validity. Furthermore, the survey was distributed via open platforms such as LinkedIn and Twitter, making the total reach unknown and preventing the calculation of an overall response rate.

## 5   Results of the Survey

In this section, we present the results of our survey study, which aimed to explore the adoption and impact of Scrum and Kanban methodologies in software startups. The questionnaire was distributed to 241 participants, resulting in 134 responses, with 121 selected for analysis based on established quality criteria (the cleaned version of the dataset, including demographic information, is available at [33]). Despite the optional nature of some core questions, the completion rate was 90%. Since the survey's dataset is ordinal, we used *Kendall's W* to measure agreement and *chi-square test* to check statistical significance. Kendall's coefficient of concordance (W) is a method to check whether there is much agreement between many people who rank the same items. It shows how similar their rankings are. This helps to understand whether people are mostly agreeing or not when rating the same things [20,34]. The Chi-square ($\chi^2$) statistic is a distribution free tool designed to analyze group differences when the dependent variable is measured at a nominal level [30]. The results indicate a strong agreement on key practices such as *Visualization of Work/Flow* (Q5: W = 0.164, $\chi^2$ = 8.37; Q6: W = 0.175, $\chi^2$ = 17.83) and *prioritization* (Q9: W = 0.149, $\chi^2$ = 15.24), suggesting that these are widely adopted and consistently interpreted practices in Agile startups. *Iterative development* and *requirement refinement practices* received moderate levels of agreement from the participants (Q1: W = 0.081; $\chi^2$ = 8.34), *Manage Workload by Limited WIP and Estimation* (Q7: W = 0.098, $\chi^2$ = 10.08; Q8: W = 0.049, $\chi^2$ = 5.08), *Pair Working/Programming* (Q12: W = 0.096, $\chi^2$ = 9.84), *Daily Events* (Q13: W = 0.053, $\chi^2$ = 5.38), and *Goal Setting* (Q14: W = 0.113, $\chi^2$ = 11.56), and *hybridize the model* (Q17: W = 0.654, $\chi^2$ = 6.67). In contrast, several areas showed weak or no agreement, including *Testing Practices* (Q10: W = 0.047, $\chi^2$ = 4.83; Q11: W = 0.069, $\chi^2$ = 7.06), *Risk Management, Team Structure*, and *Daily Work between business and technical people* (Q15: W = 0.042, $\chi^2$ = 4.31; Q16: W = 0.041, $\chi^2$ = 4.21).

Table 2 presents the principles, practices and other topics investigated in this study, along with their definitions, associated methodologies, related survey questions, and the level of agreement between the respondents, highlighting the following key observations.

*Iterative Development* and *Sustainable Pace*: In Question 1, 62% of the participants agreed (selected 5, 6, or 7) that iterative refinement of requirements and development helped them achieve more clarity and decreased uncertainty. Meanwhile, 18% were neutral (selected 4), and 20% disagreed (selected 1, 2, or 3). Furthermore, 60% (Question 2,3) stated that they were successful (selected 5, 6, or 7) in maintaining a sustainable work pace during iterations. In comparison, 18% were neutral (selected 4), and 25% disagreed (selected 1, 2, or 3).

*Iteration Size*: 60% of participants (in Question 4) outlined (selected 5, 6, or 7) based on their experiences, using shorter iterations decreased latency in their team delivery rate. At the same time, 19% were neutral (selected 4), and 21% disagreed (selected 1, 2, or 3). *Visualization and Prioritization* 80% of the respondents (Question 5,6) acknowledged (selected 5, 6, or 7) using visual task boards clarified tasks, increased completion, and improved task prioritization. While 8% disagreed (selected 1, 2, or 3) and 12% were impartial (selected 4).

*Workload Management with limited WIP*: 56% of the respondents (in Question 7) implied (selected 5, 6, or 7) that the limited work in progress helped them to have more predictable and efficient workflows. 21% selected 1, 2, or 3 and where disagree and 23% selected 4 and were neutral.

*Estimation and Prioritization*: 76% of the respondents (Questions 8,9) stated (selected 5, 6, or 7) that the estimation of tasks is helpful to prioritize work, and a prioritized backlog of tasks led to better pull up a new task after finishing the previous one. 20% selected 1, 2, or 3 and where disagree and the rest of the participants (4%) placed themselves in the middle (selected 4).

*Testing Practices*: About 50% of the respondents (by selecting 5, 6, or 7 in Question 10) conducted tests during the development cycle, and the others could not conduct tests, which is a significant share of the research sample. 30% selected 1, 2, or 3 and disagreed. The other people (20%) selected 4 and were neutral. Furthermore, with more than 60% (Question 11) favoring test-first approaches in software testing (selected 5, 6, or 7). However, 22% had no successful experience in these approaches (selected 1, 2, or 3) and 18% were impartial (selected 4).

*Collaboration and Meetings*: 69% of the participants (in Question 12) reported satisfaction with pair working and pair programming (selected 5, 6, or 7). 14% reported weak experience (selected 1, 2, or 3) and 14% where neutral (selected 4). Furthermore, 64% (in Question 13) indicated (selected 5, 6, or 7) that having short daily Scrum meetings or Kanban stand-up meetings minimized the need for unplanned gatherings. 25% disagreed (selected 1, 2, or 3) and 11% were impartial (selected 4).

*Goal Setting*: 55.8% of the respondents (in Question 14) outlined (selected 5, 6, or 7) that they could set goals during the planning events. 17.5% disagreed (selected 1, 2, or 3) and 26.7% selected 4 and were neutral.

*Team Structure and Daily Work*: In Question 15, respondents were asked to share their experience with teams formed using structure components suggested by Scrum and Kanban, how they recognize risks by business people, and how they communicate them to developers. Furthermore, Question 16 targeted one of *agile manifesto principles* on the daily work between business people and developers [5]. 44% of the respondents stated unpleasant experiences (selected 1, 2, or 3) with teams formed with a Scrum or Kanban team structure. At the same time, 38% reported successful experience (selected 5, 6, or 7) and 18% were neutral (selected 4).

*Risk Management*: Separately from the team structure, in relation to Question 15, 51.2% of the respondents stated (selected 1, 2, or 3) an undesirable experience with Scrum and Kanban methods in how they recognize risks by business people and how they communicate them with developers. 30% agreed (selected 5, 6, or 7) and 18.8 were impartial.

*Customize/Hybridize Methods*: 59% of the respondents (Question 17) outlined (selected 5, 6, or 7) their satisfaction with customizing Scrum and Kanban methods for the customization of their ideal way of working. About 20% disagreed (selected 1, 2, or 3) and 21% were neutral (selected 4).

## 6   Discussion

This research seeks to develop a nuanced understanding of the impacts of Scrum and Kanban methods on software development approaches within startup environments. The survey explores the strengths and weaknesses of both methodologies. Through the analysis of the questionnaire data and the measurement of Kendall's W and the chi-square test, we observed that certain aspects, such as the visualization of workflow and prioritization, show strong agreement between the respondents, suggesting shared understanding and consistent application. In contrast, areas such as team structure, risk management, testing practices, and daily work among business and technical people reveal low agreement, indicating

**Table 2.** Agile aspects addressing uncertainty and improve adaptability in startups

| Topics / Principles / Practices | Definition | Original Method(s) | Assoc. Q(s) | Respondents Agreement |
|---|---|---|---|---|
| Iterative Development | In complex projects, the customer may not define concrete requirements or know the end product. The iterative model allows changes [43] | Scrum | Q1 | |
| Requirement Refinement (Engineering) | Breaking down and further defining requirements daily in Kanban, or within sprints in Scrum [40,44] | Scrum / Kanban | Q1 | |
| Sustainable Pace in Development | A sustainable pace is when the team is empowered to manage their work, maintaining focus and consistency through Sprints [43,44] | Scrum | Q2 , Q3 | |
| Iteration Size Effects | Shorter Sprints can be employed to generate more learning cycles and limit risk of cost and effort to a smaller time frame [44] | Scrum | Q4 | |
| Visualization of Work / Flow | Using tools like a Kanban board to represent tasks and the process they go through [3] | Kanban | Q5 , Q6 | |
| Manage Workload by Limited Work In Progress (WIP) | A policy that constrains the amount of Work in Progress allowed in a given part of the system [3] | Kanban | Q7 | |
| Estimation | Determining required effort for doing work by all team members which use of difficulty level, scaling, numeric sizing and so on [2] | Waterfall | Q8 | |
| Prioritization | The process of ordering an emergent list of needs in the Product Backlog, guiding the Team's work to improve the product [44] | Scrum | Q9 | |
| Testing Approaches | The process of evaluating an integrated system to verify that it meets specified requirements [12]. It can involve validating software in a real setting by the intended audience through User Acceptance Testing [37]. | XP / TDD / V-Model | Q10 , Q11 | |
| Pair Working / Programming | A practice where two developers work together at one workstation. One writes the code, while the other reviews each line of code as it's written [23] | XP | Q12 | |
| Daily Events | A 15-minute event held at the same time and place each day, focusing on coordination and unblocking issues and promotes quick discussions to complete work items [3,44] | Scrum / Kanban | Q13 | |
| Goal Setting | Single or long term-objective and commitment for the Scrum team [43,44] | Scrum | Q14 | |
| Team Structure / Daily Work | Scrum's organization aspect defines team structure to deliver value [43] and team in Kanban treats work as a "service" to create a predictable flow of value [3] | Scrum / Kanban | Q15 , Q16 | |
| Risk Management | In Scrum involves the use of short sprints and the maintenance of transparency in artifacts to optimize predictability [44]. Kanban adds Risk Review Cadence to address blockers and improve delivery [3] | Scrum / Kanban | Q16 | |
| Customize / Hybridize Method | A combination of agile methods that an organization adopts and tailors to meet its specific needs [24] | None | Q17 | |

varied interpretations or implementation. In the remainder of this section, we discuss the findings, challenges, and implications for further research.

## 6.1  Key Findings and Implications

The key findings of this research can be incorporated to answer the research question on the aspects of Scrum and Kanban in addressing uncertainty and volatility to improve adaptability. Most of the respondents supported the use of Scrum and Kanban as operational frameworks in software startups. These methodologies offer valuable strengths suitable for dynamic and uncertain startup environments. Specifically, more than 80% of the respondents agreed that *Visualization* of work plays a critical role. However, there is great agreement on the endorsable impact of some aspects such as *Iterative Development, Pair Working/ Pair Programming*, and *Short Daily Meetings*. The principle of iterative and incremental work, a cornerstone of Scrum, emerges as widely adopted among respondents. Moreover, our analysis unveils a prevailing belief among participants that *shorter iterations* contribute to reduced delivery delays, aligning with the concept of shorter sprints inherent in Scrum events.

Another notable observation is the effectiveness *management of workload*, a serious challenge, particularly in startups characterized by high uncertainty. Despite these challenges, a significant portion of the respondents reported successful strategies to address workload concerns. In contrast to the revelation that many respondents *utilized visual task boards* have been asked to elucidate their work processes, it becomes apparent that elements of Kanban, such as visualizing workflow and managing flow, play a pivotal role. Although the iterative and incremental approach of the visualization and flow management capabilities of Scrum and Kanban were particularly appreciated to improve agility and productivity, approximately 60% of the participants disagreed with the *Team Structures* recommended by both Scrum and Kanban, especially with respect to the role of business people and their communication channels with developers. This issue was again reflected by around half of the respondents in the identification and *managing risks* in a fast-paced environment.

## 6.2  Challenges and Implications for Further Research

This study confirmed that software startups tend to tailor their way of working by either *customizing* Agile methods or *hybridizing* elements from multiple approaches, such as Scrum and Kanban. As shown in Sect. 5, participants expressed varying levels of agreement on the aspects investigated, revealing practical challenges and adaptations. For example, participants tended to agree with the relevance of practices like *Requirement Engineering* and *Daily Events*, suggesting that these elements align well with their work contexts.

In contrast, there was a tendency to disagree on aspects such as *Team Structure* and *Daily Work* between business and technical people, indicating potential misalignment or shortcomings in how these elements are addressed by Scrum and Kanban. Furthermore, some practices such as *Estimation* and *Pair Working/Programming* - which originate from other methodologies - were also identified by the respondents as important, reflecting the demand for broader methodological integration. These findings highlight the need for further research into how startups blend and adapt Agile practices to fit their evolving needs and constraints. Furthermore, this research identifies two extra crucial areas, including:

- *Testing Practices:* Both Scrum and Kanban are silent on software testing approaches and consider them as practices that software developers should achieve outside these methodologies. The survey results show that half of the respondents are using practices from different agile or none-agile methods such as Test Driven Development (TDD) and so on, to evolve their SDLC and test-first approaches are favored.
- *Risk Management:* Although the Kanban includes the *Risk Review Cadence* to identify and manage risks continuously [3], and Scrum claimed that the iterative incremental development approach will address risks successfully [44], around half of the respondents stated that the lack of practical attention to address it amplified uncertainty in their experience in software startups.

These areas are therefore prime targets for further research in the context of software startups.

# 7    Conclusion

This study aimed to explore the impacts of Scrum and Kanban on software development in startup environments, revealing valuable information about their practical applications and their potential for hybridization. By analyzing the survey data, several key aspects emerged as influential in shaping development practices. The findings indicate a strong consensus among the respondents on the effectiveness of certain practices. In conclusion, this study provides a nuanced understanding of how Scrum and Kanban address adaptability and uncertainty in software startups, highlighting key strengths, challenges, and the potential for hybrid models.

It underscores the importance of focusing on practices with strong consensus and low variability while approaching those with mixed results with a context-sensitive perspective. In addition, identified gaps, particularly in testing practices, daily work between business and technical people, risk management, and team structures, offer valuable opportunities for innovation in agile practices tailored to startup needs. These insights highlight how software startups navigate uncertainty and adapt Agile methodologies to their dynamic environments. Although this study identifies key elements in the management of uncertainty and adaptability issues, more research is needed to improve agility, productivity, and adaptability in dynamic and uncertain environments, such as software startups.

**Acknowledgments.** We express our sincere gratitude to all participants who contributed their valuable time and insight to our survey study. Their input was essential in enriching the findings of this research.

**Disclosure of Interests.** The authors have no competing interests to declare that they are relevant to the content of this article. This work was supported by a research grant for the GIST project (reference number 20220235) from the Swedish Knowledge Foundation.

# References

1. Abrantes, P.C., Furtado, A.P.: Agile development practices applied to software startups: A systematic mapping review. In: 16th Iberian Conference on Information Systems and Technologies, pp. 1–6. IEEE (2021)
2. Alqudah, M., Razali, R.: A comparison of scrum and kanban for identifying their selection factors. In: 6th International Conference on Electrical Engineering and Informatics (ICEEI), pp. 1–6. IEEE (2017)
3. Anderson, D.J.: Kanban: Successful Evolutionary Change for Your Technology Business. Blue Hole Press, Seattle (2010)
4. Anderson, D.J., Carmichael, A.: Essential Kanban Condensed. Blue Hole Press, Seattle (2016)
5. Beck, K., Cunningham, W., Fowler, M., et al.: Manifesto for agile software development. https://agilemanifesto.org/ [Accessed: May 2, 2024] (February 2001)
6. Berg, V., Birkeland, J., Nguyen-Duc, A., Pappas, I.O., Jaccheri, L.: Software startup engineering: a systematic mapping study. J. Syst. Softw. **144**, 255–274 (2018). https://doi.org/10.1016/j.jss.2018.06.043
7. Blank, S.: The four steps to the epiphany: successful strategies for products that win. John Wiley & Sons (2020)
8. Brühlmann, F., Petralito, S., Rieser, D.C., Aeschbach, L.F., Opwis, K.: Trustdiff: development and validation of a semantic differential for user trust on the web. J. Usability Stud. **16**(1) (2020)
9. Brunner, D., Münch, J., Kuhrmann, M.: Entrepreneurial software engineering: towards a hybrid development method for early-stage startups. WI-MAW-Rundbrief **27**(1), 5–15 (2021)
10. Cavalcante, B.H., Leal, G.C.L., Balancieri, R., de Farias Junior, I.: Technical aspects of software development in startups: A systematic mapping. In: 44th Latin American Computer Conference, pp. 100–109. IEEE (2018)
11. Dingsøyr, T., Nerur, S., Balijepally, V., Moe, N.B.: A decade of agile methodologies: towards explaining agile software development (2012)
12. Erhardsson, K., Ljungberg, O.: Team setup and ways of working at Ericsson: A study on system test teams (2017), Chalmers Univerity of Technology, Sweden
13. Gandomani, T.J., Zulzalil, H., et al.: How pre-start up assessment helps software companies in agile transition. Sci. Int. **25**, 1125–1130 (2013)
14. Giardino, C., Paternoster, N., Unterkalmsteiner, M., Gorschek, T., Abrahamsson, P.: Software development in startup companies: the greenfield startup model. IEEE Trans. Software Eng. **42**(6), 585–604 (2015)
15. Giardino, C., Unterkalmsteiner, M., et al.: What do we know about software development in startups? IEEE Softw. J. **31**(5), 28–32 (2014)

16. Iliyasu, R., Etikan, I.: Comparison of quota sampling and stratified random sampling. Biometrics Biostatistics Int. J. **10**(1), 24–27 (2021)
17. Iversen, P., Johansen, P.B., Leebeek, D., Morch, E., Olsen, E.F., Skarås, S.B.: Supporting the management of software development processes in startups (2018)
18. Jain, P., Sharma, A., Ahuja, L.: The impact of agile software development process on the quality of software product. In: 7th International Conference on Reliability, Infocom Technologies and Optimization, pp. 812–815 (2018)
19. Kemell, K.K., Nguyen-Duc, A., Wang, X., Risku, J., Abrahamsson, P.: Software startup essence: How should software startups work? In: Fundamentals of Software Startups: Essential Engineering and Business Aspects, pp. 97–109. Springer (2020)
20. Kendall, M.G.: Rank Correlation Methods. Charles Griffin, London, UK (1948)
21. Klotins, E., Unterkalmsteiner, M., Chatzipetrou, P., Gorschek, T., et al.: A progression model of software engineering goals, challenges, and practices in start-ups. IEEE Trans. Software Eng. **47**(3), 498–521 (2019)
22. Klotins, E., Unterkalmsteiner, M., et al.: Use of agile practices in start-ups. arXiv e-prints pp. arXiv–2402 (2024). https://doi.org/10.37190/e-inf210103
23. Kniberg, H., Skarin, M.: Kanban and Scrum-making the most of both. C4Media Incorporated, Research Triangle, North Carolina, United States (2010)
24. Kuhrmann, M., Diebold, P., et al.: Hybrid software and system development in practice: waterfall, scrum, and beyond. In: Proceedings of the International Conference on Software and System Process, pp. 30–39. ACM (2017)
25. Kuhrmann, M., Tell, P., Hebig, R., et al.: What makes agile software development agile? IEEE Trans. Software Eng. **48**(9), 3523–3539 (2021)
26. Kuhrmann, M., Tell, P., Klünder, J., et al.: Helena stage 2 results (2018). http://dx.doi.org/10.13140/RG.2.2.14807.52649. Accessed 2 May 2024
27. Lei, H., Ganjeizadeh, F., Jayachandran, P.K., Ozcan, P.: A statistical analysis of the effects of scrum and kanban on software development projects. Robotics Comput.-Integrated Manuf. **43**, 59–67 (2017)
28. López, L., Bagnato, A., Ahberve, A., Franch, X.: Qfl: data-driven feedback loop to manage quality in agile development. In: 43rd International Conference on Software Engineering: Software Engineering in Society (ICSE-SEIS), pp. 58–66. IEEE (2021)
29. Matthies, C.: Scrum2kanban: integrating kanban and scrum in a university software engineering capstone course. In: Proceedings of the 2nd International Workshop on Software Engineering Education for Millennials, pp. 48–55. ACM (2018)
30. McHugh, M.L.: The chi-square test of independence. Biochemia medica **23**(2), 143–149 (2013). https://doi.org/10.11613/BM.2013.018
31. Melegati, J.: What influences software startups to use lean startup? In: Proceedings of the 19th Int. Conf. on Agile Software Development, pp. 1–3 (2018)
32. Mkpojiogu, E., Hashim, N., Al-Sakkaf, A., Hussain, A.: Software startups: motivations for agile adoption. IJITEE **8**(8S), 454–459 (2019)
33. Mojabi, O.: Agile development impacts on software startups-questionnaire dataset. https://doi.org/10.5281/zenodo.15064697. Accessed 21 Mar 2025 (2025)
34. Moser, C.A., Stuart, A.: An experimental study of quota sampling. J. Roy. Stat. Soc. Series A (General) **116**(4), 349–405 (1953)
35. Nguyen-Duc, A., Kemell, K.-K., Abrahamsson, P.: The entrepreneurial logic of startup software development: a study of 40 software startups. Empir. Softw. Eng. **26**(5), 1–55 (2021). https://doi.org/10.1007/s10664-021-09987-z
36. Oliva, F.L., Kotabe, M.: Barriers, practices, methods and knowledge management tools in startups. J. Knowl. Manag. **23**(9), 1838–1856 (2019)

37. Otaduy, I., Diaz, O.: User acceptance testing for agile-developed web-based applications: empowering customers through wikis and mind maps. Syst. Softw. **133**, 212–229 (2017). https://doi.org/10.1016/j.jss.2017.01.002
38. Pantiuchina, J., Mondini, M., et al.: Are software startups applying agile practices? the state of the practice from a large survey. In: Agile Processes in Software Engineering and Extreme Programming, pp. 167–183. Springer (2017)
39. Paternoster, N., Giardino, C., Unterkalmsteiner, M., Gorschek, T., Abrahamsson, P.: Software development in startup companies: a systematic mapping study. Inf. Softw. Technol. **56**(10), 1200–1218 (2014)
40. Razali, R., Alqudah, M.: An empirical study of scrumban formation based on the selection of scrum and kanban practices. IJASEIT **8**(6), 2315–2322 (2018)
41. Ries, E.: The lean startup: How today's entrepreneurs use continuous innovation to create radically successful businesses. Crown (2011)
42. Sakikhales, M.: Nonlinear Project Management: Agile, Scrum and Kanban for the Construction Industry, pp. 227–246. Springer (2021)
43. Satpathy, T., et al.: A guide to the scrum body of knowledge (SBOK guide). A brand of VMEdu, Inc., Scrumstudy (2016)
44. Schwaber, K., Sutherland, J.: The 2020 scrum guide, November 2020. https://scrumguides.org/scrum-guide.html. Accessed 2 May 2024
45. Souza, R., Malta, K., De Almeida, E.S.: Software engineering in startups: a single embedded case study. In: IEEE/ACM 1st International Workshop on Software Engineering for Startups, pp. 17–23 (2017)
46. Souza, R., Malta, K., Silva, R., et al.: A case study about startups' software development practices: a preliminary result. In: Proceedings of the XVIII Brazilian Symposium on Software Quality, pp. 198–203 (2019)
47. Surendra, N.C., Nazir, S.: Agile development: exploring what practitioners want to know. J. Softw. Eng. Appl. **11**(1), 1–11 (2018)
48. Takahashi, H., et al.: Semantic differential scale method can reveal multidimensional aspects of mind perception. Front. Psychol. **7**, 1717 (2016)
49. Tam, C., da Costa Moura, E.J., Oliveira, T., Varajão, J.: The factors influencing the success of on-going agile software development projects. Int. J. Project Manage. **38**(3), 165–176 (2020)
50. Tegegne, E.: Software development methodologies and practices in startups: Systematic literature review (2018), Master's thesis, Faculty of Information Technology and Electrical Engineering, University of Oulu, Finland
51. Tegegne, E.W., Seppanen, P., Ahmad, M.O.: Software development methodologies and practices in start-ups. IET Software **13**(6), 497–509 (2019)
52. Tolfo, C., Wazlawick, R.S., Ferreira, M.G.G., Forcellini, F.A.: Agile practices and the promotion of entrepreneurial skills in software development. J. Softw. Evol. Process **30**(9), e1945 (2018)
53. Unterkalmsteiner, M., Abrahamsson, P., XiaoFeng, W., Nguyen-Duc, A., Edison, H., et al.: Software startups - a research agenda. e-Informatica, vol. X, pp. 2016; ISSN 1897–7979 (2016). https://doi.org/10.5277/E-INF160105
54. Verhagen, T., Hooff, B.v.d., Meents, S.: Toward a better use of the semantic differential in is research: an integrative framework of suggested action. J. Assoc. Inf. Syst. **16**(2), 1 (2015)
55. Yang, K., Banamah, A.: Quota sampling as an alternative to probability sampling? an experimental study. Sociological Res. Online **19**(1), 56–66 (2014)
56. Yordanova, S., Toshkov, K.: An agile methodology for managing business processes in an it company. Bus. Manag. **3**, 27–90 (2019)

57. Zavazava, T.: Project Management Methodologies for Software Development in Startups. Master's thesis, Stockholm University (2022)
58. Zorzetti, M., Signoretti, I., Salerno, L., Marczak, S., Bastos, R.: Improving agile software development using user-centered design and lean startup. Inf. Softw. Technol. J. **141**, 106718 (2022)

# Towards AI-Driven Organizations

Jan Bosch[1,2] and Helena Holmström Olsson[3(✉)]

[1] Department of Computer Science and Engineering, Chalmers University of
Technology, Gothenburg, Sweden
`jan.bosch@chalmers.se`
[2] Department of Mathematics and Computer Science, Eindhoven University of
Technology, Eindhoven, The Netherlands
`jbosch1@tue.nl`
[3] Department of Computer Science and Media Technology, Malmö University,
Malmö, Sweden
`helena.holmstrom.olsson@mau.se`

**Abstract.** There are few technologies, if any, that have the potential to
change the software-intensive industry to the extent that artificial intelligence (AI) is currently doing. Across industries, companies are adopting these technologies to improve productivity, to increase efficiency and
to automate tasks. In products, AI is used for optimization and mass-
customization. However, there are few examples of companies that use
AI to reinvent and fundamentally change their existing practices. In this
paper, we present results from an expert interview study in which we
explore how AI is affecting the ways in which companies operate and
what steps companies evolve through when advancing their use of AI
in their development processes, in their products and in their business
processes. The contribution of the paper is two-fold. First, we present
the interview results that reflect the adoption and use of AI technologies. As part of our interviews, we also identify a set of key challenges
that companies experience. Second, we present an inductively derived
three-pronged maturity model that describes how companies transition
from traditional towards AI-driven organizations.

**Keywords:** Software-intensive systems companies · AI-driven
development process · AI-driven products · AI-driven organizations

## 1 Introduction

During the last decade, companies across domains have experienced rapid transformations to their businesses due to artificial intelligence (AI). As recognized in
[10], AI has the potential to change the software profession more than any other
recent technology. It can improve software productivity by automating testing
processes, assist in reviewing code, analyze past project data to predict potential project risks, resource needs, and timelines, supporting project management
and planning, translate user requirements into technical specifications, provide
real-time support for developers and help in diagnosing issues in code by learning from historical debugging efforts. Several recent studies show how the use of

D. Taibi and D. Smite (Eds.): SEAA 2025, LNCS 16083, pp. 280–295, 2026.
https://doi.org/10.1007/978-3-032-04207-1_19

AI improves development of products by streamlining the software development cycle [6, 20, 27]. In many companies, tools such as e.g., Cursor GitHub and CoPilot have gained widespread usage and are considered key to reduce effort and time spent on software testing, code optimization, documentation and tasks related to quality assurance and maintenance [11]. Also, the increasingly advanced reasoning capabilities of large language models (LLMs) offer the potential to assist developers from conceptualization and code generation to project analysis [5, 13]. By automating labor-intensive tasks, AI enables engineers to focus on creative problem-solving and innovative design tasks [1].

In our experience, and based on recent interactions with companies in the software-intensive systems domain, we see similar patterns. In these companies, AI technologies are used to help people do "more of what they are already doing" and to complement teams in existing tasks. In most cases, people use AI tools to improve their own personal productivity and to automate specific steps in a process. During R&D of products, AI agents are often used to support and automate e.g., test case generation and we also see examples of AI agents being used to complement teams in areas where team members lack certain skills.

However, if looking beyond the examples of using AI for productivity and efficiency gains, we see very few examples. To the best of our knowledge, few studies report on cases in which AI is used to fundamentally reinvent existing tasks, roles, processes and organizations. Taking a critical perspective, one could argue that most organizations are using AI for relatively small and repetitive tasks while not utilizing its full potential.

In this paper, we present results from an expert interview study involving ten practitioners from different companies and representing different industry domains. The purpose of our study is to understand how AI is affecting the ways in which companies operate and what steps companies evolve through when advancing the use of AI in their development processes, in their products and in their business processes. The research question we explore is the following: *"How are AI technologies used to advance development processes, products and business processes and what are the steps that companies evolve through when transitioning towards AI-driven organizations?"*

The contribution of this paper is two-fold. First, we present the results from an exploratory interview study where we investigated the adoption and use of AI technologies in development processes, products and company-wide business processes. As part of our investigation, we also identify a set of key challenges that companies experience. Second, we present an inductively derived three-pronged maturity model that describes how companies transition from traditional towards AI-driven organizations.

The remainder of the paper is organized as follows. In Sect. 2, we present the background to this study by reviewing recent research. In Sect. 3, we describe the research method by detailing the expert interview study. In Sect. 4, we report on our empirical findings. In Sect. 5, we identify a set of key challenges that the interviewees experience in the adoption and use of AI in their organizations. In Sect. 6, we present an inductively derived three-pronged maturity model in which we outline how companies transform towards AI-driven organizations. In

Sect. 7, we discuss threats to validity. Finally, in Sect. 8 we conclude the paper and outline future research.

## 2   Background

Although Generative AI (GenAI) has been a developing field for several years, the launch of ChatGPT in late 2022 accelerated digitalization. Suddenly, there was a tool that significantly increased efficiency by automating tasks, that could enhance customer experience by providing tailored responses and recommendations, that could accelerate content creation and that could assist in data-related tasks such as interpreting large datasets, identify market trends and make data-driven decision-making more accessible to people without technical expertise. Based on what we have seen so far, it is fair to say that the introduction of ChatGPT and similar tools has forever changed software engineering and the perception of how to design and build a software-intensive system [2,17,26]. For the very first time, digital disruption has hit the software engineering field itself.

There are numerous studies exploring the potential, the use, the risks and the challenges associated with AI technologies and tools. So far, most studies take a productivity perspective when exploring how the use of e.g., Cursor and CoPilot can help reduce time and efforts spent on coding, testing and maintenance. For example, [14] study the successes and challenges of AI programming assistants, [27] explore the use of LLMs for software testing, [12] present results on using LLMs in domain-specific languages, and [31] focus on automated program repair using LLMs. In [11], the authors discuss opportunities and challenges when using AI for activities ranging from code generation, code transformation and code optimization to software testing, program analysis and maintenance. Similarly, [1] explore the potential of GenAI and how to optimize the adoption of this technology in business and development workflows. Their results show that GenAI is particularly useful for improving code quality and for reducing development time. In [21], the authors explore how Large Language Models (LLMs) can offer valuable contributions to software development and how the quality of the response from the model is dependent on the quality of the prompt given. In [28], the authors study how knowledge workers with different experience can partner with AI to gain productivity. The study shows that AI is of primary benefit for workers with greater task-based experience, and that senior workers with broader job responsibilities gain less from AI than their junior colleagues. While these studies represent only a small fraction of all recent research on GenAI, they illustrate the potential of these tools and the many ways in which they transform many of the traditional activities in software engineering. Also, they reflect the challenge in how and when to benefit from these tools and the current state-of-practice when it comes to adoption and use of these.

In our own previous research, we studied how digital technologies, i.e., software, data and AI, are rapidly transforming software-intensive systems companies [3,18,19], how AI is developed and deployed in the engineering, procurement and construction industry [7], organizational strategies for integrating AI technology into businesses [8], how to leverage AI in quantity and cost estimations

[9], the use of federated learning and federated reinforcement learning techniques in embedded systems [29,30] and deep learning text detection techniques for automation of engineering tasks [25].

# 3   Research Method

Our study employs a qualitative research design centered on expert interviews to gain insights into the ways in which companies adopt and use of AI in their development processes, in their products and in their business processes. We opted for an interview-based approach due to its capacity to generate rich, multi-perspective data that represents the experiences and perceptions of experts in the field [16,23,24]. The interviewees are experts in their fields and they have a role and a responsibility involving introducing and advancing AI in their respective organizations.

## 3.1   Data Collection

Our data collection spanned from January 2025 - April 2025, comprising semi-structured interviews with ten AI experts from eight different companies. The industry domains and roles of the interviewees are outlined in Table 1. The companies operate across various industries, including telecommunications, digital infrastructure and communication, automotive, consulting, tobacco, technology and service supply and security and surveillance. All interviews lasted for one hour and followed an interview guide organized around three themes, i.e., the use of AI in the development process, the use of AI in products and the use of AI in business processes. During the interviews, one researcher asked the questions and facilitated the conversation while the other researcher took responsibility for taking notes and for asking follow-up questions if needed. Our goal was to capture the respondents' experiences and perceptions of AI and to get their view on how AI will transform current organizations and ways-of-working. Also, we were interested in learning about the challenges the interviewees experienced in introducing and advancing the use of AI in their organizations.

## 3.2   Data Analysis

For analysis of our empirical data, we adopted a thematic analysis approach. Thematic analysis is a method for identifying and analyzing patterns of meaning in a data set and it helps illustrate which themes are important in the description of the phenomenon under study [4]. During our analysis, we followed the guidelines as provided in [15] to identify patterns in the interviews in ways that allowed us to state commonalities across interviews. As suggested in [15], the aggregation of empirical data into patterns and themes allow for putting the different pieces of our empirical insights into relation with one another.

**Table 1.** Overview of interviewees involved in our study.

| Industry | Role |
|---|---|
| Telecommunications | CI/CD expert |
| Digital infrastructure and communication | Head of AI and data |
| Consulting | AI and technology advisor |
| Automotive | AI adoption manager |
| Consulting | AI & Society expert |
| Tobacco | AI transformation expert |
| Technology and services supplier | Head of Engineering |
| Security and surveillance | Engineering manager |
| Security and surveillance | Product owner |
| Technology and services supplier | Security & Software expert |
| Defense | Chief digital officer |

## 4    Empirical Findings

### 4.1    AI in the Development Process

The use of AI in the development process is something that all interviewees are familiar with and that they see happen in their companies. Regardless of domain, interviewees report on tools such as Cursor and CoPilot being used by individual developers for tasks such as code completion, for test case generation and for documentation purposes. Typically, AI tools are viewed as "assistants" in that they help automate repetitive development tasks. This is reflected in a quote from one of the interviewees when saying: *"We see people automate some of their tasks and there is an increasing interest in learning how to use existing tools such as LLMs and agents, how to prompt and how to use and adapt existing ML models."* Similarly, another interviewee shared how people in the development organization use AI in their expertise areas: *"People use AI for tasks and in areas where they are already experts to reduce time and effort spent on certain tasks."* Also other interviewees have similar experiences and a common pattern is that AI is heavily used to simplify and automate tasks that are well-known and where AI help people to do "more of what they already do but faster". In some companies, there are examples of using AI agents to complement, and sometimes even replace, team members or entire teams. While this is not yet common practice, one interviewee shared an example of a situation in which the organization was *"...looking into multi-agent systems where AI replaces entire teams."* According to the interviewee, this would allow the organization to leverage the benefits with AI and increase productivity without having to hire additional people.

While the interviews provide several concrete examples of how AI is used in the development process, the majority of the interviewees expressed concerns about the pace of adoption. In their opinion, their organizations are not aggressive enough and hence, not reaping the full benefits of AI. In most organizations, AI is used for simpler tasks but not yet for changing the current development process. This is reflected in a quote by one of the interviewees when saying: *"We automate separate tasks, but we don't reinvent the end-to-end engineering cycle and solution development process. A worst case scenario would be that we use AI to generate test cases on source code but not much more."* In the conversation, the interviewee shared how we will get to a point where systems are generated by giving the system a prompt on which it executes. In such a scenario, fewer people will be needed to generate products and according to the interviewee this is a future we need to prepare for as development organizations. Another interviewee reflected on this when saying: *"The problem in the future is that a big part of the system is no longer code, it is no longer the software system we are used to, instead it is an ML system."* In the following discussion, the interviewee shared how the organization could free up a significant amount of resources if they would stop developing commodity software. This would allow people to instead spend their time on experimentation with differentiating functionality and advancing their skills in gathering data, training ML models and selecting, adopting and integrating third party models.

When asking the interviewees whether AI will replace people in the development of products opinions were diverse. While some interviewees believe that AI will replace what they refer to as "deep in the stack people", i.e., people in R&D who are working on very specific and narrow tasks, other interviewees view R&D as being about abstract reasoning, coordination and multi-modal knowledge and therefore, better suited for humans than for AI. What was agreed upon is that AI will be increasingly used to complement and replace developers throughout the development process. The majority of interviewees expect a future in which functionality is monitored and improved continuously during run-time. In one of the interviews, the desired state was presented as: "The best scenario would be that we use AI to generate systems based on intent." The interviewee shared how systems would no longer be built using traditional requirements but instead by defining the intent and let the system experiment and optimize for this during run-time. Similarly, another interviewee shared a scenario where new value is produced when having AI agents talking and collaborating to improve speed and quality of developing products.

## 4.2   AI in the Product

The use of AI in products vary and while some companies have automated training and multiple Machine Learning (ML) model deployments in their systems, others use static ML models that are trained on fixed data sets. The common understanding however, is that the number of ML models will only increase and that ML models and AI agents will be used to continuously adjust, improve and optimize future products.

The interviewees agree on that using AI in the product requires a skill-set involving advanced data analytics skills, the ability to build models and networks and good mathematical skills. We learnt how LLMs are used to identify memory leaks, anomalies, certain types of risks, access control and to personalize user experiences. Two of our interviewees highlighted how AI is used in almost all their products and how AI drives change throughout the product lifecycle. All interviews revealed the importance of data as the basis for successful integration of AI in their products. One interviewee described how they *"...started by building the infrastructure and training all employees in data, data platforms, data pipelines and responsible AI before "jumping" on AI and integrating AI into our products."*

In one company, there are digital solutions that can be tailored for each customer and where AI is used for mass-customization and for leveraging data. In another company, there are "smart products" that help users optimize their use and their outcomes when using the product. Overall, the interviews showed on relatively modest use of AI in products. A few cases of multiple ML model deployments were described and although the interviewees refer to a desired state in which ML is continuously used and where e.g., reinforcement learning (RL) is used to customize and optimize products, it was clear that we are not there yet.

### 4.3   AI in the Business Process

Our interviews show that there is limited use of AI at the business level and most interviewees see little use of AI in current innovation processes. This is reflected in the following quote: *"There is very little use of AI in the business and strategy layer. It is as if nobody is doing anything."* Another interviewee recognizes a similar challenge when saying: *"When thinking about what an AI use case could be, people typically think about having AI do what we already do but faster. There is very little innovation. We don't know how to unlock new value with AI nor how to use it to thrive and drive revenue."*

However, the interviewees note significant benefits of AI in terms of efficiency gains and reduced costs in business processes surrounding development of products. This is highlighted in the following quote: *"The major benefit of AI is in the business processes around the product and not in R&D itself. We use it to make it easier to extract financial data, to automate invoicing processes, to generate data from transcriptions, to produce daily reports, trend reports, and data for decision-making. Currently, we are educating managers to use AI when scanning CV's to identify mismatches and potential contradictions and also as a tool for retrieval of information."* This interviewee talked about how the organization wants to double the amount of business but not by doubling the amount of employees and mentioned the possibility to "hire" agents.

In another interview, the use of AI for business processes was also recognized: *"Business people apply tools such as Github, Copilot, ChatGPT to their own problems to create no-code solutions that reduce time and effort spent. For example, to produce documentation used to take a full working day for most people. With ChatGPT it takes minutes and people who used to be the ones writing this text can instead only check so that the information is correct."* Similarly, another interviewee shared how finance processes benefit from AI: *"In finance, we use GenAI to track how many products we sold, up-sell, cross-sell, predic-tion of sales and customers can query the data to generate their own reports. We look at shipment of products, component deliveries, and prediction of pro-duction lines."* In one interview, it was mentioned how AI is used to optimize product planning processes: *"...instead of having to have data scientists interact with market people which takes months, we can now use AI to plan and pre-dict product launches much more effectively."* Based on our interviews, we see that most companies are in a stage where individuals play around with AI tools to increase their own productivity. Also, there are several examples of success-ful automation of certain process steps in e.g., product planning processes, HR and finance. Only one interviewee mentioned an example where AI was used in the end-to-end process. When asking about the desired state and what an AI-driven organization could look like, most interviewees imagined an organization in which all business processes were redesigned from an AI-first perspective and where automation and agentic AI was used to accelerate the business.

## 5   Key Challenges

In all interviews, it was clear that the adoption and use in the development process, in the product and in the business processes is associated with several challenges. Across companies, adoption is regarded slow and all interviewees recognize hesitation, uncertainty, lack of trust and organizational cultures and hierarchies as inhibitors to AI adoption and use. Below, we summarize key chal-lenges that all interviewees experience:

- **Not in my backyard:** The interviewees highlight how a key challenge with organizing in an "AI-driven way" is that organizations are political in nature, there are power structures, reputation, etc. Typically, automation is a threat to all of these and therefore very little happens.
- **Failure is not an option:** The interviewees experience their companies as risk averse and even in areas where AI is being adopted there is "more opinions than actual work". People are afraid of failing and the uncertainty and immaturity in using the technology hold people back.
- **Just say no:** All organizations are experiencing an increasing number of regulations, laws and directives in the areas of data and AI. This causes a situation in which governance roles in organizations tend to adopt an overly careful approach with the result that little happens in adoption of new tech-nologies.
- **Don't bother me with it:** All interviewees experience a situation in which leaders in their organizations don't realize the potential of AI. A common challenge is that the management level views AI as a "technology problem" and fails in understanding that the adoption of AI is a process change that requires company-wide change management initiatives and support.

# 6  Towards an AI-Driven Organization

Although all companies involved in this study have been going through a digital transformation for a decade or more, the rapid emergence of especially generative AI (GenAI) and agentic AI took everyone by surprise and changed the course and pace of the digitalization journey. Below, we discuss the changes that the interviewees see in the development process, in the product and in the business processes. For each area, we outline the maturity steps through which companies evolve. The maturity models we present are inductively derived from our interviews and they describe how companies transition towards AI-driven organizations.

## 6.1  Maturity Model: Process

With the emergence of GenAI, we see a shift in the way software is developed in the companies. In Fig. 1, we capture the typical steps that companies evolve through when adopting GenAI in their development process.

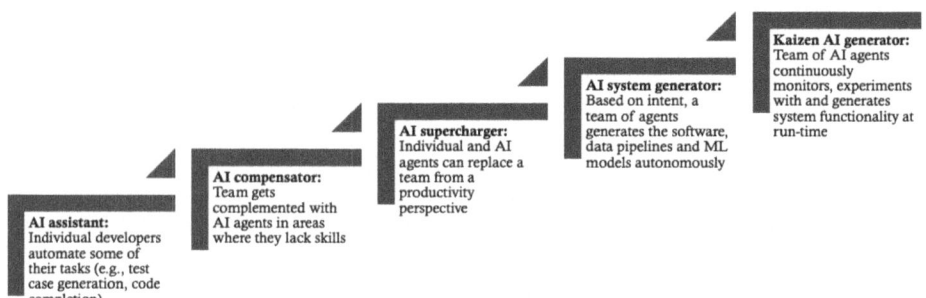

**Fig. 1.** Towards an AI-driven development process.

- **AI assistant**: The first step is concerned with improving the productivity of individual developers through automation. This often includes test case generation, code completion and other tasks that individual developers conduct and where GenAI can support or automate.
- **AI compensator**: The second step is concerned with supporting teams in areas where they lack skills and capabilities for a specific task at hand. This may be concerned with using tools or libraries that the team is not familiar with, but it may also be concerned with the functionality that the team is asked to build and where it needs more context than what is provided in the specifications. At this stage, AI is used to compensate the team in an area where it lacks expertise.

- **AI supercharger**: Once the company adopts Agentic AI, we see a step where the team is replaced by an individual, often an architect or senior engineer, complemented with a set of vertical AI agents that generate the various outputs required. In one of the interviews, an enterprise architect was complemented with a requirements agents, a design agent, a coding agent, a quality assurance agent and a documentation agent. With proper prompting and review of the generated output, the company was able to replace an entire development team.
- **AI system generator**: The fourth step is where the entire system can be generated by a set of AI agents without human oversight. Although none of the companies that we interviewed have reached this stage, it was mentioned as the next step to aspire to. Also, there are research prototypes that can generate software solutions based on a single prompt from a non-technical person, such as a product manager. In this case, the software is generated offline and then put in operation.
- **Kaizen AI generator**: The final step is where the agents and the generated system are both operating as one system at run-time where the agents monitor the system in operation, conduct experiments to improve the performance of the system and autonomously either regenerate parts of the system or use techniques such as reinforcement learning to select specific actions at run-time.

As companies evolve through the maturity steps outlined above, we see two main changes. The first is that the efficiency of development in terms of functionality generated per investment of human resources increases significantly with each stage. It is not unrealistic to replace an entire agile team with an single individual and a set of vertical AI agents. The second change is that the specification of what success looks like needs to become increasingly precise and quantitative. For a system to autonomously experiment with its own behavior, it needs quantitative metrics or a reward function to determine whether it is improving.

## 6.2   Maturity Model: Product

The companies that we interviewed have been exploring the use of ML models in a variety of use cases in their products also before GenAI was introduced. However, GenAI changed some of the ways in which AI is used in software-intensive products. As shown in Fig. 2, we again recognize five maturity steps that companies evolve through with respect to using AI in the product.

- **Static ML**: Several of the companies have been using ML models in specific, often less critical, parts of their products. Typically, this is a model that is trained offline, considered to not require updating post-deployment, and simply added to the system as a static component.
- **Dynamic ML**: The second step is where the ML model is used in a more critical context where the optimal response evolves over time. In this context,

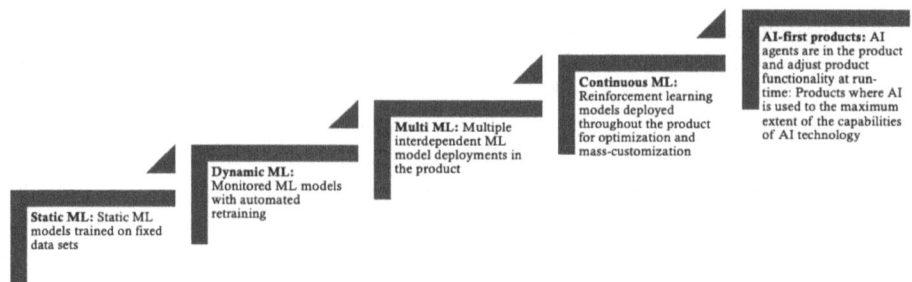

**Fig. 2.** Towards an AI-driven product.

the ML model is surrounded with monitoring solutions that determine the performance of the model. When this falls below a predefined threshold, the system triggers automated retraining based on the most recent data and subsequently deploys the newly trained model.

– **Multi ML**: When the company becomes more comfortable with using ML models, the next step is to use multiple models that have some relationship to each other. In some cases, the output of one model is used as input for the next. In other cases, two different models are used for the same task, but their output is compared so that discrepancies can be identified. This can be a way to increase the confidence in performance of the ML models.

– **Continuous ML**: Whereas the ML models in the previous steps are trained offline, typically using supervised learning, there are many use cases where reinforcement learning (RL) is the more suitable approach. In this case, the RL model has a state, a set of actions and a reward function and learns over time what action is most suitable in each state and based on earlier actions. This can, among others, be used for mass-customization of products as it allows products to adjust themselves to the specific context in which they are deployed.

– **AI-first products**: The most mature step is when the product contains both the generated functionality as well as the agents that monitor and adjust the functionality of the product (referred to as Kaizen AI generator in the development process).

In our interviews, we have seen cases of the first four steps. The last step is often discussed in aspirational terms, but it is clear from our interviews that the final step is quite achievable in the foreseeable future.

### 6.3    Maturity Model: Business Process

Our interviews also highlighted that the business processes inside the company, but outside of R&D, are affected by AI. As shown in Fig. 3, the adoption of GenAI in the business processes can be mapped to five maturity steps.

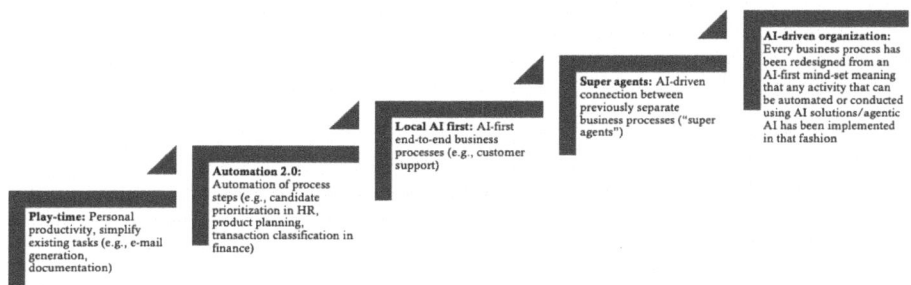

**Fig. 3.** Towards an AI-driven business process.

- **Play-time**: In the first step, similar to the first step in the product development process, individuals use GenAI solutions for personal productivity. This may include generating emails, providing documentation or other tasks typically performed by a single individual.
- **Automation 2.0**: At the second step, the focus is on process steps in business processes that have so far not been possible to automate but where GenAI can be applied. This may include tasks such as prioritization of candidates in HR, production planning in manufacturing, classification in finance, etc.
- **Local AI first**: Third, a single business process is fundamentally redesigned from an AI-first perspective. The idea is that process steps that are not necessary because these are conducted by an AI agent are removed and humans are only assigned to activities that cannot be conducted by an AI agent. This may include providing oversight, but only if it proves to be necessary.
- **Super agents**: In the fourth step, the notion of super agents is introduced as a way to connect AI-first processes that earlier were independent. The goal is to seek optimization across business processes rather than only inside each business process. For instance, R&D and procurement often are unrelated except for R&D informing procurement what to acquire from the outside for a specific product. However, product design can often be optimized significantly by incorporating commodity components that can be sourced from the outside.
- **AI-driven organization**: As the most mature step, every business process has been redesigned from an AI-first perspective. Every activity that can be conducted by AI agents has been automated and the tasks that can not (yet) be performed automatically are measured and controlled by AI agents even though the work is performed by humans.

In the interviews, we also explored the role of humans in companies that are increasingly AI-driven. A model that was discussed by several interviewees is where humans will fall into two separate categories with the first category of people being people that work *"for the algorithm"* and the second category of people being people that work *"on the algorithm"*. Here, "the algorithm" refers to all automation and AI agents that the company has assembled to provide value to customers. The tasks that cannot yet be automated are conducted by people working for the algorithm. The work of these people is often highly measured and controlled. The second category of people is concerned with continuously improving the algorithm to ensure that the efficiency and effectiveness of the company increase over time. Although this topic is not the focus of this paper, it is relevant to reflect upon as it illustrates some of the expectations people have on AI going forward.

### 6.4   Summary and Mapping of Maturity Stages

Our interviews confirm that AI is primarily used to improve efficiency and to complement teams in their existing tasks. If looking at the maturity model for development processes in Fig. 1, all companies operate at the first and second steps. There are many examples of 'AI assistants' and 'AI compensators' and people appreciate using AI to automate certain tasks and having AI add skills they lack as a team. In one interview, the interviewee shared an example of a situation in which AI agents were replacing an entire team which, in this study, is the most advanced use of AI we see in a development process. The two most mature stages, i.e., having agents generate the system ('AI system generator') and having agents continuously monitoring, experimenting and generating functionality at run-time ('Kaizen AI generator') represent what our interviewees referred to as a future and, for some, a desired state.

When discussing AI in products, our interviewees provide examples of the first four steps in Fig. 2. Static, dynamic, multi and continuous ML models are used in products to improve, to optimize and to help customization of products. The most advanced stage, i.e., 'AI-first products', were mentioned by several interviewees in more aspirational terms but it was also clear that this stage is achievable in a not too far future.

Finally, our interviews show that from a business process perspective, companies primarily operate at the first two steps in Fig. 3. We see multiple examples of what we refer to as 'Playtime'. Also, AI is commonly used to automate process steps as described in 'Automation 2.0'. In one interview, we learnt that the company had used AI to reinvent entire processes ('Local AI-first') with very promising results. The two most advanced stages where AI connects previously separate processes ('Super agents') and where every business process is redesigned from an AI-first mind-set ('AI-driven organizations') were mentioned but the interviewees had no concrete examples nor experience of these. Still, they saw the potential and everyone we talked to were highly interested in exploring what a future organization could look like if using AI to its full potential.

## 7   Threats to Validity

Throughout our study, we carefully considered the validity and trustworthiness of our results [22]. To address *construct* validity, we made sure to define key concepts and terminology in the introduction of each interview to ensure a common understanding of key concepts and to avoid misinterpretations. To address *internal* validity, we engaged with AI experts who were able to provide a deep understanding of the complexity of the phenomenon, e.g., people responsible for, and involved in, AI adoption and use within the companies. To address *external* validity, we used our interview findings to inductively derive the conceptual maturity models we present with the intention to provide value for organizations with similar characteristics and challenges as the ones we studied. Finally, to address *reliability*, we applied established practices for data collection and analysis and we made sure our results were shared and approved by the companies involved in our research.

## 8    Conclusions and Future Research

AI is disrupting industry and society to an extent that we have only seen the beginnings of. In most companies, AI is considered key to reduce effort and time spent on e.g., software testing, code optimization, documentation and tasks related to quality assurance and maintenance [11]. Typically, AI is used to enhance productivity of individuals and teams. In our experience however, there are few studies that explore how AI is used outside R&D to reinvent existing practices and transform a company towards becoming an AI-driven organization.

In this paper, we present results from an expert interview study involving ten practitioners representing different companies and industry domains. The purpose of our study is to understand how AI is affecting the ways in which companies operate and what steps companies evolve through when advancing the use of AI in their development processes, in their products and in their business processes. Based on our interviews, we derive a three-pronged maturity model that outlines the steps companies take when transitioning towards AI-driven organizations in which every business process has been redesigned from an AI-first mind-set.

In our future work, we aim to further explore the challenges companies face and identify actions that help companies advance and accelerate the use of AI with the intention to move towards AI-driven organizations.

## References

1. Banh, L., Holldack, F., Strobel, G.: Copiloting the future: How generative ai transforms software engineering. Information and Software Technology, p. 107751 (2025)
2. Bazzan, T., Olojo, B., Majda, P., Kelly, T., Yilmaz, M., Marks, G., Clarke, P.M.: Analysing the role of generative ai in software engineering-results from an mlr. In: European Conference on Software Process Improvement, pp. 163–180. Springer (2024)
3. Bosch, J., Olsson, H.H.: Digital for real: a multicase study on the digital transformation of companies in the embedded systems domain. J. Softw. Evol. Process **33**(5), e2333 (2021)

4. Braun, V., Clarke, V.: Using thematic analysis in psychology. Qual. Res. Psychol. **3**(2), 77–101 (2006)
5. Bucaioni, A., Ekedahl, H., Helander, V., Nguyen, P.T.: Programming with chatgpt: How far can we go? Mach. Learn. Appl. **15**, 100526 (2024)
6. Dakhel, A.M., Nikanjam, A., Majdinasab, V., Khomh, F., Desmarais, M.C.: Effective test generation using pre-trained large language models and mutation testing. Inf. Softw. Technol. **171**, 107468 (2024)
7. Dzhusupova, R., Bosch, J., Olsson, H.H.: Challenges in developing and deploying ai in the engineering, procurement and construction industry. In: 2022 IEEE 46th Annual Computers, Software, and Applications Conference (COMPSAC), pp. 1070–1075. IEEE (2022)
8. Dzhusupova, R., Bosch, J., Olsson, H.H.: Choosing the right path for ai integration in engineering companies: A strategic guide. J. Syst. Softw. **210**, 111945 (2024)
9. Dzhusupova, R., Ya-alimadad, M., Shteriyanov, V., Bosch, J., Olsson, H.H.: Practical software development: Leveraging ai for precise cost estimation in lump-sum epc projects. In: 2024 IEEE International Conference on Software Analysis, Evolution and Reengineering (SANER), pp. 1023–1033. IEEE (2024)
10. Ebert, C., Louridas, P.: Generative ai for software practitioners. IEEE Softw. **40**(4), 30–38 (2023)
11. Gu, A., et al.: Challenges and paths towards ai for software engineering. arXiv preprint arXiv:2503.22625 (2025)
12. Joel, S., Wu, J.J., Fard, F.H.: A survey on llm-based code generation for low-resource and domain-specific programming languages. arXiv preprint arXiv:2410.03981 (2024)
13. Khojah, R., Mohamad, M., Leitner, P., de Oliveira Neto, F.G.: Beyond code generation: an observational study of chatgpt usage in software engineering practice. Proc. ACM Softw. Eng. **1**(FSE), 1819–1840 (2024)
14. Liang, J.T., Yang, C., Myers, B.A.: A large-scale survey on the usability of ai programming assistants: Successes and challenges. In: Proceedings of the 46th IEEE/ACM International Conference on Software Engineering, pp. 1–13 (2024)
15. Lochmiller, C.R.: Conducting thematic analysis with qualitative data. The qualitative report **26**(6), 2029–2044 (2021)
16. Myers, M.D., Newman, M.: The qualitative interview in is research: examining the craft. Inf. Organ. **17**(1), 2–26 (2007)
17. Nguyen-Duc, A., et al.: Generative artificial intelligence for software engineering–a research agenda. arXiv preprint arXiv:2310.18648 (2023)
18. Olsson, H.H., Bosch, J.: Going digital: Disruption and transformation in software-intensive embedded systems ecosystems. J. Softw. Evol. Process **32**(6), e2249 (2020)
19. Olsson, H.H., Bosch, J.: Living in a pink cloud or fighting a whack-a-mole? on the creation of recurring revenue streams in the embedded systems domain. In: 2022 48th Euromicro Conference on Software Engineering and Advanced Applications (SEAA), pp. 161–168. IEEE (2022)
20. Ozkaya, I.: Application of large language models to software engineering tasks: Opportunities, risks, and implications. IEEE Softw. **40**(3), 4–8 (2023)
21. Rajbhoj, A., Somase, A., Kulkarni, P., Kulkarni, V.: Accelerating software development using generative ai: Chatgpt case study. In: Proceedings of the 17th Innovations in Software Engineering Conference, pp. 1–11 (2024)
22. Runeson, P., Höst, M.: Guidelines for conducting and reporting case study research in software engineering. Empir. Softw. Eng. **14**, 131–164 (2009)

23. Schultze, U., Avital, M.: Designing interviews to generate rich data for information systems research. Inf. Organ. **21**(1), 1–16 (2011)
24. Seaman, C.B.: Qualitative methods in empirical studies of software engineering. IEEE Trans. Software Eng. **25**(4), 557–572 (1999)
25. Shteriyanov, V., Dzhusupova, R., Bosch, J., Olsson, H.H.: Robust detection of line numbers in piping and instrumentation diagrams (p&ids). In: 2024 International Conference on Machine Learning and Applications (ICMLA), pp. 888–893. IEEE (2024)
26. Şimşek, T., Gülşeni, Ç., Olcay, G.A.: The future of software development with genai: Evolving roles of software personas. IEEE Engineering Management Review (2024)
27. Wang, J., Huang, Y., Chen, C., Liu, Z., Wang, S., Wang, Q.: Software testing with large language models: Survey, landscape, and vision. IEEE Trans. Softw. Eng. (2024)
28. Wang, W., Gao, G., Agarwal, R.: Friend or foe? teaming between artificial intelligence and workers with variation in experience. Manage. Sci. **70**(9), 5753–5775 (2024)
29. Zhang, H., Bosch, J., Olsson, H.H.: Enabling efficient and low-effort decentralized federated learning with the edgefl framework. Inf. Softw. Technol. **178**, 107600 (2025)
30. Zhang, H., Li, J., Qi, Z., Aronsson, A., Bosch, J., Olsson, H.H.: Deep reinforcement learning for multiple agents in a decentralized architecture: a case study in the telecommunication domain. In: 2023 IEEE 20th International Conference on Software Architecture Companion (ICSA-C), pp. 183–186. IEEE (2023)
31. Zhang, Q., Fang, C., Ma, Y., Sun, W., Chen, Z.: A survey of learning-based automated program repair. ACM Trans. Softw. Eng. Methodol. **33**(2), 1–69 (2023)

# BEWT: A Benchmark for End-to-End Web Testing

Dario Olianas[ID], Maurizio Leotta[✉][ID], and Filippo Ricca[ID]

Dipartimento di Informatica, Bioingegneria, Robotica e Ingegneria dei Sistemi
(DIBRIS) Università di Genova, Genova, Italy
`maurizio.leotta@unige.it`

**Abstract.** Web applications are critical to modern life and require rigorous End-to-End (E2E) testing to ensure reliability across front-end and back-end components. While recent work has improved E2E testing—reducing cost, flakiness, and increasing robustness—a common benchmark is missing, hindering fair comparison and progress.

This work introduces the first E2E benchmark dataset to address that gap: 12 Selenium WebDriver test suites for 8 web applications, packaged in Docker for easy deployment. It supports test evolution, automation, and flakiness studies, offering 389 Gherkin-based test cases, 283 Page Objects, 1,364 locators, and over 19k lines of code.

By providing a reproducible, diverse foundation, this benchmark enables consistent evaluation of testing techniques and fosters advancement in E2E testing research.

**Keywords:** End-to-End Testing · Testing Dataset · Web Testing · Selenium

## 1 Introduction

Web applications are crucial in today's society, supporting various activities. Ensuring their quality is vital to minimize errors. One effective technique is End-to-End (E2E) testing, which verifies the entire application, including both the front-end and back-end. Since web applications are complex and distributed across multiple systems, E2E testing simulates real user interactions, engaging with the GUI elements and following the application's functionalities as a human tester would. Over the years, various tools and frameworks have been proposed for implementing and executing E2E tests for web applications. Test scripts can be developed using either the Capture & Replay or Script-Based approaches [12]. Additionally, different types of locators can be used to identify and interact with elements on a web page [17, 23] (i.e., the aforementioned GUI elements). As a result, researchers have introduced numerous techniques, approaches, algorithms, and tools aimed at enhancing various aspects of E2E test suites. These efforts focus on reducing the initial cost of test script development [15], lowering long-term maintenance costs [29], improving test script resilience to changes in the web application under test [9],

© The Author(s), under exclusive license to Springer Nature Switzerland AG 2026
D. Taibi and D. Smite (Eds.): SEAA 2025, LNCS 16083, pp. 296–314, 2026.
https://doi.org/10.1007/978-3-032-04207-1_20

and minimizing test suite flakiness [26]. Whenever a new technique, algorithm, or framework is proposed, it is essential to conduct an empirical study that provides scientific evidence of its effectiveness in improving the target characteristics of the test suites. For example, in the case of a novel algorithm designed to generate locators for retrieving GUI elements during test case execution, it is important to demonstrate that these locators are more robust—particularly when considering the typical evolution of web applications—compared to those produced by state-of-the-art tools or algorithms.

A significant limitation in current web testing research is the lack of a publicly available benchmark dataset that allows researchers to effectively compare different proposed techniques. Typically, when a new technique is introduced and implemented, researchers must identify a set of test suites to evaluate its effectiveness. However, this process is challenging because readily available test suites for such purposes are scarce. Additionally, creating new test suites specifically for a study could introduce biases that may compromise the validity of the results.

This highlights the need for a publicly shared benchmark. Adopting this benchmark would not only address the challenges faced by researchers but also enable the comparison of new techniques with existing ones without the need to re-run state-of-the-art tools. Once validated on the benchmark, results can be published and directly compared with new approaches, eliminating the need for repeated execution of previous tools each time a new one is proposed.

In this work, we present a initial set of test suites that serve as a benchmark dataset for various studies in the field of E2E testing. These test suites have been carefully selected and refined to provide valuable features for evaluating new approaches in this domain. Additionally, they are accompanied by Docker containers containing the corresponding web applications, ensuring quick and effortless deployment. We plan to extend the benchmark with different versions of the test suites in order to support additional types of studies.

The paper is organized as follows: Sect. 2 provides a brief introduction to the End-to-End Web testing, Sect. 3 gives an in-depth analysis of the relevance of a E2E test suites benchmark and describes several examples of works that could make use of it. Section 4 describes the procedure adopted to create the benchmark. Section 5 presents the test suites. Finally, Sect. 6 reports the related literature while Sect. 7 concludes the paper.

## 2   End-To-End (E2E) Web Testing

End-to-End (E2E) testing for web applications is a form of black-box testing based on test scenarios [12]. Test scenarios define sequences of actions that simulate real user interactions or manual testing procedures. For example, a login test scenario might include entering a username, entering a password, clicking the login button, and verifying successful authentication.

From each test scenario, one or more test cases can be derived by specifying input data (e.g., username = "John.Doe", password = "1234") and expected outcomes, which define assertions. Test case execution can be automated through test scripts, created using various approaches [12]. The choice of approach depends on factors such as the technology stack, available tools (e.g., Selenium WebDriver, Selenium IDE), and the coding proficiency of the testers [10].

Test script development typically follows one of three main approaches: script-based testing (SBT), capture-and-replay web testing (CRT), or the more recent natural language processing-based web testing (NLT).

*Script-Based Testing* (**SBT**) relies on the development of web test scripts using programming languages like Java, Python, or Ruby, and leverages specialized libraries to manage browser execution.

*Capture and Replay Web Testing* (**CRT**) begins with a manual execution where a tester interacts with a web application, while a tool (e.g., Selenium IDE) simultaneously records the entire session. This recording captures all user actions, interactions with web elements, and keystrokes. The tool automatically generates test scripts that can be used to replay the recorded testing sessions. Typically, these recordings also include assertions, often added at the end of the test scripts, to verify the results of the replay. Testers can customize each replay by modifying input values and assertions. Depending on the tool, test scripts can be maintained using a proprietary language (e.g., Selenese, used by Selenium IDE) or exported to a common programming language like Java or Python.

*NLP-Based Web Testing* (**NLT**) leverages natural language processing techniques, enabling software testers to write test scripts using natural language. NLP, a subset of artificial intelligence, allows machines to understand and interpret human language. In NLT, testers create test cases in plain language, and specific tools then transform these descriptions into executable test scripts.

Since the aim of this work is to create a shared E2E testing benchmark, it was necessary to focus on test scripts written in programming languages accessible to all researchers and not tied to a specific proprietary tool. This criterion excluded CRT-based tools when the code is saved using a proprietary language (e.g., Selenese). Therefore, the test suites included in this benchmark are either (a) typically produced from scratch following the SBT approach or (b) created by combining the CRT approach for an initial recording followed by manual refinement of the exported test script code written in standard programming languages (more detail about this hybrid approach to E2E test suite development can be found in [15]). To further support studies and experimentation in the context of NLP-based Web Testing, we decided to provide each test script in the test suite with an equivalent Gherkin description.

## 2.1   Gherkin

Prior to creating test scripts based on a particular testing approach, it is fundamental to define the test cases to be implemented using a specification language. Gherkin[1] is a language widely used in this context [3]. More specifically, Gherkin is a Domain-Specific Language (DSL) that enables the description of software

---

[1] https://cucumber.io/docs/gherkin/reference/.

```
Feature: User management
Scenario: Creates a new user
    Given the user is on the home page
    When the user clicks the "Log in" link
        And enters "admin" in the "Username" field
        And enters "Password001" in the "Password" field
        And clicks the "Log in" button
        And clicks the "Special pages" link
        And clicks the "Create account" link
        And enters "User001" in the "Username" field
        And enters "Password001" in the "Password" field
        And enters "Password001" in the "Confirm Password" field
        And enters "Real Name 001" in the "Real Name" field
        And clicks the "Create" button
    Then "The user account for User001 (talk) has been created." is displayed

    Given the previous assertion passed
    Then the user clicks the "Log out" link
```

**Fig. 1.** Example of test case specified with Gherkin

behavior without delving into implementation specifics. Consequently, it is ideal for disseminating usage scenario descriptions among software teams and is frequently utilized as a language for specifying tests. The Gherkin language is structured and consists of a set of keywords, some of which include:

- Feature: provide a high-level description of the test
- Example/Scenario: show an example of the test
- Given: represent the initial context of the test
- When: describe an action occurred
- And: another action occurred
- Then: describe the result

The code depicted in Fig. 1 illustrates a straightforward example wherein Gherkin is employed to specify a test case for the MediaWiki test suite. The goal of the test is to verify the correct creation of a new user. These well-structured and standardized natural language descriptions are particularly useful as a starting point for studies on NLP-based Web Testing approaches (see, for instance, [16]).

## 2.2  Script-Based Web Test Automation (SBT)

Here we provide a more detailed description of the tests created following the SBT approach. As mentioned earlier, Script-Based Web Testing involves creating web test scripts using programming languages such as Java, Python, or Ruby, along with specialized libraries designed to control browser actions. Typically, these libraries enhance the programming language with user-friendly APIs, enabling commands to interact with the web application, such as clicking buttons, filling fields, or submitting forms. Test scripts are also equipped with assertions, often implemented using common libraries like xUnit (e.g., JUnit if Java is the chosen language), to verify the outcomes of the executed actions.

An example of test script is shown in Figs. 2 and 3. It provides a possible implementation for the simple test case described in Fig. 1: creating a new user

```
package mediawiki;

import java.util.concurrent.TimeUnit;

import org.junit.After;
import org.junit.Before;
import org.openqa.selenium.WebDriver;
import org.openqa.selenium.chrome.ChromeDriver;
import org.openqa.selenium.chrome.ChromeOptions;

import io.github.bonigarcia.wdm.WebDriverManager;
import po.MainPage;

public class BaseTest {

    public static WebDriver driver;

    @Before
    public void setup() {
        WebDriverManager.chromedriver().clearDriverCache().setup();
        ChromeOptions chromeOptions = new ChromeOptions();
        chromeOptions.addArguments("--no-sandbox", "--headless", "--disable-gpu",
                                   "--lang=en");
        driver = new ChromeDriver(chromeOptions);
        driver.manage().timeouts().implicitlyWait(30, TimeUnit.SECONDS);
        driver.manage().window().maximize();
        driver.get("http://localhost:8080");
    }

    protected MainPage loginAsAdmin() {
        return new MainPage(driver)
                .login()
                .setUsername("admin")
                .setPassword("Password001")
                .login();
    }

    protected MainPage loginAsUser() {
        return new MainPage(driver)
                .login()
                .setUsername("User001")
                .setPassword("Password001")
                .login();
    }

    @After
    public void tearDown() {
        driver.quit();
    }
}
```

**Fig. 2.** Example of test script for MediaWiki: base class

```
package mediawiki;

import static org.junit.Assert.assertEquals;
import org.junit.Test;
import po.CreateAccountPage;

public class CreateUserTest extends BaseTest {

    @Test
    public void createUser() {
        CreateAccountPage account = loginAsAdmin()
                .specialPages()
                .createAccount()
                .setUsername("User001")
                .setPassword("Password001")
                .confirmPassword("Password001")
                .setRealName("Real Name 001")
                .create();

        assertEquals("The user account for User001 (talk) has been created.", account.getSuccessMessage());
    }
}
```

**Fig. 3.** Example of test script for MediaWiki: code of the test script

```
package po;

import org.openqa.selenium.By;
import org.openqa.selenium.WebDriver;
import org.openqa.selenium.WebElement;
import org.openqa.selenium.support.FindBy;

public class CreateAccountPage extends PageObject {

    @FindBy(id = "wpName2")
    protected WebElement username;
    @FindBy(id = "wpPassword2")
    protected WebElement password;
    @FindBy(id = "wpRetype")
    protected WebElement confirmPassword;
    @FindBy(id = "wpRealName")
    protected WebElement realName;
    @FindBy(id = "wpCreateaccount")
    protected WebElement createAccountBtn;
    public CreateAccountPage(WebDriver driver) { super(driver); }

    public CreateAccountPage setUsername(String usr) {
        username.sendKeys(usr); return this;
    }
    public CreateAccountPage setPassword(String psw) {
        password.sendKeys(psw); return this;
    }
    public CreateAccountPage confirmPassword(String psw) {
        confirmPassword.sendKeys(psw); return this;
    }
    public CreateAccountPage setRealName(String rn) {
        realName.sendKeys(rn); return this;
    }
    public CreateAccountPage create() {
        createAccountBtn.click(); return new CreateAccountPage(driver);
    }
    public String getSuccessMessage() {
        return driver.findElement(By.xpath("//*[@id=\"mw-content-text\"]/p[1]")).getText();
    }
    public String getUsernameValidationMessage() {
        return username.getAttribute("validationMessage");
    }
}
```

**Fig. 4.** Example of test script for MediaWiki: snippet from a page object

in the MediaWiki application. Figure 2 shows the BaseTest class, which contains the common methods used by every test class. Every test class in the test suites inherits from the BaseTest class. The @Before and @After annotations are used to define commands that are executed before and after the main body of the test script, respectively, to set up and reset the test environment (e.g., initializing the WebDriver, opening the web application, and then closing the browser). The test script relies on the state-of-the-art tool Selenium WebDriver[2].

The test script shown in Fig. 3 is not complete, as it adopts the *Page Object* design pattern[3,4]. A snippet of the implementation of the class CreateAccountPage is shown in Fig. 4; however, this is not the only page object used by the test. The Page Object pattern is a popular web test design pattern that aims at improving test case maintainability and reducing code duplication [12,14], with possible benefits also during the initial development of large test suites [9].

Essentially, each Page Object (PO) is a class that represents the elements of a web page as a set of objects and encapsulates the web page's functionalities into methods. Adopting the Page Object pattern in test suite implementation allows testers to adhere to the *Separation of Concerns* design principle. This separa-

---

[2] https://www.selenium.dev/documentation/webdriver/.

[3] http://martinfowler.com/bliki/PageObject.html

[4] https://code.google.com/p/selenium/wiki/PageObjects

tion decouples test scenarios from implementation details, such as the specific locator used to identify the position of a button in the DOM. These details are relocated to the Page Objects, which serve as a bridge between web pages and test cases, with the latter primarily containing the test logic. Consequently, all functionalities for interacting with or making assertions about a web page are consolidated in a single location—the Page Object—making them easily callable and reusable across various test cases.

Figure 4 shows a code snippet from a page object used by CreateUserTest. Web elements from the page are initialized and referenced using the Page Factory pattern, which is implemented in Selenium WebDriver through the @FindBy annotation. This annotation specifies the locator that must be used to locate the element. In the @Test method body (Fig. 3), the steps are implemented by calling various methods provided by the Page Objects, such as setUsername, which contributes to the logic of the test cases (i.e., entering the name for the new user). Assertions (assertEquals condition) are used to verify the price of the product added to the cart.

The key benefit of programmable testing lies in its flexibility and potential for test script reusability. Working with programming languages empowers developers to use conditional statements, loops, logging, exceptions, and to create parameterized (data-driven) test scripts that can be executed across various browsers [6,13]. These advantages are further enhanced when adopting specific patterns such as the Page Object pattern (as in the example reported here). This approach helps reduce the coupling between web pages and test scripts, promoting greater reusability, readability, and maintainability of the test suites [12]. Nonetheless, programmable testing also has certain drawbacks [9,12], including: (i) testers need non-trivial programming skills to use it effectively; (ii) effectiveness requires adherence to programming guidelines and best practices commonly used in software development; and (iii) developing test scripts typically requires a significant initial effort.

## 3   Motivation

The primary objective of this work is to offer a valuable resource to academic and industry researchers working in the E2E Web testing domain. In particular, we aim to provide a collection of readily usable test suites to facilitate the empirical validation of proposed solutions. Indeed, research papers presenting novel E2E Web testing approaches implemented through tools often require authors to empirically assess and demonstrate the effectiveness of their proposals. However, conducting such evaluations requires researchers to access a sufficient number of test suites for their experiments. Developing these test suites themselves is impractical, as it may introduce experimental bias. Moreover, finding test suites as open-source projects associated with existing web applications is challenging.

To the best of our knowledge, there is currently no publicly available benchmark offering a comprehensive set of E2E Web test suites. This problem has been highlighted by different authors [1,21], that are proposing their own benchmarks at the time of writing this paper. In this work, we want to provide our own benchmark of carefully designed E2E Web test suites, written in Java and based on the Selenium WebDriver framework, and including different versions of some test suites to enable studies on test suite evolution. We selected Java as the reference programming language for our benchmark due to its widespread use in both industry and academia. Java is a primary language supported by many automated testing frameworks, including Selenium. We chose Selenium as the testing framework because it is the de facto standard for web automation and GUI testing [5,14]. Selenium supports a wide range of browsers and platforms, and it provides extensive documentation and community support. Its popularity and robustness makes it a natural choice for benchmarking novel E2E testing solutions.

In particular, this benchmark has been designed to support the following E2E Web testing research areas:

1. test dependencies: detection, management and elimination
2. test flakiness reduction
3. test waiting strategies optimization
4. test suite evolution effort reduction
5. test locators robustness improvement

### 3.1   Test Dependencies

In the context of an E2E test suite, an order-dependent test script is one whose outcome varies based on the sequence of previously executed test scripts. Such dependencies necessitate a strict execution order within the test suite, potentially limiting the application of techniques such as test selection, test prioritization, and test parallelization. While various tools and approaches have been suggested for identifying dependencies within a test suite, only one approach has been proposed, implemented, and validated specifically for E2E Web test suites [2]. All test suites featured in this benchmark exhibit dependencies, making them ideal candidates for validating tools designed to detect and remove test dependencies.

### 3.2   Test Flakiness

Test flakiness is a problem that affects software testing, consisting of test scripts changing their result non-deterministically when executed on the same version of the system under test. Our test suites did not exhibit flakiness at the time of publication. However, because test flakiness is a complex problem with potentially different concurrent causes, it is possible that flakiness may manifest if the suites are executed in different environments (e.g., web server/DB versions, browsers used for navigation). The test suites included in this benchmark can be employed in studies such as the one conducted by Moran et al. [22], where test suites are executed in different environments (e.g., different browser, operating system, screen size, network bandwidth) to detect the configurations that may introduce test flakiness. Moreover, they can be made flaky in several ways, for instance, by modifying the implemented waiting strategies. The test suites integrated into this benchmark are intended to be used to validate novel approaches and tools aimed at detecting and mitigating flakiness.

## 3.3  Waiting Strategies

Waiting strategies, in the context of E2E Web testing, are the mechanisms used to ensure that page elements are correctly loaded. Because E2E Web testing is asynchronous in nature, each interaction with a web page should wait for the target element to be properly loaded. The Selenium WebDriver framework offers two main categories of waiting strategies: explicit waits and implicit waits. Explicit waits are functions that can wait for complex conditions to occur for a specific element, while implicit waits are defined globally for the entire test script. Moreover, E2E testers often rely on thread sleeps to wait for page elements to load. Thread sleeps are functions offered by programming languages that pause test execution for a specified amount of time. Although thread sleeps have some contraindications, they are widely used in E2E Web testing, particularly in combination with implicit waits. According to the Selenium WebDriver documentation[5], implicit and explicit waits must not be mixed in the same test script, as this may lead to unpredictable, potentially infinite waiting times [27].

The test suites provided in this benchmark all rely on implicit waits, supplemented by thread sleeps where necessary. They will simplify the execution of comparative studies on the effectiveness and efficiency of different waiting strategies, and enable the empirical validation of novel tools for the automated management of waiting strategies [24].

## 3.4  Test Suite Evolution Effort Reduction

The primary advantages of embracing test automation include the ability to: (1) run test cases more frequently, (2) detect bugs in the early stages of development, and (3) reuse test code across subsequent releases of the web application for regression testing. However, the main drawback associated with test automation is the fragility of test cases. A fragile test is one that breaks when there are slight modifications to the web application under test. Specifically, as the web application evolves to accommodate changes in requirements, bug fixes, or additional functionalities, test cases may break. For instance, they may fail to locate certain links, input fields, or submission buttons. Repairing these test cases becomes a laborious and costly task, requiring manual intervention by software testers. The automatic evolution of test suites is an active area of research. Depending on the type of maintenance performed on the target web application, software testers must undertake a series of test case repair activities, which can be categorized into two types: logical and structural.

–  Logical Changes pertain to modifications in the functionality of the web application. To repair test cases affected by such changes, the tester needs to adjust one or more steps in the broken test scripts. For example, a change request (CR1) necessitating a logical repair activity could involve enhancing security through stronger authentication. This might entail adding a new field (in

---

[5] Selenium    WebDriver    documentation    for    waits    https://www.selenium.dev/documenta-tion/webdriver/waits/.

addition to the classic login and password) to the login form (e.g., inserting an OTP code).
- Structural Changes, on the other hand, involve alterations solely in the layout or structure of the web page. For instance, in an authentication page, the text on the login button might be changed to "Submit" (CR2), or the identifier of such a web element might be modified (e.g., from id = "UID" to id= "UserID") (CR3). Typically, the impact of a structural change is smaller than that of a logical change. To repair test scripts after a structural change, it is often sufficient to modify one or more locator lines, specifically those containing locators.

The test suites included in this benchmark will facilitate the evaluation of novel techniques focused on automatically repairing broken test scripts. This is because we selected web applications available in multiple versions. Consequently, each test suite can be executed on different versions (beyond the one for which it was created), allowing researchers to identify a set of test scripts requiring repair. At this point, the proposed approach or tools can then be employed to carry out the necessary repair activities. Additionally, for half of the web applications, we have included two test suites that operate on different application versions. These offer reference test suites, serving as a kind of ground truth for how the test suites should look after evolution.

### 3.5   Test Locators Robustness Improvement

Locators are specific structures used by test automation tools to pinpoint and identify web elements on the GUI before interacting with them. As mentioned before, locators are used, for instance, to identify and populate input sections of a web page (such as form fields), perform navigations (like locating and clicking on links), or validate the accuracy of output (such as locating web page elements displaying the results of a computation).

Research has underscored the challenges and costs associated with maintaining *locators* during the evolution of the web application under test [8,11]. Leotta et al. [11] showed that even minor modifications to the application under test can significantly impact locators. As a result, locators play a crucial role in addressing the *fragility problem* of automated test suites. When a web application undergoes changes in requirements the existing automated test code may break, necessitating manual intervention by testers to rectify the issues. This task is costly, and even minor alterations, such as changes in page layout, can cause test code to become *fragile*. The adoption of robust locators helps to alleviate the fragility problem. The generation of robust locators has been an active research area for many years [17–19,23], so, although it is part of test suite maintenance, it is important to describe it separately.

The test suites integrated into this benchmark will simplify the assessment of novel techniques focused on generating robust locators. By offering two versions of the test suite, we inherently provide a locator mapping. Each element present in both versions of the test suite is identified with a locator, say $l1$ in the first version and $l2$ in the second version. An approach or tool that effectively generates a robust locator with respect to the evolution of web applications should be able to accurately locate the same web element identified by locator $l2$ in the second version of the application, starting from the information available in the first version of the web application.

# 4   Procedure

To create the benchmark, we followed these steps. First, we gathered several existing test suites developed in the context of prior E2E testing research works [2,16,20,24,25]. Subsequently, we conducted a ***test suite selection*** process to identify the most appropriate test suites for inclusion in the benchmark. Ultimately, we ***enhanced the selected test suites*** to ensure uniformity in their code structure and compliance with the most relevant best practices in E2E web testing (e.g., adopting the Page Object (PO) pattern, the Page Factory pattern, the PO method chaining, the implicit wait strategy). The subsequent sections provided a comprehensive details of these stages.

## 4.1   Test Suites Selection

From the test suites initially collected, we selected those that adhered to the following criteria:

– The application under test must be sufficiently complex to accommodate at least 20 non-trivial test cases. Consequently, applications such as Spring Petclinic[6] and Addressbook[7], which are commonly used in E2E web testing research, were excluded due to their simplicity, making them unsuitable as examples of modern web applications.
– The application under test must have at least one version released after 2015. This criterion is essential to exclude outdated applications that are no longer maintained and, therefore, unsuitable as examples of modern web applications.
– The application under test must be open source to facilitate redistribution among researchers without licensing constraints. Additionally, open-source access allows for thorough code inspection, a crucial factor for implementing white-box testing techniques.
– The application under test must be easily deployable in one or more Docker containers, minimizing installation and configuration efforts for researchers using this benchmark.
– For half of the selected test suites, a second version of the application under test must be available, differing significantly from the original version (note that we plan to include for all in the next releases of the benchmark). This ensures that test suites can meaningfully vary between versions, enabling

---

[6] https://spring-petclinic.github.io/.
[7] https://sourceforge.net/projects/php-addressbook/.

researchers to study the evolution of test suites by comparing different versions of the same application.

## 4.2 Test Suites Refinement

The test suites we collected were originally developed for different studies with distinct objectives, resulting in variations in features, structure, and code organization. To standardize the test suites as much as possible, we applied the Page Object pattern to all of them, along with the Page Factory pattern where applicable. All page objects implement method chaining, meaning that each method of a page object returns the page object corresponding to the web application page to which the invoked method redirects.

We also standardized the waiting strategies by adopting the *implicit wait* strategy across all test suites, supplemented by thread sleeps where necessary.

For each application, we defined the Gherkin specification for a version of the base test suite.

Finally, we evolved four of the eight test suites (Joomla, MantisBT, PrestaShop, and Bludit) to provide test suites for two different versions of each application.

## 4.3 Test Suites Publish and Documentation

We published the test suites, along with the documentation, at the following URL: https://sepl.dibris.unige.it/BEWT.php. For each application, we provided installation instructions along with a recommended Docker container. For applications requiring additional installation steps after container deployment, we included an automated installer that performs these steps automatically. The installers are implemented as E2E test scripts using Selenium WebDriver, interacting with the web applications through their installation wizards.

# 5  Test Suites

In this preliminary version of the benchmark, we provide a **baseline** (Base) test suite for each application. Additionally, for four out of eight applications, we also provided a **baseline evolution** (Base+) version. This section offers a detailed description of each test suite type.

## 5.1 Baseline

The **baseline** version is the initial test suite from which all other variants are (and will be) derived. All baseline test suites adopt the Page Object pattern and, where applicable, the Page Factory pattern. The Page Object pattern can be implemented at different levels of abstraction, that go from simply encapsulating the invocations of *driver.findElement(...)* to a complex Domain Specific

Language (DSL). In this work, we chose to implement page objects with method chaining (i.e., the methods of the page objects return the page object that correspond to the page where the action performed by the method lands). Test suites are structured with one test per class.

To minimize code duplication, we used inheritance: all test classes extend a *BaseTest* class (represented in Fig. 2), which defines the setup and teardown methods, as well as the *WebDriver* objects and global variables (e.g., authentication credentials).

For waiting strategies, all baseline versions rely on implicit waits, supplemented by thread sleeps where necessary.

Table 1 provides a summary of the key characteristics of the baseline test suites.

**Table 1.** Summary of *baseline* (Base) test suites features

| App | Version | Test Cases | Page Objects | Loca-tors | Thread Sleeps | Total LOC | PO LOC | Tests LOC |
|---|---|---|---|---|---|---|---|---|
| Bludit | 2.3.4 | 23 | 16 | 77 | 5 | 1128 | 619 | 509 |
| Claroline | 1.11.10 | 40 | 22 | 130 | 3 | 1853 | 1014 | 839 |
| Expresscart | 1.19 | 31 | 25 | 105 | 19 | 1549 | 858 | 691 |
| Joomla | 3.10.11 | 35 | 29 | 136 | 5 | 1860 | 1008 | 778 |
| Kanboard | 1.2.15 | 30 | 26 | 102 | 7 | 1421 | 818 | 603 |
| MantisBT | 1.2.0 | 37 | 19 | 107 | 10 | 1662 | 792 | 836 |
| Mediawiki | 1.40.0 | 27 | 15 | 83 | 31 | 1355 | 759 | 523 |
| Prestashop | 1.6.1.23 | 35 | 31 | 135 | 5 | 1843 | 1096 | 681 |

## 5.2 Baseline Evolution

The **baseline evolution** version of the test suite is available for four applications: Bludit, Joomla, MantisBT, and Prestashop. This version is an adaptation of the original test suite to ensure compatibility with a subsequent version of the application under test. We selected application versions that displayed significant differences from the original. To determine whether two versions were sufficiently different, we executed the original test suite on the newer version and proceeded with the evolution only if a noticeable number of tests failed.

The evolved test suites retain all the structural characteristics of the original (Page Object model, use of implicit waits), introducing only the necessary changes to make them compatible with the newer version of the application (typically changes to locators or different action sequences required for certain tasks). In one case (Prestashop), the evolved test suite contains one fewer test than the baseline version, as the tested functionality was not available in the selected version.

These test suites can be used in studies focused on test suite evolution (i.e., maintaining a test suite across different versions of the application under test). Table 2 summarizes the characteristics of the evolved test suites.

**Table 2.** Summary of *baseline evolution* (Base+) test suites features

| App | Version | Test Cases | Page Objects | Loca-tors | Thread Sleeps | Total LOC | PO LOC | Tests LOC |
|---|---|---|---|---|---|---|---|---|
| Bludit | 3.13.1 | 25 | 21 | 87 | 12 | 1336 | 763 | 573 |
| Joomla | 4.2.0 | 35 | 30 | 140 | 9 | 1843 | 1044 | 779 |
| MantisBT | 2.25.4 | 37 | 19 | 105 | 8 | 1628 | 758 | 836 |
| Prestashop | 1.7.8.5 | 34 | 30 | 157 | 8 | 1863 | 1151 | 646 |

### 5.3   Future Extensions of the Benchmark

As seen in the prevision sections, in this preliminary version of our benchmark, each application includes a baseline test suite (Base). Additionally, for four out of the eight applications, we also provide an evolved version of the baseline, referred to as Base+. Over the coming months, we plan to extend the benchmark in several directions to better support a wider range of studies. Specifically, we have already outlined the addition of the following variants for each baseline (Base) test suite:

- an evolved version (Base+), completing the set by adding the four currently missing;
- a version adopting explicit waits (ExWait), which can be particularly valuable for studies focusing on waiting strategies in E2E web test scripts;
- a version that does not rely on the Page Object Pattern (No-PO), which can be useful for research investigating the Page Object model, including techniques and tools for its automatic generation;
- a version based on absolute locators (Abs-Loc), which can serve as a reference point for studies analyzing locator robustness and maintenance.

Moreover, we plan to expand the number of applications included in the benchmark, potentially with the contribution of other researchers who will be able to join and collaborate through our openly available GitHub repository. We also intend to expand the benchmark by incorporating other programming languages and testing frameworks, in addition to Java and Selenium.

## 6   Related Works

In this section, we will summarize existing research work related to this benchmark, focusing in particular on collections of E2E tests. Sanchez et al. [28] published a dataset containing six regression bugs injected into three web applications, along with the corresponding tests designed to detect these bugs. Unlike our work, the applications they used are not real-world web applications but rather purposely developed examples created specifically for their study. Furthermore, the provided tests do not follow any specific design pattern (e.g., the Page Object pattern), and each application includes only one to three tests—just enough to detect the injected regressions. Gortázar et al. [7] proposed a methodology for collecting E2E tests from GitHub projects, based on 12 criteria related to the naming of the project folders and files. While their methodology is valid, it does not include verification steps to filter out toy projects and demo applications [21]. We did not adopt their approach, since the goal of our work is not to collect existing E2E tests, but rather to provide a curated dataset of carefully designed E2E tests that incorporate different design patterns and waiting strategies, intended for use in research studies on E2E testing. Fuad et al. [4] proposed WebEV, a dataset comprised of E2E Web tests from open source projects hosted on GitHub. Differently from our work, their dataset focuses on Cypress-based test scripts, while our work focuses on Selenium WebDriver test script. For many years, Selenium has been considered the de facto tool for browser automation. However, in recent times, we have witnessed the emergence of alternative tools such as Cypress, as well as Puppeteer and Playwright. Therefore, both choices—Selenium and Cypress—can be considered interesting and relevant [5]. Moreover, at the moment of writing, their dataset is not publicly available, as the link reported in their paper leads to an empty GitHub repository. Finally, in 2025, Di Meglio et al. introduced E2EGit [21], a dataset accepted at the MSR 2025 conference and available as a pre-print at the time of writing. E2EGit contains 43,670 GUI web tests extracted from 472 GitHub repositories, along with 271 performance tests collected from 84 repositories. The performance tests rely on tools such as JMeter and Locust, while the GUI tests are built using Selenium, Playwright, Cypress, and Puppeteer, and are written in multiple programming languages, including Java, JavaScript, TypeScript, and Python. The repositories were collected using SEART[8], ensuring the exclusion of toy projects and considering only relevant open source web applications. To the best of our knowledge, at the moment of writing this is probably the most complete dataset about E2E Web testing. Although both E2EGit and our work focus on datasets for E2E web testing, they differ significantly. E2EGit is a large-scale dataset of E2E tests collected from real-world applications, covering multiple programming languages and testing technologies. Since the tests in E2EGit originate from various applications developed by different authors, the quality of the code, the structure and size of the test suites, the adopted design patterns, and the waiting strategies can vary significantly. Our dataset, on the other hand, although significantly smaller in size, consists of test suites that adhere to a uniform coding style and directory structure. This consistency makes it particularly suitable for use as a benchmark for automated tools, such as tools for Page Object generation or explicit wait insertion. Moreover, the availability of different versions of each test suite further supports studies on test suite evolution and refactoring. These

---

[8] https://seart-ghs.si.usi.ch/.

versions can also serve as valuable examples for university courses or professional training programs on E2E web testing.

# 7   Conclusion and Future Work

In this work, we addressed the need for a standardized benchmark dataset in End-to-End (E2E) web testing research by providing a comprehensive set of test suites. Our benchmark consists of 12 Java Selenium WebDriver-based test suites covering 8 different web applications, each designed to facilitate the evaluation of E2E testing techniques. By incorporating variations such as the Page Object Pattern, as well as providing test suites for different application versions, our benchmark enables studies on key challenges in web testing, including test flakiness, script resilience, and test suite evolution.

Our benchmark comprises 389 test cases distributed across multiple test suites, incorporating 283 Page Objects and 1,364 locators to facilitate research in E2E web testing. To handle asynchronous behavior, the test suites include 122 thread sleeps.

To enhance usability and reproducibility, we have packaged all test suites with Docker containers, ensuring seamless deployment. With a total of 19,341 lines of code (LOC), this dataset will support researchers in developing and comparing new approaches to E2E testing, reducing biases in experimental validation and fostering more reliable assessments of emerging techniques.

Future work will focus on expanding the benchmark with additional applications and diversifying test suite characteristics to further improve its applicability as detailed in Sect. 5.3. We plan to introduce new applications, new programming languages (Python, JavaScript) and new testing frameworks (like Cypress, Playwright or Puppeteer) to expand the applicability of our benchmark. We also aim to explore automated techniques for maintaining and evolving test suites across multiple software versions. By continuing to refine and extend this benchmark, we hope to contribute to more rigorous and effective research in web application testing.

**Acknowledgements.** This study was partially carried out within the "EndGame - Improving End-to-End Testing of Web and Mobile Apps through Gamification" project (2022PCCMLF) – Next Generation EU within the PRIN 2022 program (D.D.104 - 02/02/2022 Ministero dell'Università e della Ricerca). This manuscript reflects only the authors' views and opinions and the Ministry cannot be considered responsible for them.

# References

1. Alian, P., Nashid, N., Shahbandeh, M., Shabani, T., Mesbah, A.: Feature-driven end-to-end test generation. In: 2025 IEEE/ACM 47th International Conference on Software Engineering (ICSE), pp. 678–678. IEEE Computer Society (2025)

2. Biagiola, M., Stocco, A., Mesbah, A., Ricca, F., Tonella, P.: Web test dependency detection. In: Proceedings of the 2019 27th ACM Joint Meeting on European Software Engineering Conference and Symposium on the Foundations of Software Engineering, pp. 154–164. ESEC/FSE 2019. ACM (2019). https://doi.org/10.1145/3338906.3338948

3. Cerioli, M., Leotta, M., Ricca, F.: What 5 million job advertisements tell us about testing: a preliminary empirical investigation. In: Proceedings of 35th ACM/SIGAPP Symposium on Applied Computing (SAC 2020), pp. 1586–1594. ACM (2020). https://doi.org/10.1145/3341105.3373961

4. Fuad, M.M.N., Sakib, K.: Webev: A dataset on the behavior of testers for web application end to end testing. In: 2023 IEEE/ACM 31st International Conference on Program Comprehension (ICPC), pp. 79–83. IEEE (2023)

5. García, B., Alamo, J.M., Leotta, M., Ricca, F.: Exploring browser automation: A comparative study of Selenium, Cypress, Puppeteer, and Playwright. In: Bertolino, A., ao Pascoal Faria, J., Lago, P., Semini, L. (eds.) Proceedings of 17th International Conference on the Quality of Information and Communications Technology (QUATIC 2024), CCIS, vol. 2178, pp. 142–149. Springer (2024). https://doi.org/10.1007/978-3-031-70245-7_10

6. García, B., Ricca, F., del Alamo, J.M., Leotta, M.: Enhancing web applications observability through instrumented automated browsers. J. Syst. Softw. **203**, 111723 (2023). https://doi.org/10.1016/j.jss.2023.111723

7. Gortázar, F., Maes-Bermejo, M., Gallego, M., Contreras Padilla, J.: Looking for the needle in the haystack: End-to-end tests in open source projects. In: Paiva, A.C.R., Cavalli, A.R., Ventura Martins, P., Pérez-Castillo, R. (eds.) Quality of Information and Communications Technology, pp. 40–48. Springer International Publishing, Cham (2021)

8. Hammoudi, M., Rothermel, G., Tonella, P.: Why do record/replay tests of web applications break? In: 2016 IEEE International Conference on Software Testing, Verification and Validation (ICST), pp. 180–190 (2016). https://doi.org/10.1109/ICST.2016.16

9. Leotta, M., Biagiola, M., Ricca, F., Ceccato, M., Tonella, P.: A family of experiments to assess the impact of page object pattern in web test suite development. In: Proceedings of 13th IEEE International Conference on Software Testing, Verification and Validation (ICST 2020), pp. 263–273. IEEE (2020). https://doi.org/10.1109/ICST46399.2020.00035

10. Leotta, M., Clerissi, D., Ricca, F., Tonella, P.: Capture-replay vs. programmable web testing: an empirical assessment during test case evolution. In: Proceedings of 20th Working Conference on Reverse Engineering (WCRE 2013), pp. 272–281. IEEE (2013). https://doi.org/10.1109/WCRE.2013.6671302

11. Leotta, M., Clerissi, D., Ricca, F., Tonella, P.: Visual vs. dom-based web locators: An empirical study. In: Sven Casteleyn, Gustavo Rossi, M.W. (ed.) Proceedings of 14th International Conference on Web Engineering (ICWE 2014). LNCS, vol. 8541, pp. 322–340. Springer (2014). https://doi.org/10.1007/978-3-319-08245-5_19

12. Leotta, M., Clerissi, D., Ricca, F., Tonella, P.: Approaches and tools for automated end-to-end web testing. Adv. Comput. **101**, 193–237 (2016). https://doi.org/10.1016/bs.adcom.2015.11.007

13. Leotta, M., García, B., Ricca, F.: An empirical study to quantify the setup and maintenance benefits of adopting WebDriverManager. In: Vallecillo, A., Visser, J., Pérez-Castillo, R. (eds.) Proceedings of 15th International Conference on the Quality of Information and Communications Technology (QUATIC 2022). CCIS,

vol. 1621, pp. 31–45. Springer (2022). https://doi.org/10.1007/978-3-031-14179-9_3

14. Leotta, M., García, B., Ricca, F., Whitehead, J.: Challenges of end-to-end testing with selenium WebDriver and how to face them: a survey. In: Proceedings of 16th IEEE International Conference on Software Testing, Verification and Validation (ICST 2023), pp. 339–350. IEEE (2023). https://doi.org/10.1109/ICST57152.2023.00039

15. Leotta, M., Molinari, A., Ricca, F.: ASSESSOR: a PO-based WebDriver test suites generator from Selenium IDE recordings. In: Proceedings of 15th International Conference on Software Testing, Verification and Validation (ICST 2022), pp. 389–399. IEEE (2022). https://doi.org/10.1109/ICST53961.2022.00045

16. Leotta, M., Ricca, F., Marchetto, A., Olianas., D.: An empirical study to compare three web test automation approaches: NLP-based, Programmable, and Capture & Replay. J. Softw. Evol. Process (JSEP) **36**(5), e2606 (2024). https://doi.org/10.1002/smr.2606

17. Leotta, M., Ricca, F., Tonella, P.: SIDEREAL: Statistical adaptive generation of robust locators for Web testing. J. Softw. Testing, Verification Reliability (STVR) **31** (2021). https://doi.org/10.1002/stvr.1767

18. Leotta, M., Stocco, A., Ricca, F., Tonella, P.: Using multi-locators to increase the robustness of web test cases. In: Proceedings of 8th IEEE International Conference on Software Testing, Verification and Validation (ICST 2015), pp. 1–10. IEEE (2015). https://doi.org/10.1109/ICST.2015.7102611

19. Leotta, M., Stocco, A., Ricca, F., Tonella, P.: ROBULA+: an algorithm for generating robust XPath locators for web testing. J. Softw. Evol. Process (JSEP) **28**(3), 177–204 (2016). https://doi.org/10.1002/smr.1771

20. Leotta, M., Stocco, A., Ricca, F., Tonella, P.: PESTO: Automated migration of DOM-based Web tests towards the visual approach. J. Softw. Testing Verification Reliability (STVR) **28**(4), e1665 (2018). https://doi.org/10.1002/stvr.1665

21. Meglio, S.D., Starace, L.L.L., Pontillo, V., Opdebeeck, R., Roover, C.D., Martino, S.D.: E2EGit: a dataset of end-to-end web tests in open source projects. In: 2025 IEEE/ACM 22nd International Conference on Mining Software Repositories (MSR), pp. 836–840. IEEE Computer Society, Los Alamitos, CA, USA, April 2025. https://doi.org/10.1109/MSR66628.2025.00121

22. Moran, J., Augusto, C., Bertolino, A., De La Riva, C., Tuya, J.: Flakyloc: flakiness localization for reliable test suites in web applications. J. Web Eng. **19**(2), 267–296 (2020)

23. Nass, M., Alégroth, E., Feldt, R., Leotta, M., Ricca, F.: Similarity-based web element localization for robust test automation. ACM Trans. Softw. Eng. Methodol. (TOSEM) **32**(3) (2023). https://doi.org/10.1145/3571855

24. Olianas, D., Leotta, M., Ricca, F.: SleepReplacer: a novel tool-based approach for replacing thread sleeps in selenium webdriver test code. Softw. Quality J. (SQJ) **30**, 1089–1121 (2022). https://doi.org/10.1007/s11219-022-09596-z

25. Olianas, D., Leotta, M., Ricca, F., Biagiola, M., Tonella, P.: STILE: A tool for optimizing E2E web test scripts parallelization. J. Syst. Softw. (JSS) **222**, 112304 (2025). https://doi.org/10.1016/j.jss.2024.112304

26. Olianas, D., Leotta, M., Ricca, F., Villa, L.: Reducing flakiness in End-to-End test suites: An experience report. In: Paiva, A.C.R., Cavalli, A.R., Ventura Martins, P., Pérez-Castillo, R. (eds.) Proceedings of 14th International Conference on the Quality of Information and Communications Technology (QUATIC 2021). CCIS, vol. 1439, pp. 3–17. Springer (2021). https://doi.org/10.1007/978-3-030-85347-1_1

27. Raghavendra, S.: Waits, pp. 129–142. Apress, Berkeley, CA (2021). https://doi.org/10.1007/978-1-4842-6249-8_10

28. Soto-Sánchez, Ó., Maes-Bermejo, M., Gallego, M., Gortázar, F.: A dataset of regressions in web applications detected by end-to-end tests. In: Shepperd, M., Brito e Abreu, F., Rodrigues da Silva, A., Pérez-Castillo, R. (eds.) QUATIC 2020. CCIS, vol. 1266, pp. 439–448. Springer, Cham (2020). https://doi.org/10.1007/978-3-030-58793-2_35

29. Stocco, A., Leotta, M., Ricca, F., Tonella, P.: APOGEN: automatic page object generator for web testing. Software Qual. J. **25**(3), 1007–1039 (2016). https://doi.org/10.1007/s11219-016-9331-9

**Software Analytics: Mining Software
Open Datasets and Repositories**

# The Ground Truth Effect: Investigating SZZ Variants in Just-in-Time Vulnerability Prediction

Alfonso Cannavale[1]([envelope]) [iD], Emanuele Iannone[2] [iD], Gianluca Di Lillo[1],
Fabio Palomba[1] [iD], and Andrea De Lucia[1] [iD]

[1] Software Engineering (SeSa) Lab, University of Salerno, Fisciano, Italy
{acannavale,fpalomba,adelucia}@unisa.it, g.dilillo1@studenti.unisa.it
[2] Institute of Software Security, Hamburg University of Technology,
Hamburg, Germany
emanuele.iannone@tuhh.de

**Abstract.** Just-in-Time (JIT) vulnerability prediction is critical for proactively securing software, yet its effectiveness heavily relies on the quality of the ground truth used for training models. This ground truth is commonly established using variants of the SZZ algorithm to identify vulnerability-contributing commits (VCCs). However, the impact of choosing a specific SZZ variant on model performance remains largely unexplored. In this study, we systematically investigate the effect of eight SZZ variants on JIT vulnerability prediction across seven open-source Java projects. Our findings reveal that the choice of the SZZ variant is a non-trivial factor. Models trained with datasets labeled by variants like **B-SZZ, V-SZZ, and VCC-SZZ** achieve strong and stable predictive performance, with **median MCC scores often exceeding 0.50**. In contrast, variants such as **L-SZZ and R-SZZ** produce models that perform no better than random chance, with **median MCC scores close to 0.0**. This performance gap demonstrates that an inappropriate SZZ variant can invalidate prediction models, underscoring the necessity of a principled approach to defining *ground truth*.

## 1 Introduction

Just-in-Time (JIT) vulnerability prediction aims to identify security-introducing commits before they are integrated into a codebase, providing a first line of defense in modern software development [19,22]. The performance of the machine learning models at the core of this task depends heavily on the *ground truth*—the labeled dataset of vulnerable and clean commits used for their training. Given the infeasibility of manual labeling, researchers universally rely on automated heuristics. The most established one is the SZZ algorithm [28], which identifies *vulnerability-contributing commits* (VCCs) retroactively.

However, SZZ is not a single algorithm but a family of variants, each employing different heuristics. For instance, some variants, like **B-SZZ**, rely on basic line-level history tracing, while more advanced ones, like **V-SZZ**, implement

© The Author(s), under exclusive license to Springer Nature Switzerland AG 2026
D. Taibi and D. Smite (Eds.): SEAA 2025, LNCS 16083, pp. 317–326, 2026.
https://doi.org/10.1007/978-3-032-04207-1_21

complex logic to trace a vulnerability's origin across multiple commits. This proliferation of approaches, combined with a lack of comparative studies in the vulnerability context, creates a critical uncertainty: researchers and practitioners are left to choose a variant without understanding the downstream consequences of their choice. This raises the fundamental question of *how, and to what extent, the selection of an SZZ variant influences the resulting JIT vulnerability prediction models.*

To address this gap, we conduct a large-scale empirical study on seven Java projects, investigating the impact of eight distinct SZZ variants. We assess both the agreement between the ground truths they generate ($RQ_1$) and, more importantly, the downstream effect on the performance of JIT prediction models ($RQ_2$). Our results reveal a performance gap that depends on the chosen variant. We found that models built using ground truths from **B-SZZ, V-SZZ, and VCC-SZZ** are consistently effective, achieving high predictive power (median $MCC > 0.50$). Conversely, models relying on **L-SZZ and R-SZZ** completely fail, delivering performance equivalent to a random guess (median MCC $\sim 0.0$).

This paper provides the following contributions:

- We systematically evaluate, for the first time, the impact of eight SZZ variants on *vulnerability* prediction, demonstrating that the choice of the labeling heuristic is a critical factor.
- We provide clear, empirical evidence that certain variants (L-SZZ, R-SZZ) are unsuitable for this task and can lead to unreliable, near-random models.
- We offer actionable guidance for researchers and practitioners, identifying a set of reliable SZZ variants (B-SZZ, V-SZZ, VCC-SZZ, MA-SZZ) that provide a solid foundation for building effective JIT prediction models.

## 2    Background and Related Work

Research in vulnerability prediction has evolved from file-level analysis [27,32] to finer-grained, commit-level Just-in-Time (JIT) approaches. These JIT models, studied in works like those by Lomio et al. [19] and Nguyen et al. [22], offer immediate feedback but their effectiveness depends on reliable ground truth of *vulnerability-contributing commits* (VCCs). Since manual labeling is impractical, the de facto standard is to use the SZZ algorithm to automatically identify VCCs [28]. Our study builds on the dataset established by Lomio et al. [19] to investigate a critical, often-overlooked aspect: the impact of the SZZ variant choice on the final model.

The SZZ algorithm exists in numerous variants, each with distinct heuristics. The implementation and correctness of these variants have been systematically studied by Rosa et al. [26], who provided both a unified tool, PySZZ, and a developer-informed oracle to evaluate them. Their work highlights the concrete implementation differences between variants like **B-SZZ** [28], which uses simple line-based annotation, and more advanced ones like **V-SZZ** [2], tailored for vulnerabilities. Despite their widespread use, the relative impact of these variants on

JIT *vulnerability* prediction remains unaddressed. A full description of the eight variants we investigate, implemented through PySZZ, is available in Table 1.

The most related study to ours is by Fan et al. [11], who investigated the impact of SZZ variants on JIT *defect* prediction. They found that B-SZZ and MA-SZZ had minimal negative impact, while AG-SZZ degraded performance. Our work is different and complementary: (1) we focus on the more critical domain of **vulnerability prediction**, not general defects; (2) we analyze a broader and more modern set of **eight SZZ variants**, including those used in studies like Lomio et al.'s [19]; and (3) we evaluate not only model performance but also the **agreement** between the ground truths themselves. This study, therefore, provides the first comprehensive analysis of the *Ground Truth Effect* in the specific context of JIT vulnerability prediction.

# 3   Research Method

The *goal* of this study is to investigate how data labeling techniques impact JIT vulnerability prediction models' ground truth. The *purpose* is to understand which SZZ techniques yield better-performing and more stable JIT vulnerability prediction models. This study targets *researchers* interested in ground truth impact on JIT vulnerability prediction and *developers* who may adopt these models in their projects.

The study addresses two research questions. First, we investigate how different SZZ techniques compare in retrieving VCCs to assess their similarities, differences, and impact on ground truth construction.

Second, we assess how SZZ technique differences affect ground truth by training and validating machine learning models on resulting datasets, evaluating the impact of VCC variations on predictive performance.

> **Q RQ₁.** *How similar are the different SZZ techniques in retrieving vulnerability-contributing commits?*

> **Q RQ₂.** *How do the performances of models vary depending on the SZZ technique used to build the ground truth?*

To answer these questions, we conducted a mining software repository study, collecting VCCs using eight SZZ variants. We compared the resulting datasets to assess overlap, identify labeling discrepancies, and evaluate their impact on model performance. Figure 1 summarizes our methodology adhering to the ACM SIGSOFT Empirical Research Standards [1].

## 3.1   Ground Truth Construction and Experimental Setup

**VCC Identification.** Starting from the fixing commits identified by Lomio et al. [19], we used the **PySZZ** tool [26] to run eight distinct SZZ variants

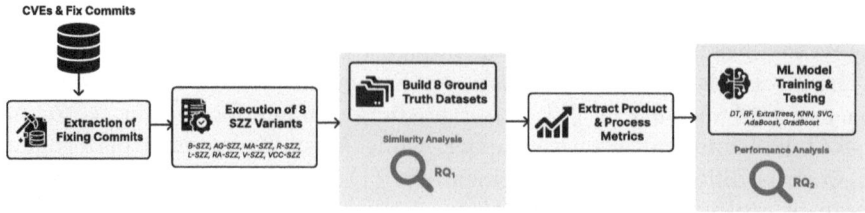

**Fig. 1.** Overview of our research methodology, from data collection to performance analysis.

**Table 1.** The eight SZZ variants analyzed in our study.

| Variant | Core Heuristic |
|---|---|
| B-SZZ [28] | Basic 'git annotate' on deleted lines |
| AG-SZZ [17] | Traverses annotation graph; ignores cosmetic changes |
| MA-SZZ [8] | Like AG-SZZ, but also ignores meta-changes |
| R-SZZ [9] | Like MA-SZZ, but only considers the most recent commit |
| L-SZZ [8] | Like MA-SZZ, but only considers the largest commit |
| RA-SZZ [21] | Like MA-SZZ, but ignores refactoring-related lines |
| VCC-SZZ [16] | Advanced filtering; ignores test/build files, blames more lines |
| V-SZZ [2] | Repeats 'git blame' until origin; vulnerability-specific filters |

and identify VCCs. The variants, summarized in Table 1, include both general-purpose (e.g., B-SZZ) and vulnerability-specific (e.g., V-SZZ) algorithms.

**Controlled Experiment Design.** For each of the eight variants, we created a distinct dataset. To isolate the effect of the labeling heuristic, these datasets differ *only* in their positive instances (the VCCs). The set of negative instances was sampled once (at a 1% ratio relative to project size, following [19]) and kept **identical** across all eight datasets. This controlled setup ensures that any observed performance difference is directly attributable to the SZZ variant used.

**Model Training and Validation.** We adopted two groups of commit-level metrics: *product metrics* capturing structural aspects of modified code (main Chidamber & Kemerer metrics [7]: LOC, WMC, CBO, RFC, DIT, NOC) and *process metrics* capturing code evolution and modification history (added and removed lines, modified files, author's prior commits, modification entropy, author's workload). These metrics, shown to be effective in prior vulnerability research [19,24,27,32], model developer context as factors like inexperience or high workload correlate with defect introduction [32]. Complete metric descriptions are in our online appendix [5].

The *target variable* is a binary label indicating whether each commit is a VCC (1) or not (0). This labeling was performed separately for each of the eight

SZZ variants, resulting in eight ground truth versions with varying VCC counts per project.

Following prior work [19,20], we selected six machine learning algorithms: Decision Tree [4], Random Forest [3], Extra Trees [15], K-Nearest Neighbors [31], Linear Support Vector Classifier [29], AdaBoost [13], and Gradient Boosting [14]. Model training involved three stages: (1) removing collinear features using Variance Inflation Factor (VIF) to reduce overfitting risk [23]; (2) addressing class imbalance through SMOTE [6] on training data; and (3) hyperparameter optimization via Random Search [18,23]. We employed Leave-One-Group-Out (LOGO) cross-validation for cross-project evaluation, where each project serves as a test set once across seven iterations. This approach better reflects operational conditions where models must generalize to unseen projects.

### 3.2   Data Analysis Protocol

To address $RQ_1$, we analyzed SZZ variant overlap using *Jaccard similarity* [25] between VCC sets for each vulnerability-fix pair, creating distributions rather than single scores. We applied Wilcoxon signed-rank tests [30] comparing these distributions against baselines of total disagreement (all zeros) and perfect agreement (all ones). A $p < 0.05$ indicates a significant difference from the baseline.

To address $RQ_2$, we evaluated model performance using the **Matthews Correlation Coefficient (MCC)**, which provides a balanced measure suitable for imbalanced datasets. We applied *Friedman tests* [10] for each ML algorithm to determine if SZZ variant choice significantly impacts performance, followed by post-hoc *Nemenyi tests* [10] when significant differences were found ($p < 0.05$).

## 4   Results and Discussion

### 4.1   $RQ_1$: How Similar Are the SZZ Variants?

To answer $RQ_1$, we measured the overlap between the VCC sets generated by each pair of SZZ variants using the Jaccard similarity. Our statistical analysis confirms that while the variants are not completely disjoint, they are also not interchangeable ($p < 0.05$ against both baselines of 0 and 1, see online appendix [5]).

The descriptive analysis reveals the practical extent of this divergence. On average, any two variants agree on only half of the VCCs they identify (mean Jaccard index ~0.50, std. dev. 0.30). The agreement ranges from a high of 0.89 for the most similar pair to a low of 0.29 for the most dissimilar.

---

### ⚡ Key Findings for $RQ_1$

SZZ variants are only moderately similar and cannot be used interchangeably. On average, two variants agree on only 50% of the identified vulnerable commits, creating substantially different ground truths for training prediction models.

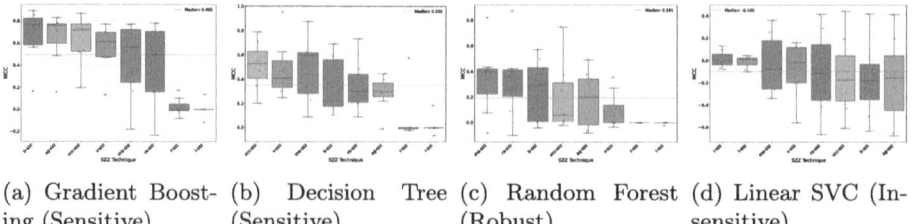

(a) Gradient Boosting (Sensitive)     (b) Decision Tree (Sensitive)     (c) Random Forest (Robust)     (d) Linear SVC (Insensitive)

**Fig. 2.** MCC distributions for four representative classifiers. Variants like L-SZZ and R-SZZ consistently yield poor models (MCC $\sim$ 0.0), while B-SZZ, V-SZZ, etc., lead to effective ones (MCC $> 0.5$).

## 4.2   RQ$_2$: What Is the Impact on Model Performance?

To answer RQ$_2$, we trained seven machine learning models on the eight distinct ground truths and evaluated their performance using the Matthews Correlation Coefficient (MCC). Figure 2 shows the MCC distributions for four representative classifiers. The results reveal a performance gap driven by the SZZ variant. A clear pattern emerges across all models: ground truths from **L-SZZ** and **R-SZZ** consistently lead to models with near-random performance, with median MCC scores close to 0.0. In contrast, variants like **B-SZZ, V-SZZ, MA-SZZ, and VCC-SZZ** consistently produce effective models, with median MCC scores often exceeding 0.50, especially for sensitive classifiers like Gradient Boosting and Decision Tree.

To validate these observations, we performed a Friedman test for each classifier. As shown in Table 2, the choice of SZZ variant has a statistically significant impact ($p < 0.05$) on the performance of the most sensitive models (e.g., Decision Tree, Gradient Boosting, Random Forest). Post-hoc Nemenyi tests (detailed in the online appendix [5]) confirm that for these models, the performance degradation caused by L-SZZ and R-SZZ is statistically significant when compared to top-performing variants like B-SZZ and VCC-SZZ.

> 🔍 **Key Findings for RQ$_2$**
>
> The choice of the SZZ variant is a factor that can make the difference between an effective prediction model and a useless one. Inappropriate variants (L-SZZ, R-SZZ) lead to models with near-random performance (MCC ~0.0), while other variants (B-SZZ, V-SZZ, VCC-SZZ, MA-SZZ) enable models to achieve high predictive power (median MCC $> 0.50$).

## 4.3   Discussion and Implications

Our findings have direct implications for researchers and practitioners. The most critical one is a clear warning: **using L-SZZ or R-SZZ for JIT vulnerability prediction is not efficient**. These variants, relying on overly simplistic

**Table 2.** Friedman test results ($p < 0.05$) on MCC scores. A ✓ indicates a significant performance difference across SZZ variants.

| Classifier | MCC Significant? |
|---|---|
| AdaBoost | NS |
| Decision Tree | ✓ |
| Extra Trees | NS |
| Gradient Boosting | ✓ |
| K-Nearest Neighbors | NS |
| Linear SVC | NS |
| Random Forest | ✓ |

heuristics, systematically produce noisy ground truths that prevent models from learning meaningful patterns.

Conversely, our results provide a set of **recommended variants: B-SZZ, V-SZZ, MA-SZZ, and VCC-SZZ**. These provide a more reliable basis for model training. Notably, the original B-SZZ remains a strong baseline, suggesting that complexity is not always a synonym for better performance in this context.

Furthermore, the impact is **mediated by the ML model**. Sensitive classifiers like Gradient Boosting amplify the differences in ground truth quality, while robust or simpler ones like LinearSVC are less affected (though often at the cost of lower overall performance). This implies that the reported performance of a new JIT prediction technique is heavily biased by the chosen SZZ variant. Comparing studies that use different SZZ variants without acknowledging this effect can lead to flawed conclusions.

## 5    Threats to Validity

VCC retrieval accuracy represents a key threat, stemming from inherent SZZ limitations rather than implementation issues. We mitigated this by selecting diverse SZZ variants, including both general-purpose (B-SZZ) and vulnerability-specific techniques (V-SZZ). This study evaluates SZZ's impact on model performance without validating absolute VCC correctness against manual ground truth; effectiveness is judged solely by downstream ML model performance.

Our ML pipeline introduces potential confounding factors. The 1% negative sampling ratio, while based on prior work [19], and SMOTE balancing, despite known weaknesses [12], could affect results. We mitigated these threats by applying consistent preprocessing across all experiments.

Our focus on open-source Java projects limits the external validity of our findings. While Java was chosen as the most studied language in SZZ research, results may not generalize to other languages or industrial settings with different development dynamics.

# 6   Conclusion and Future Work

Our findings reveal that differences in SZZ variant VCC identification lead to statistically significant variations in model performance. While variants share core VCCs ($RQ_1$), ground truth divergences affect just-in-time vulnerability prediction ($RQ_2$), particularly in data-sensitive models. B-SZZ, V-SZZ, MA-SZZ, and VCC-SZZ produce more stable models with median MCC scores often exceeding 0.50, while L-SZZ and R-SZZ yield weaker outcomes near 0.0. The impact varies by algorithm: decision trees and boosting models amplify labeling differences, while KNN shows less sensitivity but worse overall performance.

Practitioners should interpret these results cautiously, as model reliability remains tied to the unverified accuracy of SZZ ground truth labeling. Future work should investigate generalization beyond Java projects, integrate deep learning models with richer feature sets, and explore hybrid VCC retrieval techniques beyond SZZ heuristics.

**Acknowledgment.** This work was partially supported by projects SERICS (PE00000014) and FAIR (PE0000013) under the NRRP MUR program funded by the EU - NGEU, and the EU-funded project Sec4AI4Sec (grant no. 101120393).

# References

1. Ralph, P., et al.: Empirical standards for software engineering research (2021)
2. Bao, L., Xia, X., Hassan, A.E., Yang, X.: V-SZZ: automatic identification of version ranges affected by CVE vulnerabilities. In: Proceedings of the 44th International Conference on Software Engineering, pp. 2352–2364 (2022)
3. Breiman, L.: Random forests. Mach. Learn. **45**, 5–32 (2001)
4. Breiman, L., Friedman, J., Olshen, R.A., Stone, C.J.: Classification and Regression Trees. Routledge (2017)
5. Cannavale, A., Iannone, E., Di Lillo, G., Palomba, F., De Lucia, A.: The ground truth effect: dataset and materials (supplementary) (2025). https://doi.org/10.6084/m9.figshare.28788857
6. Chawla, N.V., Bowyer, K.W., Hall, L.O., Kegelmeyer, W.P.: Smote: synthetic minority over-sampling technique. J. Artif. Intell. Res. **16**, 321–357 (2002)
7. Chidamber, S.R., Kemerer, C.F.: A metrics suite for object oriented design. IEEE Trans. Software Eng. **20**(6), 476–493 (1994)
8. Da Costa, D.A., McIntosh, S., Shang, W., Kulesza, U., Coelho, R., Hassan, A.E.: A framework for evaluating the results of the SZZ approach for identifying bug-introducing changes. IEEE Trans. Software Eng. **43**(7), 641–657 (2016)
9. Davies, S., Roper, M., Wood, M.: Comparing text-based and dependence-based approaches for determining the origins of bugs. J. Softw. Evol. Process **26**(1), 107–139 (2014)
10. Demšar, J.: Statistical comparisons of classifiers over multiple data sets. J. Mach. Learn. Res. **7**(Jan), 1–30 (2006)
11. Fan, Y., Xia, X., Da Costa, D.A., Lo, D., Hassan, A.E., Li, S.: The impact of mislabeled changes by SZZ on just-in-time defect prediction. IEEE Trans. Software Eng. **47**(8), 1559–1586 (2019)

12. Fernández, A., Garcia, S., Herrera, F., Chawla, N.V.: Smote for learning from imbalanced data: progress and challenges, marking the 15-year anniversary. J. Artif. Intell. Res. **61**, 863–905 (2018)
13. Freund, Y., Schapire, R.E.: A decision-theoretic generalization of on-line learning and an application to boosting. J. Comput. Syst. Sci. **55**(1), 119–139 (1997)
14. Friedman, J.H.: Greedy function approximation: a gradient boosting machine. Ann. Stat. 1189–1232 (2001)
15. Geurts, P., Ernst, D., Wehenkel, L.: Extremely randomized trees. Mach. Learn. **63**, 3–42 (2006)
16. Iannone, E., Guadagni, R., Ferrucci, F., De Lucia, A., Palomba, F.: The secret life of software vulnerabilities: a large-scale empirical study. IEEE Trans. Software Eng. **49**(1), 44–63 (2022)
17. Kim, S., Zimmermann, T., Pan, K., James Jr, E., et al.: Automatic identification of bug-introducing changes. In: 21st IEEE/ACM International Conference on Automated Software Engineering (ASE 2006), pp. 81–90. IEEE (2006)
18. Li, L., Jamieson, K., DeSalvo, G., Rostamizadeh, A., Talwalkar, A.: Hyperband: a novel bandit-based approach to hyperparameter optimization. J. Mach. Learn. Res. **18**(185), 1–52 (2018)
19. Lomio, F., Iannone, E., De Lucia, A., Palomba, F., Lenarduzzi, V.: Just-in-time software vulnerability detection: are we there yet? J. Syst. Softw. **188**, 111283 (2022)
20. Morrison, P., Herzig, K., Murphy, B., Williams, L.: Challenges with applying vulnerability prediction models. In: Proceedings of the 2015 Symposium and Bootcamp on the Science of Security, pp. 1–9 (2015)
21. Neto, E.C., Da Costa, D.A., Kulesza, U.: The impact of refactoring changes on the SZZ algorithm: an empirical study. In: 2018 IEEE 25th International Conference on Software Analysis, Evolution and Reengineering (SANER), pp. 380–390. IEEE (2018)
22. Nguyen, S., Nguyen, T.T., Vu, T.T., Do, T.D., Ngo, K.T., Vo, H.D.: Code-centric learning-based just-in-time vulnerability detection. J. Syst. Softw. **214**, 112014 (2024)
23. O'brien, R.M.: A caution regarding rules of thumb for variance inflation factors. Qual. Quant. **41**, 673–690 (2007)
24. Perl, H., et al.: Vccfinder: finding potential vulnerabilities in open-source projects to assist code audits. In: Proceedings of the 22nd ACM SIGSAC Conference on Computer and Communications Security, pp. 426–437 (2015)
25. Rajaraman, A., Ullman, J.D.: Mining of Massive Datasets. Cambridge University Press (2011)
26. Rosa, G., et al.: Evaluating SZZ implementations through a developer-informed oracle. In: 2021 IEEE/ACM 43rd International Conference on Software Engineering (ICSE), pp. 436–447. IEEE (2021)
27. Shin, Y., Williams, L.: An empirical model to predict security vulnerabilities using code complexity metrics. In: Proceedings of the Second ACM-IEEE International Symposium on Empirical Software Engineering and Measurement, pp. 315–317 (2008)
28. Śliwerski, J., Zimmermann, T., Zeller, A.: When do changes induce fixes? ACM Sigsoft Softw. Eng. Notes **30**(4), 1–5 (2005)
29. Vapnik, V.: Support-vector networks. Mach. Learn. **20**, 273–297 (1995)
30. Woolson, R.F.: Wilcoxon signed-rank test. In: Encyclopedia of Biostatistics, vol. 8 (2005)

31. Zhang, Z.: Introduction to machine learning: k-nearest neighbors. Ann. Transl. Med. **4**(11) (2016)
32. Zimmermann, T., Nagappan, N., Williams, L.: Searching for a needle in a haystack: predicting security vulnerabilities for windows vista. In: 2010 Third International Conference on Software Testing, Verification and Validation, pp. 421–428 (2010). https://doi.org/10.1109/ICST.2010.32

# Generate with CodeXHug: A Dataset to Enhance Model Cards with Code Usage Patterns

Stefano Palombo, Claudio Di Sipio$^{(\boxtimes)}$ (ID), Juri Di Rocco (ID), and Davide Di Ruscio (ID)

University of L'Aquila, Via Vetoio, L'Aquila, Italy
{stefano.palombo,claudio.disipio,juri.dirocco,davide.diruscio}@univaq.it

**Abstract.** Pre-trained models (PTMs) are becoming increasingly popular in the software engineering community, with repositories like Hugging Face (HF) collecting and maintaining a wide range of these models. However, the actual adoption of PTMs in real-world projects remains an open question, as many models are used in toy projects or simply mirror the HF repository. Additionally, most model cards and related documentation lack explanatory code patterns, making it difficult for newcomers to understand their usage. To address this gap, we present CodeXHug, a curated dataset that includes HF PTMs used in projects stored in the GitHub ecosystem along with their related code usage patterns. The dataset is built by mining the HF repository and the GitHub ecosystem, focusing on PTMs that are characterized by a tag and a model card. We then query the GitHub ecosystem to find actual usages of these PTMs, resulting in a dataset that includes 7,325 different models and 372,063 Python files. The dataset is available on Zenodo and can be used to enhance model cards with code usage patterns, providing concrete examples of how PTMs are used in real-world projects.

To the best of our knowledge, CodeXHug is the first dataset that provides a comprehensive overview of PTM usage patterns in real-world projects, enabling researchers and practitioners to better understand how these models are used and how they can be improved.

**Keywords:** mining software repositories · pre-trained models · code generation · hugging face

## 1 Introduction

With the availability of Foundation Models (FMs), e.g., Large Language Models (LLMs) [17] or Pre-Trained Models (PTMs) [16], the Software Engineering (SE) field is experiencing a paradigm shift in how software is developed, maintained, and evolved. These models are trained on vast amounts of data and can perform various tasks, such as code generation, code summarization, bug detection, and more. PTMs can be seen as specialized off-the-shelf components supporting specialized tasks, outperforming traditional techniques in many cases [10,28,32].

D. Taibi and D. Smite (Eds.): SEAA 2025, LNCS 16083, pp. 327–344, 2026.
https://doi.org/10.1007/978-3-032-04207-1_22

The proliferation of open *model repositories* of PTMs has facilitated their usage in practice. Hugging Face (HF) is the largest model repository for SE tasks [14], providing a wide range of PTMs to support more than thirty different tasks, e.g., text generation, image classification, or code summarization. Each model is labeled with *pipeline tags*, facilitating the repository's browsing and increasing the models' discoverability given the current software engineering task.

HF permits developers to upload their models, categorize them, and give relevant information and meta-data using *model cards* [20], defined as structured documents that summarize the model's capabilities and technical details. This README-like document provides detailed instructions e.g., on how to install and execute models. Nevertheless, recent research has shown that different information is missing, e.g., carbon emission [7] or license information [26], which may hinder the adoption of PTMs in practice. Moreover, a significant limitation of model cards is the lack of concrete *code usage examples*, i.e., source code needed to import, train, or test PTMs, that demonstrate how to integrate PTMs into existing projects. This gap makes it challenging for developers, especially those who are not experts in machine learning, to understand how to use these models effectively in their applications. In this respect, platforms like GitHub can come in handy, providing a valuable codebase for those cutting edge models. Nevertheless, identifying useful code snippets for PTMs is still an open challenge, as many of them are used in toy projects or simply as a mirror for the HF repository.

In this paper, we propose CodeXHug, a curated dataset of PTMs stored in HF that have been used in GitHub repositories. To collect data, we rely on a recent HF dump made available by the HF community project [6]. We first filter out unpopular models using the number of downloads as a proxy, and then we identify GitHub repositories that make use of the elicited PTMs. To this end, we rely on a well-adopted Python library, i.e., PyGithub [3], to collect relevant data from the identified PTMs. We ended up with 7,325 different models and 372,063 Python files. In addition, we applied a set of qualitative filters to enable the generation of code usage patterns by combining KNN clustering algorithm and *Llama-3.2-3B-Instruct* model.

To the best of our knowledge, CodeXHug is the first dataset that provides a comprehensive overview of the actual usage of PTMs in the GitHub ecosystem, thus enabling different research opportunities, e.g., code assistants for developing PTMs, PTMs usage analysis, and model card generation. The contributions of this paper are threefold:

- A curated dataset, named CodeXHug, that maps existing code snippets to most popular PTMs available on HF platform, available on the Zenodo open-access research data repository [8].
- A qualitative analysis of the collected code snippets to provide developers with concrete usage examples for PTMs.
- An explanatory example of how to use CodeXHug to predict the usage of PTMs in real-world projects leveraging LLM and clustering techniques.

The paper is structured as follows. Section 2 motivates the work by discussing an explanatory example. Section 3.4 describes the data collection process, whereas Sect. 4 provides an overview of the dataset, including a statistical analysis of the collected data. A concrete usage of CodeXHug is presented in Sect. 5.3. Section 7 discusses the threats to validity of our study. Section 8.2 presents the related work and Sect. 9 concludes the paper.

## 2    Background and Motivation

Although HF provides users with several functionalities to store, maintain, and document PTMs, recent studies highlight several shortcomings related to the information available in model cards including discrepancies in the documentation [21], or missing user licenses [26]. Moreover, model cards often lack concrete code usage examples that demonstrate how to integrate models into real-world applications. This gap can make it difficult for developers, especially those who are not experts in machine learning, to understand how to effectively use PTMs in their projects.

Figure 1a shows the model card of the `deberta-largew-mnli` PTM provided by Microsoft. It is worth mentioning that the document does not contain any usage examples even though the model is very popular according to HF statistics. In contrast, Fig. 1b shows a model card related to the `all-MiniLM-L6-v2` model with code usage examples. In particular, this model card is enriched with useful scripts for installing and using the model, thus making it easier for developers to exploit it in their projects.

## 3    Data Collection

Figure 2 shows the CodeXHug data collection process. It starts with a data cleaning step leveraging the dump provided by HF community project [6], released on June 2024, where PTMs with empty content (i.e., those lacking tags or model

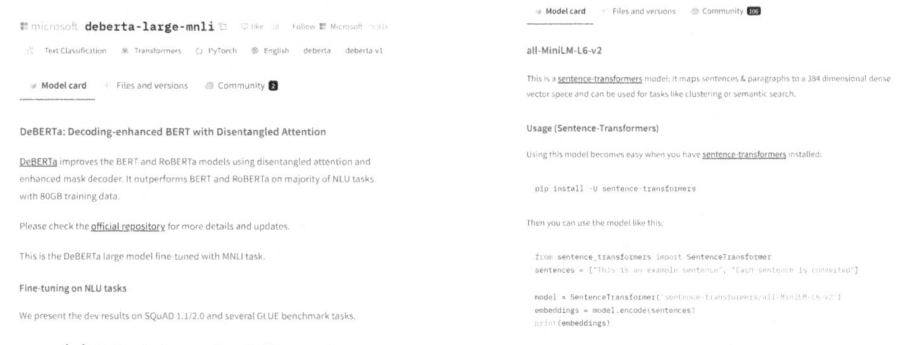

(a) Model card of *Deperta*

(b) Model card of *all-MiniLM-L6-v2*

**Fig. 1.** Model cards *with* and *without* code usage examples

cards) are filtered out. Next, we focus on selecting a sample of the most popular PTMs based on download counts. To ensure a balanced dataset, we identify the 13 most representative categories (e.g., summarization, text generation, and text classification) and then proceed to search for code usage in GitHub. In the following, we describe each step in detail.

### 3.1  CodeXHug Data Model

To collect the data, we designed a data model that captures the relevant information about PTMs and their usage in GitHub repositories. Figure 3 shows the CodeXHug data model consisting of two main entities, i.e., `HF model` and `GH repository`. The former contains the name of the PTM, the pipeline tag, the model card, and the number of likes and downloads. The latter contains the name of the repository, the topics, the description, the README content, and the number of commits, pull requests, forks, and stars. In addition, we store the files of each repository, i.e., the file name and the URL. In addition, we report the 13 different categories that are included in CodeXHug dataset as an enumeration since they refer to the pipeline tags available on HF which is a closed set of values.

### 3.2  Data Cleaning and Sampling

The first step involves the data cleaning and curation of the HF dump. To interact with the dataset, we rely on Python MySQL connector [2] to query the database and retrieve the relevant information. The dump contains 681,682 different models even though several missing entries are present, i.e., null values for tags or model cards. Since those data are relevant for our analysis, we filter out the PTMs with null content, resulting in 262,670 PTMs and the corresponding metadata, i.e., *pipeline_tag*, *model_card*, and number of likes, and download. Afterward, we select a sample of 10% the most popular PTMs in terms of download, i.e., 20,545 PTMs. The rationale behind this choice is that the most downloaded PTMs are more likely to be used in real-world projects, thus providing a more representative sample for our analysis.

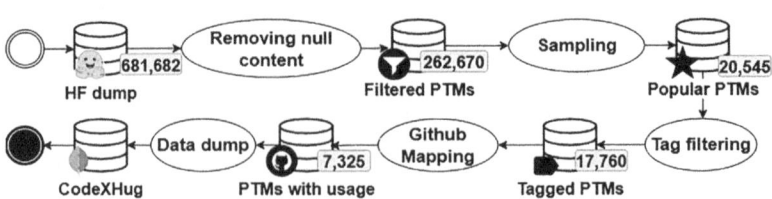

**Fig. 2.** The CodeXHug collection process

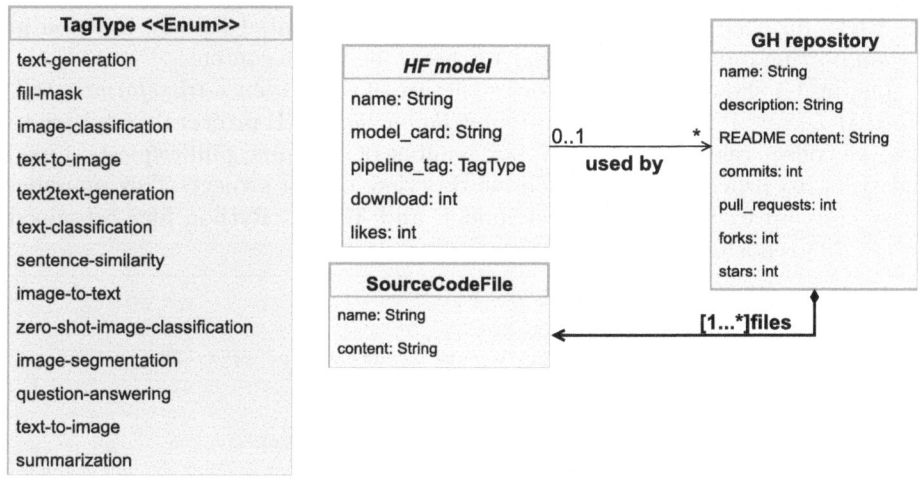

**Fig. 3.** The CodeXHug data model

## 3.3   Tag Filtering

We investigated to what categories the collected PTMs belongs to. In particular, 13 categories have been selected by including *i)* the most popular ones in terms of the number of downloads and *ii)* the less popular ones to guarantee a diverse dataset. We make sure that the number of PTMs in each category is balanced. This additional filtering step ends up with 17,760 PTMs.

## 3.4   GitHub Mapping

The final step of the data collection process is the mapping of the selected PTMs to their actual usage in GitHub repositories. To this end the PyGithub library [3] is used to interact with the GitHub API and collect the relevant data. The mapping process consists of two main phases: *i)* searching for repositories that use the PTMs and *ii)* retrieving the relevant files and metadata from those repositories.

To search for repositories that use the selected PTMs, we rely on two main strategies. First, we search the name of each PTM and limit our search to repositories written in Python, as the examined PTMs are mainly imported and tested using the HF utilities.[1] Second, we query the README file content using the *pipeline_tag* element to further remove possible false positives.

After the relevant PTMs have been identified, we retrieve the source code files, i.e., the ones ending with *.py*, by limiting the search to 1,000 for each project to avoid that big repository could lead to an unbalanced number of samples in the dataset. We collect also the README content of the project since it may contain additional usage information. In the scope of this paper, we store only

---

[1] https://huggingface.co/docs/transformers/autoclass_tutorial.

the URLs for each file even though we provide a dedicated Python function in the supporting online appendix that retrieves the whole content.

Listing 1.1 shows the explanatory structure of the *sentence-transformers/all-MiniLM-L12-v2* PTM used by *run-llama/llama_index* GH project. In addition to files, we collect relevant metadata, i.e., number of commits, pull requests, forks, and stars, to provide a comprehensive overview of the project. This mapping phase ends up with 7,325 different models and 372,063 Python files contained into 71,748 repositories.

```
1  "sentence-transformers/all-MiniLM-L12-v2": {
2  "run-llama/llama_index": {
3      ''topics": <list of GH topics>,
4      ''description": ''LlamaIndex is a data framework for your LLM
            applications",
5      ''readme": <content>",
6      ''numbers of commits:": 5494,
7      ''number of pull requests": 6146,
8      ''number of forks": 5195,
9      ''number of stars": 36388,
10     ''files": [
11         {
12             ''file_name": ''bench_embeddings.py",
13             ''file_url": ''<file_url>"
14         }
15     ]
16 }
```

**Listing 1.1.** Example of retrieved data

To further facilitate the analysis and the reproducibility of our study, we store the collected data in a MongoDB database [1] as it provides faster access compared to SQL databases. The provided dump is composed of two collections, i.e., *models* and *files*, where the former contains the name of PTM and the *pipeline_tag* while the latter contains the content of each file encoded in UTF-8 standard.

## 4   Data Overview

This section presents an overview of CodeXHug data by providing basic descriptive statistics. In particular, we aim to investigate two aspects, i.e., *the number of files* of each identified pipeline tag and *the usage of the PTMs* in the GitHub ecosystem. Concerning the first aspect, we present the distribution of the number of files for each tag in CodeXHug. As shown in Fig. 4, the file distribution is unbalanced since some tags are more used compared to others. In particular, the most popular tag is *text-generation*, followed by *fill-mask* and *image-classification*. This is quite expected since the most popular PTMs, like *gpt-2* and *RoBERTa* model, are tagged with text-generation and fill-mask, respectively. Nevertheless, we include also less popular tags to support the development of a wide range of applications based on PTMs, thus increasing the diversity of the dataset.

Concerning the popularity of the PTMs in the GitHub ecosystem, Fig. 5 shows the actual usage of the collected PTMs. In particular, we investigate the

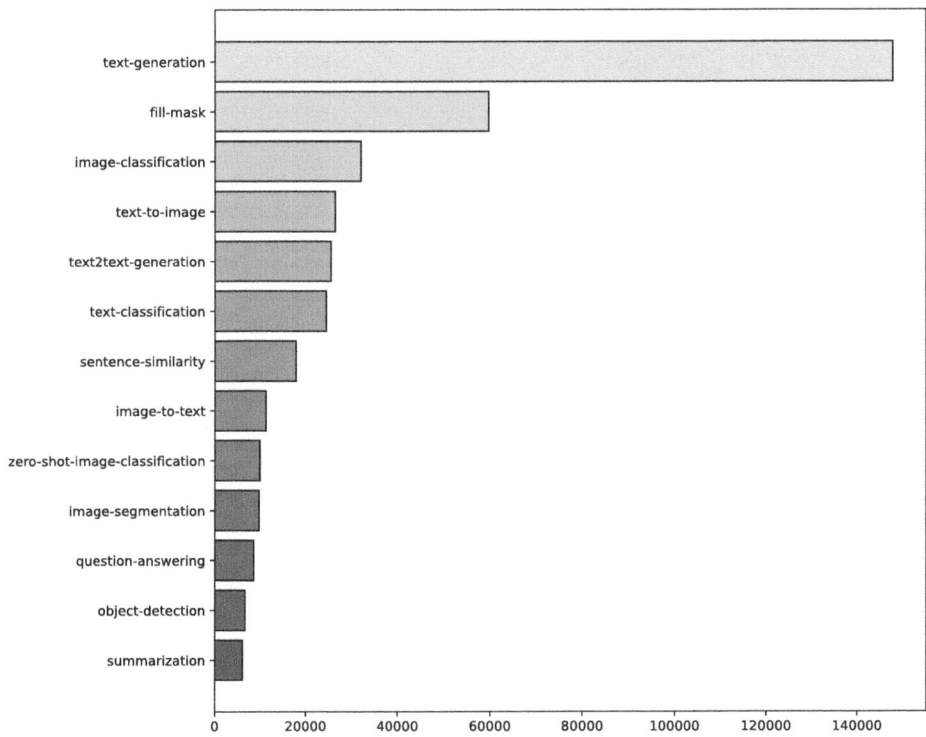

**Fig. 4.** Num. of files for each tag in CodeXHug

distribution of the number of projects for each PTM depicted in Fig. 5a. The result shows a skewed distribution that exhibits a *long-tail* effect, with a few PTMs used in many GitHub projects. By carefully inspecting the data, we discovered that the most popular PTMs are *gpt-2*, *roberta-large*, and *Salesforce/blip-image-captioning-large*, which are used in more than 800 projects. Thus, we can conclude that there are few PTMs that are widely used in the GitHub ecosystem, while the majority of the PTMs are used in some projects.

In addition, we investigated how many PTMs are used in GitHub repositories. Figure 5b shows that a considerable number of repositories (43.7%) uses more than one PTMs, meaning that developers may combine different models to support one or more tasks. Interestingly, we spot repositories that use more than 100 models, e.g., hugging-downloader.[2] By carefully investigating this, we discovered that those kinds of projects are model downloaders employed to store and test many PTMs at once.

---

[2] https://github.com/isLinXu/hugging-downloader.

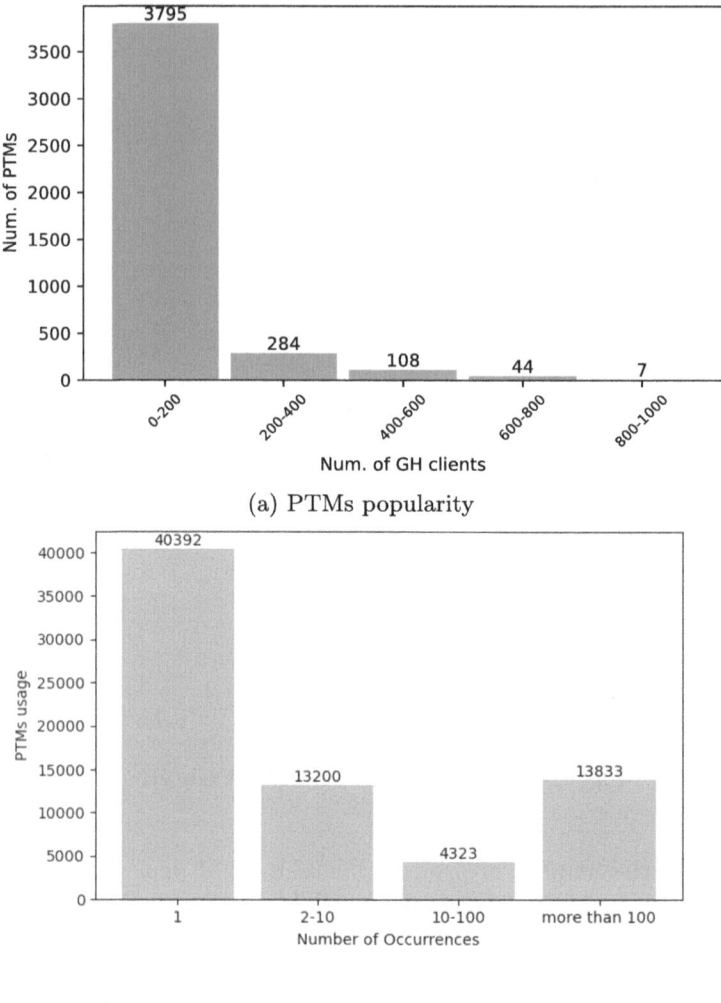

(a) PTMs popularity

(b) PTMs usage

**Fig. 5.** Distribution of PTMs in CodeXHug

## 5    Predict PTM Usage Patterns

Building upon our novel dataset that establishes a crucial link between Hugging Face model cards and their corresponding usage in publicly available source code, this section explores an illustrative application of this resource. While not the central focus of this paper, this explanatory use case demonstrates that CodeXHug can be used to support the prediction of code usage patterns. First, we filter out outliers and applied a clustering technique to identify the most suitable code patterns. Then, we exploit the Llama model to generate code snippets based on the identified patterns.

## 5.1 Outlier Filtering

As revealed by our previous analysis, the collected data presents a long-tail effect, i.e., a small subset of models is employed far more frequently than others. Thus, we filter out outliers from our analysis to those pre-trained models (PTMs) associated with more than 100 files. This criterion yielded a subset of 1,064 models, encompassing a total of 393,484 script files. Table 1 summarizes the key statistics of the original and filtered dataset.

**Table 1.** Descriptive Statistics of the Number of Files per PTM

| Metric | Original Dataset | Filtered Dataset |
|---|---|---|
| Mean | 63.99 | 369.82 |
| Median | 6.00 | 272.50 |
| Standard Deviation | 162.54 | 265.65 |
| Skewness | 3.86 | 1.17 |
| Kurtosis | 16.09 | 0.31 |

In particular, the process increases the number of supporting files for each PTM on average, from 63.99 to 369.82. In addition, skewness and kurtosis decreased to 1.17 and 0.31, respectively. Overall, this filtering step contributes to a more balanced distribution of the data, which is crucial for generating accurate snippets. To further enhance the quality of the code snippets, we applied an additional filter on the size of each snippet. On the one hand, excessively brief scripts may lack substantive content regarding a model's usage. On the other hand, long scripts often contain non-pertinent material e.g., extensive documentation or comments. Thus, we restrict our analysis to those scripts whose length, measured in lines of code, falls within a specified interquartile range (IQR) centred on the median [29], defined as follows:

$$\text{min\_length} = \max\left(\text{median} - 0.25 \cdot \text{IQR}, \ 1\right) \tag{1}$$

$$\text{max\_length} = \text{median} + 0.25 \cdot \text{IQR} \tag{2}$$

where IQR is the interquartile range, defined as the difference between the third quartile (Q3) and the first quartile (Q1) of the data distribution. This approach ensures that we retain only those snippets that are neither too short nor excessively long, thus enhancing the quality of the code patterns extracted from the dataset.

## 5.2   Clustering Analysis

After the selection of the most similar snippets, we grouped snippets that contain at least one match to the predefined keywords. However, selecting the optimal candidate requires accounting for the semantic content of the code. A similar strategy was employed by Zhong et al. [33] to improve recommendation quality by clustering code snippets according to analogous API usage patterns.

Thus, we applied the K-means algorithm from the scikit-learn library [25] to numerical representations of the snippets. Since the snippets are initially plain text, we employed the *all-MiniLM-L6-v2*[3] embedding model provided by Hugging Face via the *sentence_transformers* package.[4] This model, based on a lightweight Transformer variant of BERT, converts each snippet into a 384-dimensional vector through tokenization, attention computation, and mean-pooling across token embeddings. Although *sentence_transformers* models are primarily optimized for natural language, they nevertheless capture substantial syntactic and semantic information in code fragments, particularly when natural-language comments elucidate code structures and functions. Moreover, their relatively modest inference time and memory footprint present a favourable trade-off for processing hundreds of thousands of files, in contrast to more heavyweight alternatives such as CodeBERT [11].

The resulting embeddings are then clustered via K-means, with the number of clusters $k$ chosen empirically as the minimum of three and the total number of snippet candidates; this heuristic ensures dynamic adaptation to the available snippet set. Upon convergence, the snippet whose embedding lies closest to each cluster centroid is selected as the representative exemplar. By virtue of its proximity to the centroid, this snippet best encapsulates the shared semantic characteristics of its cluster members.

## 5.3   Code Pattern Prediction

To generate code usage patterns for given *PTMs*, we leverage the *Llama-3.2-3B-Instruct* [15] in a zero-shot prompting paradigm. This approach allows us to generate code snippets without providing explicit examples of the desired output within the input string, relying solely on the model's inherent generalization capabilities. The prompt is designed to assign the role of "Python assistant" to the model (see Listing 1.2), thereby optimizing contextual relevance and ensuring that the generated content is pertinent to Python programming. In addition, the prompt includes constraints to avoid the generation of natural-language content. Noteworthy, the dataset and the whole process can be adopted in combination with more traditional techniques, i.e., collaborative filtering [12,22] or mining usage patterns [4,30].

---

[3] https://huggingface.co/sentence-transformers/all-MiniLM-L6-v2.
[4] https://sbert.net/.

Concerning the hyperparameters, we set a temperature parameter of 0.2, the *top_p* parameter equal to 1.0, meaning that token selection considers the full probability distribution produced by the model. By avoiding the truncation inherent in lower *top_p* thresholds, which limit selection to tokens within a cumulative-probability cutoff, this configuration fully leverages the model's capabilities without prematurely excluding less probable yet potentially valid alternatives. Given that the goal is precise identification of code patterns rather than creative generation, this low temperature reduces response variance and mitigates the risk of spurious or hallucinatory outputs.

```
1   system_prompt = (
2   ''You are an AI assistant specialized in Python.
3   I will provide you with a series of code snippets extracted from various
        Python files.
4   Note that these snippets might not form a coherent or complete code
        module when combined together.
5   Your task is to analyze these snippets and extract recurring code
        patterns, such as function definitions (using 'def'), common imports,
        and other typical structures found in Python code.
6   Focus solely on identifying and returning the common patterns in the
        context of the model {snippet_model}.
7   Return ONLY the code snippets.
8   DO NOT include only the common imports.
9   Do NOT include any explanations, descriptions, or metadata.
10  Do NOT generate any summaries, bullet points, markdown formatting, or
        additional text.
11  If you are unable to find any relevant patterns, please return an empty
        string."
12  )
```

**Listing 1.2.** The zero-shot prompt used to generate model card usage patterns

Listing 1.3 presents an illustrative code excerpt generated for the model *kakaobrain/karlo-v1-alpha-image-variations*, a framework typically employed to synthesize images from natural-language prompts.[5] In particular, the generated code supports the data loading, suggesting a standard procedure for ingesting such datasets into memory (lines 1-4). Then, a preprocessing pipeline (lines 6–10) is established, by including a sequence of image transformations (i.e., resizing and normalization) to ensure that inputs conform to the model's expected dimensionality and value range. Finally, the snippet outlines the construction of a convolutional encoder–decoder architecture leveraging the Keras API[6] as shown in lines 12-24. Additionally, the code includes functions for training and evaluating the model (lines 26-35), as well as saving the trained model (lines 37–39). This comprehensive code snippet serves as a practical example of how to implement a text-to-image generation task using the *Karlo* model, providing developers with a concrete usage pattern that can be adapted to their specific needs.

---

[5] https://huggingface.co/kakaobrain/karlo-v1-alpha-image-variations.
[6] https://keras.io/.

```
 1  def load_data():
 2      # Load data from kakaobrain/karlo-v1-alpha-image-variations
 3      data = pd.read_csv('data/train.csv')
 4      return data
 5
 6  def preprocess_image(image):
 7      # Resize and normalize image
 8      image = tf.image.resize(image, (224, 224))
 9      image = tf.image.per_image_standardization(image)
10      return image
11
12  def create_model(input_shape):
13      # Create Keras model
14      model = tf.keras.models.Sequential([
15          tf.keras.layers.Conv2D(32, (3, 3), activation='relu', input_shape=
                input_shape),
16          tf.keras.layers.MaxPooling2D((2, 2)),
17          tf.keras.layers.Conv2D(64, (3, 3), activation='relu'),
18          tf.keras.layers.MaxPooling2D((2, 2)),
19          tf.keras.layers.Conv2D(128, (3, 3), activation='relu'),
20          tf.keras.layers.Flatten(),
21          tf.keras.layers.Dense(128, activation='relu'),
22          tf.keras.layers.Dense(10, activation='softmax')
23      ])
24      return model
25
26  def train_model(model, data):
27      # Train model
28      model.compile(optimizer='adam', loss='sparse_categorical_crossentropy',
                metrics=['accuracy'])
29      model.fit(data, epochs=10)
30      return model
31
32  def evaluate_model(model, data):
33      # Evaluate model
34      loss, accuracy = model.evaluate(data)
35      return loss, accuracy
36
37  def save_model(model):
38      # Save model
39      model.save('model.h5')
```

**Listing 1.3.** Generated usage example of *kakaobrain/karlo-v1-alpha-image-variations* model

# 6   Discussion

This section foreseen possible usages of the CodeXHug dataset. The primary usage of CodeXHug is generating enhanced model cards as shown in Listing 1.3, by including explanatory usage patterns for PTMs. In Sect. 2, we discussed the limitations of model cards, particularly the lack of concrete code usage examples that demonstrate how to integrate PTMs into real-world applications. CodeX-Hug addresses this gap by providing a curated dataset that maps existing code snippets to popular PTMs available on Hugging Face, thus enabling the generation of enhanced model cards with concrete usage examples. However, preprocessing and filtering steps are still needed to provide a high-quality model card as the raw data exhibited a significant long-tail effect. Subsequently, there is the need to filter out outliers and analyze the frequency of model usage across a large corpus of source code to effectively generate a useful model card. In this respect, the evaluation of our proposed approach for automated model usage recommendation relies on the insights derived from this dataset, although an in-depth analysis is needed to confirm our findings.

Besides model card generations, we believe that CodeXHug can be used to investigate how PTMs are used in real-world projects on GitHub, thus fostering applications of different automated techniques to support developers that want to implement, fine-tune, or test their own models. In particular, CodeXHug can be used to provide different types of recommendations, spanning from API function calls [12,22] to code usage pattern retrieval [4,30], providing a specific support to developers interested in integrating PTMs in their software projects.

In addition, our dataset can be used to analyze how PTMs are used in real-world projects. In particular, the retrieved code can be used to assess the overall quality of the code, e.g., code smells [24], technical debt in AI-based system [27], or antipatterns [19]. Additionally, the dataset can be used to investigate the impact of PTMs on the GitHub community, e.g., how the adoption of PTMs affects the project's popularity, its quality, and discoverability.

## 7    Threats to Validity

This section discusses threats that may hamper the quality of the collected data. The main issue is related to the dump used for collecting CodeXHug, i.e., the HF dump may not contain recently released PTMs. To mitigate this issue, we focus on popular and well-established models by selecting PTMs. In addition, we applied different quality filters to reduce the number of the outliers. Concerning the generation of usage patters scenario presented in Sect. 5.3, we acknowledge that the clustering technique used to group similar snippets may not be the most suitable for all scenarios. To mitigate this, we plan to investigate more advanced clustering techniques in future work.

Another threat is related to missing data that may not be collected during the GH mapping phase. To handle this, we rely on the GitHub query language to apply quality filters. In addition, we manually select six categories to include less popular PTMs in the final dataset. Another threat is related to the possible usage of the dataset, i.e., the PTM snippets may be not enough to train a traditional model. To mitigate this, we employ a clustering technique to group similar snippets and increase the amount of data. Another threat is related to the generalizability of the results, i.e., the dataset may not provide enough examples to support the generation of generic model cards. While we acknowledge that this can be mitigated by enlarging the dataset with additional PTMs, this goes beyond the scope of this paper as we focus on the collection and curation of the retrieved data from Hugging Face and GitHub.

## 8    Related Works

In this section, we present existing empirical studies on PTMs (see Sect. 8.1) and review existing works on recommending code usage patterns (see Sect. 8.2).

## 8.1   Empirical Studies on PTMs

Castano et al. [7] investigate the carbon footprints of 1,417 different models hosted on the platform. The measured emission correlated with different factors such as model size, dataset size, and application domains. The same authors [7] also provide an empirical investigation on the evolution of PTMs in terms of maintenance, popularity, and usage. Gong et al. [14] conducted a comprehensive study of the PTMs reuse stored in six different model repositories, including Hugging Face. After data cleaning and labeling steps, the authors propose a code contract composed of pre- and post-conditions for re-usage in software development, e.g., input data, intended usage, and performance.

Montes et al. [21] highlight discrepancies in the documentation of 36 PTMs that support image classification across four different model repositories, i.e., TensorFlow Model Garden, ONNX Model Zoo, Torchvision Models, and Keras Applications, highlighting the need for standardized documentation. Pepe et al. [26] conducted a large-scale study on 159,132 models stored on HF by focusing on the documentation, licenses, and fairness aspects. Overall, only a few PTMs provide permissive licenses and mention potential bias in the documentation. Gao et al. [13] investigate ethical concerns in HF models leveraging the API and KeyBERT model, ending up with a dedicated taxonomy. In [9] we investigate to what extent traditional ML models, namely Naive Bayesian and SVC, can classify PTM given their model card. Compared with the abovementioned works, CodeXHug provides a direct mapping between PTMs and GitHub projects that use them in practice.

## 8.2   Recommending Code Usage Patterns

FACER [5] retrieves API usage for opportunistic reuse built on top of a code fact repository, including methods' textual body, call graphs, and API usages. The approach combines clustering techniques based on Lucene and frequent pattern mining strategy to retrieve similar API compared to the developer's context.

*api2vec* [23] is an approach based on Word2Vec model to suggest relevant API patterns and usage. First, the tool mines the pairs of API elements that share the same usage relations among them. Afterward, the mined content has been used to support code translation task between Java and C# using a characteristic of the API2Vec embeddings.

Multi-HyLSTM [31] is an automated approach that exploits a modified version Short Long Term Memory (LSTM) neural network to support multi-path API prediction. The system is equipped with global dependence-enhancing learning module to accurately capture the program dependencies for an API calls.

To enhance the prediction of LLM like GPT-3 and Codex, Jain et al. propose Jigsaw [18], a tool based on program synthesis architecture to augment the input of LLM in code generation task. In particular, it contextualizes the input to the black-box language model using heuristic techniques. Afterward, a post-processing module speed up the combinatorial search space of API functions and their arguments leveraging API usage example provided by humans. Specifically trained on a Pandas dataset, Jigsaw improves the quality of the generated code of GPT-3 and Codex.

Compared to those work, CodeXHug can be seen as a curated source of knowledge to enable tailored recommendations for PTMs and their usage patterns. In particular, we provide a dataset of PTMs and their related code usage patterns, which can be used to train and evaluate different recommendation systems.

# 9    Conclusion

Motivated by the increasing usage of PTMs for software engineering tasks, we proposed CodeXHug, a curated dataset of PTMs exploited by projects stored in GitHub. We identified the most downloaded PTMs from a recent Hugging Face dump and filtered out PTMs with missing content. Afterward, we leveraged the PyGithub library to collect the actual usage of the identified PTMs in GitHub projects. We ended up with 7,325 different models and 372,063 Python files. We also presented a statistical analysis of the dataset, highlighting the most popular PTMs and the most common tasks for which they are used. In addition, we discussed a concrete application of CodeXHug, focusing on extracting representative code usage patterns for specific PTMs by combining clustering techniques and LLMs. We also discussed the research opportunities enabled by CodeXHug and the implications of our findings for the software engineering community.

We plan to extend the dataset by leveraging new dumps released by the HF community project or Hugging Face dedicated API. In addition, we plan to mine source code from additional open-source repositories, e.g., Software Heritage or GitLab, or model repositories, e.g., TensorFlow Model Garden or ONNX Model Zoo, and their usage in the GitHub platform. Concerning the prediction of PTM usage patterns, we plan to investigate the use of more advanced clustering techniques, such as deep learning-based approaches, and experiment with different LLMs to generate more accurate and relevant code usage patterns.

**Acknowledgment.** This paper was partially supported by the MOSAICO project (Management, Orchestration and Supervision of AI-agent COmmunities for reliable AI in software engineering) that has received funding from the European Union under the Horizon Research and Innovation Action (Grant Agreement No. 101189664) and Projects PRIN 2022 PNRR "FRINGE: context-aware FaiRness engineerING in complex software systEms" grant n. P2022553SL.

# References

1. Mongodb. https://www.mongodb.com/. Accessed 11 Mar 2024
2. Mysql connector/python. https://pypi.org/project/mysql-connector-python/. Accessed 11 Mar 2024
3. Pygithub documentation. https://pygithub.readthedocs.io/en/stable/. Accessed 11 Mar 2024

4. Abid, S., Shamail, S., Basit, H.A., Nadi, S.: FACER: An API usage-based code-example recommender for opportunistic reuse. Empir. Softw. Eng. **26**(6), 1–58 (2021). https://doi.org/10.1007/s10664-021-10000-w

5. Abid, S., Shamail, S., Basit, H.A., Nadi, S.: FACER: An API usage-based code-example recommender for opportunistic reuse. Empir. Softw. Eng. **26**(6), 1–58 (2021). https://doi.org/10.1007/s10664-021-10000-w

6. Ait, A., Izquierdo, J.L.C., Cabot, J.: HFCommunity: a tool to analyze the hugging face hub community. In: 2023 IEEE International Conference on Software Analysis, Evolution and Reengineering (SANER), pp. 728–732, March 2023. https://doi.org/10.1109/SANER56733.2023.00080, https://ieeexplore.ieee.org/document/10123660, iSSN: 2640-7574

7. Castaño, J., Martínez-Fernández, S., Franch, X., Bogner, J.: Analyzing the Evolution and Maintenance of ML Models on Hugging Face, November 2023. https://doi.org/10.48550/arXiv.2311.13380, arXiv:2311.13380 [cs]

8. Di Sipio, C., Di Rocco, J., Di Ruscio, D., Palombo, S.: Codexhug: a curated dataset of huggingface pre- trained models exploited in the github ecosystem, December 2024. https://doi.org/10.5281/zenodo.14267550

9. Di Sipio, C., Rubei, R., Di Rocco, J., Di Ruscio, D., Nguyen, P.T.: Automated categorization of pre-trained models in software engineering: A case study with a hugging face dataset. In: Proceedings of the 28th International Conference on Evaluation and Assessment in Software Engineering, pp. 351–356. EASE '24. Association for Computing Machinery, New York (2024). https://doi.org/10.1145/3661167.3661215

10. Ding, Z., Li, H., Shang, W., Chen, T.-H.P.: Can pre-trained code embeddings improve model performance? Revisiting the use of code embeddings in software engineering tasks. Empir. Softw. Eng. **27**(3), 1–38 (2022). https://doi.org/10.1007/s10664-022-10118-5

11. Feng, Z., et al.: Codebert: a pre-trained model for programming and natural languages (2020). https://arxiv.org/abs/2002.08155

12. Fowkes, J., Sutton, C.: Parameter-free Probabilistic API Mining Across GitHub. In: 24th ACM SIGSOFT International Symposium on Foundations of Software Engineering, pp. 254–265. ACM, New York (2016). https://doi.org/10.1145/2950290.2950319

13. Gao, H., Zahedi, M., Treude, C., Rosenstock, S., Cheong, M.: Documenting ethical considerations in open source ai models. In: Proceedings of the 18th ACM/IEEE International Symposium on Empirical Software Engineering and Measurement, ESEM '24, pp. 177–188. Association for Computing Machinery, New York (2024). https://doi.org/10.1145/3674805.3686679

14. Gong, L., Zhang, J., Wei, M., Zhang, H., Huang, Z.: What is the intended usage context of this model? an exploratory study of pre-trained models on various model repositories. ACM Trans. Softw. Eng. Methodol. **32**(3), 69:1–69:57 (2023). https://doi.org/10.1145/3569934

15. Grattafiori, A., Dubey, A., Jauhri, A., Pandey, A., et al.: The llama 3 herd of models (2024). https://arxiv.org/abs/2407.21783

16. Han, X., Zhang, Z., Ding, N., Gu, Y., Liu, X., et al.: Pre-trained models: past, present and future. AI Open **2**, 225–250 (2021). https://doi.org/10.1016/j.aiopen.2021.08.002

17. Hou, X., et al.: Large language models for software engineering: a systematic literature review. ACM Trans. Softw. Eng. Methodol. (2024). https://doi.org/10.1145/3695988. just Accepted

18. Jain, N., Vaidyanath, S., Iyer, A., Natarajan, N., Parthasarathy, S., Rajamani, S., Sharma, R.: Jigsaw: large language models meet program synthesis. In: Proceedings of the 44th International Conference on Software Engineering, ICSE '22, pp. 1219–1231. Association for Computing Machinery, New York, July 2022. https://doi.org/10.1145/3510003.3510203, https://dl.acm.org/doi/10.1145/3510003.3510203

19. Khomh, F., Penta, M.D., Guéhéneuc, Y.G., Antoniol, G.: An exploratory study of the impact of antipatterns on class change- and fault-proneness. Empir. Softw. Eng. **17**(3), 243–275 (2012). https://doi.org/10.1007/s10664-011-9171-y

20. Mitchell, M., Wu, S., Zaldivar, A., Barnes, P., Vasserman, L., et al.: Model cards for model reporting. In: Proceedings of the Conference on Fairness, Accountability, and Transparency, FAT'19, pp. 220–229. Association for Computing Machinery, New York (2019). https://doi.org/10.1145/3287560.3287596, https://doi-org.univaq.idm.oclc.org/10.1145/3287560.3287596

21. Montes, D., Peerapatanapokin, P., Schultz, J., Guo, C., Jiang, W., et al.: Discrepancies among pre-trained deep neural networks: a new threat to model zoo reliability. In: Proceedings of the 30th ACM Joint European Software Engineering Conference and Symposium on the Foundations of Software Engineering, pp. 1605–1609. ESEC/FSE 2022. Association for Computing Machinery, New York, November 2022. https://doi.org/10.1145/3540250.3560881, https://dl.acm.org/doi/10.1145/3540250.3560881

22. Nguyen, P.T., Di Rocco, J., Di Ruscio, D., et al.: FOCUS: a recommender system for mining API function calls and usage patterns. In: Proceedings of the 41st International Conference on Software Engineering, ICSE '19, pp. 1050–1060. IEEE Press, Piscataway (2019). https://doi.org/10.1109/ICSE.2019.00109

23. Nguyen, T.D., Nguyen, A.T., Phan, H.D., Nguyen, T.N.: Exploring API embedding for API usages and applications. In: 2017 IEEE/ACM 39th International Conference on Software Engineering (ICSE), pp. 438–449. IEEE, Buenos Aires, May 2017. https://doi.org/10.1109/ICSE.2017.47, http://ieeexplore.ieee.org/document/7985683/

24. Palomba, F., Bavota, G., Di Penta, M., Fasano, F., Oliveto, R., De Lucia, A.: On the diffuseness and the impact on maintainability of code smells: a large scale empirical investigation. In: Proceedings of the 40th International Conference on Software Engineering, ICSE '18, p. 482. Association for Computing Machinery, New York (2018). https://doi.org/10.1145/3180155.3182532

25. Pedregosa, F., et al.: Scikit-learn: machine learning in Python. J. Mach. Learn. Res. **12**, 2825–2830 (2011)

26. Pepe, F., Nardone, V., Mastropaolo, A., Bavota, G., Canfora, G., Di Penta, M.: How do hugging face models document datasets, bias, and licenses? an empirical study. In: Proceedings of the 32nd IEEE/ACM International Conference on Program Comprehension, ICPC '24, pp. 370–381. Association for Computing Machinery, New York (2024). https://doi.org/10.1145/3643916.3644412

27. Recupito, G., Pecorelli, F., Catolino, G., Lenarduzzi, V., Taibi, D., Di Nucci, D., Palomba, F.: Technical debt in ai-enabled systems: On the prevalence, severity, impact, and management strategies for code and architecture. J. Syst. Softw. **216**, 112151 (2024). https://doi.org/10.1016/j.jss.2024.112151

28. Tufano, R., Masiero, S., Mastropaolo, A., Pascarella, L., Poshyvanyk, D., et al.: Using pre-trained models to boost code review automation. In: Proceedings of the 44th International Conference on Software Engineering, ICSE '22, pp. 2291–2302. Association for Computing Machinery, New York, July 2022. https://doi.org/10.1145/3510003.3510621

29. Vinutha, H., Poornima, B., Sagar, B.: Detection of outliers using interquartile range technique from intrusion dataset. In: Information and Decision Sciences: Proceedings of the 6th International Conference on Ficta, pp. 511–518. Springer (2018)

30. Wang, J., Dang, Y., Zhang, H., Chen, K., Xie, T., Zhang, D.: Mining succinct and high-coverage api usage patterns from source code. In: 2013 10th Working Conference on Mining Software Repositories (MSR), pp. 319–328 (2013). https:// doi.org/10.1109/MSR.2013.6624045

31. Xiao, Y., Song, W., Qi, J., Viswanath, B., McDaniel, P., Yao, D.: Specializing neural networks for cryptographic code completion applications. IEEE Trans. Software Eng. **49**(6), 3524–3535 (2023). https://doi.org/10.1109/TSE.2023.3265362. conference Name: IEEE Transactions on Software Engineering

32. Zhang, J., Mytkowicz, T., Kaufman, M., Piskac, R., Lahiri, S.K.: Using pre-trained language models to resolve textual and semantic merge conflicts (experience paper). In: Proceedings of the 31st ACM SIGSOFT International Symposium on Software Testing and Analysis, pp. 77–88. ISSTA 2022. Association for Computing Machinery, New York, July 2022. https://doi.org/10.1145/3533767.3534396, https://dl. acm.org/doi/10.1145/3533767.3534396

33. Zhong, H., Xie, T., Zhang, L., Pei, J., Mei, H.: MAPO: mining and recommending API usage patterns. In: Drossopoulou, S. (ed.) ECOOP 2009. LNCS, vol. 5653, pp. 318–343. Springer, Heidelberg (2009). https://doi.org/10.1007/978-3-642-03013-0_15

# Investigating the Relationship Between Churning and Code Smells

Kevin Cerqueira Gomes[1], Elivelton Ramos Cerqueira[1], Gabriel Moraes[1],
Lidiany Cerqueira[2], Glauco Carneiro[3], Rodrigo Spínola[4],
Manoel Mendonça[2], and José Amancio Macedo Santos[1]

[1] State University of Feira de Santana, Feira de Santana, Bahia, Brazil
gcmorais@ecomp.uefs.br, zeamancio@uefs.br
[2] Federal University of Bahia, Salvador, Bahia, Brazil
{lidiany.cerqueira,manoel.mendonca}@ufba.br
[3] Federal University of Sergipe, São Cristovão, Sergipe, Brazil
glauco.carneiro@dcomp.ufs.br
[4] Virginia Commonwealth University, Richmond, VA 23284, USA
spinolaro@vcu.edu

**Abstract.** Code churn, the intensity of software changes, can threaten software quality and has been empirically associated with many quality attributes. However, few studies have explored its relationship with code smells, which are widely recognized as indicators of poor object-oriented design quality. This study presents a preliminary investigation into the relationship between code churn and code smells. We use the number of commits and edited lines as proxies for code churn and the presence of code smells as a measure of software quality. We mined a large software repository comprising 31 open-source projects, 749 developers, and 153,994 commits to examine how development activity intensity relates to the incidence of code smells. Our findings suggest that code churn is related to the presence of code smells. Notably, developers with lower activity levels tend to have a proportionally higher impact on the introduction or persistence of code smells. This preliminary study highlights a correlation between code churn and code smells, providing a foundation for further research. Future work may explore variations such as different types of smells or commit categories to deepen our understanding of this relationship.

**Keywords:** Code smell · software repository mining · code churning · software quality

## 1 Introduction

Software undergoes constant changes during development, encompassing maintenance and evolution activities, bringing potential threats to the software quality [35]. A term commonly used to capture the intensity of software changes

D. Taibi and D. Smite (Eds.): SEAA 2025, LNCS 16083, pp. 345–360, 2026.
https://doi.org/10.1007/978-3-032-04207-1_23

is churning [24]. Studies have linked code churn to different events in the software life cycle, such as the occurrence of bugs [21,29], technical debt risks [38], architecture flaws [27], and software vulnerabilities [35].

Code smell refers to patterns in the source code that indicate possible design problems, hindering the maintenance and negatively impacting the software evolution [15]. Code smells contribute to technical debt[1] by representing areas of the code that may require future refactoring or maintenance [9]. The early identification and removal of smells can reduce costs, prevent deterioration in the code base, and improve the efficiency of development teams. Understanding code smells is not just a matter of code maintenance. It is a proactive strategy to ensure sustainability and software quality. Studies highlight the relationship between code smells and the propensity for bugs [3,8], code complexity [16], and increased maintenance effort [25]. Considering that code smells introduces design flaws and poor programming practices, their identification and the initiatives to address them in the source code can be one of the viable ways to evaluate software quality.

Churning, which effectively reflects developers' programming pace, has been linked to various software quality attributes [21,29,35,38]. Separately, several studies have examined the relationship between code smells—often considered indicators of potential quality issues—and other software characteristics [3,8, 16,25]. However, to the best of our knowledge, no prior work has specifically explored the correlation between churning and code smells. Since both concepts offer valuable insights for understanding and managing software development, studying their relationship could contribute important empirical knowledge to the field. Previous research has also emphasized the value of linking development metrics with software quality aspects [17,39].

This study explores the relationship between churn metrics and software quality, with a particular focus on code smells. Positioned as an exploratory investigation, the study highlights how the interplay between code churn and code smells can enhance our understanding of software development processes. We aim to examine how the intensity of developer activity relates to the presence of code smells. Following Shin et al. [35], we use two common code churn metrics to represent developer activity: the number of edited lines and the number of commits. Our analysis is based on the latest version of the Technical Debt Dataset [17], positioning this work within the Mining Software Repositories (MSR) field. The dataset includes 31 software projects, 749 developers, and 153,994 commits. For the analysis, we apply both descriptive and inferential statistical techniques.

Our findings indicate that developers with greater participation tend to insert fewer code smells for each commit or edited line. This finding might indirectly aligned with the one presented by Tufano et al. [40], who concluded that more experienced developers are less prone to introducing code smells. This study also presents a complementary perspective to the results of Palomba et al. [28], which explored the relationship between development practices and the inci-

---

[1] Technical debt refers to the future cost incurred by taking shortcuts in software development [12].

dence of code smells. Our results build on the topic, supporting further in-depth investigations on the relationship between churning and code smells.

This work is organized as follows. Section 2 addresses the background, followed by a discussion of the adopted methodology (Sect. 3) and the results (Sect. 4). The discussion and limitations of the study are presented in Sect. 5. Finally, Sect. 6 presents the conclusion.

## 2 Background

This section presents the main concepts covered in the study. First, we discuss the idea of code smells, with a brief history of its evolutionary process. Next, we present studies using similar metrics to those adopted in our study as related work.

### 2.1 Code Smells: Concepts, Impacts, and Measurement

Code smells indicate potential problems in the code that could harm its maintenance and evolution. Defined by Fowler [10], the concept encompasses patterns that may reveal weaknesses in the design, especially with an impact on the readability and maintainability of the code. Fowler [10] defines 22 code smells, such as "Long Method" and "Large Class". Lanza and Marinescu [15] also present an essential work on the topic, presenting heuristics for detecting code smells based on software metrics. Since then, many studies based on automatically detecting code smells emerged [22,23]. In particular, some automatic detection tools, such as SonarQube and PMD.

Code smells indicate areas of the code that may require attention, even if they are not explicitly classified as technical debt. For instance, Yamashita et al. [43] found that the presence of code smells is associated with a higher risk of bugs. As originally noted by Cunningham [7], distinguishing between code smells and technical debt underscores the importance of addressing smells proactively to prevent future maintenance costs and preserve code quality. Further studies have investigated the detection and impact of code smells on software quality without necessarily tying them to the concept of technical debt, reinforcing the relevance of code smells as independent quality indicators [20].

Complementing    this    perspective,    the    evaluation    of    developers' contributions—through metrics such as code complexity and bug frequency— offers additional insight into software quality [13]. These contribution metrics help assess both the quantity and quality of development efforts, supporting a more comprehensive understanding of their impact on code health and maintainability. Together, code smells and contribution metrics provide valuable indicators for identifying quality issues and guiding continuous improvement in software projects.

### 2.2 Related Work

Analyzing churning as a form of developer contribution offers valuable insights into software quality. Metrics such as the number of commits, lines of code edited, and the frequency of contributions are commonly used to gauge a developer's involvement in a project [13]. Research suggests that certain contribution patterns—such as frequent, smaller commits—are often linked to a lower incidence of code smells and bugs [2]. Below, we present related studies that use similar metrics to those adopted in our work to investigate software quality.

Tsoukalas et al. [38] employed machine learning models built on software metrics to identify modules at risk of accumulating technical debt. Using data from 21 open-source projects, they classified modules as having high or low technical debt and found that code churn was one of the most influential factors in determining a class's susceptibility to high technical debt.

Ogheneovo et al. [26] explored the correlation between software complexity and maintenance costs across three operating system projects. They used changes in lines of code as a proxy for complexity, arguing that software becomes more complex as its size increases. Their cost estimation model revealed a strong correlation: as the codebase grew—reflecting higher churn—maintenance costs also increased.

Behnamghader et al. [1] investigated the impact of commits on software quality by analyzing 19,580 commits across 38 Java systems. They considered nine software quality metrics, including code smells. Notably, they found that, on average, 46% of impactful commits—those introducing significant changes—either introduced new code smells or resolved existing ones. This finding suggests that developers often engage with code affected by smells during substantial code changes.

## 3  Methodology

This study aims to investigate if the relationship between churning and code smells can enhance the understanding of the software development process. This section outlines the experimental setup, detailing the dataset, the metrics used, and the analysis strategy employed to achieve this goal.

We adopted the metrics **number of lines edited** and **number of commits** to measure churning, as [35]. We compare the differences in churning between different developers and different software projects. We also use the quantitative marker code smells.

### 3.1  Dataset and Metrics

We used version 2.0 of The Technical Debt Dataset [17]. The dataset supports studies on technical debt and has been used in other studies [18,37,39]. It provides data on several aspects of software quality, including code smells. To investigate the incidence of code smells, we rely on data that includes the developer responsible for each commit, the date and time of the contribution, and the lines of code (LOC) that were changed. The code smells present in the dataset were extracted using the SonarQube tool [4]. SonarQube is a tool widely used by researchers and practitioners for code smell detection, which lends robustness to the data. The dataset already provides the identification and categorization of the smells, enabling our analysis. We assess the intensity of developer activity using two key metrics: the number of edited lines and the number of commits. This analysis is guided by the hypothesis that a developer's level of activity can influence code quality [19, 30, 32].

We attribute a code smell to a commit—and consequently to a developer—when the developer introduces a block of code that negatively affects the software's modularization, thereby characterizing a code smell [11]. In cases where the code smell already exists, we also assign it to a commit if the developer modifies the affected code without removing the smell. This attribution is a methodological choice based on the assumption that developers are responsible both for introducing new code smells and for maintaining code quality when altering existing code. It underscores the developer's ongoing responsibility for code quality throughout the software life cycle [11, 18].

We adopt two metrics to evaluate the developer's activity: the number of commits and edited lines of code (Edited LOC). We calculate the LOC edited based on the sum of lines of code inserted and removed in each commit.

**Dataset Design and Content.** With 31 software projects containing 749 developers in total and 153,994 commits, the dataset is structured in many tables. We developed a Python script to process its tables, generating the data used in this study. The material and scripts needed to verify the processed tables and the results to develop other studies on the topic are available in GitHub[2]. Figure 1 shows the table schema:

- **AUTHOR_INFORMATION:** information related to the commits authors (the developers), such as the project, days in the project, number of edited lines, and number of code smells linked to the developer.
- **PROJECT_INFORMATION**: it is formed by information related to the analyzed projects, such as the number of commits, edited lines, and code smell information.

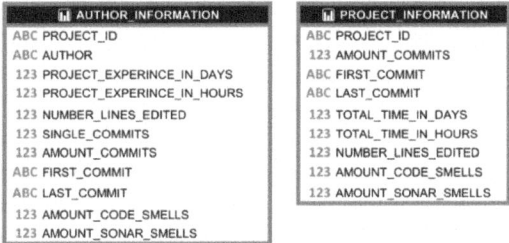

**Fig. 1.** Structure of the Dataset tables.

---

[2] https://anonymous.4open.science/r/research-smells-master-4B54/.

Additional information is provided in the tables, which support analyses we conducted or plan to explore further. We have made them available to assist future studies.

## 3.2   Data Analysis Strategy

Following previous work [18], we normalize the data to allow fair comparisons between projects and developers. We chose a two-phase analytical approach [19]. Initially, we consider all developers to determine general correlations. Subsequently, we perform a refined analysis excluding participants with low contribution volume. Figure 2 presents the analysis approach divided into two phases.

During phase 1 (top of the figure), we initially focus on percentage values and their association with specific projects to understand the distribution and incidence of code smells in a broader context. That allows an initial comparison between developers' contributions regardless of the scale of the project. This initial approach was essential to identify general patterns and trends that could be observed across different projects.

However, as we move through the analysis by carrying out hypothesis testing in phase 2 (bottom of the figure), we adopt an approach that does not distinguish between individual projects. In this phase, we carried out a hypothesis test considering the distribution of all values independent of the project context. Thus, the analysis of raw data in hypothesis tests was carried out to assess the data set in an aggregated manner, focusing on the direct relationship between the volume of commits, edited lines, and the occurrence of code smells.

**Analysis of Phase 1.** In data analysis, we normalized values and the percentage related to each observed metric (code smell, commit and edited lines). For example, consider developer X, who produced Y smells in project Z. We calculate the percentage of smells attributed to that developer using the simple rule of three, as shown in Eq. 1. Thus, we calculate the percentage of code smells related to a developer and the percentage of commits and edited lines in the project context. This is represented by the "Normalizing" rectangle in Phase 1 of Fig. 2.

$$\frac{QuantityCodeSmellDeveloperY \times 100}{QuantityTotalCodeSmellProjetoZ} \tag{1}$$

With the normalized data and developers with less than two commits removed, 232 developers remained. Then we applied the Spearman correlation test: percentage of commits X percentage of code smells; and percentage of edited lines X percentage of code smells. This is represented by the "Correlation test" rectangle in Phase 1 of Fig. 2. The choice of the test was motivated by its ability to detect monotonic relationships without the need to assume a linear relationship between the variables [31].

In addition, we initially conducted a Mann-Whitney normality test to evaluate the distribution of sample values, as recommended by Weiner [41]. We represent this test in the "Normality test" rounded rectangle in Phase 1 of Fig. 2.

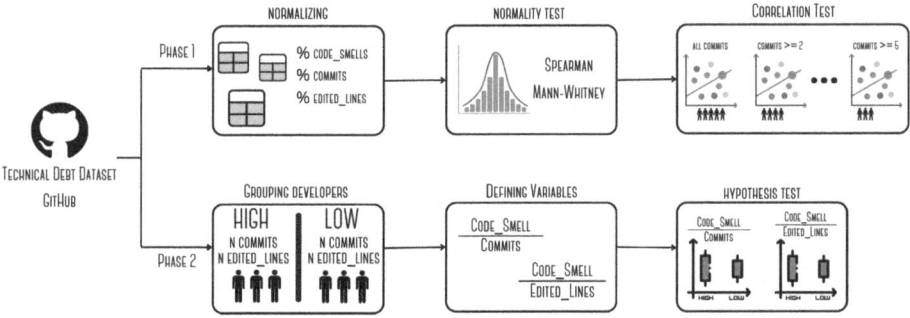

**Fig. 2.** Analysis process diagram.

The decision to exclude developers with fewer than two commits was intentional, based on a methodological choice to improve the correlations' robustness. Developers with only one commit present a limitation in the analysis, as the single contribution offers little information about the tendency to introduce or maintain code smells. The presence of many developers with a single contribution could introduce bias into the analysis, affecting the accuracy of the results, as we consider these developers to represent particular situations.

**Analysis of Phase 2.** During phase 1 (Fig. 2 top), we observed a pattern: when excluding developers with low commits, the correlation between code smells and commits stabilizes. This observation led us to a more refined analysis, focusing on developers with more active participation, defined by a minimum number of commits.

In our hypothesis, the number of commits represents a more direct indicator of the developer's involvement with the project. Although the volume of edited lines is an important metric, it is intrinsically linked to each commit made, as every commit has edited lines, and all edited lines are related to some commit. By adjusting the analysis based on the number of commits, we indirectly consider the edited lines associated with those commits.

This approach allowed us to investigate whether developers with more significant involvement (measured by the number of commits) have a proportionally greater or lesser influence on introducing code smells than those with fewer activities. This approach does not exclude the importance of edited lines but places them in a broader context, where the number of commits indicates engagement in the project.

To deepen our understanding of contribution dynamics, we grouped developers into two groups based on the median number of commits. The groups were named HIGH (most active) and LOW (least active). The "Grouping developers" rectangle in Phase 2 of Fig. 2 (bottom) represents this decision. Then, we define two variables - code smells per commit (**cspercommits**) and code smells by edited lines (**csperlinesedited**) as represented by the "Defining variables" rectangle in Phase 2 of Fig. 2. This allows us to conduct hypothesis tests for each metric to understand better the relationship between the frequency of contributions and the incidence of code smells. The hypothesis test is represented by the "Hypothesis test" rectangle in Phase 2 of Fig. 2.

In short, Fig. 2 illustrates this two-phase approach. We initially focused on percentage values during the analysis to ensure a fair comparison between projects and developers of different scales (phase 1 analysis - top of Fig. 2). However, when we observed a consistent increase in the correlation coefficient when excluding developers with fewer commits, we decided to investigate this trend further. To achieve this, we changed our approach to using raw data in hypothesis testing (phase 2 analysis - bottom of Fig. 2). This decision was made to capture the sheer magnitude of developer contributions and their direct impact on code quality. Working with raw values allowed us to more directly evaluate the relationship between the volume of commits and the occurrence of code smells without the dilution that can occur when normalizing this data about the total project size. Thus, it was possible to more clearly distinguish the impact of the most active developers (HIGH) compared to the least active (LOW) on introducing code smells. This methodological change gave us a more granular and contextualized view of the dynamics of developers' contributions and their impact on code quality.

## 4   Results

This section presents our findings. We investigate the relationship between churning, measured through the number of commits and edited lines, and the occurrence of code smells in the analyzed software projects. The results contribute to a better understanding of how the intensity of developer activity relates to software quality, using code smells as an indicator.

### 4.1   Results for the Phase 1 Analysis

In Phase 1, we investigate the correlation between the developers' activity intensity and smell incidence. We adopt the Spearman correlation test and J. Cohen's classification [5]: *Very low or no correlation* $(0.00 \leq |r| < 0.20)$; *Low* $(0.20 \leq |r| < 0.40)$; *Moderate* $(0.40 \leq |r| < 0.60)$; *Strong* $(0.60 \leq |r| < 0.80)$ ; and *Very strong perfect* $0.80 \leq |r| < 1.00)$. Considering this classification, the correlation between code smells and edited lines is strong - Spearman coefficient value 0.7627, p-value <.001. This suggests that a more significant number of edited lines is associated with an increase in the incidence of code smells. The correlation between code smells and commits indicates a moderate correlation - Spearman coefficient value 0.5621, p-value <.001. This correlation, although significant, is less intense than that observed for edited lines.

As discussed in Sect. 3.2, we also consider developers with different levels of participation. After excluding developers with fewer commits, we observe an increase in the correlation coefficient. This has been confirmed by repeated testing for groups that only have developers with more than 2, 3, and 4 commits. Table 1 presents the results considering all tests.

**Table 1.** Correlation between code smell and commit for developers with numbers of commits ≥ 2, 3, 4 and 5.

| Developer group | ($|r_s|$) coefficient | p-value |
|---|---|---|
| commits ≥ 2 | 0.5621 | <.001 |
| commits ≥ 3 | 0.6706 | .042 |
| commits ≥ 4 | 0.7047 | <.001 |
| commits ≥ 5 | 0.7142 | <.001 |

Notably, our correlation analysis between code smells and commit count relied on the raw number of commits per developer without applying proportional adjustments based on project size or scope. When we refer to developers with commits ≥ 2, 3, 4, and 5, we directly refer to the absolute number of commits linked to each developer. This methodological choice allows a direct and intuitive comparison of the impact of developer involvement, measured by the number of commits, on the incidence of code smells.

These results revealed an interesting pattern: as we increase the minimum commits threshold for including developers in the analysis, the correlation between code smells and the number of commits becomes stronger. This indicates that developers with fewer commits impact the correlation test by reducing its value (see Table 1), which suggests that the developers with few commits are related to more code smells. We performed a hypothesis test to explore this relationship, segmenting developers into two groups based on the median number of commits. This allows us to investigate the difference in behavior between the most active and least active groups of developers. We named this phase of the analysis as Phase 2.

### 4.2   Results for the Phase 2 Analysis

When analyzing the initial 232 developers in the study, we found a median of 97 commits. Therefore, we classify developers with less than 97 commits into a less active group called LOW. Developers with 97 or more commits were classified into the most active group, HIGH. From this classification, we quantify the number of smells made by committing for each group, dividing the number of code smells per commit for each developer. The idea is to quantify how many code smells a developer inserts/maintains for each commit, creating the variable:

$$cspercommits = \frac{codesmells}{commits}$$

Considering the **cspercommits** variable, it is possible to observe the distribution of the number of code smells per commit associated with developers who make more commits (HIGH group) and those who make fewer commits (LOW group). The boxplot presented in Fig. 3 shows the distribution of the variable. The objective is to observe the difference in the distribution of the number of commits/code smells between groups of developers who perform more or fewer commits; the outliers were disregarded as they bias the analysis, whose objective is to observe a general behavior. We removed outliers to capture the difference in the code distribution more clearly and smell values per number of commits between the two groups.

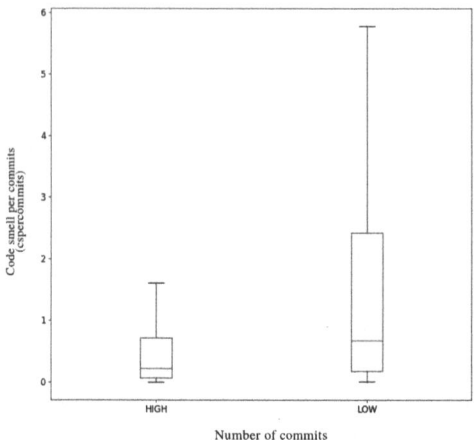

**Fig. 3.** Distribution of code smells per commit for groups of developers classified by activity level (HIGH and LOW).

Based on the data, we define the following hypotheses:

- **Null hypothesis:** There is no difference in the distribution of code smells per commit between groups of more active (HIGH) and less active (LOW) developers.
- **Alternative Hypothesis:** There is a difference in the distribution of code smells per commit between groups of more active (HIGH) and less active (LOW) developers.

As the samples do not present a normal distribution, we adopt the Mann-Whitney hypothesis test [14]. Mann Whitney is a non-parametric test suitable for comparing two independent samples of observations, considering the significance level (p-value) at 0.05. The p-value obtained was <.001 therefore, the null hypothesis was rejected, indicating that developers with fewer commits insert or maintain more code smells per commit.

We reaffirm this finding using descriptive statistics metrics: we calculated the median number of code smells/commits associated with developers. We chose to use the median instead of the mean as it offers a more robust representation and is less susceptible to distortions caused by extreme values. The values are 0.2 for the most participative group (HIGH) and 0.6 for the least participative group (LOW). In other words, the minor participative group of developers inserts/maintains 6 code smells for every ten commits made, while the most participative group inserts/maintains 2 code smells for every ten commits made. This suggests that less active developers (with fewer commits) need to make a smaller number of commits to insert/maintain more code smells if compared to more participative ones.

To evaluate efficiency in terms of code smells per edited lines, a new variable was created: *csperlinesedited = codesmells / linesedited*. Thus, observing the number of lines each group edits to insert or maintain a code smell is possible.

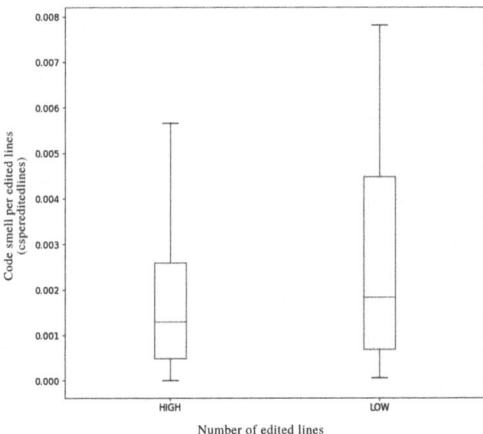

**Fig. 4.** Distribution of code smells relating to edited lines to two groups of developers.

To perform the hypothesis test, we define:

– **Null hypothesis:** There is no difference in the distribution of code smells per edited lines between groups of most active (HIGH) and least active (LOW) developers
– **Alternative Hypothesis:** There is a difference in the distribution of code smells per edited lines between groups of more active (HIGH) and less active (LOW) developers

After applying the Mann-Whitney test, the null hypothesis was rejected with a p-value of .004. Considering the median, the values are 773 for the most participative group (HIGH) and 546 for the least participative group (LOW). In other words, the minor participative group of developers inserts/maintains 1 code smell for every 546 lines edited, while the most participative group inserts/maintains 1 code smell for every 773 lines edited. This suggests that less participative developers (with fewer lines edited) need fewer lines to insert/maintain a code smell than more participative ones.

To deepen the analysis related to the distribution of code smells inserted or maintained by commits and edited lines, we performed an effect size analysis (effect size) to quantify the magnitude of the differences between the groups. The classification proposed by J. Cohen [6] was adopted: 0.1 - small, 0.3 - medium, and 0.5 - high.

The results indicate that for the group of developers classified by number of commits (cspercommits), the effect size is medium, with $r = 0.32$, pointing to a substantial difference in the proportion of code smells per commit between the HIGH and LOW groups. For the group classified by edited lines (csperlinesedited), the effect size was small ($r = 0.19$), according to the thresholds established by J. Cohen [6].

## 5   Discussion

This work emphasizes the relationship between churning and code smells. Combining both measures builds on understanding the software development process as it relates the intensity of changes with object-oriented software design quality. This supports, for example, discussions on the stability of developers in software projects [36] and work distribution.

Due to the large volume of data analyzed, we present this work as a preliminary and exploratory study. Our findings, experimental setup, and the publicly available dataset[3] provide a foundation for future in-depth investigations. Further investigations could examine different dimensions, including specific types of code smells, commit purposes (e.g., evolution vs. maintenance), and the complexity of code modifications. We are currently pursuing some of these avenues in ongoing research.

Our findings highlight the impact of developer activity intensity on code quality. Although all developers may introduce or maintain code smells, those with lower activity levels often have a proportionally more significant impact, which may negatively affect software design quality.

This finding enriches the empirical knowledge on the topic. For example, Yamashita et al. [43] highlight the correlation between development practices and the incidence of code smells, emphasizing the need for a conscious approach to code quality management. Tufano et al. [40] observe variations in the propensity to introduce code smells based on developer experience. Thus, the nonexhaustive set of software characteristics, such as developers' practices, experience, and (now) intensity of changes, composes a corpus of empirical knowledge supporting the comprehension of the relation between developers' activities and software quality.

On the other hand, by analyzing how the intensity of developer activity relates to the presence of code smells, we highlight the need to interpret code smells as design flaws and as indicators of development patterns and developer behavior. This helps in understanding how code smells can be used efficiently in measuring software quality, a demand discussed in other works, as highlighted by Santos et al. [34] and Santos et al. [33].

---

[3] https://anonymous.4open.science/r/research-smells-master-4B54/.

## 5.1   Threats to Validity

There are some threats to the validity of this work, as with any other empirical study [42]. Below, we discuss the most relevant threats to our study.

**External Validity.** It is related to using a specific dataset, which implies risks to the generalization of results. Due to the software product's characteristics and the work's exploratory bias, there is a threat related to any empirical study of this nature. However, it needs to be considered.

**Internal Validity.** That relates to the choice of analyzed code smells. We analyze the code smells whose detection heuristics were incorporated into the detection tools used by the authors of the dataset. One factor that mitigates this limitation is that the SonarQube tool extracted the code smells of "The Technical debt dataset". An aspect mitigating this threat is the SonarQube, a tool widely used by researchers and practitioners.

**Construct Validity.** One may have to consider that the data preparation depends on some choices affecting the outcomes in some way. We highlight adopting the median as a threshold to form HIGH and LOW groups: some data points may have near values. Despite this, the results of the hypothesis tests were rejected, indicating a relevant difference between the distribution of values in the HIGH and LOW groups.

**Conclusion Validity.** These risks relate to the analysis strategy. Despite adopting hypothesis tests, we need to choose groups of developers' activity intensity (HIGH and LOW groups). Furthermore, the results of the effect size test can indicate that there are points to be explored. However, this type of limitation is implicit in works of this nature. One aspect to be highlighted is that during the analysis exercise, several strategies were considered, discussed, and tested, with the result presented in this study being a small sample of the entire evolutionary process of analysis carried out in the development of the work.

## 6   Conclusion

In this work, we present a preliminary investigation of the impact of developers' actions on software maintenance and quality. We adopted "The Technical Debt Dataset Version 2.0" [17] as a data source. It comprises 31 projects, 749 developers, and 153,994 commits. Our analysis considered all 31 projects and 317 developers associated with a type of code smell. We explored the relationship between code smells, commits, and edited lines, providing insight into the influence of churning on software quality standards.

Our findings indicate that code smells are related to the intensity of developers' activity regarding the number of commits and edited lines. We observed a correlation between a more significant number of edited lines and committed, and the emergence of code smells, especially among less active developers. The results reinforce that the stability and continuity of developers in specific projects contribute to maintaining software quality. These findings are based on the use of i) information visualization, through the observation of generated graphs, as seen in Figs. 3 and 4; ii) descriptive statistics, through the observation of medians and correlation tests performed, as discussed in Sect. 3.2; and iii) inferential statistics, through hypothesis and effect size tests, also discussed in Sect. 3.2.

In future work, we plan to extend our analysis to additional datasets to improve the generalizability of our findings. We also plan to increase the number of software and developers analyzed, allowing a more global view of the relationship between development activity and software quality. Furthermore, we aim to expand the scope of metrics analyzed, such as bugs and performance indicators, to gain a more comprehensive understanding of software quality drivers. Finally, we intend to adopt feature extraction mechanisms based on machine-learning approaches to mitigate code smell detection heuristics threats.

**Acknowledgments.** This work was partially supported by UEFS-AUXPPG 2025 and CAPES-PROAP 2025 grants; by the Coordenação de Aperfeiçoamento de Pessoal de Nível Superior Brasil (CAPES) - Finance Code 001; and by the Conselho Nacional de Desenvolvimento Científico e Tecnológico (CNPq).

**Disclosure of Interests.** The authors have no competing interests to declare that are relevant to the content of this article.

# References

1. Behnamghader, P., Alfayez, R., Srisopha, K., Boehm, B.: Towards better understanding of software quality evolution through commit-impact analysis. In: QRS 2017, pp. 251–262. IEEE (2017)
2. Bird, C., Nagappan, N., Murphy, B., Gall, H., Devanbu, P.: Don't touch my code! Examining the effects of ownership on softwtowards better understanding of software quality evolution through are quality. In: Proceedings of the 19th ACM SIGSOFT Symposium and the 13th European Conference on Foundations of Software Engineering, pp. 4–14 (2011)
3. Cairo, A.S., Carneiro, G., Monteiro, M.: The impact of code smells on software bugs: a systematic literature review. Information **9**(11) (2018)
4. Campbell, G.A., Papapetrou, P.P.: SonarQube in Action. Manning Publications Co. (2013)
5. Cohen, J., Cohen, P., West, S.G., Aiken, L.: Applied Multiple Regression/Correlation Analysis for the Behavioral Sciences. Routledge (2013)
6. Cohen, J.: Statistical Power Analysis for the Behavioral Sciences. Academic Press (2013)
7. Cunningham, W.: The WyCash portfolio management system, In: OOPSLA 1992, pp. 29–30 (1992)
8. Das, T., Di Penta, M., Malavolta, I.: A quantitative and qualitative investigation of performance-related commits in android apps. In: 2016 IEEE ICSME, pp. 443–447. IEEE (2016)
9. Fontana, F., Ferme, V., Spinelli, S.: Investigating the impact of code smells debt on quality code evaluation. In: 2012 Third MTD, pp. 15–22. IEEE (2012)
10. Fowler, M.: Refactoring: Improving the Design of Existing Code. Addison-Wesley (1999)

11. Fowler, M.: Refactoring. Addison-Wesley Professional (2018)
12. Freire, S., et al.: How do technical debt payment practices relate to the effects of the presence of debt items in software projects? In: 2021 IEEE SANER, pp. 605–609. IEEE (2021)
13. Kamei, Y., et al.: A large-scale empirical study of just-in-time quality assurance. IEEE Trans. Softw. Eng. **39**(6), 757–773 (2012)
14. Kothari, C.R.: Research Methodology: Methods and Techniques. New Age International (2004)
15. Lanza, M., Marinescu, R.: Object-Oriented Metrics in Practice: Using Software Metrics to Characterize, Evaluate, and Improve the Design of Object-Oriented Systems. Springer, Heidelberg (2007). https://doi.org/10.1007/3-540-39538-5
16. Lehman, M.M.: Laws of software evolution revisited. In: Montangero, C. (ed.) EWSPT 1996. LNCS, vol. 1149, pp. 108–124. Springer, Heidelberg (1996). https://doi.org/10.1007/BFb0017737
17. Lenarduzzi, V., Saarimäki, N., Taibi, D.: The technical debt dataset. In: 15th PROMISE, January 2019
18. Lenarduzzi, V., Saarimäki, N., Taibi, D.: Some SonarQube issues have a significant but small effect on faults and changes. A large-scale empirical study. JSS **170**, 110750 (2020)
19. Li, Y., Li, D., Huang, F., Lee, S., Ai, J.: An exploratory analysis on software developers' bug-introducing tendency over time. In: SATE 2016, pp. 12–17. IEEE (2016)
20. Li, Z., Avgeriou, P., Liang, P.: A systematic mapping study on technical debt and its management. JSS **101**, 193–220 (2015)
21. Liu, J., Zhou, Y., Yang, Y., Lu, H., Xu, B.: Code churn: a neglected metric in effort-aware just-in-time defect prediction. In: 2017 ACM/IEEE ESEM, pp. 11–19 (2017)
22. Mantyla, M., Vanhanen, J., Lassenius, C.: A taxonomy and an initial empirical study of bad smells in code. In: ICSM 2003, pp. 381–384. IEEE (2003)
23. Moha, N., Guéhéneuc, Y., Duchien, L., Le M., A.F.: DECOR: a method for the specification and detection of code and design smells. IEEE Trans. Softw. Eng. **36**(1), 20–36 (2009)
24. Munson, J., Elbaum, S.: Code churn: a measure for estimating the impact of code change. In: ICSM 1998, pp. 24–31 (1998)
25. Nascimento, R., Sant'Anna, C.: Investigating the relationship between bad smells and bugs in software systems. In: 11th SBCARS, pp. 1–10 (2017)
26. Ogheneovo, E., et al.: On the relationship between software complexity and maintenance costs. J. Comput. Commun. **2**(14), 1 (2014)
27. Olsson, T., Ericsson, M., Wingkvist, A.: The relationship of code churn and architectural violations in the open source software JabRef. In: Proceedings of the 11th European Conference on Software Architecture: Companion Proceedings, ECSA 2017, pp. 152–158. Association for Computing Machinery, New York, NY, USA (2017)
28. Palomba, F., Bavota, G., Di Penta, M., Fasano, F., Oliveto, R., De Lucia, A.: On the diffuseness and the impact on maintainability of code smells: a large scale empirical investigation. In: Proceedings of the 40th ICSE, p. 482 (2018)
29. Pinzger, M., Giger, E., Gall, H.C.: Comparing fine-grained source code changes and code churn for bug prediction - a retrospective. SIGSOFT Softw. Eng. Notes **46**(3), 21–23 (2021)
30. Qiu, Y., Zhang, W., Zou, W., Liu, J., Liu, Q.: An empirical study of developer quality. In: 2015 IEEE QRS, pp. 202–209. IEEE (2015)

31. Richardson, A.: Nonparametric statistics for non-statisticians: a step-by-step approach by Gregory W. Corder, Dale I. Foreman (2010)
32. Salamea, M., Farré, C.: Influence of developer factors on code quality: a data study. In: 2019 IEEE 19th QRS-C, pp. 120–125. IEEE (2019)
33. Santos, J., Rocha-Junior, J., de Mendonça, M.: Investigating factors that affect the human perception on god class detection: an analysis based on a family of four controlled experiments. JSERD **5**, 8:1–8:39 (2017)
34. Santos, J., Rocha-Junior, J., Prates, L., Do Nascimento, R., Freitas, M., Mendonça, M.: A systematic review on the code smell effect. JSS **144**, 450–477 (2018)
35. Shin, Y., Meneely, A., Williams, L., Osborne, J.: Evaluating complexity, code churn, and developer activity metrics as indicators of software vulnerabilities. IEEE Trans. Software Eng. **37**(6), 772–787 (2011)
36. Sommerville, I.: Software Engineering. Pearson Education Inc. (2011)
37. Tsoukalas, D., Mathioudaki, M., Siavvas, M., Kehagias, D., Chatzigeorgiou, A.: A clustering approach towards cross-project technical debt forecasting. SN Comput. Sci. **2**(1), 22 (2021)
38. Tsoukalas, D., Mittas, N., Arvanitou, E.M., Ampatzoglou, A., Chatzigeorgiou, A., Kehagias, D.: Local and global explainability for technical debt identification. IEEE Trans. Softw. Eng., 1–15 (2024)
39. Tsoukalas, D., et al.: Machine learning for technical debt identification. IEEE Trans. Softw. Eng. **48**(12), 4892–4906 (2021)
40. Tufano, M., et al.: When and why your code starts to smell bad. In: 37th IEEE ICSE, vol. 1, pp. 403–414. IEEE (2015)
41. Weiner, I., Craighead, W.: The Corsini Encyclopedia of Psychology, vol. 4. Wiley (2010)
42. Wohlin, C., Runeson, P., Höst, M., Ohlsson, M., Regnell, B., Wesslén, A.: Experimentation in software engineering. Springer, Heidelberg (2012). https://doi.org/10.1007/978-3-662-69306-3
43. Yamashita, A., Moonen, L.: Do code smells reflect important maintainability aspects? In: 28th ICSM, pp. 306–315. IEEE (2012)

# An Empirical Analysis on the Use of Third-Party HTTP Clients in Open-Source Java Projects

Leif Bonorden[(✉)][iD]

University of Hamburg, Hamburg, Germany
leif.bonorden@uni-hamburg.de

**Abstract.** External communication libraries (e.g., for HTTP/REST) are static dependencies that enable dynamic dependencies in software systems. Such third-party HTTP libraries may influence the system's qualities. Thus, the selection out of numerous third-party HTTP clients needs to be taken carefully. However, the use of such clients has not been studied broadly.

We conduct a quantitative empirical study of 18,879 open-source Java repositories and analyze 259,683 configuration files. We further investigate a subset of these repositories qualitatively and in more depth. We have found that Apache HttpClient, Spring Web, and OkHttp are the most used third-party HTTP clients in Java open-source projects. Further analysis has shown that declared dependencies are often not actively managed, reference outdated versions, or are entirely unused.

**Keywords:** HTTP clients · Maven ecosystem · Repository mining · Static dependencies · Dynamic dependencies

## 1 Introduction

Build automation and dependency managers allow for the comfortable selection and integration of third-party libraries [8]. From an architectural point of view, these are executive decisions [20] during architectural synthesis [15] and the external libraries become part of the software system as *build dependencies*, a type of *static dependencies* [22]. Communication libraries take a distinctive position in this situation: They are static dependencies that enable *dynamic dependencies*, i.e., communication within the system or with external services at runtime [6].

A prevalent form of communication is the REST style using the HTTP protocol [21], while other techniques like asynchronous event-driven communication or synchronous communication via GraphQL are also used [5]. In the Java programming language, HTTP was supported initially by the `HttpURLConnection` API. However, this API was not satisfactory, which motivated a variety of third-party clients. In version 11 (released in 2018), Java added a new HTTP Client as `java.net.http` to offer a contemporary light-weight internal option [23].

© The Author(s), under exclusive license to Springer Nature Switzerland AG 2026
D. Taibi and D. Smite (Eds.): SEAA 2025, LNCS 16083, pp. 361–371, 2026.
https://doi.org/10.1007/978-3-032-04207-1_24

For Java projects, three build automation tools are widely used: *Apache Maven*[1], *Gradle Build Tool*[2], and *Apache Ant*[3] [14]. While Maven and Gradle also manage external dependencies, Ant integrates the dedicated dependency manager *Apache Ivy*[4]. Despite the name, the *Maven Central Repository*[5] is the main source of artifacts for all three tools. Artifacts in the Maven Central Repository may rely on other Maven artifacts. Thus, we distinguish a project's *direct dependencies* and *transitive dependencies*.

This study aims to broadly analyze the current use of third-party HTTP clients included in Maven, Gradle, and Ant/Ivy configuration files of open-source Java repositories. Therefore, we quantitatively study the use of build tools and declared third-party HTTP clients. Furthermore, we investigate a subset of projects in more depth to include transitive dependencies. Finally, we study a subset of projects qualitatively to characterize their use of HTTP clients. In summary, this paper provides the following contributions:

- quantitative and qualitative analyses and insights on the current use of third-party HTTP clients in Java open-source software
- a dataset comprising 259,683 build/dependency files collected from 18,879 Java repositories on GitHub [4]
- tools to re-generate or update this dataset.

## 2 Related Work

### 2.1 Architecture Evaluation and Reconstruction

Casse et al. [7] used OpenTelemetry to analyze network communication in distributed software systems and identify bottlenecks. Bonorden and van Hoorn [3] used OpenTelemetry to collected metadata about the HTTP communication itself to identify calls to deprecated APIs. Jasser [18] checks architectural security decisions that require the analysis of communication clients – e.g., "No ThirdPartyBuildingBlock can send a Message that (leaves the System)".

Genfer and Zdun [11] detected HTTP communication to identify dependencies within microservice systems and detect cyclic dependencies. Similarly, Hutcheson et al. [17] extracted REST calls to identify call graphs and reconstruct microservice architectures. Genfer and Zdun [12] further characterized data exposure through HTTP APIs in microservice systems.

### 2.2 HTTP/REST Clients in Java and Android

Rapoport et al. [25] identified the call targets of Android apps both statically and dynamically. They found that a large number of dynamic requests does not use a statically detectable URL.

---

[1] https://maven.apache.org/.
[2] https://gradle.org/.
[3] https://ant.apache.org/.
[4] https://ant.apache.org/ivy/.
[5] https://maven.org/.

Gadient et al. [10] focused the security of web communication in 160 Android apps. They found *Retrofit* and *OkHttp* to be the most used third-party HTTP libraries, and often found insecure communication protocols and other security issues. Abdellatif et al. [1] analyzed 1,595 Android apps and identified *Retrofit*, *OkHttp* and *Google Volley* as the most popularl libraries. For the year 2018, 98% of newly released apps used a third-party HTTP library.

### 2.3   Analyses of the Maven Ecosystem

Most studies on the Maven ecosystem focus on dependencies between Maven artifacts: E.g., Yoshioka et al. [31] found that *Log4j*'s deprecated versions are still used and even adopted by new projects.

Huang et al. [16] analyzed Maven dependencies retrieved from 2,216 Java repositories on GitHub. They found that the number of libraries used is correlated to the project size. Further, they identified that only a small subset of Maven artifacts is actually used in many projects.

Soto-Valero et al. [27, 28] and Keshani et al. [19] found that "bloated" dependencies, i.e., external libraries that are included but never actively used, are increasing in the Maven ecosystem. Suwanachote et al. [29] found that 52% of all projects on GitHub using Maven are declaring unused dependencies.

On the contrary, Harrand et al. [13] and Riegler et al. [26] highlight positive aspects of library diversity as they aim for automated switching between similar libraries in case of problems (e.g., security issues).

## 3   Study Design

To achieve our goal set in Sect. 1, we derive the following research questions:

**RQ 1.** Which third-party HTTP libraries are directly used in open-source Java projects?

Knowing the frequently used HTTP libraries allows researchers to refine their methods and tools, and to make reasonable assumptions.

**RQ 2.** Which versions of popular third-party HTTP libraries are directly and transitively included in open-source Java projects?

Deepening the analysis enables assessment of the number of dependencies to HTTP libraries per project and examination of outdated dependencies.

**RQ 3.** How are popular third-party HTTP libraries used in open-source Java projects?
    **RQ 3.1.** Are directly included libraries actively used?
    **RQ 3.2.** Does each project only use a single HTTP client?
    **RQ 3.2.** Are the dynamic communication targets statically provided?

The restriction to popular third-party HTTP libraries leads to a more homogeneous set of repositories for which a characterization is possible. The sub-questions address common assumptions of related work as presented in Sect. 2.

## 3.1  Data Collection

We use the *SEART GitHub Search Engine*[6] [9] to obtain a list of GitHub repositories with the following filter criteria[7]: (a) Java as repository's main language,
(b) repository with at least 10 stars,  (c) commits by at least two contributors,
(d) latest commit after 01 Jan 2024.

This selection results in a list of 18,879 GitHub repositories with an average
of 23 releases, 19 branches, and 2,506 commits by 23 contributors. Their files
comprises an average of 175,279 lines of code.

Subsequently, we filter each repository's default branch for dependency configuration files – i.e., `pom.xml` for Maven, `build.gradle` for Gradle, and `ivy.xml`
for Ant/Ivy. This yields 259,683 files for 41,336 build projects in 17,913 repositories (94.8% of all repositories analyzed). Of these build projects, 24,847 (60.1%)
use Maven, 15,979 (38.6%) use Gradle, and 510 (1.2%) use Ant/Ivy.

## 3.2  Broad Analysis of the Entire Dataset for RQ 1

To prepare this analysis, we compile a list of 146 Maven artifacts that contain
HTTP clients from scientific publications, the website MvnRepository, and a
grey literature search.

Subsequently, we extract dependencies containing an HTTP client from the
previously identified configuration files. This analysis is conducted locally and
does not require querying the Maven central repository. Thus, version information like "latest" are not resolvable.

## 3.3  In-Depth Analysis of a Subset for RQ 2

In contrast to the broad analysis, an in-depth analysis requires actually resolving
the artifacts and collecting further information from the Maven central repository to get precise version information and transitive dependencies.

To limit the processing resources required and the number of calls to the
Maven central API, we sample 100 projects from our initial list by applying
simple random sampling [2]. Subsequently, we resolve all dependencies, direct
and transitive, with the Maven build tool.

To categorize versions across libraries, we take the point of view of 01 Jan
2024 – in alignment with our filter criteria for repositories as discussed in
Sect. 3.1. We denote library versions that were released at latest three months
earlier as *up-to-date*. We further categorize versions released in the preceding
twelve months as *acceptable* as long as they don't contain a known security
issue. Versions with known security issues and versions released more than 12
months prior are labeled *outdated*. Finally, we label outdated versions *antique* if
they are two or more major release versions behind the latest version on 01 Jan
2024.

---

[6] https://seart-ghs.si.usi.ch/.
[7] For the reported analysis, we obtained a list on 08 Mar 2025.

### 3.4    Qualitative Characterization of a Subset for RQ 3

Feasibility of a manual qualitative characterization requires a smaller subset of projects to analyze. First, we limit the set of projects to those that depend on one of the most popular third-party HTTP clients: Apache HttpClient, Spring Web, and OkHttp (see Sect. 4.1). For each of these clients we select 10 projects – again by applying simple random sampling [2].

The sub-questions to RQ 3 guide our manual analysis:

RQ 3.1. We search for import statements related to the stated dependencies. Each search result is checked manually.

RQ 3.2. We check the results from RQ 1 for further declared third-party or Java-internal HTTP clients.

RQ 3.3. Within the files identified for RQs 3.1 and 3.2, we try to statically locate URsL called by the HTTP clients.

## 4    Results

### 4.1    RQ 1: Broad Analysis (Direct Dependencies)

The analysis of 259,683 configuration files from 18,879 repositories yields an overview of the popularity for third-party HTTP libraries, that is also visualized in Fig. 1.

Apache HttpClient is the most used library with 3,741 occurrences in our dataset (19.8% of all repositories). Next, the Spring Web framework accumulates 1,893 direct dependencies (10.0%), and the OkHttp client is included 1,606 times (8.5%). In total, at least one of these three dependencies is found in 38.3% of all GitHub projects we analyzed.

While OkHttp features a single client, Apache HttpClient is a collection of multiple similar clients (HttpCore, HttpClient, HttpAsyncClient), and Spring Web is a framework featuring multiple different clients (RestClient, WebClient, RestTemplate).

### 4.2    RQ 2: In-Depth Analysis (Transitive Dependencies, Versions)

While the projects included an average of 0.2 HTTP clients as direct dependencies, they also included an average of 2.1 HTTP clients transitively. We found a maximum of 4 directly included HTTP clients, but up to 22 transitively dependent HTTP clients in a single project. Their versions are shown in Table 1, categorized as described in Sect. 3.3.

Examples for outdated versions impeding security are found for Apache Http-Client and OkHttp: All Apache HttpClient versions prior to 4.5.13 (released in October 2020) are subject to CVE-2020-13956[8], i.e., the client may misread malformed parameters and contact wrong call targets. Versions of OkHttp prior to

---

[8] https://cve.mitre.org/cgi-bin/cvename.cgi?name=CVE-2020-13956.

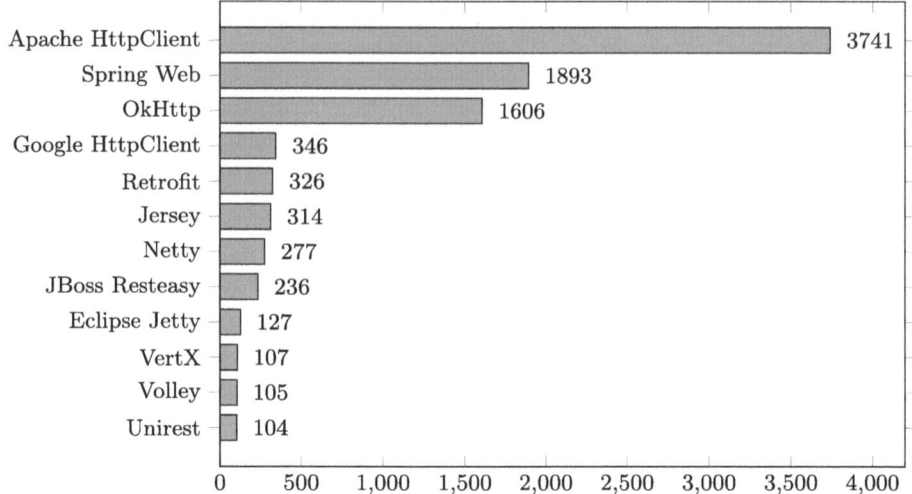

**Fig. 1.** Occurrences as direct dependencies in 18,879 GitHub repositories

4.12.0 (released in October 2023) are subject to CVE-2023-3635[9] since a Maven dependency on which OkHttp itself depends is affected. This issue may allow a denial-of-service attack using malformated gzip buffers.

**Table 1.** Classification of versions used for popular third-party HTTP clients

| Classification | Apache HttpClient | Spring Web | OkHttp | Total |
|---|---|---|---|---|
| antique | 12 (1.9%) | 6 (33.3%) | 11 (29.7%) | 29 (4.2%) |
| outdated | 318 (49.5%) | 7 (38.9%) | 6 (16,2%) | 331 (47.5%) |
| acceptable | 289 (45.0%) | — | 7 (18.9%) | 296 (42.5%) |
| up-to-date | 23 (3.6%) | 5 (27.8%) | 13 (35.1%) | 41 (5.9%) |
| Total | 642 | 18 | 37 | 697 |

### 4.3   RQ 3: Characterizing the Use of Third-Party HTTP Libraries

Regarding RQ 3.1, we found 6 of 30 cases (20.0%) that don't use a directly declared HTTP library. Furthermore, in 7 cases (23.3%), we found only a single call within the project files, and these calls did not show any noticeable necessity to declare a dependency on an external library.

Studying the use of multiple clients in a single project (RQ 3.2), we repeatedly found the combination of a third-party library and an internal API (7/30,

---

[9] https://cve.mitre.org/cgi-bin/cvename.cgi?name=CVE-2023-3635.

23.3%). Furthermore, we found projects that feature a lot of HTTP clients for good reason as they provided plugins or other tooling for as many different HTTP clients as possible, or test a setup for different HTTP clients. Regarding the use of Java-internal HTTP libraries, only 1 of 30 projects (3.3%) featured the Java HttpClient, while 9 projects used HttpURLConnection (30.0%).

Investigating call targets (RQ 3.3), we discovered hard-coded values suitable for static detection only in 2 of 30 repositories (6.7%).

## 5   Discussion

Although we analyzed only recently maintained repositories, we found dependencies to third-party HTTP clients in a generally outdated state: Declared dependencies are often unused or introduce unnecessary external dependencies. If Java-internal APIs are used, often it is the outdated HttpURLConnection. Sometimes, multiple clients are used within one project.

---

**Recommendations for Practioners**

We recommend that software developers actively maintain their dependencies to third-party HTTP libraries. This should include regular reviews to update actually required dependencies and to remove unnecessary elements.

We further recommend to check the need for third-party HTTP clients since suitable Java-internal options are available now. If Java-internal HTTP libraries are used, Java HttpClient should be preferred.

---

Comparing our results to related work, we find the focus on a small subset of HTTP libraries justified, since only few libraries are widely used. However, the common assumption that only one library is used in a system does not hold. Instead, many projects feature multiple HTTP libraries.

For another practice, the investigation of external communication based on statically determined (hard-coded) URLs, the prerequisites are not given in open-source Java projects since call targets are mostly determined only dynamically.

---

**Recommendations for Researchers**

We recommend to focus on the three most popular third-party HTTP libraries for Java: Apache Http, Spring Web (comprising RestClient, WebClient, and RestTemplate), and OkHttp. Researchers should expect a single project to feature multiple HTTP libraries.

We further advise against library-independent static approaches to identify communication, if they rely on the identification of hard-coded call targets.

---

## 6   Threats to Validity

Designing this study, we the suggestions given in [24,30]. Nevertheless, we are aware that our choices lead to limitations and possible threats to validity:

**Limitations.** By design, we study the current state of third-party HTTP libraries in Java via Maven. Thus, our study is restricted to this setting. In particular, we have not included Java's internal HTTP options.

**External Validity.** The study's selection procedure poses a threat to external validity. It comprises multiple steps that may compromise the generalizability, i.e., selecting GitHub as the only source, the selecting criteria to filter the list of repositories, and the filter criteria for the files in the collection process.

**Internal Validity.** To avoid threats to internal validity, we sampled data only where necessary and used random sampling. Furthermore, we publish the dataset and the code to update and analyze it, which allows for further verification.

**Construct Validity.** To validate the study's underlying model of constructs we opted to use broad definitions of relevant concept, e.g., HTTP libraries. In particular, we included all libraries which contain HTTP clients, even if they also provide other features. On the other hand, to avoid over-representation, we included manual analysis to validate our findings on a subset of the repositories.

**Conclusion Validity.** To ensure conclusion validity, we defined all relevant sampling, filter and search criteria a-priori. Furthermore, we explicate how our interpretative results and recommendations are based on the studies data results.

# 7 Conclusion

We collected and investigated a dataset comprising 259,683 build and dependency configuration files from 18,879 GitHub repositories. These use Maven (60.1%), Gradle (38.6%), and Ant/Ivy (1.2%). The HTTP clients Apache HttpClient, Spring Web, and OkHttp are popular in Java open-source systems.

The subsequent in-depth analysis revealed additional dependencies to HTTP clients via transitive dependencies and that 51.7% of the analyzed projects use severely outdated versions of third-party HTTP clients. Furthermore, we found that the use of internal and third-party HTTP libraries is insufficiently managed.

Several research directions follow directly from our study's design and results: First, a longitudinal analysis may include the commit histories to identify trends. Second, the study may be re-conducted for other Maven-compatible languages, in particular Kotlin, or closed-source projects to generalize the findings. And finally, this data-focused study may be complimented by human insights.

**Disclosure of Interests.** The authors have no competing interests to declare that are relevant to the content of this article.

# References

1. Abdellatif, M., Tighilt, R., Belkhir, A., Moha, N., Guéhéneuc, Y.G., Beaudry, É.: A multi-dimensional study on the state of the practice of REST APIs usage in Android apps. Autom. Softw. Eng. **27**, 187–228 (2020). https://doi.org/10.1007/s10515-020-00272-9

2. Baltes, S., Ralph, P.: Sampling in software engineering research: a critical review and guidelines. Empir. Softw. Eng. **27**(4), 94 (2022). https://doi.org/10.1007/s10664-021-10072-8

3. Bonorden, L., van Hoorn, A.: Detecting usage of deprecated web APIs via tracing. In: 21st International Conference on Software Architecture (ICSA) (2024). https://doi.org/10.1109/ICSA59870.2024.00011

4. Bonorden, L.: Third-party HTTP clients in open-source Java projects [Dataset] (2025). https://doi.org/10.5281/zenodo.15102293

5. Brito, G., Valente, M.T.: REST vs GraphQL: a controlled experiment. In: 17th International Conference on Software Architecture (ICSA) (2020). https://doi.org/10.1109/ICSA47634.2020.00016

6. Cai, H., Fu, X.: $D^2$2Abs: a framework for dynamic dependence analysis of distributed programs. IEEE Trans. Softw. Eng. **48**(12), 4733–4761 (2022). https://doi.org/10.1109/TSE.2021.3124795

7. Cassé, C., Berthou, P., Owezarski, P., Josset, S.: A tracing based model to identify bottlenecks in physically distributed applications. In: International Conference on Information Networking (ICOIN) (2022). https://doi.org/10.1109/ICOIN53446.2022.9687217

8. Cox, R.: Surviving software dependencies. Commun. ACM **62**(9), 36–43 (2019). https://doi.org/10.1145/3347446

9. Dabic, O., Aghajani, E., Bavota, G.: Sampling projects in GitHub for MSR studies. In: 18th International Conference on Mining Software Repositories (MSR) (2021). https://doi.org/10.1109/MSR52588.2021.00074

10. Gadient, P., Ghafari, M., Tarnutzer, M.A., Nierstrasz, O.: Web APIs in android through the lens of security. In: 27th International Conference on Software Analysis, Evolution and Reengineering (SANER) (2020). https://doi.org/10.1109/SANER48275.2020.9054850

11. Genfer, P., Zdun, U.: Identifying domain-based cyclic dependencies in microservice APIs using source code detectors. In: Biffl, S., Navarro, E., Löwe, W., Sirjani, M., Mirandola, R., Weyns, D. (eds.) ECSA 2021. LNCS, vol. 12857, pp. 207–222. Springer, Cham (2021). https://doi.org/10.1007/978-3-030-86044-8_15

12. Genfer, P., Zdun, U.: Avoiding excessive data exposure through microservice APIs. In: 16th European Conference on Software Architecture (ECSA) (2022). https://doi.org/10.1007/978-3-031-16697-6_1

13. Harrand, N., Durieux, T., Broman, D., Baudry, B.: Automatic diversity in the software supply chain. arXiv:2111.03154 [cs.SE] (2021). https://doi.org/10.48550/arXiv.2111.03154

14. Hassan, F., Mostafa, S., Lam, E.S., Wang, X.: Automatic building of java projects in software repositories: a study on feasibility and challenges. In: International Symposium on Empirical Software Engineering and Measurement (ESEM) (2017). https://doi.org/10.1109/ESEM.2017.11

15. Hofmeister, C., Kruchten, P., Nord, R.L., Obbink, H., Ran, A., America, P.: A general model of software architecture design derived from five industrial approaches. J. Syst. Softw. **80**(1), 106–126 (2007). https://doi.org/10.1016/j.jss.2006.05.024

16. Huang, K., et al.: Characterizing usages, updates and risks of third-party libraries in Java projects. Empir. Softw. Eng. **27**(4), 1–41 (2022). https://doi.org/10.1007/s10664-022-10131-8

17. Hutcheson, R., et al.: Software architecture reconstruction for microservice systems using static analysis via GraalVM native image. In: International Conference on Software Analysis, Evolution and Reengineering (SANER) (2024). https://doi.org/10.1109/SANER60148.2024.00008

18. Jasser, S.: Enforcing architectural security decisions. In: 17th International Conference on Software Architecture (ICSA) (2020). https://doi.org/10.1109/ICSA47634.2020.00012

19. Keshani, M., Bot, G., Rungta, P., Izadi, M., Van Deursen, A., Proksch, S.: Maven unzipped: exploring the impact of library packaging on the ecosystem. In: International Conference on Software Maintenance and Evolution (ICSME) (2024). https://doi.org/10.1109/ICSME58944.2024.00016

20. Kruchten, P., Lago, P., van Vliet, H.: Building up and reasoning about architectural knowledge. In: Hofmeister, C., Crnkovic, I., Reussner, R. (eds.) QoSA 2006. LNCS, vol. 4214, pp. 43–58. Springer, Heidelberg (2006). https://doi.org/10.1007/11921998_8

21. Lercher, A., Glock, J., Macho, C., Pinzger, M.: Microservice API evolution in practice: a study on strategies and challenges. J. Syst. Softw. **215**, 112110 (2024). https://doi.org/10.1016/j.jss.2024.112110

22. Malhotra, M., Chhabra, J.K.: Systematic review of dependencies in source code of software and their categorization. In: 2nd International Conference on Communication, Computing and Networking (ICCCN) (2019). https://doi.org/10.1007/978-981-13-1217-5_77

23. Oracle: JEP 321: HTTP Client API (2017). https://openjdk.java.net/jeps/321. Version of 27 Oct 2024. Accessed 27 Mar 2025

24. Ralph, P., et al.: Empirical standards for software engineering research (2021). https://doi.org/10.48550/arXiv.2010.03525

25. Rapoport, M., Suter, P., Wittern, E., Lhotak, O., Dolby, J.: Who You gonna call? Analyzing web requests in android applications. In: 14th International Conference on Mining Software Repositories (MSR) (2017). https://doi.org/10.1109/MSR.2017.11

26. Riegler, M., Sametinger, J., Vierhauser, M., Wimmer, M.: A model-based mode-switching framework based on security vulnerability scores. J. Syst. Softw. **200**, 111633 (2023). https://doi.org/10.1016/j.jss.2023.111633

27. Soto-Valero, C., Durieux, T., Baudry, B.: A longitudinal analysis of bloated Java dependencies. In: 29th ACM Joint Meeting on European Software Engineering Conference and Symposium on the Foundations of Software Engineering (ESEC/FSE) (2021). https://doi.org/10.1145/3468264.3468589

28. Soto-Valero, C., Harrand, N., Monperrus, M., Baudry, B.: A comprehensive study of bloated dependencies in the Maven ecosystem. Empir. Softw. Eng. **26**(3), 1–44 (2021). https://doi.org/10.1007/s10664-020-09914-8

29. Suwanachote, N., Shakizada, Y., Kashiwa, Y., Lin, B., Iida, H.: On the evolution of unused dependencies in Java project releases: an empirical study. In: 22nd International Conference on Mining Software Repositories (MSR) (2025). https://doi.org/10.1109/MSR66628.2025.00059

30. Vidoni, M.: A systematic process for mining software repositories: results from a systematic literature review. Inf. Softw. Technol. **144**, 106791 (2022). https://doi.org/10.1016/j.infsof.2021.106791
31. Yoshioka, H., et al.: Do developers depend on deprecated library versions? A mining study of Log4j. In: 22nd International Conference on Mining Software Repositories (MSR) (2025). https://doi.org/10.1109/MSR66628.2025.00057

# Lessons from Visualizing Software Architecture Structure Conformance at Thermo Fisher Scientific

Filip Zamfirov[1]([⊠]) [iD], Andrei Radulescu[2], Jacob Krüger[1] [iD],
and Michel R. V. Chaudron[1] [iD]

[1] Eindhoven University of Technology, Eindhoven, The Netherlands
{f.zamfirov,j.kruger,m.r.v.chaudron}@tue.nl
[2] Thermo Fisher Scientific, Eindhoven, The Netherlands
andrei.radulescu@thermofisher.com

**Abstract.** Modern software-intensive systems are large and complex. Therefore, well-defined software architectures are required to manage such systems. However, implementing and maintaining a software architecture can be challenging in practice. For instance, architecture erosion can cause the implemented architecture to deviate from the intended one. Industrial practitioners often lack effective tools to check that an evolving software system continues to conform to its intended architecture. In this paper, we share the lessons we learned from adopting, extending, and applying a state-of-the-art architecture visualization tool for conformance checking the structure and dependencies between intended architecture (i.e. subsystems and their relations) and implemented architecture (i.e. implemented subsytems and their dependencies in the codebase) on a large industrial software project. Specifically, we collaborated with Thermo Fisher Scientific and used a graph-based visualization tool on one of the company's systems. Using the tool, we can create a hierarchical view of layered software architectures including subsystem and component dependencies. During demonstration sessions, we presented the visualizations to 14 experts at Thermo Fisher Scientific who are involved with different subsystems to elicit their feedback. Using our tool, the experts found it easier to focus on relevant areas of the system and to detect architecture violations and anomalies. The experts expressed great enthusiasm for using the tool on their own. Our insights suggest that software architecture visualization tools can aid software architects in maintaining the conformance between intended and actual software architectures. However, applying existing tools faces challenges regarding scalability, usability, and the integration into company workflows. Our lessons highlight opportunities for future research and improvements in (open-source) software architecture tools.

**Keywords:** Software Architecture Conformance · Software Architecture Erosion · Dependency Analysis · Reference Architecture · Experience Report

D. Taibi and D. Smite (Eds.): SEAA 2025, LNCS 16083, pp. 372–389, 2026.
https://doi.org/10.1007/978-3-032-04207-1_25

# 1    Introduction

Software-intensive systems have become a key enabler of innovative high-tech systems in all areas of society. The growing size and complexity of software in such systems make it increasingly difficult to develop and maintain them [8]. To deal with growing software, defining and implementing a suitable architecture is key [21]. A software architecture defines the organization of a software system from various perspectives, including its structure (how the system is decomposed into subsystems) and behavior (how these subsystems interact) [9]. Consequently, software architectures are key instruments for managing the complexity of a software system.

One practical problem of software architectures is their erosion [17,21]. Architecture erosion is a multifaceted phenomenon that occurs when the implemented architecture violates the intended one, when the internal structure of a system is compromised by a faulty design, or when the design of the system becomes increasingly difficult to modify. Architecture erosion can be analyzed from different perspectives (e.g., quality, structure, evolution), but is most commonly described in terms of violations [17].

In this perspective, architecture erosion represents the violation of design principles, architectural constraints, or architectural rules; all of which lead to poor maintainability of a system [21]. Previous research has proposed different solutions for detecting architectural violations and applied these solutions to open-source software [17]. In contrast, little research has been conducted in industrial settings, which limits the generalizability of the findings [17,25,26]. Furthermore, Wan et al. [26] performed an interview survey with industry practitioners in which they found that they are challenged by a lack of feasible tool support for monitoring architecture conformance and violations.

In this paper, we explore the benefits and challenges of adopting tooling to support software architecture structural conformance checking in practice and to provide industrial insights. To this end, we share an experience report with lessons learned on visualizing and analyzing the architecture conformance of an industrial software system. More precisely, we focus on a specific aspect of software architecture conformance, namely the conformance of the structural aspects of an architecture: The dependencies between architectural subsystems and components and their implemented structural dependencies in the codebase. To do so, we extended and tailored the ARViSAN tool that was developed by Kakkenberg et al. [10]. We used ARViSAN to create interactive views and analyses of industrial software-intensive systems developed at Thermo Fisher Scientific. Through our work, we contribute:

1. We report on our ongoing development of the ARViSAN tool to meet the needs for checking structural architecture conformance.
2. We discuss the challenges, benefits, and insights of applying our extended ARViSAN at Thermo Fisher Scientific, including feedback from 14 software engineering professionals.
3. We share an anonymized dataset detailing the structure and dependencies of an industrial software-intensive system [28].

4. We publish our extended version of ARViSAN, including its parser [27], frontend [12] and backend [11] that we developed.

Through these contributions, we aim to foster future research on checking architecture conformance in practice. Specifically, researchers and practitioners can reuse our tooling and use the shared dataset as ground truth representing a real-world industrial system.

## 2    Context and Related Work

In this section, we introduce Thermo Fisher Scientific and discuss related work.

### 2.1    Thermo Fisher Scientific

Thermo Fisher Scientific is a global supplier of analytical instruments and services for laboratories, pharmaceuticals, and biotechnology. In 2024, Thermo Fisher Scientific had an annual revenue of $ 42.9 billion, and employed around 125,000 people. At Eindhoven, Thermo Fisher Scientific develops its Transmission Electron Microscopy (TEM) technology for sample analyses at ultra-high resolutions, reaching sub-Angstrom levels.

TEM microscopes are software-intensive systems composed of various complex instruments. Such instruments include, for instance, detector, sample-handling, vacuum, electromagnetic, and electrostatic devices, which work together through a coordinated software architecture. Each type of device is managed by its own software subsystem, which captures the specific functionalities of the device. This architecture creates a complex multi-level and multi-technology software ecosystem, consisting of several architectural layers. The most basic layer represents components, each of which can contain one or more software projects that contribute to an executable or a library. Related components are grouped into (higher layer) subsystems, each encapsulating the functionalities of a device in the TEM. Finally, subsystems are clustered into subsystem groups providing a family of related functionality.

The software architects at Thermo Fisher Scientific have developed architecture documentation and a reference architecture to ensure the quality of the software architecture on all levels. Both of these resources define architectural rules that shall be applied to subsystems and their dependencies. However, due to the complexity, size, and the speed at which the overall system evolves, architects lack a straightforward way to obtain an overview of the current architecture. Often, they have to piece together information from scattered or outdated sources. Also, it can be challenging to assess and ensure conformance between the reference architecture and the latest implementation. For instance, as for any larger system, the question can arise whether the actual architecture must be aligned to the reference, or vice versa. Lastly, the limited tool support for monitoring architecture and implementation conformance increases the manual effort required to gather the necessary information. To address such challenges, we have initiated a research-industry collaboration in which we started to explore how to apply state-of-the-art solutions for checking structural software-architecture conformance.

## 2.2   Related Work

**Industrial Studies of Architecture Conformance and Violations.** Sas et al. [25] conducted a study on the evolution of architecture smells at ASML, in which they extended ARCAN [4] to support the proprietary C/C++ used by the company. Using the extended ARCAN, Sas et al. detected architecture smells across releases for nine projects from one of the company's software systems. They also interviewed developers and architects to learn about maintenance issues the interviewees were experiencing with the projects. Their findings show that architecture smells can spread over time to more artifacts, and that some of the artifacts may suffer from multiple smells. The interviewees linked the affected components with frequent changes, the presence of severe bugs, and general maintenance issues.

Martini et al. [19] studied the impact and refactoring costs of architecture smells to aid practitioners prioritize architectural technical debt. They used ARCAN on multiple industrial systems written in Java to identify three architecture smells. The authors then conducted a survey with the developers to investigate how they prioritize architectural technical debt and how they perceive its impact. Martini et al. report that the practitioners found it useful to automatically detect architecture smells, even low-priority ones. The study emphasizes the impact and refactoring costs of code smells, with the hub-like dependency being the easiest to detect and refactor.

Fontana et al. [3] conducted a study akin to that of Martini et al., utilizing ARCAN on three systems from a software consulting company. Through surveys, they gathered developer feedback on architecture smells identified by the tool. The respondents acknowledged the impact of smells on maintainability, but were unfamiliar with the definitions of many of the eight smells examined. Similar to Martini et al., the findings indicate that developers consider hub-like dependencies as primary candidates for refactoring. Additionally, some of the smells were deemed relevant only within a layered architecture.

Mo et al. [20] explored architecture maintainability in a study of nine industrial systems. They considered two metrics and architectural "hotspots" linked to high maintenance costs. Mo et al., analyzed the systems using their DV8 tool suite and conducted interviews with practitioners. They report that DV8 was key for pinpointing hotspots for refactoring, and DV8 was adopted in the respective company to quantify maintenance costs.

Groot at al. [7] report an interview survey with 17 software developers at ASML. They focused on unintended software dependencies, which represent violations of architecture rules, in multi-lingual software systems. They contribute a catalog of eight unintended dependencies and discuss their overlap with architecture smells and other signs of architecture erosion. An important insight is that resolving unintended dependencies is often delayed, even though they challenge developers' comprehension, because the system still works, other tasks are perceived as more important, and due to the costs involved.

Such studies motivate the need for more advanced tooling to facilitate architecture conformance checking. Unlike such studies, which rely on code parsing to derive the implemented architecture or interviews, we start from a documented reference architecture. We use this specification to construct a detailed view of a system's intended architecture, providing a baseline against which the implemented architecture can be compared. Then, we extract dependencies from the implemented system to visualize violations of the reference architecture. So, besides contributing complementary experiences to the previous work, we also propose a different way of checking architecture conformance: combining the perspectives of intended reference and actually implemented architecture.

**Tools for Visualizing and Checking Software Architecture.** Previous works have proposed various tools for analyzing and checking implemented software architectures. Azadi et al. [1] and Li et al. [17] provide detailed overviews of such tools, which we summarize. Some tools, such as JArchitect [17], ARCAN [4], DV8 [20], NDepend [16], and Lattix [16], offer graph-based or matrix-based visualizations of an implemented architecture. Other tools, for example, Understand [17], the Renaissance approach [2], and Axivion [17], aim to facilitate dependency analyses. Some tools have been extended to visualize, particularly the evolution of architecture smells [5,6]. All these tools provide powerful capabilities, but they typically derive architectural information by parsing source code. This limits their applicability to specific languages and technologies, with extensions requiring to design new parsers. Moreover, we are not aware of any tool that takes a reference architecture into account. In contrast, our tooling is designed not to require language-specific code parsing and uses a reference architecture. So, we complement existing tools, particularly to help architects reflect on the mapping between reference and implemented architecture.

## 3   Visualizing the TEM Architecture

Next, we describe the TEM system and explain how we adjusted ARViSAN to visualize its architecture.

### 3.1   TEM Components and Dependencies

TEM is a complex embedded software system comprising 31 subsystems (cf. Fig. 1), each of which provides self-contained functionality. Moreover, each subsystem can be further decomposed into multiple individually built components. To facilitate the build process, each component must contain a metadata file specifying its dependencies to other components.

Originally, a simple solution existed to visualize the TEM software architecture. Specifically, a full component dependency graph was constructed during the system's build process to collect information about its dependencies. As a

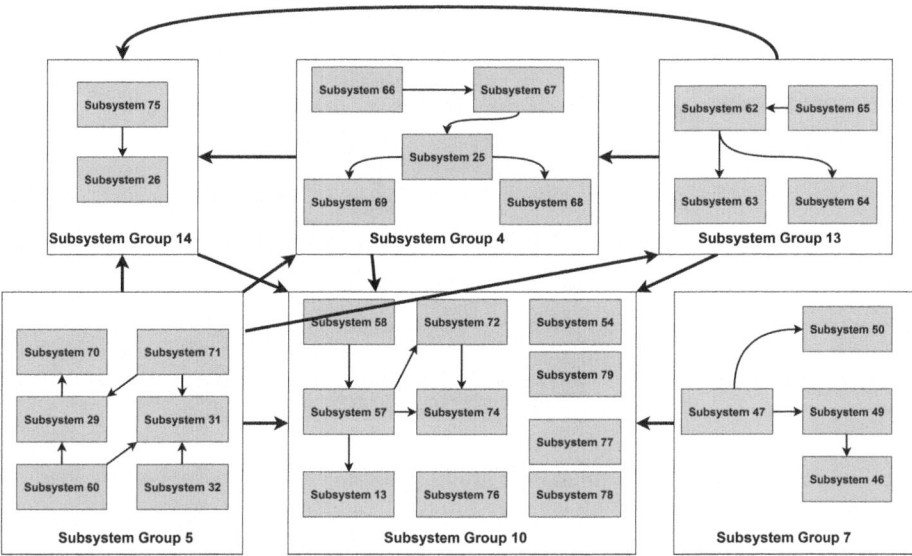

**Fig. 1.** Anonymized dependency graph depicting the expected high-level dependencies defined in the TEM reference architecture.

component was built, its dependencies were gathered from the metadata file. A script then generated a Graphviz[1] dependency graph. Due to the complexity and size of the TEM software, the graph contained over 200 components and more than 6,000 dependencies, making it very difficult to interpret.

## 3.2   TEM Reference Architecture

For TEM, Thermo Fisher Scientific architects have defined a reference architecture using the 4+1 architectural view model [13]. To achieve full architecture conformance, all the different views would have to be considered. However, in the context of this work, we focus on the structural aspects of the software system. Therefore, we consider the logical view, which describes the functionality that a system provides to end-users. In this logical view, the architects have specified dependencies on two levels to simplify how dependencies are defined and maintained:

1. dependencies between subsystems within a subsystem group and
2. dependencies between subsystem groups.

In Fig. 1, we display an anonymized graph of the intended dependencies in the TEM system.

Using the list of components gathered during the build process and the reference architecture, we created a specification containing all the components

---

[1] https://graphviz.org/.

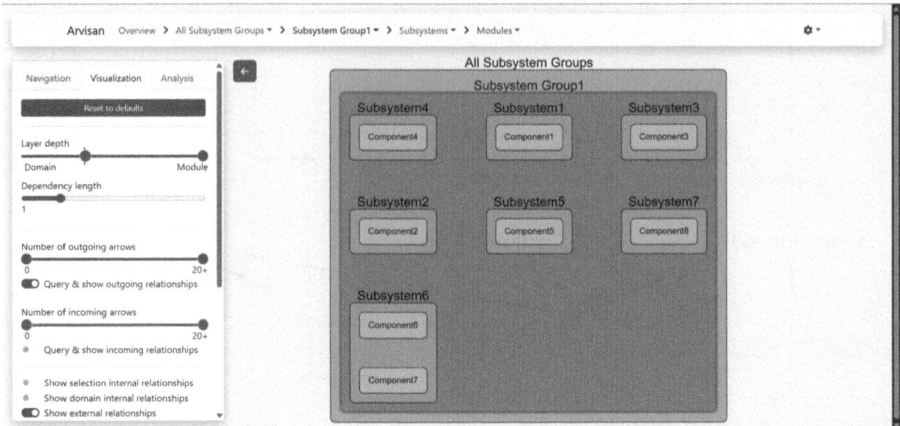

**Fig. 2.** An anonymized TEM subsystem group (dark green) as displayed in our adapted ARViSAN. The subsystem group includes seven subsystems (green) with one subsystem comprising two components, while the others have one component each (light green). (Color figure online)

mapped to a subsystem and a subsystem group. As subsystem interfaces are contained in individual components, the specification also contained metadata about the presence and types of interfaces in a component. We share the anonymized version of this specification to allow other researchers to work with it.[3]

### 3.3   Visualizing the Architecture

To create an overview of the TEM architecture, we adapted ARViSAN [10]. ARViSAN allows users to interactively explore a graph-based visualization of a target system and its dependencies. We chose to build on ARViSAN because it provides a hierarchical view in which users can explore the system architecture and dependencies at different levels of abstraction. So, ARVISAN was already capable of representing the multiple levels of components, subsystems, and subsystem groups that are relevant for TEM.

Our adapted ARViSAN uses a simple input format: Two `.csv` files of which one defines the logical entities, such as subsystems, and the other defines the implemented dependencies after validation against the reference architecture. These entities and dependencies are the respective nodes and edges that ARViSAN shall visualize. Nodes can be flat or hierarchical, and we distinguish three types of nodes: subsystem groups, subsystems, and components.

Additionally, the input files contain containment relations between the (hierarchical) nodes. This containment information allows to use a slider in ARViSAN to simplify or expand the graph to show higher-level nodes (e.g., subsystem groups) or lower-level nodes (e.g., components). In Fig. 2, we exemplify how the containment of components and subsystems in a subsystem group is rendered in our adapted ARViSAN. The processing of the implemented and the reference architecture dependencies is described in our parser repository and can be replicated using the anonymized data that we share.

### 3.4 Visualizing Architecture Violations

The reference architecture provided to ARViSAN defines the original baseline architecture of a system with its intended dependencies. To enable engineers to identify violations more easily, we integrated a parser into ARViSAN that compares the dependencies between the two architectures and marks differences. Using optional interface information from the specification, we identify dependencies between subsystems in which a component relies directly on the implementation of another subsystem's functionality, rather than its interface. In other words, we check for dependencies that bypass defined interfaces and mark them as potentially degrading.

We extended ARViSAN to display three types of dependencies through colored arrows in the user interface (cf. Fig. 3):

**Black** for conforming dependencies.
**Red** for non-conforming dependencies (i.e., violations).
**Orange** for potentially degrading dependencies.

Furthermore, we implemented three coloring modes that change the color of nodes to show component information. Such information includes, for example, the presence of interfaces, their deployment platforms, and their instability. As these coloring modes require company data, not all of them are available in the version of ARViSAN that we share. Finally, we modified ARViSAN to allow nodes to be enriched with custom information like metrics (e.g., instability [18]). Such custom information can be inserted into ARViSAN's input and can be used to better support different architecture analyses.

Through these visualizations and additional interactivity features, we support users of ARViSAN in identifying where the reference- and actual architecture do not conform. For example, a user can focus on an individual node (e.g., a subsystem) by right-clicking it. This renders only those dependencies that are relevant to this node. Furthermore, users can lift the visualized depth to a higher level (e.g., from component to subsystem level) to simplify the view. To illustrate this, we display a circular dependency between two subsystems caused by an unintended dependency in Fig. 3 and in Fig. 4. In Fig. 3, we show the dependencies on the component level, where the circular dependency may be overlooked due to the number of components and dependencies. Considering Fig. 4, the dependencies are lifted to the subsystem level, and the circular dependency becomes easier to identify.

## 4    Evaluation

In this section, we report our evaluation of our tooling.

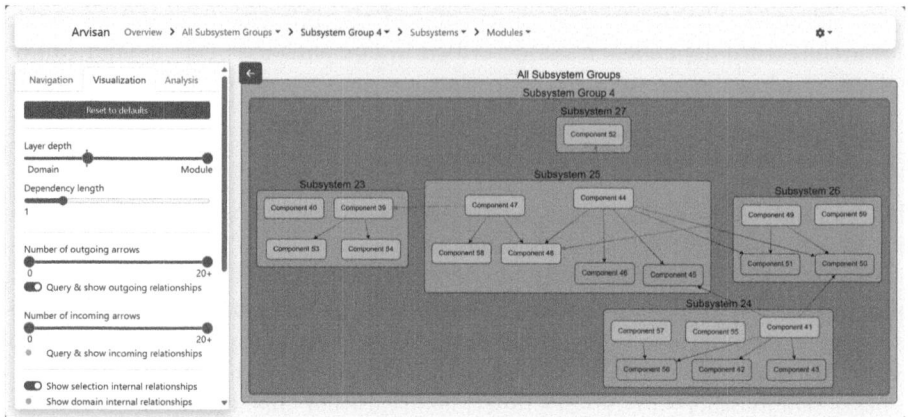

**Fig. 3.** The dependencies within **Subsystem Group 4** on the level of components. A circular dependency exists between **Subsystem 25** and **Subsystem 26**, because of an unintended dependency (red arrow) from **Component 49** to **Component 48**. The components colored in orange contain subsystem interfaces. (Color figure online)

## 4.1   Study Design

We conducted a formative assessment of our adapted ARViSAN by employing it at Thermo Fisher Scientific on the TEM software. The goal of this evaluation was to identify the benefits of our solution in addressing the needs of the TEM architects and developers. Specifically, these needs included a clear overview of the TEM software architecture and support for monitoring the structural conformance between the reference and implemented architecture. Additionally, we aimed to collect challenges or unintended consequences of our tooling. For this purpose, we parsed and visualized the dependencies of the latest release of the system and conducted five 30-min demonstrations with groups of company architects. In Table 1, we present an overview of the participants in these demonstrations (in order of conduct). Some of the architects were involved in subsystem architectures ($S_1$, $S_2$, $S_4$), and some in the overall TEM architecture ($S_3$). Additionally, we demonstrated our visualizations to two architects responsible for a separate Thermo Fisher Scientific system to diversify our set of participants ($S_5$).

We started each demonstration by showing the reference architecture diagram (cf. Fig. 1) and the Graphviz graph created with the old tooling available at Thermo Fisher Scientific. Then, we presented the visualization we created in ARViSAN and allowed the architects to explore the dependencies most relevant to them. We asked the participants to report on their perceptions of ARViSAN and the visualizations we integrated, particularly compared to any tools they used for the same purpose so far. Each demonstration was led by the first author, who answered questions and documented the participants' feedback.

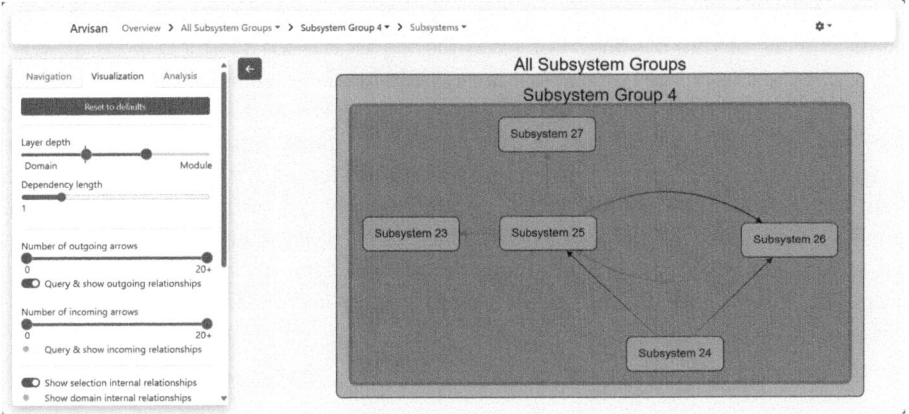

**Fig. 4.** The dependencies within **Subsystem Group 4** on the level of subsystems. Because dependencies are lifted to the subsystem level, the circular dependency between **Subsystem25** and **Subsystem26** is clearly visible—in contrast to Fig. 3.

## 4.2    Results

Next, we present our observations from the demonstrations.

**ARViSAN Compared to Other Tools Used.** Our participants reported that they had access to various quality-related tools and dashboards. However, only a few of them reported using these tools to monitor architecture violations. Two participants ($p_2$, $p_{12}$) mentioned using tools for visualizing and verifying violations. Interestingly, $p_2$ relied on custom scripts, which were simplistic and required significant manual effort. In contrast, $p_{12}$ had previously used NDepend, which is limited to software written in C# and .NET. They noted that they appreciated the flexibility and technology independence of our adapted ARViSAN; even though the required preprocessing of dependency data makes it less convenient. Lastly, $p_3$ used a search engine capable of cross-referencing source code. They pointed out that this engine lacked comprehensive dependency information, demanding extensive manual reviews.

**Visualizing Violations.** During the demonstrations, participants were able to identify unexpected and unintended dependencies. Specifically, in $S_1$, $p_1$ and $p_2$ noticed two unexpected dependencies to other subsystems. One was an unnecessary dependency. The cause for the second dependency remained unclear. In turn, $p_1$ indicated that being able to see dependencies is a positive initial step towards understanding and addressing architecture violations. During $S_2$, $p_3$ and $p_4$ quickly identified a circular dependency between two subsystems, which was distinctly visible. This dependency was already scheduled for refactoring, but the participants appreciated that our visualization made it immediately recognizable.

**Visual Appeal.** Several participants across the demonstrations appreciated the visual aspects of our tooling. For example, $p_8$ expressed that *"looking at a red edge immediately triggers you to start thinking about it and whether you can improve it."* All participants found the tool intuitive and easy to use, particularly because it did not require learning complex query languages. Both $p_1$ and $p_4$ appreciated the ability to focus on specific nodes and to constrain the visualization to relevant dependencies. More generally, $p_3$ and $p_5$ emphasized the benefits of a visualization, with $p_5$ stating: *"The biggest added value to have a tool is to point it out [when people avoid following the architecture constraints], because it is hard to see, sometimes you find it by accident."*

**Table 1.** Overview of our demo sessions and participants.

| Session ID | Participant ID | Role | Assignment |
|---|---|---|---|
| $S_1$ | $p_1$ | Software Engineer | Subsystem49 |
| | $p_2$ | Domain Architect | |
| $S_2$ | $p_3$ | Domain Architect | Subsystem25 |
| | $p_4$ | Domain Architect | Subsystem26 |
| $S_3$ | $p_5$ | Software Engineer | Entire system |
| | $p_6$ | Staff Architect | |
| | $p_7$ | Staff Architect | |
| | $p_8$ | Senior Staff Architect | |
| | $p_9$ | Senior Staff Architect | |
| | $p_{10}$ | Senior Staff Architect | |
| $S_4$ | $p_{11}$ | Software Engineer | Subsystem7 |
| | $p_{12}$ | Domain Architect | |
| $S_5$ | $p_{13}$ | Senior Staff Architect | Other system |
| | $p_{14}$ | Senior Staff Architect | |

**Scope and Depth.** Given the layered architecture of the TEM system, several participants were interested in the scope and depth that can be visualized. Three participants ($p_3$, $p_4$, $p_{12}$) expressed a need for in-depth visualizations, though their preferences varied: from project-level details within a component to fine-grained code-level information, such as classes and functions. Additionally, $p_3$ noted that information on interface-level dependencies would be particularly useful, since they currently had to verify them manually—which is time-consuming due to a large number of interfaces. In contrast, $p_5$ and $p_8$ expressed concerns about expanding the visualization depth. For instance, $p_5$ explained: *"Going to code level makes the visualization too big, overloads you with too much data. This is a simple tool that shows where we are, and we can simply say 'fix these' [violations], we can have a different tool on a lower level, because optimizing* *language-specific dependencies is a different story.*" Participant $p_8$ stated they had a preference for other professional tools when it comes to the code level.

**Suggested Use Cases.** Participants in all demonstrations expressed enthusiasm for gaining access to our tooling and using it on their own. Several potential use cases emerged during our discussions, especially in $S_2$, $S_3$, and $S_4$. In $S_2$ and $S_3$, participants were interested in using the tool to analyze dependencies across software releases. Although ARViSAN currently does not support direct visualizations and comparisons of multiple graphs, such analyses can be performed manually and can be automated in future work. During $S_3$, one participant suggested deploying the tool to development teams, so that it can be used in planning to improve the visibility and organization of refactoring tasks. In $S_4$, participants identified an opportunity to use the tool for onboarding new developers by providing a visual and interactive representation of the system architecture, which is in line with previous research [14,15].

**Limitations.** Through the demonstrations, we identified limitations of our visualizations that we will tackle in the future. First, due to the diverse technologies used across the TEM system, dependencies are defined in different ways. As a result, some dependencies were missing from our visualizations. While a unification on how to declare dependencies is underway at Thermo Fisher Scientific, $p_8$ suggested that dependencies missing in the visualizations could also help identify where such unification is needed (i.e., an additional use case). Second, $p_5$ was concerned that when the entire TEM system is rendered in ARViSAN on the component level, violations can exist or may be introduced without being noticed (e.g., Fig. 3 versus Fig. 4). Currently, our solution can be used to interactively explore and display dependency violations. However, there is no functionality that prevents developers from introducing violations, which is also out of the scope of this work.

**Tool Adoption.** Adopting our tooling at Thermo Fisher Scientific was also a topic of interest among our participants. Previously, another open-source tool for architecture analysis was introduced within the company [2]. While the tool allowed to derive the implemented system architecture and facilitated large-scale refactoring, it required resource-intensive and time-intensive source code parsing. A dedicated team was assigned to maintain it, but due to high maintenance efforts and limited adoption, the tool was eventually discontinued.

Our solution does not depend on source code parsing and is meant to provide a visual and interactive architecture view. Still, because of their experiences with the previous tool, some participants were cautious about introducing another tool for architecture analysis. Currently, our extended version of ARViSAN and dependency processing scripts have been forked into an internal repository of Thermo Fisher Scientific, along with the parsed TEM system data as well as user and developer documentation. This enables developers and architects at Thermo Fisher Scientific to explore our tool within their workflows and for other systems.

# 5    Discussion

In the following, we discuss our results, distinguishing between implications for researchers, practitioners, and both.

## 5.1    Implications for Researchers

**Improving Usability and Performance.** When applied to large industrial software systems, dependency visualizations tend to become overly complex with hundreds of nodes and edges (e.g., the graph produced by Graphviz). We observed that while such a view contains rich information, participants found it overwhelming and unusable. Our participants valued the ability to simplify views by lifting dependencies to a higher level or by focusing on its relevant parts. Such functionalities and visually distinguishing violations (e.g., with different colors) made it easier to identify violations. We believe that:

> *The trade-offs between visual simplicity and depth of information should be further investigated to optimize the usability of software architecture visualization tools and to avoid overwhelming users.*

**Studying Architecture Evolution.** Several participants expressed interest in analyzing and visualizing subsystem dependencies across system releases. Recent research has explored this direction regarding the evolution of architecture smells and violations [5,6,24]. We believe that there is a need to also provide such evolution-based techniques for other properties of software architectures:

> *Researchers should investigate and compare existing techniques and solutions for studying the evolution of software architectures across releases to facilitate long-term software maintenance.*

## 5.2    Implications for Practitioners

**Unifying Dependency Management Across Technologies.** Implementing software that uses different programming languages and technologies can result in varying methods for declaring dependencies. Such differences hinder collecting and analyzing dependencies automatically, with some companies implementing their own techniques for declaring multi-lingual dependencies to mitigate such problems [7]. Declaring dependencies in a uniform way enables further automation, so that:

> *Companies may benefit from standardizing dependency-declaration practices or from applying tools that aggregate dependencies from multiple sources. This can facilitate the application of analysis and visualization tools, and can reduce the need for manual validation.*

**Using Architecture Visualizations for Onboarding.** Several participants saw value in using our visualizations for planning refactorings and onboarding new developers. This aligns with our prior work on developers' preferences for documentation [14,15] and software architecture explanations [22]. However, we [22] also observed that architecture visualization tools are rarely used when onboarding new developers in practice. Therefore, we suggest:

> *Organizations should explore embedding architecture visualizations into the onboarding of new developers and in the planning of development work to facilitate better architectural decisions.*

### 5.3 Implications for Researchers and Practitioners

**Validating Reference Against Implemented Architecture.** We used a reference architecture as a baseline against which the implemented architecture can be validated. However, we observed that not all the latest developments of the TEM system were reflected in the reference architecture. For example, some documented subsystem groups were implemented as subsystems. Moreover, several implemented subsystems were not covered in the reference architecture. Therefore, we conclude that:

> *To improve architecture conformance, both the intended and the implemented architecture must be validated and revised if necessary. Future research should investigate how to synchronize the documentation and implementation of evolving architectures.*

**Reducing Efforts of Architecture Data Preparation.** To construct the reference architecture, we relied on documentation prepared by the software architects. Although this documentation provided valuable insights, certain architectural details, such as the mapping of components to subsystems, were not included. To fill these gaps, we conducted several meetings with the architects to collect and validate the missing information. We recognize that in other settings the effort required to obtain such architectural data may differ significantly. Based on our experience, we suggest the following recommendation to practitioners:

> *Assign clear ownership of architectural knowledge and documentation to support its maintenance and ongoing validation.*

For researchers, we argue:

> *Future research should examine not only the costs and efforts of repairing architecture conformance violations, but the efforts of gathering and maintaining architectural data as well as optimizing such efforts.*

**Simplifying the Adoption of Tools.** Our participants were enthusiastic about using our tool themselves. However, they raised concerns about the adoption due to experiences with previous tools. Specifically, some participants were concerned because a previously adopted open-source tool was discontinued due to high maintenance efforts that were coupled with limited use. Such concerns raise the question of what factors drive or hinder the adoption of (open-source) architecture tools in practice. For researchers, we argue that:

*Future research should examine organizational and technical barriers to sustainably adopting and maintaining (open-source) tools in industrial settings.*

For practitioners, we suggest that:

*Companies should assign clear ownership and support mechanisms for tool adoption. Integrating tools into existing workflows and developer environments, rather than providing stand-alone solutions, could improve tool adoption.*

## 6   Threats to Validity

We are aware of different threats to the validity of our work and discuss them according to the classification proposed by Runeson et al. [23] for case studies.

**Construct Validity.** Construct validity concerns the constructs we aimed to study. Since we investigated architecture conformance, a possible threat is that the violations our tool identified were incorrect. To mitigate this threat, we used a specification derived from the documented Thermo Fisher Scientific reference architecture to distinguish violations. We created and refined this specification with architects at Thermo Fisher Scientific.

**Internal Validity.** Internal validity concerns whether the observations in our study truly resulted from our proposed solution and not from other factors. One potential threat to the internal validity arises from the sample of participants who attended the demonstrations. They were invited by the second author as the company representative in our project. So, our participants may not fully represent the broader user population, since they are from one company, and we may have missed other interested stakeholders. To mitigate this threat, we invited experts from various roles and supplemented our demonstrations with a session ($S_5$) involving experts from a different Thermo Fisher Scientific system.

**External Validity.** Threats to the external validity concern the extent to which the study findings can be generalized. An inherent threat of industry reports is that, although our visualization tool is technology-independent, we designed our tooling with the specifics of Thermo Fisher Scientific in mind and evaluated it within the company only. However, a layered architecture may not be applicable or translate to paradigms like microservices. Additionally, using Thermo Fisher Scientific's reference architecture and tooling limits the generalizability if other companies do not have these resources—but using these is also a new idea of our work. Lastly, Thermo Fisher Scientific's context seems representative of (larger) industrial settings, but further studies are needed to validate the broader applicability of our tool in other organizations. Finally, a potential threat to the external validity is the lack of feedback on the long-term use of our tool. While the feedback from the demonstrations illustrates our tool's capabilities, we have not evaluated how ARViSAN performs or is perceived over an extended period. For this reason, the long-term impact and generalizability of our findings must be further verified in future work.

# 7  Conclusion

In this paper, we presented our experiences of extending and applying a visualization tool to support the needs of software architects by visualizing architectures and checking architecture conformance. We collaborated with experienced software architects and developers at Thermo Fisher Scientific and jointly evaluated the benefits and challenges of using our tool on the company's software systems. ARViSAN creates a hierarchical view of the software architecture, and visualizes violations of the intended architecture, such as unexpected and circular dependencies. The feedback from 14 software experts at Thermo Fisher Scientific indicated that the visualizations made it easier to focus on relevant system areas and to effectively detect architecture violations. These experts expressed great enthusiasm for using the tool in their daily work. Our insights suggest that existing software architecture visualization tools can aid software architects in maintaining conformance between the intended and the implemented software architectures. In the future, we will extend and improve our tooling, including its evaluation on other paradigms, other systems, and over time.

**Acknowledgments.** This work has received funding from Eindhoven University of Technology's IMPULSE program (COMARIC project, grant RVO-TKI2212P17).

**Data Availability Statement.** We publish our anonymized dataset [28] and tooling [11,12,27] through persistent open-access repositories.

**Disclosure of Interests.** Michel R. V. Chaudron and Filip Zamfirov have received funding from Eindhoven University of Technology and Thermo Fisher Scientific through the COMARIC project, which is funded from the Holland High Tech IMPULSE program. Andrei Radulescu works for Thermo Fisher Scientific.

# References

1. Azadi, U., Fontana, F.A., Taibi, D.: Architectural smells detected by tools: a catalogue proposal. In: TechDebt (2019)
2. Dams, D., Mooij, A., Kramer, P., Rădulescu, A., Vaňhara, J.: Model-based software restructuring: lessons from cleaning up COM interfaces in industrial legacy code. In: SANER. IEEE (2018)
3. Fontana, F.A., Locatelli, F., Pigazzini, I., Mereghetti, P.: An architectural smell evaluation in an industrial context. In: ICSEA. IARIA (2020)
4. Fontana, F.A., Pigazzini, I., Roveda, R., Tamburri, D., Zanoni, M., Di Nitto, E.: Arcan: a tool for architectural smells detection. In: ICSAW. IEEE (2017)
5. Gnoyke, P., Schulze, S., Krüger, J.: On developing and improving tools for architecture-smell tracking in Java systems. In: SCAM. IEEE (2023)
6. Gnoyke, P., Schulze, S., Krüger, J.: Evolution patterns of software-architecture smells: an empirical study of intra- and inter-version smells. J. Syst. Softw. (2024)
7. Groot, T., Ochoa Venegas, L., Lazăr, B., Krüger, J.: A catalog of unintended software dependencies in multi-lingual systems at ASML. In: ICSE-SEIP. ACM (2024)

8. Hölzl, M., Rauschmayer, A., Wirsing, M.: Engineering of software-intensive systems: state of the art and research challenges. In: Wirsing, M., Banâtre, J.-P., Hölzl, M., Rauschmayer, A. (eds.) Software-Intensive Systems and New Computing Paradigms. LNCS, vol. 5380, pp. 1–44. Springer, Heidelberg (2008). https://doi.org/10.1007/978-3-540-89437-7_1

9. ISO/IEC/IEEE: Systems and software engineering–architecture description. Technical report. ISO/IEC/IEEE 42010: 2011 (E)(Revision of ISO/IEC 42010: 2007 and IEEE Std 1471-2000), ISO/IEC/IEEE (2011)

10. Kakkenberg, R., Rukmono, S.A., Chaudron, M.R.V., Gerholt, W., Pinto, M., de Oliveira, C.R.: Arvisan: an interactive tool for visualisation and analysis of low-code architecture landscapes. In: MODELS. ACM (2024)

11. Kakkenberg, R., Zamfirov, F.: Software-analytics-visualisation-team/Arvisan-backend: Arvisan backend v1.0.0, July 2025. https://doi.org/10.5281/zenodo.15848517

12. Kakkenberg, R., Zamfirov, F.: Software-analytics-visualisation-team/Arvisan-frontend: Arvisan frontend v1.0.0, July 2025. https://doi.org/10.5281/zenodo.15848538

13. Kruchten, P.B.: The 4+ 1 view model of architecture. IEEE Softw. **12**(6), 42–50 (1995)

14. Krüger, J., Hebig, R.: What developers (care to) recall: an interview survey on smaller systems. In: ICSME. IEEE (2020)

15. Krüger, J., Hebig, R.: To memorize or to document: a survey of developers' views on knowledge availability. In: Kadgien, R., Jedlitschka, A., Janes, A., Lenarduzzi, V., Li, X. (eds.) PROFES 2023. LNCS, vol. 14483, pp. 39–56. Springer, Cham (2024). https://doi.org/10.1007/978-3-031-49266-2_3

16. Kumar, N.: Software architecture validation methods, tools support and case studies. In: Shetty, N.R., Prasad, N.H., Nalini, N. (eds.) Emerging Research in Computing, Information, Communication and Applications, pp. 335–345. Springer, New Delhi (2016). https://doi.org/10.1007/978-81-322-2553-9_32

17. Li, R., Liang, P., Soliman, M., Avgeriou, P.: Understanding software architecture erosion: a systematic mapping study. J. Softw. Evol. Process (2022)

18. Martin, R.: OO design quality metrics: an analysis of dependencies (1994)

19. Martini, A., Fontana, F.A., Biaggi, A., Roveda, R.: Identifying and prioritizing architectural debt through architectural smells: a case study in a large software company. In: Cuesta, C.E., Garlan, D., Pérez, J. (eds.) ECSA 2018. LNCS, vol. 11048, pp. 320–335. Springer, Cham (2018). https://doi.org/10.1007/978-3-030-00761-4_21

20. Mo, R., Snipes, W., Cai, Y., Ramaswamy, S., Kazman, R., Naedele, M.: Experiences applying automated architecture analysis tool suites. In: ASE (2018)

21. Perry, D.E., Wolf, A.L.: Foundations for the study of software architecture. ACM SIGSOFT Softw. Eng. Notes (1992)

22. Rukmono, S.A., Zamfirov, F., Ochoa, L., Chaudron, M.R.V.: From expert to novice: an empirical study on software architecture explanations (2025). https://arxiv.org/abs/2503.08628

23. Runeson, P., Höst, M., Rainer, A., Regnell, B.: Case Study Research in Software Engineering: Guidelines and Examples. Wiley (2012)

24. Sas, D., Avgeriou, P., Fontana, F.A.: Investigating instability architectural smells evolution: an exploratory case study. In: ICSME. IEEE (2019)

25. Sas, D., Avgeriou, P., Uyumaz, U.: On the evolution and impact of architectural smells—an industrial case study. Empirical Softw. Eng. (2022)

26. Wan, Z., Zhang, Y., Xia, X., Jiang, Y., Lo, D.: Software architecture in practice: challenges and opportunities. In: ESEC/FSE, pp. 1457–1469. ACM (2023)
27. Zamfirov, F.: Software-analytics-visualisation-team/arvisan- dependency-parser: Arvisan dependency parser v1.0.0, July 2025. https://doi.org/10.5281/zenodo.15848528
28. Zamfirov, F., Andrei, R., Krüger, J., Chaudron, M.: Software subsystem dependencies: anonymized industrial dataset (2025). https://doi.org/10.5281/zenodo.15075337

# Does Context Matter? An Exploratory Study on God Class Distribution Based on Contextual Attributes

Elivelton Ramos Cerqueira[1], Gabriel Moraes[1], Lidiany Cerqueira[2], Glauco Carneiro[3], Rodrigo Spínola[4], Manoel Mendonça[2], and José Amancio Macedo Santos[1]([⊠])

[1] State University of Feira de Santana, Feira de Santana, Bahia, Brazil
elivelton.cerq@gmail.com, gcmorais@ecomp.uefs.br, zeamancio@uefs.br
[2] Federal University of Bahia, Salvador, Bahia, Brazil
{lidiany.cerqueira,manoel.mendonca}@ufba.br
[3] Federal University of Sergipe, São Cristovão, Sergipe, Brazil
glauco.carneiro@dcomp.ufs.br
[4] Virginia Commonwealth University, Richmond, VA 23284, USA
spinolaro@vcu.edu

**Abstract.** The evaluation of software quality has traditionally focused on internal design characteristics, such as cohesion and complexity. However, recent studies have shown that contextual factors may also be associated with quality-related attributes. In this study, we investigate whether the incidence of the god class code smell varies according to different development contexts. We define context based on the combination of four software attributes: system size, number of commits, number of contributors, and development time. Using data from 419 Java systems extracted from GHTorrent, we classified the projects into distinct contexts and analyzed the distribution of the god class smell within each. The results reveal statistically significant variations in smell incidence across contexts, suggesting that contextual attributes should not be overlooked in the assessment of design quality. This work contributes by presenting an empirical analysis of god class incidence across distinct development contexts, introducing a methodological strategy for context formation based on measurable software attributes, providing empirical evidence that supports a contextualized understanding of design quality, and making the experimental package publicly available to foster further research on the topic.

**Keywords:** Code smells · God class · Software attributes · Software context · Mining software repositories

## 1 Introduction

Software quality is commonly assessed through its internal characteristics, such as cohesion, complexity, and adherence to design principles [6]. However, recent

D. Taibi and D. Smite (Eds.): SEAA 2025, LNCS 16083, pp. 390–406, 2026.
https://doi.org/10.1007/978-3-032-04207-1_26

studies suggest that contextual factors, including technical [5] and operational aspects [4], may also influence software quality. This highlights the importance of considering the development context in predicting software quality, which in turn requires a clear and operational definition of the concept.

The software community has addressed defining context. Kirk and MacDonell [11,12] define context as any factor affecting software project practice effectiveness or objective achievement that lies outside the development team's direct control (e.g., organizational processes, policies, resources).

In this study, we adopt a complementary context definition based on the observation of measurable technical attributes which, although resulting from the development process, can serve as proxies for the context in which software systems are built. We consider four key attributes: *system size, number of commits, number of contributors*, and *development time*. Although these are shaped throughout the project, they reflect decisions made from the early stages and directly influence the system's structure and organization.

This methodology goes beyond merely measuring isolated software attributes; it enables the combination of attributes across diverse contextual scenarios, supporting a large-scale, data-driven investigation into how these scenarios relate to software quality. Moreover, rather than contradicting Kirk's definition, it operationalizes it as the attributes are easily measured. Zhang et al. [34] also adopt this perspective, treating technical attributes as representations of software development context.

There are studies investigating how these contextual factors relate with software quality. Zhang et al. [34] report variations in maintainability depending on the context. Fontana et al. [8] suggest adapting code smell detection tools to system-specific contexts, and Alkharabsheh et al. [3] demonstrate that attributes such as project size and domain significantly influence the effectiveness of god class detection algorithms.

Despite these advances, systematic empirical studies that examine the relationship between different contexts and specific code smells remain scarce. This work addresses this gap by adopting an analytical strategy defining multiple contexts through combinations of the four considered attributes (*system size, number of commits, number of contributors*, and *development time*).

The study focuses on the god class code smell as a quality indicator, given its prominence and extensive documentation in the literature [14,27]. A god class constitutes a violation of the principle of separation of concerns, aggregating excessive complexity and functionality within a single class [20]. This smell is associated with challenges in maintenance, testing, and system evolution, and is considered one of the most harmful to software architecture [15,24].

We analyze 419 Java systems from GHTorrent [10], grouped by combinations of the four context-defining attributes, to compare god class distribution across different contexts.Main contributions include: i) empirical analysis of god class incidence across diverse contexts; ii) a methodological strategy for context formation based on four measurable attributes; iii) empirical evidence strengthening contextual understanding through measured attributes; and iv) open availability of the experimental package, supporting further research.

The article is organized as follows: Sect. 2 presents background and related work; Sect. 3 describes the dataset, context methodology, and analysis procedures; Sect. 4 presents empirical results; Sect. 5 discusses findings and limitations; Sect. 6 concludes with future work.

## 2    Background

### 2.1    Context and Software Quality

Software Engineering literature increasingly acknowledges context's role in quality metrics and development practice effectiveness. Kirk and MacDonell [11,12] define context as any factor affecting project practice effectiveness or goal achievement, not under direct team control (a 'hard constraint'). They structure this concept into What (product), When (time/maturity), and How (execution mode) dimensions, offering a useful conceptual model.

Zhang et al. [34] reinforce this, demonstrating, through a study of over 300 projects, that contextual attributes like system size (LOC), number of changes, and project domain significantly influence maintainability metric distribution. Their results suggest direct metric comparison across projects may be biased without proper context.

Complementing this, Ogheneovo [23] shows larger systems incur higher maintenance costs, suggesting technical attributes accumulated throughout the software lifecycle directly associate with perceived quality. Behnamghader et al. [4] argue historical aspects (e.g., evolution measured by commits) reveal context-sensitive quality patterns. These studies support attributes like LOC, commits, and development time as operational bases for large-scale quality analyses, despite being project evolution outcomes.

These studies support the idea that attributes such as LOC, number of commits, and development time, although resulting from project evolution, are observable manifestations of contextual decisions made early in the software life cycle. Therefore, such attributes provide a valid operational basis for large-scale analyses of software quality.

### 2.2    Code Smell as Software Quality Metric

Code smells are structural indicators suggesting potential design problems. Introduced by Fowler [9], they signify weaknesses hindering code maintenance and evolution, rather than functional defects.

Marinescu [18–20] significantly contributed to systematizing code smell detection, proposing metric-based strategies for identifying design flaws like god class, feature envy, and data class.His approach combines heuristic rules with metric thresholds to detect structures that violate fundamental principles of object-oriented design.

Lanza and Marinescu [16] reinforce metric usefulness for structural system assessment. Palomba et al. [24] explore code smell diffusion and its correlation with maintainability, showing direct impact on perceived system quality. Santos et al. [27] investigate how varying god class conceptualizations impact detection, highlighting clear, consistent definition importance.

These studies position code smells as relevant metrics for assessing design quality, especially in empirical studies analyzing multiple systems or establishing comparative patterns.

### 2.3   Related Work

The relationship between code smells and context has been studied to adapt detection processes to system characteristics. Fontana et al. [8] argue fixed metric thresholds yield inconsistent results across contexts; to mitigate this, they propose automatic threshold derivation based on metric distribution within contextually similar groups.

Tufano et al. [31] reinforce this by evaluating code smell detection tool reliability under different configurations, finding performance varies significantly with project domain, size, and characteristics, suggesting standardized approaches are insufficient.

More recently, Alkharabsheh et al. [3] demonstrated, using ML algorithms for god class detection, that contextual information (e.g., project domain, system size in LOC) directly affects detection effectiveness. They show model accuracy varies by system size category, indicating contextual attributes are decisive even for automated techniques.

These studies strengthen the notion that context should be explicitly incorporated into design quality analyses, via heuristic tool adaptation or customized data-driven approaches like ML algorithms.

## 3   Methodology

This section details the experimental setup, covering the research question, software attributes forming contexts, data selection/collection/classification processes (including god class measurement), and the adopted analysis strategy.

### 3.1   Research Question

We define the following research question:

RQ: Is there a difference in god class incidence among software systems developed in different contexts?

This question guides our exploratory, quantitative study, seeking preliminary evidence on the relationship between software attributes (grouped as contexts) and god class incidence, without assuming causality. Its relevance lies in building empirical evidence for a knowledge *corpus* on how development context relates to design quality, requiring iterative evidence construction due to large data volumes. This study presents our initial results.

## 3.2  Dataset and Extraction of Software Attributes

This work adopts GHTorrent [10] as the original data source, a project collecting public GitHub repository names and addresses[1]. We downloaded GHTorrent data in May 2021 (when GitHub had over 200 million repositories and 65 million developers), provided to support the software engineering research community. At collection, GHTorrent contained 6,760,351 software systems.

Only Java software was considered, as it is widely used and most code smell detection tools accept Java input [7]. By applying this restriction, a dataset of 631,274 software systems was selected.

From this dataset, we extracted attributes to form contexts using a Python script with the Pydriller framework [30], a tool for mining Git repository data. The extracted attributes are:

- **System size:** We considered the total number of lines of code. Since this information is not directly accessible through Pydriller, we calculated it by summing the lines added and subtracting the lines deleted across all commits.
- **Number of commits:** Total commits in the repository.
- **Number of contributors:** Total developers who made commits in the repository.
- **Development time:** We calculated the time elapsed between the first and the last commit in the repository, measured in hours.

Since the GHTorrent dataset was created in 2015, it was necessary to verify the availability of the repositories. To perform this verification and collect the attributes, we used 10 virtual machines hosted on DigitalOcean[2], where the Python script using Pydriller was executed on different parts of the GHTorrent dataset. The scripts were executed and successfully retrieved project attribute data for 452,843 software systems. For the remaining 178,431 systems, it was not possible to retrieve the data because they were unavailable on GitHub. These were excluded from the selection.

## 3.3  Grouping Software Into the Contexts

After collecting attributes from 452,843 software systems, we analyzed each attribute's individual distribution. We discarded software with attribute values in the 1st quartile, suspecting they were toy or unfinished systems (e.g., system size $\leq$ 1,300 lines, four times smaller than the median of 4,829 lines). Similarly, 1st quartile development time systems had fewer than 269 h, compared to the median of 3,316 h.

The strategy of focusing on software whose attribute values fell into the 2nd (LOW) and 4th (HIGH) quartiles was deliberately adopted. Our objective is to elucidate how the development 'context' relates to software quality, specifically the incidence of god classes. To achieve this goal, it was fundamental to maximize

---

[1] https://github.com/.
[2] https://www.digitalocean.com/.

the contrast between the analyzed software groups. By selecting systems with distinctly lower (2nd quartile) or higher (4th quartile) attribute characteristics, we sought to identify and analyze patterns that could be obscured in a sample with less contextual variability.

This approach allows a clearer observation of potential associations between different contexts and the incidence of god classes, which is crucial for an exploratory investigation. The exclusion of the 3rd quartile and outliers contributes to increasing contrast and forming purer contexts, where differences in software characteristics are more pronounced. It is important to note that the selection criteria were defined *a priori* and applied systematically to mitigate biases in the sampling process.

Thus, the analyzed sample includes only software with attribute values in the 2nd or 4th quartiles (based on median distribution). Each of the four attributes received a quartile label: HIGH for 4th quartile, LOW for 2nd. Figure 1 illustrates this classification and Fig. 2 summarizes these values.

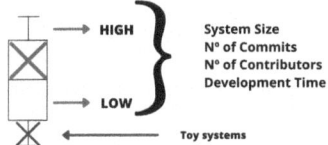

| Contextual Factor | *LOW* | | *HIGH* | |
|---|---|---|---|---|
| | From | To | From | To |
| System size | 1363 | 4829 | 28642 | 69560 |
| Number of commits | 7 | 25 | 148 | 359 |
| Number of contributors | 1 | 2 | 7 | 16 |
| Development time | 269 | 3316 | 16421 | 40647 |

**Fig. 1.** Schematic view of the classification for each software attribute

**Fig. 2.** Collected values of contextual factors

Next, we considered only software where all four attributes were labeled HIGH or LOW (i.e., *system size, number of commits, number of contributors,* and *development time*). Applying this criterion yielded 9,058 systems.

The combination of four attributes allows 16 different contexts ($2^4$). For example, the intersection of sets in the Venn diagram in Fig. 3 represents one of the formed contexts. In this case, the context consists of software with LOW *system size,* HIGH *number of commits,* HIGH *number of contributors* and LOW *development time.*

### 3.4 Software Selection and Extraction of God Classes

Due to resource constraints, it was not feasible to download all 9,058 systems. We selected 30 software systems for each of the 16 generated contexts. During selection, we identified and removed potentially biasing characteristics, such as software names including 'test' or 'demo'. These were removed as potentially incomplete or non-final versions.

While aiming for 30 systems per context (480 total), some combinations had fewer than 30 (commonly LOW commits and HIGH contributors), likely because repositories with many contributors tend to have many commits. In total, 419 randomly selected software systems were downloaded.

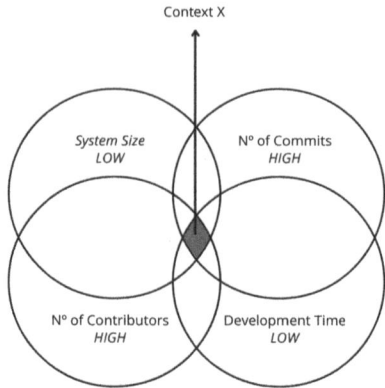

**Fig. 3.** Schematic view of one context as defined in this work

God classes were extracted using the Repository Miner tool [22], which mines software repositories and detects god classes based on Lanza and Marinescu's heuristics[16].

### 3.5 Analysis Procedure

To perform the analysis, we calculated the percentage of god classes in relation to the total number of classes for each software system. This percentage was used to normalize the data, as the number of classes varies greatly between systems. We created a variable called *percentClassesWithGodClass*, which was associated with each software system. Based on this data, we conducted analyses to identify whether there are differences in the incidence of god classes across different contexts.

For result presentation, attributes were grouped into less specific contexts for two reasons: i) to obtain more meaningful statistical test results with larger samples; ii) to simplify interpretation by reducing data volume.

Thus, in the first stage we considered only one attribute to observe differences in the incidence of god classes, forming a context based on that attribute. For example, we formed two contexts related to the *system size* attribute, grouping software systems with HIGH and LOW values for this attribute. Figure 4 shows the contexts formed based solely on the *system size* attribute. We compared the differences in the distribution of god class incidence between these two contexts. The same procedure was applied for the other attributes: *number of commits*, *number of contributors*, and *development time*.

When we found significant differences in the distribution of god class incidence between the observed contexts, we considered an additional attribute in the analysis. For example, if there was a significant difference in god class incidence between software with HIGH and LOW *system size*, we then checked whether this difference is also significant in a more specific context—that is,

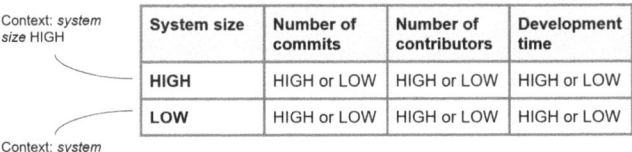

**Fig. 4.** *System size* context based

among software with HIGH *number of commits*. Next, we examined the difference for software with LOW *number of commits*. Figure 5 represents this comparison strategy: first, comparing whether software with HIGH *number of commits* shows a significant difference in god class incidence between HIGH and LOW *system size* (first two rows of the figure); second, repeating the comparison for software with LOW *number of commits* (last two rows of the figure). The same strategy was used for *number of contributors* and *development time*.

| | System size | Number of commits | Number of contributors | Development time |
|---|---|---|---|---|
| Context: *number of commits* HIGH, *system size* HIGH | HIGH | HIGH | HIGH or LOW | HIGH or LOW |
| Context: *number of commits* HIGH, *system size* LOW | LOW | HIGH | HIGH or LOW | HIGH or LOW |
| Same idea for *number of commits* LOW | HIGH | LOW | HIGH or LOW | HIGH or LOW |
| | LOW | LOW | HIGH or LOW | HIGH or LOW |

**Fig. 5.** *System size* and *number of commits* context based

We performed two statistical tests to compare differences of god classes between software grouped into different contexts. First, we analyzed the difference in the distribution of god classes using a hypothesis test. Second, we measured the magnitude of the difference among the sample values using an effect size test. Both the hypothesis test and the effect size test are discussed below.

**Hypothesis Test.** We applied the Mann-Whitney test (U Test) using a 5% significance level (p-value = 0.05). This choice was made after applying the Shapiro-Wilk normality test, which showed that the context distributions are not normal in all cases[3]. The Mann-Whitney test is used to determine whether two independent samples, which may be unmatched, come from the same population by checking for median equality [13]. As a non-parametric test, it does not assume normal distribution, aligning with the characteristics of the study samples.

**Effect Size Test.** We adopted Hedges's G test. Among the family of effect size tests including Hedges'G, Cohen's d, and Glass's test, we selected Hedges'G because it includes a correction factor for samples of different sizes [26].

---

[3] The Shapiro-Wilk test is one of the most powerful tests for checking normality [33].

# 4   Results

As previously mentioned, we created the variable *percentClassesWithGodClass* to represent the percentage of classes labeled as *god class* within each software system. We then compared the distribution of this variable across systems developed in different contexts to assess whether significant differences exist. Accordingly, we define the following null and alternative hypotheses:

*H0: There is no significant difference in the distribution of percentClassesWithGodClass between software systems developed into different contexts.*

*HA: There is a significant difference in the distribution of percentClassesWithGodClass between software systems developed into different contexts.*

## 4.1   Analysis of Contexts Defined by a Single Software Attribute

Table 1 presents the results of the Mann-Whitney test, considering contexts defined by a single software attribute. The attributes are abbreviated. The columns "# of HIGH software" and "# of LOW software" indicate the number of data points in each sample, i.e., the number of systems grouped under each context. Each data point corresponds to the value of the *percentClassesWithGodClass* variable. The columns "H0 is false" and "p-value" highlight the rows where the null hypothesis was rejected. For the attributes *system size*, *number of commits*, and *development time*, the null hypothesis was rejected, indicating a significant difference in the distribution of god classes between systems developed under different conditions.

**Table 1.** Mann Withney result for contexts formed by one atribute

| Software attribute | # of HIGH systems | # of LOW systems | H0 is false | *p-value* |
|---|---|---|---|---|
| SSiz | 191 | 228 | Yes | **6,10e-08** |
| NCom | 240 | 179 | Yes | **0,0272** |
| NCon | 179 | 240 | No | 0,7748 |
| DevT | 201 | 218 | Yes | **0,0009** |

Effect sizes for all comparisons were small (Rosenthal's classification [26]). These values are omitted due to space, but their implications are revisited in Sect. 5.1.

## 4.2   Analysis Considering More Specific Contexts

This section examines god class incidence variation across more specific contexts. We focus on *system size*, *number of commits*, and *development time*, as they showed significant god class incidence differences (Table 1). Results for *number of contributors* are omitted due to their non-significance in specific contexts.

Table 2 presents Mann-Whitney test results comparing god class incidence between HIGH and LOW *system size* systems within specific contexts (*NCom, NCon, DevT*). The *'System size'* column indicates the attribute tested. *'H0 is false'* and *'p-value'* columns report Mann-Whitney results, highlighting statistically significant differences in god class distribution.

**Table 2.** Mann-Whitney test comparing god classes incidence for the *system size* attribute in specific contexts

| Specific context | | | System size context | H0 is false | *p-value* |
|---|---|---|---|---|---|
| NCom | NCon | DevT | | | |
| HIGH | - | - | | Yes | **5,56e-09** |
| LOW | - | - | | No | 0,2542 |
| - | HIGH | - | **HIGH X LOW** | Yes | **0,0001** |
| - | LOW | - | | Yes | **8,64e-05** |
| - | - | HIGH | | Yes | **0,0026** |
| - | - | LOW | | Yes | **3,90e-06** |

For example, the first row in Table 2 indicates that for systems developed under a context with HIGH *number of commits*, there is a significant difference in god class incidence comparing systems with HIGH and LOW *system size*. In contrast, the second row shows that the null hypothesis could not be rejected, suggesting no significant difference in god class distribution between systems with HIGH and LOW *system size* when developed under a LOW *number of commits* context. In the remaining rows, the null hypothesis was rejected, suggesting that *system size* is an attribute that consistently reflects differences in god class incidence across various contexts.

Tables 3 and 4 follow the same structure. Table 3 analyzes god class incidence based on *number of commits*, with significant differences only for HIGH*system*

**Table 3.** Mann-Whitney test comparing god classes incidence for the *number of commit* attribute in specific contexts

| Specific context | | | Number of commits | H0 is false | *p-value* |
|---|---|---|---|---|---|
| SSiz | NCon | DevT | | | |
| HIGH | - | - | | Yes | **0,0007** |
| LOW | - | - | | No | 0,3425 |
| - | HIGH | - | **HIGH X LOW** | No | 0,6049 |
| - | LOW | - | | Yes | **0,0151** |
| - | - | HIGH | | No | 0,4578 |
| - | - | LOW | | No | 0,0543 |

*size* and LOW *number of contributors* (rows 1 and 4). Other cases did not reject the null hypothesis, indicating *number of commits* is a less decisive attribute for god class incidence variation.

Table 4 presents results for comparisons based on differences in *development time*. Except for systems with HIGH *system size*, all other specific contexts showed a significant difference in the distribution of god classes. These findings suggest that *development time* plays a relevant role in shaping the distribution of god classes, as significant differences were observed in most contexts.

**Table 4.** Mann-Whitney test comparing god classes incidence for the *development time* attribute in specific contexts

| Specific context | | | Development | H0 is | *p-* |
| SSiz | NCom | NCon | time context | false | *value* |
|---|---|---|---|---|---|
| HIGH | - | - | | No | 0,0609 |
| LOW | - | - | | Yes | **0,0054** |
| - | HIGH | - | **HIGH X LOW** | Yes | **0,0241** |
| - | LOW | - | | Yes | **0,0161** |
| - | - | HIGH | | Yes | **0,0152** |
| - | - | LOW | | Yes | **0,0233** |

## 5   Discussion

The results of this study empirically demonstrate the relationship between contextual attributes and software quality, in terms of object-oriented design measured by god class code smell. This supports the ongoing discussion on how the context in which software is developed can assist in predicting quality-related attributes.

Different sets of contextual and quality attributes have been considered by other researchers, highlighting the importance of conducting empirical research to advance understanding in this area. For instance, Zhang et al. [34] investigate whether the distribution of software maintenance metrics is affected by contextual factors such as domain, programming language, age, *development time*, *number of changes*, and number of downloads. Another example is the study by Alkharabsheh et al. [3], which examined how the domain and *system size* impact god class detection algorithms.

Our study presents evidence that, in software systems developed under contexts with varying *system size*, *number of commits*, or *development time*, the distribution of god classes differs more significantly than in systems with varying *number of contributors* (see Table 1). Moving beyond these overall findings, a detailed analysis of each contextual attribute reveals specific patterns in god class incidence.

When examining **system size**, our findings reveal a pronounced difference: projects categorized with HIGH system size consistently exhibit a higher median and a broader spread of *percentClassesWithGodClass* compared to those with LOW system size. This pattern is strongly aligned with our statistical results (p-value of 6.10e-08 from Table 1), indicating that larger systems are significantly more prone to the god class smell. This suggests that as software systems grow in scale, their inherent complexity increases, creating fertile ground for the accumulation of responsibilities in central classes if not rigorously managed. This can be a natural outcome of organic growth, where new functionalities are incrementally added, and existing classes absorb more logic over time without adequate refactoring.

Similarly, for **development time**, projects with HIGH development time show a distinctly higher median percentage of god classes compared to projects with LOW development time. This visual trend is supported by a significant statistical difference (p-value of 0.0009 from Table 1). Over long durations, different developers or teams might contribute, incrementally adding functionalities to existing classes without strictly adhering to initial design principles, which can result in the proliferation of god classes over time.

The analysis of **number of commits** presents a more nuanced picture. While our statistical test indicates a significant difference (p-value of 0.0272 from Table 1), the visual separation in the distribution of *percentClassesWithGodClass* between projects with HIGH and LOW commit counts is less pronounced compared to system size or development time. The central tendencies of both groups show more overlap. This suggests that the sheer volume of changes might not be as strong a sole predictor of god classes as the overall scale or duration of the project. A high number of commits could indicate an active development environment which, if coupled with robust development practices (e.g., continuous integration, frequent code reviews), might not necessarily lead to a higher incidence of smells.

Conversely, our study found no statistically significant difference in *percentClassesWithGodClass* based on the **number of contributors** (p-value of 0.7748 from Table 1). This is a particularly insightful finding, indicating that the number of contributors alone does not directly influence the incidence of god classes. Instead, factors such as the quality of collaboration within the team, adherence to established coding standards, effective communication channels, strong architectural governance, and the maturity of the development process should also be considered when assessing design quality and addressing code smells, beyond just the number of contributors.

This analytical strategy enhances the understanding of how contextual observation relates to software quality. Recognizing that the conditions under which a software system is developed affect its quality is not a trivial task [11,12]. Our work presents a focused set of empirical evidence on this topic, emphasizing the relationship between *system size, number of commits, number of contributors*, and *development time* with the god class smell. The contextual groupings formed using these attributes may serve as a starting point for supporting the consolidation of context definitions in this domain.

Finally, we believe this study also contributes to the discussion surrounding the use of the code smell metaphor within software development environments. Generally, previous studies have explored the relationship between smells and software size, indicating that larger systems are naturally more prone to having classes with numerous methods, high complexity, or low cohesion [21,25]. Our study specifically focuses on the god class smell. Several works aim to understand god classes from different perspectives, ranging from detection processes to their effects on code quality [1,2,17,28]. In this work, we associate god classes with contextual attributes, contributing to the understanding of how this smell can be used to predict software design issues. This point is particularly relevant because the smell reflects problems in one of the main principles of object-oriented programming—class cohesion [20]—and is also associated with other issues related to software maintainability and evolution [15,24].

## 5.1   Threats to Validity

The analysis of threats to the validity of this study follows the classification proposed by [32].

**Internal Validity:** The main threat to internal validity concerns the selection of the analyzed software systems. Although the study relies on a well-established dataset [10], the analysis was restricted to Java systems for which data was available. The exclusion of systems within the 1st and 3rd quartiles may impact representativeness. However, this methodological choice was deliberately made to increase the contrast between contexts and, crucially, was directly aligned with the exploratory objective of the study: to elucidate how 'context' can be related to software quality. By focusing on the extremes (LOW and HIGH), we aimed to identify the most evident patterns of association, which is fundamental for the exploratory nature of this investigation. The selection criteria were defined a priori and applied systematically to mitigate bias.

**External Validity:** The generalization of the findings is limited due to the number of software systems in the sample. However, one may have to consider that this study still present a large set of software, in comparison with other works in the area. Moreover, the generalization to software systems developed in other programming languages or domains may be limited. Nonetheless, the choice of Java systems is justified by the language's widespread use in software engineering research and the availability of mature analysis tools, including those for detecting code smells [7]. Another potential threat is the study's exclusive focus on the god class code smell, which restricts the breadth of the conclusions. We acknowledge this limitation but argue that the observed patterns are likely applicable to other types of code smells as well. Indeed, we conducted preliminary analyses involving other smells, but due to space constraints, this paper addresses only god class smells, selected for their high prevalence and theoretical relevance in the literature [24].

**Construct Validity:** The study defines development contexts using four attributes: *system size, number of commits, number of contributors*, and *development time*. While these are output-oriented metrics, prior research has employed them as proxies for characterizing technical development contexts [34]. God class detection was performed using the Repository Miner tool [22], a well-recognized tool in the literature, which is based on established heuristics [29]. Although false positives or negatives are possible, the use of a consistent detection method helps ensure standardization across analyses.

**Conclusion Validity:** All possible combinations of context attributes were tested; however, only a subset of the results is reported due to space limitations. In cases where no significant differences were found in broader contexts, further refinement by combining additional attributes rarely altered the observed patterns, suggesting consistent results. The statistical analyses employed, such as the Mann-Whitney test [13,33], were appropriate for the non-parametric nature of the data and were complemented by effect size calculations [26]. Although effect sizes indicated small differences between groups, potentially weakening the conclusions, it is important to emphasize that small effect sizes do not invalidate the outcomes of hypothesis testing. Moreover, this study is framed as an exploratory investigation aimed at enhancing understanding of the relationship between development context and software quality, rather than offering definitive conclusions on the topic.

Overall, the methodological choices, the use of validated tools, and the public availability of the dataset contribute to mitigating validity threats and provide a robust foundation for future research.

# 6  Conclusion

This study aimed to investigate the relationship between software development context and the incidence of the god class code smell, considering four observable technical attributes: *system size, number of commits, number of contributors*, and *development time*. By analyzing 419 Java systems extracted from GHTorrent [10], grouped into distinct contexts defined by the combination of these attributes, we observed statistically significant variations in the distribution of god classes across different contextual scenarios.

The results indicate that the context in which a system is developed is associated with the presence of structures that violate fundamental design principles, such as the excessive concentration of responsibilities in a single class [20,24]. These findings reinforce the importance of considering contextual attributes as part of design quality assessment [3,8,34], especially in large-scale empirical studies and in the development of code smell detection tools [9,16].

This work provides four main contributions. First, we present an empirical analysis of god class incidence in real-world systems, considering contextual variation. Second, we propose a systematic methodological strategy for context formation based on the combination of four contextual attributes. This approach operationalizes the concept of context in a practical and scalable manner, enabling its application in large-scale, data-driven studies. Third, we provide empirical evidence that contributes to consolidating the understanding of context as an explanatory variable in the evaluation of design quality. Finally, we publicly made available the experimental package used in this study to verification; to foster scientific reproducibility; and to support further research on the relationship between contextual attributes and software quality. The experimental package includes: i) the downloaded software systems; ii) tables with measurements of contextual attributes and data about god classes; iii) tables with contextual attribute measurements for all observed software in GHTorrent; and iv) scripts for the statistical tests performed. The experimental package is available at: https://zenodo.org/record/7374205#.ZBiFSnbMJD8

As future work, we intend to expand the analysis to include other code smells beyond god class, evaluate the impact of combining different contextual attributes, and explore predictive approaches based on machine learning for adaptive smell detection, incorporating context as a key variable in model construction.

**Acknowledgments.** This work was partially supported by UEFS-AUXPPG 2025 and CAPES-PROAP 2025 grants; by the Coordenação de Aperfeiçoamento de Pessoal de Nível Superior Brasil (CAPES) - Finance Code 001; and by the Conselho Nacional de Desenvolvimento Científico e Tecnológico (CNPq).

**Disclosure of Interests.** The authors have no competing interests to declare that are relevant to the content of this article.

# References

1. Alkharabsheh, K.: An empirical study on the co-occurrence of design smells in the same software module: god class case study. In: 2021 IEEE JEEIT, pp. 1–6 (2021)
2. Alkharabsheh, K., et al.: Prioritization of god class design smell: a multi-criteria based approach. J. King Saud Univ.-Comput. Inf. Sci. (2022)
3. Alkharabsheh, K., Crespo, Y., Fernández-Delgado, M., Viqueira, J.R., Taboada, J.A.: Exploratory study of the impact of project domain and size category on the detection of the god class design smell. Sw Qual. J. **29**, 197–237 (2021)
4. Behnamghader, P., Alfayez, R., Srisopha, K., Boehm, B.: Towards better understanding of software quality evolution through commit-impact analysis. In: 2017 IEEE International Conference QRS, pp. 251–262. IEEE (2017)
5. Di Pompeo, D., Tucci, M.: Quality attributes optimization of software architecture: research challenges and directions. In: 2023 IEEE 20th International Conference on Software Architecture Companion (ICSA-C), pp. 252–255. IEEE (2023)
6. Fernandes, E., Kalinowski, M.: On the perceived relevance of critical internal quality attributes when evolving software features. In: IEEE/ACM 16th CHASE, pp. 13–24 (2023)
7. Fernandes, E., Oliveira, J., Vale, G., Paiva, T., Figueiredo, E.: A review-based comparative study of bad smell detection tools. In: Proceedings of the 20th EASE, pp. 1–12 (2016)

8. Fontana, F.A., Ferme, V., Zanoni, M., Yamashita, A.: Automatic metric thresholds derivation for code smell detection. In: 2015 IEEE/ACM 6th International Workshop on Emerging Trends in Software Metrics, pp. 44–53. IEEE (2015)
9. Fowler, M.: Refactoring: improving the design of existing code. In: 11th European Conference. Jyväskylä, Finland (1999)
10. Gousios, G.: The ghtorent dataset and tool suite. In: 2013 10th Working Conference on Mining Software Repositories (MSR), pp. 233–236. IEEE (2013)
11. Kirk, D.: Software development context: critiquing often used terms. In: ENASE, pp. 340–347 (2021)
12. Kirk, D., MacDonell, S.: Categorising software contexts (2014)
13. Kothari, C.R.: Research methodology: methods and techniques. New Age Int. (2004)
14. Kovačević, A., et al.: Automatic detection of long method and god class code smells through neural source code embeddings. Exp. Syst. Appl. **204** (2022)
15. Lacerda, G., Petrillo, F., Pimenta, M., Guéhéneuc, Y.G.: Code smells and refactoring: a tertiary systematic review of challenges and observations. J. Syst. Softw. **167**, 110610 (2020)
16. Lanza, M., Marinescu, R.: Object-oriented metrics in practice: using software metrics to characterize, evaluate, and improve the design of object-oriented systems. Springer (2006)
17. M Santos, J.A., de Mendonça, M.G., dos Santos, C.P., Novais, R.L.: The problem of conceptualization in god class detection: agreement, strategies and decision drivers. J. Softw. Eng. Res. Dev. **2**(1), 1–33 (2014). https://doi.org/10.1186/s40411-014-0011-9
18. Marinescu, R.: Detecting design flaws via metrics in object-oriented systems. In: Proceedings 39th TOOLS, pp. 173–182. IEEE (2001)
19. Marinescu, R.: Measurement and quality in objectoriented design (2002)
20. Marinescu, R.: Detection strategies: metrics-based rules for detecting design flaws. In: 20th IEEE ICSM, 2004. Proceedings, pp. 350–359. IEEE (2004)
21. Martins, J., Bezerra, C., Uchôa, A., Garcia, A.: Are code smell co-occurrences harmful to internal quality attributes? a mixed-method study. In: Proceedings of the XXXIV Brazilian Symposium on Software Engineering, pp. 52–61 (2020)
22. Mendes, T., Novais, R., Mendonca, M., Carvalho, L., Gomes, F.: Repositorymineruma ferramenta extensível de mineração de repositórios de software para identificação automática de dívida técnica. CBSoft **2017**, 12 (2017)
23. Ogheneovo, E.E., et al.: On the relationship between software complexity and maintenance costs. J. Comput. Commun. **2**(14), 1 (2014)
24. Palomba, F., Bavota, G., Di Penta, M., Fasano, F., Oliveto, R., De Lucia, A.: On the diffuseness and the impact on maintainability of code smells: a large scale empirical investigation. In: Proceedings of the 40th ICSE, pp. 482–482 (2018)
25. Palomba, F., Bavota, G., Di Penta, M., Oliveto, R., Poshyvanyk, D., De Lucia, A.: Mining version histories for detecting code smells. IEEE TSE **41**(5) (2014)
26. Rosenthal, R., Rosnow, R.L.: Essentials of behavioral research: methods and data analysis (2008)
27. Santos, J.A.M., de Mendonça, M.G., Silva, C.V.: An exploratory study to investigate the impact of conceptualization in god class detection. In: Proceedings of the 17th EASE, pp. 48–59 (2013)
28. Santos, J.A.M., Rocha-Junior, J.B., de Mendonça, M.G.: Investigating factors that affect the human perception on god class detection: an analysis based on a family of four controlled experiments. J. Softw. Eng. Res. Dev. **5**(1), 1–39 (2017). https://doi.org/10.1186/s40411-017-0042-0

29. Santos, J.A.M., Rocha-Junior, J.B., Prates, L.C.L., do Nascimento, R.S., Freitas, M.F., de Mendonça, M.G.: A systematic review on the code smell effect. J. Syst. Softw. **144**, 450–477 (2018)

30. Spadini, D., Aniche, M., Bacchelli, A.: Pydriller: python framework for mining software repositories. In: 26th ACM Joint Meeting on European Software Engineering Conference and Symposium on the Foundations of Software Engineering, pp. 908–911 (2018)

31. Tufano, M., et al.: When and why your code starts to smell bad (and whether the smells go away). IEEE TSE **43**(11), 1063–1088 (2017)

32. Wohlin, C., Runeson, P., Höst, M., Ohlsson, M., Regnell, B., Wesslén, A.: Experimentation in Software Engineering. Springer, Berlin, Heidelberg (2012)

33. Yap, B.W., Sim, C.H.: Comparisons of various types of normality tests. J. Stat. Comput. Simul. **81**(12), 2141–2155 (2011)

34. Zhang, F., Mockus, A., Zou, Y., Khomh, F., Hassan, A.E.: How does context affect the distribution of software maintainability metrics? In: 2013 IEEE International Conference on Software Maintenance, pp. 350–359. IEEE (2013)

# Emerging Computing Technologies

# Towards a Defense-in-Depth Approach for Securing Collaborative Cloud Infrastructures

Dimosthenis Natsos[1,2]([✉]) [iD] and Andreas L. Symeonidis[1,2] [iD]

[1] School of Electrical and Computer Engineering, AUTH, 54124 Thessaloniki, Greece
{dcnatsos,symeonid}@ece.auth.gr
[2] Cyclopt PC, 55535 Thessaloniki, Greece
{dnatsos,asymeon}@cyclopt.com

**Abstract.** Data is wealth and this is indisputable. The one that owns the data may perform data analytics, understand the domain and the existing problems, propose solutions, even generate innovation. This is the reason why data ownership is so important and data owners have been reluctant in sharing their data. However, the last decade, cloud infrastructure solutions that enable collaborative data processing are increasingly adopted in research and industry, allowing data owners to make their datasets available for computation without directly exposing them, thus preserving confidentiality and acknowledging ownership, while harnessing the power of collaborative analytics and comparative analysis. Obviously, this paradigm introduces new challenges: protecting sensitive data from potentially malicious code, ensuring code execution integrity, and securing the underlying infrastructure. Existing approaches only partially address these issues. Some approaches focus on protecting the execution environment, others rely on pre-attested code—limiting exploratory research—and some adopt confidential computing techniques that shield data but assume both code and data are inherently trustworthy. In this conceptual work, we examine a more open and collaborative cloud infrastructure that executes unattested code directly on private data without requiring pre-approval. To address the resulting security and privacy challenges, we propose a Defense-in-Depth architecture that integrates static code analysis, dynamic behavioral monitoring, and container-based sandboxing. Our architecture aims to secure the execution environment, preserve data confidentiality, and ensure computational integrity—even in multi-tenant settings where neither code or data can be trusted. This work lays the foundation for secure, privacy-preserving, and flexible collaborative cloud systems.

**Keywords:** Collaborative Cloud · Defense-in-Depth · Privacy · Security · Trust

## 1 Introduction

Among collaborative cloud platforms, a growing subset enables unattested code execution—allowing users to remotely run custom scripts and programs on

D. Taibi and D. Smite (Eds.): SEAA 2025, LNCS 16083, pp. 409–418, 2026.
https://doi.org/10.1007/978-3-032-04207-1_27

hosted infrastructure. Platforms like Google Colab [6] and Amazon SageMaker [2] offer such capabilities, empowering researchers and developers to offload computationally intensive tasks. While these platforms protect the infrastructure using sandboxing or virtualization techniques [8], their security model is designed around single-party trust: they assume that both the code and data are provided by the same trusted user. As a result, they do not aim to protect data from potentially malicious code, or to ensure the correctness or integrity of computations across untrusted participants. To address such issues, several platforms like Azure Confidential Computing [13], PySyft [26], and Ocean Protocol's Compute-to-Data [12] introduce privacy-preserving computation by separating data owners from code providers. These platforms rely on confidential computing principles to isolate data during processing and protect the execution environment. For example, PySyft utilizes techniques like federated learning, secure multi-party computation and differential privacy to ensure data confidentiality while enabling data processing. On the other hand, Azure Confidential Computing encrypts data in memory in hardware-based trusted execution environments and processes it only after the cloud environment is verified. Finally, Ocean Protocol's Compute-to-Data enables data owners to retain control over which algorithms are allowed to run on their data, enforcing strict approval mechanisms to protect sensitive content.

While such platforms enhance data privacy by enforcing execution controls, they typically allow only pre-approved or statically attested code to run on sensitive data [19], limiting the range of possible data-driven operations, ultimately hindering exploratory research and experimentation. Furthermore, they provide no visibility into the software's behavior at runtime, assuming instead that statically attested code will behave securely. This assumption may not always hold true: vulnerabilities such as race conditions or runtime logic errors can still lead to data leaks or system instability. Moreover, malicious behavior—such as logic bombs or conditional exfiltration triggered at runtime—can evade static attestation [3]. Furthermore, many applications are confidential or proprietary, making third-party audits infeasible [14]. Finally, the threat models of these platforms often overlook infrastructure-level risks, placing the burden of securing code execution on the host environment. In summary, by focusing narrowly on data privacy and relying solely on pre-attested code, these platforms neglect both the integrity of runtime execution and the security of the underlying infrastructure. In contrast, RAISE [16] supports a more flexible and open model: unattested code can be submitted by users and executed on private datasets, without exposing raw data to the code providers. Crucially, RAISE nodes that host these datasets and perform the code execution can be deployed by any participating entity, in any location. This approach increases flexibility but raises a critical security question: *How can we secure such a complex collaborative environment that enables unattested code execution on private, sensitive data, where both the code and the data can not be trusted?*

In this short, work-in-progress paper, we lay the foundations for a collaborative cloud architecture that ensures (a) the protection and integrity of the execution environment, (b) the privacy of the data, and (c) the integrity of the code execution. We achieve this by designing a Defense-in-Depth (DiD) architecture that combines lightweight software sandboxing with static code analysis and dynamic, behavioral monitoring during execution. To the best of our knowledge, this is the first solution to introduce a comprehensive Defense-in-Depth architecture specifically tailored to secure privacy-preserving, cloud-based collaborative environments that support unattested code execution, where both the code and the data can not be trusted.

## 2  Literature Review

Existing works that address privacy and integrity in collaborative cloud environments typically fall into three categories: confidential computing, virtualization-based isolation, and behavioral monitoring.

Confidential computing approaches, such as those using Trusted Execution Environments (TEEs), isolate sensitive data within hardware-protected enclaves to prevent infrastructure-level access [23]. While recent extensions support data sharing across enclaves [24], these systems remain hardware-bound and incur high initialization costs, making them unsuitable for scalable, on-demand cloud deployments [10]. Software-based alternatives, such as Multi-Party Computation frameworks, avoid hardware dependencies and protect data privacy across non-colluding providers [11], but assume trusted code and lack defenses against unsafe or malicious software inputs.

To protect the execution environment, tools like Kata Containers, Firecracker, and gVisor isolate untrusted workloads through virtualization or syscall-level sandboxing [1, 7, 17]. These methods offer strong host protection but provide limited safeguards against runtime data misuse or attacks arising from adversarial inputs.

Behavioral monitoring techniques add a dynamic layer of defense. Taint-based models track data flows to block unauthorized propagation [22], while newer approaches employ Transformer-based models to detect anomalous process behavior based on system-level signals [15]. Hybrid systems have begun combining sandboxing with runtime monitoring into DiD architectures [25], but often omit static analysis, leaving critical blind spots.

In contrast, our work assumes mutual distrust between code, data, and infrastructure, treating the execution environment as an exposed attack surface. We propose a hardware-agnostic, multi-layer DiD architecture that unifies static analysis, dynamic monitoring, and sandboxing to ensure secure, privacy-preserving code execution in multi-tenant cloud settings.

## 3  System Requirements

The RAISE platform is a public cloud infrastructure that enables secure, collaborative computations between mutually untrusted parties. In this context, a *collaborative cloud* refers to an environment where data owners and code providers interact via a shared execution platform, without directly sharing data or source code with each other. The platform supports remote execution of user-submitted code on private datasets, enabling data-driven experimentation while preserving data privacy and ensuring computational integrity. Data owners upload datasets and code providers upload code to run experiments, where software is executed against data within the infrastructure. To protect sensitive information, code providers never access the original datasets; instead, they receive synthetic data with matching structure for local development. During execution, only the code interacts with the real data, within a controlled environment with internet access. Results are returned after execution. The execution environment is multi-tenant, meaning concurrent user jobs may share the same physical host. Our work focuses on securing this environment. Accordingly, we define three core non-functional requirements (NFR):

- **NFR1:** The system must be able to protect and ensure the integrity of the execution environment.
- **NFR2:** The system must be able to preserve the privacy of user data during the experiment phase.
- **NFR3:** The system must be able to guarantee the integrity of the executed code.

Example use cases that highlight the importance of the aforementioned NFRs and the sensitivity of the processed data include executing epidemiological experiments on private hospital datasets using externally provided models, or running financial fraud detection algorithms on proprietary banking logs—without exposing internal systems or revealing the code logic.

## 4   Trust and Threat Model

Our trust model comprises three distinct parties:

- **Data Owners (DOs):** Provide sensitive datasets and expect their data to remain confidential throughout the execution process. They do not trust Code Providers, whose code may attempt to leak or misuse data, and they rely on the Execution Environment (EE) to enforce strict data protection.
- **Code Providers (CPs):** Upload software for processing data and expect the code to run without interference or manipulation. They do not trust Data Owners, whose datasets may be adversarial or exploit vulnerabilities in the code, and depend on the EE to provide a fair and secure execution context.
- **Execution Environment (EE):** Executes code on private data and is assumed to be trusted by both DOs and CPs. However, it does not trust either party, as code may contain malware or sandbox escapes, and data may include malicious payloads. Therefore, it must be hardened as a potential attack surface.

The proposed threat model includes potential attacks during the code execution phase. Overall, three vectors of attacks are identified and some of the potential exploits are presented next.

## 4.1    Attacks Against the Execution Environment

The execution environment is the primary attack surface, targeted by adversaries seeking to break isolation, disrupt co-resident workloads, or launch anonymous attacks using cloud resources. Numerous studies have analyzed such threats in cloud settings, particularly in containerized and multi-tenant environments [8, 20]. Threats include privilege escalation, logic bombs, obfuscated malware, and backdoors—delivered through unverified code, or crafted datasets designed to exploit software vulnerabilities during execution. As the platform allows unattested code and data, both known and zero-day exploits are considered plausible. Robust isolation and runtime detection are essential to identify and contain such threats, while ensuring accountability in the event of compromise.

## 4.2    Attacks Against the Data

Since original datasets are accessed during runtime, malicious code may attempt to exfiltrate them. Data leakage attacks are among the most prevalent threats in cloud environments, and adversaries may employ a variety of techniques to achieve them [18]. Direct exfiltration may occur via web protocols (HTTP, sockets), while indirect methods may hide sensitive data in output files, logs, or metadata. These covert channels can bypass detection unless strict data flow and output inspection mechanisms are in place. Therefore, robust security measures are essential to preserve the confidentiality, integrity, and privacy of the data throughout its lifecycle within the execution environment.

## 4.3    Attacks Against the Data Processing Software

These include direct attacks, such as adversarial inputs that manipulate output or poison models, and indirect attacks that exploit code vulnerabilities to escalate privileges or hijack sessions. For example, a dataset may exploit deserialization flaws such as CVE-2020-14343 in unpatched PyYAML libraries[1], enabling arbitrary code execution. Such attacks underscore the need for pre-execution vulnerability assessment and runtime safeguards.

# 5    Defense-in-Depth Architecture

To fortify the infrastructure and meet the proposed requirements, we introduce a Defense-in-Depth architecture that integrates static analysis, dynamic monitoring, and sandboxing (Fig. 1). This layered approach is essential because no single mechanism can simultaneously safeguard data confidentiality, execution integrity and environment security. Often relying on a single defense makes the system vulnerable to a single point of failure [8]; if it is bypassed, the system is compromised. In contrast, combining multiple layers increases resilience: if one is evaded, others can still detect or mitigate the threat. Moreover, as modern malware is designed to evade static or dynamic techniques, layering both improves detection and narrows the attack surface.

---

[1] https://nvd.nist.gov/vuln/detail/CVE-2020-14343, Accessed on July 6, 2025.

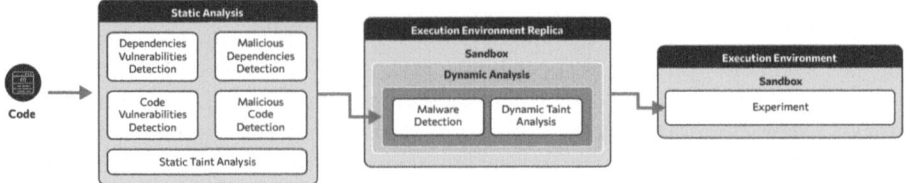

**Fig. 1.** Defense-in-Depth Architecture

Static analysis is performed immediately after code upload and before execution, enabling early detection of threats and preventing potential damage or data leaks. By halting the pipeline when issues are found, it also conserves computational resources that would otherwise be spent on dynamic analysis. Attacks targeting the code typically exploit vulnerabilities either in the code itself or its dependencies. To address this, the first step involves scanning the code and its dependencies for known vulnerabilities. By blocking the use of vulnerable software components, the infrastructure mitigates attacks that exploit such weaknesses. In addition, the system assesses the maliciousness of both the code and its dependencies by identifying known malicious libraries and inspecting code patterns that violate the platform's policies or signal harmful intent. For instance, patterns indicative of malware—such as attempts to encrypt local files, escalate privileges, or generate excessive network traffic for a denial-of-service (DoS) attack—can be detected early. Static taint analysis is also applied to evaluate how the code intends to use the provided data and whether it might leak sensitive information to external or covert channels. This can be implemented using pattern matching, and static taint analysis software, like Semgrep [9] and CodeQL [5]. Unlike general-purpose code scanners, the novelty lies in the customization of detection rules to address threats that are unique in collaborative cloud scenarios where source code is not vetted beforehand, such as data exfiltration, obfuscated logic bombs, and unauthorized outbound channels.

After passing static analysis, the code is matched with the associated dataset and deployed into the dynamic analysis environment. This environment is designed to closely replicate the production execution context and includes all necessary dynamic analysis tools. The rationale behind this design is that the more accurately the environment mimics production, the more reliably malware will exhibit its intended behavior. As a result, detection accuracy of logic bombs and time-based or condition-based malware—that traditional sandboxes often miss—will be enhanced. Furthermore, this similarity serves to counteract obfuscation and evasion techniques, which often rely on environmental cues to detect whether the code is being analyzed. By minimizing the observable differences between analysis and production, it becomes significantly harder for malware to distinguish between the two and alter its behavior accordingly.

Dynamic analysis runs in isolated sandboxes, following the same multi-tenant model as production. The sandbox serves as a critical security layer, isolating untrusted code both from the host system and from other co-tenant executions. This isolation is essential, as even with advanced detection measures in place, an undetected threat could still cause damage if not properly confined. Additionally, sandboxes enforce strict resource constraints, limiting the memory, CPU, and network access granted to each analysis. This mitigates resource exhaustion attacks impacting the host or tenants. In order to ensure that the execution environment remains scalable, efficient, and hardware-agnostic, container-based isolation is employed. Specifically, the combination of gVisor and Docker preserves the lightweight nature, rapid startup, and scalability of containers while enhancing host isolation through gVisor's user-space kernel protection mechanisms [21].

Finally, the dynamic analysis process comprises two key components. The first is a real-time malware detection mechanism that monitors behavioral characteristics—such as resource usage and process activity—to identify potentially malicious behavior. Powered by Transformers, this recent approach has shown promising results in detecting both known and zero-day threats [15]. The second component is dynamic taint analysis, which labels sensitive data and then tracks their flow through memory, processes, and system-level operations, such as file writes or network transmissions, during execution. This technique helps identify unauthorized data leaks or misuse by detecting instances where tainted data reaches unauthorized or covert channels [4,22]. It is important to note that, during dynamic analysis, synthetic data are served to the code instead of real user data. This precaution prevents the leakage of actual sensitive information while still enabling the detection of malicious behavior, as leakage attempts are visible through interactions with the synthetic data. Overall, detection of harmful or unauthorized behavior reinforces accountability and supports the non-repudiation principle, while also acting as a deterrent by increasing the likelihood that malicious actions will be traced back to their origin.

The aforementioned defenses are integrated into a DiD pipeline, collectively designed to fulfill the NFRs of the cloud infrastructure's execution environment. First, vulnerability assessment strengthens the code against exploitation via maliciously crafted inputs, thereby ensuring that the code operates as intended and maintaining its integrity *(NFR3)*. It also protects the execution environment from vulnerability-based attacks, such as regular expression denial of service, insecure deserialization and arbitrary code exection *(NFR1)*. Second, detecting malicious dependencies and code patterns helps defend the infrastructure against embedded threats. When combined with static taint analysis, this stage further mitigates the risk of data leakage through direct or covert channels, thus contributing to data privacy *(NFR1, NFR2)*. However, because static analysis alone cannot fully capture the runtime behavior of software—especially in the presence of obfuscation techniques—dynamic analysis serves as the next layer of defense. Here, real-time malware detection and dynamic taint tracking identify malicious behavior and prevent data leakages during execution, further safeguarding both the environment and user data *(NFR1, NFR2)*. Together, these layers form a cohesive DiD architecture that collectively satisfies all three system requirements.

## 6    Conclusion and Future Work

In this short concept paper, we presented a Defense-in-Depth architecture for cloud infrastructures that support collaborative data processing through the execution of unattested code. Our approach combines multiple layers of defense—namely static analysis, dynamic analysis, and sandboxing—into a practical framework aimed at ensuring infrastructure security, code integrity, and data privacy. We have already begun implementing this architecture and plan to test and validate it in a production environment using real-world malware and adversarial scenarios. Our broader vision is to enable the creation of secure, trusted, and collaborative cloud infrastructures that support diverse data processing through unattested code execution—without imposing strict limitations on inputs. This, in turn, fosters a more open form of collaboration while still respecting the privacy and security requirements of modern cloud systems.

**Acknowledgments.** Parts of this work have been supported by the Horizon Europe projects Nostradamus (Grant Agreement No 101134888) and Research Analysis Identifier SystEm (Grant Agreement No. 101058479), funded by the European Union.

**Disclosure of Interests.** The authors have no competing interests to declare that are relevant to the content of this article.

## References

1. Agache, A., et al.: Firecracker: lightweight virtualization for serverless applications. In: 17th USENIX Symposium on Networked Systems Design and Implementation (NSDI 20), pp. 419–434. USENIX Association, Santa Clara, CA, February 2020, https://www.usenix.org/conference/nsdi20/presentation/agache
2. Amazon: Amazon sagemaker (2025), https://aws.amazon.com/sagemaker/, Accessed 10 April 2025
3. Bulazel, A., Yener, B.: A survey on automated dynamic malware analysis evasion and counter-evasion: Pc, mobile, and web. In: Proceedings of the 1st Reversing and Offensive-Oriented Trends Symposium. ROOTS, Association for Computing Machinery, New York, NY, USA (2017). https://doi.org/10.1145/3150376.3150378
4. Enck, W., et al.: Taintdroid: an information-flow tracking system for realtime privacy monitoring on smartphones. ACM Trans. Comput. Syst. **32**(2) (2014). https://doi.org/10.1145/2619091
5. GitHub: Codeql - semantic code analysis engine (2025), https://codeql.github.com/, Accessed 10 April 2025
6. Google: Google colaboratory (2025), https://colab.research.google.com/, Accessed 10 April 2025

7. Google: gvisor - application kernel for containers (2025), https://gvisor.dev/, Accessed 10 April 2025

8. He, Y., et al.: Cross container attacks: the bewildered eBPF on clouds. In: 32nd USENIX Security Symposium (USENIX Security 23), pp. 5971–5988. USENIX Association, Anaheim, CA, August 2023, https://www.usenix.org/conference/usenixsecurity23/presentation/he

9. Inc., S.: Semgrep - lightweight static analysis for many languages (2025), https://semgrep.dev/, Accessed 10 April 2025

10. Li, M., Xia, Y., Chen, H.: Confidential serverless made efficient with plug-in enclaves. In: 2021 ACM/IEEE 48th Annual International Symposium on Computer Architecture (ISCA), pp. 306–318 (2021). https://doi.org/10.1109/ISCA52012.2021.00032

11. Liagouris, J., Kalavri, V., Faisal, M., Varia, M.: SECRECY: secure collaborative analytics in untrusted clouds. In: 20th USENIX Symposium on Networked Systems Design and Implementation (NSDI 23), pp. 1031–1056. USENIX Association, Boston, MA, April 2023, https://www.usenix.org/conference/nsdi23/presentation/liagouris

12. McConaghy, T.: Ocean protocol: tools for the Web3 data economy, pp. 505–539. Springer, Cham (2022). https://doi.org/10.1007/978-3-031-07535-3_16

13. Microsoft: Azure confidential computing (2025), https://azure.microsoft.com/en-us/solutions/confidential-compute, Accessed 10 April 2025

14. Mulligan, D.P., Petri, G., Spinale, N., Stockwell, G., Vincent, H.J.M.: Confidential computing—a brave new world. In: 2021 International Symposium on Secure and Private Execution Environment Design (SEED), pp. 132–138 (2021). https://doi.org/10.1109/SEED51797.2021.00025

15. Natsos, D., Symeonidis, A.L.: Transformer-based malware detection using process resource utilization metrics. Results Eng. **25**, 104250 (2025). https://doi.org/10.1016/j.rineng.2025.104250, https://www.sciencedirect.com/science/article/pii/S2590123025003366

16. RAISE: Raise infrastructure (2025), https://portal.raise-science.eu/, Accessed 10 April 2025

17. Randazzo, A., Tinnirello, I.: Kata containers: an emerging architecture for enabling mec services in fast and secure way. In: 2019 Sixth International Conference on Internet of Things: Systems, Management and Security (IOTSMS), pp. 209–214 (2019). https://doi.org/10.1109/IOTSMS48152.2019.8939164

18. Salih, B.M., Jasim Mohammad, O.K.: Cloud data leakage, security, privacy issues and challenges: review. Procedia Comput. Sci. **242**, 592–601 (2024). https://doi.org/10.1016/j.procs.2024.08.113, https://www.sciencedirect.com/science/article/pii/S1877050924018325, 11th International Conference on Information Technology and Quantitative Management (ITQM 2024)

19. Sardar, M.U., Fetzer, C.: Confidential computing and related technologies: a critical review. Cybersecurity **6**(1), 10 (2023). https://doi.org/10.1186/s42400-023-00144-1

20. Tomar, A., Jeena, D., Mishra, P., Bisht, R.: Docker security: a threat model, attack taxonomy and real-time attack scenario of dos. In: 2020 10th International Conference on Cloud Computing, Data Science & Engineering (Confluence), pp. 150–155 (2020). https://doi.org/10.1109/Confluence47617.2020.9058115

21. Wang, X., Du, J., Liu, H.: Performance and isolation analysis of RunC, gVisor and Kata Containers runtimes. Clust. Comput. **25**(2), 1497–1513 (2021). https://doi.org/10.1007/s10586-021-03517-8

22. Wu, Z., Chen, X., Yang, Z., Du, X.: Reducing security risks of suspicious data and codes through a novel dynamic defense model. IEEE Trans. Inf. Forensics Secur. **14**(9), 2427–2440 (2019). https://doi.org/10.1109/TIFS.2019.2901798

23. Xu, R., Fang, Z.: Tempo: Confidentiality preservation in cloud-based neural network training. In: 2024 International Joint Conference on Neural Networks (IJCNN), pp. 1–10 (2024). https://doi.org/10.1109/IJCNN60899.2024.10650731

24. Xu, Y., Pangia, J., Ye, C., Solihin, Y., Shen, X.: Data enclave: a data-centric trusted execution environment. In: 2024 IEEE International Symposium on High-Performance Computer Architecture (HPCA), pp. 218–232 (2024). https://doi.org/10.1109/HPCA57654.2024.00026

25. Yang, Z., Xiao, J.: A dynamic sandbox detection technique in a private cloud environment. Scalable Comput. Pract. Exp. **25**(6), 4995–5004 (2024). https://doi.org/10.12694/scpe.v25i6.3412

26. Ziller, A., et al.: PySyft: a library for easy federated learning, pp. 111–139. Springer, Cham (2021). https://doi.org/10.1007/978-3-030-70604-3_5

# QuTiP-MRL: A Library for Multiple-Valued Reversible Logic Simulations

Fabio Pievani, Asma Taheri Monfared[ID], Andrea Bombarda[✉][ID], and Angelo Gargantini[ID]

University of Bergamo, Bergamo, Italy
f.pievani1@studenti.unibg.it,
{asma.taherimonfared,andrea.bombarda,angelo.gargantini}@unibg.it

**Abstract.** Reversible logic is a key technology for low-power and quantum computing, as it allows computation without information loss and minimizes energy dissipation. Meanwhile, multiple-valued logic offers advantages such as reduced circuit complexity and improved data representation compared to binary systems. Combining the benefits of multiple-valued logic and reversibility opens new possibilities for efficient and scalable computing architectures. However, there has been a lack of tool support for designing and simulating multiple-valued reversible circuits. In this paper, we present QuTiP-MRL, a Python-based library for designing and analyzing multiple-valued reversible logic circuits, with current support for ternary and quaternary logic. Built on top of the QuTiP (Quantum Toolbox in Python) framework, QuTiP-MRL addresses this gap by providing a set of well-defined multiple-valued reversible gates and tools to construct and simulate multiple-valued circuits. This library offers an environment for exploring the behavior and properties of multiple-valued reversible systems, supporting research and development in emerging computational paradigms.

**Keywords:** Multiple-Valued Logic · Reversible Circuits · Circuit Simulation · Circuit Visualization

## 1 Introduction

Reversible computation has become a key paradigm in modern computing, particularly in the domains of low-power design and quantum information processing. Unlike conventional logic circuits that lose information during computation, reversible logic ensures bijective transformations, allowing outputs to be traced back to their original inputs [1]. This information-preserving property is essential for quantum computing, where all operations must be unitary and reversible by nature [17]. Additionally, reversible logic minimizes energy dissipation, in accordance with Landauer's principle, which states that the erasure of a single bit of information results in an energy cost of at least $kT \ln 2$ joules [16].

D. Taibi and D. Smite (Eds.): SEAA 2025, LNCS 16083, pp. 419–427, 2026.
https://doi.org/10.1007/978-3-032-04207-1_28

In parallel, there has been growing interest in Multiple-Valued Logic (MVL), which extends binary logic to systems with more than two states. MVL, especially ternary and quaternary logic, offers several theoretical and practical advantages, such as reduced circuit complexity, lower interconnect overhead, and increased data density [3,10,14]. In the context of quantum computing, these benefits are particularly compelling, as physical implementations of qudits (quantum digits with $d > 2$ levels) are becoming increasingly feasible on platforms such as trapped ions, photonic systems, and superconducting circuits. Ternary and quaternary quantum logic are also known to exhibit better noise resilience and fault tolerance compared to binary approaches [8].

Despite these advantages, the practical development, simulation, and analysis of multiple-valued reversible logic circuits remain a major challenge. Most existing quantum circuit design and simulation tools, including widely-used frameworks like Qiskit [11], Cirq [18] and QuTiP [12] focus exclusively on binary systems and qubit-based gates. Researchers interested in non-binary reversible logic have to resort to low-level mathematical modeling or custom simulations, which are error-prone and time-consuming. There is currently no well-supported library that enables users to design, simulate, and visualize ternary or quaternary reversible logic circuits in an accessible and modular way [20].

To address this gap, we introduce QuTiP-MRL, a Python-based simulation library for Multiple-Valued Reversible Logic (MRL), with current support for both ternary and quaternary logic systems. Built on top of the QuTiP (Quantum Toolbox in Python) framework, QuTiP-MRL enables users to define multi-valued reversible gates, build custom circuits, and simulate their behavior using quantum mechanical state vectors and operators. The library includes a growing set of built-in gates for ternary logic, along with utilities for constructing larger systems, visualizing circuit behavior, and analyzing quantum cost metrics.

QuTiP-MRL is designed to support both research and educational applications. It provides a high-level, modular API for simulating multiple-valued reversible logic, and it is open-source to encourage collaboration and extensibility. By making the simulation of multiple-valued reversible circuits more accessible, this library aims to accelerate the exploration of emerging computational paradigms that go beyond the limitations of binary logic.

This paper is structured as follows: Sect. 2 describes the library implementation, including the overall structure, supported gate sets, and the functionalities offered by QuTiP-MRL. Section 3 provides a detailed demonstration of the library. Section 4 discusses related works and comparison. Finally, the conclusion of this work is given in Sect. 5.

## 2  Library Implementation

In this section, we describe our QuTiP-MRL library and the operations it supports. It is based on QuTip [15] and it is available at https://github.com/foselab/QuTiP-MRL. To minimize the effort required for users familiar with Qiskit [11], we designed QuTiP-MRL with an interface that closely resembles that of Qiskit and with similar visualization modes.

The main class of this library is QuditCircuit, which provides all the core functionalities for gate addition, circuit simulation, and visualization in a unified interface. The library is qutrit ready, therefore it includes the matrices used by ternary reversible logic gates and their specific visualization, but it also works with general qudits through user-specified matrices, making QuTiP-MRL compatible with any basis states qudits. In the following, we describe QuTiP-MRL functionalities in terms of circuit construction (Sect. 2.1), simulation backends (Sect. 2.2), and visualization (Sect. 2.3).

## 2.1  Internal Circuit Structure

The first step the user must perform when using QuTiP-MRL is the circuit initialization through the QuditCircuit class. When instantiating a QuditCircuit object, users must specify the number of qudits in the modeled circuit and, possibly, the number of states. By default, QuTiP-MRL works with qutrits, thus it assumes working with ternary logic. For example, the call q = QuditCircuit(4) creates a ternary circuit with 4 qutrits, while q = QuditCircuit(3, 4) creates a quaternary circuit with 3 qudits, each with 4 states.

When an instance q of a QuditCircuit is available, users can add quantum gates. QuTiP-MRL supports ternary *shift* gates, ternary *Muthukrishnan–Stroud* gates, and *custom* gates, in the case in which more than 3 states or different gates are required.

Concerning *shift* gates, we provide functions for all ternary gates (id, plus1, plus2, one_two, zero_one, zero_two). All of them require as input parameter the index of the target qutrit. For example, q.plus2(0) adds a +2 gate to the qutrit 0. Concerning controlled gates, i.e., *Muthukrishnan–Stroud* gates, QuTiP-MRL provides functions for all quantum multiple valued gates (i.e., c_plus1, c_plus2, c_one_two, c_zero_one, c_zero_two). Similarly to shift gates, controlled gates require a parameter indicating the target qudit and, in addition, they require the index of the control qudit. For example, The command q.c_plus2(3,0) represents a controlled +2 gate, where the first argument (3) is the control qudit and the second argument (0) is the target qudit.

Finally, when working with quaternary logic, more than 4 states, or not available gates are needed, two additional methods are provided: custom_gate and c_custom_gate. These two functions allow for defining alternative shift or controlled gates. Both functions follow the same structure as those for ternary gates. Additionally, users must input a matrix in the form of numpy.array and optionally the name of the gate for visualization purposes. For example, the command q.c_custom_gate(np.array([...]), 3,0, "CG1") adds a new gate, corresponding to the matrix specified as the first parameter to the qudit 0, controlled by the qudit 3. The gate is called, for visualization purposes, "CG1".

## 2.2  Simulation Backends

QuTiP-MRL allows users to simulate MVL circuits by using two backends, namely the one based on *full matrix* simulation and the one *einsum-based*.

Once a QuditCircuit instance q is available, the full matrix simulation can be performed by using the q.simulate_fullmatrix() command. QuTiP-MRL initializes the system in the $|0\rangle$ state for each qudit, applies each gate to the system state, and calculates and prints the density matrix for each individual qudit, as well as the probability for each possible final measurement. During this operation, the system state is evolved step by step by performing matrix multiplication, for each gate, on the full quantum state. As a result, the data size grows rapidly, and simulation becomes computationally expensive: The bigger the number of states, the less qudits can be used in the circuit. For example, when using ternary it is recommended to limit the circuit to a maximum of 8 qutrits. Note that, when using this simulation mode, unlike other available libraries, QuTiP-MRL supports superposition [5].

Similarly, for the einsum-based simulation [19], once a QuditCircuit instance q is available, it can be performed by using the q.simulate_einsum() command. This method evolves the state of the circuit with tensor contractions using NumPy's einsum, which performs string manipulation, with index-wise operations. It allows the simulation of circuits with a relatively large number of qudits, as it avoids explicit matrix multiplication, which depends on the number of states of the qudit. For example, in ternary logic, 17 qutrits can be used with this kind of simulation. The quantum state is represented as a multidimensional tensor with shape $[d_1, d_2, \ldots, d_m]$ where $d$ is the number of states and $m$ is the number of qudits. The main limitation of this approach is that it only provides the marginal probability distributions of each qudit, losing quantum information in the process.

An example of the output obtained with each of the simulation backends will be shown in Sect. 3.3.

## 2.3  Rendering and Visualization

Rendering and visualizing logic circuits is of paramount important, as it allows for visually checking whether the circuit has been designed correctly and all gates have been connected to the correct qudits.

QuTiP-MRL offers, for circuit rendering, the same interface as Qiskit. Once a QuditCircuit instance q is available, multiple-valued circuits can be visualized by calling the q.draw() method. It offers two different visualization methods: ASCII and Matplotlib-based. In ASCII mode the circuit is displayed as plain text, making it suitable for quick inspection in command-line interfaces or automatic post-processing. In Matplotlib mode [2], the circuit is rendered as a structured and color-coded diagram, allowing for a clearer visualization of gate placement, control lines, and circuit depth. The former is triggered when no parameter is passed to the draw method, while the latter is triggered by passing 'mpl'. Note that the Matplotlib library is required to use this functionality.

Regardless of the chosen visualization technique, users may want to visually separate input preparation gates from the rest of the circuit. For this reason, the QuTiP-MRL library provides the q.barrier() method to draw input barriers.

An example of mpl visualization is reported and discussed in Sect. 3.2.

# 3   Demonstration

To showcase the capabilities of QuTiP-MRL, we present the construction and simulation of a reversible ternary full adder circuit [8]. This example highlights key features of the library, including gate-based circuit design, visualization modes, and simulation backends. We emphasize that, while this example focuses on a ternary logic circuit, QuTiP-MRL is designed to support reversible circuits in both ternary and quaternary logic. Further examples can be found in our GitHub repository at https://github.com/foselab/QuTiP-MRL/tree/main/examples.

## 3.1   Circuit Design

We report the Python code designing the circuit in Listing 1.1. Initially, we instantiate a circuit with four qutrits. Since we do not specify the number of possible dimension values, qutrits are used by default. The first two qutrits ($q_0$ and $q_1$) represent the ternary inputs; After circuit simulation, $q_0$ will contain the final sum, while $q_2$ and $q_3$ will be used to store the carry-in and the carry-out, respectively.

To initialize the inputs, we apply shift gates. The command plus2(0) applies a cyclic increment by two modulo 3 to the state of $q_0$. This operation shifts the current state by two. Similarly, plus2(1) applies the same shift to $q_1$. These are 1-qutrit shift (uncontrolled) gates that modify the qutrit's value.

After setting the initial inputs, we use the barrier() method to insert a vertical separator in the circuit. This barrier acts as a visual and logical boundary between the input initialization and the main computation. It does not affect the circuit's functionality but improves readability in both ASCII and graphical visualizations.

Muthukrishnan and Stroud gates (Controlled Shift gates) are used for conditional logic. For instance, c_plus2(1, 0) applies a +2 shift to $q_0$ only if $q_1$ is in the $|2\rangle$ state. In this command, the first argument (1) refers to the *control* qutrit, and the second (0) is the *target* qutrit. Another example is c_one_two(0, 1), which swaps the $|1\rangle$ and $|2\rangle$ states of $q_1$, but only if $q_0$ is in state $|2\rangle$. These controlled operations are crucial for expressing reversible conditional logic.

The commands reported in Listing 1.1 implement the full adder logic using only reversible ternary gates, ensuring no information loss during computation.

## 3.2   Visualization

The code we use to visualize the circuit, in the two available modes, is reported in Listing 1.2. Figure 1 reports the Matplotlib-based visualization of the full adder.

```
full_adder = QuditCircuit(4)          full_adder.plus1(1)
# Set initial input states            full_adder.c_plus1(1, 0)
full_adder.plus2(0) # Q0 = |2>        full_adder.plus2(1)
full_adder.plus2(1) # Q1 = |2>        full_adder.c_plus2(2, 0)
full_adder.barrier()                  full_adder.c_one_two(0, 2)
# Full adder logic                    full_adder.c_plus1(2, 3)
full_adder.c_plus2(1, 0)              full_adder.c_one_two(0, 2)
full_adder.c_one_two(0, 1)            full_adder.plus1(2)
full_adder.c_plus1(1, 3)              full_adder.c_plus1(2, 0)
full_adder.c_one_two(0, 1)            full_adder.plus2(2)
```

**Listing 1.1.** Python code describing the implementation of a reversible ternary full adder with QuTiP-MRL

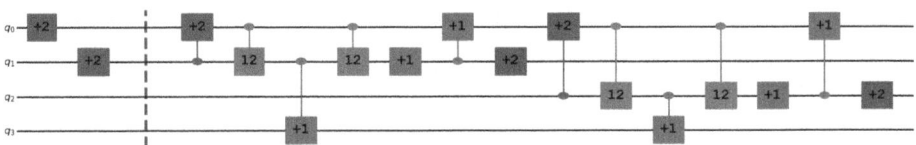

**Fig. 1.** Matplotlib-based visualization of the ternary full adder circuit.

## 3.3   Simulation

As described in Sect. 2, QuTiP-MRL provides two simulation engines [13] optimized for different circuit sizes. In our demonstration example, both modes are suitable as we only have four qutrits. The two modes can be invoked as in Listing 1.5. Both simulation modes start from the $|0000\rangle$ state and apply gates sequentially. The full matrix method outputs individual density matrices, while the einsum method provides final-state probabilities. More specifically, the full matrix method provides detailed information about each qutrit state in the form of $3 \times 3$ density matrices as well as the probabilities for each final possible measure, as shown in Listing 1.3, while the einsum-based simulation produces the state probabilities in the computational basis, as reported in Listing 1.4.

## 4   Related Works and Comparison

The increasing complexity of quantum algorithms and architectures has driven the development of a variety of libraries and frameworks for the design, simulation, and visualization of quantum circuits [9]. These tools aim to facilitate efficient prototyping, correctness verification, and performance optimization across diverse quantum computing models.

```
full_adder.draw() # ASCII representation
full_adder.draw('mpl') # Matplotlib visualization
```

**Listing 1.2.** Python code for the visualization of a circuit with QuTiP-MRL

```
Qudit 0 Density Matrix:
[[0.+0.j 0.+0.j 0.+0.j]
 [0.+0.j 1.+0.j 0.+0.j]
 [0.+0.j 0.+0.j 0.+0.j]]
Qudit 1 Density Matrix: [...]
Final measurement probabilities:
|1201>: 100.00
```

**Listing 1.3.** Full matrix simulation

```
Qudit 0 state probabilities:
0
1
0


Qudit 1 state probabilities:
[...]
```

**Listing 1.4.** Einsum-based simulation

```
full_adder.simulate_fullmatrix() # Prints qutrit density matrices
full_adder.simulate_einsum() # Prints qutrit state probabilities
```

**Listing 1.5.** QuTiP-MRL simulation of the quantum ternary full adder

When it comes to quantum circuits, the most used library is Qiskit [11], developed by IBM. Similarly, Quantum++ is a high-performance C++11 library that supports simulation of arbitrary quantum processes, including classical reversible logic operations, making it suitable for mixed classical-quantum circuits [6]. Qibo [4] is a Python-based framework providing hardware-accelerated simulation capabilities with usability across CPUs, GPUs, and multi-GPU systems. However, all these libraries do not have a proper means to deal with multiple-valued circuits and with their simulation.

Lambert et al. [15] introduced QuTiP, an open-source software designed for simulating the dynamics of open quantum systems. Although it offers a robust simulation framework, its logic and syntax differ significantly from Qiskit, which is more familiar to most users. To address this, we present QuTiP-MRL in this work—a tool that enhances QuTiP by offering a more user-friendly interface and circuit visualization similar to that of Qiskit. In [7], the authors extended the Cirq [18] open-source framework from Google to support multiple-value logic. Similar to QuTiP, its visualization capabilities lack in a proper graphical representation, such as the one we support in QuTiP-MRL. Moreover, the tool proposed in [7] supports circuits of up to 14 qutrits, while QuTiP-MRL allows users to work with 17 qutrits. Additionally, the existing tool does not support superposition, while our tool does.

To the best of our knowledge, despite the recent advancements in the quantum circuits field, few frameworks directly support multi-valued quantum circuits. Moreover, none of these frameworks offers simulation capabilities for circuits of the same size as those supported by QuTiP-MRL or provides visualization similar to the well-known Qiskit's style and the one allowing the simulation of bigger circuits.

# 5   Conclusion

This work addresses the current lack of tools for quantum multi-valued logic circuits by introducing a comprehensive environment for their design, simulation, and visualization—an essential step toward enabling more effective circuit development and supporting critical activities such as validation and analysis. In this paper, we have presented QuTiP-MRL, a Python library for the design, simulation, and visualization of multi-valued reversible quantum circuits. It is, to the best of our knowledge, the only available tool supporting the design, simulation, and visualization of multiple-valued quantum circuits by keeping the same structure and logic of Qiskit. We have demonstrated how to use QuTiP-MRL with a simple ternary full-adder circuit, starting from its design, to the simulation and visualization. Future improvements could include further code optimization allowing users to deal with even bigger and more complex circuits.

**Acknowledgments.** This work has been partially funded by project ANTHEM (AdvaNced Technologies for Human-centrEd Medicine) - Grant PNC0000003 – CUP: B53C22006700001 and by project PRIN 2022 SAFEST (Trust assurance of Digital Twins for medical cyber-physical systems), funded by the EU - NGEU, Mission 4, Component 2, Investment 1.1, CUP F53D23004230006, under the National Recovery and Resilience Plan (NRRP).

**Disclosure of Interests.** The authors have no competing interests to declare that are relevant to the content of this article.

# References

1. Bennett, C.H., Shor, P.W.: Quantum information theory. IEEE Trans. Inf. Theory **44**(6), 2724–2742 (1998). https://doi.org/10.1109/18.720553
2. Bisong, E.: Matplotlib and Seaborn. In: Building Machine Learning and Deep Learning Models on Google Cloud Platform, pp. 151–165. Apress, Berkeley, CA (2019). https://doi.org/10.1007/978-1-4842-4470-8_12
3. Dong, H., Lu, D., Li, C.: A novel qutrit representation of quantum image. Quantum Inf. Process. **21**(3), 1–29 (2022). https://doi.org/10.1007/s11128-022-03450-8
4. Efthymiou, S., Ramos-Calderer, S., et al.: Qibo: a framework for quantum simulation with hardware acceleration. Quantum Sci. Technol. **7**(1), 015018 (2021). https://doi.org/10.1088/2058-9565/ac39f5
5. Friedman, J.R., Patel, V., et al.: Quantum superposition of distinct macroscopic states. Nature **406**(6791), 43–46 (2000). https://doi.org/10.1038/35017505
6. Gheorghiu, V.: Quantum++: a modern c++ quantum computing library. PLoS ONE **13**(12), e0208073 (2018). https://doi.org/10.1371/journal.pone.0208073
7. Gokhale, P., Baker, J.M., et al.: Asymptotic improvements to quantum circuits via qutrits. In: Proceedings of the 46th International Symposium on Computer Architecture, pp. 554–566. ISCA '19. ACM, New York (2019). https://doi.org/10.1145/3307650.3322253
8. Haghparast, M., Wille, R., Monfared, A.T.: Towards quantum reversible ternary coded decimal adder. Quantum Inf. Process. **16**(11), 1–25 (2017). https://doi.org/10.1007/s11128-017-1735-3

9. Hamid, M., Alam, B., Pal, O.: Comparative study of quantum computing tools and frameworks. In: Innovation and Emerging Trends in Computing and Information Technologies, pp. 87–104. Springer Nature Switzerland, Cham (2025). https://doi.org/10.1007/978-3-031-80842-5_8

10. Hurst: Multiple-valued logic—its status and its future. IEEE transactions on Computers **100**(12), 1160–1179 (1984). https://doi.org/10.1109/TC.1984.1676392

11. Javadi-Abhari, A., Treinish, M., Krsulich, K., et al.: Quantum computing with qiskit (2024). https://doi.org/10.48550/ARXIV.2405.08810

12. Johansson, J.R., Nation, P.D., Nori, F.: Qutip: an open-source python framework for the dynamics of open quantum systems. Comput. Phys. Commun. **183**(8), 1760–1772 (2012). https://doi.org/10.1016/j.cpc.2012.02.021

13. Jozsa, R.: On the simulation of quantum circuits. https://doi.org/10.48550/ARXIV.QUANT-PH/0603163

14. Klimov, A., Guzmán, R., et al.: Qutrit quantum computer with trapped ions. Phys. Rev. A **67**(6), 062313 (2003). https://doi.org/10.1103/PhysRevA.67.062313

15. Lambert, N., Giguère, E., et al.: Qutip 5: The quantum toolbox in python (2024). https://doi.org/10.48550/ARXIV.2412.04705

16. Landauer, R.: Irreversibility and heat generation in the computing process. IBM J. Res. Dev. **5**(3), 183–191 (1961). https://doi.org/10.1147/rd.53.0183

17. Nielsen, M.A., Chuang, I.L.: Quantum computation and quantum information. Cambridge University Press (2010). https://doi.org/10.1017/CBO9780511976667

18. Omole, V., Tyagi, A., et al.: Cirq: A python framework for creating, editing, and invoking quantum circuits (2020). https://github.com/quantumlib/Cirq

19. Pan, F., Gu, H., Kuang, L., Liu, B., Zhang, P.: Efficient quantum circuit simulation by tensor network methods on modern gpus. ACM Trans. Quantum Comput. **5**(4) (Nov 2024). https://doi.org/10.1145/3696465

20. Taheri Monfared, A., Ciriani, V., Haghparast, M.: Qutrit representation of quantum images: new quantum ternary circuit design. Quantum Inf. Process. **23**(8), 288 (2024). https://doi.org/10.1007/s11128-024-04484-w

# Design Decisions for Architecting Digital Twins of Microservices-Based Systems

Aurora Macías[1] ⓘ, Evangelos Ntentos[2] ⓘ, Uwe Zdun[2] ⓘ, and Elena Navarro[1](✉) ⓘ

[1] LoUISE Research Group, University of Castilla-La Mancha, Albacete, Spain
Aurora.Macias@alu.uclm.es, Elena.Navarro@uclm.es
[2] Research Group Software Architecture, University of Vienna, Vienna, Austria
uwe.zdun@univie.ac.at

**Abstract.** Architecting Digital Twins (DTs) that model and monitor microservice-based (MS-based) systems is challenging due to the lack of both design approaches and knowledge among practitioners. To address these shortcomings, we conducted a qualitative study of the patterns and practices applied by practitioners using a Straussian grounded theory-based methodology. After analyzing twenty-three sources of grey literature, we identified three Architectural Design Decisions (ADDs) with twenty-four decision options and their relationships, as well as seventeen key decision drivers based on quality (sub)characteristics from a standard model. We also evaluated the impact of the decision drivers on the ADDs. This resulted in a UML-based ADD model that provides practitioners with guidance for building distributed DT-based systems, including information often omitted or inconclusive in other scientific works on DTs and even on Application Programming Interfaces (API) design. Among the main findings are the intricacies and impact of decisions regarding the granularity of DTs, as well as the seamless integration both among DTs and between DTs and other systems. Additionally, we identified strong similarities between architecting DTs and MS-based systems.

**Keywords:** Architectural Design Decisions · Digital Twins · Microservices · Software Architecture · Grey Literature · Grounded Theory

## 1 Introduction

Digital Twins [1] have emerged as a transformative approach to enhancing the design, operation, and maintenance of complex systems across multiple domains, such as manufacturing, smart cities, or healthcare among others. A Digital Twin (DT) is defined as "a virtual representation of real-world entities and processes, synchronized at a specified frequency and fidelity, that uses real-time and historical data to represent present and past states and simulate predicted future" [2]. DTs generally consist of three components: a physical counterpart (PT), a virtual counterpart, and the integration of both [3, 4]. The PT can be either a physical entity, a software entity, or even a software process [3].

The properties of DTs make them ideal candidates for the real-time monitoring and continuous assessment of microservice-based (MS-based) systems [5]. MS-based systems inherently involve distributed components, dynamic interactions and contexts [5, 6], and a high degree of complexity [7, 8]. These characteristics can hinder their ability both to provide reliable services [9] and to prevent service failures beyond acceptable limits [5].

There are three aspects to consider when architecting a DT, just as with any other system [4, 3, 10]:

- *Granularity* refers to the degree of abstraction or detail in the design [11], considering not only the functional requirements but also the non-functional ones [12]. The granularity level determines the boundaries, size, and complexity of the software components of the MS-based system to be twined, and consequently, of the DTs that will be developed based on control needs. Thus, granularity is key aspect in the development of DTs [25].
- An *Interface* defines an interaction point between two components or systems and specifies how they communicate with each other, including the methods, protocols, and data formats used. Interfaces are used when architecting DTs to facilitate their control, governance, and orchestration or for simple querying the DTs [3].
- *Integration* refers to the combination, coordination, and collaboration of different components to enable their seamless interaction. Different DTs can be integrated into a composite DT, so that both composite and individual DTs can be observed and controlled to meet specific requirements. DTs can also be integrated with other convenient services or systems for simulation, analysis, and other purposes, as needed to achieve specific business goals [3].

Implementing DT architectures is a challenging task [3, 4], especially when the twinned element is a complex MS-based system [5]. Thus, architecting DTs of MS-based systems considering the three architectural aspects stated is both critical and non-trivial. Although various architectural patterns and practices for architecting DTs have been identified [3, 4, 7, 8], they neither explicitly address these architectural aspects nor are they well documented or formalized. Moreover, there is limited research on their interrelations and the factors driving and influencing their selection. Practitioners often lack both a systematic understanding of how to apply these concepts and a comprehensive framework to guide their decision-making [3, 13, 14]. This knowledge gap challenges them in making informed architectural design decisions (ADDs) when designing robust and scalable DT architectures. This leads to suboptimal implementations that may not meet quality requirements such as compatibility, maintainability, or performance efficiency [15]. These issues also affect the design of DTs of MS-based architectures that should meet the properties expected from DT [23]. Considering this, this work aims to answer the following Research Questions (RQs):

- **RQ1**. Which ADDs and corresponding patterns and practices are used by practitioners while architecting DTs of MS-based systems with respect to the aspects of granularity, interfaces, and integration?
- **RQ2**. What are the relations between the identified patterns and practices?
- **RQ3**. Which decision drivers are relevant to the identified patterns and practices and in what degree?

To answer these RQs, we conducted a qualitative Grey Literature Study (GLS) [16, 17] based on Straussian Grounded Theory (GT) [18, 19, 20, 21], with the aim of formalizing the current understanding and architectural concepts of practitioners when architecting DTs of MS-based systems. The study focused on three key aspects: granularity, interfaces, and integration. Other aspects of DT design were excluded due to space constraints. We analysed 23 knowledge sources to identify established industrial patterns and practices. Based on our findings, we developed a formal ADD model comprising 3 decisions, 24 decision options, and 17 decision drivers.

This paper is organized as follows: Sect. 2 compares this work with related studies. Section 3 presents the research methods applied in this study and summarizes the knowledge sources. Section 4 details the resulting reusable ADD model for architecting DTs of MS-based systems, focusing on the aspects of granularity, interfaces, and integration. Section 5 discusses the results. Subsequently, Sect. 6 considers potential threats to the validity of this study, and Sect. 7 summarizes the findings and outlines directions for future work.

## 2 Related Work

Few studies focusing on patterns and practices for architecting DTs can be found. Furthermore, existing research often lacks detail about which patterns or practices are used for architecting DTs with respect to granularity, interfaces, and integrations. For instance, Ferko et al. [15] presented a systematic mapping study on architecting DTs, capturing architectural solutions including reference architectures and architectural styles, as well as quality attributes based on those proposed by the ISO 25010 standard. They examined the correlations between those architectural styles and quality attributes. This work explores architecting DTs from a high-level perspective and does not consider more specific architectural patterns or practices.

Some studies [13, 14, 22] review academic works analysing key enabling technologies for DTs. They identify the use of communication protocols and APIs as interfaces for enabling the integration among DTs and other systems as well as their interactions. Besides defining a high-level architecture for DTs or their execution platform, they do not provide information about more specific architectural patterns or practices. Furthermore, none of these works provide precise information about common decision drivers. A similar work [3] posing similar issues, identifies the key properties that a DT should satisfy and thoroughly defines them. It also identifies different patterns and practices related to the interaction that mainly include interfaces defined based on well-formed APIs and structured data, meeting the key technical features and properties of DTs. This work does not consider standard quality attributes as decision drivers.

Although different studies have explored the definition of patterns for architecting DTs, they do not detail how these patterns support the DT properties or do not explore the correlation between the patterns and standard quality attributes. Some of those works, such as [23], document the use of patterns for DTs, such as digital shadow. Other works propose using well-known design patterns. For example, [24] documents the use of the façade pattern for integration. Some proposals, however, identify patterns that could meet the DT properties [3] and propose the definition of interfaces such as APIs for management and data querying. For instance, [10] proposes design patterns mostly popularized in the field of microservices, such as ambassador, sidecar, or adapter, to balance complexity and manage costs. This work assumes that DTs are monolithic services or decomposed in multiple components, which are deployed as a distributed network of containerized entities. Another work [4] proposed a domain-independent approach inspired by Domain-Driven Design (DDD), suitable for architecting DTs [25] [S3]. It includes the use of various patterns, such as open host service (OHS), messaging, or integration services, and discusses how they support the DT properties.

Recent works address the design of DTs of complex systems with MS architectures that are cloud-native or deployed on Kubernetes-based platforms. For example, Borsatti et al. [7] define a message queue pattern for the interaction among DTs as well as between DTs and other systems, exploiting APIs as an alternative. This work does not study how these practices or patterns may satisfy any DT property, although the DT should present functional correctness. A message queue pattern is also used in [8], considering accuracy, precision, and performance as the main driving factors of the design. In both works, the impact of those driving factors is not formally specified.

Our study addresses the gap identified by systematically examining practitioners' methods and techniques, resulting in a formal model that includes ADDs, patterns and practices, decision drivers based on a quality standard, and their relationships. This model offers valuable insights to help practitioners effectively architect DTs of MS-based systems. To the best of our knowledge, this is the first study of its kind in this area.

## 3   Research Method

We conducted a systematic GLS of practitioners' sources such as blog posts, system documentation and practitioners' reports [16, 17, 26], to obtain information about practitioners' views on architecting DTs of MS-based systems in terms of the granularity of DTs and their components, their interfaces, and integrations among the DTs and of DTs with other convenient services or systems. GLS combined with Straussian GT was successfully applied in previous studies [27, 28].

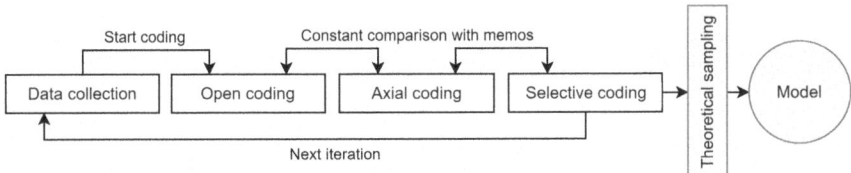

**Fig. 1.** Research method steps.

The research method consists of the steps shown in Fig. 1. As part of *data collection*, following Kitchenham's guidelines [29], the search terms and string were defined. The initial search string was <"digital twin*" AND microservice*>. We added alternative terms to the initial search string in subsequent searches, as done in <"digital twin*"

AND microservice* AND granularity>, based on concepts included in Sect. 1 and other related concepts found during the analysis. The search for practitioner sources was conducted using search engines such as Google, Bing, Yahoo, DuckDuckGo, and StartPage, since they keep around 95% of the market share, as well as widely used technology topic portals such as DZone and InfoQ, among others. The practitioners' articles found were carefully read by the authors to determine their eligibility based on the criteria for evaluation and critical appraisal of grey literature defined by [30], namely authority, accuracy, coverage, objectivity, date, and significance. For instance, articles including patterns and practices for DTs of MS-based systems had to be at least recent (date), relevant to the topic (significance) and not marketing a business or product (objectivity) to be considered candidate sources. All authors reviewed and approved other author's selection of sources. Knowledge sources are summarised in Table 1 (the link to a copy of each source in a web archive is included in the replication package, which is publicly accessible at https://zenodo.org/uploads/15514330). Then, GT coding practices and constant comparison were repeatedly and iteratively applied to identify concepts, categories, drivers, and relations. The identified entities were modelled using a diagramming tool. The types of coding activity proposed by GT [21] were conducted. *Open coding* was used to translate conceptual details into labels. *Axial coding* was applied to group recurring terms, synonymous, and related concepts into categories. Each source was examined line by line, with thought processes, interpretations, and argumentation documented in memos for traceability. Through *selective coding* concepts were refined, and the theory's core ideas were extracted. The final theory was presented as a formal UML-like model already used in previous studies [27, 28]. The process was iterated until *theoretical saturation* [31] was achieved, that is, when five to seven additional sources no longer yielded any new insights.

**Table 1.** Knowledge sources included in the study.

| ID | Title | Reference |
|----|-------|-----------|
| S1 | The Role of Digital Twins in Unlocking the Cloud's Potential | https://tinyurl.com/2r4epny8 |
| S2 | Webinar: Putting the 'I' in IoT – building digital twins with Akka microservices | https://tinyurl.com/3mneknnu |
| S3 | Digital Twins: A digital counterpart for a new concept of Product | https://tinyurl.com/yc85jcfj |
| S4 | Microservice Twins in Kubernetes - breaking new grounds | https://tinyurl.com/yeyj7837 |
| S5 | How Kubernetes supports digital twins | https://tinyurl.com/332u36jh |
| S6 | Building Digital Twins of Software Systems with Generative AI: A Practical Approach | https://tinyurl.com/y35j89f7 |
| S7 | Kafka at the Core of any Digital Twins Architecture | https://tinyurl.com/55c9898b |
| S8 | Digital twins to virtualise the world | https://tinyurl.com/4kfnxfu9 |
| S9 | Digital Twins Event Gateway | https://tinyurl.com/993ra83k |

(*continued*)

**Table 1.** (*continued*)

| ID | Title | Reference |
|----|-------|-----------|
| S10 | Using Digital Twins | https://tinyurl.com/b44c8xsh |
| S11 | Challenges of Creating Digital Twins in the Transition to Industry 4.0 | https://tinyurl.com/5rj2ru8z |
| S12 | IoT Architectures for Digital Twin with Apache Kafka | https://tinyurl.com/33ppzvvf |
| S13 | Apache Kafka as Digital Twin in Industrial IoT | https://tinyurl.com/dvu8efuc |
| S14 | Building the digital representation with digital twin using AWS stack | https://tinyurl.com/y2pr38mn |
| S15 | Building the digital representation with Digital Twin using Microsoft stack | https://tinyurl.com/mr4837pr |
| S16 | HiveMQ and Eclipse Ditto: Friends or Foes? | https://tinyurl.com/4xrh4f7c |
| S17 | Understanding digital twin environments | https://tinyurl.com/mu7yf29z |
| S18 | Hands-on Guide to Using MQTT and Eclipse Ditto for Digital Twins | https://tinyurl.com/uwekb2cy |
| S19 | Digital Twin Platform Stack Architectural Framework | https://tinyurl.com/48zbdj8j |
| S20 | Building Digital Twins for DFDS With Cross plane and Kubernetes | https://tinyurl.com/5bz52kuk |
| S21 | How Digital Twins and IoT Work Together [With Example] | https://tinyurl.com/4d8f987r |
| S22 | A Comprehensive Guide on Digital Twins | https://tinyurl.com/3z7bjfdn |
| S23 | Building a Digital Twin with MQTT and Hasura Streaming Subscriptions | https://tinyurl.com/yh7wdch5 |

## 4   ADD Model for Architecting Digital Twins of MS-Based Systems

The ADD model derived includes practitioners' views, patterns, and practices extracted from GL related to architecting DT(s) of MS-based systems. The ADD model was specified as an instance of the metamodel shown in Fig. 2, defined in [28] and used in previous studies [27, 28].

According to this metamodel, a Category groups Decisions that are closely related to a specific aspect. A Decision also has a Context: a domain object that denotes the system part or aspect for which the decision is applied. An Option can be a Pattern or a Practice as a possible Solution to the design problem expressed and modelled as a set of design Decisions. An Option has influencing factors driving the decisions called Forces, which can have a force impact. Forces identified in this work are expressed as quality (sub)characteristics of the software product quality model ISO/IEC 25010 [32]. An Option can be related to another Option using a Relation. Possible Relations are 'is-a', 'uses', 'can be combined with', 'realizes', etc. All Options must be linked directly or via other Options to a Decision. Decisions and Options can have 'next' decision Relations as well, and they can be 'mandatory' or 'optional'.

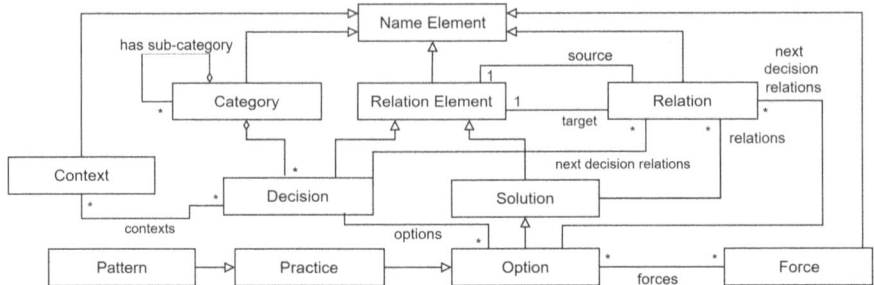

**Fig. 2.** Meta-model for ADD model.

As Fig. 3 depicts, the ADD model presented in this work consists of a single decision Category: *Architecting DTs of an MS-based system*. This has three top-level Decisions related to the architecting aspects of DTs considered in this study (see Sect. 1). Some secondary decisions have been excluded due to space restrictions. Although all the decisions of the ADD model represent a crucial aspect, the last one has an optional character depending on whether the DT is composite and whether it interacts with other systems and services. For each mandatory Decision, one of the modelled Options should be chosen.

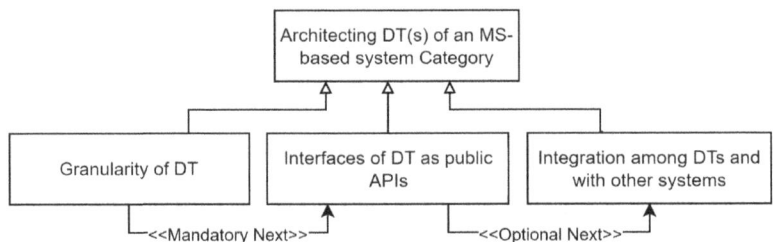

**Fig. 3.** ADD model on architecting DTs of MS-based systems: overview.

## 4.1 ADD: Granularity of DT

When designing DTs of MS-based systems, it is essential to determine the granularity level: the unit of operational control structure that the DT will represent. This decision plays a critical role in supporting stakeholders, such as engineers and operators [S1, S3, S9, S7, S10], in monitoring system performance and detecting issues or anomalies [33]. It is heavily influenced by the specific goals and requirements of these stakeholders.

Granularity impacts on composability and interactions, as the number of DTs representing the MS-based system(s) and their integrations will vary accordingly [S2]. Four main options for the granularity of DTs have been identified (see Fig. 4).

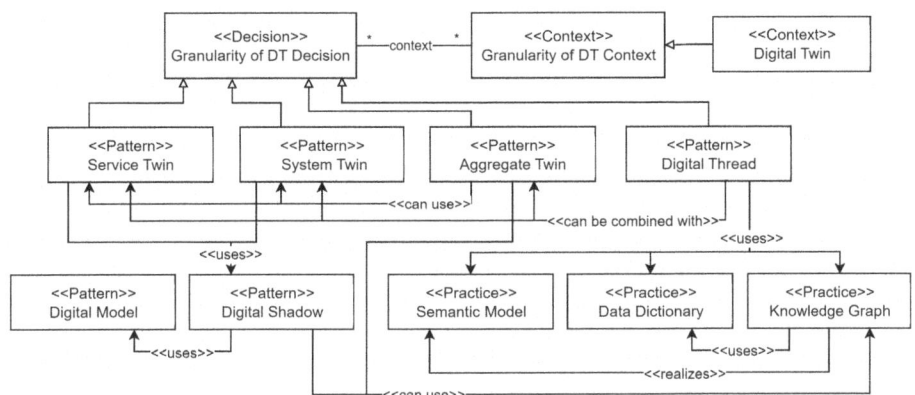

**Fig. 4.** Granularity of DT decision (the forces have been extracted to Table 2).

It is straightforward to use the *System Twin* pattern [S7, S3, S9, S10] to represent a (sub)system composed of interconnected components or services. This pattern can meet the operational requirements when monitoring and modelling a traditional monolithic or a simple MS-based system. Therefore, the degree of *adaptability* provided is **medium**. This pattern offers a **low** level of *modularity*, *reusability*, and *modifiability* due to the high level of combination of system components in the DT, which implies that changes to one component may affect the entire DT of a system. It also offers a **medium** degree of *resource utilization* and *time behaviour,* since the performance of the DT is efficient only at the (sub)system-level when it is simple, and a **low** degree of *scalability*, as handling variable workloads for the entire DT of a (sub)system can be complex.

Another option is the *Service Twin* pattern [S1, S4, S7, S3, S9, S10, S13] when a DT twins a component or service of a (sub)system. Since services are the primary units of MS-based systems, this pattern helps stakeholders to accomplish their tasks at the service level. It is suitable when interactions among different services do not need to be represented. This pattern requires designing multiple DTs for modelling an entire MS-based system, as it follows a one-to-one mapping between an MS and its corresponding DT. The Service Twin pattern provides a **medium** degree of *adaptability*, and, since DTs of individual services can be modified independently, a **very high** level of *modularity*, *reusability*, and *modifiability*. It also offers a **high** degree of *resource utilization*, *time behaviour*, and *scalability*.

When either the System Twin or the Service Twin are applied, then, the *Digital Shadow* (DS) pattern [S3, S10, S12] can be used. This pattern creates an up-to-date and accurate virtual replica, including properties and state, of an MS or MS-based system, depending on the main pattern that uses it. It involves one-way data flow from the twinned system to the DS to monitor its changes without commanding it. The DS can use multiple Digital Models (DMs), especially when used along with the System Twin, typically one per component or service of the system. Different types of DMs can be used to reflect different perspectives of the system (e.g., infrastructure, software, etc.) [S3, S7, S10], **positively** impacting the degree of *modularity* and *reusability*, and increasing the representation fidelity and the degree of *functional correctness.*

The third option is the *Aggregate Twin* pattern [S7, S3, S9]. It represents a composition or aggregation of DTs designed using the system or service twin patterns. It is used to interconnect DTs of components or subsystems of a complex system, including its IT infrastructure [S3]. It is also used to aggregate DTs of several independent (sub-) systems that are interconnected as part of a supply chain or broader organizational process. This pattern implies high complexity and offers a **high** degree of *modularity*, and a **medium** degree of *reusability, modifiability,* and *adaptability,* since modifications of a DT of the aggregation may have widespread effects. It also offers a **medium** degree of *resource utilization* and *time behaviour* as aggregating DTs of multiple systems can lead to resource overhead and increase latency, and a **high** degree of *scalability*, as it has been designed for complex, interconnected systems, although scaling DTs of multiple systems simultaneously can be challenging.

The last option is the *Digital Thread* pattern [S12, S14, S15, S20] [33], which offers the highest level of granularity and complexity. It represents and enables the monitoring of the lifecycle, including design, of a service or system modelled by one or more DTs based on any of the previous patterns. This pattern interconnects the DTs of all relevant components or services, systems, and functional processes as appropriate to enable efficient collaboration and decision-making across all the stages of a business process and to optimize traceability. It allows the seamless modification of the DTs network as the systems evolve and can connect to (almost) any other enterprise system. The degree of *adaptability* provided is therefore **very high,** as it supports the ability of the DT(s) to evolve alongside the system(s) represented across different stages. This pattern offers a **high** degree of *modularity* and *reusability*, since it spans across the entire lifecycle and multiple systems. Additionally, it provides a **high** degree of *modifiability,* as it allows for continuous updates across the entire lifecycle. It also offers a **low** degree of *resource utilization* and *time behaviour,* due to the high complexity and data volume, and a **very high** degree of *scalability*, as it supports scaling across different stages and systems.

Practices like Semantic model [S14, S15, S16], Data dictionary [S14, S15, S16] and Knowledge graph [S14, S15, S16] are used to contextualize data, mainly by the Digital Thread pattern. A *Knowledge Graph* [34] represents a collection of interlinked descriptions of objects, events or concepts, using semantic metadata. Knowledge Graphs can also be used by the DS and the Aggregate Twin patterns to link DMs and DTs, respectively [S15]. In general, the use of the patterns DS and DM and the practices Semantic Model, Data Dictionary and Knowledge Graph **positively** impact the degree of *modularity* and *reusability,* but it also increases the complexity and **negatively** impacts the level of *modifiability.* The degrees of *resource utilization* and *time behavior* also suffer a **negative** impact.

**Table 2.** Forces for the Architectural and representation granularity of DT decision (extracted from the ADD model).

|  | Option | Forces (Degree/Impact) |
|---|---|---|
| Main | Service Twin | ADAPT (M), MODUL (M), REUSA (M), MODIF (H), SCALA (M), RUTIL (H), TBEHA (H) |
|  | System Twin | ADAPT (M), MODUL (L), REUSA (L), MODIF (H), SCALA (L), RUTIL (VH), TBEHA (VH) |
|  | Aggregate Twin | ADAPT (M), MODUL (H), REUSA (H), MODIF (M), SCALA (H), RUTIL (M), TBEHA (M) |
|  | Digital Thead | ADAPT (VH), MODUL (VH), REUSA (VH), MODIF (L), SCALA (VH), RUTIL (L), TBEHA (L) |
| Additional | Digital Shadow | MODUL (+), FCORR (+), REUSA (+), MODIF (-), TBEHA (-), RUTIL (-) |
|  | Digital Model | MODUL (+ +), FCORR (+ +), REUSA (+ +), MODIF (- -), TBEHA (- -), RUTIL (-) |
|  | Knowledge graph | MODUL (+), REUSA (+), MODIF (-), TBEHA (-), RUTIL (-) |

**Forces Codes**: **FCORR**: Functional correctness, **FAPPR**: Functional appropriateness, **TBEHA**: Time behavior, **RUTIL**: Resources utilization, **OPERA**: Operability, **MODUL**: Modularity, **REUSA**: Reusability, **MODIF**: Modifiability, **ADAPT**: Adaptability, **SCALA**: Scalability
**Degree scale** *(main options)*: **L**. Low, **M**. Medium, **H**. High, **VH**. Very High. **Impact scale** *(additional options)*: +: positive, −: negative

Table 2 presents the forces identified for the different options of this ADD, extracted from the model for clarity. Each force's degree or impact value on a given option is shown in parenthesis. Values are based on authors' interpretation of the GL sources and of the well-known descriptions of patterns and practices. The legend explains the abbreviations and scales used. The force degree of the main options is aligned with the definitions provided by the quality standard and is rated from Low (negative) to Very High (positive) to facilitate decision-making, while the impact of forces of the additional options is represented by plus (+) or minus (−) signs depending on whether their impact on the main option(s) is positive or negative. An extended version of this table and the tables for the other decisions can be found in the replication package.

## 4.2 ADD: Integrations of DTs and Between DTs and Other Systems

The decision related to interfaces involves six options for exposing DT functions and/or data (Fig. 5), based on the endpoints design and influenced by common API design bests practices expressed as standard quality aspects.

The first option identified is the Action-oriented API pattern [S2, S4, S5, S6]. Endpoints are designed to expose and perform specific complex custom actions or operations, often encapsulated into single API calls made using verbs. The degree of *modularity* provided is **low**, since these APIs are often tightly coupled to specific actions. They offer a **low** degree of *adaptability*, as they are designed for specific tasks. They often have clear, descriptive endpoints, so they provide a **high** degree of *self-descriptiveness*. The degree of *installability* offered is **medium**, as they may require specific configurations. They provide a **high** degree of *operability* due to their straightforward nature. The degree of *interoperability* offered is **medium**, depending on how well they integrate with other systems.

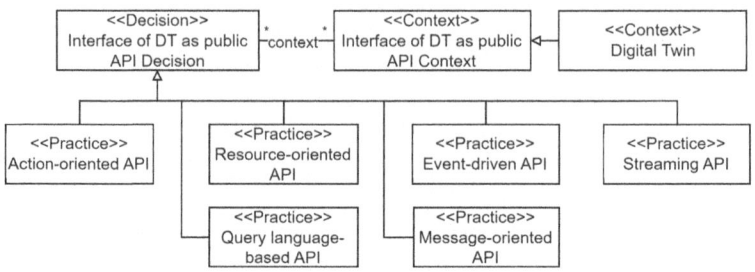

**Fig. 5.** Interfaces of DT as public APIs decision.

Another common option is the use of a Resource-oriented API pattern [S2, S4, S5, S6]. Endpoints are designed for exposing resources and support standard CRUD operations over resources mapped to standard HTTP methods to manipulate them. Endpoints are typically invoked using resource names. The degree of *modularity* provided is **high**, since these APIs are often loosely coupled to specific actions (they are resource-centric). They offer a **high** degree of *adaptability*, as they can be extended to new resources. They follow widely understood principles, so they provide a **high** degree of *self-descriptiveness*. The degree of *installability* offered is **high**, due to their standardized nature. They provide a **high** degree of *operability* as they are intuitive and easy to use. The degree of *interoperability* offered is **high**, due to adherence to API standards.

Another option is the *Query language-based API* [S2, S4, S5, S6] pattern. It involves endpoints designed to be invoked by sending queries written in a flexible query language that allows clients to specify exactly what data they need and how it should be formatted. The degree of *modularity* provided is **high**, since these APIs allow fine-grained data access. They offer a **high** degree of *adaptability*, as queries can be modified as needed without changing the API. Understanding the query language is required, so they provide a **medium** degree of *self-descriptiveness*. The degree of *installability* offered is **medium**, as they may require additional setup for the query language. They provide a **high** degree of *operability* since they offer flexibility for data retrieval. The degree of *interoperability* provided is **high** when the query language is widely supported.

A variety of options that reduce the need for clients to repeatedly poll for updates, typically used in event-driven architectures, have been identified. For example, *Event-based APIs* [S2, S4, S5, S6] are designed to handle events, triggering actions in response to specific occurrences. Notifications to subscribers are usually pushed from the server to the client, using callbacks or other push mechanisms. Another option is the use of the *Message-oriented API* [S2, S4, S5, S6] pattern, involving an API designed to exchange messages between producers and consumers to facilitate the communication between different systems or components. An additional option is the use of the *Streaming API* [S2, S4, S5, S6] pattern, in which the API is designed to provide a continuous data flow from a source to a subscriber client, that consumes and processes the data, often in real-time. These three types share the same driving forces degrees. The degree of *modularity* provided is **high**, since these APIs are decoupled from the main application logic. They offer a **high** degree of *adaptability*, as new events, types of messages or data streams can be added. Understanding event triggers and messaging and streaming protocols is necessary, so they provide a **medium** degree of *self-descriptiveness*. The degree of *installability* offered is **medium**, as they may require event handling, messaging, and streaming infrastructure like event bus, (message) broker, and streaming data pipeline, respectively. They provide a **high** degree of *operability* since they offer real-time responsiveness. The degree of *interoperability* provided is **high** when they follow standard event, messaging and streaming protocols, respectively.

### 4.3  ADD: Integrations of DTs and Between DTs and Other Systems

An important aspect of architecting DTs, or any other software system, is to identify and model the required interactions among components [4] [S16], bearing in mind that they do not always share the same interface [S12] [4] (see Sect. 4.B). Eight main decision options have been identified to support the integration of DTs and other systems for their seamless interaction (see Fig. 6).

The straightforward option is the *Direct communication* pattern [S12, S14, S17]: a DT acts as a client that can make requests directly to the public endpoint of other DTs, systems, or services, that act as servers (clients can act servers at the same time). Since it lacks built-in *fault tolerance* mechanisms, the degree of this quality attribute is **low**. This option involves a high degree of coupling and, therefore, a **low** degree of *modularity* and *modifiability*, which complicates the addition and handling of mandatory cross-cutting security concerns, resulting, for example, in a **low** degree of *authenticity* of the services involved, since there is no mechanism to verify the identity of the interacting entities. All the interacting DTs, systems, and services must be exposed to the "external world", which increases the attack surface compared to that offered when internal components are hidden. For that reason, the degrees of *confidentiality* and *integrity* are **low**. This pattern offers a **high** degree of *resources utilization* and *time behaviour*. However, the operation of complex composite DTs might require several calls to other DTs, services, or systems, which may result in multiple network round trips among them, adding significant latency. This option could be good enough for DTs twining small MS-based systems but not for large and complex MS-based systems. Therefore, the degree of *scalability* and *adaptability* is **low**.

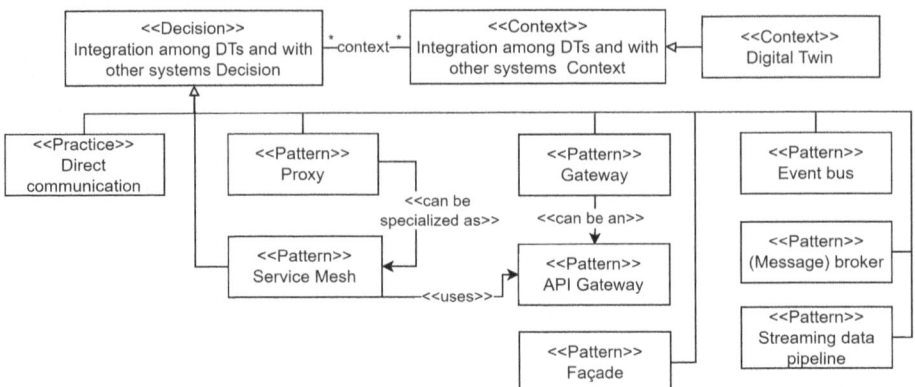

**Fig. 6.** Integration of DTs and between DTs and other systems.

A common option for integration is the *Proxy* pattern [S11, S12, S17]. It involves the use of an intermediary object between a client component of the DT and an invoked or server component that share the same protocol. It controls the access by executing additional functionality related to Load balancing, Catching, or Security before forwarding the request with small overhead. Similarly to Direct Communication pattern, the degree of *adaptability, modularity* and *modifiability* offered is **medium**, although the degree of *fault tolerance, authenticity, confidentiality*, and *integrity* is **high**. This pattern offers also a **medium** degree of *resources utilization, time behaviour*, and *scalability*.

Another option, based on proxies, is the *Service mesh* pattern [S1, S3, S4], commonly used as an infrastructure layer to support the interaction among service-based DTs and other services, and when numerous cross-cutting concerns such as traffic management, security, and observability, need to be (dynamically) implemented. The Service mesh pattern offers a **high** degree of *adaptability, modularity* and *modifiability, fault tolerance, authenticity, confidentiality, integrity, time behaviour*, and *scalability*, although the degree of *resource utilization* is **medium**.

A well-known option is the use of the *Gateway* pattern [S4, S5, S8, S16, S12, S13, S14], which constitutes a single-point-of-entry and encapsulates access to external services, systems or resources. A common type of Gateway identified is *API gateway* [S18, S13, S14] that provides application-level functionalities to manage API requests such as routing, rate limiting, and security. This pattern also offers a **high** degree of *adaptability, modularity, modifiability, fault tolerance, authenticity, confidentiality, integrity, time behaviour*, and *scalability*, but a **medium** degree of *resource utilization*. API gateway aspects are used by the Service Mesh pattern.

An additional option identified is the *Façade* pattern [S17, S13, S14] that provides a simplified interface to a complex subsystem although introducing some overhead. It is commonly used to provide a unified point of access to legacy systems [S16]. This pattern offers a **high** degree of *adaptability, modularity* and *modifiability, fault tolerance, time behaviour*, and *scalability*, but a **medium** degree of *resource utilization*. This pattern enforces security aspects, however, since it relies on the underlying subsystems for that, it offers a **medium** degree of *authenticity, confidentiality, integrity*.

A group of options used in even-driven architectures have been also identified. The *Event-bus* pattern [S3, S4, S8, S16, S13, S14, S15] facilitates asynchronous, decoupled communication between components when a change in a component state triggers an event that is consumed by other component(s). Another well-known option is the *Broker* pattern [S3, S4, S8, S16, S13, S14, S15] that handles the delivery of messages among components. It often enables queueing, topic-based routing, or persistence. The last option is the *Streaming data pipeline* pattern [S3, S4, S8, S16, S13, S14, S15], used to continuously process incoming data from a DT in real time. It may enrich, transform, filter, and feed such data into analytics or storage systems. All these three patterns offer a **high** degree of the ten quality aspects previously identified.

Common combinations of some of the main options identified and with additional patterns are not documented in this work due to space constraints.

## 5 Discussion

The ADD model presented to support the design of DTs of (complex) MS-based systems is closely aligned with the selected sources and has been systematically developed. The point of theoretical saturation in GT [32] was reached after integrating information from 23 sources. While reading the first 10 sources, frequent adjustments to the identified codes and categories were necessary. However, in the subsequent 8 sources, such modifications became less frequent, and no further alterations were required for the remaining sources. In the following, the main results of each RQ are discussed.

**RQ1:** The 24 patterns and practices identified as decision options were modelled in association with 3 different ADDs, as we observed that they could be grouped based on the aspects defined in Sect. 1. The resulting models and their descriptions help clarify and define, from a practical perspective, these three aspects paramount for the design of DTs [4]. It is worth noting that that the decision options related to the second ADD provide significantly more detail than descriptions found in existing works on DT design [3, 4] and on API design [35], which primarily refer to public APIs with either an action-oriented or a data-oriented role. Our work documents a total of 6 options, focusing on the endpoint design and highlighting their invocation methods, thereby enabling more informed design decisions. Another remarkable finding is that some of the identified decision options associated with the third ADD correspond to well-known and documented patterns, such as the integration-related patterns API Gateway or Service Mesh. Some of those patterns are also commonly used in the design of MS architectures. The design of both DTs and MS-based architectures share some challenges, such as defining boundaries (first ADD) and communication across them (second and third ADD) [35]. These aspects are also addressed as part of the strategic design activity defined by the DDD-inspired approach for architecting DTs [4] (see Sect. 2).

**RQ2:** The study reveals relations between ADDs and decision options that are generally clear. Although additional relations have not been specified in the diagrams, due to the modular structure of the ADD model, most of them have been mentioned in the text or can be derived from the descriptions provided. For instance, potential correlations may exist between certain API types outlined in the second ADD and the corresponding integration mechanisms proposed in the third ADD. Another noteworthy aspect is that the third ADD, although modelled as an "optional next" decision, plays a crucial role in the success of DTs of complex MS-based systems, particularly when DTs must interact among them and with other systems, and when business-oriented stakeholders are expected to benefit from DT adoption through the Digital Thread pattern.

**RQ3:** The research identified a total of 17 forces, including sub-characteristics of maintainability and flexibility, that are common to most of the ADDs and decision options. The forces identified correspond to standard quality characteristics and their impact factors are expressed using well-defined rating scales. This allows practitioners to easily select the most convenient options based on specific requirements. It is worth noting that the first ADD, related to granularity, and the third ADD, related to integration, are the decisions influenced by the highest number of forces: 10. The ADDs are mainly driven by maintainability and flexibility aspects, and the rest of forces appear to play a complementary role. Furthermore, the third ADD is the only decision driven by forces related to security and reliability, which highlights its importance in DT design despite its optional nature.

# 6  Threats to Validity

In the following, the threats to validity identified by Wohlin et al. [36] are discussed.

*Construct validity* ensures that the measurements accurately reflect what is intended. To mitigate potential biases, the research was not limited to specific sources. Instead, it followed well-defined inclusion and exclusion criteria, pulling from a wide range of relevant materials. Despite searches were exhaustively conducted, some sources may have been unintentionally overlooked.

*Internal validity* deals with factors that impact causality. To mitigate this threat, the study used independently created practitioner reports, ensuring objectivity but potentially missing insights from interviews. To address this, we reviewed more sources than necessary to reach theoretical saturation, reducing the risk of missing critical perspectives.

*External validity* concerns the applicability of findings beyond this work. While the inclusion of diverse sources supports generalization to DT architectures for MS-based systems, the exclusive use of grey literature, despite its practical value, may introduce bias due to the lack of peer review. Although strict selection criteria and data triangulation were applied, this limitation may affect the model's reliability. Additionally, focusing on three architectural aspects (granularity, interfaces, and integration) enabled depth but may restrict applicability to other concerns. Future work should explore broader architectural dimensions.

*Conclusion validity* ensures that the relationships identified between treatments and outcomes are sound. The sources were assessed based on objectivity, significance, and other relevant criteria, and were reviewed by all the authors prior to their consensual inclusion. Theoretical saturation was reached, and additional sources were even analysed beyond that threshold to be extra cautious. Since GT focuses on real-world phenomena, the main risk is misinterpreting concepts. Extensive sourcing minimizes that risk, but findings are intended the defined scope.

# 7 Conclusions and Future Work

This work presents a GL study using Straussian GT to develop an ADD model for patterns and practices adopted by practitioners when architecting DT(s) for (complex) MS-based systems. These DTs are designed to continuously and automatically monitor, model, and enhance its operation. The model encompasses 3 ADDs, 24 decision options, 18 relations, and 17 driving forces defined by an international standard on software quality. The impact of these forces is represented using well-defined rating scales, allowing practitioners to easily choose the most convenient options based on specific requirements. The work reveals that the main ADDs are defined around the architectural aspects of granularity of DTs and integration, including the use of interfaces of DTs as public APIs. It provides information on patterns and practices that support these aspects, often omitted or inconclusive in other scientific works on DTs and even on API design. These findings contribute to a clearer and more practical understanding of the foundational concepts that underpin DT architecture. They emphasize the unique complexity of determining DT granularity (a decision specific to DTs) and highlight the critical importance of integration, both among DTs and between DTs and external systems. Although formally categorized as optional, integration decision has proven essential for the effective deployment of DTs of complex microservice-based systems. Although the findings are based on a specific group of practitioners, they align with widely accepted standards, suggesting potential applicability to other domains. However, further validation in diverse industrial settings is needed to confirm the model's broader relevance.

As future work, we plan to explore the use of DDD design principles in the design of DT architectures, considering the similarities found, as well as patterns mentioned in scientific papers that could be applied to DTs design despite not being identified in practitioners' sources.

**Acknowledgments.** This paper has been partially funded by the 2024 predoctoral mobility grant for research stays at international universities and research institutions for PhD students from the University of Castilla-La Mancha, and two Erasmus+ grants for short-term doctoral stays 2025 (reference numbers 2024-1-ES01-KA131-HED-000206822-MOB-0053 and 2023-1-ES01-KA131-HED-000113966-MOB-0733), all of them awarded to Aurora Macías. It is also part of the R+D+i project PID2022-140907OB-I00 funded by MICIU/AEI/https://doi.org/10.13039/501100011033 and ERDF, EU. It has also been partially supported by Junta de Comunidades de Castilla-La Mancha/ERDF (SBPLY/21/180501/000030) and by the University of Castilla-La Mancha (2023-GRIN-34436). Evangelos Ntentos' and Uwe Zdun's work was supported by the FFG (Austrian Research Promotion Agency) project MODIS (no.\ FO999895431).

**Disclosure of Interests.** The authors have no competing interests to declare that are relevant to the content of this article.

# References

1. Grieves, M., Vickers, J.: Digital twin: mitigating unpredictable, undesirable emergent behavior in complex systems. In: Kahlen Franz-Josef, S., Flumerfelt, A.A., (eds.) Transdisciplinary Perspectives on Complex Systems: New Findings and Approaches, pp. 85–113. Springer, Cham (2017). https://doi.org/10.1007/978-3-319-38756-7_4

2. Turner, J., Ferris, R., Eckhardt, S.: Infrastructure digital twin maturity: a model for measuring progress (2021). https://www.digitaltwinconsortium.org/wp-content/uploads/sites/3/2022/06/Infrastructure-Digital-Twin-Maturity-Model.pdf. Accessed 16 Dec 2023

3. Minerva, R., Lee, G.M., Crespi, N.: Digital twin in the IoT context: a survey on technical features, scenarios, and architectural models. Proc. IEEE **108**(10), 1785–1824 (2020). https://doi.org/10.1109/JPROC.2020.2998530

4. Macías, A., Navarro, E., Cuesta, C.E., Zdun, U.: Architecting digital twins using a domain-driven design-based approach. In: IEEE 20th International Conference on Software Architecture (ICSA), pp. 153–163 (2023). https://doi.org/10.1109/ICSA56044.2023.00022

5. Grassi, V., Mirandola, R., Perez-Palacin, D.: A conceptual and architectural characterization of antifragile systems. J. Syst. Softw. **213**, 112051 (2024). https://doi.org/10.1016/j.jss.2024.112051

6. Avritzer, A., Camilli, M., Janes, A., Russo, B., Trubiani, C., van Hoorn, A.: Continuous dependability assessment of microservice systems. In: Software Architecture. ECSA 2022 Tracks and Workshops, pp. 138–147. Springer, Cham (2023). https://doi.org/10.1007/978-3-031-36889-9_11

7. Borsatti, D., et al.: KubeTwin: a digital twin framework for Kubernetes deployments at scale. IEEE Trans. Netw. Serv. Manage. **21**(4), 3889–3903 (2024). https://doi.org/10.1109/TNSM.2024.3405175

8. Bhardwaj, A., Benson, T.A.: KubeKlone: a digital twin for simulating edge and cloud microservices. In: Proceedings of the 6th Asia-Pacific Workshop on Networking, in APNet '22. New York, NY, USA, pp. 29–35. Association for Computing Machinery (2023). https://doi.org/10.1145/3542637.3542642

9. Avizienis, A., Laprie, J.-C., Randell, B., Landwehr, C.: Basic concepts and taxonomy of dependable and secure computing. IEEE Trans. Dependable Secure Comput. **1**(1), 11–33 (2004). https://doi.org/10.1109/TDSC.2004.2

10. Bellavista, P., Bicocchi, N., Fogli, M., Giannelli, C., Mamei, M., Picone, M.: Requirements and design patterns for adaptive, autonomous, and context-aware digital twins in industry 4.0 digital factories. Comput. Ind. **149**, 103918 (2023). https://doi.org/10.1016/j.compind.2023.103918

11. Spijkman, T., Molenaar, S., Dalpiaz, F., Brinkkemper, S.: Alignment and granularity of requirements and architecture in agile development: a functional perspective. Inf. Softw. Technol. **133**, 106535 (2021). https://doi.org/10.1016/j.infsof.2021.106535

12. Medhat, N.: Granularity in Software Architecture. nadermedhatthoughts.medium.com

13. Fuller, A., Fan, Z., Day, C., Barlow, C.: Digital twin: enabling technologies, challenges and open research. IEEE Access **8**, 108952–108971 (2020). https://doi.org/10.1109/ACCESS.2020.2998358

14. Qi, Q., et al.: Enabling technologies and tools for digital twin. J. Manuf. Syst. **58**, 3–21 (2021). https://doi.org/10.1016/j.jmsy.2019.10.001

15. Ferko, E., Bucaioni, A., Behnam, M.: Architecting Digital Twins. IEEE Access **10**, 50335–50350 (2022). https://doi.org/10.1109/ACCESS.2022.3172964

16. Garousi, V., Felderer, M., Mäntylä, M.V.: Guidelines for including grey literature and conducting multivocal literature reviews in software engineering. Inf. Softw. Technol. **106**, 101–121 (2019). https://doi.org/10.1016/j.infsof.2018.09.006

17. Garousi, V., Felderer, M., Mäntylä, M.V., Rainer, A.: Benefitting from the grey literature in software engineering research. In: Felderer, M., Travassos, G.H. (eds.) Contemporary Empirical Methods in Software Engineering, pp. 385–413. Springer, Cham (2020). https://doi.org/10.1007/978-3-030-32489-6_14

18. Glaser, B., Strauss, A.: Discovery of Grounded Theory: Strategies for Qualitative Research, 1st edn. Routledge, New York (1999)

19. Corbin, J., Strauss, A.: Basics of Qualitative Research (3rd ed.): Techniques and Procedures for Developing Grounded Theory. SAGE Publications, Inc., Thousand Oaks, California (2008). https://doi.org/10.4135/9781452230153

20. Charmaz, K.: Constructing Grounded Theory: A Practical Guide Through Qualitative Analysis. Sage Publications, London; Thousand Oaks, Calif (2006). http://www.amazon.com/Constructing-Grounded-Theory-Qualitative-Introducing/dp/0761973532

21. Corbin, J.M., Strauss, A.: Grounded theory research: procedures, canons, and evaluative criteria. Qual. Sociol. **13**(1), 3–21 (1990). https://doi.org/10.1007/BF00988593

22. Liu, M., Fang, S., Dong, H., Xu, C.: Review of digital twin about concepts, technologies, and industrial applications. J. Manuf. Syst. **58**, 346–361 (2021). https://doi.org/10.1016/j.jmsy.2020.06.017

23. Tekinerdogan, B., Verdouw, C.: Systems Architecture design pattern catalog for developing digital twins. Sensors **20**(18) (2020). https://doi.org/10.3390/s20185103

24. Sulaiman Khail, W., Schnizer, P.: Patterns in digital twin development. In: Proceedings of the 29th European Conference on Pattern Languages of Programs, People, and Practices, in EuroPLoP '24. New York, NY, USA. Association for Computing Machinery (2024). https://doi.org/10.1145/3698322.3698325

25. Abrahão, S., Staron, M., Insfran, E., Muccini, H.: Modeling and architecting of complex software systems. IEEE Softw. **41**(3), 76–79 (2024). https://doi.org/10.1109/MS.2024.3363541

26. Rainer, A., Williams, A.: Using blog-like documents to investigate software practice: Benefits, challenges, and research directions. J. Softw. Evol. Process. **31**(11) (2019). https://doi.org/10.1002/smr.2197

27. Zdun, U., Stocker, M., Zimmermann, O., Pautasso, C., Lübke, D.: Guiding architectural decision making on quality aspects in microservice APIs. In: Pahl, C., Vukovic, M., Yin, J., Yu, Q.: Service-Oriented Computing, pp. 73–89. Springer, Cham (2018). https://doi.org/10.1007/978-3-030-03596-9_5

28. Ntentos, E., Warnett, S.J., Zdun, U.: Supporting architectural decision making on training strategies in reinforcement learning architectures. In: IEEE 21st International Conference on Software Architecture (ICSA), pp. 90–100 (2024). https://doi.org/10.1109/ICSA59870.2024.00017

29. Kitchenham, B., Charters, S.: Guidelines for performing Systematic Literature Reviews in Software Engineering (2007)

30. Tyndall, J.: AACODS Checklist (2010)

31. Johnson, R.B., Christensen, L.: Educational Research: Quantitative, Qualitative, and Mixed Approaches. SAGE Publications (2019)

32. ISO/IEC 25010. ISO/IEC 25010:2011, Systems and software engineering — Systems and software Quality Requirements and Evaluation (SQuaRE) — System and software quality models (2011)

33. C. R. China: Digital twin vs. digital thread: Two complementary ways to digitally replicate assets. www.ibm.com/think/topics. https://www.ibm.com/think/topics/digital-thread-vs-digital-twin#:~:text=A%20digital%20thread%20is%20a,all%20aspects%20of%20the%20life cycle. Accessed 26 Jan 2025

34. Hunt, C.: Semantic Model vs Ontology vs Knowledge Graph: Untangling the latest data modeling terminology," medium.com/@cassihunt. https://medium.com/@cassihunt/semantic-model-vs-ontology-vs-knowledge-graph-untangling-the-latest-data-modeling-terminology-12ce7506b455. Accessed 27 Jan 2025

35. Zimmermann, O., Stocker, M., Lübke, D., Zdun, U., Pautasso, C.: Patterns for API Design: Simplifying Integration with Loosely Coupled Message Exchanges (2022)

36. Wohlin, C., Runeson, P., Hst, M., Ohlsson, M.C., Regnell, B., Wessln, A.: Experimentation in Software Engineering. Springer, Heidelberg (2012). https://doi.org/10.1007/978-3-642-290 44-2

# Author Index

## A

Abbasi, Mateen Ahmed   I-164
AbdElhameed, Marwan   II-371
Abrahamsen, Kristian Degn   II-23
Abrahamsson, Pekka   II-143, II-178
Abughazala, Moamin   I-130
Afkhami, Mohammad Mehdi   I-46
Ait, Adem   I-367
Ali, Nauman bin   II-389
Alonso, Silvio   I-79, II-350
Alves, Antonio Pedro Santos   I-79
Andrada-Mihaela-Nicoleta, Moldovan   II-219
Angelis, Lefteris   II-32, III-121
Araújo, Júlia   II-425
Araújo, Marina   II-425
Ardito, Luca   I-383
Arvidsson, Simon   III-245
Ashoori, Mohammad Hossein   I-46
Axell, Johan   III-245

## B

Barcomb, Ann   III-174
Barner, Simon   I-201
Barros, Glauber   II-405
Batista, Thais   II-405
Bauer, Tim   II-90
Baumann, Lars   II-159
Bazmandegan, Hossein   I-46
Becker, Jürgen   I-64
Bezerra, Carla Ilane   II-188
Blincoe, Kelly   III-155
Bluemke, Ilona   II-49
Bombarda, Andrea   III-419
Bonorden, Leif   III-361
Borgmann, Joshua   II-159
Börstler, Jürgen   II-389
Bosch, Jan   II-270, II-298, III-280
Bousson, Kouamana   II-3
Breu, Ruth   I-329
Bulhakov, Vladyslav   I-349

## C

Cabot, Jordi   I-367
Cabrero-Daniel, Beatriz   I-183
Calefato, Fabio   II-334
Calinescu, Radu   I-273, I-290
Cámara, Javier   I-273
Camilli, Matteo   I-219
Cannavale, Alfonso   III-317
Caporuscio, Mauro   III-231
Carlson, Jan   I-393
Carneiro, Glauco   III-345, III-390
Cerqueira, Elivelton Ramos   III-345, III-390
Cerqueira, Lidiany   III-345, III-390
Chabridon, Sophie   II-405
Chaudron, Michel R. V.   III-372
Cihan, Umut   III-201
Conan, Denis   II-405
Coppola, Riccardo   I-383
Costa, Heitor   II-188
Cruz, Marcos Vinicius   III-57

## D

d'Aloisio, Giordano   I-349
Dakkak, Anas   II-199
Daniele, Piero   II-199
de Abreu Aguiar, Maria Fernanda   II-324
De Luca, Marco   III-137
De Lucia, Andrea   II-361, III-39, III-317
de Paula Filho, Pedro Luiz   I-3
de Souza Santos, Ronnie   III-85, III-174
de Souza, Érica Ferreira   II-324
De Stefano, Manuel   III-39
Decker, Christian   II-235
Della Porta, Antonio   III-105
Demirors, Onur   III-14
Di Lillo, Gianluca   III-317
Di Marco, Antinisca   I-349
Di Martino, Sergio   III-137
Di Meglio, Sergio   III-137, III-191
Di Rocco, Juri   III-327
Di Ruscio, Davide   I-349, III-327

D. Taibi and D. Smite (Eds.): SEAA 2025, LNCS 16083, pp. 447–450, 2026.
https://doi.org/10.1007/978-3-032-04207-1

Di Sipio, Claudio   I-349, III-327
Dogramadzi, Sanja   I-290
Donner, Justus   II-159
Drews, Paul   III-23

**E**
Egyed, Alexander   I-3
Eibl, Florian   II-90
Elahi, Ehsan   I-219
Elnouby, Yahya   III-201
Engeln, Ulrike   I-309
Engström, Emelie   II-389
Erdogmus, Hakan   III-201
Eriksson, Erik   I-113
Etaiwi, Layan   II-298

**F**
Fasolino, Anna Rita   III-137
Felizardo, Katia Romero   II-324
Fernandes, Gabriel Zoéga   II-313
Ferrucci, Filomena   III-39, III-105
Freire, Sávio   II-253, III-85
Friberg, David   III-75
Fronchetti, Felipe   III-85
Fuchß, Daniel   II-159

**G**
Garaccione, Giacomo   I-383
García-Valls, Marisol   II-108
Gargantini, Angelo   III-419
Georgiou, Konstantinos   II-32, III-121
Giordano, Giammaria   III-105, III-155,
     III-214
Giussani, Samuele   III-231
Gomes, Felipe   II-253
Gomes, Kevin Cerqueira   III-345
Gomes, Otávio Santos   II-313
Groner, Raffaela   II-280
Grünbacher, Paul   I-3

**H**
Halak, Marko   I-201
Hammes, Sascha   I-329
Hartkopf, Melanie   II-159
Hasan, Md. Toufique   II-143, II-178
Hayat, Sodaba   II-159
Hemati Moghadam, Iman   I-46
Herda, Tomas   II-178
Heumüller, Robert   I-37

Hierons, Robert M.   I-290
Hryszko, Jarosław   II-80, II-125

**I**
Iannone, Emanuele   III-317
Ibiyo, Motunrayo   I-130
Ihantola, Petri   I-164
Indykov, Vladislav   I-97, I-113
Ismaili, Gino   II-159
Izquierdo, Javier Luis Cánovas   I-367

**J**
Johansson, Emil   II-270
Jongeling, Robbert   I-393
Joosten, Jan   II-298

**K**
Kalinowski, Marcos   I-79, II-350, II-425
Kassab, Mohamad   II-371
Kavargyris, Dimitrios Christos   II-32
Kazman, Rick   III-155
Kelter, Christopher   I-329
Kemell, Kai-Kristian   II-143, II-178
Khan, Ayman Asad   II-143
Kirschner, Maximilian   I-64
Kitchen, Martin   I-393
Klös, Verena   I-237, II-280
Kreutzer, Marius   I-64
Krüger, Jacob   III-372
Kuhrmann, Marco   II-235
Kulyabin, Mikhail   II-298
Kurkchi, Yelyzaveta   I-254

**L**
L. Symeonidis, Andreas   III-409
Labay, Ben   III-23
Laiq, Muhammad   II-389
Lakshminarayanan, Sadhana   II-63
Lambiase, Stefano   III-39
Langer, Theo   I-37
Lanubile, Filippo   II-334
Leotta, Maurizio   III-296
Liebel, Grischa   III-57
Lopes, Hélio   I-79
Lotze, Maurice   II-159

**M**
Macedo Santos, José Amancio   III-390
Machado, Ivan   II-188

Macías, Aurora III-428
Magalhaes, Cleyton III-174
Mäkitalo, Niko I-164
Mallardi, Giulio II-334
Maraki, Iosifina II-32
Martino, Vincenzo De III-214
Martins Pacheco, Nuno Miguel II-298
Martins, Luana II-188
Mauro, Jacopo II-23
Meiertöns, Tim II-159
Mendes, Thiago II-253
Mendonça, Manoel II-253, III-345, III-390
Michael, Judith I-329
Mikkonen, Tommi I-164
Mirandola, Raffaela I-219
Misslisch, Jonathan II-90
Mittas, Nikolaos II-32, III-121
Mnich, Michał II-80
Mohamad, Mazen I-183
Mojabi, Omid III-263
Moldovan, Vasilica I-20
Monteiro, Bruno II-3
Moraes, Gabriel III-345, III-390
Motogna, Simona I-20
Muccini, Henry I-130
Munaro, Tiziano I-201
Muzikants, Caroline II-199

N
Natsos, Dimosthenis III-409
Navarro, Elena III-428
Neumann, Michael II-90, II-159
Nissen, Lars Peter Torp I-393
Ntaoulas, Vasileios III-121
Ntentos, Evangelos I-148, III-428

O
Olausson, Joel I-113
Olianas, Dario III-296
Oliveira, Romeu II-350, II-425
Olsson, Helena Holmström II-270, II-298, III-280
Ortmeier, Frank I-37

P
Palomba, Fabio II-361, III-39, III-105, III-155, III-214, III-317
Palombo, Stefano III-327
Parziale, Alessandra III-214

Patcas, Rares I-20
Pentangelo, Viviana III-214
Perdigão Batista, César II-405
Perez-Palacin, Diego III-231
Petrescu, Manuela III-3
Petrescu, Paul Razvan III-3
Petridis, Filippos II-298
Pievani, Fabio III-419
Pombo, Nuno II-3
Pontillo, Valeria III-155, III-191
Porta, Antonio Della III-214
Preuner, Matthias I-3
Przybyłek, Adam II-90

Q
Quaranta, Luigi II-334

R
Radulescu, Andrei III-372
Rafiq, Yasmin I-290
Rasheed, Zeeshan II-178
Rasku, Jussi II-178
Rebelo, Luciana II-313, II-324
Recupito, Gilberto III-214
Ricca, Filippo III-296
Rocha, Larissa II-188
Roman, Adam II-80, II-125
Romao, Lucas I-79, II-350, II-425
Ronanki, Krishna III-245
Röse, Kerstin II-298
Ryttegård, Fredric II-199

S
Saari, Mika II-143
Sabando-Alonso, Gonzalo II-108
Sami, Malik Abdul II-178
Santana, Railana II-188
Santos, José Amancio Macedo III-345
Schön, Eva-Maria II-90, II-159
Schupp, Sibylle I-309
Schwab, Alex II-159
Sharaf, Mohammad I-130
Sheykina, Alexandra II-361
Sihler, Florian II-280
Silva, Gláucia Braga e II-313
Sotolani, Rodrigo III-85
Souza, Érica Ferreira de II-313
Spalazzese, Romina II-63
Spanke, Julia II-90, II-159

Spínola, Rodrigo    II-253, III-345, III-390
Spinola, Rodrigo    III-85
Starace, Luigi Libero Lucio    III-137, III-191
Staron, Miroslaw    III-75
Stefanakos, Ioannis    I-273
Stotz, Nils    III-23
Straub, Philipp    II-235
Straub, Raphael    II-280
Strøm, Niels Jørgen    I-393
Strüber, Daniel    I-97, I-113
Strzelczyk, Tom    II-159
Sun, Simin    III-75
Svahnberg, Mikael    III-263

**T**

Taheri Monfared, Asma    III-419
Tamburri, Damian A.    III-155
Tichy, Matthias    II-280
Torbati, Ali    I-237, II-280
Tramontana, Porfirio    III-137
Trubiani, Catia    I-254
Turalija, Matko    I-201
Tüzün, Eray    III-201

**U**

Ulan Uulu, Choro    II-298
Unlu, Huseyin    III-14
Unterkalmsteiner, Michael    III-263
Urdih, Francesco    I-148
Uysal, Selen    III-201

**V**

Vázquez, Gricel    I-290
Verma, Pragya    III-57
Vermeer, Lukas    III-23
Vijaykumar, Nandamudi L.    II-313
Villamizar, Hugo    II-350
Voria, Gianmario    III-214
Vu, Quoc Trung    II-159

**W**

Wang, Cong    I-237, II-280
Waseem, Muhammad    II-143, II-178
Wesemann, Lars    II-159
Wessel, Mairieli    III-174
Wohlrab, Rebekka    I-97, I-113
Woźny, Ewa    II-125

**Y**

Yenel, Melih    III-14

**Z**

Zamfirov, Filip    III-372
Zaytsev, Vadim    I-46
Zdanowski, Arkadiusz    II-49
Zdun, Uwe    I-148, III-428
Zech, Philipp    I-329
Zhang, Haotian    III-155
Zhang, Qi    I-273
Zhang, Zheying    II-178